T0321931

Research Anthology on Strategies for Using Social Media as a Service and Tool in Business

Information Resources Management Association
USA

Volume III

Published in the United States of America by
    IGI Global
    Business Science Reference (an imprint of IGI Global)
    701 E. Chocolate Avenue
    Hershey PA, USA 17033
    Tel: 717-533-8845
    Fax: 717-533-8661
    E-mail: cust@igi-global.com
    Web site: http://www.igi-global.com

Library of Congress Cataloging-in-Publication Data

Names: Information Resources Management Association, editor.
Title: Research anthology on strategies for using social media as a service
  and tool in business / Information Resources Management Association,
  editor.
Description: Hershey, PA : Business Science Reference, [2021] | Includes
  bibliographical references and index. | Summary: "This book of
  contributed chapters provides updated information on how businesses are
  strategically using social media and explores the role of social media
  in keeping businesses competitive in the global economy by discussing
  how social tools work, what services businesses are utilizing, both the
  benefits and challenges to how social media is changing the modern
  business atmosphere,"-- Provided by publisher.
Identifiers: LCCN 2021016024 (print) | LCCN 2021016025 (ebook) | ISBN
  9781799890201 (hardcover) | ISBN 9781799890218 (ebook)
Subjects: LCSH: Social media--Economic aspects. | Marketing. | Branding
  (Marketing) | Customer relations. | Customer services--Technological
  innovations.
Classification: LCC HM742 .R4678 2021 (print) | LCC HM742 (ebook) | DDC
  302.23/1--dc23
LC record available at https://lccn.loc.gov/2021016024
LC ebook record available at https://lccn.loc.gov/2021016025

British Cataloguing in Publication Data
A Cataloguing in Publication record for this book is available from the British Library.

The views expressed in this book are those of the authors, but not necessarily of the publisher.

For electronic access to this publication, please contact: eresources@igi-global.com.

List of Contributors

Table of Contents

Section 2
Development and Design Methodologies

Section 4
Utilization and Applications

Volume III

Section 5
Organizational and Social Implications

Volume IV

Section 6
Managerial Impact

Section 7
Critical Issues and Challenges

Preface

Since its conception, social media has become an integral part in how society communicates. As with the development of any other important piece of communication, business and industry must adapt to utilize this tool to reach its vast audiences to survive. Moreover, social media can be applied for internal processes for organizations and should be considered by human resources managers. Through this transition, it is essential for businesses to be aware of how to best utilize these tools and services in order to best promote themselves within the social sphere. The *Research Anthology on Strategies for Using Social Media as a Service and Tool in Business* provides these strategies for businesses to grow under this new era of communication.

Staying informed of the most up-to-date research trends and findings is of the utmost importance. That is why IGI Global is pleased to offer this four-volume reference collection of reprinted IGI Global book chapters and journal articles that have been handpicked by senior editorial staff. This collection will shed light on critical issues related to the trends, techniques, and uses of various applications by providing both broad and detailed perspectives on cutting-edge theories and developments. This collection is designed to act as a single reference source on conceptual, methodological, technical, and managerial issues, as well as to provide insight into emerging trends and future opportunities within the field.

The *Research Anthology on Strategies for Using Social Media as a Service and Tool in Business* is organized into seven distinct sections that provide comprehensive coverage of important topics. The sections are:

1. Fundamental Concepts and Theories;
2. Development and Design Methodologies;
3. Tools and Technologies;
4. Utilization and Applications;
5. Organizational and Social Implications;
6. Managerial Impact; and
7. Critical Issues and Challenges.

The following paragraphs provide a summary of what to expect from this invaluable reference tool.

Section 1, "Fundamental Concepts and Theories," serves as a foundation for this extensive reference tool by addressing crucial theories essential to understanding the concepts of social media in multidisciplinary settings. Opening this reference book is the chapter "The Role of Social Media in Public Involvement: Pushing for Sustainability in International Planning and Development" by Prof. Tooran Alizadeh of University of Sydney, Australia and Profs. Reza Farid and Laura Willems of Griffith

University, Australia. This chapter explores social media's potential to enhance public involvement to pursue sustainable practices on an international scale across planning and development projects. This first section ends with the chapter "Social Media and Social Identity in the Millennial Generation" by Prof. Guida Helal of American University of Beirut, Lebanon and Prof. Wilson Ozuem of University of Cumbria, UK, which focuses on theoretical implications and managerial implications. The concluding section offers some significant roles that social media and social identity may play in keeping up with the design and development of marketing communications programs.

Section 2, "Development and Design Methodologies," presents in-depth coverage of the design and development of social media strategy for its use in different applications. This section starts with the chapter "An Absorptive Capacity Perspective of Organizational Learning Through Social Media: Evidence From the Ghanaian Fashion Industry" by Profs. Richard Boateng, Edna Owusu-Bempah, and Eric Ansong from University of Ghana, Ghana, which examines the role social media has played on brand perceptions in the fashion apparel and accessories industry from a social identity theory perspective. This section ends with the chapter "CommuniMents: A Framework for Detecting Community Based Sentiments for Events" by Prof. Muhammad Aslam Jarwar of Quaid-i-Azam University, Pakistan & Hankuk University of Foreign Studies (HUFS), South Korea; Prof. Rabeeh Ayaz Abbasi of King Abdulaziz University, Saudi Arabia & Quaid-i-Azam University, Islamabad, Pakistan; Prof. Mubashar Mushtaq of Forman Christian College (A Chartered University), Pakistan & Quaid-i-Azam University, Pakistan; Prof. Onaiza Maqbool of Quaid-i-Azam University, Pakistan; Prof. Naif R. Aljohani of King Abdulaziz University, Saudi Arabia; Prof. Ali Daud of King Abdulaziz University, Saudi Arabia & International Islamic University, Pakistan; Prof. Jalal S. Alowibdi of University of Jeddah, Saudi Arabia; Prof. J.R. Cano of University of Jaén, Spain; Prof. S. García of University of Granada, Spain; and Prof. Ilyoung Chong of Hankuk University of Foreign Studies (HUFS), South Korea, which proposes a framework CommuniMents that enables us to identify the members of a community and measure the sentiments of the community for a particular event. CommuniMents uses automated snowball sampling to identify the members of a community, then fetches their published contents (specifically tweets), pre-processes the contents, and measures the sentiments of the community.

Section 3, "Tools and Technologies," explores the various tools and technologies used in the implementation of social media for various uses. This section begins with the chapter "Social Networking Data Analysis Tools and Services" by Prof. Gopal Krishna of Aryabhatt Knowledge University, India, which explains the methods and tools used for the analysis of the huge amount of data produced by social networks. This section ends with the chapter "Social Media as a Tool to Understand Behaviour on the Railways" by Prof. David Golightly of University of Nottingham, UK and Prof. Robert J. Houghton of Griffith University, Australia, which highlights important factors such as the broad range of issues covered by social media (not just disruption), the idiosyncrasies of individual train operators that need to be taken into account within social media analysis, and the time critical nature of information during disruption.

Section 4, "Utilization and Applications," describes how social media is used and applied in diverse industries for various technologies and applications. The opening chapter in this section, "Adoption of Web 2.0 Marketing: An Exploratory Study About the Nigerian SMEs," by Prof. Maryam Lawan Gwadabet of IT and Business School, Blue Sapphire E-Solutions ltd, Kano, Nigeria, explores the value which Web 2.0 marketing adds to the Nigerian SME's. The final chapter in this section, "An Evaluation of Toronto's Destination Image Through Tourist Generated Content on Twitter," by Profs. Hillary Clarke and Ahmed Hassanien of Edinburgh Napier University, Edinburgh, UK, evaluates the cognitive, affective, and conative components of destination image from the perception of tourists on social media.

Section 5, "Organizational and Social Implications," includes chapters discussing the impact of social media on society and shows the ways in which social media is used in different industries and how this impacts business. The first chapter, "An Empirical Evaluation of Adoption and Diffusion of New ICTs for Knowledge Sharing in IT Organizations," by Profs. Srinivasan Vaidyanathan and Sudarsanam S. Kidambi of VIT Business School, VIT University, Chennai, India, describes how knowledge is one of the most important assets in organizations which should be carefully managed and is continuously generated throughout an organization. The last chapter, "Fast-Fashion Meets Social Networking Users: Implications for International Marketing Strategy," by Prof. Tehreem Cheema of Clark University, USA, contributes to the existing literature on the influence of digital marketing on fast fashion, and it provides a number of pertinent marketing recommendations in regard to the practice of apparel retailers.

Section 6, "Managerial Impact," presents the uses of social media in industry and management practices. Starting this section is "Management and Marketing Practices of Social Media Firms" by Prof. Abdulaziz Alshubaily of University of Liverpool, Jeddah, Saudi Arabia, which examines the key variances in application and strategy between different social media management strategies and its effective marketing. Ending this section is "Tweeting About Business and Society: A Case Study of an Indian Woman CEO" by Profs. P. Vigneswara Ilavarasan, Ashish Kumar Rathore, and Nikhil Tuli of Indian Institute of Technology Delhi, India, which examines the social media content posted by a woman Indian chief executive officer (CEO) on Twitter.

Section 7, "Critical Issues and Challenges," highlights areas in which social media provides challenges for the industries utilizing it. Opening this final section is the chapter "E-Reputation in Web Entrepreneurship" by Profs. Sylvaine Castellano and Vincent Dutot of Paris School of Business, France, which gives to web-entrepreneurs the key elements in order to manage their e-reputation efficiently by presenting what e-reputation is, what its main components are, how to measure it, and what tools exist. The final chapter, "Ethical Dilemmas Associated With Social Network Advertisements," by Prof. Alan D. Smith of Robert Morris University, USA and Prof. Onyebuchi Felix Offodile of Kent State University, USA, explains the three hypotheses dealt with the interplay of online social networking, advertising effectiveness, gender and age trends, and remaining the interplay with positive comments of the use of the "like" function and its impacts on consumer behavior, as derived from the review of relevant operations literature and from applying the basic tenants of uses and gratification theory.

Although the primary organization of the contents in this multi-volume work is based on its seven sections, offering a progression of coverage of the important concepts, methodologies, technologies, applications, social issues, and emerging trends, the reader can also identify specific contents by utilizing the extensive indexing system listed at the end of each volume. As a comprehensive collection of research on the latest findings related to social media, the *Research Anthology on Strategies for Using Social Media as a Service and Tool in Business* provides researchers, instructors, social media managers, IT consultants, business managers, students, executives, practitioners, industry professionals, social media analysts, and all audiences with a complete understanding of the applications and impacts of social media. Given the vast number of issues concerning usage, failure, success, strategies, and applications of social media in modern industry, the *Research Anthology on Strategies for Using Social Media as a Service and Tool in Business* encompasses the most pertinent research on the applications, impacts, uses, and development of social media as a tool in business.

Chapter 46

The Emergence of Social Media and Its Impact on SME Performance

Ignatius Ekanem
Middlesex University, UK

Kayode Samuel Erukusin
Middlesex University, UK

ABSTRACT

This study aims to critically analyze the emergence of social media (SM) and its impact on Small- and Medium-sized Enterprise (SME) performance. This study employs a qualitative methodology for gathering information which has been able to provide clear insights, good quality, and rich data from the direct source. The evidence from this study suggests there is a relationship between the growth of a company's market share and the adoption of social media. There is also evidence that SM helps to improve sales figure, brand image and awareness. The findings in this study also suggest that SM helps to improve communication between companies and customers. The main implication of these findings is that SMEs should be encouraged to establish their presence on different social media networks in order to enhance their performance.

INTRODUCTION

In recent years, social media has increasingly attracted the attention of academics, researchers, practitioners, companies, and customers due to its affordability and the fact that it is a global tool (Aula, 2010). Social network sites can be defined as web-based applications on smart devices such as phones, tablets, iPads, lap tops and computers that allow users or organisations to create a public or semi-public profile about themselves, compile a list of users with whom they share a connection with in the case of individuals and a target market in the case of a company (Boyd & Ellison, 2008).

DOI: 10.4018/978-1-7998-9020-1.ch046

The introduction of social media tools such as Twitter, Bebo, YouTube, and Facebook. has been able to attract millions of users, many of which have integrated their daily practices with these sites and, therefore, giving businesses the chance of targeting and reaching millions of people through these sites with minimal cost. The first social network site launched in 1997 was called SixDegrees.com. This was followed by others such as AIM and ICQ, Hi5, MySpace, Friendster, and LinkedIn (Armelini & Villanuev, 2011). The various formats of social media include: photo sharing, blogs, wikis, social networks, video sharing, virtual worlds, social bookmarking sites and micro-blogging. These numerous formats have created a shift from the traditional one-way communication system according to Qualman (2012) and has changed, expanded, and broken the barrier of communication between companies and their respective consumers.

Social media is the latest invention which companies, consumers, businesses, Non-Government Organizations (NGOs) and government agencies are moving towards as it has the tendency to reach millions of people by just one click (Sunden, 2003). Sunden (2003) argues that despite the adoption of the Internet by companies and customers, SMEs are still struggling with how to effectively adopt and integrate social media into their business models and strategies.

The Internet has significantly changed the world and so has social media. In the early days of social media, MySpace was one of the emerging social media networks that supported celebrity activities in terms of promoting music and videos and it also made an impact on the entertainment world and businesses at large from music to movies. MySpace was later displaced by Facebook, which offered more features and benefits such as uploading photos, creating fan page, direct communication and interactions between celebrities and fans (Mandelli & Mari, 2012). The arrival of Facebook united millions of people around the globe, thereby giving organisations the insight and the realisation of being able to potentially capitalise on the fact that customers are just a few mouse clicks away (Mandelli & Mari, 2012).

The aim of this study is to critically analyse and assess the rapid emergence of social media and its impact on SME performance. Although performance indicators may vary between companies, depending on their priorities or performance criteria and may include profit, earning per share, and revenue per employee, but for the purposes of this study performance is defined as how well organisations are doing in terms of sales figures, market share and the value they deliver for customers and other stakeholders. In other words, to assess the true nature of a company's performance with reference to social media, the criteria used in this study include, market share, reduced cost and improved sales, and brand building and awareness.

The study also aims to fill the gap in this area of study, as most of the previous studies have used quantitative method to gather information from companies whilst this study employed a qualitative approach consisting of face-to-face interviews with companies which engage with social media. Past studies also focused on big or multinational companies whilst this study focuses on small and medium sized companies. The study explores three research questions:

RQ1: Is there a relationship between the growth of SMEs' market share and the adoption of social media?
RQ2: Do social media aid SMEs to improve sales figure?
RQ3: Do social media help SMEs build or improve brand image and awareness?

The chapter is structured as follows. Our conceptual discussion starts with a review of the extant literature regarding the concepts of the impact of social media on company performance. After describing our research context and methodology, we discuss the findings of the seven empirical case studies. We conclude with the implications and limitations of the study and suggest new avenues for future research.

LITERATURE CONTEXT

Social Media Evolution

Social media has numerous definitions and descriptions. According to Cohen (2011, p. 17), social media has been defined as: "Digital content and network based interaction that are developed and maintained by and between people". Whilst Kaplan and Haenlein (2010, p/22) defined social media as: "A group of Internet – based applications that build on the ideological and foundations of Web 2.0, and that allow the creation and exchange of User Generated Content".

In just a matter of a few years, the use of social media has become a sweeping cultural, social and economic phenomenon (Chui *et al.*, 2012). Hundreds of millions of people have adopted new behaviours using social media. They are now conducting social activities on the Internet, creating and joining virtual communities and organising political activities. All the rituals and rites in which individuals and groups in society participate – from personal events such as wedding or daily gossip, to global happenings such as the Arab Spring – play out on social platforms (Chui *et al.*, 2012). As a matter of fact, much behaviour that sociologists study – forming, maintaining, and breaking social bonds – are now occurring online (Ainin, Parveen, Moghavvvemi, Jaafar, & Shuib, 2015).

Social media have literally changed how millions of people live. People rely on their online social connections – often including friends and associates they have never met in person – for everything from advice on what movie to watch to positive reinforcement for behaviour modification (e.g., diet and weight loss) (Chui *et al.*, 2012). The report also points out that on social media, writers who have never been published and musicians who have never performed in public are now contributing to blogs and posting videos to YouTube. Social platforms have the potential to tap the great "cognitive surplus" of society by using leisure time for creating content and collaborating, rather than consuming (Ainin et al., 2015).

Businesses are changing their behaviour as well. The evolution of social media has been rapid with more than 80% of the *Fortune* 500 companies adopting some form of social media tool in order to connect and interact with their consumers (Naylor, Lamberton, & West, 2012). As a result of this rapid development, it has been reported that 87% of the *Fortune* Global 100 companies are using at least one social media platform to interact with their consumers (Burson-Marsteller, 2012). The same report has indicated that while Twitter remains the most popular platform for Global 100 companies, by far the largest growth in corporate social media use occurred on YouTube, which jumped from 39% to 79% in just one year. The report shows that companies have taken to social media in order to reach and deliver a better service to their customers considering the fact that social media are emerging to be the new trend both for businesses and customers.

About 1.5 billion people around the globe have an account on social networking sites, and almost one in five online hours is spent on social networks – increasingly via mobile devices (Chui *et al.*, 2012). The study indicates that by 2011, a total of 72% of companies surveyed reported using social media technologies in their businesses and 90% of those users reported that they are seeing benefits. The findings in this study suggest another encouraging opportunity available on social media for companies as far as increasing sales figure is concerned.

Non-profit organisations are also embracing the opportunities and the use of social media with 92% of their websites including at least one social media link (Mashable Social Media, 2011). Just as many companies are currently adopting the use of various social media platforms to develop stronger consumer-brand relationships, non-profit organisations are also realising that social media provides a great opportunity to engage and foster conversations and interactions. It is also relatively cheaper in terms of advertisements as compared to the traditional means such as radio or TV advertisements, billboards etc. (Mashable Social Media, 2011).

The Emergence of Social Media and Potential Growth in Company's Market Share

As these relatively emerging powerful social media technologies establish their presence, they have rapidly become popular amongst consumers faster than previous technologies; hence the reasoning behind why a lot of organisations are moving towards this trend (Bughin, Chui, & Manyika, 2012). According to Bughin *et al.* (2012), it took 13 years for commercial television to reach a mark of 50 million users or households and only three years for Internet service providers to reach same figures in terms of reaching 50 million subscribers. However, it took Facebook a year to reach the same 50 million mark while Twitter required nine months to sign on the same figures. This rapid development in such a short time has been associated and accelerated with the sweeping and fast growing cultural, economic and social changes adopted by consumers worldwide (Bughin *et al.*, 2012).

The rapid growth of social media represents potential opportunities for companies to grow and increase their market share as evidence shows that social media has been able to capture more subscribers in a shorter time compared to traditional means of commercial media such as television. Therefore, the technology may change the way companies conducts their businesses in terms of going digital in order to take advantage of the over 50 million subscribers that are already registered on social media. This exciting news will enable companies to formulate strategies of maintaining the subscribers on social media as opposed to stressing or finding ways of attracting new customers as a whole (Kirpatrick, 2011).

Over the past few years, social media has emerged as an integral part of many organisations communication strategies (Wilcox & KyungOk, 2012). As a result, over $2 billion was spent on social media advertising in 2012 and there is a forecast that indicates that the spending will increase to US$9 billion by 2015 (Chui *et al.*, 2012). This huge spending represents the fact that organisations are investing more into social media as it is a means to capture the attention of users globally at a cheaper rate as compared to TV or radio advertisements, billboards etc. (Chui *et al.*, 2012).

Moreover, the investments which organisations have made into social media has experienced growth with the likes of Facebook, Twitter, and YouTube and more importantly, these investments have also accounted for the growth in company's market share (Protalinski, 2011; Kirpatrick, 2011). With Facebook accounting for over 800 million active subscribers and over 175 million registered and consistent users on Twitter, social media has not only been integrated into a consumers' everyday life but most importantly increasing the chances of improved and increased sales activities, reduction of cost associated with marketing and advertising and finally enhancing the way companies connect with their consumers (Protalinski, 2011; Kirpatrick, 2011).

Social Media and the Potential to Increase Sales Figure

As stated earlier, research shows that although organisations have adopted social media technologies, they have only generated a small fraction of the potential value they can create (Bughin *et al.,* 2012). A study and an in-depth analysis on four major companies that represents almost 20 percent of the global industry sales also supports the fact that organisations are yet to maximize the full potential of social media and technologies (Chui et al., 2012). The same study suggests that social media platforms have the ability and business potential to unlock US$900 billion to US$1.3 trillion in value. This represents a massive value in monetary terms considering the fact that this is a study on just four business sectors (Bughin *et al.,* 2012). However, the study shows that two-thirds of this value creation lies in the improvement of communication and in partnership across and within enterprises (Bughin *et al.,* 2012).

These improvements have extended beyond the imagination and areas many companies have focused on in the past and are currently focusing on in their social media efforts (Chui *et al.,* 2012). Chui *et al.* (2012) also highlight that companies are currently focusing their efforts on connecting and interacting with consumers, deriving customer insights on marketing and product development, and providing customer service.

In terms of sales figures, the emergence of social media has captured the attention of organisations especially the sales people and managers of organisations and there is an increase in the role that social medial plays in buying process of consumers (Featherstonebaugh, 2010). At the same time, social media-supported transaction has emerged as an important means through which people buy and review products (Stephen & Toubia, 2010). Social media network has also become an integral facilitator of a closer relationship between consumer and an organisation (Tedeschi 2006). As a result, it is evident that organisations and individuals gain both social and professional benefits from social media (Tedeschi 2006).

Communication and Improved Brand Image and Awareness

One of the main advantages associated with social media is improved communication between a company and consumers (Chui *et al.*, 2012). However, Mandelli and Mari (2012) have also stressed that if social media is not properly managed, it can also be a disadvantage as illustrated by their Toyota case study. Toyota suffered from a wide spread negative media communication when consumers wrote bad reviews about the company on their social media platform during a recall of 3.8 million vehicles in September, 2009.

Toyota's sales decreased by 8.7% and its reputation was seriously damaged with the news spreading quickly around the world through traditional media and even more so through social media as it has more capacity to reach more people (Mandelli & Mari, 2012). The report indicates that the first tweets about Toyota appeared towards the end of 2009 when they recalled over four million of its cars, and by January, 2010 the buzz had skyrocketed from less than 100 posts to over 3,200 in just a matter of four days.

Even though Toyota's reputation was harmed due to the fast spread of information through social media during the recall of some of its vehicle, they acted immediately to rectify the problem. This was done by creating an "online newsroom" and a "social media response team" to organize and coordinate its communication strategies and processes. Toyota's social media expert response team was able to monitor and listen to their customer's complaints and was able to respond aggressively and effectively to the concerns and issues raised and most importantly in a timely manner (Rao, 2010).

Toyota's National Social Media and Marketing Integration Manager pointed out that social media is an important and critical element in their communication-mix. He further said that how a company "responds and reacts to those [social-media] conversations really has become perhaps the most important platform for dealing with a crisis like this" (Rao, 2010, p.11). In terms of tangible results, Toyota has successfully been able to grow it Facebook fan base by more that 10% and more importantly as Toyota's social media presence has grown, so has customer loyalty and sales compared to the initial stages of the recall (Mandelli & Mari, 2012).

RESEARCH CONTEXT AND METHODOLOGY

In this chapter we subscribe to a qualitative research methodology by employing a multiple case study approach which is in line with the suggestion that a qualitative approach is the appropriate methodology as the starting point in theory building (Gummesson, 2005; Yin, 2009). We agree with Merriam (1998) that a qualitative methodology is required when the research objective is to understand phenomena or interpret the uniqueness of an event. In practice, we undertook a comprehensive and critical review of the literature to identify gaps about the impact of social media on the performance of SMEs. This approach is a departure from "traditional" research in this area of study where quantitative measures are sought from a deductive approach. This study is novel for this reason.

We chose to use multiple case studies because extant literature indicates that it is an appropriate method for having a clear understanding of observable phenomena (Gummesson, 2005; Yin, 2009; Wison, 2010). The choice of seven firms was influenced by Eisenhardt (1989, p. 545) which argue that "...while there is no ideal number of cases to include in the sample, a number between 4 and 10 usually works well. With fewer than 4 cases it is often difficult to generate theory..., with more than 10 cases it quickly becomes difficult to cope with the complexity and volume of the data".

Research Approach

Although one of the researchers used to work for one of the case study firms, the rest were purposively selected through snowballing to provide data pertinent to understanding the research questions (Shaw, 1999). To be included in the study, the firms had to be in existence for five years; be independently owned; employ less than 250 employees; and must have adopted social media for at least a year. Archival documents (e.g., ledgers and financial statements) were also examined to see how use of social media has impacted on company performance over the years and case material built up on each company.

In-depth interviews and observations were conducted with business owners and sales managers of the seven case study companies. These interviews were exploratory in nature and each interview was between one hour and one and half hours. The interviews started by establishing initial boundaries for the study and moved on to provide details on company information such as age of the company, education, training and experience. The interview was also able to establish the objectives of the business, progress, challenges, and future plans.

These interviews were semi-structured and followed a detailed interview plan starting with icebreakers, giving room for flexibility, and a relaxed and comfortable atmosphere. The questions asked enabled the business owners and sales managers to touch on other areas, which eventually provided further insights into the study. The importance of conducting interviews with these companies is that it provided the opportunity to ask and unravel new clues, open up new dimension of problems and get a vivid and accurate answer directly from the source (Burgess, 1982).

Table 1. List of interviewees in each case

Case	Company Sector	Number of Respondents
1	Electronic cigarette	2
2	Drinks (Fruit smoothies and juice)	2
3	IT project management and branding	2
4	Photography	2
5	Catering (food and services)	2
6	Sales of phone gadgets	2
7	Training and development (IT courses and training)	2

Apart from asking questions, the researcher watched, listened, and learned because not all information is produced by informants responding to questions: they may be unsolicited (Ekanem, 2007). The presence of the researcher during interviews provided the opportunity for direct observations of some of the relevant behaviour, and such observations served as yet another source of evidence in the case study (Yin, 2009). They were carried out through interrupted involvement (Easterby-Smith *et al.*, 2008) which allowed access not only to what owner-managers said during the interview but also how they said it through symbolic language, including body language. Non-verbal language was found to be of equal importance as real feelings were constantly communicated, in addition to verbal language, in the language of behaviour.

Data Analysis

The qualitative data were collected and analysed using an inductive process of recording, tabulation, coding, and constantly comparing emerging codes and categories with data until meaningful ideas emerged (Yin, 2009; Ekanem, 2007). Categories were allowed to emerge according to the topics emphasised by each participant relating to the impact of social media on their business performance. The process of analysing the data began as soon as the researcher started collecting data. It was ongoing and inductive as the researcher was trying to make sense of the data collected (Shaw, 1999).

While interviews were recorded on tape for later verbatim transcription, data collected during observation were not recorded until the researcher had left the business premises and his notes were written up. The combination of interviews and observation provides triangulation because it enabled the researchers to explore respondents' accounts from different angles, thus offering a degree of verification. It also permitted detailed comparison between respondents' accounts and the identification of common features. The data being qualitative were convincing enough to allow a conceptual rather than descriptive analysis particularly focusing on how the respondents evaluated the impact of social media on their performance.

The data analysis utilised a set of techniques such as content analysis, pattern-matching, and explanation-building technique (Yin, 2009; Ekanem, 2007). Content analysis involved listening to and transcribing the tapes, reading the transcripts to list the features associated with the learning behaviour of each owner-manager and establishing categories which were then developed into systemic typology. These features included market shares, reduced cost and improved sales, brand building and awareness, and effective target markets.

Pattern-matching technique involved examining whether there were any interesting patterns and how the data related to what was expected on the basis of common sense or previous theory (Yin, 2009). The length of time the company has been on social media, which social media and its effectiveness were examined for each company and matched. This involved comparing sales figures, market share and costs of each participant case study company and the types of social media used. It also involved examining whether there were inconsistencies or contradictions between owner-managers' accounts. When a pattern was established, the transcriptions were read again in order to make further comparisons with different respondents to identify stable features (Shaw, 1999).

Explanation-building technique allowed series of linkages to be made and interpreted in the light of the explanations provided by each respondent on attractiveness of social media to customers and the re-lationship of such platforms to cost. Explanations were also collated about the impact of social media on company image and the correlation with sales figure. This technique allowed explanation of the findings to be built around the stories of business owners and sales manager. For example, body language and tone of voice on certain answers were put into consideration when analysing the information gathered from the interviews. The aim was to build a general explanation based on a cross-case analysis.

Table 2. Interview themes and guide related to associated research questions

Research Questions	Interview Themes
RQ1: Is there a relationship between the growth of SMEs' market share and the adoption of social media?	• General discussion on profile of business • Identify length of time company has been on social media • Identify which social media company has established presence
RQ2: Does social media aid SMEs to improve sales figure?	• Identify which social media is effective and efficient for the company • Identification of attractiveness of social media to customers • Identification of the relationship of social media with cost • Identification of correlation between social media and increase in sales figure
RQ3: Does social media help build or improve brand image and awareness?	• Assessment of impact of social media on image and awareness • Identification of how social media help in targeting primary customers

ANALYSIS AND DISCUSSION OF FINDINGS

The summarised findings from the qualitative methodology are presented from the empirical study subject to the constraints of presentation.

Exploring RQ1

In response to the first research question, it was found that the company's presence on social media has attracted customers and therefore increases their market share. The respondents in Companies 1, 4, 5, and 6 further went on to express their opinions of the innovation and ease with which social media adds to the growth of their company. They were all of the opinion that non-presence on social media would have made it more difficult for their companies to advertise their products and services to their consumers. For example, the Company 1 sales manager emphasized the following:

in as much as the type of products we sell are best shown to our customers on a face-to-face demonstrations, social media however, still helps to put our products out there and we would have struggled or found it harder to be able to reach our customers without the help of social media. Yes, our market share has increased substantially.

The above quote demonstrates the effectiveness of using social media to gain market share without which companies would struggle to reach customers. It also supports the concept of social dimensions of interactive advertisement (Sohn & Leckenby, 2002). The owner-manager of Company 4 commented, "not to be present on social media is neglecting the opportunity of growing and adding to one's consumer list or numbers". He explained that it is unwise not to subscribe or establish a company's presence on social media considering it is free to sign up.

However, he also pointed out that being on social media requires monitoring social media activities which can be time consuming. He emphasised, "Not monitoring these social media activities or replying to customer enquiries or complaints can lead to a company getting a bad reputation due to bad or negative review from customers and these reviews can be seen by all." Despite these potential negative setbacks, he is still enthusiastic about his company's presence on social media as it increases the chances of reaching more consumers thereby increasing market share. He also remarked in a jovial way that:

life is full of risk; business is fierce, and with social media, the challenges that come with it are no different especially with the opportunities it offers.

This means that the benefit of using social media far outweighs any challenges the company may face. However, the response from the owner-manager of Company 7 was different. He indicated that social media has not been able to add directly to its market share. The business owner explains that because of the type of business he runs which is organizing professional training courses in business analysis and project management, he tends to attract customers by word of mouth as opposed to social media. However, he stressed the fact that he receives many reviews on social media about his business, but 90% of his customers are mainly through word-of-mouth while the remaining 10% may be through social media.

All the companies in this study agreed there is more to gain than to lose in establishing their company's presence on social media as it enhances the opportunity to reach more customers. They also agreed it is inexpensive to be involved with social media compared to other means of advertising and marketing. When asked to identify which social media was more effective the owner-managers of the case study firms indicated that Facebook was more effective for them followed by Twitter and YouTube. This finding contradicts the literature which suggests YouTube to be more popular followed by Twitter for Global 100 companies (Burson-Marsteller, 2012).

Social media also facilitated transactions by adding purchasing function to a seller's social platform or by adding social features to an e-commerce site. For example, Company 6 allows visitors to sign in with their Facebook accounts to see what phones gadgets their friends liked and recommend some of them to certain friends, thus creating online parts of the social experience of going shopping with friends.

These findings have shown that social media is a viable environment for companies to do their business as the opportunity to reach and target consumers are realistic and achievable considering the fact that they are already on these platforms. As a result, this will save companies the advertising and marketing funds that can be used for other purposes. This provides an answer to research question 1 that there is a relationship between a company's performance in terms of growth and market share due to the adoption of social media. These findings support Bughin *et al.* (2012)'s argument that companies are yet to fully maximize the business potential and monetary value that social media offers.

Exploring RQ2

With respect to the second research question, a correlation between company's presence on social media and increase in sales figure was established. For example, the owner of Company 1 explained that although face-to-face demonstration of their product works for them,

Social media puts the company out there on a larger scale hence we are able to get our primary customers through social media after which we can go out to demonstrate our products to them.

In other words, social media is a major tool through which they contact customers before a product demonstration can take place. The respondent in Company 5 explained that 70% of its customers get to know about her business through the company's presence on social media. She emphasized: "This definitely adds to and increases the company's sales figure." She stressed that social media has really helped her business and as a result has experienced an increase in both customers and sales figure. She said the best thing about social media for her is the fact that "it is totally free."

The owner-manager of Company 4 explained that considering his type of business which is photography, social media has been a perfect tool. He described it as a "match made in heaven." The business owner said social media has been able to help show case his photographic skills and as a result it has been able to attract a lot of customers, thus increasing his company's sales figure.

The body language of the owner-managers of Companies 4 and 5 (beaming with smiles and excitement) also suggested that social media has proved to be a success for their business. They were also excited about the technology due to the fact that they spend minimal amounts on marketing and advertising yet they still get through to their primary targets. The response from Company 7, however, does not show a direct relationship between social media advertising and increase in sales figure because social media does not directly add to the company's market share as explained earlier.

Again with excitement and pride, the owner-manager of Companies 2, 4, and 6 indicated that they use social media to improve customer service in the their organisations, thus taking some of the work usually performed on the phone (e.g., answering routine questions about product features). When asked how this was done, the owner-manager of Company 6 responded:

We set up a social platform as a dedicated customer service channel. We recruit enthusiastic customers to be featured on our company home page and they help answer each other's questions. Believe you me, it is very effective.

The books of the case study companies were examined to see how the use of social media actually affected sales figures and increased the number of customers. There was evidence of huge increase in both sales figures and number of customers compared to the period when their presence was not established on social media. The finding revealed that more than a third of consumer spending was influenced by social shopping and highlighted in the company's annual report.

The result suggests the enormous business opportunities available to companies especially with the growth of sales figures. Companies can specifically target part of their resources on consumers that have signed on to their service or product page(s). With customers signed on to company pages, it saves time and increases the chances of sales figure soaring high. Again, this is another positive revelation for companies as the findings suggest that customers are visiting their pages to read more about the company and obtain information on their products and services.

It has also been demonstrated by Chui et al. (2012) that the information they obtain from social media platforms has influenced customers' decision to buy a product or use a service. Social media multiply the potential sources of information about demand, adding another level of granularity to improve distribution efficiency and responsiveness. Based on information shared on social networks by customers or people in the distribution network (e.g., retail store staff), suppliers were able to respond to localised variations in demand and detect stock-outs earlier. Companies were also able to use information derived from social platform to improve inventory control. The findings in this study suggest another encouraging opportunity available on social media for companies as far as increasing sales figure as indication of performance is concerned.

Exploring RQ3

From the analysis of the seven cases, we found that social media helps to develop or improve brand image and awareness which enhance a high level of performance. For example, the owner of Company 3 emphasized that being on social media has helped in promoting his events and building his brand image from the scratch. He reflected:

I can't really imagine how I would have gone about building my brand considering the fierce business environment and the competition it faces.

The above quote means that social media has a significant impact on image and awareness. Similarly, the owner of Company 4 explained that social media has helped to increase his brand awareness, but warned, "one has to be careful with the type of services it offers because one bad review from a customer can easily be seen by all and this could be a nightmare for any company as there is nothing worse than a bad reputation for any company."

Company 1 sales manager's body language of excitement also demonstrated the positive impact of social media on their brand image and awareness. An examination of these companies' social media platforms confirmed the significance of this social technology in creating brand image and awareness.

From the findings it is evident that social media offer a way to achieve efficient distribution of messages (i.e., communicate directly with customers at very low costs and with highly targeted messages and content, such as special pricing or other promotions for certain customers and markets). They offer more ways to create more engagements with customers e.g. to promote certain products through interactive media. They were also used to build customer communities, which were tapped for marketing and product development. In this role, social media helps customers to communicate with one another in a way in which companies actively or passively participate.

Social media also give the case study firms a way to listen to customer conversation, identify customer service issues, and act on them before they harm sales or reputations. For example, the owner of Company 6 spoke of a customer who used his twitter account to complain about one of their products not being of a merchantable quality and the company responded immediately with tweets of its own, apologising and offering to refund to the customer, thereby defusing what could have become a much more negative situation.

The literature (e.g. Chui *et al.,* 2012) indicates that a huge number of consumers go on social media sites or platforms to read reviews about products or services before making a buying decision. This could be a positive or a negative attribute for a company. The positive feature about customers reading reviews before making a buying decision will definitely work for a company that does what it has advertised, such as providing after-sale care or exceptional customer service. This helps to increase their brand image or improve their reputation and possibly increase their customer base due to positive reviews written by other customers that have used the company's products or services.

On the other hand, one bad review could ruin a company's reputation. As seen earlier in the literature review with the case study of Toyota, bad reviews will dent a company's reputation regardless of how long they have maintained that reputation. In light of this information, it is important for companies to monitor their reputation and probably respond to every customer enquiry or issues as Toyota did when repairing their reputation and as Company 6 did when a customer complained about the quality of one of its product.

CONCLUSION

The aim of this study was to analyse the impact of social media on SME performance using case studies, interviews, and observation. The evidence from this study suggests there is a relationship between the growth of a company's market share and the adoption of social media, resulting in high performance. There is also evidence that social media aids or improves sales figure, brand image and awareness, which lead to high performance. The findings in this study also suggest that social media helps to improve communication between companies and customers, leading to increased performance. The findings also confirm the untapped value creation potential of social media within SMEs (Chui *et al.*, 2012).

As demonstrated in this study, social media has been used to gather insights about products and brands, opinions, about competitors and perceptions of market segments. These insights have been used as inputs for product requirements and design, advertising campaigns, pricing, packaging and other marketing and product development activities with significant impact on firms' performance.

The implications of these findings are threefold: First, SMEs should be encouraged to establish their presence on different social media networks in order to enhance their performance. Therefore, it can be suggested that business owners should adopt a learning approach (i.e., being ready to experiment with new things and adapting as they learn from experience of what works and what does not work). The second implication of the study is for business owners to endeavour to maintain data security without limiting the ways in which social media can be used. One way of maintaining security is to prevent unauthorised disclosure of confidential information through social media. The third implication of this study is for both business owners and policy makers to ensure that personal and property rights are protected in online communities without undermining the essential strength of social media.

This study makes contribution to the growing body of literature on the impact of social media on companies' performance. It also sheds lights on the different aspects of effects of social media such as market share, reduced cost and improved sales, brand building and awareness. The qualitative methodology adopted for gathering information has provided clear insights, good quality and rich data from the business owners themselves, thereby leading to a better understanding and knowledge of SME's strategy and attitude to social media as opposed to a quantitative means of collecting data.

The qualitative methodology is unique in terms of the combination of the different threads such as in-depth, semi-structured interviews and direct observation which are lacking in any single method. The direct observation allowed the researcher to explore the differences between what the participants said and how they said it. The approach is novel as it enabled the researcher to get beyond a one-dimensional picture by allowing different shades of meaning to be captured and creating a solid foundation for drawing valid conclusions about the impact of social media on SME performance.

The study has several limitations which suggest the implications for further research. The major limitation of the study is the extent to which the study can be generalised to wider population of small firms since it was based on only seven case studies drawn from different sectors, which was not randomly selected. Therefore, a large-scale study of businesses would be necessary to test the research results to a wider, less heterogeneous population.

REFERENCES

Ainin, S., Parveen, F., Moghavavvemi, S., Jaafar, N. I., & Shuib, N. L. (2015). Factors influencing the use of social media by SMEs and its performance outcomes. *Industrial Management & Data Systems*, *115*(3), 1–25. doi:10.1108/IMDS-07-2014-0205

Armelini, G., & Villanuev, A. (2011). Adding Social Media to the Marketing Mix. *IESE Insight*, *9*(9), 29–36. doi:10.15581/002.ART-1968

Aula, P. (2010). Social media, reputation risk and ambient publicity management. *Strategy and Leadership*, *38*(6), 43–49. doi:10.1108/10878571011088069

Boyd, D., & Ellison, N. (2008). Social Network Sites: Definition, History, and Scholarship. *Journal of Computer-Mediated Communication*, *13*(1), 210–230. doi:10.1111/j.1083-6101.2007.00393.x

Bughin, J., Chui, M., & Manyika, J. (2012). Capturing business value with social technologies. *The McKinsey Quarterly*, *4*, 72–80.

Burgess, R. (1982). *Field Research: A Source Book and Field Manual*. London: Allen and Unwin. doi:10.4324/9780203379998

Burson-Marsteller. (2012). *Global Social Media check-up*. Retrieved on May 12, 2012, from: http://www.burson-marsteller.eu/innovation-insights/global-social-media-studies

Chui, M., Manyika, J., Bughin, J., Dobbs, R., Roxburgh, C., Saaazin, H., ... Westergren, M. (2012, July). *The Social Economy: Unlocking value and productivity through social technologies*. McKinsey Global Institute.

Cohen, H. (2011). *30 Social Media Definitions.* Retrieved on July 17, 2013, from: http://heidicohen. com/social-media-definition/

Easterby-Smith, M., Thorpe, R., & Jackson, P. R. (2008). *Management Research.* London: Sage Publications.

Eisenhardt, K. M. (1989). Building Theories from Case Study Research. *Academy of Management Review, 14*(4), 532–550.

Ekanem, I. (2007). Insider Accounts: A qualitative research method for small firms. *Journal of Small Business and Enterprise Development, 14*(1), 105–117. doi:10.1108/14626000710727926

Featherstonebaugh, B. (2010). *The Future of Selling: It's Social.* Retrieved on July 17, 2013, from http://:www.forbes.com/2010/12/03/future-of-selling-leadership-sales-leader-shipogilvyone.html

Gummesson, E. (2005). Qualitative research on marketing: Road-map for a wilderness of complexity and unpredictability. *European Journal of Marketing, 39*(3/4), 309–327. doi:10.1108/03090560510581791

Kaplan, A. M., & Haenlein, M. (2010). Users of the World, Unite! The Challenges and Opportunities of Social Media. *Business Horizons, 53*(1), 59–68. doi:10.1016/j.bushor.2009.09.003

Kirpatrick, M. (2011). *Twitter confirms it has passed 200 million accounts, 70% of traffic now international.* Retrieved on July 20, 2013, from: http://www.readwriteweb.com/archives/twitter_confirms_it_has_passed_200_million_account.php

Mandelli, A., & Mari, A. (2012). The relationship between social media conversations and reputation during a crisis: The Toyota case. *International Journal Of Management Cases, 14*(1), 456–489. doi:10.5848/APBJ.2012.00041

Marriam, S. B. (1998). *Qualitative Research and Case Study Applications in Education. Revised and Expanded from Case Study Research in Education.* San Francisco: Jossey-Bass.

Mashable Social Media. (2011). *How non- profits are using social media.* Retrieved on July 18, 2013, from: http://www.mashable.com/2011/10/14/how-non-profits-use-social-media/

Naylor, R., Lamberton, C., & West, P. (2012). Beyond the like button: The impact of mere virtual presence on brand evaluations and purchase intentions in social media setting. *Journal of Marketing, 76*(6), 105–120. doi:10.1509/jm.11.0105

Protalinski, E. (2011). *Facebook is not 20 times the size of Google+; it's even bigger* [WWW document]. Retrieved on July 20, 2013, from: http://www.zdnet.com/blog/facebook/facebook-is-not-20-times-the-size-of-google- its-even-bigger/4654

Qualman, E. (2012). *Socialnomics: How Social Media Transforms the Way We Live and Do Business.* John Wiley & Sons.

Rao, L. (2010). *Toyota turns to twitter to repair its image.* Retrieved on July 18, 2013, from: http://techcrunch.com/2010/03/02/toyota-turns-to-twitter-to-repair-its-image/

Shaw, E. (1999). A guide to the qualitative research process: Evidence from a small firm study. *Qualitative Market Research: An International Journal, 2*(2), 59–70. doi:10.1108/13522759910269973

Sohn, D., & Leckenby, J. D. (2002). Social dimensions of interactive advertising, *Proceedings of the Annual Conference of the American Academy of Advertising.*

Stephen, A. T., & Toubia, O. (2010). Deriving Value from Social Commerce Networks. *JMR, Journal of Marketing Research, 47*(2), 215–228. doi:10.1509/jmkr.47.2.215

Sunden, J. (2003). *Material Virtualities.* New York: Peter Lang.

Tedeschi, B. (2006). Like Shopping? Social Networking? Try Social Shopping. *New York Times.* Retrieved on July 20, 2013, from: http://www.nytimes.com/2006/09/11/technology/11ecom

Wilcox, G. & KyungOk, K. (2012). Multivariate time series use for the measurement of social media effects. *Marketing Management Journal, 22*(2), 90–101.

Wilson, J. (2010). *Essentials of Business Research: A Guide to Doing Your Research Project.* London: Sage Publications.

Yin, R. (2009). *Case Study Research: Design and Methods.* London: Sage.

This research was previously published in Technological Integration as a Catalyst for Industrial Development and Economic Growth; pages 132-150, copyright year 2017 by Business Science Reference (an imprint of IGI Global).

Chapter 47
Exploring the Relationship Between Social Media and Social Influence

Ali Usman
University of the West of Scotland, UK

Sebastian Okafor
University of Cumbria, UK

ABSTRACT

Online behavioral tailoring has become an integral part of online marketing strategies. Contemporary marketers increasingly seek to create an influential environment on social media to empower online users to participate in online brand communities. By interacting in this way, online communities hosted by brands marketers can enhance the nature of the complex interactions that occur amongst those that participate. Such online interactions lead to three different types of social influence compliance, internalization, and identity, which develop the consumers' purchase intentions. This chapter explains how the social influence support the change in beliefs, attitude, and intentions of the online consumers in the user-generated social media networking sites (SNSs). Furthermore, it discusses the functional impact of such online social influence that enables companies to understand the perceptions and needs of online users making sense of how multiple levels of social influence phenomenon on social media impact on consumers purchase intentions.

INTRODUCTION

The transition from traditional modes of marketing to a consumer-centric marketing approach in B2C environments has had an explicit impact on the psychological behaviours of consumers. Such developments have captured the attention of marketers and academic researchers (Michaelidou et al., 2011). The shift to an integrated marketing communication paradigm from traditional media to internet based multi-channel marketing has revolutionised the concept of integrated marketing communication (Huang

DOI: 10.4018/978-1-7998-9020-1.ch047

& Benyoucef, 2013). Furthermore, the continuous development of online media from computer mediated marketing applications to more sophisticated Web 2.0-based social media has dramatically transformed the purchase behaviours of online users by enhancing the speed of communications between businesses and consumers and reducing the costs associated with doing so (Tsai & Men, 2013). The development of social media has become one of the prime tools of online marketing, and this has captured the attention of stakeholders due to its significant impact on promotional communications between businesses and consumers, as well as amongst consumers (Ansarin & Ozuem, 2014). However, the empirical efforts for online consumers behavioural modelling on social media could result in its greater acceptability, making it a real-time online marketing tool for transforming online users into potential customers through change of behaviour via valuable information exchange. The extent to which social media and the development of behavioural modelling based on networked online social interactions can determine changes to purchase intentions and decision making behaviour lacks empirical understanding (Zhu & Chen, 2015). The aim of this chapter is to explain recent changes in the beliefs, opinions, attitudes and intentions of individuals as a result of complex heterogenic online social interactions among online users. Such interactions take place to expedite exchange information. They are valued for facilitating collaborative learning and circulating vital information about products and services (Lim & Heide, 2015). Further, this chapter also reveals how group-based online social interactions develop multiple levels of social influence to create behavioural uniformity among members of online social groups based on social influence.

The development of appropriate marketing and communication strategy on the basis of impartial changes to integrated marketing communication helps businesses to establish a direct connection with end-consumers at relatively low cost, and in an efficient timely manner. Such exchanges can socially influence the purchase behaviour of online users (Bhatli & Mehri, 2015). Businesses can exert significant influence by taking advantage of interactions between online members who join communities to satisfy a need to belong. This is achieved when they associate themselves with certain brand communities to feel socially connected and recognised after interacting with similar, like-minded online users (Bamberg et al., 2007; Zhang et al., 2015). Such an enhanced sense of belonging increases the desire of online users to become part of an online brand community. It also significantly increases the level of trust that exists between online users in financial services and enhances interactions and information sharing between group members who engage with financial services brands. Such online users feel more valued and recognised when associating with certain brands, and this is a direct result of engagement which significantly influences purchase intentions (Zhou, 2011).

Social media is facilitated by Web 2.0 technologies and is based on user-generated content. This is also known as user-generated media since it enables active participation amongst online users allowing them to communicate with, and respond to, promotional content that they interact with on social media (Nelson-Field et al. 2012). User-generated content has changed the layout of social media which helps in shaping the behaviour of customers by making social media a prevalent information source which, as a result, creates positive Electronic Word of Mouth (EWOM) (Ozuem et al. 2015). User-generated media has transformed communication tools and strategies in such a way as to control information and the speed of information that is exchanged. Such control rests with consumers rather than with marketing experts (Gallaugher & Ransbotham, 2010). This phenomenon not only supports two-way communication between consumers and businesses, but also transforms online users into active participants rather than passive recipients of promotional communications based on traditional models of media. For example, on a Social Networking Site (SNS) an online user can actively express his or her views at an individual level or in a group setting. They can circulate messages and evaluate information on the basis of informational exchanges and knowledge sharing. The use of social networking sites for business has greatly enhanced the adaptability of social media as a vital source of promoting products and services and has transformed the behaviour of consumers through education. In this way, online social media users gain more information and knowledge through socialisation.

THEORETICAL CONTEXT

Most previous researchers have approached social media as a vital tool for online marketing communications due to its clear significance within marketing discussions (Holsapple et al., 2018; Yankova & Ozuem, 2014; Brengarth & Mujic, 2016). However, a widely recognised empirically-based definition of social media is still lacking in academic literature. The term social media is defined as the collection of internet-based applications purposely built for the exchange and creation of digital content within the technological foundations of Web 2.0 (Kaplan & Haenlein, 2010). Such technologies are built with the intention of helping companies engage in two-way communications with customers, such as listening to customers and responding appropriately.

Furthermore, Safko & Brake (2009,p.6) defined social media in their research as:

Activities, practices and behaviour among communities of people who gather online to share information knowledge, and opinions using conversational media. Conversational media are Web-based applications that make it possible to create and easily transmit content in the form of words, pictures, videos, and audios.

Constantinides & Fountain (2008) interpret the term social media as a synonym for Web 2.0, suggesting both terms can be used interchangeably. Cox et al. (2008), suggest the term social media means "user-generated content websites" that explain and promote digital content produced by users in the form of podcasts and blogs. Endress (2014) defines social media as social software that enables online users to undertake social networking, including photo sharing, blogging and instant messaging. Social media facilitates instant communication, providing an easy interface for the sharing of digital information to help online users to achieve quick access by removing the barriers to, and inherent time constraints of, traditional media (Azemi & Ozuem, 2014). Social media is a hub and can be simply described as a starting point for acquiring intelligence on the buying behaviour of consumers using social media marketing strategies (Stokinger & Ozuem, 2014). A variety of explanations and definitions have been propounded by various scholars but a universally accepted definition of social media is unavailable in the academic world. The issue of how these scholars have contributed to social media marketing and explained the phenomenon of social media and its implications for social media marketing has been investigated by a number of key authors in the field of digital marketing (Helal & Ozuem, 2017; Hlebec et al., 2015; Carr et al., 2016).

Developments in technology have enabled individuals to interact online and exchange communications through computer mediated online social media. Online social media of the type developed across Web 2.0-based technologies offers online users the ability to communicate and instantly exchange information through multiple forms of social media social networks, social bookmarking and blogs (Holsapple et al., 2018). Online social media has facilitated joint learning through collaboration and social networking which has enabled millions of online individuals to enhance their communication within their social circles. Such users have also been able to communicate promotional and marketing messages to entire populations of online consumers on a consumer-to-consumer communication exchange basis (Muñiz & Schau, 2007). Compared with traditional media and the integrated marketing communication paradigm, new computer-mediated online social media have empowered consumers to communicate, not just amongst themselves, but with companies as well (Dolan & Goodman, 2017). This type of online social communication and the speedy exchange between members of the online platforms it supports strengthens participation by connecting populations of online members. This significantly impacts on their behaviour and mindset (Sinha et al., 2012).

Online social media enables the creation, alteration and modification of user-generated content that is publicly available to online consumers and end-users (Jiang et al. 2009; Herget & Mader, 2009; Litvin et al. 2008). The development of internet-based information technologies and communications platforms facilitated by Web 2.0-based technologies has enabled, not just the publication of user-generated content on social media, but it has also dramatically improved the aesthetics of websites (Brengarth & Mujic, 2016). Depending on the usage and influence of the associated technologies, Web 2.0 offers a unique technological set-up to enhance the use of online applications developed with and based on these technologies. For example, enhancing social networking amongst individuals, collaborative learning and the rapid exchange of information facilitates a form of two-way communication which not only enables online users to receive user-generated content-based messages, but also enables such users to respond to and interact with the sender at the same time (Hearn et al., 2009). This further enables online consumers to potentially engage in communication, information sharing and empowerment in anticipation of some kind of economic exchange between the companies involved and consumers in the form of consumer purchase intentions (Sinha et al., 2012; Zhu et al., 2016). Li & Bernoff (2008) explained that the significance and outcome of online social media from a business perspective differs considerably from the traditional communication paradigm where marketers have been able to control promotional content. This high degree of contrast has implications for businesses in multiple dimensions. First, it allows marketers to communicate promotional content to a wide audience on social media quicker than ever before. Secondly it has supported the efficiency of an integrated marketing communications strategy through cost reduction based on inexpensive, direct engagement and communication with clients on the basis of two-way communication. This is achieved with greater efficiency and a sharper focus greater than any other integrated marketing communication tool (VanMeter et al., 2015; Felix et al., 2017).

Within the context of social media, marketing is understood to be planned and based on an online, inbound consumer-centric strategy that uses social media networking sites as tools to facilitate online interactions and the consumption of user-generated content in the form of blogs, micro-blogs, product ratings, product reviews, group discussions and social book-marking. This creates a two-way communication process between marketers and online consumers (Dang et al. 2014; Bojārs et al. 2008). Social media marketing has been widely used in the context of integrated marketing communications through social networking. Such marketing is considered to be discrete and different from its long-standing existence in the field of sociology (Qi et al., 2018). The term 'social network' is a subset of online communities, platforms, or group pages where users interact and share their ideas and choices with others (Jansen et al., 2009). It is important to note that the terms 'social media' and 'social networking sites' cannot be used interchangeably, as the former is a broader term compared with the latter, which is a component of 'social networking sites'.

Chan & Guillet (2011, p. 347) define Social Media Marketing (SMM) as

A set of Internet-based applications that enable interaction, communication, collaboration of user-generated content and hence, sharing of information such as ideas, thoughts, content, and relationships.

Understanding social media marketing as a platform for the promotion and communication of products and services on social networking sites through user-generated content using Web 2.0 provides a fundamental basis upon which to establish two-way conversation and communications between companies and customers (Kaplan & Haenlein, 2010). User-generated content is the material generated by online members of social media websites, comprising information in the form of blogs, product reviews, videos, micro blogs and informational content, based on experiences of products. Examples include Facebook and YouTube. Cox et al. (2008), note that online users interact with online social media in three ways i.e.: i) by consuming social media, ii) by participating in social media and iii) by producing social media content. Consuming social media involves a range of activities such as using social media to read information and view interactive content without participating in it. Participation concerns user-to-user and user-to-content interactions in which users share their personal experiences about content use. They share content socially and evaluate content on the basis of its value proposition to the public (Jia et al., 2018). Finally, producing user-generated content entails the creation, modification and publication of content generated by a user on social media, such as pictures, videos or podcasts. Such user-generated content on social media sites has drawn the attention of many customers and it plays a significant role in modifying perceptions of, and awareness about, products and services (Füller, 2006).

Malthouse et al. (2013), state that since social media is all about users sharing user-generated content for information and knowledge-sharing purposes, the creation of such content on social media could limit a company's control over its promotional and advertising messages which are accessible to the general public. Such user-generated content and information exchange activities cannot be isolated and limited to a certain group of people on social media, as it is viewed in multiple contexts on social media (Lee, 2018). Thus, whenever a company designs a promotional campaign to target certain users with specific needs, this phenomenon necessarily signifies that the campaign will hit users on social media who are not specifically targeted (Arrigo, 2014). In real-time practice it is almost impossible for organisations to limit the audience of a marketing promotional campaign based on specific needs and requirements (Hajli, 2015). In almost every case, whenever a company launches a promotional campaign directed at a certain group of specific users on social media with defined needs, such promotions must make provision for the high probability of users sharing such advertising information with fellow online social media users regardless of whether they share their specific needs and/or requirements with others. This phenomenon has created a positive impact on viral marketing as part of social media marketing strategies because a considerable audience can be reached with promotional advertisements, encouraging information-sharing amongst social media members (Miller & Lammas, 2010)

Social media explicitly emphasises user-generated communication between consumers and consumers and companies. The importance of web-based technologies, such as Web 2.0, functions is based on the principle of user-generated content and the instant creation and sharing of content amongst communities and groups (Harrysson et al. 2012). The transition of marketing strategies from a company-centric matrix has influenced the target audiences of marketing strategies with the elaboration of the mechanism of online value creation (Lee, 2018). The phenomenon of two-way communications between users, and users and marketers as a function of user-generated content has increased the scope of marketing online due to its extensive influence and ability to target wide audiences within a short time span (Hajli, 2015). Broadly, users participate in value creation by creating innovative activities on the social medium. The vital aspect of users' innovation in terms of online content by adding value to it stems from online engagement with content, where users actively participate in value addition to the online content of promotional campaigns (Weinberg & Pehlivan, 2011). Such a process of adding value can include value creation in the context of a company's promotional campaign achieved when consumers share their personal experiences (Ozuem & Tan, 2014). In so doing they demonstrate loyalty to a certain brand by helping other online users with product evaluation, generating new ideas or sharing information on specific problems (Scott, 2012). Such a process of content modification by users on behalf of the company on social media helps the company to reach increasing numbers of potential customers online. To achieve this they harness contributions made by online users and incorporate value into their promotional campaigns, subsequently changing the online behaviour of consumers (Qualman, 2009). Technological developments in social media fit with the current marketing landscape and challenge the usefulness of traditional media as an influencing agent that can shape consumer behaviour.

Marketers use this phenomenon as a cushion for their online marketing strategies by purposely engaging online users in promotional content, and by further empowering them to share information and knowledge with fellow-users in order to achieve a maximum population of online users exposed to promotional content (Hajili, 2015). However, the limitations related to social media marketing can impose restrictions on the use of social media for marketing purposes. Predominantly, there are two major perspectives that clearly indicate the limitations of social media. The first factor defines the limitations of the social medium on a platform in terms of information exchange and knowledge-sharing, which completely overlook self-expression amongst users. The second factor indicates a limitation of social media as an online social interaction platform where information exchange, knowledge-sharing and online interactions with content are exchanged in a marketing environment inextricably connected to consumption-related activities (Iankova et al. 2018). On social media, social influence stems from social interactions which triggers the development of new attitudes and intentions due to significant changes to consumer behaviour and makes social media an intensely valuable medium for marketing in the current business environment (Qualman, 2009). With particular reference to the emergence of social media websites, user-generated content has undergone a tremendous development whereby online members not only consume but create content and share it on social media. This kind of creation of digital content on social media, and the concurrent consumption of user-generated content has created the phenomenon of "prosumers"; a term used to describe the members of online media who create and at the same time consume digital content (Laestadius & Wahl, 2017). Fuchs (2010) describes the mechanism of prosumers as a process that merges the creation and consumption of user-generated content simultaneously on social media. Such prosumers are both the creators and consumers of content on social media.

Online users interact with social media in multiple ways. For example, the way users participate in the content creation process as active consumers, and the way they act as passive consumers consuming such online content is significant. So too is the process of users acting as facilitators in sharing content and information with fellow-users online. The interactive motive of online users on social media is categorised into two major groups based on the nature of the interaction. The first view holds that online social interactions are based on rational motivation, for example knowledge-sharing and/or advocacy. Similarly, the second view approaches online user interactions as an emotional motivation. An example might be developing social networking by interacting with more social media members and expressing personal views, thereby gaining confidence and identity (Li et al., 2017). Further, the integration of online user interactions combined with complex internet tools and technologies creates electronic word-of-mouth (Balaji et al., 2016). However, this phenomenon is limited in the sense that, when confronted with such an output on certain occasions due to extensive overloading of information, online users face difficulty in choosing the promotional campaign they would like to participate in. In the majority of cases, consumers are drawn to those companies that are most familiar to them.

Contemporary academic research has mainly focused on consumer responses to social media marketing, although significant research has yet to be undertaken regarding the optimisation of social media, which would significantly explain how firms attain greater numbers of customers with rapid customer responses using social networking websites as a trade platform (Chong et al., 2018). Hoffman & Novak (1997) first used the term 'digital medium' as a platform for online marketing to sell goods and services. They used the term "hyper-mediated computer environments" to explain the behavioural targeting of consumers by firms as the root cause of the origin of digital media. They suggested that marketing trends are shifting, with more emphasis on the digital-based marketing of products and services. They affirmed that the traditional communication paradigm, fundamentally based on the traditional promotional mix strategies of integrated marketing communications strategies, must be replaced with a new communication paradigm which explicitly relies on computer-mediated environments and platforms. These must include all forms of social media and potential tools for creating an IMC strategy in online B2C marketing settings (Ozuem et al., 2016). For example, in a computer-mediated environment and in terms of a technological setup, web pages hold key information and are composed of banners and other forms of advertising through which marketers reach customers by tailoring their behaviour when a customer clicks on their details and passes on their information (Chang & Wang, 2008).

Most importantly, this phenomenon speaks to the specific manner of change that impacts on digital searches and online search decision aids in computer-mediated environments (Wu & Chang, 2005). Hoffman *et al.*, (2013) indicate that the development of such computer-mediated environments, with the explicit development of social media, is an evolution of the type of electronic commerce that highlights the impact of social media and social networking on online marketing. This creates a new dimension of online social media marketing called 'social commerce'. Such social commerce is a notable platform for providing online shopping information with the help of social media and social networking sites by engaging the maximum possible number of customers with social network ties, enabling them at the same time to develop a social identity by sharing, recommending, and discovering online financial services information (Vemuri, 2010; Sciglipaglia & Ely, 2006). Such an adaptive process based on technologies elicits the true capabilities of firms in computer mediated environments and creates value for customers in the retail banking industry (Walsh et al. 2004).

Hau & Kim (2011) explained that the concept of social media marketing became operational in the middle of the last decade, when the growing use of these social networking sites made them an important platform for online trade (Sashi, 2012). This created a change for consumers and led them to rely more on online shopping using social media and social networking sites. The most popular of this social networking and social media sites are Facebook, Twitter or Instagram, YouTube & LinkedIn. Chan & Ngai (2011), argue that the motivation of users and their interactions with online promotional messages depends on their perceptions of online advertising and the participation of consumers in online communities. This takes place through discussion and the sharing of advertised information with peers on social networks. This also includes the self-disclosure of behaviour and attitudes in online social communities amongst the participants of a social group (Ouirdi et al. 2015; Chen & Li, 2017). Such self-disclosure and intentional involvement in social media, and engagement with communication, can influence buying decisions (Lin & Utz, 2017). This self-disclosure by consumers on social media takes place in various forms of online media where users create content and share it. The nature of how this takes place depends on their level of engagement and interactivity. This creates a form of social capital based on personal or mutual interactions on social media. It creates common knowledge in relation to consumer-to-consumer information sharing and it encourages discussions and personal experiences through interactions and the sharing of promotional messages. This helps marketers to communicate with online clients using a B2C approach (Iankova et al., 2018). Chang & Zhu (2011) found that individual, personal interactions on any social medium define the personality influences and so-called self- presentation of users. In this way, users share their thoughts, feelings and ideas and are motivated to help develop a relationship and, crucially, an identity, in social circles on social media. Kaplan & Haenlein (2010) classified such individual self-presentation and disclosure which triggers a level of engagement with online users on social media as a form of social media based on individual social presence which is shaped by various levels of self-disclosure and self-presentation.

DEVELOPMENT OF SOCIAL MEDIA

To comprehensively understand the concept of social media, it is first essential to understand the background of its development and the wider implications of Web 2.0, since the concepts of social media and Web 2.0 are closely related and are often used in the same context (Berthon et al. 2012). The term Web 2.0, which is used to describe a subset of the internet, comprises websites on the internet which operate on the principle of user-generated content. These sites facilitate users on the internet and help them to actively participate in altering and editing web content for ease of use (Kang, 2016). Web 2.0 is the composition of images, graphics and texts on the internet based on user-generated content (Ho & Chang, 2010). Jansen *et al.* (2009) argue that Web 2.0 has revolutionised the world on the internet, based on the active participation of users. These users create digital content online rather than act as passive recipients of such content, as was the case in the era of Web 1.0 (Constantinides & Fountain, 2008). They further stated that the development of Web 2.0 has had a considerable impact on the world of the internet. For example, the internet has undergone certain modifications which have led to the development of new internet-based applications and new categorisations of internet-based applications. The most valuable transformation that the internet has undergone with the development of Web 2.0 is the facilitation of user-generated content which has led to the development of social media and other interactive communicational platforms as contributions to the electronic economy (Cox et al., 2008). Further, Web 2.0 categorises internet-based applications as: user-generated content applications which run on Web 2.0 platforms such as social media; digital content communities; online forums; blogs and micro blogs.

Webs 1.0 was based on the arrangement that online users were passive recipients of web content and were unable to alter or create content due to its limited functionality (Newman et al., 2016). The term "Web 2.0" came into focus in 2004 when online network developers integrated Web 2.0 platforms with user-generated content (Newman et al., 2016; Cox et al., 2008). Such user-generated content relaunched the World Wide Web as a platform harnessed by end-users to alter and modify online content and share it on the internet. This sat in stark contrast to first-generation Web 1.0, where users had limited access as passive viewers of content on a website (Rodriguez-Ardura et al., 2010). Further, Web 2.0 evolved as an open foundation platform, supporting the sustainable development of innovative technological applications through the generic features of royalty-free technologies (De Valck et al., 2009). This enabled the establishment of unlimited web-based links to web pages and unrestricted, instant access to those webpages. McQuail (2005), stated that, for the majority of prominent search engines which run on Web 2.0, the smallest unit is a webpage. This is particularly the case with social media, also referred to as Web 2.0 by the majority of users. The smallest entity of social media is considered to be content bits, altered or created by active online social media users in real time. These are commonly known as "user-generated content units". This explains why Web 2.0 and social media differ, as each webpage has several content entries created or altered by users or companies and is greater than the smallest entity on a social medium (Newman et al., 2016).

The development of Web 2.0 is also linked with the evolution of the development of the internet serving as a medium to help share and alter user-generated content online. Jansen et al., (2009), affirmed that the purpose of the development of the internet with subsequent Web 2.0 development is primarily concerned with enabling online feasibility for the general public to more actively engage with the internet to communicate and interact, to form a new era of development towards online democracy (Rainie & Wellman, 2012). As a step further from the development of the internet, the development of Web 2.0 means it is friendlier and easier to use where user-generated content is concerned. This has empowered users and revolutionised the process for marketers and companies to interact and share information with each other (Newman, 2018). Furthermore this second-generation web service has also led to the exchange of digital content in many ways, for example between one-to-many, many-to-many consumers on digital platforms.

Focussing on the basics of the multi-dimensional functionality of Web 2.0, marketers consider it a prime medium for the development of internet-based applications developed using digital content creation. Web 2.0 has become a mass medium, since it encompasses a much wider role than traditional Web 1.0, as it has modernised the structure of online communications, giving a clearer focus regarding the transfer of promotional messages. It has enabled the polarisation of social and digital content-based interactions (Murugesan, 2007). The modernisation of such a mass medium in the form of Web 2.0 has out-performed traditional marketing and communications methods, thanks to instant two-way communication and the ability to reach a far wider audience with quick customer responses (Fuchs et al., 2010). Additionally, it has enabled a power shift on the internet from sender to receiver with more emphasis on information acquisition leading to the transition of the landscape of the marketing mix and orientation of marketing strategies from push to pull (Faci et al., 2017). This seismic change in the paradigm of marketing communications has enabled the communication and interaction processes among online users to enhance the credibility and vitality of online promotions. This is enabled through confident user exchange of information initiated by organisations in an expeditious and convenient way (Newman, 2018). Changes to the behaviour of online stakeholders are an explicit function of Web 2.0 and its interactive features which have made online applications more user-friendly. Consumer interaction-based applications such as social media have empowered consumers to interact as individuals or in communities to seek information and gain wide acceptance in social media circles to create content (Brengarth & Mujkic, 2016; Walther et al., 2012)

Web 2.0 has made social interactions easier through the technologically innovative development of online social communities connecting online users all over the globe. Such users have formed a sophisticated platform of human interaction in a virtual online environment (Al-ghamdi & Al-ghamdi, 2015). Predominantly, Web 2.0 has proven to be the key medium for the development of online communications, linking users around the world and supporting interaction-based applications development such as social media networking sites. An explicit feature of Web 2.0 is its user-friendly interface which has enabled online users to participate in, and control, online interactions, social information sharing, and the promotion of products and services (Dang et al. 2014). With such a user-friendly interface, the development of online communities where consumers become members sharing a common interest and similar characteristics of membership has also been made possible. Such online communities represent evolution in this sense, enabling content consumption by online users who achieve satisfaction by reading and sharing valuable content which enables them to shape their buying behaviour. This in turn has had a subsequent impact on their online purchase decision(s) (Berthon et al. 2012), who noted that, with the development of social networking sites running explicitly on user-generated content, the internalisation of content information shared on social media can be used for both commercial and non-commercial purposes. Within this scenario, consumers use digital content which has originated, not from a commercial source, but from a reference group on a social networking site, in the form of product reviews, experiential product reflections and online user recommendations on Web 2.0 (Michopoulou & Moisa, 2018). The advancement and development of technology such as the development of online search engines, sophisticated mobile communication devices, online social networks and websites for peer-to-peer communications and online group discussions has helped marketers to extend their capacity to form a detailed understanding of online communities, social trends and user preferences regarding buying branded products and services advertised online (Habibi et al., 2014). This has led to the development of social networking sites on the web that has made it easier for online users to develop a greater understanding about how to make a rational choice when it comes to electronically available products and services. Such developments lead to consumer engagement which has a subsequent impact on purchase intentions based on the creation of a sense of loyalty and affiliation between consumers and the brand (Hollebeek et al. 2014). However, the question that remains salient in the literature is whether social media has a direct influence on consumer engagement and interactions. It is not yet known how useful social media is when it comes to boosting the sales revenue of companies by transforming the psychological behavior of online users, or if it has a long-term influence over post-purchase related behavior (Muntinga et al., 2011).

Social Media and Social Influence

Arguably social networking sites such as Facebook, twitter and Instagram transform consumer perceptions and preferences through online social interactions. These include group discussions, information exchange among members. Such group based online interaction together with gratification features of social media such as interactivity and entertainment result in development of social influence through significant change in members' knowledge, attitude and intentions as a result of informational content exchange and increase in value perception (Bagozzi & Lee, 2002). The term social influence is explained as a product of individual group-based online social interactions which are determined by individual attitudes towards perspective social behaviour and value systems (Dholakia et al., 2004). Changes to the behaviour and intentions of individuals are an explicit outcome of the acceptance of social influence in online network-based communities. Hutter et al. (2013) note that such online social interactions and group-based mutual social actions on social media develop social influence which significantly impacts on decision making amongst online members. Furthermore, the consumers' engagement with promotional content together with individual or group level social exchange explicitly add aesthetic value towards developing a rational mindset for making a buying decision (Kozinets et al., 2010).

Previous research has established the connection between social media and the purchase intentions of consumers but there exists a knowledge gap in terms of how social media influences the psychology of consumers and how it motivates consumers to make purchases (Erkan & Evans, 2016; Zhu et al., 2016;

Wang et al., 2012; Hutter et al., 2013). In particular, the role of social influence in transforming consumer behaviour and decision-making in terms of social media has yet to be conceptualised on an empirical basis, leaving an extensive knowledge gap. There is scope, therefore, to develop a conceptual framework in relation to social influence and consumer purchase intentions in academic literature. (Dholakia et al., 2004) argued that social influence provides a more subjective understanding of the direct connection between social media and consumer purchase intentions. Social influence is related to the attitude and behaviour of online consumers.

The consumer social influence model includes three fundamental components which are value perceptions, social identity and group norms. These share some similarity with the initial framework of social influence (Kelman, 1958) which includes compliance, internalisation and identity. Kelman (1958), explained that social influence develops at various levels in society; and each level has a unique outcome associated with it. Social influence develops based on mutual agreement to adopt the common attitude and behaviours of the group. An individual either conforms to the new behaviour by accepting it to gain acceptance, or finds a match between his/her personal value system, norms, attitude and behaviour with the group's norms, values and attitudes (Zhou, 2011). In addition, identity-based influence determines self-defined relationships and the acceptance of group behaviour by individuals. In this way an individual can become recognised and accepted by other members in the online media (Shen et al., 2011).

Dholakia et al., (2004) used the social influence theory (Kelman 1958) to determine to measure the participative behaviour of individuals in network based online social communities. The social influence model introduced by Dholakia et al. (2004) contains three components which are: consumer value perceptions; social influence predictors; and decision-making variables. Consumer value perceptions or antecedents of the model include the five-factor framework in relation to the use and gratification paradigm framework which incorporate purposive and self-discovery values as well as the maintenance of interpersonal connectivity, social enhancement and entertainment values (Shen et al., 2011). Consumer value perceptions act as antecedents to the main predictors, group norms and social identities in terms of determining changes in attitude and intention in the form of group based social actions known as we-intentions (Zhou, 2011). The antecedents and social influence framework (group norms and social identity) impact on the mediator variable of desire, which leads to the we-intentions that create changes in participative behaviour (Cheung, 2011). There are two component parts belonging to the social influence group norms of mutual agreement and mutual accommodation, and the three components of social identity and online social communities which are affective identity, evaluative identity and cognitive identity.

However, Dholakia et al.'s (2004) social influence model, the compliance factor (subjective norms) which develops normative social influence has not been included since it is less useful in determining 'we-intentions' in online communities. Furthermore, the value perceptions of consumers are psychological triggers of engagement with online groups on the social media. Such value perception serves as an antecedent and reveals potential clues as to the change in group members' beliefs, intentions and norms. (Dellarocas et al., 2007). Tsai & Bagozzi (2014), argued that individuals accept influence either by becoming active members of online groups by sharing their opinions, ideas and thoughts in group based online interactions or by acting as passive members who receive information and knowledge and accept social influence.

CONCLUSION AND MANAGERIAL IMPLICATIONS

The explicit role of social media in transforming the psychological behaviours of online users and in helping them to make purchase decisions adds economic value to the marketing communications that take place between consumers and companies (Hutter et al., 2013). In addition to the socialisation perspective, social media also helps marketers to promote brands, thereby helping companies to create online brand identity and brand communities (Hajli & Sims, 2015). As a platform of exchange of user-generated content, companies endorse the features and use of brand related products and services with an embedded message of brand value to improve the lifestyle of customers or to meet more specific needs. This is also true of the retail financial services industry where social media has played a prominent role in disseminating information-sharing about the value of financial services. Such data is shared amongst online members on social media (Liang & Chen, 2009).

Developments on social media networking sites gained popularity when the practices of different forms of user-generated content became available on different websites created by end-users. However, in order to qualify as a social networking website, some basic features and regulations must be recognised in order to meet the criteria and requirements. For example, the website must contain online users' profiles, personal content and information in order to enable users to develop a unique identity on a social network and to be able to participate in online communities and establish a connection with other online users. This enables users to post online in online communities and seek out information by reading online blogs and expert testimonials on social media (Alarcón et al., 2018). According to the OECD (2007) for a user-graphic interface to be considered as an online social exchange platform it should fulfil certain requirements. First of all, the content needs to be available online as published content available to a group of online users to access and alter. Secondly, it needs to demonstrate innovation in containing vital information for online users. These characteristics perfectly support the development of social media, which is explained by many researchers as the internet-based applications developed on Web 2.0, helping online users to exchange user-generated content (Dang et al., 2014; Faci et al., 2017). The most recognised forms of user-generated content exchange include micro blogs, weblogs, podcasts, social blogs, ratings and bookmarks, especially on Facebook, which supports group discussions amongst members.

Kietzmann et al., (2011) explained that such interactions reveal the human behavioural matrix on online social platforms. For example, online social networking and group discussions on a Web 2.0-based application increase human exposure to the desired content and information related to consumption, initiating the transition process from ordinary user to potential online consumer (Fu et al., 2018). Such a behavioural matrix supported by online interactions and active membership has dominated Web 2.0 with extensive online traffic enlarging the overall function of user-generated content applications in online behavioural change (Ozuem et al., 2015). Online user traffic on Web 2.0-based applications is based on the act of participation by online users and the heterogeneous nature of interaction. For example, on social networking sites, online users create digital content and interact simultaneously to share information and knowledge. They actively participate in group discussions or become members of a group associated with specific content related to information concerning a product or services, such as product reviews, personal experiences, or post-purchase behaviour. Cheema (2017) argues that, today the exchange of user-generated content on Web 2.0 has enabled the development of many potential social networking websites that provide extensive benefits to online users, such as Facebook, Wikipedia, or LinkedIn.

Such a social influence has unique implications for change in individuals' mindsets on online social medium. Similarly, modification in Dholakia et al.'s (2004) social influence model could enhance the vitality and credibility of its use in determining the purchase intentions in the financial services industry. From a managerial perspective, the framework of the consumers' social influence model has potential significance in explaining the behavioural and attitudinal change of consumers interacting through social media networking sites such as Facebook. Indeed, the research model of this study also functions as an integrated marketing communication process, especially while promoting financial services online (Friedkin & Johnsen, 2011; Mason et al., 2007). Such a cumulative social influence supported by social identity, group association and the value perceptions of consumers will enhance consumer trust in information about financial services in online, group-based social interaction.

REFERENCES

Alarcón, C. N., Sepúlveda, A. N., Valenzuela-Fernández, L., & Gil-Lafuent, J. (2018). Systematic mapping on social media and its relation to business. *European Research on Management and Business Economics*, *24*(2), 104–113. doi:10.1016/j.iedeen.2018.01.002

Ansarin, M., & Ozuem, W. (2014). Social media and online brand communities. In Computer-Mediated Marketing Strategies: Social Media and Online Brand Communities. IGI Global.

Arrigo, E. (2014). Social media opportunities for market-driven firms. In Integrating social media into business practice, applications, management, and models. IGI Global.

Azemi, Y., & Ozuem, W. (2014). Social media and SMEs in transition countries. In Computer-mediated marketing strategies: social media and online brand communities. IGI Global.

Bagozzi, R. P., & Lee, K.-H. (2002). Multiple Routes for Social Influence: The Role of Compliance, Internalization, and Social Identity. *Social Psychology Quarterly*, *65*(3), 226–247. doi:10.2307/3090121

Balaji, M. S., Khong, K. W., & Chong, A. Y. L. (2016). Determinants of negative word-of-mouth communication using social networking sites. *Information & Management*, *53*(4), 528–540. doi:10.1016/j.im.2015.12.002

Bamberg, S., & Hunecke, M., & Blöhbaum. (2007). Social context, morality and the use of public transportation: Results from two field studies. *Journal of Environmental Psychology*, *27*, 190–203. doi:10.1016/j.jenvp.2007.04.001

Berthon, P. R., Pitt, L., & Campbell, C. (2008). Ad lib: When customers create the ad. *California Management Review*, *50*(4), 6–31. doi:10.2307/41166454

Berthon, P. R., Pitt, L. F., Plangger, K., & Shapiro, D. (2012). Marketing meets Web 2.0, social media, and creative consumers: *Implications for international marketing strategy. Business Horizons*, *55*(3), 261–271. doi:10.1016/j.bushor.2012.01.007

Bhatli, D., & Mejri, C. A. (2015). The Influence of Social Media on Consumption Practices. In *Ideas in Marketing: Finding the New and Polishing the Old. Developments in Marketing Science: Proceedings of the Academy of Marketing Science*. Springer. 10.1007/978-3-319-10951-0_289

Bojãrs, U., Breslin, J. G., Finn, A., & Decker, S. (2008). Using the Semantic Web for linking and reusing data across Web 2.0 communities. *Journal of Web Semantics, 6*(1), 21–28. doi:10.1016/j.websem.2007.11.010

Brengarth, L. B., & Mujkic, E. (2016). Web 2.0: How social media applications leverage non-profit responses during a wildfire crisis. *Computers in Human Behavior, 54*, 589–596. doi:10.1016/j.chb.2015.07.010

Carr, C. T., Wohn, Y. D., & Hayes, R. A. (2016). As social support: Relational closeness, automaticity, and interpreting social support from paralinguistic digital affordances in social media. *Computers in Human Behavior, 62*, 385–393. doi:10.1016/j.chb.2016.03.087

Chan, N. L., & Guillet, B. D. (2011). Investigation of Social Media Marketing: How Does the Hotel Industry in Hong Kong Perform in Marketing on Social Media Websites? *Journal of Travel & Tourism Marketing, 28*(4), 345–368. doi:10.1080/10548408.2011.571571

Chan, Y. Y. Y., & Ngai, E. W. T. (2011). Conceptualising electronic word of mouth activity: An input-process-output perspective. *Marketing Intelligence & Planning, 29*(5), 488–516. doi:10.1108/02634501111153692

Chang, H. H., & Wang, I. C. (2008). An investigation of user communication behaviour in computer mediated environments. *Computers in Human Behavior, 24*(5), 2336–2356. doi:10.1016/j.chb.2008.01.001

Chang, Y. P., & Zhu, D. H. (2011). Understanding social networking sites adoption in China: A comparison of pre-adoption and post-adoption. *Computers in Human Behavior, 27*(5), 1840–1848. doi:10.1016/j.chb.2011.04.006

Cheung, C. M. K., Chiu, P.-Y., & Lee, M. K. O. (2011). Online Social Networks: Why Do Students Use Facebook? *Computers in Human Behavior, 27*(4), 1337–1343. doi:10.1016/j.chb.2010.07.028

Chong, A. Y. L., Lacka, E., Boying, L., & Chan, H. K. (2018). The role of social media in enhancing guanxi and perceived effectiveness of E-commerce institutional mechanisms in online marketplace. *Information & Management, 55*(5), 621–632. doi:10.1016/j.im.2018.01.003

Constantinides, E., & Fountain, S. (2008). Web 2.0: Conceptual foundations and marketing issues. *Journal of Direct. Data and Digital Marketing Practice, 9*(3), 231–244. doi:10.1057/palgrave.dddmp.4350098

Cox, C., Burgess, S., Sellitto, C., & Buultjens, J. (2008). *Consumer-Generated Web-based Tourism Marketing*. Queensland, Australia: Sustainable Tourism Cooperative Research Centre.

Dang, Y., Zhang, Y., Hu, P. J.-H., Brown, S. A., Ku, Y., Wang, J.-H., & Chen, H. (2014). An integrated framework for analysing multilingual content in Web 2.0 social media. *Decision Support Systems, 61*, 126–135. doi:10.1016/j.dss.2014.02.004

De Valck, K., Van Bruggen, G., & Wierenga, B. (2009). Virtual communities: A marketing perspective. *Decision Support Systems, 47*(3), 185–203. doi:10.1016/j.dss.2009.02.008

Dellarocas, C., Zhang, X., & Awad, N. (2007). Exploring the value of online product reviews in forecasting sales: The case of motion pictures. *Journal of Interactive Marketing, 21*(4), 23–45. doi:10.1002/dir.20087

Dholakia, U. M., Bagozzi, R. P., & Pearo, L. K. (2004). A social influence model of consumer participation in network- and small-group-based virtual communities. *International Journal of Research in Marketing, 21*(3), 241–263. doi:10.1016/j.ijresmar.2003.12.004

Dolan, R., & Goodman, S. (2017). Succeeding on social media Exploring communication strategies for wine marketing. *Journal of Hospitality and Tourism Management, 33*, 23–30. doi:10.1016/j.jhtm.2017.09.001

Endress, T. (2014). Digital Governance and Social Media Engagement. In Computer-mediated marketing strategies: social media and online brand communities. IGI Global.

Erkan, I., & Evans, C. (2016). The influence of eWOM in social media on consumers' purchase intentions: An extended approach to information adoption. *Computers in Human Behavior, 61*, 47–55. doi:10.1016/j.chb.2016.03.003

Faci, N., Maamar, Z., Buregio, V., Uglijanin, E., & Benslimane, D. (2017). Web 2.0. Applications in the workplace: How to ensure their proper use? *Computers in Industry, 88*, 1–11. doi:10.1016/j.compind.2017.03.003

Felix, R., Rauschnabel, P. A., Gallaugher, J., & Ransbotham, J. (2010). Social media and customer dialog management at Starbucks. *MIS Quarterly Executive, 9*(4), 197–212.

Habibi, M. R., Laroche, M., & Richard, M.-O. (2014). The roles of brand community and community engagement in building brand trust on social media. *Computers in Human Behavior, 37*, 152–161. doi:10.1016/j.chb.2014.04.016

Hajli, N. (2015). Social commerce constructs and consumer's intention to buy. *International Journal of Information Management, 35*(2), 183–191. doi:10.1016/j.ijinfomgt.2014.12.005

Hajli, N., & Sims, J. (2015). Social commerce: The transfer of power from seller to buyers. *Technological Forecasting and Social Change, 94*, 350–358. doi:10.1016/j.techfore.2015.01.012

Harrysson, M., Metayer, E., & Sarrazin, H. (2012). How 'social intelligence' can guide decisions. *The McKinsey Quarterly*, 1–9.

Hau, Y. S., & Kim, Y. G. (2011). Why Would Online Gamers Share Their Innovation-Conducive Knowledge in the Online Game User Community? Integrating Individual Motivations and Social Capital Perspectives. *Computers in Human Behavior, 27*(2), 956–970. doi:10.1016/j.chb.2010.11.022

Hearn, G., Foth, M., & Gray, H. (2009). Applications and implementations of new media in corporate communications: An action research approach. *Corporate Communications, 14*(1), 49–61. doi:10.1108/13563280910931072

Helal, G., & Ozuem, W. (2017). Social Identity Matters: Social Media and Brand Perceptions in the Fashion Apparel and Accessories Industries. In W. Ozuem & Y. Azemi (Eds.), *Digital Marketing Strategies for Fashion and Luxury Brands* (pp. 326–361). Hershey, PA: IGI Global.

Herget, J., & Mader, I. (2009). Social software in external corporate communications – a conceptional approach towards measuring, assessment and optimization of Web 2.0 activity [Social Software in der externen Unternehmenskommunikation – ein Gestaltungsansatz zur Messung, Bewertung und Optimierung von Web 2.0-aktivita¨ten]. *Information-Wissenschaft und Praxis, 60*(4), 233–240.

Hlebec, V., Manfreda, K. L., & Vehovar, V. (2015). The social support networks of internet users. *New Media & Society*, *8*(1), 9–32. doi:10.1177/1461444806058166

Ho, H. Y., & Chang, C. P. H. (2010). Influence of message trust in online word-of-mouth on consumer behaviour - By the example of food blog. In *International conference on electronics and information engineering*. Los Alamitos, CA: IEEE.

Hoffman, D.L., & Novak, T. (2013). *Online Experience in Social Media: Two Paths to Feeling Close and Connected*. Academic Press.

Hollebeek, L. D., Glynn, M. S., & Brodie, R. J. (2014). Consumer brand engagement in social media: Conceptualization, scale, development and validation. *Journal of Interactive Marketing*, *28*(2), 149–165. doi:10.1016/j.intmar.2013.12.002

Holsapple, C. W., Hsiao, S.-H., & Pakath, R. (2018). Business social media analytics: Characterization and conceptual framework. *Decision Support Systems*, *110*, 32–45. doi:10.1016/j.dss.2018.03.004

Huang, Z., & Benyoucef, M. (2013). From e-commerce to social commerce: A close look at design features. *Electronic Commerce Research and Applications*, *12*(4), 246–259. doi:10.1016/j.elerap.2012.12.003

Hutter, K., Hautz, J., Dennhardt, S., & Fuller, J. (2013). The impact of user interactions in social media on brand awareness and purchase intention: The case of MINI on Facebook. *Journal of Product and Brand Management*, *22*(5/6), 342–351. doi:10.1108/JPBM-05-2013-0299

Jansen, B. J., Zhang, M., Sobel, K., & Chowdury, A. (2009). Twitter power: Tweets as electronic word of mouth. *Journal of the American Society for Information Science and Technology*, *60*(11), 2169–2188. doi:10.1002/asi.21149

Jia, A. L., Shen, S., Li, D., & Chen, S. (2018). Predicting the implicit and the explicit video popularity in a User-generated Content site with enhanced social features. *Computer Networks*, *140*, 112–125. doi:10.1016/j.comnet.2018.05.004

Jiang, Z., Chan, J., Tan, B. C. Y., & Chua, W. S. (2009). Effects of interactivity on website involvement and purchase intention. *Journal of the Association for Information Systems*, *11*(1), 34–59. doi:10.17705/1jais.00218

Kang, I. (2016). Web 2.0 UGC, and citizen journalism: Revisiting South Korea's Oh my News model in the age of social media. *Telematics and Informatics*, *33*(2), 546–556. doi:10.1016/j.tele.2015.07.007

Kaplan, A. M., & Haenlein, M. (2010). Users of the world, unite! The challenges and opportunities of Social Media. *Business Horizons*, *53*(1), 59–68. doi:10.1016/j.bushor.2009.09.003

Kaplan, A. M., & Haenlein, M. (2011). The early bird catches the news: Nine things you should know about micro-blogging. *Business Horizons*, *54*(2), 105–113. doi:10.1016/j.bushor.2010.09.004

Kelman, H. C. (1958). Compliance, identification, and internalization: Three processes of attitude change. *The Journal of Conflict Resolution*, *2*(1), 51–60. doi:10.1177/002200275800200106

Kietzmann, J. H., Hermkens, K., McCarthy, I. P., & Silvestre, B. S. (2011). Social Media? Get Serious! Understanding the Functional Building Blocks of Social Media. *Business Horizons*, *54*(1), 241–251. doi:10.1016/j.bushor.2011.01.005

Kozinets, R., de Valck, K., Wojnicki, A., & Wilner, S. (2010). Networked narratives: Understanding word-of-mouth marketing in online communities. *Journal of Marketing, 74*(2), 71–89. doi:10.1509/jmkg.74.2.71

Laestadius, L. I., & Wahl, M. M. (2017). Mobilizing social media users to become advertisers: Corporate hashtag campaigns as a public health concern. *Digital Health, 3*, 1–12. doi:10.1177/2055207617710802 PMID:29942600

Li, C., & Bernoff, J. (2008). *Groundswell: Winning in a world transformed by social technologies.* Boston: Harvard Business Press.

Li, H., Zhang, Z., Meng, F., & Janakiraman, R. (2017). Is peer evaluation of consumer online reviews socially embedded? – An examination combining reviewer's social network and social identity. *International Journal of Hospitality Management, 67*, 143–153. doi:10.1016/j.ijhm.2017.08.003

Liang, C., & Chen, H. (2009). How to lengthen, deepen and broaden customer-firm relationships with online financial services. *Journal of Financial Services Marketing, 14*(3), 218–231. doi:10.1057/fsm.2009.20

Lim, Y.-S., & Heide, B. V. D. (2015). Evaluating the Wisdom of Strangers: The Perceived Credibility of Online Consumer Reviews on Yelp. *Journal of Computer-Mediated Communication, 20*(1), 67–82. doi:10.1111/jcc4.12093

Litvin, S. W., Goldsmith, R. E., & Pan, B. (2008). Electronic Word-of-Mouth in Hospitality and Tourism Management. *Tourism Management, 29*(3), 458–468. doi:10.1016/j.tourman.2007.05.011

Malthouse, E. C., Haenlein, M., Skiera, B., Wege, E., & Zhang, M. (2013). Managing Customer Relationships in the Social Media Era: Introducing the Social CRM House. *Journal of Interactive Marketing, 27*(4), 270–280. doi:10.1016/j.intmar.2013.09.008

Mason, W. A., Conrey, F. R., & Smith, E. R. (2007). Situating Social Influence Processes: Dynamic, Multidirectional Flows of Influence within Social Networks. *Personality and Social Psychology Review, 11*(3), 279–300. doi:10.1177/1088868307301032 PMID:18453465

McQuail, D. (2005). *McQuail's Mass Communication Theory* (5th ed.). London Sage publishers.

Michaelidou, N., Siamagka, N. T., & Christodoulides, G. (2011). Usage, barriers and measurement of social media marketing: An exploratory investigation of small and medium B2B brands. *Industrial Marketing Management, 40*(7), 1153–1159. doi:10.1016/j.indmarman.2011.09.009

Michopoulou, E., & Moisa, D. G. (2018). (in press). Hotel social media metrics: The ROI dilemma. *International Journal of Hospitality Management.*

Miller, R., & Lammas, N. (2010). Social media and its implications for viral marketing *Asia Pacific. The Public Relations Journal, 11*(1), 1–9.

Muntinga, D. G., Moorman, M., & Smit, E. G. (2011). Introducing COBRA: Exploring motivations for brand-related social media use. *International Journal of Advertising, 30*(1), 13–46. doi:10.2501/IJA-30-1-013-046

Muñiz, A. M. Jr, & Schau, H. J. (2007a). Vigilante marketing and consumer-created communications. *Journal of Advertising, 36*(3), 35–50. doi:10.2753/JOA0091-3367360303

Murugesan, S. (2007). Understanding Web 2.0. *IT Professional, 9*(4), 34–41. doi:10.1109/MITP.2007.78

Nelson-Field, K., Riebe, E., & Sharp, B. (2012). What's not to "like?": Can a Facebook fan base give a brand the advertising reach it needs? *Journal of Advertising Research*, 1–8.

Newman, M. C. (2018). Evidence in Social Networks. In M. Newman (Ed.), *The Nature and Use of Eco toxicological Evidence Natural Science* (pp. 219–243). Statistics, Psychology, and Sociology.

Newman, R., Chang, V., Walters, R. J., & Wills, G. B. (2016). Web 2.0—the past and the future. *International Journal of Information Management, 36*(4), 591–598. doi:10.1016/j.ijinfomgt.2016.03.010

OECD. (2007). *Participative Web: user-created content - OECD*. Available online: http://www.oecd-ilibrary.org/science-and-technology/participative-web-and-user-created-content_9789264037472-en

Ouirdi, M. E., Segers, J., Ouirdi, A. E., & Pais, I. (2015). *Predictors of job seekers self-disclosure on social media*. Computers in Human Behaviour.

Ozuem, W., & Tan, K. (2014). Reconciling Social Media with Luxury Fashion Brands: An Exploratory Study. In L. Aiello (Ed.), *Handbook of Research on Management of Cultural Products: E-Relationship Marketing and Accessibility Perspectives* (pp. 257–285). IGI Global. doi:10.4018/978-1-4666-5007-7.ch013

Ozuem, W., Pinho, C. A., & Azemi, Y. (2016). User-Generated Content and Perceived Customer Value. In W. Ozuem & G. Bowen (Eds.), *Competitive Social Media Marketing Strategies* (pp. 50–63). IGI Global. doi:10.4018/978-1-4666-9776-8.ch003

Ozuem, W., Kerry, H., & Geoff, L. (2008). Communicating in the new interactive marketspace. *European Journal of Marketing, 42*(9/10), 1059–1083. doi:10.1108/03090560810891145

Ozuem, W., O'Keeffe, A., & Lancaster, G. (2015). Leadership Marketing: An exploratory study. *Journal of Strategic Marketing*. doi:10.1080/0965254X.2014.1001867

Ozuem, W., Borrelli, M., & Lancaster, G. (2015). Leveraging the co-evolution of offline and online video games: An empirical study. *Journal of Strategic Marketing*. doi:10.1080/0965254X.2015.1076883

Qi, J., Monod, E., Fang, B., & Deng, S. (2018). Theories of Social media Philosophical Foundations. *Engineering, 4*(1), 94–102. doi:10.1016/j.eng.2018.02.009

Qualman, E. (2009). *Socialnomics: How social media transforms the way we live and do business.* Hoboken, NJ: John Wiley & Sons.

Rainie, L., & Wellman, B. (2012). *Networked: the new social operating system.* MIT Press.

Rodriguez-Ardura, I., Martinez-Lopez, F. J., & Luna, P. (2010). Going with the consumer towards the social web environment: A review of extant knowledge. *International Journal of Electronic Marketing and Retailing, 3*(4), 415–440. doi:10.1504/IJEMR.2010.036885

Safko, L., Brake, D., & David, K. (2009). *The Social Media Bible: Tactics, Tools, and Strategies for Business Success*. Wiley.

Sashi, C. M. (2012). Customer engagement, buyer-seller relationships, and social media. *Management Decision*, *50*(2), 253–272. doi:10.1108/00251741211203551

Sciglipaglia, D., & Ely, D. (2006). Customer account relationships and e-retail banking usage. *Journal of Financial Services Marketing*, *10*(4), 109–122. doi:10.1057/palgrave.fsm.4760026

Scott, J. (2012). *Social network analysis*. Thousand Oaks, CA: Sage.

Shen, A. X. L., Cheung, C. M. K., Lee, M. K. O., & Chen, H. (2011). How Social Influence Affects We-Intention to Use Instant Messaging: The Moderating Effect of Usage Experience. *Information Systems Frontiers*, *13*(2), 157–169. doi:10.100710796-009-9193-9

Sinha, K. S., Subramanian, S., & Bhattacharya, K. C. (2012). The contemporary framework on social media analytics as an emerging tool for behaviour informatics, HR analytics and business process. *Journal of Contemporary Management Issues*, *17*(2), 65–84.

Stokinger, E., & Ozuem, W. (2014). Social media and customer retention: Implication for luxury beauty industry. In Computer-mediated marketing strategies: social media and online brand communities. IGI Global.

Tsai, H.-T., & Bagozzi, R. P. (2014). Contribution Behaviour in Virtual Communities: Cognitive, Emotional, and Social Influences. *Management Information Systems Quarterly*, *38*(1), 143–163. doi:10.25300/MISQ/2014/38.1.07

Tsai, W. S., & Men, L. R. (2013). Motivations and Antecedents of Consumer Engagement with Brand Pages on Social Networking Sites. *Journal of Interactive Advertising*, *13*(2), 2. doi:10.1080/15252019.2013.826549

Vanmeter, R. A., Grisaffe, D. B., & Chonko, L. B. (2015). Of "Likes" and "Pins": The Effects of Consumers' Attachment to Social Media. *Journal of Interactive Marketing*, 70–78.

Vemuri, A. (2010). Getting social: Bridging the gap between banking and social media. *Global Finance*, *24*(5), 20–21.

Walsh, S., Gilmore, A., & Carson, D. (2004). Managing and implementing simultaneous transaction and relationship marketing. *International Journal of Bank Marketing*, 22(7), 468–483. doi:10.1108/02652320410567908

Walther, J. B., Liang, Y. J., Ganster, T., Wohn, D. Y., & Emington, J. (2012). Online reviews, helpfulness ratings, and consumer attitudes: An extension of congruity theory to multiple sources in Web 2.0. *Journal of Computer-Mediated Communication*, *18*(1), 97–112. doi:10.1111/j.1083-6101.2012.01595.x

Wang, X., Yu, C., & Wei, Y. (2012). Social Media Peer Communication and Impacts on Purchase Intentions: A Consumer Socialization Framework. *Journal of Interactive Marketing*, *26*(4), 198–208. doi:10.1016/j.intmar.2011.11.004

Weinberg, B. D., & Pehlivan, E. (2011). Social Spending: Managing the Social Media Mix. *Business Horizons*, *54*(1), 275–282. doi:10.1016/j.bushor.2011.01.008

Wu, J. J., & Chang, Y. S. (2005). Towards understanding members' interactivity, trust, and flow in online travel community. *Industrial Management & Data Systems*, *105*(7), 937–954. doi:10.1108/02635570510616120

Yankova, I., & Ozuem, W. (2014). Social Media and its Implications for Marketing Communications. In Computer-mediated marketing strategies: social media and online brand communities. IGI Global.

Zhang, L., Tam, V. C., Wan, W. W., Wu, P., & Luk, C. L. (2015). An exploratory study on school children's intent attributions for parental structuring behaviours. *Psychological Reports*, *116*(1), 249–273. doi:10.2466/21.PR0.116k17w3 PMID:25668329

Zhou, T. (2011). Understanding online community user participation: A social influence perspective. *Internet Research*, *21*(1), 67–81. doi:10.1108/10662241111104884

Zhu, Y. Q., & Chen, H. G. (2015). Social media and human need satisfaction: Implications for social media marketing. *Business Horizons*, *58*, 335–345.

Zhu, Z., Wang, J., Wang, X., & Wan, X. (2016). Exploring factors of user's peer-influence behaviour in social media on purchase intention: Evidence from QQ. *Computers in Human Behavior*, *63*, 980–987. doi:10.1016/j.chb.2016.05.037

KEY TERMS AND DEFINITIONS

B2C: The business environment where firms directly communicate and promote their products and services to the consumers through adopting multiple media and using integrated marketing communication strategies.

Purchase Intention: The willingness of a customer to buy a product or service in a certain condition.

Social Influence: The phenomenon which explains the change in the individuals' beliefs, attitudes, and intentions occurs at different levels because of social interaction between an individual and another individual or a group of individuals.

Social Interaction: The communication or contact of an individual with another individual or a group of individuals in the society for purpose of information exchange, entertainment, or to maintain essential social connection.

Social Media: Web 2.0-based application that runs on the principles of user-generated content, facilitating the online users to create, share, modify, and alter the digital content enabling the two-way communication on internet.

User-Generated Content: UGC represents all the ways by which users create and exchange digital content and use social media on the technological basis of Web 2.0.

Web 2.0: Web 2.0 is a platform in which software and digital content are not only produced and published by individual companies and people but are also produced and developed by different participants in a continuous and collaborative manner.

Chapter 48
Emoji in Advertising

Marcel Danesi
University of Toronto, Toronto, Canada

ABSTRACT

Emoji have become an ipso facto universal language that fit in perfectly with informal routine digital communications, especially on mobile devices and on social media. Marketers and advertisers have taken notice of this communicative phenomenon and have started tapping into the emotive power of the emoji code since at least 2010. But is emoji advertising truly effective? Almost no study exists to examine this question. This article thus has a two-fold purpose. First, it looks at the use of emoji in advertising generally and then it presents a pilot study that aims to assay if such advertising is indeed effective. The overall conclusion is that effectiveness relates to the increase in interpretations, or connotations, that emoji ads seem to generate. The use of emoji in advertising is, thus, a field laboratory for gauging where emoji writing is heading and what it entails more broadly for communication.

INTRODUCTION

It is now a well-known, but still remarkable, fact that in 2015 The Oxford Dictionary's "Word of the Year" was an emoji (in this paper this term is used both as a singular and plural noun)—the "face with tears emoji." The rationale for this selection was, simply, that the emoji was one of the most used new "words," and thus meritorious of its word-of-the-year status (see Figure 1).

This event signaled that a shift in how we view what a word is had taken place, at least in digital forms of communication. A word written with alphabet characters is designed to represent its phonemic structure, so as to match the spoken word. On the other hand, emoji are essentially pictograms that stand for referents directly, often replacing alphabetic words. In most informal written texts, such as tweets and text messages, emoji are used in tandem with the alphabet, producing what can be called a "hybrid writing code," which allows interlocutors to use both the traditional alphabet and emoji symbols to create messages that effectively blend phonemic with iconic-pictographic referential systems.

Since 2010, Unicode has made a large repertory of emoji signs available for installation on mobile device keyboards and on apps, making emoji use a matter of routine. Unicode is an international encoding standard for use with different scripts.

DOI: 10.4018/978-1-7998-9020-1.ch048

Figure 1. Face with tears emoji

Emoji now constitute a pictographic writing system, complementing alphabetic writing and, in some contexts, substituting it completely. This new kind of hybrid writing system harbors a broad range of implications within it for the future of writing and even language, which are beyond the purpose of the present study (Danesi, 2016). For the present purposes, it is sufficient to focus on the use of emoji in advertising. As argued elsewhere (Danesi, 2006), advertisers are always at the avant-garde when it comes to understanding the role of new sign systems in evolving social contexts. The question becomes: Is the incorporation of emoji in advertising truly effective psychologically, or is it just an example of a cooption strategy that may have minimal psychological force? This paper thus has two purposes: (1) to take an overall look at the use of emoji in advertising, and then (2) to attempt an initial answer to this question by presenting the results of an informal study with 100 undergraduate students at the University of Toronto who were asked to evaluate the appeal of 3 ads with emoji and 3 without them on a scale of 1 to 7. They were also asked to interpret each ad in their own words. The ideas was to measure the so-called connotative index of the ads, a model which suggests that the more connotations that are embedded into an ad text the more likely it is to be effective (Beasley & Danesi, 2002). The underlying subtext of this paper is that advertising is a guide to trends in sign systems and thus a gauge of how these are evolving generally.

THE EMOJI CODE

To use David Olson's (1977) terminology, there is a difference between "utterance meaning," which is comprehensible only in the context where the utterance occurs, and "text meaning," which entails dislocation from the context and greater control of language and content. Today's text messages, tweets, and ads have essentially an utterance function. The textual functions of writing are still realized through traditional writing styles, as can be seen in all kinds of formal texts, such as scientific papers, essays, and the like, where emoji have no role to play. Emoji serve the utterance function of informal texts, providing visual imagery that adds emotional tone and semantic nuances through pictographic representation. In other words, emoji allow for the prosodic and emotive features of oral expression to be semiotized in writing.

Most emoji are essentially stylized iconic signs similar to sketches. The iconicity varies in degree, of course. For example, a cloud emoji is a visual iconic sign that suggests the outline of a cloud. A sunrise emoji, on the other hand, is an ideographic iconic form, showing the shape of a sun as it rises up from a background (see Figures 2 and 3).

Figure 2. Cloud emoji

Figure 3. Sunrise emoji

Other suggestive iconic modalities of emoji include value, color, and perspective. Value refers to the darkness or lightness of a line or shape. It plays an important role in portraying contrasts of various kinds. Color conveys various modalities of meaning. In the cloud emoji, the grayish-white color stands for the actual color of clouds (as we perceive it); in some emoji, however, it can suggest various emotions (such as boredom). Perspective refers to a simulative mode of representation, intended to evoke some feature of perception, such as movement. The sunrise emoji is designed to impart a sense of the sun moving upwards, this possessing indexical qualities. In effect, emoji are rarely just iconic; in many cases they blend several semiotic modalities, such as indexicality and symbolism, at once, with one or the other being foregrounded on the basis on the meaning context.

It is relevant to note here that, although emoji surfaced as a means to enhance a broader comprehension of written texts in an age of instant communications across the globe, culturally-stylized emoji have nonetheless emerged for various reasons. Even facial emoji (or smileys) have undergone modification based on culture-specific needs. The creators of smileys attempted to make them as culturally-neutral as possible. The use of yellow to color the smiley was an obvious stylistic ploy to remove recognizable facial features associated with race or ethnicity. Roundness also seems to attenuate specific details of facial structure that would otherwise suggest personality or identity (see Figure 4).

Figure 4. Typical smiley emoji

But, almost right after their spread into common usage, new emoji were constructed that embedded culturally-based meanings, either explicitly or unwittingly. So, different colors to represent the face have now become common. It is perhaps more accurate to say, therefore, that some emoji are higher on a culturally-neutral "universality scale" of interpretation than others. The smiley, with or without color modifications, can be located higher up on the scale than can, for example, a golf cart emoji which is likely to have mid-scale comprehensibility; and others still, such as the live long and prosper emoji, are likely to have a lower-scale comprehensibility. The latter emoji alludes to a pop culture referent—the 1960s *Star Trek* program on American network television where it was used as the Vulcan peace sign. Although the sign has become somewhat of a common symbol in many parts of the world, its interpretation is constrained by various factors, such as the age of the emoji user and his or her geo-historical background.

The smiley and face with tears emoji are found on virtually all mobile device keyboards, no matter what language is involved. They are stylized, almost comic-book-like, pictograms that can (and do) replace words and phrases. As mentioned, their main function seems to be to add utterance meaning to a written text. They are meaning-enhancing devices that are amalgamated with alphabetic writing in a hybrid fashion, although there are now texts that are composed entirely of emoji. It is not certain, however that this "emoji-only" mode of writing is spreading broadly. The hybrid system continues to be the most prominent one in informal settings.

The ever-broadening research on emoji use (Miller, Thebault-Spieker, Chang, Johnson, Terveen, & Hecht, 2016; Moschini, 2016; Vidal, Ares, & Jaeger, 2016; Alshenqeeti, 2016) suggests that emoji have indeed become commonplace writing symbols across all social variable structures, including age and social class. Above all else, emoji have assumed common discourse functions, such as the phatic one (Malinowski, 1923; Jakobson, 1960). For example, a smiley used at the beginning of a text message has largely replaced opening protocols such as "Hello," "Dear so-and-so," and the like. The smiley provides an opening interpretive frame for imbuing the tone of the message with positivity, thus ensuring that a phatic bond between interlocutors is established.

An analysis of common text messages shows that three phatic functions are now part of systematic emoji usage (Danesi, 2016):

1. **Utterance Opener:** The smiley is used in place of opening salutations such as "Hi!" allowing the sender to strengthen or maintain friendly bonds with the interlocutor even when a message may have some negativity in its contents;
2. **Utterance Ending:** The smiley and similar sentiment emoji (such as hearts in the case of intimate messages) are used typically as the good-bye function in a message;
3. **Silence Avoidance:** In written messages, the equivalent of silence gaps occurs when the reader expects more information about something, whereas the writer wishes to avoid it. By putting emoji in such content gaps, the intent is to counteract the uncomfortableness that may result from such silence gaps.

In addition to the phatic function, emoji usage entails a considerable level of emotivity (Jakobson, 1960). This is defined as the use of discourse structures to portray one's state of mind and to raise the level of emotions in the context of the text. In face-to-face communication, people use interjections, intonation, and other prosodic strategies, alongside specific keywords and phrases, to convey their feelings, explicitly or implicitly. In hybrid messages these are typically replaced by emoji forms. While emotivity may seem to be additive or annotative to the main written message, and thus easily removable from it, research has shown that this is not the case (Danesi, 2016).

There are also other utterance functions with respect to emoji usage that need not concern us here. The main point is that emoji are hardly randomly-used visual devices to embellish a written text. They now form a "placement grammar," as it can be called—that is, emoji are used systematically in texts. This grammar is not a replica of linguistic grammar with visual symbols; it has its own syntax, or system for organizing the emoji to create coherent and meaningful sequences or combinations.

A perfect example is PETA's (People for the Ethical Treatment of Animals) 2014 mobile-based campaign calling for social action against the mistreatment of animals. The campaign was known, rather appropriately, as "Beyond Words." The campaign featured texts created entirely with emoji. Figure 5 is one of the original texts used in it.

Figure 5. PETA emoji campaign (https://www.peta.org/blog/one-emoji-can-save-animals/)

The message begs a young woman (the left-most emoji) to reconsider (shown by the thought cloud above her) that the items she might wish to buy (dress, shoes, purse, lipstick, boots), laid out in that order to become a "princess" (the right-most emoji), are all animal products and thus destructive of animal life for purely casual lifestyle reasons. Interpreting the text requires more than just knowledge of the semantic possibilities of the emoji. It also requires knowledge of how they are combined and laid out and, thus, how these are connected to each other syntactically. This aspect raises several immediately obvious issues vis-à-vis the relation between the text layout and the message. First, emoji texts of this kind require significant referential background knowledge and a particular frame of mind for interpreting them. Not everyone who sees the text will, in fact, make the association between the products and animal killings; nor does the text take into account the fact that everyone across the world buys such products. In other words, the contextualization of this text is embedded primarily in a specific kind of interpretive frame and aimed at a specific demographic—white, young Anglo-American-European women. As some critics of the campaign pointed out, this is a rather stereotypical portrayal of womanhood, and highly restricted to commercial cultures. But it turned out to be an effective campaign nonetheless. Since then, emoji-based texts in advertising have spiraled.

EMOJI VARIATION: A PROBLEM FOR ADVERTISTING

The widespread use of emoji became practicable in 2010 when hundreds of emoji characters were standardized by Unicode. The standardized emoji lexicon consisted of smileys, heart emoji, and a few other pictographic forms still found across keyboards and apps (with minor variations in detail), implying that people likely use the lexicon in similar ways. Additional characters are created on a daily basis, and these are accessed primarily on online dictionaries and inventories that allow for selection and, in some cases, even modification of emoji for personalized or specialized use.

It is the standardized lexicon that has allowed the emoji code to migrate broadly and used by virtually anyone in the world. But its popularity and spread has caused pressure to add culture-sensitive designs into the Unicode standard to meet the demands of different nations and their languages. There is a constant ongoing amplification of the emoji lexicon to include variation of all kinds. Emoji of sports equipment, culturally-based food items, symbols for places of worship and the like require culture-specific interpretation. Nonetheless, it seems that the diversity of interpretations in emoji, when compared with the diversity found typically in the corresponding words, is somewhat attenuated. One of the primary dangers to the use of emoji especially in advertising, in addition to culture-specific variation, is the constant potential for ambiguity and misinterpretation. For example, the nail polish emoji has been found to have a whole array of unwanted sexual connotations that users in some non-English speaking countries want to avoid, finding the emoji offensive (see Figure 6).

Figure 6. Nail polish emoji

The thumbs-up emoji is another problematic one (see Figure 7).

This gesture is offensive in parts of the Middle East, West Africa, Russia, and South America. In many of these areas, it is the equivalent of using the middle finger in the western world. The list of such culturally-coded emoji is an extensive one, and need not concern us here. The point is that ambiguity, misinterpretations, and cultural-coding are likely unavoidable in emoji-based discourse. The emoji of an airplane could refer to the plane itself, flying, traveling, or an airport. One cannot assume an isomorphic relation between the emoji and its interpretation. It is in taming these variable factors, veering the interpretation mode towards a standardized one, that advertising has been attempting to do since adopting emoji as part of its new rhetorical code. In other words, the aim in advertising seems to be to develop a kind of largely invariable emoji code that can be seen transcend variation, but remain highly suggestive, thus raising what has been called the "connotative index" higher—that is, the number of positive connotations that an ad text aims to generate (Beasley and Danesi, 2002). The higher the connotative index, the higher the efficacy. And this seems to be achieved by utilizing symbols from the standardized lexicon or creating ones for specific advertising purposes.

Figure 7. The thumbs-up emoji

EMOJI IN ADVERTISING

Overall, the emoji code has two advantages over alphabetic codes that vary from language to language—it is based on visual signs that have, arguably, a better chance at being interpreted more consistently across cultures and second, it injects tone and mood, especially happiness, into the textuality of messages. It can of course add other emotive connotations, from irony to sarcasm, but the happiness one is a common one in advertising. It is perhaps for this reason that emoji have become so common and diffuse in advertising, where graphics, images, and graphic design guide the making of texts (Skaggs, 2017). Raising the connotative index is also a primary goal of advertisers. This has been achieved in the past with effective images blended with text (Beasley and Danesi, 2002, Polak, 2015). The theory of the connotative index implies that the higher the number of connotations evoked by an ad text, in a suggestive rather than explicit manner, the more effective the ad. Emoji appear to raise the connotative index considerably.

The ad in Figures 8 for Bud Light is an example of how the suggestiveness of emoji can raise the connotative index. It has reconstructed the American flag to celebrate the Fourth of July holiday with fireworks emoji in place of the stars, and beer glasses with flags in place of the stripes.

The ad is transparently evocative of Andy Warhol's serial silkscreen painting technique, where an object, such as a flag, would be reproduced over and over to mirror the assembly-line manufacturing process that produced it. Indeed, many of emoji ads are imitative of pop and comic-book art, with their pastiche style (Danesi 2016). Arguably, these patriotic connotations give the ad a different tone and texture than would be possible with an ad portraying a July 4 celebration with a different imagery—actual people celebrating with a beer in hand. It is, in fact, a primary aim here to assay if this type of suggestiveness is effective, as will be discussed below. If it is, it means that emoji have an inbuilt high connotative index allowing advertisers to create effective ads.

Figure 8. Bud Light emoji ad (https://twitter.com/budlight/status/485050295517335552?lang=en)

The marketing world has even expanded the emoji code on its own, to get around the limitations imposed by the preset Unicode system. There are now custom branded emoji keyboards and sticker campaigns allowing brands to reach their consumers much more directly. The question of whether emoji enhance product recognition and marketability has rarely been approached. In a pioneering study, Yakin and Eru (2017) measured the attitudes of advertisers and interpreters towards emoji usage in social marketing campaigns (campaigns based on the use of social media). Their results indicate that emoji advertising is indeed effective. They put it as follows (Yakin and Yu, 2017, p. 230):

According to the results of the study, it has been concluded that emojis are effective for social advertising campaigns. Participants expressed that, usage of emojis in advertising campaigns is suitable for social campaigns. And using emojis in advertising campaigns explains the Project successfully. They expressed that the transmitted message of the campaign is informative and effective. And also participants expressed that these kinds of campaigns are attractive, creative and innovative.

Of particular relevance to advertising is the incorporation of emoji as vicarious spelling forms, as shown in the title page of an emoji phrase book by Fred Benenson, *How to speak emoji* (2015), where the "o" of "emoji" is replaced by an emoji face that has the outline of the letter (see Figure 9).

Figure 9. Title page of Benenson's 2015 book (http://publishing.andrewsmcmeel.com/books/detail?sku=9781449478025)

Basically, an alphabet character may be replaced by an emoji that looks similar to it. This strategy is a basic part of emoji advertising, as we shall see below (Balasuriya, Doran, Sheth, & Wijeratne, 2016). Moreover, as Leung C-H & Chan (2017) indicate, this allows advertisers to overcome several hurdles posed by culture-coding, ambiguity, and counterproductive misinterpretations. At the very least, the use of emoji as letter replacements lowers the possibility of misinterpretation, while at the same time allowing for emotivity to go up.

Projecting brands into emoji discourse practices is a powerful strategy. Recently the online emoji-construction site, Emogi, launched Wink, a new platform allowing brands to present branded emoji, stickers or GIFs as options to consumers through the text fields on several of the world's most popular messaging apps. Wink identifies the unique context of messages where brands can introduce their content, without requiring a separate keyboard or app.

RESULTS OF AN INFORMAL STUDY

In January of 2017, 100 undergraduates at the University of Toronto were asked to assess the appeal and meanings of six ads in order to establish a framework for assessing the effects of emoji ads in comparison to non-emoji ads. It constituted an informal study whose results clearly need further investigation and replication to corroborate them beyond the study's limited scope. The university students were divided equally into an experimental group, A, called the emoji group, and a control group, B, called the non-emoji group. The selection of the subjects was totally random, producing an asymmetry in the gender constitution of each group, whereby there were more females overall, 2-to-1 than males, not to mention similar asymmetries in background ethnicity and the like. So, the study was an uncontrolled one and was meant simply to provide an initial answer to the question of whether or not emoji ads are connotatively more powerful than other ads.

Clearly, a follow-up quantitative study, enlarging the sample size to include the assessment of emoji use across the normal social variables (age, class, education, gender, and so on), is needed. This research project was simply a starting point. The 50 subjects in group B were shown the three ads below and asked simply to rate them from 1 to 7 according to intuitive appeal, with 1 indicating the lowest appeal and 7 the highest. At the same time each subject was asked to say what it conveyed to him/her in an open fashion. The latter was a means of compiling the number of different distinctive interpretations, in order to calculate the connotative index—in this case measured as a percentage. To contextualize the experiment, only hypothetical ads for Pepsi were used, thus making it easier to constrain the domain of product meaning. These were created by Megan Lorraine (http://www.artofmeganlorraine.com/pepsi-hypothetical-ads.html).

In Figure 10 are the average appeal ratings for the Pepsi ads without emoji as indicated by the 50 subjects in group B.

Figure 10. Pepsi ads without emoji

B-1: average rating = 4.1   B-2: average rating = 5.2   B-3: 2.9

  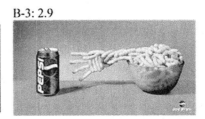

The cumulative average of the B-evaluations was 4.0, with standard deviation of 0.9, Below are the average appeal ratings for the Pepsi ads constructed with emoji as indicated by the 50 subjects in group A (see Figure 11).

The cumulative average of the A-evaluations was 6.0, with standard deviation of 0.3, Applying a simple t-test to check for any initial significance showed that the results were indeed significant. The purpose was, to reiterate, simply to get an initial glimpse into the effectiveness of emoji ads, and there seems to be an indication that they are indeed effective.

Figure 11. Pepsi ads with emoji

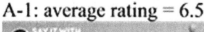

A-1: average rating = 6.5

A-2: average rating: 5.3

A-3: average rating = 6.4

The interview of the informants, about the meaning of each ad produced interesting and relevant results as well. For example, one interpretation of B-1 was "it evokes happiness," another one was "it shows friendship with the three bottles together." Overall, for B-1 there were 4 distinct connotations, with 42 of the subjects explaining it as a "happiness-producing" ad. So, its connotative index (CI) is calculated as 4. On the other hand, A-1 produced 15 distinct interpretations, ranging from "happiness" and "funniness" to "cute" and "cool." So, its CI is 15. To ensure that the connotations were minimally distinct we asked a control group of 5 other students if they themselves could see a difference in meaning to each interpretation.

Results for CIs

A-1 = 15
A-2 = 7
A-3 = 10
B-1 = 4
B-2 = 3
B-4 = 3

Thus, on average the A-ads produced a cumulative connotative index of 10.7 and the B-ads a cumulative index of 3.3. Using a t-test detected, again, the presence of significance. These raw initial results thus suggest that emoji advertising, at least among young people (the average age of the 100 subjects was 19.7), is a contemporary effective mode of delivering brand image.

A schematic semiotic analysis of the A-ads shows that there is an ingenious use of emoji at various levels. A-1 equates the smiley with the actual face of the Pepsi drinker. This facial isomorphism is re-inforced by the fact that the drinker puts his glasses on over the emoji, thus fusing the smiley with the face—a perfect iconic blend. The logo reinforces this by equating the Pepsi drink with the face. A-2, which was less effective than the other two A-ads, represents the bubbles emanating from the Pepsi can as different emoji, all of them associated with a vibrant and active lifestyle. But unlike A-1 many subjects said that it was "too cluttered" for specific interpretations to emerge. Finally, A-3 was connotatively effective because the smiley was part of the presentation of the bottle, equating the bottle with a facial expression of happiness. Now, while all 6 ads revolved around a basic core interpretation of happiness, the ways in which the A-ads represented this state allowed for the CI to increase considerably.

It is also to be noted that the placement of emoji is not random or decorative. In A-1 it is the subject of the ad syntax, so to speak, since it blends with the human subject. It seems to be in an adjunct relation with the emoji on the bottle in the bottom corner. So, the syntax would read exactly like the tagline at the top, "Say it with Pepsi," with the "Say it" coming from the emoji face and the "with Pepsi" coming from the bottom bottle. In other words, the left-to-right syntax of the tagline is mirrored in the syntax of the emoji layout.

As the study revealed, emoji advertising is based on an ingenious use of the standard emoji lexicon. The suggestiveness of an emoji ad is raised through a syntactic juxtaposition of the emoji characters on faces and products, which appears to generate higher CIs than comparable non-emoji ads.

CONCLUSION

The emoji trend within advertising mirrors the larger trend of emoji usage in the contemporary Internet Age. In effect, the emoji code has found a special communicative niche in advertising, which is always a gauge for larger communicative trends. Advertisers, politicians, pop celebrities and the like tend to see the emoji code as an opportunity to establish contact with specific audiences so as to portray themselves as friendly, trustworthy, and *au courant*. But there is a negative aspect to all this—if the emoji code is ever to become a true universal language, it cannot become constrained through commercial usages, since these are bound to have a rebound effect on communicative trends generally.

A number of brands have systematically tapped into the power of emoji advertising from Burger King, Dove, Gatorade, Pepsi and Taco Bell. But marketers have no idea what the future holds for emoji advertising, or for the shelf-life of the emoji code itself. What will happen when the emoji novelty wears off, as argued in a previous work (Danesi 2016)? Only time will tell, as the cliché goes.

REFERENCES

Alshenqeeti, H. (2016). Are emojis creating a new or old visual language for new generations? A socio-semiotic study. *Advances in Language and Literary Studies, 7,* 56–69.

Balasuriya, L., Doran, D., Sheth, A., & Wijeratne, S. (2016). EmojiNet: A machine-readable emoji sense inventory. *PubMed*, *10*, 527–541. PMID:28736776

Beasley, R., & Danesi, M. (2002). *Persuasive signs: The semiotics of advertising*. Berlin: Mouton de Gruyter. doi:10.1515/9783110888003

Benenson, F. (2015). *How to speak emoji*. London: Ebury Press.

Danesi, M. (2006). *Brands*. London: Routledge.

Danesi, M. (2016). *The semiotics of emoji: The Rise of visual language in the age of the Internet*. London: Bloomsbury.

Jakobson, R. (1960). Linguistics and poetics. In T. A. Sebeok (Ed.), *Style and language* (pp. 34–45). Cambridge, Mass.: MIT Press.

Leung, C.-H., & Chan, W. (2017). Using emoji effectively in marketing: An empirical study. *Journal of Digital & Social Media Marketing*, *5*(1), 76–95.

Malinowski, B. (1923). The problem of meaning in primitive languages. In C. K. Ogden & I. A. Richards (Eds.), *The meaning of meaning* (pp. 296–336). New York: Harcourt, Brace and World.

Miller, H., Thebault-Spieker, J., Chang, S., Johnson, I., Terveen, L., & Hecht, B. (2016). "Blissfully happy" or "ready to fight": Varying interpretations of emoji. In *Proceedings of the Tenth International AAAI Conference on Web and Social Media (ICWSM 2016)* (pp. 259-268).

Moschini, I. (2016). The "face with tears of joy" emoji: A socio-semiotic and multimodal insight into a Japan-America mash-up. *Hermes: Journal of Language and Communication in Business*, *55*, 11–25.

Olson, D. (1977). *Media and symbols: The forms of expression, communication and education*. Chicago: University of Chicago Press.

Polak, K. (2015). When a product becomes a brand. *Marketing w Praktyce, February*. Retrieved June 2017 from http://semiotyka.com/en/cultural-branding.html

Skaggs, S. (2017). *Fire signs: A semiotic theory of graphic design*. Cambridge: MIT Press.

Vidal, L., Ares, G., & Jaeger, S. R. (2016). Use of emoticon and emoji in tweets for food- related emotional expression. *Food Quality and Preference*, *49*, 119–128. doi:10.1016/j.foodqual.2015.12.002

Yakin, V., & Eru, O. (2017). An application to determine the efficacy of emoji use on social marketing ads. *International Journal of Social Sciences and Education Research*, *3*(1), 230–240. doi:10.24289/ijsser.270652

This research was previously published in the International Journal of Semiotics and Visual Rhetoric (IJSVR), 1(2); pages 1-12, copyright year 2017 by IGI Publishing (an imprint of IGI Global).

Chapter 49
Shopping via Instagram:
The Influence of Perceptions of Value, Benefits and Risks on Purchase Intentions

Chayada Apiraksattayakul
Newcastle University Business School, Newcastle upon Tyne, UK

Savvas Papagiannidis
 https://orcid.org/0000-0003-0799-491X
Newcastle University Business School, Newcastle upon Tyne, UK

Eleftherios Alamanos
Newcastle University Business School, Newcastle upon Tyne, UK

ABSTRACT

This study presents an empirical investigation as to the key determinants of purchase intention towards clothing on Instagram. A conceptual model has been created, based upon the relevant literature and research questions of this study, which has subsequently been evaluated through a quantitative methodology. A convenience sample of 200 Thai customers was selected in order to complete the questionnaire. The accumulated data was analysed via multiple regression in order to test the study's hypotheses. The results suggest that four aspects contribute positively towards customer purchase intentions (perceived social value, perceived price value, perceived quality value and perceived benefits) while, in contrast, risk perceptions have been found to adversely impact upon customer purchase intentions. Two other aspects, perceived emotional value and electronic word of mouth, have been found to have no significant influence upon purchase intentions.

1. INTRODUCTION

In recent years, social media have become a part of everyday life. Consumers are increasingly using the Internet to search for information related to products and services and social networking sites for vale co-creation related activities (Paredes, Barrutia, & Echebarria, 2014). On the other hand, many

DOI: 10.4018/978-1-7998-9020-1.ch049

e-marketers and e-sellers have begun to offer their products and services via social networking sites. Social networks can enhance online marketing by providing an effective advertising platform (Duffett, 2015) as well as by offering up-to-date information, products and services, which can be very important for fast-moving industries the rely on trend-setting, such as fashion (Kang & Johnson, 2013; Kim & Ko, 2010; Park & Cho, 2012)

A number of studies have discussed online customer purchase intentions in relation to fashion. While previous studies have investigated the purchase intentions held by online customers towards apparel, most research has focused on e-commerce websites (Almousa, 2010; Almousa & Brosdahl, 2013; Dawson & Kim, 2010; Erdil, 2015; Kim & Kim, 2004; Kwon & Noh, 2010; Loan, Fah, & Samadi, 2015; Rodriguez & Fernandez, 2016). While a small number of previous studies have investigated the relationship between purchase intentions and social media sites such as Facebook (Duffett, 2015; Kwahk & Ge, 2012; Nadeem, Andreini, Salo, & Laukkanen, 2015; Napompech, 2014), studies on other social networks that have a different scope and function remain scarce.

Consequently, this study examines what factors influence customer intentions towards buying apparel via Instagram. More specifically, the study's research objectives are, first, to examine which factors among various perceptions have a significant influence upon Thai customer purchase intentions towards apparel available to buy on Instagram and, secondly, how various perceptions towards apparel as given on Instagram impact upon customer intentions. To this end, this study examines seven potential antecedents of online purchase intentions, namely, perceived social value, perceived price value, perceived quality value and perceived emotional value as well as perceived risk, perceived benefits and, finally, the impact of electronic word of mouth.

2. LITERATURE REVIEW

2.1. Social Commerce

Social commerce is an evolution of e-commerce and a new way of undertaking online business, available as a result of the dramatic growth of social media sites and their active users. Social commerce uses a Web 2.0 infrastructure and social media applications to support online interactions and user contributions for the acquisition of products and services (Liang & Turban, 2011; Liang & Turban, 2012). Yadav et al (2013) define social commerce as "...exchange-related activities that occur in, or are influenced by, an individual's social network in computer-mediated social environments, where the activities correspond to the need recognition, pre-purchase, purchase, and post-purchase stages of a focal exchange..." The unique features that differentiate social commerce from e-commerce are that the former makes it possible for consumers and sellers to generate content and for both to interact with each other at any time and from anywhere (Kim & Park, 2013). Web 2.0 applications enable the interactions of online users, with the information shared among users being able to help in the decision-making in relation to products and services (Hajli, 2014). Aside from assisting users in seeking and exchanging information, social media also facilitate the sharing of opinions and the purchasing of products and services online (Constantinides, 2014). This makes social commerce a powerful channel for online businesses while simultaneously supporting customer-centric contexts, such as customer services and understanding customer personae (Liang & Turban, 2012).

2.2. Conceptual Framework & Hypothesis Development

According to Ajzen (1991) intention refers to an individual's behaviour, attitudes and purpose in regard to their motivations. Purchase behaviour occurs when a customer plans to purchase a particular product or service (Jin & Kang, 2011; Laroche, Kim, & Zhou, 1996). Purchase intentions relate to the possibility of a customer desiring to buy a particular product or service (Schiffman & Kanuk, 2000). The higher the consumer purchase intention rate, the more a customer intends to buy the given product or service. Hong and Cho (2011) argue that a strong relationship exists between purchase decisions and brand loyalty, with this relationship being considered to be purchase intention. Purchase intentions can determine the incentives that drive individuals with regard to buying a particular product or service through the Internet (Chen, Hsu, & Lin, 2010). Consequently, when customers look for a product, their purchase intentions are affected by the perceptions they hold towards the available products and services. In other words, they will have specific reasons and a positive attitude that they wish to satisfy, instigating their purchase intention (Hong & Cho, 2011).

According to Sinha and Desarbo (1998), "…perceived value is clearly a multi-dimensional construct derived from perceptions of price, quality, quantity, benefits and sacrifice…" In line with this view, Sweeney and Soutar (2001) have developed a multi-dimensional construct of perceived value, identifying this as consisting of: price, quality, social and emotional value. Studies have previously shown that perceived value has a positive correlation with customer purchase intentions, but mainly in the offline business (Akdeniz, 2012; Sweeney & Soutar, 2001; Wang, 2010). In online commerce, perceived risk is a crucial factor directly impacting upon customer intentions to buy. According to Manzano et al. (2009) perceived risk can reduce customer anxiety as to the outcome of an online transaction while increasing customer confidence towards buying products and services online. Also, customers' perceived benefits are affected by their perceived risks (Kim, Ferrin, & Rao, 2008; Loan et al., 2015). In addition, the reduction of risk for customers influences their perceptions of electronic word of mouth (Lin, Wu, & Chen, 2013). The opinions and past experiences of other customers will enhance the trust in online transactions and customer purchase intentions. Therefore, in order to explore which factors impact upon customer purchase intentions in relation to apparel on Instagram, the variables shown in Figure 1 will be considered within this study.

2.2.1. Social Value

Social value is associated with hedonic value, namely in that it enhances the ability of people to interact and communicate with other people, it increases their social status and connects them with wider groups (Williams, 2002). Social value has been defined as "…the utility derived from the product's ability to enhance social self-concept…" (Sweeney & Soutar, 2001). Customers note the link between a product and the groups associated with the product in order to classify their individualism, thereby promoting their preferences, by imbuing the products with symbolic value (Park, Jaworski, & MacInnis, 1986). Perceived social value impacts upon a customer's evaluation and suppositions as to the judgement of others, consequently comparing their own outcome with that of others (Tynan, McKechnie, & Chhuon, 2010). In other words, consumers weigh the consequence of their choices against the choice of others prior to making their selection as to which products and services they are going to buy. Hence, customers intend to purchase and use products that reside within categories that can clearly personify their value in society (Wang, 2010).

Figure 1. Conceptual model of this study

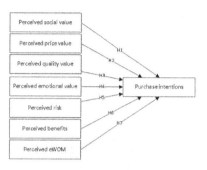

In the past few years, several studies have been undertaken on perceived social value and purchase intention and have focused upon both the retail and service industry. Chia and Kilduff (2011) found that perceived social value positively and significantly affected the purchase intentions of US customers when it came to selecting casual sportswear. Kakkos et al. (2015) undertook an analysis of purchase intentions of Greek customers as held towards private label brands and found that this is correlated with perceived social value. Social value can also be seen to impact upon purchase intentions held in relation to fashion products (Bai, Li, & Niu, 2016; Yoh, Damhorst, Sapp, & Laczniak, 2003). Specifically, previous research suggests that social value mediates the effect of materialism on purchase intentions of luxury products (Sun et al., 2017). The positive relationship between perceived social value and purchase intention has also been found in a number of Far-East studies in the context of luxury products, e.g. for Taiwanese (Li, Robson, & Coates, 2013), Chinese (Zhang & Kim, 2013) and Korean customers (Park, Rabolt, & Jeon, 2008). Thus, a hypothesis can be proposed as:

H1: Perceived social value has a positive impact upon purchase intentions.

2.2.2. Price Value

Price value refers to the value a product has for a customer rather than the actual value of the product. Perceived price value can help identify when a customer hesitates in paying for a good or service (Akdeniz, 2012). Given that customers examine prices across a range of similar products available, price relates particularly to the brand choice (Chang & Wang, 2011). Perceived price is one of the major considerations in purchase decision-making, and most consumers evaluate value (combined price and quality) when deciding to purchase (Chiang & Jang, 2007). Perceived price becomes a less efficient value if a customer accepts the product quality and is willing to purchase it at the set price (Erdem, Zhao, & Valenzuela, 2004). Most previous studies have related to perceived price value and purchase intentions in regard to offline shopping, demonstrating that they have a positive relationship. As shown by Bhaduri and Ha-Brookshire (2011), customers consider price to be an important factor when purchasing private label wine brands. Perceived price value influences the purchase intentions in relation to technology products (Coelho, Meneses, & Moreira, 2013; Ozen & Kaya, 2013). Perceived price value has also been seen to impact upon the purchase intention of Indian customers towards private label brands (Patel & Barad, 2016). Previous literature also suggests that in the case of luxury products, such as gold ornaments that consumers consider as a type of investment, the expected future monetary value of such products can affect purchase intentions (Chaisuriyathavikun and Punnakitikashem, 2016). Hence, from the available literature, the perceptions as given towards price appear to be a crucial factor in regard to the purchase intentions of customers.

H2: Perceived price value has a positive impact upon purchase intentions.

2.2.3. Quality Value

Quality relates to the ability of a product to fulfil the expectations of customers (Sweeney & Soutar, 2001). In this sense, the quality of a product is often used to assess its value (Omar, 1994). Product quality is a crucial factor in determining the image of a brand, with this therefore relating to customer preferences for certain brands (Akdeniz, 2012). In the case of luxury products, the perceived quality and therefore consumers' purchase intentions are influenced by the item's country of origin (Vijaranakorn and Shannon, 2017). High quality goods will enhance the reputation of a brand and also affect the purchase intentions of customers (Tee, Gharleghi, Chan, Samadi, & Balahmar, 2015).

The relationship between perceived quality value and purchase intentions has been explored in relation to various types of product by several researchers. For example, luxury products were investigated by Li, Robson and Coates (2013), who found that perceived quality has a direct impact upon the purchase intentions of Chinese customers towards buying brand name handbags. In addition, it has been found that quality value is related to customer purchase intention in relation to sport shoes (Eunju, Kim, & Zhang, 2012; Tsiotsou, 2006). Prior studies have found that perceived quality significantly and positively impacts upon the purchase intentions of Jordanian (Tee et al., 2015) and Indian customers (Kumar, Kim, & Pelton, 2009) as held towards fashion products.

H3: Perceived quality has a positive impact upon purchase intentions.

2.2.4. Emotional Value

Sweeney and Soutar (2001) define emotional value as "...the benefit derived from the feeling or affective states that a product generates..." LeBlanc and Nguyen (2001) have described emotional value as the power of a product to provoke and affect a customer's sentiments. Marketers desire to achieve a competitive advantage by engaging with the sentiments of consumers, seeking to do this by encouraging high value to be given towards the emotional relationship each customer has with the given product/brand (Lojacono & Zaccai, 2004). Sentimental value relates to customer satisfaction in this sense, a significant component in enhancing business profits and customer loyalty (Rich, 2000). Hence, perceived emotional value is one factor that affects purchase intentions whereby a product can trigger positive sensations in customers (Wen & Noor, 2015). Previous literature has identified how perceived emotional value has a significant impact upon the process of purchasing (Kim, Knight, & Pelton, 2009; Lee, Kim, Pelton, Knight, & Forney, 2008; Lojacono & Zaccai, 2004; Shah, Shahzad, Ahmed, & Ahmed, 2012) as well as on engagement in social commerce activities (Herrando, Jiménez-Martínez, & Martín-De Hoyos, In Press). Hedonic values appear to be an important factor in regard to the buying intentions of Chinese customers (Li, Li, & Kambele, 2012). Previous research also suggests that for luxury products hedonic value derives from the satisfaction of consumers' need for uniqueness (Latter et al., 2012). Hedonic value also influences customers' purchase intention towards digital products through social networking (Kim, Gupta, & Koh, 2011).

H4: Perceived emotional value has a positive impact upon purchase intentions.

2.2.5. Risk

Dowling and Staelin (1994) define perceived risk as "…the consumer's perceptions of the uncertainty and adverse consequences of buying a product or service…" Put differently, upon making a payment, customers are often not confident in taking this action as they cannot ensure that this payment will fulfil their objectives (Corbitt, Thanasankit, & Yi, 2003). Although online shopping is convenient and saves transportation costs, research has found that purchasing through non-retail store channels can negatively affect the risk perceived by customers (Chang & Tseng, 2013). Bhatnagar and Ghose (2004) reported that customers will perceive a higher degree of risk when they purchase products online, in particular when using mobile devices (Cozzarin & Dimitrov, 2016), rather than when they purchase through traditional stores. Similar results have been presented by studies in other ecommerce and apparel contexts (Chang, Chih, Liou, & Yang, 2016; Parke, 2005; Pires, Stanton, & Eckford, 2004). Additional risks identified in relation to online purchase also include the accidental purchase of counterfeit products (Mavlanova and Benbunan-Fich, 2010).

H5: Perceived risk has a negative impact upon purchase intentions.

2.2.6. Benefits

Perceived benefits involve positive outcomes as correlated with an individual's behaviour and activities (Chandon, Wansink, & Laurent, 2000). In the online context, perceived benefits represent what customers gain from doing online shopping and undertaking online transactions on a particular website. Here, the perceptions held as to such benefits will improve customer satisfaction by forming a key aspect of the shopping process (Liu, Brock, Shi, Chu, & Tseng, 2013).

Recent research has found that customers tend to purchase online as they perceive several benefits of this method over shopping in physical stores – including, but not limited to, convenience in relation to being able to shop whenever they want, the time-saving and cost-saving nature of online shopping and the wider range of products available (Kim et al., 2008; Lim & Dubinsky, 2004). Such convenience thereby relates to purchasing behaviour being easier. Online shopping also involves savings in relation to the expenditure of transportation costs and the time expenditure of travelling to physical retail stores (Wolfinbarger & Gilly, 2001). Online shopping also contributes to the wellbeing of consumers who perceive themselves as socially excluded (Dennis et al., 2016). Therefore, perceived benefits have a positive relationship with customer purchase intention towards the online shopping context (To, Liao, & Lin, 2007) and social media (Coker, Boostrom, & Altobello, 2014). According to Chiu et al. (2014), perceived benefits also influence repeat purchase intention through e-commerce sites.

H6: Perceived benefits have a positive impact upon purchase intentions.

2.2.7. Electronic Word of Mouth

Electronic word of mouth (eWOM) is an effective method of gaining an appreciation as to the opinions of other customers via the Internet. eWOM refers to any online statements, be they positive or negative, as given by Internet users in relation to given products and services (Hennig-Thurau, Gwinner, Walsh, & Gremler, 2004). eWOM can be more useful than traditional word of mouth in terms of spreading and sharing information, as customers prefer to read the suggestions of those with personal experience of a given product/service before they decide whether to buy that product/service as well (Chatterjee, 2001). eWOM is a more credible and trustworthy source in terms of providing information as it is unbiased and has been provided for non-commercial purposes (Bickart & Schindler, 2001). Electronic word of mouth is one of the key drivers of social commerce (Ahmad and Laroche, 2017). Consequently, it can influence customers when using the Internet to search for information as to particular products and services. There are three dimensions of perceived eWOM: perceived eWOM credibility (Cheung, Luo, Sia, & Chen, 2009), perceived eWOM quantity (Bhattacherjee & Sanford, 2006) and perceived eWOM quality (Mangold & Faulds, 2009), which can have a positive relationship with purchase intention. Scholars have studied the multiple dimensions of perceived eWOM in relation to various types of product. Fan and Miao (2012) found that perceived eWOM credibility influences the intention of Taiwanese customers in regard to buying electronic products online, while perceived eWOM quality also affects the purchase intentions towards products through online shopping websites (Lee & Lee, 2009). Park, Lee and Han (2007) have found that perceived eWOM has a direct impact upon the purchase intentions of Koreans in relation to purchasing products online. Also, the type of eWOM platform moderates the influence of eWOM quality on eWOM credibility and purchase intention (Tsao & Hsieh, 2015). Finally, Bataineh's (2015) exploration as to the perceived eWOM on social media and its impacts upon the purchase intentions of Jordanian customers found a correlation between the two.

H7: Electronic word of mouth has a positive impact upon purchase intentions.

3. METHODOLOGY

The data collected was provided through an online questionnaire. The questionnaire was provided in English and consists of two parts. In the first part, the general demographic information about the participants (including their gender, age, occupation, monthly income, frequency of Internet use and average time they spent purchasing clothes online) was sought. The questions in the second part related to the research variables, aiming to measure the impact of the seven factors hypothesised on purchase intentions, namely perceived emotional value, perceived social value, perceived price value, perceived quality value, perceived risk, perceived benefits and electronic word of mouth. The categories of the questions asked in the questionnaire, the items used to measure each construct and their sources can be seen in Table 1. Some of the original items were dropped to improve the reliability and validity of the model. The respondents were requested to note their agreement with each statement using a 7-point Likert scale.

Thailand is an excellent choice of location to undertake such research as a National Statistical Office (2013) study has indicated that 23.3% of Thais purchase fashion products online. The sample included individuals who possessed both an Instagram account and had experience of buying apparel online within the preceding three months. The questionnaire was posted on and was available across many social media platforms (such as Facebook, Twitter and Google+) for approximately two weeks. Ultimately, while 233 respondents participated in the study, due to incomplete answers only 200 valid responses were used for the analysis. Table 2 summarises the main demographic characteristics of the participants.

Table 1. Constructs

Construct	Variable	Statement	Source
Perceived Emotional Value	EM01	The clothes on Instagram give me pleasure.	(Sweeney & Soutar, 2001)
	EM02	I am comfortable purchasing clothes on Instagram.	
	EM03	The clothes on Instagram make me feel good.	
Perceived Social value	S01	The clothes on Instagram make me feel accepted.	(Wang, 2010)
	S02	The clothes on Instagram increase positive perception when other people look at me.	
	S03	The clothes on Instagram ensure social acceptance of users in the community.	
Perceived Price	P01	The clothes on Instagram are suitably priced.	(Akdeniz, 2012; Sweeney & Soutar, 2001)
	P02	The clothes on Instagram are good quality for their price.	
Perceived Quality	Q01	The clothes on Instagram are well-produced.	(Akdeniz, 2012; Sweeney & Soutar, 2001)
	Q02	The clothes on Instagram are of an acceptable quality.	
Perceived Risk	R01	Purchasing clothes on Instagram is risky because the delivered products may fail to meet my expectations.	(Corbitt et al., 2003)
	R02	Purchasing clothes on Instagram is risky because the delivered products may be of inferior quality.	
	R03	Purchasing clothes on Instagram is risky because the delivered products may be unusable.	
Perceived Benefits	B01	Shopping for clothes on Instagram is convenient.	(Kim et al., 2008)
	B02	Shopping for clothes on Instagram accomplishes a shopping task more quickly than if using traditional stores.	
	B03	Shopping for clothes on Instagram increases productivity in shopping (e.g., it quickens purchase decisions and the finding of product information).	
Perceived eWOM	EW01	The reviews/comments on Instagram are credible.	(Lin et al., 2013)
	EW02	The quantity of reviews/comments on Instagram suggest that the product has good sales.	
	EW03	I think that the customers who provided reviews/comments on Instagram are experienced.	
Purchase Intention	INTEN01	I am willing to buy the products of this apparel brand via Instagram.	(Akdeniz, 2012; Wang, 2010)
	INTEN02	I am likely to recommend apparel brands on Instagram to others.	

Table 2. Demographics of the respondents (n = 200)

Variable	Option	Frequency	%
Gender	Male	63	31.5
	Female	137	68.5
Age	18-21	32	16.0
	22-25	109	54.5
	26-29	47	23.5
	30-35	12	6.0
Monthly Income (฿)	Less than ฿10000	29	14.5
	฿10000 - ฿20000	53	26.5
	฿20001 - ฿30000	69	34.5
	฿30001 - ฿40000	22	11.0
	More than ฿40001	27	13.5
Occupation	Student	84	42.0
	Office Worker	55	27.5
	Self-Employed	29	14.5
	Other	32	16.0
Time Spent Online Per Day	Less Than 1 Hour	2	1.0
	2-3 Hours	37	18.5
	4-7 Hours	107	53.5
	8-12 Hours	39	19.5
	More Than 12 Hours	15	7.5
Frequency of Shopping Online via Instagram	2-3 Times a Week	1	0.5
	Once a Week	11	5.5
	Every Two Weeks	19	9.5
	Monthly	25	12.5
	Occasionally	144	72.0
Money Spent On Each Shopping Occasion (฿)	Less than ฿2000	155	77.5
	฿2000 - ฿5000	42	21.0
	฿5001 - ฿10000	3	1.5

4. RESULTS

4.1. Analysis of Reliability and Validity

Confirmatory factor analysis was used to test the reliability and validity. All items load significantly under their respective factors, demonstrating good reliability of the scales (Table 3). The results indicated that discriminant and convergent validity were satisfactory (Table 4).

Table 3. Construct validity

Construct	Variable	Loading	Composite Reliability
Perceived Emotional Value	EM01	.837	.875
	EM02	.855	
	EM03	.816	
Perceived Social value	S01	.822	.872
	S02	.741	
	S03	.928	
Perceived Price	P01	.821	.862
	P02	.917	
Perceived Quality	Q01	.865	.860
	Q02	.872	
Perceived Risk	R01	.909	.925
	R02	.927	
	R03	.852	
Perceived Benefits	B01	.853	.864
	B02	.808	
	B03	.811	
Perceived eWOM	EW01	.798	.869
	EW02	.824	
	EW03	.868	
Purchase Intention	INTEN01	.780	.798
	INTEN02	.848	

Method: ML; Model fit: $\chi2(161) = 314.687$, CMIN/DF = 1.955, CFI = .951, RMSEA = .069

Table 4. Discriminant validity and average variance explained

Construct	AVE	PeW	PEV	PSV	PP	PQ	PR	PB	PI
Perceived eWOM (PeW)	.690	.831							
Perceived Emotional Value (PEV)	.699	.700	.836						
Perceived Social Value (PSV)	.695	.509	.429	.834					
Perceived Price (PP)	.757	.753	.570	.469	.870				
Perceived Quality (PQ)	.754	.720	.737	.455	.797	.869			
Perceived Risk (PR)	.804	-.639	-.484	-.470	-.612	-.514	.897		
Perceived Benefits (PB)	.679	.716	.605	.402	.792	.814	-.488	.824	
Purchase Intention (PI)	.664	.695	.626	.632	.762	.751	-.627	.781	.815

The diagonal of the table presents the square root of AVE. Numbers below the diagonal represent the correlations between the factors.

4.2. Regression Analysis

The factor scores of the constructs were employed in multiple regression analysis to examine the relationships between the independent and the dependent variables. The model explained 59% of the variance ($R^2 = 0.59$), and no multicollinearity issues were found between the variables (Table 5).

Table 5. Collinearity statistics for independent variables

Construct	VIF
Perceived Social Value	1.382
Perceived Price Value	2.581
Perceived Quality Value	2.742
Perceived Emotional Value	1.943
Perceived Risk	1.655
Perceived Benefits	2.464
Perceived eWOM	2.485

The results of the regression analysis suggest that perceived social value has a positive effect on purchase intentions (H_1 supported). H_2 is also supported as a positive effect of price value on purchase intentions was found. The effects of perceived quality value and perceived emotional value on purchase intentions were not statistically significant (H_3 and H_4 respectively not supported). Perceived risk was found to have a significant negative impact upon purchase intentions (H_5 supported). Perceived benefits were also found to have a significant and positive effect upon purchase intention (H_6 is supported). Finally, the relationship between eWOM and purchase intention was found not to be significant (H_7 not supported) (Table 6).

Table 6. Coefficients of regression analysis

Model	Unstandardised Coefficients		Standardised Coefficients		
	B	Std. Error	Beta	t	Sig.
(Constant)	-3.200E-16	.046		.000	1.000
Perceived Social Value	.220	.054	.220	4.050	.000
Perceived Price Value	.200	.074	.200	2.700	.008
Perceived Quality Value	.099	.077	.099	1.296	.197
Perceived Emotional Value	.089	.064	.089	1.388	.167
Perceived Risk	-.160	.059	-.160	-2.698	.008
Perceived Benefits	.251	.073	.251	3.459	.001
Perceived eWOM	-.022	.073	-.022	-.298	.766

5. DISCUSSION

The findings of this research indicate that perceived social value has a positive effect on purchase intentions towards apparel on Instagram, this being similar to the findings of previous research as to how perceived social value impacts upon the intention of customers to buy given products (Li et al., 2013; Zhang & Kim, 2013). According to Hofstede (2015), Thailand is highly collectivist and Thai people prefer to act as a member of society rather than in an individualist manner. Thus, the findings show that they will consider the types of clothing they wear as a way of improving their self-esteem, while also purchasing items that make it possible for them to belong to a societal group and enhance the way others perceive them.

The findings also show that perceived price has a positive effect on purchase intentions, as customers will often consider price when shopping. The results of this study are consistent with the findings of previous research on traditional retail shopping (Bhaduri & Ha-Brookshire, 2011; Wang, 2010). However, in this study it has been found that perceived price also influences online purchase intention. As Instagram allows customers to search for the kind of clothes they desire, they can easily compare the offered price with that advertised by other shops. Offering a reasonably-priced acceptable quality product can therefore encourage purchase decisions.

The analysis of the collected data suggested that perceived quality value has a non-significant impact upon the purchase intentions of customers. This is in contrast to the findings of previous studies relating to perceived quality value and offline purchase intentions (Li et al., 2013; Tee et al., 2015). Thai customers are concerned as to the performance of clothing products, the materials used and the quality of their construction (Ackaradejruangsri, 2013). However, in this study, quality was not emphasised in regard to their preference for one apparel shop over another as the customers are not able to touch or observe the raw material of products when they do online shopping.

In addition, this study found that there is no significant relationship between perceived emotional value and purchase intention in the online setting. This contradicts previous literature that has argued that perceived emotional value plays an important role in relation to purchase intentions (Lee et al., 2008; Li et al., 2012; Lojacono & Zaccai, 2004). The results of this study are consistent with Sarker (2011), who found that customers with a high emotional value tend to avoid online shopping, as they cannot interact with the sellers directly. Here, customers prefer to buy in traditional stores rather than via online stores. This may explain why, when Thai customers want to pay for clothes online, they rely on reason rather than sentiment. The plausible reason is the limited condition of online shopping as the customer cannot ensure that the real product is the same as what they are paying for. Thus, they will consider the reason to purchase more than the need. This means that emotional aspects or hedonic considerations do not impact upon the buying intentions of Thai customers towards apparel shopping undertaken via Instagram.

It is unsurprising that this study confirms the significant impact of perceived risk upon purchase intentions, this being congruent with many prior studies (Almousa, 2010; Erdil, 2015; Pires et al., 2004). The more a customer perceives risk, the less likely they will be to intend to buy a product/service. Instagram can facilitate interactions between users in that the customers can make inquiries before they consider purchasing the products/services from the online retailers. This means that the risk perceptions held by online customers might be reduced through their increased confidence in buying products/services online (Drennan, Mort, & Previte, 2006). In addition, Niemela-Nyrhinen (2007) points out that members of the younger generation are more likely to perceive a lower degree of risk than people of an older generation – the former/latter being the age range of this study's participants (18-35). As far as Thai customers perceiving less risk is concerned, they seem to accept the uncertainty of purchasing online, particularly in regard to the purchased product/service potentially failing to meet their expectations.

Moreover, the findings of this study also demonstrate the positive impact of perceived benefits upon the purchase intentions of Thai customers towards apparel shopping via Instagram. These results are in line with previous research as to the key role of perceived benefits on the purchase intentions held towards online clothing in different countries (Kim et al., 2008; Loan et al., 2015). One explanation for this is offered by Changchit (2006), who suggested that customers perceive more benefits in online shopping than in conventional retail shopping. According to Cheawkamolpat (2009), the benefits of online shopping for Thai customers relate to time and cost saving, which is consistent with the outcomes of this study.

Finally, perceived electronic word of mouth has no direct impact upon the purchase intentions of Thai customers when shopping online. The findings of this study are not in line with a number of previous studies (Bataineh, 2015; Fan & Miao, 2012; Lee & Lee, 2009; Park et al., 2007). According to Bataineh (2015), there is a positive correlation between perceived electronic word of mouth on social media and the purchase intentions of Jordanian customers. Nevertheless, the findings of this study reflect the fact that reviews, likes or the opinions of other customers towards particular clothes on Instagram do not impact upon the purchase intentions of Thai customers. One plausible reason for this is given by Chu and Kim (2011), who proposed that on social media people generally do not develop strong ties and thus do not know each other well enough to have such trust.

6. CONCLUSION

The aim of this study was to test a number of factors that influence Thai customers' perceptions towards having purchase intentions in relation to apparel promoted on Instagram. This study has examined seven variables, namely perceived social value, perceived price value, perceived quality value, perceived emotional value, perceived risk, perceived benefits and perceived eWOM. According to the findings, three of the perceptions (social, price, and benefits) were found to have a positive and significant impact upon the purchase intentions of Thai customers towards shopping for clothing via Instagram. In contrast, perceived risk has been found to have an adverse impact upon such purchase intentions. This means that the purchase intentions of Thai customers will decrease upon there being a reduction in the risk perceived by such customers. On the other hand, three other dimensions (perceived emotional value, perceived quality and perceived electronic word of mouth) were found not to have a significant relationship with the purchase intentions of Thai customers. It can thus be concluded that neither emotions, feelings nor the opinions of other buyers directly influence the purchase intentions of Thai consumers when it comes to purchasing clothing via Instagram.

From the analysis presented in this study, a number of managerial implications can be derived. For example, the findings indicate that if sellers desire to attract customers, they will have to follow fashionable trends that appeal to their followers. The visual nature of the hosted content is conducive to advertising products in an attractive manner. The social network can also make the marketplace more transparent when it comes to pricing, which can render customers more sensitive to price variations among sellers. In addition, enhancing customer confidence is a determinant of purchase intentions, which sellers could approach by offering one-to-one conversations, guaranteed satisfaction pledges and return policies. Also, sellers should enhance the convenience of online shopping via Instagram by providing transaction support and a wide range of products in order to improve the shopping experience. Instagram and similar platforms can provide the necessary functionally to better integrate feeds with sellers' systems so that purchasing is as easy as possible. This appears to be a direction Instagram is already following, judging from recently introduced changes.

6.1. Limitations and Recommendations for Future Research

While this study contributes important insights as to the perceptions that impact upon the purchase intentions of Thai customers, limitations nonetheless exist that should be addressed in future research. Firstly, the data was collected from a single province of Thailand, Bangkok. Future studies could examine a more representative sample of the population and / or, more broadly speaking, of Instagram users. Secondly, only one product category has been explored in this research, that of clothing. Further studies could consider other types of products and the impact this might have on customer purchase intentions. Finally, this study has utilised a relatively small number of independent factors and thus may not have captured all of the variables that affect the purchase intentions of customers when shopping online. Consequently, future studies may wish to incorporate additional independent variables in order to gain a more holistic understanding of consumer behaviour.

REFERENCES

Ackaradejruangsri, P. (2013). The effect of product quality attributes on Thai consumers' buying decisions. *Ritsumeikan Journal of Asia Pacific Studies*, *33*, 14–24.

Ahmad, S. N., & Laroche, M. (2016). Analyzing electronic word of mouth: A social commerce construct. *International Journal of Information Management*, *37*(3), 202–213. doi:10.1016/j.ijinfomgt.2016.08.004

Ajzen, I. (1991). The Theory of Planned Behavior. *Organizational Behavior and Human Decision Processes*, *50*(2), 179–211. doi:10.1016/0749-5978(91)90020-T

Akdeniz, A. (2012). Effect of perceived values on the brand preference and purchase intention. *European Scientific Journal*, *8*(17), 1–17.

Almousa, M. (2010). Perceived Risk in Apparel Online Shopping: A Multi Dimensional Perspective. *Canadian Social Science*, *7*(2), 23–31.

Almousa, M., & Brosdahl, D. J. C. (2013). Online apparel purchasing: A cultural comparison of Saudi Arabian and U.S. consumers. *Journal of International Business and Cultural Studies*, *13*(7).

Bai, Y., Li, C., & Niu, J. (2016). Study on Customer-Perceived Value of Online Clothing Brands. *American Journal of Industrial and Business Management*, *6*(8), 914–921. doi:10.4236/ajibm.2016.68088

Bataineh, A. Q. (2015). The Impact of Perceived e-WOM on Purchase Intention: The Mediating Role of Corporate Image. *International Journal of Marketing Studies*, *7*(1), 126–137. doi:10.5539/ijms.v7n1p126

Bhaduri, G., & Ha-Brookshire, J. (2011). Do transparent business practices pay? Exploration of transparency and consumer purchase intention. *Clothing & Textiles Research Journal*, *29*(2), 135–149. doi:10.1177/0887302X11407910

Bhatnagar, A., & Ghose, S. (2004). Journal of Business Research. *Segmenting Consumers Based on the Benefits and Risks of Internet Shopping*, *57*(12), 1352–1360.

Bhattacherjee, A., & Sanford, C. (2006). Influence process for information technology acceptance: An elaboration likelihood model. *Management Information Systems Quarterly*, *30*(4), 805–825.

Bickart, B., & Schindler, R. (2001). Internet forums as influential sources of consumer information. *Journal of Interactive Marketing*, *15*(3), 31–40. doi:10.1002/dir.1014

Chaisuriyathavikun, N., & Punnakitikashem, P. (2016). A study of factors influencing customers' purchasing behaviours of gold ornaments. *Journal of Business and Retail Management Research*, *10*(3), 147–159.

Chandon, P., Wansink, B., & Laurent, G. (2000). A Benefit Congruency Framework of Sales Promotion Effectiveness. *Journal of Marketing*, *64*(4), 65–81. doi:10.1509/jmkg.64.4.65.18071

Chang, E.-C., & Tseng, Y.-F. (2013). Research note: E-store image, perceived value and perceived risk. *Journal of Business Research*, *66*(7), 864–870. doi:10.1016/j.jbusres.2011.06.012

Chang, H. H., & Wang, H.-W. (2011). The moderating effect of customer perceived value on online shopping behaviour. *Online Information Review*, *35*(3), 333–359. doi:10.1108/14684521111151414

Chang, S., Chih, W., Liou, D., & Yang, Y. (2016). The mediation of cognitive attitude for online shopping. *Information Technology & People*, *29*(3), 618–646. doi:10.1108/ITP-08-2014-0172

Changchit, C. (2006). Customer perception of online shopping. *Issues in Information Systems*, *7*(2), 177–181.

Chatterjee, P. (2001). Online reviews: Do consumers use them? *Advances in Consumer Research. Association for Consumer Research (U. S.)*, *28*(1), 129–133.

Cheawkamolpat, P. (2009). Online shopping behavior: A study of consumers in Bangkok. *AU journal of management*, *7*(2), 1-11.

Chen, Y. H., Hsu, I. C., & Lin, C. C. (2010). Website attributes that increase consumer purchase intention: A conjoint analysis. *Journal of Business Research*, *63*(9-10), 1007–1014. doi:10.1016/j.jbusres.2009.01.023

Cheung, M., Luo, C., Sia, C., & Chen, H. (2009). Credibility of electronic word-of-mouth: Informational and normative determinants of on-line consumer recommendations. *International Journal of Electronic Commerce*, *13*(4), 9–38. doi:10.2753/JEC1086-4415130402

Chia, T., & Kilduff, P. P. D. (2011). Understanding consumer perceived value of casual sportswear: An empirical study. *Journal of Retailing and Consumer Services*, *18*(5), 422–429. doi:10.1016/j.jretconser.2011.06.004

Chiang, C.-F. (2007). The Effects of Perceived Price and Brand Image on Value and Purchase Intention: Leisure Travelers Attitudes Toward Online Hotel Booking. *Journal of Hospitality & Leisure Marketing*, *15*(3), 49–69. doi:10.1300/J150v15n03_04

Chiu, C., Wang, E.T.G., Fang, Y., & Huang, H. (2014). Understanding customers' repeat purchase intentions in B2C e-commerce: the roles of utilitarian value, hedonic value and perceived risk. *Information Systems and e-Business Management, 24*(1), 85–114.

Chu, S.-C., & Kim, Y. (2011). Determinants of consumer engagement in electronic word-of-mouth (eWOM) in social networking sites. *International Journal of Advertising, 30*(1), 47–75. doi:10.2501/IJA-30-1-047-075

Coker, K. K., Boostrom, R. E., & Altobello, S. A. (2014). What Makes Social Shoppers Click? The Role of Social Rewards in Social Shopping. *The Marketing Management Journal, 24*(1), 66–79.

Constantinides, E. (2014). Foundations of Social Media Marketing. *Procedia: Social and Behavioral Sciences, 148*(2), 40–57. doi:10.1016/j.sbspro.2014.07.016

Corbitt, B. J., Thanasankit, T., & Yi, H. (2003). Trust and e-commerce: A study of consumer perceptions. *Electronic Commerce Research and Applications, 2*(3), 203–215. doi:10.1016/S1567-4223(03)00024-3

Cozzarin, B. P., & Dimitrov, S. (2016). Mobile commerce and device specific perceived risk. *Electronic Commerce Research, 16*(3), 335–354. doi:10.100710660-015-9204-5

Dawson, S., & Kim, M. (2010). Cues on apparel web sites that trigger impulse purchases. *Journal of Fashion Marketing and Management: An International Journal, 14*(2), 230–246. doi:10.1108/13612021011046084

Dennis, C., Alamanos, E., Papagiannidis, S., & Bourlakis, M. (2016). Does social exclusion influence multiple channel use? The interconnections with community, happiness and well-being. *Journal of Business Research, 69*(3), 1061–1070. doi:10.1016/j.jbusres.2015.08.019

Dowling, G. R., & Staelin, R. (1994). A Model of Perceived Risk and Intended Risk-Handling Activity. *The Journal of Consumer Research, 21*(1), 119–134. doi:10.1086/209386

Drennan, J., & Mort, G. S. (2006). Privacy, Risk Perception, and Expert Online Behavior: An Exploratory Study of Household End Users. *Journal of Organizational and End User Computing, 18*(1), 1–22. doi:10.4018/joeuc.2006010101

Duffett, R. G. (2015). The influence of Facebook advertising on cognitive attitudes amid Generation Y. *Electronic Commerce Research, 15*(2), 243–267. doi:10.100710660-015-9177-4

Duffett, R. G. (2015). Facebook advertisings influence on intention-to-purchase and purchase amongst Millennials. *Internet Research, 25*(4), 498–526. doi:10.1108/IntR-01-2014-0020

Erdem, T., Zhao, Y., & Valenzuela, A. (2004). Performance of Store Brands: A Cross-Country Analysis of Consumer Store-Brand Preferences, Perceptions, and Risk. *JMR, Journal of Marketing Research, 41*(1), 86–100. doi:10.1509/jmkr.41.1.86.25087

Erdil, T. S. (2015). Effects of Customer Brand Perceptions on Store Image and Purchase Intention: An Application in Apparel Clothing. *Procedia: Social and Behavioral Sciences, 207*, 196–205. doi:10.1016/j.sbspro.2015.10.088

Eunju, K., Kim, K. H., & Zhang, H. (2012). A Cross Cultural Study of Antecedents of Purchase Intention for Sports Shoes in Korea and China. *Journal of Global Academy of Marketing Science, 18*(1), 157–177. doi:10.1080/12297119.2008.9707281

Falcão e Cunha, J., Snene, M., & Nóvoa, H. (Eds.). Coelho, Dany C., Meneses, Raquel F. Ch., & Moreira, Maria R. A. (2013). Factors Influencing Purchase Intention of Private Label Products: The Case of Smartphones. In J. Falcão e Cunha, M. Snene & H. Nóvoa (Eds.), *Exploring Services Science: 4th International Conference, IESS 2013, Porto, Portugal, February 7-8, 2013. Proceedings* (pp. 313-321). Berlin, Heidelberg: Springer Berlin Heidelberg.

Fan, Y. W., & Miao, Y. F. (2012). Effect of electronic word-of-mouth on consumer purchase intention: The perspective of gender differences. *International Journal of Electronic Business Management, 10*(3), 175–181.

Hajli, M. N. (2014). The role of social support on relationship quality and social commerce. *Technological Forecasting and Social Change, 87*, 17–27. doi:10.1016/j.techfore.2014.05.012

Hennig-Thurau, T., Gwinner, K. P., Walsh, G., & Gremler, D. D. (2004). Electronic word of mouth via customer-opinion platform: what motivates consumers to articulate themselves on the internet? *Journal of Interactive Marketing, 18*(1), 38–52. doi:10.1002/dir.10073

Herrando, C., Jiménez-Martínez, J., & Martín-De Hoyos, M. J. (in press). Passion at first sight: How to engage users in social commerce contexts. *Electronic Commerce Research*.

Hofstede, G. (2015). Thailand Retrieved 10th August 2016, from https://geert-hofstede.com/thailand.html

Hong, I. B., & Cho, H. (2011). The impact of consumer trust on attitudinal loyalty and purchase intentions in B2C e-marketplaces: Intermediary trust vs. seller trust. *International Journal of Information Management, 31*(5), 469–479. doi:10.1016/j.ijinfomgt.2011.02.001

Jin, B., & Kang, J. H. (2011). Purchase intention of Chinese consumers toward a US apparel brand: A test of a composite behavior intention model. *Journal of Consumer Marketing, 28*(3), 187–199. doi:10.1108/07363761111127617

Kakkos, N., Trivellas, P., & Sdrolias, L. (2015). Identifying Drivers of Purchase Intention for Private Label Brands. Preliminary Evidence from Greek Consumers. *Procedia: Social and Behavioral Sciences, 175*(3), 522–528. doi:10.1016/j.sbspro.2015.01.1232

Kang, J. Y. M., & Johnson, K. K. P. (2013). How Does Social Commerce Work for Apparel Shopping? Apparel Social E-Shopping with Social Network Storefronts. *Journal of Customer Behaviour, 12*(1), 53–72. doi:10.1362/147539213X13645550618524

Kim, A. J., & Ko, E. (2010). Impacts of Luxury Fashion Brands Social Media Marketing on Customer Relationship and Purchase Intention. *Journal of Global Fashion Marketing, 1*(3), 164–171. doi:10.1080/20932685.2010.10593068

Kim, D. J., Ferrin, D. L., & Rao, H. R. (2008). A trust-based consumer decision-making model in electronic commerce: The role of trust, perceived risk, and their antecedents. *Decision Support Systems, 44*(2), 544–564. doi:10.1016/j.dss.2007.07.001

Kim, E. Y., & Kim, Y. K. (2004). Predicting online purchase intentions for clothing products. *European Journal of Marketing, 28*(7), 883–889.

Kim, E. Y., Knight, D. K., & Pelton, L. E. (2009). Modeling Brand Equity of a U.S. Apparel Brand as Perceived by Generation Y Consumers in the Emerging Korean Market. *Clothing & Textiles Research Journal, 27*(4), 247–258. doi:10.1177/0887302X08327085

Kim, H., Gupta, S., & Koh, J. (2011). Investigating the intention to purchase digital items in social networking communities: A customer value perspective. *Information & Management, 48*(6), 228–234. doi:10.1016/j.im.2011.05.004

Kim, S., & Park, H. (2013). Effects of various characteristics of social commerce (sCommerce) on consumers trust and trust performance. *International Journal of Information Management, 30*(2), 318–332. doi:10.1016/j.ijinfomgt.2012.11.006

Kumar, A., Kim, Y., & Pelton, L. (2009). Indian consumers purchase behavior toward US versus local brands. *International Journal of Retail & Distribution Management, 37*(6), 510–526. doi:10.1108/09590550910956241

Kwahk, K. Y., & Ge, X. (2012, January 4-7). The Effects of Social Media on E-Commerce: A Perspective of Social Impact Theory. *Paper presented at the 2012 45th Hawaii International Conference on System Science (HICSS).*

Kwon, W. S., & Noh, M. (2010). The influence of prior experience and age on mature consumers perceptions and intentions of internet apparel shopping. *Journal of Fashion Marketing and Management: An International Journal, 14*(3), 335–349. doi:10.1108/13612021011061825

Laroche, N., Kim, C., & Zhou, L. (1996). Brand familiarity and confidence as determinants of purchase Intention: An empirical test in a multiple brand context. *Journal of Business Research, 37*(10), 115–120. doi:10.1016/0148-2963(96)00056-2

Latter, C., Phau, I., & Marchegiani, C. (2010). The roles of consumers need for uniqueness and status consumption in haute couture luxury brands. *Journal of Global Fashion Marketing, 1*(4), 206–214. doi:10.1080/20932685.2010.10593072

LeBlanc, G., & Nguyen, N. (2001). An exploratory study on the cues that signal value to members in retail co-operatives. *International Journal of Retail & Distribution Management, 29*(1), 49–59. doi:10.1108/09590550110366361

Lee, J., & Lee, J.-N. (2009). Understanding the product information inference process in electronic word-of-mouth: An objectivity–subjectivity dichotomy perspective. *Information & Management, 46*(5), 302–311. doi:10.1016/j.im.2009.05.004

Lee, M.-Y., Kim, Y., Pelton, L., Knight, D., & Forney, J. (2008). Factors affecting Mexican college students purchase intention toward a US apparel brand. *Journal of Fashion Marketing and Management: An International Journal, 12*(3), 294–307. doi:10.1108/13612020810889263

Li, G., Li, G., & Kambele, Z. (2012). Luxury fashion brand consumers in China: Perceived value, fashion lifestyle, and willingness to pay. *Journal of Business Research, 65*(10), 1516–1522. doi:10.1016/j.jbusres.2011.10.019

Li, N., Robson, A., & Coates, N. (2013). Chinese consumers purchasing: Impact of value and affect. *Journal of Fashion Marketing and Management: An International Journal, 17*(4), 486–450. doi:10.1108/JFMM-03-2013-0030

Liang, T. P., & Turban, E. (2011). Introduction to the special issue: Social commerce: A research framework for social commerce. *International Journal of Electronic Commerce, 16*(2), 5–14. doi:10.2753/JEC1086-4415160201

Liang, T. P., & Turban, E. (2012). Introduction to the Special Issue Social Commerce: A Research Framework for Social Commerce. *International Journal of Electronic Commerce, 16*(2), 5–13. doi:10.2753/JEC1086-4415160201

Lim, H., & Dubinsky, A. J. (2004). Consumers" perceptions of e-shopping characteristics: An expectancy-value approach. *Journal of Services Marketing, 18*(7), 500–513. doi:10.1108/08876040410561839

Lin, C., Wu, Y., & Chen, J. (2013, May 29-31). Electronic Word-of-Mouth: The Moderating Roles of Product Involvement and Brand Image. *Paper presented at the International Conference on Technology Innovation and Industrial Management*, Phuket.

Liu, M. T., Brock, J. L., Shi, G. C., Chu, R., & Tseng, T. H. (2013). Perceived benefits, perceived risk, and trust: Influences on consumers group buying behaviour. *Asia Pacific Journal of Marketing and Logistics, 25*(2), 225–248. doi:10.1108/13555851311314031

Loan, K. T. M., Fah, B. C. Y., & Samadi, B. (2015). Exploring Customer Purchasing Intention over Online Store. *International Journal of Business and Social Research, 5*(5), 15–23.

Lojacono, G., & Zaccai, G. (2004). The evolution of the design-inspired enterprise. *MIT Sloan Management Review, 45*(3), 75–79.

Mangold, W. G., & Faulds, D. J. (2009). Social media: The new hybrid element of the promotion mix. *Business Horizons, 52*(4), 357–365. doi:10.1016/j.bushor.2009.03.002

Manzano, J. A., Navarré, C. L., Mafé, C. R., & Blas, S. S. (2009). The role of consumer innovativeness and perceived risk in online banking usage. *International Journal of Bank Marketing, 27*(1), 53–75. doi:10.1108/02652320910928245

Mavlanova, T., & Benbunan-Fich, R. (2010). Counterfeit products on the internet: The role of seller-level and product-level information. *International Journal of Electronic Commerce, 15*(2), 79–104. doi:10.2753/JEC1086-4415150203

Nadeem, W., Andreini, D., Salo, J., & Laukkanen, T. (2015). Engaging consumers online through websites and social media: A gender study of Italian Generation Y clothing consumers. *International Journal of Information Management, 35*(4), 432–442. doi:10.1016/j.ijinfomgt.2015.04.008

Napompech, K. (2014). Factors Driving Consumers to Purchase Clothes through E-commerce in Social Networks. *Journal of Applied Sciences, 14*(17), 1936–1943. doi:10.3923/jas.2014.1936.1943

National Statistical Office. (2013). The Survey of e-Commerce Status in Thailand. Retrieved August 3, 2016 from http://web.nso.go.th/en/survey/ict/data_ict/560514_Electric_13.pdf

Niemelä-Nyrhinen, J. (2007). Baby boom consumers and technology: Shooting down stereotypes. *Journal of Consumer Marketing*, *24*(5), 305–312. doi:10.1108/07363760710773120

Omar, O. E. (1994). Comparative Product Testing for Own-label Marketing. *International Journal of Retail & Distribution Management*, *22*(2), 12–17. doi:10.1108/09590559410054086

Ozen, H., & Kaya, I. (2013). How Value Perception Affects Buying Intentions of Online Consumers? *Bogazici Journal: Review of Social, Economic & Administrative Studies*, *27*(2), 11–29.

Paredes, M. R., Barrutia, J. M., & Echebarria, C. (2014). Resources for value co-creation in e-commerce: A review. *Electronic Commerce Research*, *14*(2), 111–136. doi:10.100710660-014-9135-6

Park, C. W., Jaworski, B. J., & MacInnis, D. J. (1986). Strategic brand concept/image management. *Journal of Marketing*, *50*(4), 135–145. doi:10.2307/1251291

Park, D. H., Lee, J., & Han, I. (2007). The Effect of On-Line Consumer Reviews on Consumer Purchasing Intention: The Moderating Role of Involvement. *International Journal of Electronic Commerce*, *11*(4), 125–148. doi:10.2753/JEC1086-4415110405

Park, H., & Cho, H. (2012). Social network online communities: Information sources for apparel shopping. *Journal of Consumer Marketing*, *29*(6), 400–411. doi:10.1108/07363761211259214

Park, H. J., Rabolt, N. J., & Jeon, K. S. (2008). Purchasing global luxury brands among young Korean consumers. *Journal of Fashion Marketing and Management: An International Journal*, *12*(2), 244–259. doi:10.1108/13612020810874917

Parke, F. I. (2005). Lower cost spatially immersive visualization for human environments. *Landscape and Urban Planning*, *73*(2-3), 234–243. doi:10.1016/j.landurbplan.2004.11.009

Patel, V., & Barad, K. (2016). Factors Affecting Consumers' Intention to Purchase Private Labels in India. *Amity Business Review*, *16*(2), 91–99.

Pires, G., Stanton, J., & Eckford, A. (2004). Influences on the perceived risk of purchasing online. *Journal of Consumer Behaviour*, *4*(2), 118–131. doi:10.1002/cb.163

Rich, M. K. (2000). Emotional Value: Creating Strong Bonds with Your Customers. *Journal of Business and Industrial Marketing*, *5*(6), 458–460. doi:10.1108/jbim.2000.15.6.458.1

Rodriguez, T. E., & Fernandez, R. B. (2016). Analysing online purchase intention in Spain: fashion e-commerce. *Information Systems and e-Business Management, 14*(54), 1-24.

Sarker, A. (2011). Impact of Utilitarian and Hedonic Shopping Values on Individual's Perceived Benefits and Risks in Online Shopping. *International Management Review*, *7*(1), 58–65.

Schiffman, L. G., & Kanuk, L. L. (2000). *Consumer Behavior* (7th ed.). New Jersey: Prentice-Hall, Inc.

Shah, S. L., Shahzad, A., Ahmed, T., & Ahmed, I. (2012). Factors Affecting Pakistan's University Student's Purchase Intention Towards Foreign Apparel Brands. *Management*, *17*(1), 1–14.

Sinha, I., & DeSarbo, W. S. (1998). An Integrated Approach toward the Spatial Modeling of Perceived Customer Value. *JMR, Journal of Marketing Research*, *35*(2), 236–249. doi:10.2307/3151851

Sun, G., Wang, W., Cheng, Z., Li, J., & Chen, J. (2017). The Intermediate Linkage Between Materialism and Luxury Consumption: Evidence from the Emerging Market of China. *Social Indicators Research*, *132*(1), 475–487. doi:10.100711205-016-1273-x

Sweeney, J. C., & Soutar, G. N. (2001). Consumer perceived value: The development of a multiple item scale. *Journal of Retailing*, *77*(2), 203–220. doi:10.1016/S0022-4359(01)00041-0

Tee, P. K., Gharleghi, B., Chan, B., Samadi, B., & Balahmar, A. A. (2015). Purchase Intention of International Branded Clothes Fashion among Younger's in Jakarta'. *International Journal of Business and Social Research*, *5*(8), 8–17.

To, P., Liao, C., & Lin, T. (2007). Shopping motivations on Internet: A study based on utilitarian and hedonic value. *Technovation*, *27*(12), 774–787. doi:10.1016/j.technovation.2007.01.001

Tsao, W.-C., & Hsieh, M.-T. (2015). eWOM persuasiveness: Do eWOM platforms and product type matter? *Electronic Commerce Research*, *15*(4), 509–541. doi:10.100710660-015-9198-z

Tsiotsou, R. (2006). The role of perceived product quality and overall satisfaction on purchase intentions. *International Journal of Consumer Studies*, *30*(2), 207–217. doi:10.1111/j.1470-6431.2005.00477.x

Tynan, C., McKechnie, S., & Chhuon, C. (2010). Co-creating value for luxury brands. *Journal of Business Research*, *63*(11), 1156–1163. doi:10.1016/j.jbusres.2009.10.012

Vijaranakorn, K., & Shannon, R. (2017). The influence of country image on luxury value perception and purchase intention. *Journal of Asia Business Studies*, *11*(1), 88–110. doi:10.1108/JABS-08-2015-0142

Wang, E. S.-T. (2010). Impact of Multiple Perceived Value on Consumers Brand Preference and Purchase Intention: A Case of Snack Foods. *Journal of Food Products Marketing*, *16*(4), 386–397. doi:10.1080/10454446.2010.509242

Wen, T. C., & Noor, N. A. M. (2015). What Affects Malaysian Consumers' Intention to Purchase Hybrid Car? *Asian Social Science, 11*(26), 52-63.

Williams, T. G. (2002). Social class influences on purchase evaluation criteria. *Journal of Consumer Marketing*, *19*(3), 249–276. doi:10.1108/07363760210426067

Wolfinbarger, M., & Gilly, M. (2001). Shopping online for freedom, control, & fun. *California Management Review*, *43*(2), 34–56. doi:10.2307/41166074

Yadav, M. S., de Valck, K., Hennig-Thurau, T., Hoffman, D. L., & Spann, M. (2013). Social Commerce: A Contingency Framework for Assessing Marketing Potential. *Journal of Interactive Marketing*, *27*(4), 311–323. doi:10.1016/j.intmar.2013.09.001

Yoh, E., Damhorst, M. L., Sapp, S., & Laczniak, R. (2003). Consumer Adoption of the Internet: The Case of Apparel Shopping. *Psychology and Marketing*, *20*(12), 1095–1118. doi:10.1002/mar.10110

Zhang, B., & Kim, J.-H. (2013). Luxury fashion consumption in China: Factors affecting attitude and purchase intent. *Journal of Retailing and Consumer Services*, *20*(1), 68–79. doi:10.1016/j.jretconser.2012.10.007

This research was previously published in the International Journal of Online Marketing (IJOM), 7(4); pages 1-20, copyright year 2017 by IGI Publishing (an imprint of IGI Global).

Chapter 50

Is Anybody Out There?
Using Application Statistics and Web Analytics to Assess Social Media Reach

Junior Tidal

New York City College of Technology (CUNY), USA

ABSTRACT

This chapter will explore how social media assessment is used for library marketing. It will build upon existing literature on how other libraries quantify social media impact in promoting their services. This includes methods on how libraries can gather native application statistics from popular platforms such as Facebook, Twitter, YouTube, and Instagram. An exploration into web analytics will also be explored as evidence of social media impact. The chapter will use case-studies of the Ursula C. Schwerin Library of the New York City College of Technology (City Tech), CUNY, and how social media platforms are used to advertise library events and disseminate news.

INTRODUCTION

In the last few years, social media has made impacts in culture, politics, and most notably, libraries. Libraries and librarians are known as early technology adopters, with over 1,300 libraries possessing Twitter accounts (Emery & Schifeling, 2015). After observing 6 Midwest academic libraries, Harisson et al., make the claim that libraries "must use social media in order to retain legitimacy in today's college environment (2017)." This make sense as 68% of Americans use Facebook accessing the service on a daily basis (Smith & Anderson, 2018). As libraries utilize social media it is important to analyze if these networks are making an impact in providing their services.

This chapter will explore how social media assessment is used for library marketing. It will build upon existing literature on how other libraries quantify social media impact in promoting their services. This includes methods on how libraries can gather native application statistics from popular platforms such as Facebook, Twitter, YouTube, and Instagram. An exploration into web analytics will also be explored as evidence of social media impact. The chapter will use case-studies of the Ursula C. Schwerin Library

DOI: 10.4018/978-1-7998-9020-1.ch050

of the New York City College of Technology (City Tech), CUNY, and how social media platforms are used to advertise library events and disseminate news.

BACKGROUND

There has been an enormous amount of literature related to the development of social media in libraries in the last few years. As of this writing, there are over 7,400 articles related to social media in the Library & Information Science Source electronic database. 86% of public libraries are using social media to connect with users (Dowd, 2013). It can be used for collaborative work and opens opportunities for advertising library services (Delaney & Bates, 2015). Social media tools can be a "useful discovery tool for scanning and finding users' comments" of an organization (Koontz & Mon, 2014).

Social media is useful as it can help build an online community around the library. Montana State University utilized its Twitter feed to creating more interactive postings by developing an internal social media guide, developing plans to focus on the audience, and intentional and frequent posting (Young & Rossman, 2015). Facebook was used to specifically cater to a community of young adults, by promoting materials, programming, and services, for those particular patrons (Philips, 2015). In China, libraries specifically target users of the WeChat app, a popular social media mobile chat platform, to boost and promote library services (Xu et al. 2014).

Although there is an abundance of scholarly literature on social media, there is a gap in focusing specifically on social media assessment in libraries. There are, however, articles in the larger literature that do touch upon it. Burclaff notes that when assessing social media it is important to create a strategy that identifies goals so quantifiable metrics, like click-throughs and student feedback, can be measured (2014). Libraries can also use influence, the amount of sway an organization has on its followers, or engagement, the amount of conversation a post generates, to measure the effectiveness of social media (Blowers, 2012).

MAIN FOCUS OF THE CHAPTER

The City Tech Library uses multiple social media platforms, including Facebook, Twitter, Instagram, YouTube, Flickr, and Pinterest. Each of these platforms has their own form of built-in statistics. This ranges from the complex, such as Facebook's page insights or Twitter's built-in analytics tools, to the more the simplistic like Instagram's number of likes. This chapter will look specifically at Facebook, Twitter, and Instagram.

Facebook

Facebook is a social media platform that allows its users to share information between one another, groups, and online communities. It offers a wide variety of statistics on followers visiting a library's Facebook page, using an analytics tool called Facebook Insights (see Figure 1). Administrators can access Insights through the top menu of the Facebook page.

Figure 1. Facebook Insights displays a variety of metrics of users

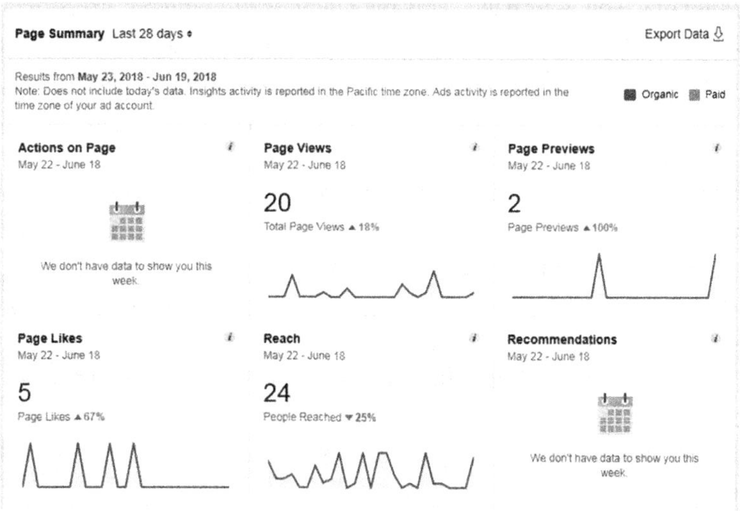

Statistics such as page views, likes, reach, recommendations, engagements, and more are displayed. Information can be cross-referenced by date (today, yesterday, past week, and past 28 days) for comparison. There are several different metrics that Insights uses. Page views are self-explanatory. Likes indicates how many people have "liked" your page. It also displays posts from your page that appear in the user's feed that are liked. Reach is the number of people who have seen posts from your page (see Figure 2). The recommendations metric indicate which users have shared your page with others. Engagement is the number of times users have liked, commented, or shared your posts.

Figure 2. A display of Facebook posts and the number of users each reach

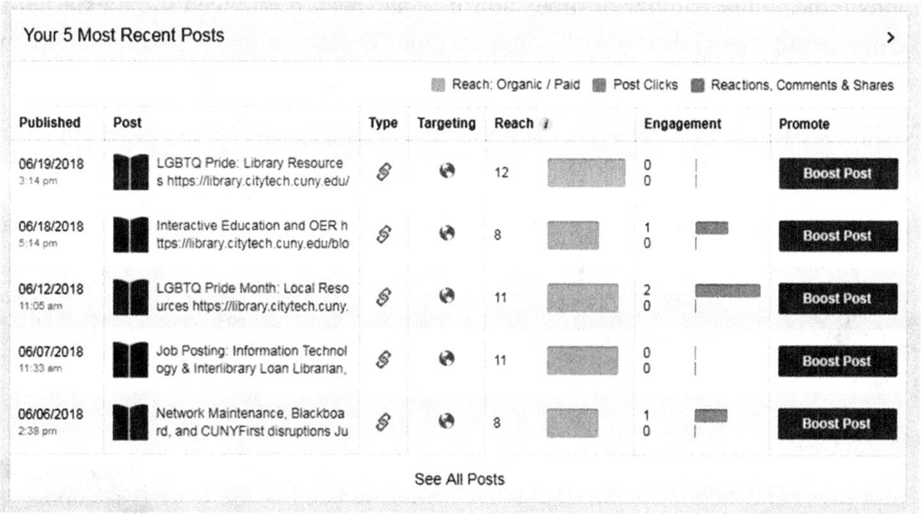

There are other metrics that Facebook Insights records in relation to your page. Actions are user interactions that are taking place on your page. This may include clicking on directions, external websites, or phone numbers. Posts displays all the posts published on a page. It indicates when fans are online and the different types of posts, such as links, that are on your page. Thronbill and Houk point out that postings should be frequent, be highly visual, and be posted at the peak times that pages are visited (2013).

The other metric that Insights displays for posts include the top posts of pages that you are watching. This allows the comparison of your page with others that you are viewing. For example, you may be part of a consortium or branch library and you want to see what other posts they are displaying. It can also be a way to share posts from other pages you are watching.

The videos and stories categories show statistics when that type of media on your page are viewed. The people category displays demographic information about followers, as well as what country and city that they originate from. This section of Insights also shows what languages they use. The last category of the Insights page is messages, which presents active conversations between your page and users of Facebook Messenger. Facebook also has an analytics tool (https://analytics.facebook.com) that can be used to track users from your website to your Facebook page.

Twitter

Twitter is a microblogging social media platform where posts are known as "tweets." Tweets can be replied to, favored (liked), or retweeted. It is a microblogging service because the number of characters that can be posted are finite. Twitter has an analytics tool that librarians can use to see how well tweets are received. This tool also gives information on an account's followers, users who actively monitor an account.

Much like Facebook Insights, Twitter Analytics (TA) displays metrics such as the monthly number of tweets produced, tweet impressions, profile visits, mentions, and followers (see Figure 3). It can be found here - https://analytics.twitter.com/about. Impressions are the collected number of views of a tweet or conversation. Profile visits, similar to page views, are the number of times a profile has been seen by a user. Mentions indicate the number of times a profile has been referenced in an external tweet. Followers are the number of users following a Twitter account. TA also provides more in-depth information through various tabs, including the audience tab, events tab, and video and conversion tabs. All of this collected data can be exported into other formats for further manipulation.

Figure 3. The Twitter Analytics dashboard gives a snapshot of metrics related to a Twitter account

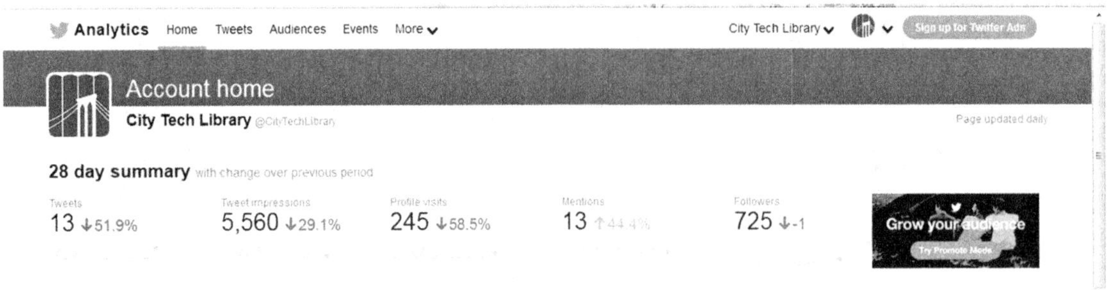

The tweets tab displays the number of impressions a tweet has earned over a given time period. These can be filtered to display the top tweets, replies, and promoted tweets. Impressions, engagements, and engagement rate are also available for further analysis. Link clicks, retweets, likes, and replies also provides information to see interactivity between an account and its followers.

The audience tab shows information on followers of a Twitter account. Users can be filtered by all Twitter users, an account's followers, or organic audiences. These different types of users can then be compared in real-time within TA. This tab lists users' top interests, demographic information, lifestyle (interests), consumer behavior, and mobile footprint. Interests represent what topics the majority of your users favor. This can be useful for crafting specific tweets. Demographic information lists gender, household income, languages used, what country they are tweeting from, and which region or state they are from. This tab also displays what mobile carriers followers use. The consumer behavior tab displays the top products audience users have purchased.

The events tab displays trending events that are popular on the platform. Drilling down into specific events, events can show the demographics of a popular event, the number of tweets, impressions, and reach, the top tweets, and the countries that event is popular in. TA can also be used as a jumping board to create a social media campaign in relation to these events. Events can also display recurring actions. For example, the events can display #FBF. #FBF, or flashback Friday, is a popular hashtag where users post or repost a moment in their past.

In addition to those tabs, TA can also display analytics for videos posted on Twitter and conversion tags. The video tab shows the reach of an account's video. The conversion tag system is much like Google Analytics (GA), where user behavior can be tracked on a website by embedding Twitter's tracking code. This can be used to place a dollar amount to the interactions of a Twitter account on a website.

Instagram

Instagram is a photo-based social media platform which is designed specifically for mobile devices, such as smartphones and tablets. Using the built-in camera of these devices, users are able to take photos and videos posting them to their accounts along with a caption. Users can also post "stories," which disappear from the platform after 24 hours. Followers of an Instagram account can "like" posts on their feed or comment. Accounts can be made private or public, and the platform has seamless integration with Facebook and Twitter. Unless it is private, accounts do not necessarily need to be following one another to view each other's posts. These posts can be followed using hashtags, or Instagram's search interface. Instagram has also launched IGTV, which provides users with longer-format videos.

Owned by Facebook, Instagram's analytics tool is called Instagram Insights. Insights provides statistics on individual posted photos. It provides information regarding the overall interactions of an account. This feature, however, is only available for business accounts. It should be noted that standard accounts can be converted to business accounts. So, if a library has a standard Instagram account it can be altered to become a business account.

Instagram Insights, like the other native analytics tools discussed, provides numerous metrics. Individual photo metrics include the number of likes, comments, and saves of a post. Insights displays information such as interactions, discovery, reach, and impression. Interactions are similar to those in Facebook Insights. This metric is the total number of likes and comments on a post. Discovery is the number of accounts that had seen a post, including those that do not follow your account. Reach is the number of unique users that have seen your post. Impressions is the number of times a post or story has been seen.

Insights also presents the top posts based on impressions. Engagement is the total number of accounts that have liked, saved, or commented on a post. Instagram users, known as the "audience," is also analyzed within Instagram Insights. Audience metrics include age, gender, location, active hours, active days, story impressions, and top followers. These metrics are self-explanatory, but indicates an account's overall audience. They are useful for developing strategic social media campaigns, which will be discussed later.

SOLUTIONS AND RECOMMENDATIONS

Web Analytics

Application statistics are not the only tools that the modern-day social media engaged librarian has at their disposal. Google Analytics, which can be found at https://analytics.google.com and its open-source counterpart, Matomo (formerly known as Piwik and is located at https://matomo.org/) are two web analytics tools that can track social media traffic coming into a library website. This data can be used to better understand user engagement. Wright notes that "statistics provide an excellent start for assessing whether or not social campaigns are successful, but they may not give much information about problems or reasons why campaigns are not successful (2015)."

Google Analytics

In a nutshell, GA is used to gather information on web traffic for a specific website. Developed by Google, GA provides a number of metrics ranging from user engagement, referrals (where traffic is originating from), what pages on a site are visited, what pages users are exiting from, and much more. The system works by adding JavaScript to the header of a webpage. This script triggers the analytics server to record interaction data from that page. This is then processed and centralized on the GA website, where administrators can login and view the data collected from the website over a period of time.

There is an abundance of literature related to GA. Vecchione et al. used GA to better understand their users by identifying the navigation pathways used inside and out of the site (2016). It has been used to improve the design and content of library websites (Fang, 2007, Turner, 2010), develop learning objects (Betty, 2009), and understand LibGuides usage (Griffin and Taylor, 2018). There has also been literature criticizing GA due to privacy concerns. McKenzie argues that GA should not be used within libraries due to ethical and privacy concerns (2017). Cornell has replaced their installation of GA stating, "for privacy-related reasons alone, Piwik is a better web analytics solution for libraries. (Chandler and Wallace, 2016)."

GA can be used to evaluate social media reach. GA has a "Social" reports tab under the "Acquisitions" menu, that displays data from 8 different categories. This includes overview, network referrals, data hub activity, landing pages, trackbacks, conversions, plugins, and user flow.

The overview tab is the main dashboard for the social reports tab. It shows the social value of the website. It lists network referrals, the number of overall sessions of a site, and how many of those sessions originate from social media. Network referrals displays the sources and pages that users utilize on your site through social media (see Figure 4). These can be used to develop navigation schemes or prioritize campaigns for users originating from specific platforms. For instance, it can display all the sessions that had originated from Twitter and landed your blog URL. By clicking on a specific social media network within this tab, it can display the URLs that users entered through. Knowing this information, content on that page can be catered specifically for Twitter users.

Figure 4. The social media page in Google Analytics show what networks are used to connect to the website

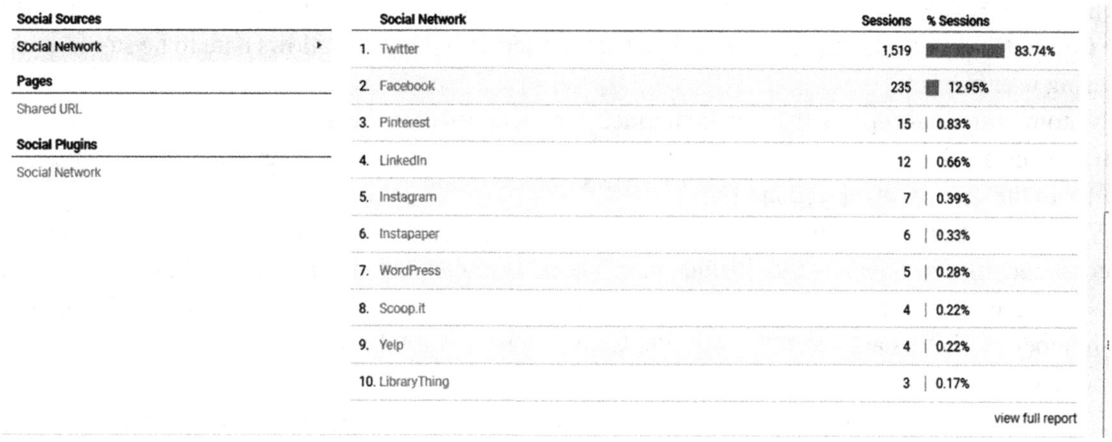

Social Sources		Social Network	Sessions	% Sessions
Social Network	▸	1. Twitter	1,519	83.74%
Pages		2. Facebook	235	12.95%
Shared URL		3. Pinterest	15	0.83%
Social Plugins		4. LinkedIn	12	0.66%
Social Network		5. Instagram	7	0.39%
		6. Instapaper	6	0.33%
		7. WordPress	5	0.28%
		8. Scoop.it	4	0.22%
		9. Yelp	4	0.22%
		10. LibraryThing	3	0.17%
				view full report

Landing pages is a metric that shows what pages social media users "land" on. For example, if a user connects to the library website homepage through Facebook, this metric will display this. GA can be used to cross-reference these statistics, so it is also possible to see which of those users visited the homepage using a tablet or mobile device. With this in mind, specific webpages, if not the whole site already, could be rendered mobile friendly. Again, this can be used to target specific users. In this scenario, it could potentially be Facebook users using a Smartphone.

Conversions is an analytics report show the return of investment (ROI) in social media using monetary measurements. This function requires a goal to be setup through the admin menu, where administrators can set a dollar amount. For example, one could setup a goal to have GA track every time the electronic resources page on a library website is accessed via social media and assign a dollar value to that conversion. This may be useful to show the budgetary value of social media and to justify subscriptions for electronic resources.

The social plugins is a category that displays information regarding social media buttons on the website. This system tracks when users click a social media link through that button on a webpage. If your website has a Twitter button or icon it will record the number of clicks that button receives. This is useful to see how many users are utilizing the library website to access social media platforms.

The users flow is a visualization of traffic navigating a site. It records how users enter the site, the pages they traversed, and how they exited the site. This can be useful to better understand bulk traffic. One scenario could be how successful a social media campaign is to promote a group of electronic resources. A group of electronic resources could be promoted via Twitter, and this visualization could see which specific resource is being traversed to.

Matomo

Matomo is a popular open-source alternative to GA. It offers similar features to that of GA, yet it is open-source and cost-free. It does require some technical know-how for installation. The prerequisite of running a Matomo server include a web server installed with PHP, a web parsing language, and MySQL, a popular database language. It works on the same technical principles as its Google based counterpart. A line of JavaScript code is installed into each web page of a site to track users. Matomo can be hosted, like GA, but users can install the software on the web server itself. This allows data to be stored locally ensuring user privacy.

Matomo provides reports that can be applied for social media assessment. This widget can display metrics such as visits, actions, unique visitors, users, conversions, and total revenue. Many of these are similar to the metrics displayed in GA.

Visits are defined as the number of new users accessing a site for more than 30 minutes. Actions that Matomo records users conducting include page views, site searches, downloads or clicking on external links. Unique visitors are the number of users visiting the website, omitting multiple visits. Users is the number of visitors active on the website. Conversions and total revenue are parallel to the metrics found in GA.

Visualizations of visitors cross referenced to social media can be displayed as a bar graph, pie graph (see Figure 5), a table, and even a tag cloud. This will display the most visited social media platforms within a given time-frame. This can extremely useful, as it can give comparisons to the data reported in GA. For example, GA may display uncommonly used social media platforms (see Figure 6) in their statistics, whereas Matomo may not.

The analytics system can also display insights of social media, which displays the changes in visits over a period of time. Matomo also allows URLs to be "tagged," much like GA, so specific URLs can be tracked to see what links users are clicking on to reach the site. In addition, Matomo has exporting capabilities, rendering data in CSV, XML, PHP, RSS, TSV, JSON, and HTML. This can be helpful for sharing information with other librarians and administrators. Even further, this data can be parsed for data dashboards which may be useful for annual reporting.

Figure 5. A display of visits from social media networks to the website using Matomo

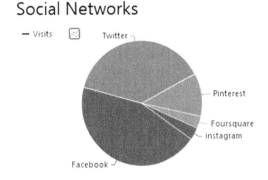

This is a subset of the Websites report to the left. It filters out other websites so you can compare your social network referrers directly.

Figure 6. Matomo shows less used social media platforms

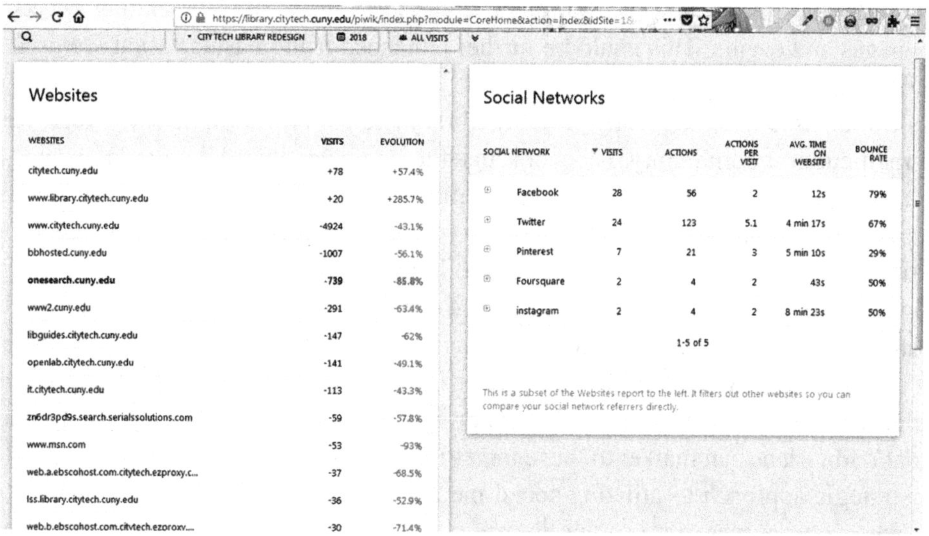

City Tech Analytics

The Ursula C. Schwerin Library has not used social media statistics to formally evaluate marketing and promotional reach. It is used more as a guideline of how things could improve. Burclaff mentions that "determining success is dependent on what you're trying to achieve" when it comes to social media (2014). Social media strategies and goals should be developed prior to evaluating analytics. It would be difficult, if not impossible, to effectively assess a social media campaign if there were no benchmarks determined before the campaign.

Despite not using formal analytics analysis, the City Tech Library has utilized other methods to understand users' behavior with social media. An online poll on the library website was used to determine which social media platforms the community uses. The anonymous poll was on the website for a full academic year. Although the result was a small sample of respondents (n=20), it was found that Instagram was the most popular platform, followed by Facebook, Twitter, and LinkedIn. It should be noted, however, that this does not necessarily mean our users were utilizing those platforms to visit our social media accounts. Instead, this information was used to initiate campaigns on Instagram, the most used platform.

Every semester, platforms are evaluated on an ad hoc basis. This coincides with the marketing and promotion of specific library events. The library does not have a designated social media librarian, but a formal internal committee known as the public relations, outreach, and marketing (PROM) committee. The PROM committee occasionally reviews social media statistics, such as the number of likes and which platforms referring to the library website.

GA and Matomo provides much more information that can be used to drive broad or specific social media campaigns. Some examples include better understanding website users, promoting library events, or reaching social media users not visiting the library website.

Social media analytics can find users' preferences. Using the City Tech library's analytics data, there are a number of generalities that can be derived. Over the course of a calendar year, GA and Matomo indicate that Twitter is our most referred social media network. This information can be used to target users from other platforms, such as sharing Instagram photos on Twitter or sending tweets with links to Facebook pages and events. This could be further enhanced using hashtags that are used to index a post or tweet.

Analytics can be used to strategically promote library events. For example, City Tech serves a very diverse and multicultural community. Facebook Insights indicates that there are languages other than English that users speak. This information can be useful to promote a library event specifically to speakers of those other modern languages. Inclusive library programs and events could be developed to cater to those particular users based on the statistics found in analytics.

Assessing this library event scenario is simple. Attendees can be asked how they heard about the event. A post-event survey, either through email, social media, or in-person, could enquire if they had heard about the event through a specific platform or if they speak another language. This information can be coupled with analytics information for the promotion of future events. By combining analytics and survey data, librarians can market to these target library users.

Another strategic approach to utilizing social media analytics for libraries is to reach those social media users who don't necessarily use the library at all. Twitter analytics provides a multitude of information that could be used to develop personas. Personas are a common usability method to develop archetypes based on real data. Ward notes that "personas can help us see user needs more clearly as we make decisions about how to provide services (2010)."

Deriving a persona from a combination of analytics tools can be useful to reach users who do not visit the library's website. In Figures 7 and 8, this image displays the Twitter analytics audience insight page of the City Tech Library. For instance, we can create a persona named Bob who lives in New York, speaks English and Spanish, is interested in science and uses an iPhone to access the Internet. We can also describe Bob as a male student, aged 17-22. Bob is active on social media with his mobile device, yet is easily distracted juggling a job and student life. He doesn't use the library.

Figure 7. Twitter reveals information about users through the audience insight page, such as interests

Figure 8. Audience insight shows what countries Twitter users are using the social media platform, based on IP

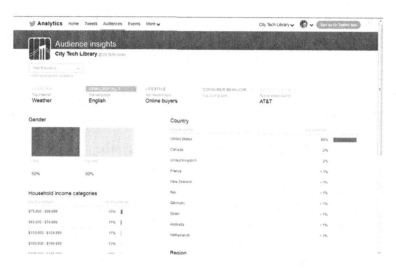

Since we have an idea of who "Bob" is, we can develop scenarios to market specifically to him. The end goal is to have Bob utilize the library website. Tweets that cater to Bob's interest in science could be one avenue to connect with him. We can construct a tweet promoting a new science-based electronic resource with hashtags that are used among City Tech students. We may also want to explore creating a bilingual tweet, since our persona speaks both English and Spanish. If there is an iPhone app for that electronic resource, which too can be promoted with a shortened URL to where it can be downloaded for Bob's consumption.

Assessing this campaign that has been developed using the Bob persona can be done by comparing it with real-world users. Similar to the event scenario above, surveys and questionnaires can be used to test users' reaction of our tweet with Bob. This can help determine if the campaign has been successful or not. For example, if these systems report that a majority of users are utilizing Facebook the most in comparison to other platforms, then campaigns can be designed to target other networks to promote library resources.

FURTHER RESEARCH DIRECTIONS: ANALYTICS IS JUST THE TIP OF THE ICEBERG

Statistics and analytics are not the only methods that a library's social media impact can be measured. These measures only provide one dimension of technological use, and at times can be quite limiting. Surveys, focus groups, and usability studies, can provide further insights into how patrons utilize social media. It is important to investigate the human aspect of how users truly engage social media to access library happenings and resources.

There are other usability techniques that can assess the performance of social media usage in libraries. As mentioned above, this can include questionnaires and surveys, focus groups, and usability testing. These research methods help round out the full picture of social media assessment. They can confirm or disprove assumptions made from analytics. More importantly, they can be used to find information that cannot be found through analytics data.

Questionnaires and surveys are useful because they can collect both quantitative and qualitative information from respondents. Likert scales can be used to discover the frequency, ease of use, and engagement of social media platforms. Besides using a persona as a point of reference for analytics data, questionnaires can be used to uncover information behind data. Data collected from surveys can be used to enhance personas and even make them more accurate. Our Bob example above notes that he doesn't use the library, but by asking a large sample of users, we can have a better understanding of why they don't use the library.

Another method of understanding users are focus groups. Focus groups are interviews with a collective of people facilitated by a stakeholder. A stakeholder could be a librarian, an administrator, a developer, or anyone who represents the library or institution. It can be beneficial for stakeholders to conduct a focus group, as interacting with users can prove or disprove assumptions about them. There is an immediacy in focus groups which may provide additional feedback with multiple participants (Battleson, Booth, and Weintrop, 2001). Focus groups may reveal insights on users' experiences with a library's social media plan, as they have with discovery systems (Brett, Lierman, & Turner, 2016), library based tutorials (Held & Gil-Trejo, 2016), and websites (Duncan, & Durrant, 2015).

Usability testing, specifically cognitive walkthroughs, can show librarians how their website works in conjunction with social media platforms. Cognitive walkthroughs are task-based heuristic evaluations of a website. Typically, a proctor will sit with a participant and have them complete a predetermined task. For example, the task could be identifying and interacting with the library's link to Facebook. The proctor can see first-hand how the user will navigate to that link and observe any obstacles from completing that task. This is coupled with the "think-aloud protocol" or TAP, where the user will discuss what they are thinking and feeling as they are navigating and attempting the task.

The TAP protocol can uncover not just usability obstacles, but can give opinions on social media embedded in the library website. Imagine a situation where users may say that the placement of social media icons in the footer is not effective. If users cannot see links to the library's social media platforms on the website, then they may be less likely to interact with them.

Once testing has ended, the website is updated to repair any usability obstacles or errors that the participant had encountered. This is re-tested again using the same task scenario, to observe the performance of the site with the repairs in place. Rubrics of success and failure rates can be applied for individual tasks to determine the effectiveness of a website in supporting a user.

Social media assessment is useful to better understand users. Utilizing it with the data gathered from usability and user experience studies can augment it to increase users, cater to their preferences, and ultimately understand them. These tools can be used to market library events and meet users where they are.

CONCLUSION

Social media assessment is an important aspect for libraries, as they digitally market their services. Native analytics within Instagram, Twitter, and Facebook can provide statistics about individual posts and generalities about users. Web analytics can further enhance this data to show how well a library's website interacts with its associated platforms. This data is useful as it can help direct campaigns, create personas, and be used to strategically communicate with users. However, analytics can only provide one piece of the bigger puzzle of how users use these services. Using other methods such as focus groups, surveys, and interviews, librarians can truly see how their community interacts with their digital presence.

REFERENCES

Battleson, B., Booth, A., & Weintrop, J. (2001). Usability testing of an academic library web site: A case study. *Journal of Academic Librarianship, 27*(3), 188–198. doi:10.1016/S0099-1333(01)00180-X

Betty, P. (2009). Assessing homegrown library collections: Using Google Analytics to track use of screencasts and flash-based learning objects. *Journal of Electronic Resources Librarianship, 21*(1), 75–92. doi:10.1080/19411260902858631

Blowers, H. (2012). Measuring social media and the greater digital landscape. *Computers in Libraries, 32*(7), 27–29.

Brett, K. R., Lierman, A., & Turner, C. (2016). Lessons learned: A primo usability study. *Information Technology and Libraries, 35*(1), 7–25. doi:10.6017/ital.v35i1.8965

Burclaff, N., & Johnson, C. (2014). Developing a social media strategy: Tweets, pins, and posts with a purpose. *College & Research Libraries News, 75*(7), 366–369. doi:10.5860/crln.75.7.9156

Chandler, A., & Wallace, M. (2016). Using Piwik Instead of Google Analytics at the Cornell University Library. *The Serials Librarian, 71*(3-4), 173–179. doi:10.1080/0361526X.2016.1245645

Delaney, G., & Bates, J. (2015). Envisioning the academic library: A reflection on roles, relevancy and relationships. *New Review of Academic Librarianship, 21*(1), 3–51. doi:10.1080/13614533.2014.911194

Dowd, N. (2013). Social media: Libraries are posting, but Is anyone listening? *Library Journal.*

Duncan, A. P., & Durrant, F. (2015). An assessment of the usability of the University of the West Indies (Mona, Jamaica) Main Library's website. *The Electronic Library, 33*(3), 590–599.

Emery & Schifeling. (2015). Libraries Using Twitter Better: Insights on Engagement from Food Trucks. In *Creating Sustainable Community The Proceedings of the ACRL 2015 Conference* (pp. 593-604). Association of College and Research Libraries: Chicago.

Fang, W. (2007). Using Google Analytics for improving library website content and design: a case study. *Library Philosophy and Practice*, 1-17.

Griffin, M., & Taylor, T. I. (2018). Employing Analytics to Guide a Data-Driven Review of LibGuides. *Journal of Web Librarianship*, 1–13.

Harrison, Burress, R., Velasquez, S., & Schreiner, L. (2017). Social media use in academic libraries: A phenomenological study. *Journal of Academic Librarianship, 43*(4), 248–256. doi:10.1016/j.acalib.2017.02.014

Held, T., & Gil-Trejo, L. (2016). Students Weigh In: Usability Test of Online Library Tutorials. *Internet Reference Services Quarterly, 21*(1/2), 1–21. doi:10.1080/10875301.2016.1164786

Houk, K. M., & Thornhill, K. (2013). Using Facebook page insights data to determine posting best practices in an academic health sciences library. *Journal of Web Librarianship*, *7*(4), 372–388. doi:10.1080/19322909.2013.837346

Koontz, C., & Mon, L. (2014). *Marketing and social media: A guide for libraries, archives, and museums*. Lanham, MD: Rowman & Littlefield.

McKenzie, J. (2017). *Ethics of using Google Analytics*. Presented to the User Experience Interest Group. Retrieved from http://summit.sfu.ca/item/17107

Phillips, A. L. (2015). Facebooking it: Promoting library services to young adults through social media. *Public Library Quarterly*, *34*(2), 178–197. doi:10.1080/01616846.2015.1036710

Turner, S. J. (2010). Website statistics 2.0: Using Google Analytics to measure library website effectiveness. *Technical Services Quarterly*, *27*(3), 261–278. doi:10.1080/07317131003765910

Smith, A., & Anderson, M. (2018, March 1). *Social Media Use in 2018*. Pew Internet Research Center. Retrieved from http://www.pewinternet.org/2018/03/01/social-media-use-in-2018/

Vecchione, A., Brown, D., Allen, E., & Baschnagel, A. (2016). Tracking user behavior with Google Analytics events on an academic library web site. *Journal of Web Librarianship*, *10*(3), 161–175. doi:10.1080/19322909.2016.1175330

Ward, J. L. (2010). Persona development and use, or, how to make imaginary people work for you. In *Building Effective, Sustainable, Practical Assessment* (pp.477 - 483). Academic Press.

Wright Joe, J. (2015). Assessment of social media in the library: Guidelines for administrators. *Journal of Library Administration*, *55*(8), 667–680. doi:10.1080/01930826.2015.1085251

Xu, J., Kang, Q., Song, Z., & Clarke, C. P. (2014). Applications of mobile social media: WeChat among academic libraries in China. *Journal of Academic Librarianship*, *41*.

Young, S. W. H., & Rossman, D. (2015). Building library community through social media. *Information Technology and Libraries*, *34*(1). doi:10.6017/ital.v34i1.5625

ADDITIONAL READING

Al-Daihani, S. M., & Abrahams, A. (2018). Analysis of Academic Libraries' Facebook Posts: Text and Data Analytics. *Journal of Academic Librarianship*, *44*(2), 216–225. doi:10.1016/j.acalib.2018.02.004

Dority Baker, M. L. (2013). Using Buttons to Better Manage Online Presence: How One Academic Institution Harnessed the Power of Flair. *Journal of Web Librarianship*, *7*(3), 322–332. doi:10.1080/19322909.2013.789333

Foster, M., Wilson, H., Allensworth, N., & Sands, D. T. (2010). Marketing Research Guides: An Online Experiment with LibGuides. *Journal of Library Administration*, *50*(5/6), 602–616. doi:10.1080/01930826.2010.488922

Guza, T. A. (2011). Washington Libraries Reveal Social Media Secrets. *Alki*, *27*(1), 19–21.

Konkiel, S., & Guichard, S. (2018). Altmetrics: "big data" that map the influence of New Zealand research. *Library Hi Tech News*, *35*(4), 1–5. doi:10.1108/LHTN-04-2018-0021

Mahmood, K., & Richardson, J. V. Jr. (2013). Impact of Web 2.0 technologies on academic libraries: A survey of ARL libraries. *The Electronic Library*, *31*(4), 508–520. doi:10.1108/EL-04-2011-0068

Rivosecchi, M. (2014). Social Media in an Academic Library: One Piece of the Puzzle. *Feliciter*, *60*(4), 45–46.

Stewart, B., & Walker, J. (2018). Build It and They Will Come? Patron Engagement Via Twitter at Historically Black College and University Libraries. *Journal of Academic Librarianship*, *44*(1), 118–124. doi:10.1016/j.acalib.2017.09.016

Sutton, S., Miles, R., & Konkiel, S. Q. (2018). Awareness of Altmetrics among LIS Scholars and Faculty. *Journal of Education for Library and Information Science*, *59*(1/2), 33–47. doi:10.3138/jelis.59.1-2.05

Vucovich, L. A., Gordon, V. S., Mitchell, N., & Ennis, L. A. (2013). Is the Time and Effort Worth It? One Library's Evaluation of Using Social Networking Tools for Outreach. *Medical Reference Services Quarterly*, *32*(1), 12–25. doi:10.1080/02763869.2013.749107 PMID:23394417

This research was previously published in Social Media for Communication and Instruction in Academic Libraries; pages 85-99, copyright year 2019 by Information Science Reference (an imprint of IGI Global).

Chapter 51

Understanding How Mexican and U.S. Consumers Decide to Use Mobile Social Media:
A Cross–National Qualitative Study

Kenneth C. C. Yang
https://orcid.org/0000-0002-4176-6219
The University of Texas at El Paso, USA

ABSTRACT

This chapter investigated cross-national consumer behaviors in adopting mobile social media among U.S. and Mexican samples. Using a combination of Extended Technology Acceptance Model (TAM2) and consumer behavior theories to describe the decision-making process of mobile and social media platform adoption. Three thematic insights are identified after analyzing their adoption decision narratives. This book chapter concluded with a summary of current academic research on multi-platforms and their advertising applications. This chapter further identified major theoretical concepts, frameworks, and methodological approaches that may help advertising and marketing communications researchers and practitioners to better understand the planning, execution, and assessment of multi-platform advertising campaigns.

INTRODUCTION

Since its introduction in the late 20th century, multi-platform advertising and marketing communications activities have played an indispensable part in the pervasive digital economy as part of the contemporary human experiences (Neijens & Voorveld, 2015; Nielsen, 2014). These multi-platform technologies have become an integral part in the life of many younger consumers around the world (Pew Research Center, 2012). They have shown similarly significant impacts on consumers with different demographic attributes as reported by Pew Internet Research Project (2014, January). For many young consumers, they began

DOI: 10.4018/978-1-7998-9020-1.ch051

their early multi-platform experiences with relatively simple mobile phones, and has progressed into avid users of feature-rich cell phones and hand-held computers (Stempel & Hargrove, 1996).

The evolution of multi-platform advertising technologies (for example, mobile or social media platforms) have affected advertising and marketing communications strategies and practices (Dreyer, 2013). In this com.Score report, Dreyer (2013) also identified the following five strategies to take advantage of the advent of multi-platform advertising practices: 1) to focus on platform-centric marketing strategies; 2) to create integrated, yet consistent, user experiences with platforms; 3) to maximize multi-platform campaign effectiveness through the leveraging synergies; 4) to collect and analyze users' demographic data to increase targeting efficiencies; 5) to select the most appropriate and relevant metrics to measure campaign ROI. Given the significant impacts of multi-platform advertising on consumers, advertising and marketing communication industry, and technology firms, this book chapter reports a cross-national qualitative study of Mexican and U.S. consumers to provide a rich and thorough exploration of their decision-making process to adopt mobile social media—a potentially feasible advertising media. This book chapter concludes by reviewing the current state of multi-platform advertising research to show its impacts on advertising, marketing, and consumer research. This study attempts to demonstrate what this multi-platform phenomenon have affected advertising research and methods.

BACKGROUND

The United States: Country Profile

The United States is a country with about 324 million people (UNData, 2016a). Its population density is 35.14 (International Telecommunications Union, 2016a). GDP per capita in 2014 is USD$54,306 (UNData, 2016a). Various ICT indices show that the United States is a developed country. Its fixed (wired)-broadband subscriptions are 31.53 per 100 inhabitants (or 31.53%), while those for active mobile-broadband are 109.23 per 100 inhabitants (or 109.23%) (International Telecommunications Union, 2016a). Its mobile-cellular subscription has grown to 117.59 per 100 inhabitants (or 117.59%) (International Telecommunications Union, 2016a) and individuals using the Internet is about 87.4% (International Telecommunications Union, 2016a; UNData, 2016a). Percentage of households with Internet access is 82.20 (or 82.20%) (International Telecommunications Union, 2016a).

Mexico: Country Profile

Mexico is a country with about 128 million people (UNData, 2016b). Its population density is 65.34 (International Telecommunications Union, 2016b). GDP per capita in 2014 is USD$10,325 (UNData, 2016b). As seen in Figure 2 below, several ICT indices have shown that Mexico is a developing country (International Telecommunications Union, 2016b). Subscriptions of fixed telephone is 15.88 per 100 inhabitants (or 15.88%), while mobile-cellular telephone subscriptions are far more popular among Mexican consumers (85.30 per 100 inhabitants) (International Telecommunications Union, 2016b). Its mobile-cellular subscription is about 98.4% and individuals using the Internet is about 87.4% (UNData, 2016b). Access to the Internet through fixed (wired)-broadband is 11.65 per 100 inhabitants, while active mobile broadband subscriptions are 50.36 per 100 inhabitants (or 50.36%) (International Telecommunications Union, 2016). In 2014, 82.5% of its population has subscribed to mobile and cellular devices

(UNData, 2016b). Internet penetration in Mexico is about 44.4% in 2014 (UNData, 2016b). Individuals using the Internet are about 57.43 per 100 inhabitants (or 57.43%) (International Telecommunications Union, 2016b).

Figure 1. ICT indices of the United States
Source: International Telecommunications Union (2016a)

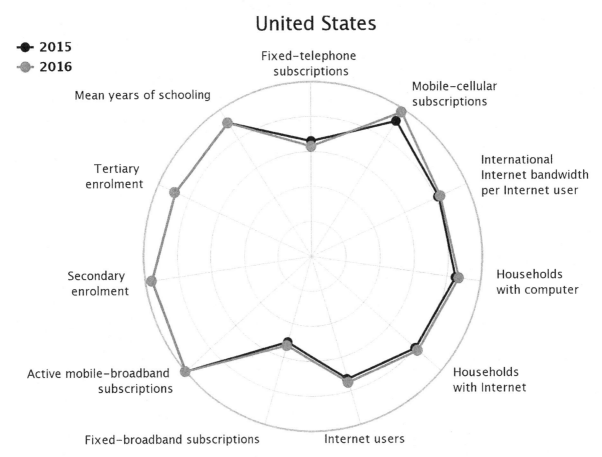

In recent years, cross-platform media and their applications have seen exponential growth in both the United States and Mexico. Lella and Lipsman (2016) observe several multi-platform trends in the United States in 2016. Driven by smartphone apps, digital media usage has accounted for 50% of all digital media time spent by U.S. consumers. Consumers in the U.S. have increasingly relied on mobile devices for shopping activities (Lella & Lipsman, 2016). Similar trends are also observed in Mexico, which leads to the development of multi-platform measurements (Merchant, 2016). For example, many Mexican consumers also use a combination of desktop, smartphone, and tablet. Multi-devices are also used by consumers to access contents (Merchant, 2016). As a result, comScore in Mexico launched its MMX Multi-Platform® to better understand multi-platform media usage behaviors and audience insights (Merchant, 2016).

Figure 2. ICT indices of Mexico
Source: International Telecommunications Union (2016b)

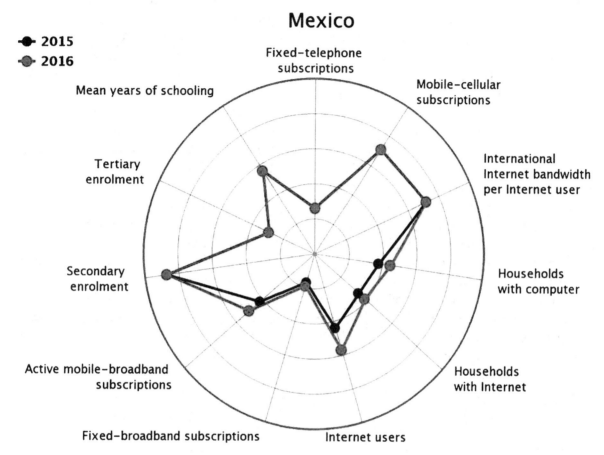

Popularity of Mobile and Social Media Platforms in the U.S. and Mexico

According to the Pew Internet Research Project report (2014, January), 58% of American adults own a smartphone. Many adults also own Wi-Fi enabled e-Readers (32%) and tablets (42%). Related to mobile social media adoption, cell phone ownership in the U.S. is also correlated with their age, education level, and household income (Pew Internet Research Project, 2014). In the same research report, household income is positively correlated with users' cell phone ownership. In the same report, it is found that over 90% of those who receive college education and with a higher household income ($50,000 above) tend to own cell phone (Pew Internet Research Project, 2014).

Similar demographics of mobile social media users can be found in Mexico and many other countries around the world. In Mexico, smartphone use has grown to 33.3 million in 2014, or more than 25% of the population (eMarketer, 2014). Smartphone users has increased to 51.7 million in 2017, and is expected to grow to 57.9 million in 2018 and 62.4 million in 2019 (eMarketer, 2015a). The demographic breakdowns also demonstrate that Mexican smartphone users clearly skew toward young and male segments (eMarketer, 2015b). The overall penetration of smartphone among male users is 57.5%, while 42.0% of female users adopt smartphone (eMarketer, 2015b). Young Mexicans between 18 and 24 years old have the highest adoption rate (58.1%) of smartphone when compared with 15.0% of the older segments (65 years old and above) (eMarketer, 2015c). The tilt toward the younger and male segments is expected to continue till 2019 (eMarketer, 2015c). While penetration rate among high income segments is higher, future growth is predicted among lower income segments when cheaper devices are available (eMarketer, 2015c). According to Consejo Nacional de Población (CONAPO), 40.5 million millennials (born between 1981 and 2000) account for 2/3 of social media and smartphone users in Mexico (cited in eMarketer, 2015c). Another usage behavior statistics published by the Competitive Intelligence Unit (CIU) also found that 96% of the millennial segment used social network (cited in eMarketer, 2015c).

Mobile devices and mobile-enabled advertisements have attracted attention among multi-platform researchers and practitioners because "marketers and researchers seek to understand how to achieve a balance between permissible and effective" (Romaniuk, 2015, p. 353). Therefore, this study is likely to provide a potential assessment of how cross-national consumers will respond to multi-platform advertising as an innovation. With the popularity of mobile devices, social media have obtained their mobility by allowing users to check their social media applications anytime they prefer. Adding to the increasingly interconnected and multi-screen media ecosystem is the exponential growth of mobile social media as a new communication platform (Duggan, 2015). As Lee (2014) observes, the convergence of smartphone and social networking services (henceforth, SNSs) has enabled users to access their Facebook and other social media platforms anywhere and anytime, which is likely to increase overall usage. The latest report on digital, social and mobile media (We Are Social, 2015) confirms this diffusion trend at a global scale. A recent Statista data (2017) found that the North America (i.e., Canada and the U.S.) has the highest penetration rate (57%) of mobile social media, when compared with that of Central America (including Mexico) is 46%. The growing popularity of mobile social media has been observed as one of the main catalysts to generate new applications and activities.

MAIN FOCUS OF THE CHAPTER

Existing literature on the adoption decision of new information-communication technologies often derives its theoretical foundation from diffusion of innovation (Rogers, 2003), consumer behavior (Villarrel, 2014), and information systems research (Vannoy & Palvia, 2010). This book chapter investigates the decision-making process of cross-national consumers in the United States and Mexico when considering adopting mobile social media. Therefore, theoretical frameworks that explain consumer decision-making processes in the context of technology adoption are most suitable to explore this phenomenon. Among many theoretical models that investigate the decision-making process, Technology Acceptance Model (TAM) (Davis, 1989) and its extended version (TAM2) (Venkatesh & Davis, 2000) provides one of the most parsimonious, yet rigorous, theoretical models in explaining technology characteristics and their effects on consumer adoption/use behaviors (Yang, 2005).

The following sections review theoretical frameworks that are pertinent to study mobile social media adoption, and can be potentially extended to study how consumers will adopt and respond to multi-platform advertising. These predictor variables in these theoretical frameworks can be extended to predict how consumers are likely to respond to multi-platform advertising messages. The first theoretical framework is the widely-used Technology Acceptance Model (TAM) and its extended version (TAM2). The original TAM was proposed by Davis (1989) and aims to account consumer technology adoption behavior. This theoretical model has been widely used to explain and understand external and internal determinants of consumer acceptance and adoption of technologies (Davis, 1989; Joo & Sang, 2013). Past TAM literature has been used to empirically test consumer intention and actual usage behaviors of a variety of technologies both by individuals and organizations (Yang, 2005). Venkatesh and Davis's seminal study (2000) observes that this model consistently explains 40% of variance in predicting the relationship between consumer attitudes, consumer usage intention and behaviors. Among many factors identified in the TAM and TAM2, two salient belief factors, "Perceived Usefulness" (PU) and "Perceived Ease of Use" (PEOU), are often included to explain subsequent behavioral intention and actual use (Joo & Sang, 2013; Yang, 2005). Subsequent TAM model, or its more extended version (TAM2) (Venkatesh & Davis, 2000) has added social-level influence (such as subjective norms and image) and work-related variables (such as job relevance, output quality, and result demonstration) to account for external and social-level variables in predicting people's technology adoption behavior. Soura-Koury and Yang (2009) applied the TAM2 model and social norms theory to study the predictable power of PU and PEOU in mobile advertising use. The linear relationships of these predictors are represented in both TAM (See Figure 3) and TAM2 (See Figure 4).

Figure 3. Technology Acceptance Model
Source: (Davis, 1989)

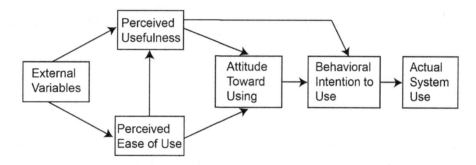

The growth of mobile social media has prompted communication scholars to employ TAM and TAM2 to empirically test determinants of consumer adoption of these technologies (Verkasalo, López-Nicolás, Molina-Castillo, & Bouwman, 2010). Verkasalo et al. (2010) extends the TAM2 model to examine actual usage of mobile applications. Extracting insights from a panel of 579 smartphone users in Finland who took part in a web-based questionnaire survey, their study found that consumers' perceived usefulness and enjoyment of mobile technologies affect their intention to use mobile apps among users and non-users of the technology (Verkasalo et al., 2010).

Another theoretical foundation related to this study will be based on consumer behavior research that offer significant insights into how consumers make their adoption decision (Blackwell, Engel, & Miniard, 2005). This popular consumer behavior model as shown in Figure 5 below is made up of two sub-components: information processing model on the left, and consumer decision-making process on the center, and ecological and psychology factors on the right side of the model. The information processing model explains how consumers are exposed to advertising/marketing communication messages and how they process these messages. On the other hand, the decision-making model demonstrates a linear explanation of how consumers' needs are activated, leading to information search, and actual purchase.

Figure 4. Extended Technology Acceptance model (TAM2)
Source: *Venkatesh & Davis, 2000, p. 188*

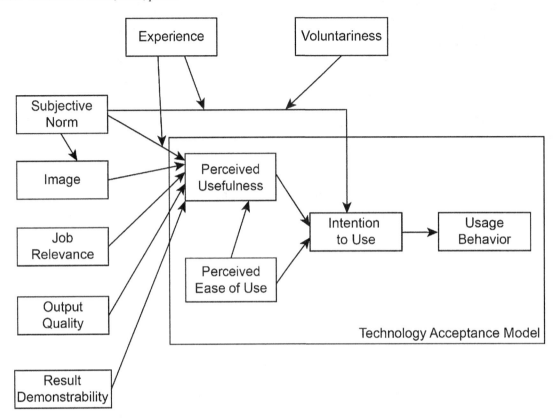

Relevant to the study of multi-platform advertising, Neijens and Voorveld (2015) extensively reviewed existing literature from both academic journals and trade publications and identified the following consumer behavior variables and models: encoding variability, forward encoding, backward retrieval, and Central Processing/Elaboration Likelihood Model. These variables and models mainly focus on how consumers process multi-platform advertising messages, but do not allow researchers to understand the adoption decision process as shown in TAM2 (Venkatesh & Davis, 2000; Verkasalo et al., 2010).

Research Questions

The interpretative frameworks of the in-depth interview data were based on a combination of the Extended Technology Acceptance Model (TAM2) (Venkatesh & Davis, 2000) and consumer behavior theories (Blackwell et al., 2005) to answer the following research questions:

- Research Question 1: Why do cross-national consumers decide to use mobile social media applications in the U.S. and Mexico?
- Research Question 2: On the basis of these theories what are the most important external or internal factors to understand cross-national consumers' decision to adopt emerging mobile social media applications?

Figure 5. Consumer Decision-making model
Source: Wood, 1970

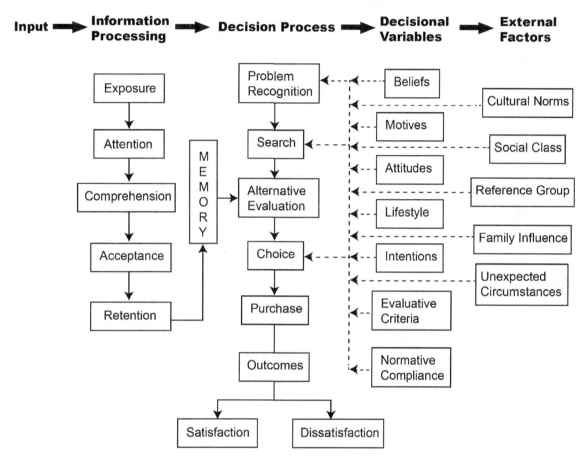

RESEARCH METHODS

The In-Depth Interview Method: Justifications and Procedures

The study used an in-depth interview method to understand the decision-making processes undertaken by Mexican and the U.S. consumers when adopting and using mobile social media platforms. A list of in-depth interview questions approved by the Institution Review Board was developed to standardize the data collection process and to avoid any biases. Research assistants also used audio and/or video recording devices to facilitate the data collection process. Responses from the interviews were analyzed using a qualitative thematic analysis to identify repetitive themes identified in participants' narratives.

Among many qualitative research methods used in advertising and marketing research, in-depth interviewing has been a widely-used research method (Hausman, 1984; Morrison, Haley, Sheehan, & Taylor, 2002; Sayre, 2001). Recent interests in mobile and social media platforms have extended qualitative methods to study consumer decision-making processes in various contexts (Pelet & Papadopoulou, 2014). Their qualitative study also found that design (e.g., perceived ease of use), privacy, reputation, and security are important to explore m-commerce, social media adoption and use (Pelet & Papadopoulou, 2014). Boyce and Neale (2006) further explained that the in-depth interview method refers to "a qualitative research technique that involves conducting intensive individual interviews with a small number of respondents to explore their perspectives on a particular idea, program, or situation" (p. 3). The in-depth interviewing technique has increasingly been used in new technology adoption research (Abdullah, Wahab, & Shamsuddin, 2013; Kindberg, Spasojevic, Fleck, & Sellen, 2005). Abdullah et al. (2013) employed an in-depth interview method to study factors affecting technology adoption decision-making processes among small to mid-size enterprises in Malaysia. Their study evaluated the effects of external, internal, and business owners' demographics on their adoption process. This research method has often been also used to understand how cross-national consumers make decisions to adopt mobile social media. However, four major limitations are commonly associated with this technique: 1) the data collection process is time-intensive; 2) the need to train research assistants in interviewing techniques; 3) data are not generalizable; 4) bias as a result of data collection process (Boyce & Neale, 2006).

To standardize the data collection procedures, an interview protocol, or "interview guide" (Morrison et al., 2002, p. 48) was developed for research assistants who also received one-hour intensive training before initiating the data collection process. The protocol was composed of the following questionnaire sections: 1) demographic questions (e.g., age, ethnicity, educational background, marital status, occupation, etc.); 2) a standardized VALS2 online questionnaire (http://www.strategicbusinessinsights.com/vals/surveynew.shtml); 3) social media usage behaviors (e.g., types of social media applications, frequency, amount of time, location, types of devices to access social media applications, most favorite, and least favorite mobile social media applications, etc); 4) ecological and psychological determinants to affect their decision-making processes (e.g., attitudes, knowledge, beliefs, social, cultural, and family influence, word-of-mouth communication, information search behaviors, and product evaluation, etc.). Probing questions were developed to avoid leading questions to solicit more narratives from the respondents (Sayre, 2001).

A group of research assistants conducted the in-depth interview in a setting comfortable to the participants—an important advantage of using this method (Morrison et al., 2002; Parmelee, 2014). The settings included participants' homes, coffee shops and on-campus locations. At the beginning of the in-depth interview, research assistants recorded the location, data, and duration of the interview. Participants were advised to read and sign the consent form. The use of audio and/or video devices to record the interview was first consulted with the participants to grant their permission. At the end of the data collection, research assistants would thank all participants and ensure the confidentiality of their interviews. On average, the in-depth interview took about 30 to 50 minutes to allow participants to answer all interview questions and to respond research assistants' probing questions.

Profile of Participants

The in-depth interviews were conducted by a team of research assistants in 2014. A total of 39 cross-national participants were interviewed using a structured interview protocol. Twenty-nine of the participants were from the U.S., while 10 of them were Mexicans. Among the U.S. participants, 16 of them were females, while 13 participants were males. Age of these U.S. participants ranges from 20 to 31 years old among male participants, while that of female participants' ranges from 21 to 52 years old. In comparison, six Mexican participants were males (aged between 18 and 35 years old), while four of them were females between 18 and 26 years old. While some are students, working professionals and retired seniors are also part of our participants. Marital status of the participants ranges from being single, married with children, to recently widowed. Occupations of the participants include student, university staff, accountant, housewife, consultant, etc. In terms of their psychographic profiles using the VALS2 segmentation, various psychographic types are represented in the sample, ranging from *Strivers*, *Experiencers*, *Believers*, *Innovators*, and *Achievers*. However, the majority of the participants in this in-depth interview study belong to *Experiencers* and *Innovators* categories.

In terms of their mobile social media usage behaviors, *Facebook* is the most frequently used applications, followed by *Instagram* and *Snapshot*. Among the Mexican participants, 7 have indicated that they used *Facebook* most frequently, followed by *Instagram* (N = 2) and *Snapshot* (N = 1). Among the U.S. participants, *Facebook* was selected as the most favorite mobile social media applications (N=18), followed by *Instagram* (N = 7), *WhatsApp* (N = 4), *Pinterest* (N = 2), *Snapchat* (N = 2), *Twitter* (N = 1), and *Imgur* (N = 1). The least popular mobile social media applications are *LinkedIn*, *Pinterest*, *Tumblr*, and *MySpace*. As shown by the cross-national data, while participants who are currently students prefer *Facebook* over other types of mobile social media applications, older and working participants used *LinkedIn* more. On average, the participants spent one hour per day using these mobile social media applications. Students and housewives tend to use mobile social media more, while working professionals use these applications less. Many participants have indicated that they access these social media applications through their mobile devices (such as smartphone, I-Pad, or laptop).

FINDINGS

The interview narratives were recorded and transcribed by the research team to allow thematic content analysis at the next phase of the research project. The author used a thematic (content) analysis method, a commonly-used method to categorize and interpret qualitative interview data (Abdullah et al., 2013; Wahl, McBride, & Schrodt, 2005). Wahl et al. (2005) explained the thematic analysis procedures that include three major stages: identification of broad themes, subthemes, and their naming. To help identify broad themes, attention will be paid to forcefulness, recurrence, and repetition in the interview data (Wahl et al., 2005). Sub-themes can be analyzed and identified when there are multiple meanings within a particular broad theme (Wahl et al., 2005). Once both broad and subthemes are identified, identifiers and labels will be assigned to each theme and sub-theme to describe their meaning (Wahl et al., 2005). This research followed the thematic analysis procedures employed in Wahl et al. (2005).

Major Themes Identified in the Data

Three broad and recurrent themes have emerged after reviewing the transcripts of these cross-national participants: 1) family and peer influence in the decision-making process to adopt mobile social media; 2) functional benefits of mobile social media (such as PEOU and PU) play critical roles; 3) cultural and sub-cultural influence on the adoption decision-making process. In general, these themes correspond to the recurrent topics in participants' narratives as to how they determine to adopt and use mobile social media.

Theme 1: Family and Peer Influence on Cross-National Consumers' Adoption to Use Mobile Social Media

These interview narratives show that these cross-national consumers decide to adopt mobile social media because they consider many family members and friends around them are using them and they considered suggestions and recommendations from these members in their social networks to be a critical factor in their decision-making processes. Many of these participants go to their family and friends for information in the adoption process.

A female U.S. participant in her 20's mentioned how her decision to adopt Facebook is related to her family members.

Absolutely I think that the people around me, the experiences I have to go through definitely encourage and almost require the use of social media. Without it most of the time I can't.

In addition to the first sub-theme identified above, the second sub-theme is the perceptions of social media as a trend to create a "bandwagon effect," which further strengthens the family and peer influence in the adoption decision among both Mexican and U.S. participants. A 35-years-old female participant from Mexico suggested the perception of social media as a trend and influence from existing social network of relationships affect her decision to use mobile social media.

I think so, just because I work here at the university, so social media is everywhere, all of the departments have a Facebook account, that is the way to get your information out there...through social media. TV is too expensive, radio is very expensive, Facebook is free, it's word of mouth, it is really easy to use and really convenient.

Gender of the participants does not seem to affect the perceived trend to adopt mobile social application as the narratives of a male respondent demonstrates below:

Mmmm well influenced because of all my family and friends, I mean they have it.

Umm and especially going into the whole sales aspect, I mean that's a good promotion for yourself. I mean you just can't keep relying on passing out your business cards over to people. So that another way to get yourself out there.

Several participants, regardless of their gender and nationality, below reveal this "bandwagon effect" to follow the crowd as the underlying reasons of why they use social media:

Because it got popular and it is easy to use, beside is fun because you can interact with any contact you have or only with one. (from a female participant from the U.S.)

I realize that I have to use Facebook because everyone at school was using that method. It was almost impossible for me to communicate with my peers without Facebook. (from a female participant from the U.S.)

Well everyone in my circle of friends was using them so I wanted to see what the fuss was about. (from a female participant from Mexico)

I notice that a lot of people were creating an account, so I just sign up for one. As well as I wanted to be in touch with people that I care. (from a female participant from Mexico)

Well because I saw everyone was using it so, I thought it was a really good idea to use them. (from a male participant from the U.S.)

The third sub-theme is the influence of words of mouth from strangers and unknown sources can exert strong impacts on consumers' decision-making process, given the strong social milieu to adopt:

So I heard word by mouth from a couple of people, and that's when I realized I should check it out. And that is when I started using it. (from a female participant from the U.S.) My friends they would talk about it all the time, and even like one of my friends got me and said "oh, open your Instagram account. (from a male participant from Mexico)

As demonstrated in the narratives above, it is clear that participants decision-making process were greatly influenced by their friends, family, coworkers, classmates, relatives, or even strangers, regardless of their nationality. In addition to the fourth sub-theme of receiving recommendations and suggestions from family and friends, another sub-theme has emerged after analyzing the interview narratives; that is, many consumers use mobile social media to be integrated into existing networks of relationships for a variety of activities.

As demonstrated below to support sub-theme five to maintain interconnectivity with other functional and social groups, for example, one of the participants stated that her decision to use Facebook is to take part in class activities:

I actually was not in social media for a very long time, and last year I took a class and we had to sign up on Facebook because we were like part of a group discussion and we had to do, as part of the class assignment, so I have to create a Facebook account, and then after the class I stop using it, and then one of my very good friends moved away and she was on Facebook so then I pick it up again, and the I started using it just for social media purposes instead of class purposes.

Staying connected with other family members can be seen as an example of how Mexican consumers use social media to maintain social relationship with family members and friend as shown in the narratives below:

Sometimes. I have a lot of family who live out of town, like in Juarez, so we don't get to see each other very often, and it is nice to be able to stay up to date with the things that are happening in our lives.

Another female participant from the U.S. shared her thoughts on how family affects her decision to use social media:

I do feel that my family affects my decision to use social media because this is a way to communicate with them. I have family that lives across the country and these apps make it easy for me to share and communicate things with them.

The following narrative is another clear demonstration of showing how the decision to adopt social media is affected by peer and family influence to stay connected with them. This sub-theme to connect with distant friends is particularly noticeable among female respondents in this study. Regardless of participants' gender and nationality, recommendations from family members also play a role in facilitating the decision-making process:

Yes, most of the friends that were actually using Facebook, and then I started using it. I talked to friends and family before using it... It does, because I have a bunch of family and I cannot keep in contact with them because it is too expensive to do it, and that is where social media (Facebook) makes the good part. (from a female participant from the U.S.) Well, I was used to use MySpace and my friend told me that it was more easy to use and more efficient to use Facebook. (from a male participant from Mexico)

Regardless of participants' gender and nationality, peer pressure to adopt social media plays a critical factor in affecting consumer's decision to adopt as evidenced in the narrative below:

Ummm I'm not a big technology freak so a lot of my friends were pushing me, common get Instagram, get Instagram, but then I was like for what? I'm not going to really use it... but now I actually see a good purpose on it ... umm Facebook as well... all my family had it before me. Umm and then it's a really good tool to communicate with people from out of town especially family members ...or people that you haven't seen in a while ...umm so yeah I did talk to them and umm well they gave me a good review overall... (from a female Mexican participant in her 20s)

A male American student in his 20s also voiced his decision to adopt is affected by his peers:

Everyone at the time was talking about it, Myspace fallout and switched to Facebook, I didn't want to be left behind with the crowd so I switched over from and outdated social media and choose to switch over.

However, older consumers seem to place more emphasis on the function aspects of mobile social media when it comes to their adoption decision. For example, when asked about his decision-making processes, a 31-year-old Mexican male consumer in a managerial position shows a different aspect of the adoption process below:

It is good tool for keeping updated with news, keep in contact with people, have interaction with them and helps the radio station's ratings. No, personally I believe that using social media is a personal choice. I don't think that culture affects its usage.

Lin and Shang-Yi Liu (2009) studied the adoption of mobile video services and concluded that adopters' perceived critical mass contributed most significantly to shaping consumers' intention to adopt the new technology. As suggested in the interview narratives above, many participants mentioned the number of family members, colleagues, and friends who have been using the mobile social media are an important factor to shape their decision to adopt. It is likely that such perceptions of critical mass contribute to both Mexican and U.S. consumers' decisions to adopt mobile social media. However, Lin and Shang-Yi Liu (2009) also found that perceived usefulness, price, and enjoyment are also important contributing factors, which will be examined in the next theme.

Theme 2: Perceived Usefulness (PU) and Perceived Ease of Use (PEOU) of Mobile Social Media (Functionality)

With the growing numbers of functions available on mobile social media, users not only stay connected with their family members and friends, social commerce functions are made widely available to users. According to TAM2 (Venkatesh & Davis, 2000), consumers' decision to adopt a new technology is affected by factors such as subjective norms, images, job relevance, output quality, result demonstrability, experience, and voluntariness, as well as their perceptions of a technology (such as PEOU or PU) and intention to use. On the basis of the narratives below, two recurrent sub-themes emerged: 1) perceived usefulness of mobile social media; 2) perceived ease of use of mobile social media.

Gender does not seem to account for any variations of opinions in the participants' narratives. For example, a female participant in this study have stated that Facebook's perceived usefulness (PU) is to locate personal information:

Mmmm, you don't really receive information. For me it is more developing a habit. If you had a pending conversation with someone you will log into Facebook to keep on talking with that person, or if you want to find out something about someone it is more likely for someone to consider first looking into that person's Facebook account than on actually asking to the person.

Another female participant shows that she is aware of various benefits each social media application offers.

I knew that Facebook provides worldwide news and information. And it keeps me in touch with everybody. On the other hand, Pinterest helps me to get inspired because of all the things that are showed of people that I follow. Instagram just kept me in touch with celebrities, friends and family that I follow by looking at the pictures that they post.

However, a male American participant focuses on the functional differences of various social media applications in his adoption process and this emphasis is seen across national borders:

When I took pictures I realized that filters looked good, and Instagram gives you a variety of filters.

A Mexican male in his 30s also shows the similar emphasis on functions.

Because Facebook is a great tool for work and be able to communicate the latest news in a large scale with people that are interest to the radio station.

Clearly shown in the following narratives, another participant was using Instagram to learn more about a brand and a company. The same perceived usefulness of providing information was shown below:

To be honest, probably like. I mean I use Instagram just because you could have an insight on presence and visual perspective on things. I really only like different thing that inspire me the most like I have my friends and stuff, but I like following bands and companies that I care about because they provide me with information that there is no way I can live without seen that.

Another participant's narrative was related to the sub-theme that PU is essential to account for female consumer's adoption of social media, however, in a reverse direction. In other words, the lack of perceived usefulness of Twitter accounts for why this participant (as well as other participants in this study) feels that Twitter is their least favorite.

Those are probably, Twitter for sure, I mean I do not use it at all, anymore, but twitter does have a lot of good things if you follow, I mean if you just follow strictly like news pages, for things that you care about, like record labels or that stuff that you are into. So, you could find out a lot about music and stuff and things that you are interested in, but sometimes people that you follow they go overboard with that and only post every other minute about what their doing and stuff and if you are following a lot of people like that, it just builds and builds and it is tired to scroll, to like, a lot of pages of thing that do not mean anything. (from a female participant)

The second sub-theme identified in participants' interview data addresses that female consumers need to perceive if social media are easy to use before they adopt the technologies. As one of the participants simply put it to explain why she is not using Twitter:

I think Twitter [is my least favorite social media] because I do not get it.

Another participant said that the ease of use to use messaging on Facebook affects her adoption decision.

Well, it was just a lot of fun when I started using it with my friends because I would have conversations online and things like that. I was never really into Messenger, or anything like that, so when I started sending messages on Facebook it was just really easy to communicate. That's the thing that I like about Facebook, that it is really easy to use, it's really easy to communicate.

Another participant emphasizes the ease of communication through Facebook:

I basically use fb trough the chat they have and it is very useful to communicate.

As revealed in several participants' narratives, the perceptions of ease of use (PEOU) and usefulness (PU) are two major reasons why they determine to adopt a variety of social media:

I like it. I am on Facebook every day, so it has just become something that I automatically check at night, checking my friends, my family. Now, I actually started using it to communicate a little bit more with co-workers by Facebook Messenger. I have some of my student assistant who live in Juarez, so it is really easy to communicate with them via Facebook.

Another participant who is married with kids and spent less time on social media also echoes how PEOU and PU of Facebook affects her decision to adopt:

I think so, just because I work here at the university, so social media is everywhere, all of the departments have a Facebook account, that is the way to get your information out there…through social media. TV is too expensive, radio is very expensive, Facebook is free, it's word of mouth, it is really easy to use and really convenient.

In general, regardless of their gender, participants in this interview recognize their needs to use mobile social media because they want to be constantly communicating with their family, friends and other people around them. Both Mexican and U.S. consumers are also aware of various functions provided and thus are able to make an informed adoption decision that matches their needs. In the interview data, consumers also admit to use mobile social media for different purposes depending on the social media such as *Instagram* for self-expression and *Whatsapp* for communication.

Theme 3: Influence of Culture and Sub-Culture on the Decision to Adopt Mobile Social Media

Several recurrent sub-themes have emerged after analyzing the interview data. The first sub-theme addresses how culture and sub-culture affects the perceptions of adopting social media as shown below:

I believe that beyond culture, what affects your decision towards social media is society. I opened my Facebook account because of peer pressure; I don't regret it but my friend was almost obligating me to do it and so I did. Culture is also a factor because it influences our perception of right or wrong, or if something will bring us benefit, and all of these are important when you take the decision of using social media; but in my case, it was more of a social effect.

The second sub-theme reveals the emergence of social media culture/sub-culture prompts consumers to adopt these technologies as voiced by a married participant with kids from the U.S.:

Yea, we do a ton of invites on social media and I don't ever remember doing that before. I guess with the way culture is now, it seems like I get invites for everything and it's almost not personal anymore.

The narrative from one 18 years old student participant from the U.S. who uses social media heavily (over 8 hours per day) best describes the impact of this cultural trend that permeates Millennials' daily life:

Yes. An example of this is when I have a group project, everybody needs to know what we need to do or how, and with social media we can talk about it and how to collaborate from our own house. Or just socially, when you're invited to a party, you don't get a paper invitation anymore, right? Everything is easier just creating an invitation on Facebook.

The emergence of social media sub-culture seems to affect the student population more to affect their adoption decisions. As shown by a female American student participant, she expresses the peer pressure she experiences:

Nowadays everyone is in the computer, the phone, and they are constantly using Facebook, Instagram, twitter, so you can feel the pressure to actually go ahead and start doing it yourself just to fit in.

Regardless of participant's gender, the sub-cultural influence is persistent. The following narrative from a 22-year-old male college student:

Yes, because people here are all about social media, and [city name concealed] is like the Twitter capitol of the world, so yeah I guess like peer pressure, so [city name concealed] is like out there posting where you go, so that's what it is.

The emphasis of family value among both American and Mexican consumers (see Villarrel, 2014 for a review) may also interact with the emergence of social media sub-culture to affect consumer's decision-making process. As voiced by a married participant, she decides to use social media to be united with her family to share her thoughts and pictures:

I do believe so because my culture taught me to be united with my family, and using social media allows me to share thoughts and pictures with family that lives out of town.

CONCLUSION

The convergence of mobile and social media platforms presents a promising opportunity for the advertising industry (Bradbury, 2013). As many industry pundits have predicted, the merger of these two platforms have generated new applications that "[l]ocation-based advertising and mobile games are bringing a whole new layer to social media marketing" (Bradbury, 2013). Increasingly, consumers have used mobile devices to access social media whenever they are free. According to Twitter, 60% of its 200 million active users in the United States check their Twitter account through their mobile device at least once each month (Bradbury, 2013). Multi-platform usage behaviors have apparently become a pervasive contemporary human experience. Cohen (2014) cited that about 107 million adults over 18 years old in the U.S. have used at least two or more social media platforms. Consumers also make conscious decisions to use different platforms to meet their interests (Cohen, 2014). Because of the evolving usage behaviors, multi-platform advertisers have employed a variety of media platforms to tailor their messages for different consumer segments (Cohen, 2014).

Current multi-platform advertising research has mainly focused on two areas: 1) synergy effects through the integration of multiple channels, media, or touchpoints (Neijens & Vooreld, 2015; Romaniuk, 2015; Varan et al., 2013); 2) measuring consumer responses to this advertising practice (Romaniuk, 2015; Treutler et al. 2010; Varan et al., 2013). Neijens and Voorveld's (2015) literature review study provides a very thorough assessment of what academic researchers and industry practitioners should do to contribute to the development of multi-platform advertising. They state, "Academics and practitioners should come out of their separate worlds and make a serious effort to collaborate. Our literature study shows that academic and industry research are not connected. (Neijens & Voorveld, 2015, p. 336 for a review of current state of multi-platform advertising). This book chapter provides insights into how cross-national consumers decide to adopt and use mobile social media. Results from this in-depth interview study hopes to shed lights on consumers' decision-making process to adopt mobile and social media platforms.

FUTURE RESEARCH DIRECTIONS

This study used a qualitative in-depth interview method to collect narratives about how and why these 39 cross-national consumers from Mexico and the U.S. make their decisions to use mobile social media. The same qualitative interview method can be used to generate insights into how consumers respond to multi-platform advertising, in addition to the prevalent quantitative experimental study published in many academic journals (Neijens & Voorveld, 2015). The in-depth interview method employed in this cross-national study demonstrates how this qualitative data collection method can be useful to study multi-platform advertising.

Although these interview data have shaded lights on the decision-making process of cross-national consumers to adopt mobile and social media platforms, research findings reported in this book chapter allow researchers to explore recurrent factors and themes affecting their decision-making processes by asking the following research directions. First, generational variations are likely to affect mobile social media adoption and likely to account for the emergence of multi-platform advertising usage among various generational segments. Nielsen's (2017) report on Millennials has observed that younger/Millennial users (18-34 years old) are less likely to change the channel during commercials (less than 2%), when compared with viewers older than 55 years old (8%) and 35-54 years old. Furthermore, 18-24 years old Millennials will respond to mobile advertising (51%) if the contents are free, when compared with the response likelihood of viewers above 55 years old (33%) (Nielsen, 2017). The consumer characteristics is expected to have profound impacts on consumer behaviors, media landscape, and business practices. For example, 83% of Millennial consumers is expected to use mobile consumers in the next 12 months (InMobi, 2013). Around 88% of these consumers are said to pay attention to mobile advertising (InMobi, 2013). Therefore, generation variations and other demographic variables are likely to be useful predictors to explore the effectiveness of multi-platform advertising campaigns.

The second research direction and question demands the exploration of other theoretical frameworks to understand the decision-making process of technology adoption (See Li & Zeng, 2011 for review). Despite the popularity and rigor of TAM and TAM2, scholars have questioned whether the models are able to explain all technology adoption behaviors in numerous settings (Baaren, Wijngaert, & Huizer, 2011; Soroa-Koury & Yang, 2009). Barren et al. (2011) further suggest whether additional constructs (i.e., knowledge and user-technology match, and temporary dynamical contexts in the adoption decision-making process) should be taken into consideration. Barren et al. (2011) also recommend the inclusion of consumers' uses (of a technology) and gratifications, characteristics of technologies, and individual personality traits should be included. Furthermore, Li and Ze (2011) and Barren et al. (2011) include a social utility of media use construct to examine how the judgement of media use and adoption influences consumers' decision to adopt Podcast. In the context of multi-platform advertising, the interaction between users' information processing and media/channel/device has begun to attract researchers' attention (Romaniuk, 2015; Treulter, Levin, & Marci, 2010; Varan, Murphy, Hofacker, Robinson, Potter, & Bellman, 2013).

LIMITATIONS

Research findings reported in this study were based on a series of in-depth interviews from a non-random sample of cross-national consumers. While this qualitative research method enables researchers to collect more in-depth and thorough narratives in a dynamic data collection process, biases accompanied this research method should be taken into consideration (Cook, 2008). The thematic (content) analysis approach might not be as objective as computer-assisted content analysis of the interview transcripts. Future research should explore how these factors contribute to consumers' perceptions to better understand their decision-making process to adopt mobile social media and other emerging technologies (such as multi-platform advertising).

REFERENCES

Abdullah, N. H., Wahab, E., & Shamsuddin, A. (2013). Exploring the common technology adoption enablers among Malaysian SMES: Qualitative findings. *Journal of Management and Sustainability*, *3*(4), 78–91. doi:10.5539/jms.v3n4p78

Baaren, E., Wijngaert, L., & Huizer, E. (2011). Understanding technology adoption through individual and context characteristics: The case of HDTV. *Journal of Broadcasting & Electronic Media*, *55*(1), 72–89. doi:10.1080/08838151.2011.546257

Blackwell, R. D., Miniard, P. W., & Engel, J. F. (2005). *Consumer behavior* (10th ed.). Cincinnati, OH: South-Western College Publisher.

Boyce, C., & Neale, P. (2006, May). *Conducting in-depth interviews: A guide for designing and conducting in-depth interviews for evaluation input*. Retrieved April 7, 2015 from http://www2.pathfinder.org/site/DocServer/m_e_tool_series_indepth_interviews.pdf

Bradbury, D. (2013, August 1). When mobile and social meet. *The Guardian*. Retrieved April 24, 2017 from https://www.theguardian.com/technology/2013/aug/2001/when-mobile-and-social-meet

Cohen, H. (2014, June 23). Are you ready for multi-platform social media use? Retrieved April 24, 2017 from http://heidicohen.Com/multi-platform-social-media-use/

Cook, K. E. (2008). In-depth interview. In L. M. Given (Ed.), *The Sage encyclopedia of qualitative research methods* (pp. 423–424). Thousand Oaks CA: Sage Publications, Ltd.

Davis, F. D. (1989). Perceived usefulness, perceived ease of use, and user acceptance of information technologies. *Management Information Systems Quarterly*, *13*(2), 319–340. doi:10.2307/249008

Dreyer, K. (2013, October 24). Five strategies for effectively marketing to the multi-platform majority, Retrieved December 1, 2016 from https://www.comscore.com/Insights/Blog/Five-Strategies-for-Effectively-Marketing-to-the-MultiPlatform-Majority

Duggan, M. (2015, August 19). *Mobile messaging and social media 2015*. Pew Research Center. Retrieved January 1, 2017 from http://www.pewinternet.org/2015/08/19/mobile-messaging-and-social-media-2015/

eMarketer. (2014, February 11). *Hispanic women connect with friends, brands and news via social.* Retrieved April 3, 2015 from http://www.emarketer.com/Article/Hispanic-Women-Connect-with-Friends-Brands-News-via-Social/1010597#sthash.ELe3Zmtb.dpuf

eMarketer. (2015a, September 16). Latin America is home to a robust mobile market. Retrieved January 1, 2017 from https://www.emarketer.com/Article/Latin-America-Home-Robust-Mobile-Market/1012985

eMarketer. (2015b, October 16). Mexico's smartphone user base reaches 62.5 million. Retrieved January 1, 2017 from https://www.emarketer.com/Article/Mexicos-Smartphone-User-Base-Reaches-625-Million/1013113

eMarketer. (2015c, February 19). Nearly all millennials in Mexico use social media, instant messaging. Retrieved January 1, 2017 from https://www.emarketer.com/Article/Nearly-All-Millennials-Mexico-Use-Social-Media-Instant-Messaging/1012075

Hausman, A. (1984). A multi-method investigation of consumer motivations in impulse buying behavior. *Journal of Consumer Marketing*, *17*(5), 403–426. doi:10.1108/07363760010341045

InMobi. (2013, February). *Global mobile media consumption reaching millennials.*

International Telecommunications Union (ITU). (2016a). *ICT development index 2016: United States.* Geneva, The Switzerland: International Telecommunications Union. Retrieved on April 26, 2017 from https://www.itu.int/net4/ITU-D/idi/2016/#idi2016countrycard-tab&USA

International Telecommunications Union (ITU). (2016b). *ICT development index 2016: Mexico.* Geneva, The Switzerland: International Telecommunications Union. Retrieved April 26, 2017 from https://www.itu.int/net4/ITU-D/idi/2016/#idi2016countrycard-tab&MEX

Joo, J., & Sang, Y. (2013). Exploring Koreans' smartphone usage: An integrated model of the technology acceptance model and uses and gratifications theory. *Telematics and Informatics*, *29*, 2512–2518.

Kindberg, T., Spasojevic, M., Fleck, R., & Sellen, A. (2005, April-June). The ubiquitous camera: An in-depth study of camera phone use. *Pervasive Computing*, *4*(2), 42–50. doi:10.1109/MPRV.2005.42

Lee, S. Y. (2014). Examining the factors that influence early adopters smartphone adoption: The case of college students. *Telematics and Informatics*, *31*(2), 308–318. doi:10.1016/j.tele.2013.06.001

Lella, A., & Lipsman, A. (2016, March 30). *2016 U.S. Cross-platform future in focus.* com.Score. Retrieved April 26, 2017 from http://www.comscore.com/Insights/Presentations-and-Whitepapers/2016/2016-US-Cross-Platform-Future-in-Focus

Li, X., & Zeng, L. (2011, Fall). Technology attributes, perceived value of information, and social utility: Predicting podcast adoption and use. *Southwestern Mass Communication Journal*, 83-69.

Lin, J. C.-C., & Shang-Yi Liu, E. (2009). The adoption behaviour for mobile video call services. *International Journal of Mobile Communications*, *7*(6), 646–666. doi:10.1504/IJMC.2009.025536

Marchant, I. (2016, May 10). *Multi-platform measurement in Mexico.* comScore. Retrieved April 26, 2017 from http://www.comscore.com/Insights/Presentations-and-Whitepapers/2016/Multi-platform-Measurement-in-Mexico

Morrison, M. A., Haley, E., Sheehan, K. B., & Taylor, R. (2002). Using qualitative research in advertising: Strategies, techniques, and applications. Thousand Oaks, CA: Sage Publications. doi:10.4135/9781412986489

Nielsen. (2014, May 29). *The 8%_ unleashing the power of cross-platform advertising*. Retrieved on July 7, 2016from http://www.nielsen.com/content/corporate/us/en/insights/news/2014/the-8-percent-unleashing-the-power-of-cross-platform-advertising.html

Neijens, J., & Voorveld, R. (2015). Cross-platform advertising: Current practices and issues for the future. *Journal of Advertising Research, 55*(3), 55-60. doi:. doi:10.2501/JAR-2016-2042

Pelet, J., & Papadopoulou, P. (2014). Consumer Behavior in the Mobile Environment: An Exploratory Study of M-Commerce and Social Media. *International Journal of Technology and Human Interaction, 10*(4), 36–48. doi:10.4018/ijthi.2014100103

Nielsen. (2017, March 2). Millennials on millennials: A look at viewing behavior, distraction and social media stars. Retrieved March 15, 2017 from http://www.nielsen.com/us/en/insights/news/2017/millennials-on-millennials-a-look-at-viewing-behavior-distraction-social-media-stars.html

Pew Internet Research Project. (2014, January). *Mobile technology fact sheet*.

Pew Research Center. (2012, December 12). *Social networking popular across globe Arab publics most likely to express political views online*. Retrieved from http://www.pewglobal.org/2012/12/12/social-networking-popular-across-globe/

Rogers, E. M. (2003). *Diffusion of innovations* (5th ed.). New York, N.Y.: Free Press.

Romaniuk, J. (2015, September). Coming in December: How cross-platform advertising works. *Journal of Advertising Research*. doi:10.2501/JAR-2015-2014

Sayre, S. (2001). Qualitative methods for marketplace research. Thousand Oaks, C.A.: Sage Publications. doi:10.4135/9781412985543

Soroa-Koury, S., & Yang, K. C. C. (2010). Factors affecting consumers responses to mobile advertising from a social norm theoretical perspective. *Telematics and Informatics, 27*(1), 103–113. doi:10.1016/j.tele.2009.06.001

Statista. (2017, January). Global mobile social network penetration rate as of January 2017, by region. Retrieved February 2, 2017 from https://www.statista.com/statistics/412257/mobile-social-penetration-rate-region/

Stempel, G. H. I., & Hargrove, T. (1996). Mass media audiences in changing media environment. *Journalism & Mass Communication Quarterly, 77*, 71–79. doi:10.1177/107769900007700106

Treutler, T., Levine, B., & Marci, C. D. (2010, September). Biometrics and multi-platform messaging: The medium matters. *Journal of Advertising Research, 5*(3), 243-249. doi:10.2501/S0021849910091415

Vannoy, S. A., & Palvia, P. (2010, June). The social influence model of technology adoption. *Communications of the ACM, 53*(6), 149–153. doi:10.1145/1743546.1743585

Venkatesh, V., & Davis, F. D. (2000). A theoretical extension of the technology acceptance model: Four longitudinal field studies. *Management Science, 46*(2), 186–204. doi:10.1287/mnsc.46.2.186.11926

Verkasalo, H., López-Nicolás, C., Molina-Castillo, F. J., & Bouwman, H. (2010). Analysis of users and non-users of smartphone applications. *Telematics and Informatics, 27*(3), 242–255. doi:10.1016/j.tele.2009.11.001

Varan, D., Murphy, J., Hofacker, C. F., Robinson, J. A., Potter, R. F., & Bellman, S. (2013). What works best when combining television sets, pcs, tablets, or mobile phones? How synergies across devices result from cross-device effects and cross-format synergies. *Journal of Advertising Research, 53*(2), 212–220. doi:10.2501/JAR-53-2-212-220

Wahl, S. T., McBride, M. C., & Schrodt, P. (2005). Becoming point and click parents: A case study of communication and online adoption. *Journal of Family Communication, 5*(4), 279–294. doi:10.120715327698jfc0504_3

We Are Social. (2015). *Digital, social and mobile in 2015 report*. Retrieved April 3, 2015 from http://wearesocial.sg/blog/2015/01/digital-social-mobile-2015/

Yang, K. C. C. (2005). Exploring factors affecting the adoption of M-commerce in Singapore. *Telematics and Informatics, 22*(3), 257–277. doi:10.1016/j.tele.2004.11.003

UNData. (2016a, July). United states of America. World Statistics Pocketbook. Retrieved April 26, 2017 from http://data.un.org/CountryProfile.aspx?crName=United%20States%20of%20America

UNData. (2016b, July). Mexico. World Statistics Pocketbook. Retrieved April 26, 2017 from http://data.un.org/CountryProfile.aspx?crName=Mexico

ADDITIONAL READING

Assael, H. (2011). 50th Anniversary Supplement)). From silos to synergy: A fifty-year review of cross-media research shows synergy has yet to reach its full potential. *Journal of Advertising Research, 51*(1), 42–58. doi:10.2501/JAR-51-1-042-058

Crain, R. (2001, May 21). Multiplatform buys can lead to disruption for buyer, seller. *Advertising Age, 72*, 19.

Doyle, G. (2010). From television to multi-platform less from more or more for less? *Convergence: The International Journal of Research into New Media Technologies, 16*(4), 431-449. doi:10.1177/1354856510375145

Enoch, G., & Johnson, K. (2010). Cracking the cross-media code. *Journal of Advertising Research, 50*(2), 125–136. doi:10.2501/S0021849910091294

Erdal, I. J. (2009). Cross-media (re)production cultures. *Convergence: The International Journal of Research into New Media Technologies, 15*(2), 215-231. doi:10.1177/1354856508105231

Feit, E. M., Wang, P.-Y., Bradlow, E. T., & Fader, P. S. (2013, June). Fusing aggregate and disaggregate data with an application to multiplatform media consumption. *JMR, Journal of Marketing Research, 50*(3), 348–364. doi:10.1509/jmr.11.0431

Fulgoni, G. M. (2015, December). Is the grp really dead in a cross-platform ecosystem? In a cross-platform ecosystem? Why the gross rating point metric should thrive in today's fragmented media world. *Journal of Advertising Research*, 358-361. doi:10.2501/JAR-2015-2019

Havlena, W., Ardarelli, R. C., & Ontigny, M. D. M. (2007). Quantifying the isolated and synergistic effects of exposure frequency for TV, print, and internet advertising. *Journal of Advertising Research, 47*(3), 215–221. doi:10.2501/S0021849907070262

Kim, S. J. (2016). A repertoire approach to cross-platform media use behavior. *New Media & Society, 18*(3), 353-372. doi:10.1177/1461444814543162

Ksiazek, T. B. (2011). A network analytic approach to understanding cross-platform audience behavior. *Journal of Media Economics, 24*, 237-251. doi:10.1080/08997764.08992011.08626985

Marks, R. (2016, May). Challenges and opportunities in cross platform media measurement. *Research World, 2016*(58), 9–13. doi:10.1002/rwm3.20366

McIntyre, P. (2006). Cross-media deals expected to double to $600m a year; alliance mulls multi-platform package. *Australasian Business Intelligence, 33*, Retrieved on June 31, 2016 from https://www.highbeam.com/doc/2001G2001-154865588.html

McNeal, & Marguerite. (2013, Summer). Solving the multiplatform puzzle. *Marketing Insights,* pp. 41-47.

Nielsen. (2014, May 29). *The 8% unleashing the power of cross-platform advertising*. Retrieved July 7, 2016 from http://www.nielsen.com/content/corporate/us/en/insights/news/2014/the-8-percent-unleashing-the-power-of-cross-platform-advertising.html

Legris, P., Ingham, J., & Collerette, P. (2003). Why do people use information technology: A critical review of the technology acceptance model. *Information & Management, 40*, 191–204.

Lopez, M. H., Gonzalez-Barrera, A., & Patten, E. (2013, March 7). *Closing the digital divide: Latinos and technology adoption*. Washington, D.C.: PEW Research Center. Retrieved March 30, 2015 from http://www.pewhispanic.org/2013/03/07/closing-the-digital-divide-latinos-and-technology-adoption/

Parmelee, J. H. (2013). Political journalists and twitter: Influences on norms and practices. *Journal of Media Practice, 14*(4), 291–305. doi:10.1386/jmpr.14.4.291_1

Parmelee, J. H. (2014). The agenda-building function of political tweets. *New Media & Society, 16*(3), 434–450. doi:10.1177/1461444813487955

Precourt, G. (2015, December). How does cross-platform advertising work? *Journal of Advertising Research*, 356-357. doi:10.2501/JAR-2015-2018

Snyder, J., & Garcia-Garcia, M. (2016, December). Advertising across platforms: Conditions for multimedia campaigns a method for determining optimal media investment and creative strategies across platforms. *Journal of Advertising Research*, 352-367. doi:10.2501/JAR-2016-2042

Taylor, J. R., Kennedy, C., McDonald, N., Haddad, Y., Ouarzazi, E., & Larguinat, L. (2013). Is the multi-platform whole more powerful than its separate parts? Measuring the sales effects of cross-media advertising. *Journal of Advertising Research*, *53*(2), 200–211. doi:10.2501/JAR-53-2-200-211

Wood, H. (1970, January 01). Day to Day Insight. Retrieved from http://harrywood93.blogspot.com/2012_04_01_archive.html

Zelenkauskaite, A. (2016). Remediation, convergence, and big data: Conceptual limits of cross-platform social media. *Convergence*. doi:10.1177/1354856516631519

KEY TERMS AND DEFINITIONS

Ad Audience: The total number of consumers that are exposed or are likely to view an ad during any specific period of time. This concept is also equivalent to reach.

Bandwagon Effect: The term refers to a psychological phenomenon that describes people's decisions to follow the crowd, regardless their individual beliefs or attitudes. This concept has been widely applied in political science, business, and consumer behavior research.

Consumer Behavior Theories and Models: A systematic study of the processes that demonstrate how consumers make decisions to select, secure, use, and dispose of products or services. Consumer behavior theories and models aim to examine psychological, social, cultural, regulatory, and other ecological factors in affecting their decision-making process.

Cross-Device Targeting: This term describes when the same group of consumers or target audience is offered the ad through multiple platforms or devices. This technique enables advertisers to deliver advertising messages through a variety of platforms to the target audience in a sequential, repetitive, and strategic manner.

Diffusion of Innovation: A sociological conceptualization of how an innovation diffuses in society. Developed by Dr. Everett Rogers in his book, *Diffusion of Innovations* (2005), he proposed four key components to explain how and why an innovation is diffused through specific channels among participants in a social system over a period of time. These four components include the innovation, communication channel, time, and a social system. A popular typology in the diffusion theory includes five adopter types to explain how individual characteristics affect the decision to adopt an innovation: Innovators, Early Adopters, Early Majority, Late Majority, and Laggards.

Extended Technology Acceptance Model (TAM2): An extended and revised version of the popular Technology Acceptance Model (TAM) that includes variables such as subjective norms, images, job relevance, output quality, result demonstrability, experience, and voluntariness, in addition to individual's perceptions of a technology. As an extended model of the original TAM, this extended model is often referred to as TAM2,

In-Depth Interview Method: A qualitative research method or technique to investigate a small and intentionally selected number of respondents through intensive inquiry and probing to explore their views on a particular idea or a situation related to the research topic. Using this method in a face-to-face setting or through a telephone or a computer network (such as Skype), researchers ask open-ended questions to record the respondent's answers through various types of data collection tools.

Mobile Social Media: A term to refer to the popular social media platforms such as Facebook, Foursquare, Instagram, Pinterest, Twitter, etc., that are delivered via mobile devices such as smartphone, tablet, or laptop computer to allow users to launch these applications.

Multi-Platform Advertising: Also known as cross-media, cross-platform, cross-channels, cross-touchpoints, multi-channels, and multi-touchpoints, advertising/marketing, this popular advertising practice is expected to grown globally from $15.13 billion in 2013 to $76.57 billion in 2018. This term or its equivalents often refer to an emerging practice that employs "a multitude of combinations of TV spots or sponsorship, online, OOH, print, radio and so on." It describes what contemporary media users have often experienced when they increasingly depend on multi-screens and platforms ranging from computers, laptops, smartphones, tablets, and smart TV, etc.

Perceived Ease of Use (PEOU): An important belief component in TAM and TAM2. The term is defined by Davis (1989) as "the degree to which a person believes that using a particular system would be free from effort."

Perceived Usefulness (PU): A key belief component in TAM and TAM2. The term is defined by Davis (1989) as "the degree to which a person believes that using a particular system would enhance his or her job performance."

Social Media: According to Andreas Kaplan and Michael Haenlein (2010), social media are defined as "a group of Internet-based applications that build on the ideological and technological foundations of Web 2.0, and that allow the creation and exchange of user-generated content." Social media include collaborative projects (such as Wikipedia), microblogs and blogs, contents (such as YouTube), social networking services (such as Facebook), virtual games, and virtual social life (such as Second Life).

Thematic (Content) Analysis: A qualitative research method to describe and analyze textual data from interview transcripts or other qualitative data.

This research was previously published in Multi-Platform Advertising Strategies in the Global Marketplace; pages 168-198, copyright year 2018 by Business Science Reference (an imprint of IGI Global).

Chapter 52
Top Museums on Instagram:
A Network Analysis

Vasiliki G. Vrana
International Hellenic University, Serres, Greece

Dimitrios A. Kydros
International Hellenic University, Serres, Greece

Evangelos C. Kehris
International Hellenic University, Serres, Greece

Anastasios-Ioannis T. Theocharidis
International Hellenic University, Serres, Greece

George I. Kavavasilis
International Hellenic University, Serres, Greece

ABSTRACT

Pictures speak louder than words. In this fast-moving world where people hardly have time to read anything, photo-sharing sites become more and more popular. Instagram is being used by millions of people and has created a "sharing ecosystem" that also encourages curation, expression, and produces feedback. Museums are moving quickly to integrate Instagram into their marketing strategies, provide information, engage with audience and connect to other museums Instagram accounts. Taking into consideration that people may not see museum accounts in the same way that the other museum accounts do, the article first describes accounts' performance of the top, most visited museums worldwide and next investigates their interconnection. The analysis uses techniques from social network analysis, including visualization algorithms and calculations of well-established metrics. The research reveals the most important modes of the network by calculating the appropriate centrality metrics and shows that the network formed by the museum Instagram accounts is a scale–free small world network.

DOI: 10.4018/978-1-7998-9020-1.ch052

INTRODUCTION

Instagram, the social photo and video sharing mobile application, now owned by Facebook, Inc., was launched in October 2010 (Gillen, Freeman, and Tootell, 2017) and since then it has enjoyed impressive growth. Instagram provides its users an instantaneous way to capture and share their life moments with their followers through pictures, videos and stories which can be edited with various filters, organized with tags and location information and accompanied by a textual caption (Weilenmann, Hilliman, and Jungselius, 2013). Nowadays Instagram community counts more than 800 million monthly active users, 500 million of daily active users and 300 million of Instagram Stories Daily Active Users (Aslam, 2018).

As social media platforms are growing in popularity, organizations and corporations are moving quickly to integrate them into their marketing strategies (Constantinides, Romero, and Gómez Boria, 2018). Instagram and the other social media platforms provide to museums, galleries and other cultural institutions, new opportunities to widen the distribution of their cultural offer in ways that were unthinkable and accessible only in person before (Ciasullo, Gaeta, Monetta, and Rarità, 2015). Thus, social network platforms allow cultural institutes and museums to present their collections, demonstrate their core values, communicate their activities and exhibitions directly, reach people, increase public engagement (Spiliopoulou, Mahony, Routsis, and Kamposiori, 2014; Gonzalez 2017), connect with other museums, build relationships and establish networks (Lazaridou, Vrana, and Paschaloudis, 2015).

Museums are increasingly investing in human resources, money and time to create and maintain a high profile social media presence (Adamovic, 2013). However, up to now, little research effort has been devoted to investigate how museums are using Instagram in exploiting its features and possibilities with the existing studies mainly focusing on visitors (Budge, 2018; Budge and Burness, 2018; Suess, 2014; Suess 2018; Weilenmann, Hilliman, and Jungselius, 2013) and museum performance (Lazaridou, Vrana, and Paschaloudis, 2015), while the structure of Instagram virtual museum communities formed are understudied. The paper at first investigates the use of Instagram by the most visited museums worldwide by recording and analyzing performance characteristics like number of followers, following and number of posts, and number of likes of the ten last posts. All indexes provide evidence of the popularity and the activity of the accounts.

Instagram users form social networks since an Instagram account (user) can follow the activity of other Instagram accounts (users). An Instagram social network is asymmetric (directed), in the vein that if an Instagram user A follows user B, B need not follow A back (Hu, Manikonda, and Kambhampati, 2014). Social network analysis can help to explore the nature of interconnected accounts (Wasserman, and Faust, 1994). Next, the paper performs a topological analysis of the network of the Instagram accounts of the most visited museums at two stages. At the macroscopic analysis museums' communication patterns are revealed. Park, and Jankowski (2008, p. 62) mentioned that, this is important, since "the discovery of information networks among web sites or among site producers through the analysis of link counts and patterns, and exploration into motivations or contexts for linking, has been a key issue in this social science literature." At the microscopic analysis of the network the study identifies the central accounts that may have important implications as they act as leaders where probably the most interesting conversation and exchange of information occurs. To our knowledge, no research on the study of the social networks formed by museum Instagram accounts has been reported, thus this paper attempts to fill this gap.

The rest of the paper is structured as follows. The next section presents a literature review on the use of Instagram by museums while the third section provides a short introduction to social network analysis. The fourth section presents the methodology applied and the fifth section discusses the findings of the study and more specifically the performance of the accounts, the macroscopic view of the museums' network and the node level analysis of the network. Finally, conclusions and limitations of the study are as well as future research directions are presented.

MUSEUMS AND INSTAGRAM STUDIES

Social media have enhanced the capability of museums to increase public engagement, build communities of interest around them, create "many-to-many" relationships, reach communities and individuals, connect with visitors in a more meaningful way, perform marketing activities, get more audience and communicate their exhibitions and activities (Angus, 2012; Fletcher, and Lee, 2012; Kidd, 2011; Langa, 2014; Osterman, Thirunarayanan, Ferris, Pabon, and Paul, 2012; Spiliopoulou et al., 2014; Tuğbay 2012). Few studies have focused on investigating how museums are using Instagram and exploiting its features and possibilities and on visitors and connection to exhibition content through Instagram.

One of the first studies in the field is that of Weilenmann, Hilliman, and Jungselius (2013) who investigated how Instagram is used to communicate visitors' experiences while they are visiting a natural history museum. Instagrammers work to construct their own narratives from their visits and when they communicate their experiences using Instagram, they extend the reach of the museum beyond its walls.

Suess (2014) explored the motivations of people using Instagram while visiting art galleries. Through a case study of the Queensland Gallery of Modern Art, he found that when art exhibition visitors use Instagram, they may share, promote and endorse the event to others and highlighted that visitors "use Instagram in complex and meaningful ways" (p. 62). Later on, Suess (2018) investigated the use of Instagram by visitors to an art gallery and the role it plays in their experience and found that the use of Instagram at the gallery engaged visitors in a manner that transcended the physical space and extended their aesthetic experience.

Studies have also focused on visitors and their connection to exhibition content through Instagram. Budge (2017) investigated how museum visitors are using Instagram as part of their experience. His investigation was based on a case study of an exhibition and employed visual content analysis to frame, explore and interpret visual and textual posts by museum visitors using Instagram as part of their experience. Findings suggest that museum's visitors record details of their experience and draw attention to exhibition content and specially to objects. Budge and Burness (2018) studied how visitors engage with objects through Instagram. They recorded the visitors' desire to communicate and share their perspective and experience through photography. Arias (2018) using posts tagged to the Museum of Islamic Art geolocation, identified graphic trends in the visiting narrative, situating the visiting experience not only within the museum's collection, but also within the social and cultural fabric of the country and claims that visual media has the capacity to create preconceptions and expectations about museum visiting experiences.

At a different approach Lazaridou, Vrana, and Paschaloudis (2015) investigated the use of Instagram by the most visited museums worldwide; they described the activity and the performance of museum accounts' and recorded performance differentiations among the museums Instagram accounts.

To our knowledge, no research on the study of the social networks formed by museum Instagram accounts has been reported. Thus, the originality of the paper lies in the study of the network formed by museums interconnections using Social Network Analysis for first time while the limitations of the study are associated to the sample, as the paper only investigates the list of the most visited museums.

SOCIAL NETWORK ANALYSIS

Network theory or social network analysis (SNA) theory is a mature theory which can help exploring the nature of interconnected unities (Wasserman, and Faust, 1994). The theory first emerged by Moreno, a field anthropologist. Ever since the early 70's, SNA is being studied within Graph Theory, a branch of pure mathematics originated from Euler. Social Network Analysis has been one of the fields with exploding research in the past twenty to thirty years, yielding considerable literature, both in textbooks and journals. SNA ideas and results have been extensively used in many applications and cases, ranging from structural anthropology to marketing and banking and from viral infection to sociology.

Social networks can be defined as "a collectivity of individuals among whom exchanges take place that are supported only by shared norms of trustworthy behavior" (Liebeskind, Oliver, Zucker, and Brewer, 1996). In social media applications like Instagram, new online social networks emerge, linking people, organizations, companies and knowledge and new ties are developed among people sharing interests (Wellman, 2001).

Social networks can be represented by graphs (also called networks). A graph/network depicts useful relationships (Kydros, and Oumbalis, 2015). According to this approach, entities are represented as nodes and any kind of interaction between two entities is shown by a line which connects the two nodes that represent the interacting entities. A graph is thus comprised of a set of nodes (or vertices or points) and a set of lines (or arcs, links, edges). The total volume of a network depends on the absolute number of its vertices and edges. The density of a network is the actual number of edges divided by the total number of edges that would completely connect all pairs of vertices. A network is connected if a path exists between every pair of vertices; otherwise it is disconnected in components. The shortest path between two vertices is the smaller number of 'hops' needed to travel from one vertex to the other. The degree of a vertex is the total number of its neighbors and it is the sum of in-degree (neighbors that point to) plus the out-degree (neighbors pointed to) the vertex. The clustering coefficient of a vertex is a measurement that computes the total number of edges within a node neighborhood divided by the maximum possible edges in this neighborhood. Finally, a number of very useful metrics on nodes, such as centrality measurements (degree, closeness, betweenness, PageRank, etc.) can show different aspects of importance of a node among others.

Social network analysis can be used to identify patterns of interaction among the nodes and knowledge flows within a social network, boundary spanners, gatekeepers, knowledge bottlenecks, under- and over- utilized nodes (Ryan, 2007), along with central nodes that can act as hubs, leaders, or bridging different communities (Albert, Jeong, and Barabási, 2000). Mead (2001) mentioned that Social Network Analysis makes the invisible work visible. Moreover, the discovery of inherent community structures can help understand networks deeply and reveal interesting properties shared by the nodes (Zhao, Feng, Wang, Huan, Williams, and Fan, 2012).

METHODOLOGY

The paper at first investigates the use of Instagram by the most visited museums worldwide. The ranked list of the top most visited museums was searched. Data about sixty-nine top museums according to the annually number of visitors were recorded between the 1st and the 3rd of July 2018. For each museum of the ranked list its Instagram account was located and visited and the Number of Followers, Number of Following, Number of Posts and Number of Likes of the Ten Last Posts were recorded as shown in Table 1. All indexes provide evidence of the popularity and the activity of the accounts.

Table 1. Top museums and their Instagram accounts

Museum	City	Followers	Following	Posts	Likes 10
Palace Museum	Beijing	275	1	1	74
Louvre	Paris	1.7m	260	1.486	392,258
National Museum of China	Beijing	48	0	2	14
National Air and Space Museum	Washington, D.C.	162.3k	67	1.113	12,060
Palace of Versailles	Versailles	0	0	6	0
Metropolitan Museum of Art	New York City	199	3	6	64
Vatican Museums	Vatican City	7.203	34	11	3,960
National Museum of Natural History	Washington, D.C.	676.4k	79	1.029	48,348
British Museum	London	1.1m	424	1.512	174,637
Tate Modern	London	2.2m	247	1.757	129,567
National Gallery of Art	Washington, D.C.	273.4k	717	1.664	22,084
Peterhof State Museum-Reserve	Saint Petersburg	25.5k	144	554	7,301
National Gallery	London	859.7k	118	1.378	76,433
American Museum of Natural History	New York City	232.9k	112	1.812	21,040
Natural History Museum	London	221.7k	395	1.602	31,539
State Hermitage Museum	Saint Petersburg	218.1k	484	2.944	36,208
Reina Sofía	Madrid	54.5k	398	604	7,622
National Museum of American History	Washington, D.C.	184.4k	733	2.97	14,212
Victoria and Albert Museum	London	780.7k	216	2.187	48,103
Tsarskoe Selo State Museum-Reserve	Saint Petersburg	30k	256	1.399	8,019
National Museum of Korea	Seoul	15.5k	102	1.285	2,110
Centre Pompidou	Paris	677.8k	199	1.449	19,640
London Science Museum	London	163.1k	211	1.112	7,685
Somerset House	London	98k	317	1.919	2,292
Musée d'Orsay	Paris	459.3k	137	306	82,340
National September 11 Museum	New York City	41.6k	104	1.192	11,756
Museum of King John III's Palace at Wilanów	Warsaw	1.785	162	324	774
Nanjing Museum	Nanjing	100	63	56	145
Museo del Prado	Madrid	278.6k	145	294	102,059
National Museum of Natural Science	Taichung	99	0	18	30
Kazan Kremlin State Museum-Reserve	Kazan	2.111	3.7	1.013	186
Museum of Modern Art	New York City	3.7m	648	3.174	116,438
National Gallery of Victoria	Melbourne	211.1k	1.368	4.222	20,311

continues on following page

Table 1. Continued

Museum	City	Followers	Following	Posts	Likes 10
National Art Center	Tokyo	16.6k	3	133	4,990
Royal Museums Greenwich	London	10.4k	815	545	1,589
Russian Museum	Saint Petersburg	98.3k	157	924	14,194
Mevlana Museum	Konya	470	680	225	1,101
Cité des Sciences et de l'Industrie	Paris	5.519	2.658	687	416
National Museum of African American History and Culture	Washington, D.C.	149.9k	81	691	15,621
Battle of Stalingrad State Museum	Volgograd	1.44	107	598	1,212
National Museum of Anthropology	Mexico City	29.1k	31	564	3,722
Houston Museum of Natural Science	Houston	28.9k	498	2.226	2,257
Galleria degli Uffizi	Florence	147.9k	1.862	836	25,933
Rijksmuseum	Amsterdam	215.3k	485	911	34,388
National Museum of Scotland	Edinburgh	24.2k	1.503	992	1,428
National Museum of History	Mexico City	43.3k	70	573	4,065
Shanghai Museum	Shanghai	152	1	1	35
Van Gogh Museum	Amsterdam	749k	269	1.27	157,389
California Science Center	Los Angeles	11.8k	52	481	1,188
Tretyakov Gallery	Moscow	182.9k	497	1.495	14,582
Topkapý Palace	Istanbul	2.154	21	84	1,808

Likes 10: The likes of the last 10 posts

The following museums belong to the list of the top visited museums, but they do not have an Instagram account and therefore they are not included in Table 1: Shanghai Science and Technology Museum (Shanghai), National Palace Museum (Taipei), China Science and Technology Museum (Beijing), Zhejiang Museum (Hangzhou), Chongqing Museum of Natural History (Chongqing), National Folk Museum of Korea (Seoul), Shaanxi History Museum (Xi'an), Chongqing Science and Technology Museum (Chongqing), China Art Museum (Shanghai), National Science and Technology Museum (Kaohsiung), New Taipei City Gold Museum (New Taipei), National Museum of Natural Science (Tokyo), Victoria Memorial (Kolkata), Auschwitz-Birkenau Memorial and Museum (Oświęcim), Royal Łazienki Museum (Warsaw), Three Gorges Museum (Chongqing), Fujian Museum (Fuzhou).

The network studied in this work has as nodes the museum Instagram accounts; if a museum Instagram account follows another museum Instagram account then a directed line (arc) is drawn from the node that represents the first Instagram account to the node that represents the second Instagram account.

In order to construct this network, a java program was developed that found for each Instagram museum account its Instagram followings that are included in the top museum list. The program logic as pseudocode is the following:

- For each museum m of the top museums list:
  ○ Record the Number of Followers;
  ○ Record the Number of Following;
  ○ Record the Number of Likes of the Last Ten Posts;

- Construct the set of the museums that:
  - Belong in the top museums list AND follow museum m.

The network of museum Instagram accounts was represented by an adjacency matrix A. In our case, A is a 69 × 69 non-symmetric binary data matrix, where the number 1 is placed in cell Aij if the Instagram account i follows the Instagram account j; otherwise the number 0 is placed in the cell. By using the adjacency matrix, the article performs a topological analysis of the network. The open source package Gephi (Bastian, Heymann, and Jacomy, 2009) was used for the construction of the directed graphs while NodeXL was used for calculating the community structures. At the macroscopic analysis museums' communication patterns are revealed. At the microscopic analysis of the network the study identifies the central accounts that may have important implications as they act as leaders where probably the most interesting conversation and exchange of information occurs.

PERFORMANCE OF THE ACCOUNTS

Eighteen out of the sixty-nine most visited museums worldwide (26%) do not have an Instagram account. Skewness is recorded both at the numbers of followers and following implying that there is a tendency for some museums to have high values of the indexes while most museums have low values.

The number of followers of an account shows how many other Instagram accounts have subscribed to see the photos/videos/stories posted by the account and it is an indicator of success of the account. This metric implies that the more followers an account has, the more impact the account has, as the account seems to be more popular. De Veirman, Cauberghe, and Hudders (2017) studying Instagram influencers referred to them as "people who have built a sizeable social network of people following them" (p.798) while Jin and Phua (2014) mentioned that accounts that have a larger network of followers are perceived to be more credible and popular. The number of following of a museum account m, on the other hand, shows how many other museum accounts the account m has been subscribed to follow. The number of others that an account follows is as equally important as the number of followers when estimating the importance of an account in the sphere of the medium (Saito & Masuda, 2013), like the Instagram-sphere in this case. In previous studies it was found that museums are following a relatively small number of Instagram accounts, a fact that indicates museums do not engage with the museum visitors (Lazaridou, Vrana, and Paschaloudis, 2015). However, the number of followers and following provide an indication of the network expansion of an Instagram account.

Table 2 shows the descriptive statistics for the Posts, Number of Followers and Number of Following indexes.

Table 2. Descriptive statistics of Instagram accounts

	Mean	sd	Skewness	n
Posts	1,191.177	897.945	1,33	45
Number of Followers	357,621.822	682,604.800	3,61	45
Number of Following	406.644	524.719	2,7	45

Museum accounts with low activity in Posts (Posts<10) or Followers (Followers<100) were excluded from the analysis. More specifically, the museums: Palace Museum, National Museum of China, Palace of Versailles, Metropolitan Museum of Art, National Museum of Natural Science and Shanghai Museum where excluded from the analysis and the resulting dataset consisted of 45 museums.

The Museum of Modern Art New York has the maximum number of followers. Its network has been continually expanding since the number of followers increased from 1,200,000 in 2014 (Lazaridou, Vrana, and Paschaloudis, 2015) to 3,700,000 in 2018. Tate Modern, the Louvre and British Museum follow with 2.2, 1.7 and 1.1 million followers respectively. The mean number of followers for a museum Instagram account is 357,621.822 and the Std. Deviation is 682,604.800. As the standard deviation is much larger than the mean, there is a great dispersion of this particular index among the museum accounts.

Figure 1. Number of followers (on the left) and numbers of following (on the right)

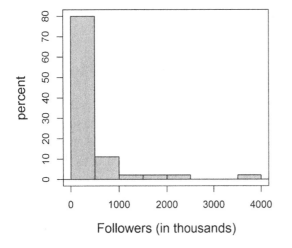 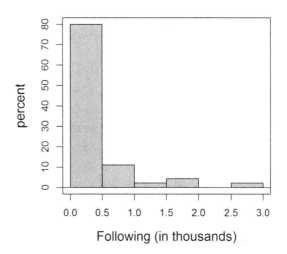

The Number of Following range from 0 to 2,658. The mean is 406.644 and the Std. Deviation 524.719. From Table 2 it is evident that museums accounts follow only few other Instagram accounts. This finding is in accordance with the findings of Lazaridou, Vrana, and Paschaloudis (2015).

The Number of Posts is an indication of the activity of the account. National Gallery of Victoria Melbourne is the most active account with 4,222 post followed by Museum of modern art New York with 3,174 posts, while the mean number of posts is 1,191.177 (Figure 1).

The Number of Followers shows the maximum potential reach of an account, as the Instagram algorithmic selection of posts may lead to a significantly smaller audience (Issac, 2016). Lazaridou, Vrana and Paschaloudis (2015) also claimed that "not all the followers really "follow" the account by means that they need not see and read labels of every post." (p. 80) thus a large number of interactions may indicate engaging and interesting content (Gräve, and Greff, 2018). The number of likes an account receives can be a strong measure of persuasion. Therefore, the Number of Likes at Ten Last Posts was recorded as an indication of engagement. Louvre is the museum account that engages Instagram users and attracts a larger number of likes along with British Museum, Van Gogh Museum, Tate Modern, Museum of Modern Art New York and Prado.

Figure 2 presents number of followers, posts and mean of likes at the ten last posts.

Figure 2. Number of followers, posts and mean of likes of the ten last posts

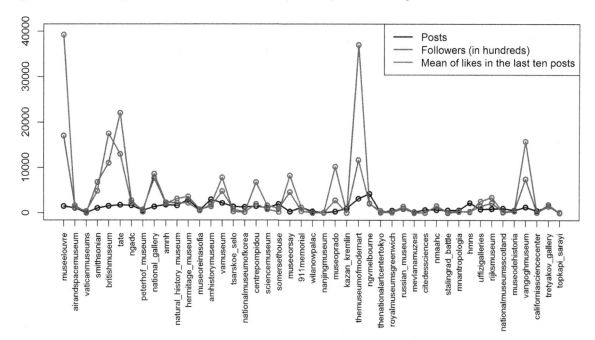

The following correlation matrix indicates significant bivariate coefficients mainly between Followers and Mean of Likes and less between Followers and Posts.

The above relation (Table 3) is depicted in the scatter diagram of Figure 3.

Table 3. Correlation matrix

	Posts	**Mean of Likes**	**Followers**	**Following**
Posts	1.00	0.19	0.42	0.24
Mean of likes	0.19	1.00	0.65	-0.08
Followers	0.42	0.65	1.00	-0.03
Following	0.24	-0.08	-0.03	1.00

MACROSCOPIC VIEWS AND ANALYSIS

The network formed among the museum Instagram accounts is investigated in this section. Some museums do not follow and are not followed by any other museum. These museums correspond to isolated nodes and each one of them constitutes one network component. Isolate notes create "a kind of noise in computations regarding the network as a whole, so it is a common practice to be removed" (Kydros, 2017). Figure 4 presents the network in a circular format. The nodes at the upper right of the figure have no connections to other nodes while the vertices in the bottom area are more connected since their edges are denser. This is a first hint for the existence of a non-random interconnection between nodes and thus the network needs further investigation.

Figure 3. 3D Scatter diagram between the number of followers, the posts and the mean of the likes of the ten last posts

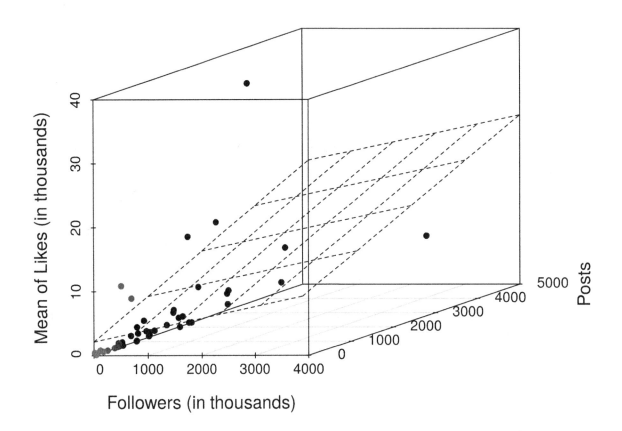

The network has 51 vertices that create 12 connected components. The larger component of the network contains 40 vertices while the 11 isolated museum accounts correspond to single-vertex connected components as shown in Table 4.

The Diameter, D, of the network is 4 and is the longest distance over all pairs of nodes. The Average Geodesic Distance is 1.69, which is relatively small due to the fact that the network is small. However, the coexistence of an Average Clustering Coefficient less than 1 (0.339) is an indication that the network is a small world.

Reciprocated Vertex Pair Ratio is 0.215 and it is "the number of vertex pairs that have edges in both directions divided by the number of vertex pairs that are connected by any edge" (Ranjan and Sood, 2016, p.326) As the relationship "following" in Instagram is not mutual an "asymmetric" model relationships exist (Zafiropoulos, Antoniadis, and Vrana, 2016) and only 21.5% of the relations in the network are mutual.

Figure 4. The network in a circular format

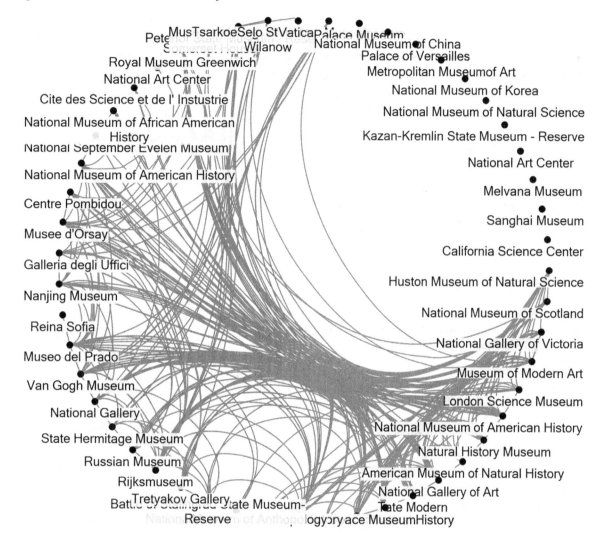

Table 4. Overall network metrics

Graph Metric	Value	Graph Metric	Value
Graph Type	Directed	Single-Vertex Connected Components	11
Vertices	51	Max Vertices in a Connected Component	40
Unique Edges	350	Max Edges in a Connected Component	350
Edges With Duplicates	0	Maximum Geodesic Distance (Diameter)	4
Total Edges	350	Average Geodesic Distance	1.69
Reciprocated Vertex Pair Ratio	0.215	Graph Density	0.137
Connected Components	12	Modularity	0.146
		Average Clustering Coefficient	0.339

Grouping by Country

We now proceed in grouping the museums based on the country they are located. The resulting network is shown in Figure 5. Not all countries are represented. There are a lot of interconnections between countries.

In Figure 6 Country Groups are collapsed and vertex size is proportional to the number of museums per group. Important information about the edges between the countries is shown in Table 4. Based on the network shown in Figure 6 and taking into account Table 4 we notice that:

- Some edges between countries do not exist. For example, China only points out but is not pointed by anyone while France is pointed by many but only points to Japan;
- U.S.A. museums are the most connected followed by U.K. museums. These museums tend to follow each other but they are also following others;
- Top museums in UK follow museums in France and USA and USA museums follow museums in France.

Figure 5. Museums grouped by country

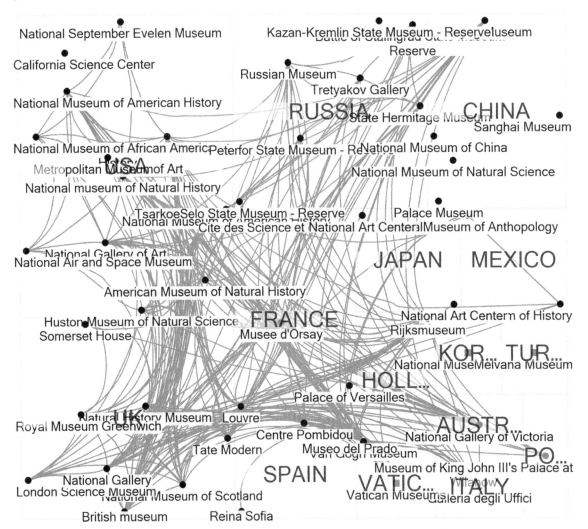

Figure 6. Country groups are collapsed

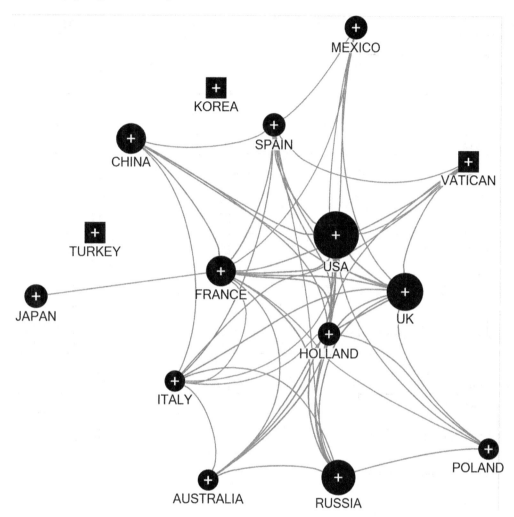

These comments are based on the data in Table 5.

Communities

In Social Network Analysis, different groupings of nodes have been extensively used (Kydros, and Anastasiadis, 2017) in order to investigate the "sub-structures" that may be present in a network. These grouping usually follow quite strict rules and are rather hard to calculate (Wasserman, and Faust, 1994). Girvan and Newman (2002) proposed the idea of communities of nodes. A group of nodes belongs to the same community if more links exist between them than with other nodes outside of this community.

Table 5. Edges within and between countries

From	To	Edges	From	To	Edges	From	To	Edges
USA	USA	40	China	USA	5	Italy	USA	1
	UK	22		UK	3		UK	2
	Russia	1		France	3		Russia	1
	France	8		Holland	2		Spain	1
	Holland	2		Spain	1		Australia	1
	Australia	3		Italy	1		Vatican	1
UK	USA	28	Mexico	USA	2	Poland	USA	2
	UK	30		UK	2		UK	2
	Russia	3		France	1		Russia	1
	France	11		Mexico	2		France	1
	Holland	9		Holland	1		Holland	2
	Spain	1	Holland	USA	11	Vatican	USA	1
	Australia	2		UK	9		UK	2
	Italy	2		Russia	1		France	2
Russia	USA	7		France	6		Holland	2
	UK	8		Holland	2		Spain	1
	Russia	13		Spain	2		Italy	1
	France	8		Australia	2	France	USA	11
	Holland	5		Italy	1		UK	7
	Italy	1	Spain	USA	4		France	5
	Poland	1		UK	4		Holland	4
Australia	USA	6		Russia	1		Spain	1
	UK	4		France	3		Japan	1
	Russia	2		Mexico	1		Australia	1
	France	1		Holland	2		Italy	1
	Holland	2		Spain	1		Vatican	1
				Italy	1			

The metric of modularity has been introduced as a measurement that corresponds to the quality of grouping (Blondel, Guillaume, Lambiotte, and Lefebvre, 2008). Modularity measures the strength of division of a network into modules. Networks with high modularity have dense connections between the nodes within modules but sparse connections between nodes in different modules. Modularity quantifies the quality of a given division of a network into communities thus it is often used for detecting community structure in networks. The value of the modularity for the network of museum Instagram accounts is $0.14 > 0$, showing that the number of edges within groups exceeds the number expected on the basis of chance (Li, and Schuurmans, 2011). The density, d, of a network is the number of arcs in the network divided by the possible number of arcs (Faust, 2006). Figure 7 presents the five communities identified in the network:

- All isolates are in one group (Group 3);
- Group 2 is the most interconnected group, with a density of 0.394. This group is consisted of History and Natural History Museums. Thus, a tendency is recorded that this type of museums tries to connect each other;
- Group 1 contains the Top Art Museums such as Louvre, Vatican Museums, Gelleria degli Uffici and Russian museums;
- Group 4 contains Museums in the U.K, Paris, Japan and Holland;
- Group 5 contains museums from Mexico and Spain.

Figure 7. Communities

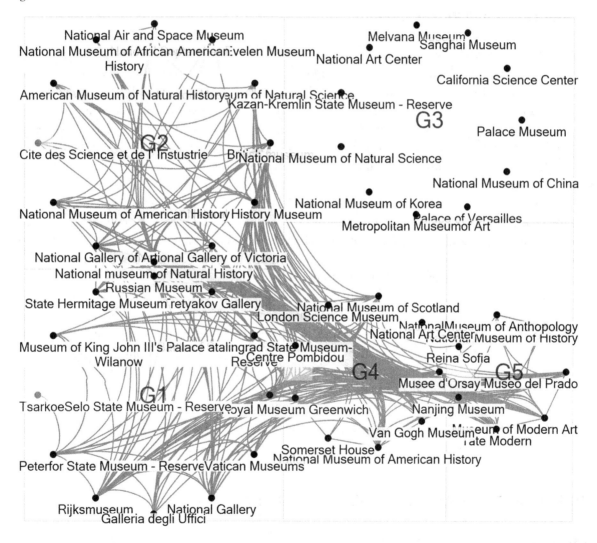

Table 6. Communities after Clauset-Newmann algorithm

Label	Vertices	Unique Edges	Maximum Geodesic Distance (Diameter)	Average Geodesic Distance	Graph Density
G1	12	45	3	1.361	0.341
G2	12	52	2	1.250	0.394
G3	11	--	--	--	--
G4	9	25	3	1.284	0.347
G5	7	13	3	1.265	0.310

Scale-Free (Small World) Testing

Watts and Strogatz (1998) and Barabási and Albert (1999) proposed 'small-world networks' and 'scale-free networks' respectively in an effort to define models of network structures differing from regular and random networks (Erdös, and Rényi, 1959). Small world networks exhibit a small average path length between pairs of nodes and a high local clustering coefficient. Scale-free networks are characterized by a highly heterogeneous degree distribution, which follows a "power-law" (Barabási, and Albert, 1999). By zooming in on any part of the distribution does not change network's shape, in the vein that there is a small, but significant number of nodes with a lot of connections and there is a trailing tail of nodes with a very few connections at each level of magnification.

In order to obtain the small world property, clustering coefficient should be between 0 and 1 and the average shortest path length should be smaller to that of a random network. For the museum network the clustering coefficient is 0.339 and the average shortest path length (average geodesic) is 1.69, which in turn is smaller to that of a random network with the same volume. In a small world it is very easy to navigate from one node to another, with a small number of hops.

On the scale-free property, one needs to calculate the degree distributions and check whether they follow the power-law. Pajek and R were used for this purpose and the outcome is presented in Figure 8. Parameter x-min is set to 2 and alpha coefficient is computed to exactly 2, which lies on the upper limit value. Thus the network is very close to a scale free network. In Figure 8 we present the degree distributions (left side) and fit them in the power-law on the right side. The almost straight line on the right side implies that the network follows indeed the power-law property. Such networks have the very interesting property of resilience to attacks, meaning that if a number of vertices are removed, then the resulting network will still be connected. Such a network will be disconnected if many high-degree nodes are removed for some reason.

MICROSCOPIC (NODE LEVEL) VIEWS AND ANALYSIS

In directed networks, like the one under investigation, it is important to rank vertices, in order to identify the "important" individuals within the network as asymmetry in networks is assumed to be linked to social prestige. Centrality measures capture a node's position in the network. Well-established centrality metrics are:

- **In-degree:** The number of links going to a node (inbound links). It is a measure of high prestige or a proof that others try to imitate the node and they represent support or influence;
- **Out-degree:** The number links leaving a node (outbound links). Less important vertices or vertices that have a very active but new social networking team do that;
- **Betweenness Centrality:** Described as the number of shortest paths from all the vertices to all the other vertices in the network that pass through the node in consideration (Brandes, 2001). It is an indicator of a node's centrality or importance in the network and shows the degree to which the node mediates in information or controls the most information paths;
- **Pagerank:** The former google-ranking algorithm for the popularity of web pages. It is a graph-based ranking algorithm used to determine the importance of a vertex within a network by considering both its inbound links and outbound links (Ding, Yan, Frazho, and Caverlee, 2009).

Figure 8. Scale free testing

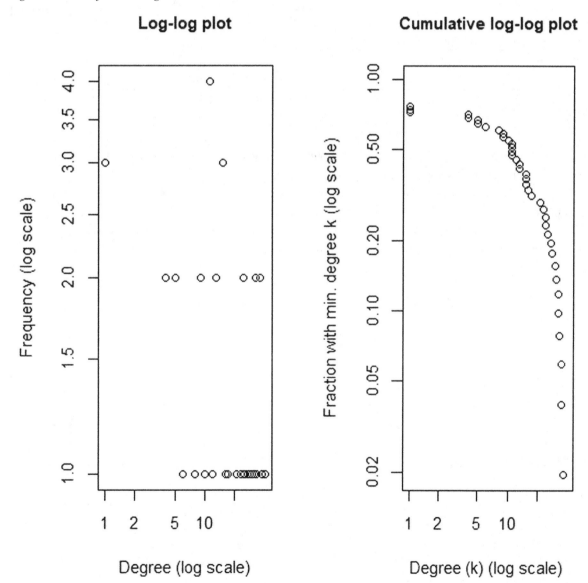

The metrics can show the most important variables in the network, according to the exact definition of the metric (Newman, 2002, pp. 1-12).

Table 7 shows the museums with in-degree larger than 10. British museum, Museum of Modern art and Louvre are the three most prominent museums since more than 20 other museums seek to direct ties to them. These "elite" accounts act as "focal points" encouraging other influential museums to congregate around them and thus attract audience to their account.

Table 7. Museums ranked by their in-degree metric

Museum	In-Degree	Museum	In-Degree
British museum	24	Van Gogh Museum	17
Museum of Modern Art	24	Rijksmuseum	16
Louvre	23	National Museum of American History	16
Tate Modern	21	Musee d'Orsay	13
National Museum of American History	20	Centre Pombidou	12
National museum of Natural History	20	London Science Museum	11
National Gallery of Art	18	American Museum of Natural History	11
National Gallery	18	State Hermitage Museum	11

Figure 9 visualizes the graph taking into account the In-degree metric. Vertices with small in-degree are smaller while vertices with high in-degree are larger.

Table 8 presents the museums with out-degree larger than 10. Natural History Museum, National Museum of Scotland and Rijksmuseum are the top three museums with the higher out-degree. These museums serve as nodes of useful information in the network as they may be relatively able to exchange with others, or disperse information quickly to many others, and are often characterized as influential.

Table 8. Museums ranked by their out-degree metric

Museum	Out-Degree	Museum	Out-Degree
Natural History Museum	21	Musee d'Orsay	15
National Museum of Scotland	19	Louvre	14
Rijksmuseum	19	Huston Museum of Natural Science	13
Royal Museum Greenwich	18	Russian Museum	13
Museo del Prado	17	Peterfor State Museum - Reserve	13
British museum	16	National Museum of American History	12
National Gallery of Victoria	15	National Gallery	12
National Gallery of Art	15	Museum of Modern Art	11
Van Gogh Museum	15	National museum of Natural History	11
Nanjing Museum	15		

Figure 9. In-degree visualization

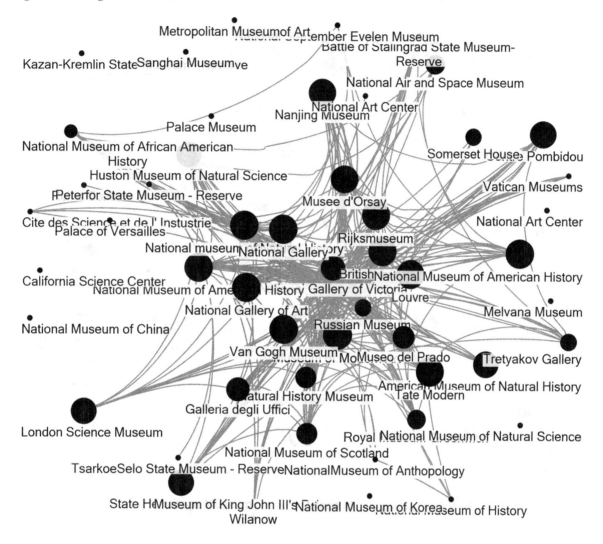

Figure 10 is the out-degree visualization. Again, larger vertices correspond to museums with greater out-degree.

A number of museums accounts such as the Rijksmuseum, Louvre, National Museum of American History, National museum of Natural History, National Gallery of Art, National Museum of American History and National Gallery serve both as good hubs and good authority accounts. A good hub account is one that points to many good authorities; a good authority account is one that is pointed to by many good hub accounts.

Table 9 presents the museums with betweenness centrality above 10. Musee d'Orsay, British museum, Museum of Modern Art, Museo del Prado and Peterfor State Museum – Reserve are the nodes with higher betweenness centrality and have more control over the network, because more information passes through that nodes.

Figure 11 is the visualization of the network according to the betweenness centrality measure. Higher betweenness centrality is shown by larger vertices.

Figure 10. Out-degree visualization

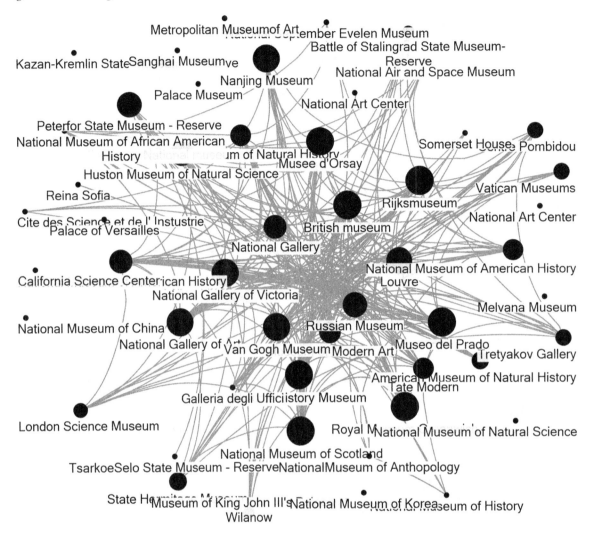

Table 9. Betweenness centrality above 10

Museum	Betweenness Centrality	Museum	Betweenness Centrality
Musee d'Orsay	116.922	Van Gogh Museum	42.760
British museum	113.470	Natural History Museum	41.323
Museum of Modern Art	112.819	National Gallery	39.622
Museo del Prado	100.561	National Gallery of Art	38.469
Peterfor State Museum - Reserve	82.407	Tate Modern	33.318
National Museum of American History	70.321	National Gallery of Victoria	29.295
National museum of Natural History	67.812	National Museum of American History	28.262
Louvre	61.240	Royal Museum Greenwich	19.118
Rijksmuseum	57.484	National Museum of Scotland	17.866

Figure 11. Betweenness centrality

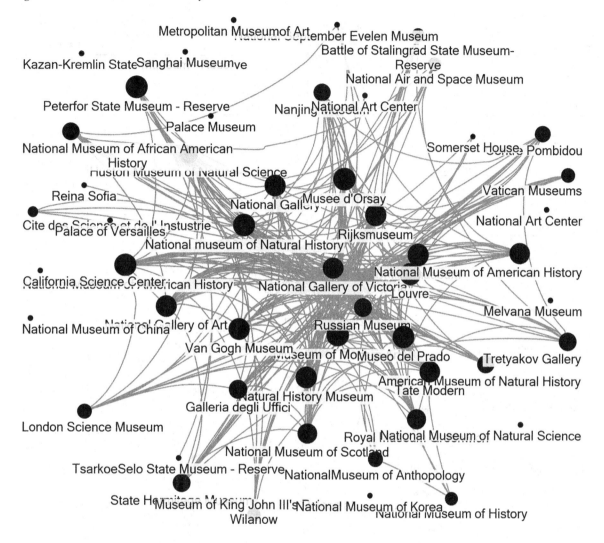

According to Pagerank, British museum, Museum of Modern Art, Rijksmuseum and Louvre are the most important nodes in the museums network. Table 10 and Figure 12 present modes having Pagerank larger than 1.0; these nodes are the community leaders and have huge influence on museums' Instagram community (Wang, Zhang, Deng, Wang, Miao, and Zhao, 2013).

In Figure 9 the graph is visualized taking into account the In-degree metric. Vertices with small Pagerank are smaller while vertices with high Pagerank are larger.

CONCLUSION AND IMPLICATIONS

The paper at first aims to describe the performance of Instagram accounts of the sixty-nine most visited museums worldwide. The methodology makes use of a prior original idea proposed to measure Twitter accounts' and blogs' performance, so it transfers the relative knowledge to the field of Instagram.

Table 10. Pagerank larger than 1.0

Museum	Page Rank	Museum	Page Rank
British museum	1.889	Natural History Museum	1.434
Museum of Modern Art	1.839	Museo del Prado	1.433
Rijksmuseum	1.722	Tate Modern	1.376
Louvre	1.679	National Museum of Scotland	1.290
National Museum of American History	1.676	National Gallery of Victoria	1.256
Musee d'Orsay	1.666	Royal Museum Greenwich	1.187
National museum of Natural History	1.584	National Museum of American History	1.102
Van Gogh Museum	1.553	Peterfor State Museum - Reserve	1.028
National Gallery	1.486	Nanjing Museum	1.000
National Gallery of Art	1.482		

Figure 12. Pagerank

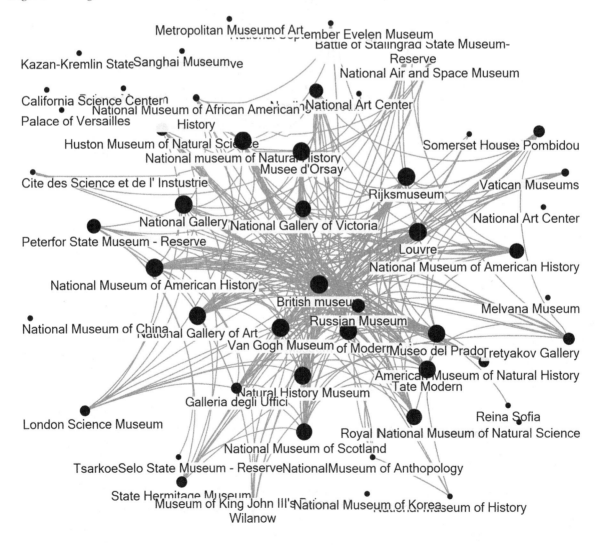

From the sixty-nine most visited museums that were examined, fifty-one have an Instagram account and were included in the research. Skewnness is recorded both at the numbers of followers and number of following implying that there is a tendency for some museums to have high values of the indexes while most museums have low values. This finding is in accordance with findings on other social networks were skewnness has been recorded in some indexes (Antoniadis, Vrana, and Zafiropoulos, 2014; Drezner, and Farrell, 2008; Theocharidis et al., 2015). Significant differentiations regarding activity have also been recorded, implying that some accounts are very active, while others are only partially involved in spreading information and attracting users.

Next, the article investigated the properties of the network that is formed between the museum accounts. The analysis uses techniques from Social Network Analysis, including visualization algorithms and the calculation of well-established metrics. Investigation of connections in a social network is crucial as they are the substrate over which information flows, which makes their flow partially dictated by the network structure (Cardoso et al., 2017).

The network of the museums on Instagram is not mutual and an "asymmetric" model of relationships exists. The network is very close to a scale free network. It turns out that the major museum accounts are closely followed by smaller ones. These smaller museums accounts, in turn, are followed by other museum accounts with an even smaller degree and so on. This hierarchy allows for a fault tolerant behavior. As the network grows over time, museum accounts that already have a high number of followers are more likely to see new followers (other museums in this case) established to them, compared with other museum accounts with a lower number of followers. For a museum account it is attractive to be connected to other museum accounts that are already highly connected.

The network of the museums on Instagram is a small world if isolates are removed. That means that any museum account is on average connected to any other museum account in a small number of steps. As museums network of acquaintances form a small world network, this has implications for the spread of information, knowledge and ideas. Information, knowledge and ideas spread much more rapidly in a small world network than they would through a network that does not have the small world property. Small world properties enable museum networks to achieve great reach, high bandwidth, and accelerate rate of knowledge creation.

Communities are formed in the network showing a tendency of museums to connect each other according to their type (History and Natural History Museums) or to their location. Thus, museums' tend to interact with those museums with which they share similar traits and create ties with museums that are similar to themselves in significant ways. Thus, information reaches museums of the same type or the same location more quickly than the other museums.

Centrality metrics reveal the most important nodes in the network. Thus, the British museum, Museum of Modern art and Louvre are the most prominent museums. If other museums Instagram accounts congregate around them, and cooperate with authority museums will be closer to the centers of community; may boost their Instagram visibility; attract more attention and audience to their own account.

Natural History Museum, National Museum of Scotland and Rijksmuseum are the museums that serve as nodes of useful information in the network, as they may be relatively able to exchange with others, or disperse information quickly to many others. These museums serve as hubs in the network, in the vein that they cite many related authorities, thus they are a useful resource for finding authorities. They are influential and they play a key role in spreading information. This has obvious implications on "word of mouth" and viral marketing, which in turn makes influential museums important for the promotion and endorsement of new ideas.

Musee d'Orsay, British museum, and Museum of Modern Art, have more control over the network as more information passes through them. Finally, according to Pagerank, the most important nodes in the museums network are the British museum, Museum of Modern Art, Rijksmuseum and the Louvre. Other museums should follow them in order to be aware of the information that flows in the network and also to be motivated and inspired by them.

These distinct classes of measures assume different models of information flow on the network. Museums may consider which measures are the most appropriate for them according to their strategy and make their acquaintances and informed decisions based on them.

The limitations of the study are associated to the set of museums taken into account as the paper only investigates the list of the most visited museums. Further research is needed taking in to consideration all the museums that have an Instagram account.

REFERENCES

Adamovic, M. (2013). *Social media and art museums: Measuring success* [Arts Administration Master's Media Management Concentration]. University of Oregon, Retrieved from https://core.ac.uk/download/pdf/36687473.pdf

Albert, R., Jeong, H., & Barabási, A. H. (2000). Error and Attack Tolerance of Complex Networks. *Nature, 406*(6794), 378–382. doi:10.1038/35019019 PMID:10935628

Angus, J. (2012). Innovations in practice: An examination of technological impacts in the field. *Journal of Museum Education, 37*(2), 37–46. doi:10.1080/10598650.2012.11510729

Antoniadis, K., Vrana, V., & Zafiropoulos, K. (2014). Promoting European countries destination image through Twitter. *European Journal of Tourism. Hospitality and Recreation, 5*(1), 85–103.

Arias, M. P. (2018). Instagram Trends: Visual Narratives Of Embodied Experiences At The Museum Of Islamic Art. *Paper presented at MW18: Museums and the Web 2018*, Vancouver, Canada.

Aslam, S. (2018). Instagram by the Numbers: Stats, Demographics and Fun Facts. *Omnicore Agency*. Retrieved from https://www.omnicoreagency.com/instagram-statistics/.

Barabási, A. L., & Albert, R. (1999). Emergence of scaling in random networks. *Science, 286*(5439), 509–512. doi:10.1126cience.286.5439.509 PMID:10521342

Bastian, M., Heymann, S., & Jacomy, M. (2009). Gephi: an open source software for exploring and manipulating networks. *Paper presented at International AAAI Conference on Weblogs and Social Media*, San Jose, CA.

Blondel, V. D., Guillaume, J.-L., Lambiotte, R., & Lefebvre, E. (2008). Fast Unfolding of Communities in Large Networks. *Journal of Statistical Mechanics*, (10), P10008. doi:10.1088/1742-5468/2008/10/P10008

Brandes, U. A. (2001). Faster Algorithm for Betweenness Centrality. *The Journal of Mathematical Sociology, 25*(2), 163–177. doi:10.1080/0022250X.2001.9990249

Budge, K. (2017). Objects in Focus: Museum Visitors and Instagram. *Curator (New York, N.Y.), 60*(1), 67–85. doi:10.1111/cura.12183

Budge, K., & Burness, A. (2018). Museum objects and Instagram: Agency and communication in digital engagement. *Continuum, 32*(2), 137–150. doi:10.1080/10304312.2017.1337079

Cardoso, F.M., Meloni, S., Santanchè, A., & Moreno, Y. (2017). Topical homophily in online social systems.

Ciasullo, M. V., Gaeta, M., Monetta, G., & Rarità, L. (2015). E-Cultural Value Co-Creation. A Proposed Model for the Heritage Management. In *Proceedings of 18th Toulon-Verona International Conference, "Excellence in Services"* (pp. 139-158).

Constantinides, E., Romero, C.-l., & Gómez Boria, M. (2018). Social Media: A New Frontier for Retailers? *European Retail Research, 22*, 1–28.

De Veirman, M., Cauberghe, V., & Hudders, L. (2017). Marketing through Instagram influencers: The impact of number of followers and product divergence on brand attitude. *International Journal of Advertising, 36*(5), 798–828. doi:10.1080/02650487.2017.1348035

Ding, Y., Yan, E., Frazho, A., & Caverlee, J. (2009). PageRank for ranking authors in co-citation networks. *Journal of the American Society for Information Science and Technology, 60*(11), 2229–2243. doi:10.1002/asi.21171

Drezner, D., & Farrell, H. (2008). The power and politics of blogs. *Public Choice, 134*, 15–30.

Erdös, P., & Rényi, A. (1959). On random graphs. *Publicationes Mathematicae, 6*, 290–297.

Faust, K. (2006). Comparing Social Networks: Size, Density, and Local Structure. *Metodološki zvezki, 3*(2),185-216.

Fletcher, A., & Lee, M. J. (2012). Current social media uses and evaluations in American museums. *Museum Management and Curatorship, 27*(5), 505–521. doi:10.1080/09647775.2012.738136

Gillen, J. J., Freeman, M., & Tootell, H. (2017). Human behavior in online social networks. In *Proceedings of the 2017 IEEE International Symposium on Technology and Society (ISTAS)*, Sydney, Australia (pp. 1-6). doi:10.1109/ISTAS.2017.8318979

Girvan, M., & Newman, M. E. J. (2002). Community Structure in Social and Biological Networks. *Proceedings of the National Academy of Sciences of the United States of America, 99*(12), 7821–7826. doi:10.1073/pnas.122653799 PMID:12060727

Gonzalez, R. (2017). Keep the conversation going: How museums use social media to engage the public. *The Museum Scholar, 1*(1). Retrieved from http://articles.themuseumscholar.org/vol1no1gonzalez

Gräve, J. F., & Greff, A. (2018) A Good KPI, Good Influencer? Evaluating Success Metrics for Social Media Influencers. *In Proceedings of the 9th International Conference on Social Media and Society (SMSociety '18)*. New York: ACM, 10.1145/3217804.3217931

Hu, Y., Manikonda, L., & Kambhampati, S. (2014). What we instagram: A first analysis of instagram photo content and user types. In *Proceedings of the 8th International Conference on Weblogs and Social Media, ICWSM 2014* (pp. 595-598). The AAAI Press.

Isaac, M. (2016). Instagram may change your feed, personalizing it with an algorithm. *New York Times.* Retrieved from https://www.nytimes.com/2016/03/16/technology/instagram-feed.html

Jin, S., & Phua, J. (2014). Following Celebrities' Tweets About Brands. *Journal of Advertising, 43*(2), 181–195. doi:10.1080/00913367.2013.827606

Kidd, J. (2011). Enacting engagement online: Framing social media use for the museum. *Information Technology & People, 24*(1), 64–77. doi:10.1108/09593841111109422

Kydros, D. (2017). Twitting bad rumours - the Grexit case. *International Journal of Web Based Communities, 14*(1), 4–20. doi:10.1504/IJWBC.2018.090933

Kydros, D., & Anastasiadis, A. (2017). Greek Political Language during the Economic Crisis – A Network Analytic Approach. *Social Networking, 6*(02), 164–180. doi:10.4236n.2017.62010

Kydros, D., & Oumbalis, V. (2015). A network analysis of the Greek Stock Market. *Procedia Economics and Finance, 33*, 340–349. doi:10.1016/S2212-5671(15)01718-9

Langa, L. (2014). Does Twitter help museums engage with visitors? In *iConference 2014 Proceedings, iSchools* (pp. 484-495). doi:10.9776/14130

Lazaridou, K., Vrana, V., & Paschaloudis, D. (2015). Museums + Instagram. In V. Katsoni, A. Upadhya, & A. Stratigea (Eds.), *Tourism, Culture and Heritage in a Smart Economy* (pp. 73–84). Cham: Springer.

Newman, M. (2002). *The mathematics of networks.* Ann Arbor, MI: University of Michigan.

Li, W., & Schuurmans, D. (2011). Modular Community Detection in Networks. *IJCAI Proceedings, 22*(1). doi:10.5591/978-1-57735-516-8/IJCAI11-231

Liebeskind, P., Oliver, A. L., Zucker, L., & Brewer, M. (1996). Social networks, learning and flexibility: Sourcing scientific knowledge in new biotechnology firms. *Organization Science, 7*(4), 428–443. doi:10.1287/orsc.7.4.428

Mead, S. P. (2001). Using Social Network Analysis to Visualize Project Teams. *Project Management Journal, 32*(4), 32–38. doi:10.1177/875697280103200405

Osterman, M., Thirunarayanan, M. O., Ferris, E. C., Pabon, L. C., & Paul, N. (2012). Museum and Twitter: An exploratory qualitative study of how museums use Twitter for audience development and engagement. *Journal of Educational Multimedia and Hypermedia, 21*(3), 241–255.

Park, H.W., & Jankowski, N. (2008). A hyperlink network analysis of citizen blogs in South Korean politics. *Javnost—The Public, 15*(2), 57-74.

Ranjan, S., & Sood, S. (2016). Exploring Twitter for Large Data Analysis. *International Journal of Advanced Research in Computer Science and Software Engineering, 6*(7), 325–330.

Ryan, C. (2007). *Performance of Public-Private Collaborations in Advanced Technology Research Networks: Network Analyses of Genome Canada Projects* [Doctoral Dissertation]. University of Saskatchewan, Saskatchewan.

Saito, K., & Masuda, N. (2013). Two types of Twitter users with equally many followers. In *Proceedings of the IEEE/ACM International Conference on Advances in Social Networks Analysis and Mining*, Niagar Falls, Canada, August 25–28 (pp. 1425–1426). 10.1145/2492517.2492575

Spiliopoulou, A. Y., Mahony, S., Routsis, V., & Kamposiori, C. (2014). Cultural institutions in the digital age: British Museum's use of Facebook Insights. *Participations*, *11*(1), 286–303.

Suess, A. (2014). Art Gallery Visitors and Instagram [Masters thesis]. University of Arts London. Retrieved from https://www.academia.edu/12086365/Art_Gallery_Visitors_and_Instagram

Suess, A. (2018). Instagram and art gallery visitors: Aesthetic experience, space, sharing and implications for educators. *Australian Art Education*, *39*(1), 107–122.

Theocharidis, A. I., Vrana, V., Michailidis, E. N., Zafiropoulos, K., Paschaloudis, D., & Pantelidis, P. (2015). Social Influence in online social networks. *Paper presented at International Conference on Internet Studies (NETs2015)*, Tokyo, Japan.

Tuğbay, S. (2012). *Museums and visitors on the web. A comparative study of visitor engagement on social media in Dutch and Turkish museums* [Master Thesis]. Erasmus University Rotterdam.

Wang, R., Zhang, W., Deng, H., Wang, N., Miao, Q., & Zhao, X. (2013). Discover Community Leader in Social Network with PageRank. In Y. Tan, Y. Shi, & H. Mo (Eds.), *Advances in Swarm Intelligence. ICSI 2013 (LNCS)* (Vol. 7929, pp. 154–162). Berlin, Germany: Springer. doi:10.1007/978-3-642-38715-9_19

Watts, D. G., & Strogatz, S. (1998). Collective dynamics of 'small-world' networks. *Nature*, *393*(6684), 440–442. doi:10.1038/30918 PMID:9623998

Wasserman, S., & Faust, K. (1994). *Social Network Analysis: Methods and Applications*. Cambridge, UK: Cambridge University Press. doi:10.1017/CBO9780511815478

Weilenmann, A., Hilliman, T., & Jungselius, B. (2013). Instagram at the museum: Communicating the museum experience through social photo sharing. *Paper presented at CHI 2013: Changing Perspectives*, Paris, France. 10.1145/2470654.2466243

Wellman, B. (2001). Computer Networks as Social Networks. *Science*, *293*(5537), 2031–2034. doi:10.1126cience.1065547 PMID:11557877

Zafiropoulos, K., Antoniadis, K., & Vrana, V. (2014). Sharing Followers in e-Government Twitter Accounts: The Case of Greece. *Future Internet*, *6*(2), 337–358. doi:10.3390/fi6020337

Zhao, Z. Y., Feng, S. H., Wang, Q., Huan, J. Z., Williams, G., & Fan, J. P. (2012). Topic Oriented Community Detection through Social Objects and Link Analysis in Social Networks. *Knowledge-Based Systems*, *26*, 164–173. doi:10.1016/j.knosys.2011.07.017

This research was previously published in the International Journal of Computational Methods in Heritage Science (IJCMHS), 3(2); pages 18-42, copyright year 2019 by IGI Publishing (an imprint of IGI Global).

Chapter 53
Using Online Data in Predicting Stock Price Movements:
Methodological and Practical Aspects

František Dařena

Mendel University in Brno, Czech Republic

Jonáš Petrovský

Mendel University in Brno, Czech Republic

Jan Přichystal

Mendel University in Brno, Czech Republic

Jan Žižka

Mendel University in Brno, Czech Republic

ABSTRACT

A lot of research has been focusing on incorporating online data into models of various phenomena. The chapter focuses on one specific problem coming from the domain of capital markets where the information contained in online environments is quite topical. The presented experiments were designed to reveal the association between online texts (from Yahoo! Finance, Facebook, and Twitter) and changes in stock prices of the corresponding companies. As the method for quantifying the association, machine learning-based classification was chosen. The experiments showed that the data preparation procedure had a substantial impact on the results. Thus, different stock price smoothing, the lags between the release of documents and related stock price changes, levels of a minimal stock price change, different weighting schemes for structured document representation, and classifiers were studied. The chapter also shows how to use currently available open source technologies to implement a system for accomplishing the task.

DOI: 10.4018/978-1-7998-9020-1.ch053

INTRODUCTION

A lot of research has been focusing on incorporating the vast amount of data available online into models of various social and economic phenomena in miscellaneous fields of science. The data, which is generated not only by domain experts but also by regular people, can provide new perspectives and potentially complementary information to conventional quantitative and objective evidence (Kearney & Liu, 2014). The data often comes from non-traditional and contemporary information sources and environments, like social networks or microblogging sites. The data typically has a form of unstructured texts that are published by different types of subjects, without the time and spatial limits.

On one hand, there are many logical reasons for this trend: there is a lot of data freely available, many different sources can be combined together, the data is often accessible immediately, in real time, and the variety of data items, opinions, and perspectives can be great. On the other hand, collecting, storing, and processing such data relate to several problems: tools for collecting the data need to be available, it is necessary to handle multiple systems and data formats, it is necessary to consider differences in data quality, reliability, objectivity etc.

One of the domains, where using online data is very topical and plays an important role in analyzing the studied systems, is the field of capital markets. Here, the data provided by digital media can help, e.g., in explaining less rational factors such as investors' sentiment or public mood as influential for asset pricing and capital market volatility (Bukovina, 2016).

One of the greatest advantages of using online resources for decision making support in the domain of capital markets is the timeliness of the information, which is particularly important for investment decisions. The quality of the messages posted in online environments (such as microblogs or discussions in social networks) is, however, generally low. That is why Internet postings have been the least frequently studied source of textual sentiment (Kearney & Liu, 2014). Despite all difficulties, content generated by web users has become a widely accepted resource for determining sentiment or opinions related to different aspects of the public mood (Tumasjan et al., 2011). It has been also shown that a large number of people participating in a content generation process enables the creation of artifacts that are of equal or superior quality than those made by experts in the respective field (Gottschlich & Hinz, 2014). Messages from millions of people are also unlikely to be biased (Mostafa, 2013).

There exist numerous studies focusing on the usefulness of textual data for predictions related to stock prices. Majority of them focused on an aggregate level (e.g., the level of a stock market index), worked with a single source of texts (e.g., newspaper articles or financial reports), or required additional expert knowledge (e.g., a list of words or expressions that are usually related to positive and negative stock price movements).

In our work, we focus on analysis at the micro level, namely at the level of individual companies. The goal is to determine whether there are some associations between the content of online texts related to a company and the movements of the stock prices of that company. We also wanted to avoid the necessity of using various lexicons provided by domain experts, which might perform poorly in previously unknown situations (Eisenstein, 2017). In our research, we also combine documents from three different sources, Yahoo! Finance, Facebook, and Twitter collected over a period of about 8 months. A machine learning-based approach is applied in order to find out whether the content plays an important role in revealing the document-stock price movement association.

Section Background gives a brief overview of the current state of research in the field of capital markets where text data is used as one of the possible sources of data. The Experimental Procedure Background section describes the considerations related to individual aspects of the problem that include the data and its processing. Section Experiments contains a detailed characterization of the conducted experiments together with their variable parameters. In section Results, specific values obtained from all conducted experiments and some statistical measures derived from them are presented and discussed. The last section, Implementation of the Procedure, focuses on the technological background of the research and describes the technologies and tools used in the research.

BACKGROUND

Most of the past research in the domain of capital markets utilized structured data, which is often objective, to analyze the impact of volatile data on business (Groth & Muntermann, 2011). Including other information sources and types into various models can provide another insight and potentially complementary information to quantitative data. This supplementary information source is typically unstructured texts as the textual form is the most typical form used by people to convey messages. The texts are published by different types of subjects, in many forms, with different frequency, quality, quantitative characteristics etc.

Decisions of investors in capital markets are based on information that is available to them. The investors can behave both rationally and irrationally, depending on the availability of information and the mental state of every person. It might be expected that rational decisions are based on objective and often quantitative facts coming from reliable sources. Irrational actions can be a result of sudden decisions, affect caused by opinions of other people, or when working with imprecise, incomplete, or irrelevant information. Thus, both objective and subjective resources are interesting and should be taken into consideration.

Objective facts, good writing style, argumentation, or reliability are mostly typical for newspaper articles, books, scientific papers, annual reports, theses, or other professional texts. On the other hand, texts like blog posts, personal e-mails, customer reviews, or questions to open-ended questions in a marketing survey are written informally by normal people, without the time and spatial limits, are shared with their friends or interest groups, and often contain a certain portion of subjective information.

It can be assumed that subjective information, such as the sentiment and mood of the public can influence financial decisions to a similar extent as news. Bollen, Mao and Zheng (2011) found that the collective mood in Twitter messages correlates to the value of the Dow Jones Industrial Average.

Wuthrich et al. (1998) investigated whether the content of newspaper articles can predict changes in selected composite indices of major stock markets in Asia, Europe and America. Their approach is based on training data from 100 days and a set of more than four hundred phrases (like "bond strong", "dollar falter", or "property weak") provided by a human expert. Knowledge of the phrases that are related to an index movement can thus also explain the movement. The achieved prediction accuracy of the proposed approach was between 40 and 47%. However, a great portion of additional outcomes was only slightly wrong, which enabled achieving a trading strategy comparable to or better than human managers.

Schumaker and Chen (2007) studied 484 companies from the S&P 500 for five weeks in 2005. They analyzed the impact of slightly more than 9,000 financial news articles on stock price movements. In their experiments, a Support Vector Machine derivative was used to predict a stock price after the publication of a newspaper article. Three different representations of textual data (Bag of Words, Noun Phrases, and

Named Entities) were used separately or combined with stock price information. The achieved directional accuracy lied in the interval 56 to 58%.

Rao & Srivastava (2014) studied several characteristics of Twitter messages in a period of 14 months and their relation to stock price movements for 13 major stock market indices. They found a strong correlation (up to 0.88) between returns and twitter sentiments. The sentiment was determined using Twittersentiment API provided by the Stanford NLP research group (Go, Bahyani & Huang, 2009). To validate the causative effect of tweet feeds on stock movements they used the econometric technique of Granger's Causality Analysis (Granger, 1969).

Most of the studies analyzed sentiment primarily at an aggregate level, based on the existence of specific words or expressions identified by rules or lexicons. Despite numerous attempts and application areas summarized by Hagenau, Liebmann and Neumann (2013), prediction accuracies for the direction of stock prices following the release of corporate financial news rarely exceeded 58%. The same authors achieved the accuracy of about 76% for one data set by employing a particular combination of advanced feature generation and selection methods together with exogenous market feedback.

Compared to other research, we analyze data from multiple sources using a common methodology employing both the dictionary-based and content-based approaches. Besides popular newspaper articles, we employ also data from Twitter and Facebook. On Facebook, we distinguish two types of documents – posts created by company representatives, and comments created by other Facebook users. Unlike other studies, that focus on an aggregate value representing stock price movements we focus on the level of individual companies.

THE EXPERIMENTAL PROCEDURE BACKGROUND

To be able to make a conclusion whether there exists or there does not exist an association between stock prices and texts published online different approaches might be applied. The most straightforward one would require a human expert who will thoroughly read all of the documents, look at the corresponding stock prices and their movements, and assess how the objective and subjective facts from the documents are related to stock prices. To be able to prove such an association, enough quantitative evidence must be ideally given. Obviously, it is usually not feasible to choose this approach from many reasons (unavailability of human experts, time constraints, mental limits etc.). Instead, an automated procedure based on algorithmic steps where the findings can clearly be substantiated by undeniable facts is favorable. In order to make the results more reliable, it is good to support them with a sufficient amount of data.

Data Used in the Experiments

In the experiments, we used data related to so-called blue chip (large and famous) companies because there is a higher probability of availability of a sufficient amount of related data. The analyzed companies were selected from Standard & Poor's 500 and FTSEurofirst 300 indices as they contain a sufficient number of listed, both US-based and European, companies.

In order to analyze the relationship between stock price movements and facts and opinions expressed by Internet users, two types of data were needed – stock prices at desired moments in time, and texts containing information related to the selected companies.

The information about stock prices can be obtained at stock exchanges or in specialized Internet data sources. For the research, only historical data is needed (no live feeds). Table 1 contains several sources that of such data. The differences are in prices of the data, covered stock exchanges, the length of the history, and others. It is generally quite a complicated task to obtain reliable and high-quality data so banks and hedge funds spend thousands of dollars a month to get it (Lukebuehler, 2013). Although sometimes contains some mistakes, Yahoo! Finance is relatively credible and reliable source that enables obtaining the stock price data free of charge (Caltech, 2017). It contains daily data for many stock exchanges around the world, with a long history. For every working day and company, opening, highest, lowest, closing, and adjusted closing stock prices are available together with traded volumes.

Texts related to the investigated companies may be found in many different sources. Usually, the objective ones are typically found on news servers. Examples of them can be found in Table 2. It is obvious that not all servers are focused on news related to European companies. Also, their popularity expressed in terms of Alexa rank (http://alexa.com) is different. It can be assumed that more visited ones can influence a higher number of investors. From the available financial news servers Yahoo! Finance was selected. It contains news aggregated from several sources (unlike, e.g., Reuters.com), is one of the most visited servers (measured by the Alexa rank), contains also recommendations of financial analysts, and is accessible free of charge.

Texts containing also subjective opinion are usually located in places where the content is created by individuals without many constraints imposed on the content. These places include social networks, microblogging sites, instant messaging platforms, sites for multimedia sharing, or discussion forums. A list of most popular can be found in Table 3.

Some of the listed sites focus on users from China. The content is not expected to be related to western companies so the sites can be eliminated. Instant messaging services are not able to provide data and are thus useless as well as services enabling photo and video sharing. From the remaining ones, Facebook, Tumblr, Twitter, LinkedIn, and a Google+, Facebook and Twitter seem to be a reasonable choice for obtaining a sufficient amount of relevant text data from enough users. The data is freely also available through an API with sufficient search capabilities.

Table 1. Selected sources containing information about stock prices

Name	Price	Frequency	History	Area
Yahoo! Finance	free	Daily	max	World
Quant Quote Free	free	Daily	1998	S&P 500
CSI data	paid	Daily	10/30 years	World
Quant Quote	paid	minutes, seconds, tick	1998	USA
Tick Data	?	minutes, tick	?	World
NYSETAQ	paid	Tick	1993	USA
Compustat	paid	Daily	1960	?
CRSP	?	Daily	100 years	USA
Xignite	?	Daily	1993 USA, 2000 other	World
Nanex	paid	Tick	2004	USA

(Caltech, 2017; lukebuehler, 2013)

Table 2. Selected news servers together with their characteristics in March, 2016 (Alexa – global Alexa rank of a server; Europe – indicates whether a server provides information about stocks in Europe; RA – shows whether a server contains recommendations of analysts).

Source Name	URL	Alexa	Europe	RA
Bloomberg Business	http://www.bloomberg.com	338	no	no
CNBC International	http://www.cnbc.com	704	no	no
CNNMoney	http://money.cnn.com	85	no	yes
FINVIZ.com	http://finviz.com	4,857	no	yes
Google Finance	https://www.google.com/finance	1	yes	no
MarketWatch	http://www.marketwatch.com	784	no	yes
Motley Fool	http://www.fool.com	1224	no	yes
Morningstar	http://www.morningstar.com	2,660	no	yes
MSN Money	http://www.msn.com/en-us/money/markets	15	no	no
Reuters.com	http://www.reuters.com/finance/markets	398	yes	yes
Seeking Alpha	http://seekingalpha.com	1,402	no	no
Wall Street Journal	http://www.wsj.com/news/markets	384	no	yes
Yahoo! Finance	http://finance.yahoo.com	5	yes	yes

Table 3. Selected social networks and similar sites containing opinions of people

No.	Name	Users	Area	Type
1	Facebook	1,550	World	social network
2	WhatsApp	900	World	instant messaging (IM)
3	QQ	860	Asia	instant messaging
4	Facebook Messenger	800	World	instant messaging
5	Qzone	653	China	social network
6	WeChat	650	China	instant messaging
7	Tumblr	555	World	microblogging site
8	Instagram	400	World	photo and video sharing
9	Twitter	320	World	microblogging site
10	Baidu Tieba	300	China	communication platform
11	Skype	300	World	video, VoIP, instant messaging
12	Viber	249	World	VoIP, instant messaging
13	Sina Weibo	222	China	microblogging site
14	LINE	212	World	video, VoIP, instant messaging
15	Snapchat	200	World	photo and video sharing, inst. messaging
16	YY	122	China	social network
17	VKontakte	100	Russia	social network
18	Pinterest	100	World	photo sharing
19	BlackBerry Messenger	100	World	video, IM
20	LinkedIn	100	World	professionals' social network

(Statista, 2016)

On Facebook, companies have their profile pages. From the investigated companies, only 55% had such a page. There is a sequence of documents, called posts, arranged according to the time of their publishing in a timeline. The company representatives create these short postings. Other Facebook users may comment the posts on at any moment. The comments, however, do not have necessarily relate to a particular post (e.g., users are just complaining about company products/services). Twitter is a microblogging site enabling users to publish short messages (up to 140 characters), called tweets. Other users may follow their favorite users (i.e., receive their tweets), answer them, or send them new messages. Twitter provides a searching capability with quite a lot of possibilities. In this work, tweets containing the user name of a company (a query contains, e.g., "@google"), mentioning a company (e.g., "Google"), replies to the tweets of a company (e.g., "to: google"), and tweets from the company timeline were used. Because the amount of data on Twitter is extremely massive, only 21 representative companies from different industries were investigated.

The data was collected in the eight-month period in years 2015 and 2016. Together with them, the 100 most liked comments from Facebook pages were retrieved, too. Twitter data was collected every six hours because the amount of generated data is quite large and Twitter does not allow retrieving more than 100 tweets at a time. Table 4 contains the total and average numbers of data items analyzed in the experiments.

Table 4. Amounts of data from different sources (from 2015-08-01 to 2016-04-04).

Document Type	Total Number	Daily Average/Company	Monthly Average/Company
Yahoo! Finance articles	81,519	0.40	12.55
Facebook posts	134,941	0.71	21.97
Facebook comments	2,222,362	17.59	545.43
Tweets	3,887,527	774.29	24,003.00

Quantifying the Association Between Stock Prices and Texts

The presented problem belongs to a group of tasks that are described by series variables whose values are recorded over a period of time. A simple time series can be described as a discrete function Y taking its values y_t at certain time points t, $Y = \{y_t: t \in T\}$, where T stands for an index set of a given stretch of time. Except for the scalar values, the general function Y may also return vectors y_t, which is here a case of text comments that accompany the stock-price time series.

The content and meaning of the documents written in a natural language is given by the words and their combinations included in them. It is expected that the documents' content is somehow related to the values of the stock prices and a method for quantification of such mutual dependency needs to be found.

The stock price values can be expressed as a time series $S = \{s_t: t \in T\}$, and similarly the content of the documents as $D = \{w_t: t \in T\}$, where w_t stands for a vector from term-document matrix (Eldén, 2007). Words are included in the vocabulary, which is shared by the all investigated documents. Both time series, i.e., S and D share the same time dimension.

However, it is not clear when the values of one series react to the values of the other. It can be assumed that the time series are shifted in time relative to each other, which is known as a lagged relationship. In this chapter, we study how financial markets react to news, which is a long-lasting question in finance (Wong, Liu & Chiang, 2014).

For quantification of the possible interdependency between values returned by two functions Y_1 and Y_2, the statistical theory offers computations of so-called correlation values provided by a correlation function $C(Y_1, Y_2)$. Statistical methods include several possibilities for the calculation of correlation between series of values, for example, perhaps the most popular Pearson's correlation coefficient (Benesty et al., 2009) based on the rate between the covariance of two variables and the product of their standard deviation.

However, the problem is complicated by the fact that w_i is not a scalar value and it is not clear how to transform it into just one number. This chapter suggests a viable procedure, which is heavily applied in the machine learning domain. We might hypothesize that there exists a function that is mapping values of one variable to the values of another variable. In our case, S and D represent the variables. However, the function is not known and has to be found in a process generally known as the training. A critical aspect is to quantify how well (i.e., with what correctness or error) the found function performs because a correct mapping for all instances is usually not found for many reasons. If the performance of the function approaches to some ideal (errorless) performance, there can be supposed that there exists a clear association between the two variables. This association is then expressed by the found function. On the other hand, when the found function is not able to correctly assign an appropriate value, the association probably does not exist or cannot be expressed by the selected function at all or under given circumstances.

The problem can belong to the class of classification or regression problems (Matloff, 2017) depending on the properties of the target variable, i.e., the stock prices. When considering continuous values, the problem is referred to as the regression. In case of categorical/discrete values, we talk about classification.

The absolute values of stock prices are not of the highest importance for our task because stocks can be traded at different price levels. Rather, the price changes between certain moments in time are more interesting. Because the absolute changes can be again proportional to the price levels, relative changes can be considered. In order to simplify the problem even more, the stock price changes can be divided into several classes depending on their movement direction, i.e., increase, decrease, or invariable behavior. Having, for example, these three types of stock price movements it is quite easy to interpret the task of quantifying the association between documents' content and stock price movements as a classification problem. For the quantification of the association, the performance of the function, which is known as a classifier, can be used. Such a performance might be measured, e.g., by classification accuracy which is a number between 0.0 (totally wrong) and 1.0 (totally right).

To find the classifier, so-called training data (Witten, Frank & Hall, 2011) is needed. The training set must contain instances of documents where a previously known stock price movement type is available. The movement type of a stock price will be later used as a label for the document. During training, i.e., the process of building a classifier, rules that enable mapping documents with a similar content to the same labels are expected to be found.

To create the training set of documents and train a classifier, the data needs to be converted to a form suitable for a given algorithm. The following sections, focusing on texts and stock prices (that are the basis for determining labels) describe this process.

Handling Stock Price Data

Stock price values are numbers expressing the prices (for example, in US dollars) at which stocks are sold and purchased at stock exchanges in certain time moments. Because the prices are usually volatile, which means that they are changing very quickly during trading periods (opening hours of a stock exchange), only some of the values are important, especially for historical data. Typically, the prices at the beginning and end of a trading day (opening and closing prices), minimal (low), and maximal (high) prices in a day are considered (Ang, 2015). Sometimes, a market price doesn't give a true picture about a firm's equity value because some corporate actions, such as stock splits, that occurred at any time before opening the next day affect a stock price. The price then needs to be adjusted, especially when working with historical data (http://www.investopedia.com/terms/s/splitadjusted.asp).

In an investigated period, the stock prices can increase or decrease or, which is very rare, remain on the same level. Naturally, the prices change very quickly, although often at small rates, reflecting many different events, habits, or sentiment (Blau & Griffith, 2016). These movements can have a reason but there is also evidence that price movements might be completely random (Borch, 1963). Than it is not necessary to include them in reasoning about the data.

Not all changes are, however, important. Instead, trends, cycles, or their combinations are more interesting (Patel et al., 2015). These movements can be revealed by smoothing, i.e., replacing the original values by other values not showing that high volatility. After application of a smoothing, the "noise" is eliminated and the data better represents real and significant changes.

Good candidates for smoothing are moving averages that substitute the original data by sequences of averages calculated from subsets of the data sets. Moving averages of different types have been widely used in technical analyses studying stocks markets (Chen, Su & Lin, 2016; Huang & Ni, 2017).

A moving average calculation can work with sequences of subsequent values of different lengths. Short moving averages are more sensitive to changes than long ones (Wang et al., 20014). Generally, there are two distinct groups of smoothing methods – averaging methods, and exponential smoothing methods. Both method calculate a new value based on n last original values. In our problem, n stands for a number of days since only one stock price value of a given type per day is available.

Simple Moving Average – SMA, an averaging method, relies on calculating the simple arithmetic mean of n successive values of past data. The Exponentially Weighted Moving Average – EWMA, an exponential smoothing method, assigns exponentially decreasing weights to older values. The values can be calculated according to the following formulas (NIST, 2016):

$$SMA_t = (price_t + price_{t-1} + \ldots price_{t-n+1}) / n$$

$$EWMA_t = \lambda \bullet price_t + (1 - \lambda) \bullet EWMA_{t-1}, \lambda = 2 / (n+1)$$

In our experiments, besides working with the original stock prices, both types of moving averages based on two different periods, 5 and 20 days, were considered for calculations in order to include averages with different sensitivities.

Changes in these average values are then better indicators of the important changes in prices, see Figure 1. On the left side of the graph, the price is decreasing with a small increase followed by an even bigger decrease. Both moving averages, here SMA working with 5 and 20 days, express the same though the latter is smoother. On the right side of the graph, the price is oscillating quite significantly while a slightly decreasing trend is noticeable at the beginning and an increasing trend is apparent at the end. The shorter moving average, SMA(5), was able to capture both trends whereas the longer moving average captured only the increasing trend of the entire part of the time series.

Figure 1. A graph showing stock price development and its smoothing (using Simple Moving Average, SMA, working with 5 and 20 days). The smoothing can better reveal trends in the data. Here, the trend derived from SMA(5) is expressed by the arrows. Three trend types (increase, stagnation, and decrease) based on a minimal price change are shown.

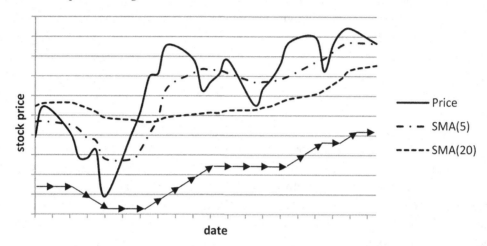

At any time, a change that has occurred since the previous moment can be detected. Obviously, very small changes, e.g., in the order of tenths or hundredths of a percent, are usually not important. The question is how big a change needs to be to be considered significant? Wuthrich et al. (1998) found that appreciation and depreciation take place when the market moves up or down by at least 0.5%. However, the same authors observed that the average change in market indices is often much more, about 1.5%. A certain threshold can be then determined to distinguish between important and unimportant movements. Positive and negative changes above this threshold, in other words, price increases and price drops (decreases), respectively, can then represent the classes (categories) for the stock prices data set.

Preparing the Text Documents

Text documents generally contain some information that has a relationship to reality. The reality is described, evaluated, judged, or compared. Understanding the messages conveyed in the documents helps with understanding or predicting the world without explicitly observing and studying it. This then has a strong impact on decisions made by people.

For example, reading customer reviews of a product might influence purchase behavior (Weisstein et al., 2017) or looking at customer reviews of a hotel accommodation at a travelers' website might predict the business performance of a hotel (Ye, Law & Gu, 2009).

Information that can contain objective facts, but also personal attitudes, feelings, assumptions, current mood, etc. is generally expressed by the words contained in the text and their combinations. In order to have an impact on decisions, the message needs to be understood by a person. In case of computers, the situation is quite different. A perfect understanding of the meaning of a text and its relation to reality is, though, a complicated task. Such a task is often not faultlessly accomplished even by human experts.

However, for many problems, a perfect and complete comprehension of the text is not needed. It is, for example, possible to determine the main topic of a scientific paper on the basis of the presence of some keywords in the text (Conway, 2009). Similarly, according to a few properties (contained words, number of words, text visibility, the presence of hyperlinks, etc.) an e-mail can be classified as spam or non-spam (Aski & Sourati, 2016).

In the last years, a lot of research has been devoted to extracting useful knowledge (e.g., sentiment or included topics) from texts written in natural languages. This discipline, known as text mining (Feldman & Sanger, 2007), is a branch of computer science that uses techniques from data mining, information retrieval, machine learning, statistics, natural language processing, and knowledge management (Berry & Kogan, 2010). The discipline focuses not only on the specification of some general classes of problems, but also on methods for representation of text data, application or adaptation of existing algorithms, development of new algorithms, and finding new applications in many scientific fields.

Many text mining methods today rely on the availability of a sufficient amount of suitable data from which a model representing a real-world problem can be learned. These data-driven methods often use an algorithmic approach that tries to find a new function that models the data. This approach, referred to as called *machine learning*, can be successfully used on large complex data sets and as a more accurate and informative alternative to data modelling on smaller data sets (Breiman, 2001). At the end of the last century, machine learning gained its popularity and became a dominant approach to text mining.

Textual documents contain mostly unstructured information, which is not suitable, in terms of effectivity and efficiency, for most of the knowledge discovery procedures. Texts are therefore usually converted to a more appropriate structured representation.

The quality of text mining outputs heavily relies on the application of various text preprocessing techniques. Their goal is to infer or extract structured representations from unstructured plain text data (Feldman & Sanger, 2007). Preprocessing methods include, e.g., online text cleaning, white space removal, case folding, spelling errors corrections, abbreviations expanding, stemming, stop words removal, negation handling, and feature selection (Carvalho & Matos, 2007; Clark, 2011; Haddi & Liu, 2013). Some of the natural language processing techniques, such as tokenization (including stemming) or part-of-speech tagging, are a subset of these methods requiring knowledge of the language to be processed (Feldman & Sanger, 2007). The application of these techniques influences what will be the features characterizing the documents and what will be their quality.

A widely used structured format is the vector space model proposed by Salton & McGill (1983). Every document is represented by a vector where individual dimensions correspond to the features (terms) and the values are the weights (importance) of the features. All vectors then form so-called term-document matrix where the rows represent the documents and the columns correspond to the terms in the documents. The values in the matrix correspond to the importance of words contained in the documents. Such a simple approach, known as the bag-of-words approach, is popular because of its simplicity and straightforward process of creation while providing satisfactory results (Joachims, 2002). The terms might be, however, also multi-word expressions or be derived from the original words.

The weight w_{ij} of every term i in document j is given by three components (Salton & McGill, 1983):

- A local weight lw_{ij} representing the frequency of terms in every single document,
- Global weight gw_i reflecting the discriminative ability of the term, based on the distribution of the term in the entire document collection,
- A normalization factor n_j correcting the impact of different document lengths.

Popular weights include *term frequency* (the number of occurrences of a term in a document) and *term presence* (1 if a term is included in the document, 0 otherwise; this is, in fact, a binary weight) for the local weight (Singhal, 1997), *inverse document frequency* for the global weight (Robertson, 2004), and the *cosine normalization* (Chisholm & Kolda, 1999) as the normalization factor.

The texts of collected documents were modified in the way that all HTML tags, @ and # characters (denoting user names and hashtags), and other non-alphanumeric characters were removed, selected emoticons were replaced by artificial terms representing positive and negative sentiment, all URLs were replaced by a single artificial term, and the text was converted to lower case. The minimal length of processed words was 2, and the minimal document frequency of terms (the number of documents where a term occurred) was 10 for Yahoo! Finance articles and 5 for the other collections.

The texts were converted to vectors using the bag-of-word approach to become acceptable for machine learning algorithms. As for weighting schemes, three possibilities were investigated – simple term presence, term frequency with the inverse document frequency weight (tf-idf), and tf-idf with cosine normalization. In order not to bias a classifier against one bigger class the numbers of documents from both classes (increase and decrease) were balanced in terms of instance numbers.

EXPERIMENTS

For the training phase of the experiments, a sufficiently large amount of training instances (text documents) had to be prepared and appropriately labeled (using the information about stock price movements). For each text document, the date of its publication and a related company was known. It was then possible to determine the stock price movement trend (increase, decrease, or stagnation) for that company for a corresponding date and use it as a label for the document. Generally, the publication date and the date related to a stock price movement do not have to be the same, which enables to consider also a time lag.

Then, a classifier mapping the document features to the labels derived from stock price movements is learned. To measure the quality of the induced classifiers, i.e., their ability to assign correct labels for unknown documents, they are examined on test samples that are distinct from the training ones and for which correct answers are known. The strength of the relationship between the input (the content of documents) and output (the label representing stock price movements) might be then expressed by some classification performance measures because they contain information on how well a classifier is able to assign a correct label to a document based on the values of its attributes. High values of these measures demonstrate that there exist attributes or their combinations that are accurately able to distinguish between instances of different classes.

The values representing correctly and incorrectly classified examples are used to compute measures of classifier effectiveness. In the two-class classification, the classes are often labeled as positive and negative. The positive and negative examples that are classified correctly are referred to as true positive (TP) and true negative (TN), respectively. False positive (FP) and false negative (FN) represent misclassified positive and negative examples.

Commonly accepted classifier performance evaluation measures include accuracy, precision, recall, and F-measure combining the values of TP, TN, FP, and FN into a single measure (Sokolova, Japkowicz & Szpakowicz, 2006).

Experimental Parameters

Four different data sources (Yahoo! Finance newspaper articles, Facebook posts and comments, and tweets) were processed separately. Because of the computational complexity, a manageable amount of documents was selected – a maximum 200 most retweeted tweets and 40 most liked Facebook comments for every company in every day. A number of Facebook posts and Yahoo! Finance articles was not that high and no preselection was thus performed.

The stock price data needed to be transformed using moving averages and a suitable class label for training a classifier was assigned to every text. In order to transform the stock price data and to determine a class label of a document D_i related to company C_i, released at time T_r, representing a change in stock price of company C_i at time T_c the following aspects and parameters needed to be determined:

- Concrete values of stock prices to be considered – here, adjusted closing values, simple moving average (SMA) and exponential moving average (EWMA), both based on 5 and 20 days were analyzed (the methods are later referred to as SMA(5), EWMA(5), SMA(20), and EWMA(20)); for days when no value was available (weekends, holidays), the price was calculated as the arithmetic average of the last closing value and the first following opening value.
- The lag between publication of texts at date T_r and a stock price movement at T_c – lags of 1, 2, and 3 days were investigated.
- The minimal relative difference in stock prices at T_c and T_{c-1} to be considered significant – changes of 1, 2, 3, 4, and 5 percent were investigated. If a price change is within the percentage limit it is considered constant and all documents related to the specific date are labeled by the stagnation class label. If the price change is above the limit in the positive direction, i.e., increased more than, e.g., 3%, documents are labeled as increase. In the remaining case, the price decreased significantly and the corresponding documents are labeled by the decrease label.

The data was massively unbalanced in terms of class labels distributions. The reason is that a large majority of documents belonged to days when no significant change in stock prices occurred. Unbalanced data biased or useless results in terms of accuracy would be achieved without further data set adjustment (Kubat, Holte & Matwin, 1998). Because significant increases or decreases in prices are more interesting than remaining approximately on the same level, documents labeled as stagnation were excluded from further processing and the interdependence between texts and stock price movements was analyzed only in periods with significant price changes. In order not to bias a classifier against one bigger class, the numbers of documents from the remaining classes (increase and decrease) were balanced.

The data was split into training and test sets in the proportion 65:35 percent. This means that 65% of the documents were randomly selected and used for inducing a classifier. The remaining 35% documents were then supplied to the classifier and the assigned label was compared to the real label.

Many different classifiers can be trained on the data. We focused on six of them that are often used in sentiment analysis and text classification (Pang, Lee & Vaithyanathan, 2002; Žižka & Dařena, 2015a) and are implemented in Python's scikit-learn package (Lorica, 2015): Multinomial Naïve Bayes (with α=1, i.e., Laplace smoothing), Bernoulli Naïve Bayes, Maximum entropy (Logistic regression), CART decision tree, Random forest, and Linear SVC (Support vector machine with a linear kernel).

RESULTS AND THEIR DISCUSSION

Using combinations of all possible parameters of the class label assignment procedure, i.e., five options for stock price value transformation (adjusted close, simple and exponential moving averages working with 5 and 20 days), three options for the lag between publication of a document and related stock price movement (1, 2, or 3 days), and five options for class determination (change 1-5 percent), 75 data sets were prepared. These data sets containing documents labeled differently were then encoded using the three weighing schemes (term presence, tf-idf, and tf-idf with cosine normalization) into three different representations which were subsequently supplied to six classifiers. The correctness of class label assignment was recorded and selected classification performance metrics were calculated. To achieve sufficiently general results, collections of less than 500 documents were excluded from detailed analyses of the experiments.

Selected measures of the most important classification performance metrics and data set properties for all experiments can be found in Table 5. The values are based on experiments using all possible combinations of parameters and classifiers. Because the collections were almost perfectly balanced in terms of class distribution in the data sets, the values of accuracy, precision, recall, and F-measure reached almost the same values. Thus, in the following text, only the values of accuracy are presented.

Table 5. Classification performance and data set characteristics for all experiments with data from all sources.

	Average Accuracy	Min. Accuracy	Max. Accuracy	Accuracy Variance	Average Number of Documents	Average Number of Attributes
Yahoo! Finance articles	0.637	0.543	0.814	0.003	10,911	13,597
Facebook posts	0.582	0.502	0.694	0.001	14,191	6,743
Facebook comments	0.604	0.523	0.786	0.003	43,037	10,456
Tweets	0.666	0.553	0.839	0.002	35,768	8,459

It is obvious that the classification accuracy varies quite considerably from its minimal to maximal values, e.g., from 0.543 to 0.814 in case of Yahoo! Finance articles. Because the same data was processed in all experiments, the difference must be caused by different values of parameters of the proposed procedure. A detailed exploration of the used algorithms and all parameters was therefore conducted in order to reveal how individual parameters influence the classification process. For every variable parameter, average accuracies for all experiments where the value of the parameter was fixed were calculated. For example, the average accuracy for all experiments where the smoothing method was *AdjClose* was calculated. Then, the average accuracy for all experiments where the smoothing method was *SMA(5 days)* was calculated etc. If the average accuracy for *SMA(5)* was higher than for *AdjClose*, we can assume that *SMA(5)* is a better method for handling stock price values.

It was found that only the smoothing method and classification algorithm had a significant impact on accuracy values. Higher accuracies were achieved for *SMA(20)* and *EWMA(20)* and for *Linear SVC*, *Maximum Entropy*, and *multinomial Naïve Bayes* classifiers across all data sources. The average accuracies from all experiments using the combinations containing only these values for respective parameters increased from 0.64 to 0.72 for Yahoo! Finance articles, from 0.85 to 0.61 for Facebook posts, from 0.60 to 0.67 for Facebook comments, and from 0.67 to 0.70 for tweets.

The remaining parameters did not have a significant impact on the classification accuracy. For example, for all possible values of the minimal price change (1-5%), the average accuracy achieved for Yahoo! Finance articles ranged from 0.631 to 0.644.

For further detailed analysis, aiming at better evaluation of the impact of the remaining parameters, only the experiments where *SMA(20)* and *EWMA(20)* were used for smoothing and *Linear SVC, Maximum Entropy*, and *multinomial Naïve Bayes* were used for classification were considered. The values of the achieved average accuracies can be found in Table 6a-6e.

Table 6a. Classification performance and data set characteristics for all experiments with data from all sources: Lag in Days

	1	2	3
Yahoo! Finance	0.741	0.718	0.713
Facebook comments	0.671	0.675	0.655
Facebook posts	0.645	0.598	0.596
Tweets	0.676	0.699	0.705

Table 6b. Classification performance and data set characteristics for all experiments with data from all sources: Minimal Price Change

	1	2	3	4	5
Yahoo! Finance	0.696	0.733	0.714	0.728	0.747
Facebook comments	0.629	0.663	0.668	0.686	0.719
Facebook posts	0.601	0.607	0.600	0.603	0.636
Tweets	0.714	0.713	0.704	0.654	0.660

Table 6c. Classification performance and data set characteristics for all experiments with data from all sources: Classifier

	LinearSVC	MaxEnt	NB-multi
Yahoo! Finance	0.725	0.721	0.710
Facebook comments	0.659	0.667	0.670
Facebook posts	0.599	0.606	0.615
Tweets	0.702	0.695	0.693

Table 6d. Classification performance and data set characteristics for all experiments with data from all sources: Vector Type

	tf-idf-cos	tf-idf-no	tp-no-no
Yahoo! Finance	0.711	0.728	0.717
Facebook comments	0.668	0.665	0.664
Facebook posts	0.582	0.585	0.585
Tweets	0.691	0.700	0.699

Table 6e. Classification performance and data set characteristics for all experiments with data from all sources: Smoothing Method

	sma(20)	ewma(20)
Yahoo! Finance	0.720	0.718
Facebook comments	0.665	0.666
Facebook posts	0.607	0.607
Tweets	0.702	0.691

The stock price data is generally highly volatile and the movements are sudden, unanticipated, and sometimes random. Thus, trends that are more meaningful can be discovered with an application of a smoothing. This has proven to be a reasonable step in improving the classification accuracy for most of the data sources significantly. Moving averages based on 20 days had more positive impact than moving averages based on 5 days, which means that a greater smoothing had a more positive impact than a smaller one. The type of the moving average used in calculations (simple or exponential) was not considerably important.

When looking at the distance between the moments of publication of documents and related stock price changes, the strongest correlation was found for shorter time spans for the Yahoo! Finance articles and Facebook posts and comments (1 day, or 1-2 days, respectively) and longer (2-3 days) for tweets. The source of the documents is thus another interesting factor. A possible explanation of the finding might be in the nature of the documents and their sources. As it takes some time to publish a newspaper article, the time distance between an article and a related price movement is rather short. Texts that are published very quickly, such as tweets, might anticipate a price movement earlier. Facebook posts that are often prepared by company representatives are usually not published timely so their nature is in this respect more similar to newspaper articles. In addition, the comments written by other people can sometimes be immediate but sometimes are delayed.

For all data sources, except Twitter, a higher considered minimal stock price changes lead to better results in terms of classification accuracy. We can assume that substantial changes are accompanied by an exceptional content of documents making them more distinguishable from the documents published when no or small price changes happened. From all of the experimental parameters, the minimal percentage of stock price change was the one that influenced the size of data set the most. When a higher minimal relative change was considered a smaller number of documents labeled as increase or decrease were available, which is quite natural (there are fewer periods with large changes than periods with small changes). Thus, a meaningful threshold should be used in practical applications in order to balance the accuracy of predictions and a number of cases to be considered relevant.

The impact of different weighting methods was very low; the average accuracies lied in an interval of about 1%. Thus, the weighting scheme can be considered an unimportant factor of data preprocessing.

IMPLEMENTATION OF THE PROCEDURE

The chapter should not only describe the theoretical background of the domain and methods and simply present some results, but also show how to use currently available open source technologies to implement a system for accomplishing the task. The activities, technological considerations, and tools related to data collection and analysis are thus presented in this section.

The complete source code implementing the tasks can be found on Github (see https://github.com/jontesek/mendelu-finance-analyzer). It is divided into three basic modules:

- **DataGetter:** Retrieving data from Yahoo! Finance, Facebook, and Twitter, and storing it to a database.
- **DataProcessor:** Reading data from the database and generating text files for further processing.
- **AnalyzingPipeline:** Converting texts to their structured representation (vectors) and performing classification.

Data Collection

Firstly, the chosen data sources and possibilities they provide are described.

Yahoo Finance

There is a homepage for each company listed on the stock exchange (e.g. for 3M Company it is https://finance.yahoo.com/quote/MMM) on Yahoo! Finance. The page contains a lot of information, such as price charts, financial ratios and statements, analysists recommendations, and other. News articles are located directly on the homepage and consist of a headline and a short description. They both link to a full version of the article, which is either placed directly on Yahoo! Finance or on another service (in total more than 42 different services present their articles on Yahoo! Finance). In the first case, the structure of a generated HTML web page is always the same, so it is possible to acquire the text using web scraping. In the second case, the situation is more complicated, because each service has a unique HTML structure and therefore cannot be parsed in a common way. Therefore, we chose to examine only the articles fully available on Yahoo! Finance. We also downloaded the number of shares on Facebook by querying a public API (http://graph.facebook.com/<article url>).

Yahoo! Finance also provides historical stock prices (https://finance.yahoo.com/quote/MMM/history), which can be downloaded as a CSV file by sending a HTTP GET command in format:

```
http://realchart.finance.yahoo.com/table.csv?s=ABT&d=3&e=9&f=2016&g=d&a=3&b=6&
c=1983&ignore=.csv
```

where s determines the stock symbol (ticker) of a company, a, b, c an initial month, day, and year, and d, e, f a final month, day, and year for the period of data collection. The data contain only values for working days. We saved all available values: Open, High, Low, Close, Adjusted Close (close price adjusted by dividends and splits) price, and Volume – the number of company stocks traded on the exchange during the day.

Facebook

Because Facebook offers no search capability, we decided to focus on fan pages of the examined companies. We wanted to download company posts and user comments. Data from Facebook may be downloaded using the Graph API, which enables applications to read and write into "social graph" of Facebook. The API is based on REST (Richardson & Ruby, 2007) and returns data in the JSON format (Bray et al., 2014). We are interested in the node *Page,* which offers many fields including the posts. You can get at maximum 100 posts per one request. For requesting data from the API, it is necessary to use an access token. It can be obtained on the basis of an APP_ID and APP_SECRET after creating an Application in Facebook Developers section.

We downloaded posts by sending the following HTTP GET request:

```
https://graph.facebook.com/2.3/intel/posts/?limit=90&date_format=u&si
nce=<timestamp>&fields=id,created_time,message,shares,likes.limit(0).
summary(true),comments.limit(100).summary(true)
```

It means to get 90 (limit) newest posts from page *"intel"* which were created since *<timestamp>* (a UNIX timestamp – a number of seconds passed since 00:00 UTC 1. 1. 1970). We wanted to get the following fields for each post: ID, publication time, text, number of shares and likes. We also wanted to retrieve the most 100 popular comments (ordered by the number of likes).

Twitter

Statuses from Twitter may be obtained by using two types of API. The first is a classical REST API, which is limited by a number of requests an application can send to Twitter servers. For search, it is 450 requests per 15 minutes. The second option is to use a Streaming API, which is focused on processing tweets in real-time. It is based on a long-term HTTP connection and can be used to bypass the limits of REST API. We decided to download Twitter data only for a small amount number of companies (21). The reason is that we wanted to focus also on other sources of data and that downloading tweets for all companies would require a huge amount of storage space. Therefore, we decided to use REST API, because its limits did not hold us back.

The Twitter API provides many different endpoints from which the desired data can be accessed via an URL in the format https://api.twitter.com/<version>/<endpoint>. For authentication, OAuth protocol is used – we used an application token. The Search API enables the access to tweets at maximum one week old and a response may contain at maximum 100 tweets. We used the following HTTP GET request (an example for searching tweets about the Google company):

```
https://api.twitter.com/1.1/search/tweets.json?q=Google&lang=en&result_
type=mixed&count=100&since_id=123
```

The example means that we wanted to get 100 (*count*) tweets corresponding to the given query (*q*) that are written in English (*lang*). Popular as well as recent tweets (*result_type*), whose ID is larger than 123 (*since_id*), are included. For downloading tweets from company profiles, another endpoint, by which it is possible to get last 3200 tweets while one response may contain at most 200 tweets, is used. The limit is 300 requests per 15 minutes. We used the following HTTP GET request:

```
https://api.twitter.com/1.1/statuses/user_timeline.json?count=200&since_
id=123&screen_name=google
```

That means that 200 (*count*) newest tweets from the profile of Google (*screen_name*) which have their ID higher than 123 are retrieved. Requests to the Twitter API return data in the JSON format and contain many different fields (see https://dev.twitter.com/overview/api/tweets). We saved the following: ID, text, publication time, number of likes and shares (so-called "retweets"), if it is a response to another tweet, location, and information about the author: ID, location, number of followers, number of users he follows, and number of published tweets.

Data Downloading

Downloading of the data may be performed by various programming languages and tools. We chose Python mainly because of the presence of many available packages for working with data from the Web. We used the object-oriented approach so the resulting program module consists of classes defining methods for data manipulation. The scripts using these classes for downloading the data were periodically (once a day) run by the CRON (Unix-like task scheduler) on a Linux server.

Text-Preprocessing Using Python

We used three parameters influencing the values of training data vectors – a minimal percentage of a price change, a delay in days, and a smoothing method. Based on the combination of their values, a class (*decrease* or *increase*) was assigned to a document according to a stock price movement of the related company.

We thus had 75 versions of training sets where texts. The textual part of the data was a subset of all available texts based on the presence of a significant price movements related to the texts; individual sets also differed in the values of class labels associated to the texts.

Each data source was processed separately. To assign a correct label, the following steps needed to be performed for every company:

- Getting values of stock prices: for every day in the observed period, a given price type (Adjusted Close, SMA(5), SMA(20), EWMA(5), or EWMA(20)) was assigned to every date.
- Calculating the percent difference of stock prices in subsequent days and assigning a label according to the intensity of the movement.
- Retrieving all documents from the database.

- Looking at a date in a desired distance from the publication of every document and assigning a label according to the respective stock price movement.
- Preprocessing the documents (removing non-alphanumeric characters, replacing emoticons, URLs, transforming to lower case etc.).
- Writing the data to a text file with the name matching the following template:

```
<source>_<all|company>_<smoothing>_<lag>_<minimal price change>.text
```

Converting Texts to Vectors Using VecText

For converting text data to vector numerical data, VecText (https://sourceforge.net/projects/vectext/) was used. The application has many options that influence the conversion process and results. The minimal word length was set to 2 and the minimal document frequency 10 for Yahoo! Finance articles, and 5 for the remaining documents. The program was called for each text file. The following example shows generating a vector file from a set containing Yahoo! Finance articles. The parameters were generated by the script (AnalPipeline/src/docs_to_vectors_bulk.py):

```
params = '--logarithm_type="natural" --min_document_frequency="10"
--input_file="article_all_ewma_1_1.text" --output_format="SVMlight"
--min_word_length="2" --encoding="utf8" --normalization="none" --case="lower
case"
--subset_size="100000" --output_decimal_places="6" --create_dictionary="no"
--output_file="article_all_ewma_1_1_tp-no-no" --class_position="1"
--local_weights="Binary (Term Presence)" --global_weights="none" --n_grams="1"
--output_dir="\outputs\vec_text\article" --sort_attributes="none" --print_sta-
tistics'
command = 'perl vectext-cmdline.pl ' + params
return_code = subprocess.call(command, shell=True)
```

Output files had a SVMlight (sparse matrix) format. The values of all specific parameters were included in the file name (e.g., *article_all_ewma_1_1_tp-no-no*).

Classification Using Scikit-Learn

The resulting files in the SVMlight format were then automatically processed by the following machine learning algorithms available in the scikit-learn Python library: Multinomial Naïve Bayes, Bernoulli Naïve Bayes, Logistic Regression, Decision tree (CART), Random Forest Classifier, and Linear SVC.

Each file was loaded and the data was divided into training (65%) and testing (35%) sets:

```
data_matrix = load_svmlight_file(' article_all_ewma_1_1_tp-no-no')
X_train, X_test, y_train, y_test = cross_valida-
tion.train_test_split(data_matrix[0], data_matrix[1],
test_size=0.35, random_state=38)
```

The split (training and test set) is random, but a parameter *random_state* was specified, so the result will be identical on the same data and platform.

Each classifier was then trained and tested:

```python
def classify_data(clf_obj, X_train, X_test, y_train, y_test, save_model_
filepath=False):
    # Train model.
    start_time = time.time()
    clf_obj.fit(X_train, y_train)
    train_runtime = round(time.time() - start_time, 6)
    # If desired, save model to disk.
    if save_model_filepath:
        joblib.dump(clf_obj, save_model_filepath)
    # Test model.
    start_time = time.time()
    y_predicted = clf_obj.predict(X_test)
    test_runtime = round(time.time() - start_time, 6)
    # Evaluate model.
    accuracy = metrics.accuracy_score(y_test, y_predicted)
    precision = metrics.precision_score(y_test, y_predicted,
average='weighted', pos_label=None)
    recall = metrics.recall_score(y_test, y_predicted, average='weighted',
pos_label=None)
    f1_score = metrics.f1_score(y_test, y_predicted, average='weighted', pos_
label=None)
    # Get the number of tested samples for class 1 and 2.
    conf_matrix = metrics.confusion_matrix(y_test, y_predicted, labels=[1, 2])
    cl_1_count = conf_matrix[0][0] + conf_matrix[0][1]
    cl_2_count = conf_matrix[1][0] + conf_matrix[1][1]
    # Return data.
    tested_counts = [cl_1_count, cl_2_count]
    results = [accuracy, precision, recall, f1_score, train_runtime, test_run-
time]
    eval_data = [y_test, y_predicted]
    return results, eval_data, tested_counts
```

The results of classification of the test data were evaluated using the metrics *Accuracy*, *Precision*, *Recall* and *F1 score*. Except the first one, the values were weighted by the support (the number of instances for a given class). The output is a CSV file where every row represents an experiment (the application of a classification algorithm) on a data file and every column represents the characteristics of the experiment:

```
timestamp, input file name, document type, company, smoothing method, lag in
days, minimal price change, vector, type, total, samples, number of features,
```

number of class 1 test samples, number of class 2 test samples, algorithm
name, accuracy, precision, recall, F1 score, training time, testing time

Analyzing Experimental Parameters Using MS Excel

The CSV with the experimental results was imported to Microsoft Excel 2017 spreadsheet calculator and further analyzed to evaluate the impact of individual parameters. We used the *Pivot Table* tool that allows users extract the significant characteristics from a large, detailed data set and to cross-analyze data from different perspectives. The pivot table allows the user place selected attributes to columns and rows and analyze the observed values on their intersection in the data field. In Figure 1, different smoothing methods, lag in days, and minimal price change in rows are combined with different classifiers in columns and the values of accuracy in the data field of the pivot table. The bold values are the averages of the subordinate values. The overview of the whole dataset gives the pivot chart on the right side. The highest values of accuracy for EWMA(20), 1 or 2 days lag, and 2 or 4 percent of a price change for the Multinomial Naïve Bayes classifier can be identified.

Figure 2. The application of Pivot Tables in MS Excel for analyzing the experimental results.

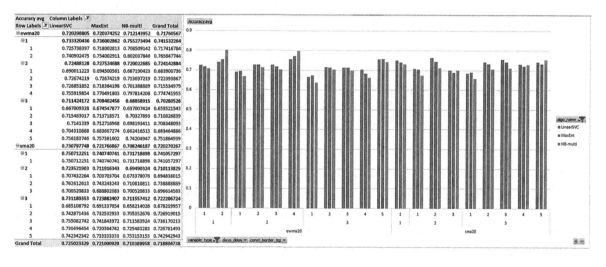

This tool helped us to identify the best combinations of classifiers and smoothing methods. For further analysis, we used only the filtered dataset (with the selected values of experimental parameters). The selected statistical characteristics of the results for the classification of Yahoo! Finance articles can be found in Figure 3.

CONCLUSION

The paper presented the result of experiments that were designed with the goal of revealing the association between texts published online and changes in stock prices of the corresponding companies at a micro level. To make the association quantifiable, the two time-series (texts and stock prices) needed to be transformed so quantitative analysis was possible. We considered four different methods of stock prices smoothing, three different lags between the release of documents and related stock price changes, five levels of a minimal stock price change to consider the change as significant, and three different weighting schemes for structured document representation used in the machine learning procedure. From these parameters, the smoothing method played the most important role. It was found that smoothing the stock price data with moving averages based on the 20 preceding days led to better results than in the case of using only 5 days. Such smoothing removed excessive price oscillations which are quite typical for this type of data. On the other hand, some of the important changes, especially when followed by another change in the opposite direction might be lost.

Figure 3. Obtaining important statistical characteristics of the experimental results using MS Excel.

Row Labels	Accuracy max	Accuracy avg	Accuracy min	Accuracy varp
LinearSVC	0.792349727	0.725023329	0.660536836	0.000917653
MaxEnt	0.779202279	0.721000929	0.62295082	0.001321222
NB-multi	0.81420765	0.710389958	0.626156482	0.001863961
Grand Total	**0.81420765**	**0.718804738**	**0.62295082**	**0.001405713**
Row Labels	Accuracy max	Accuracy avg	Accuracy min	Accuracy varp
tf-idf-cos	0.794759825	0.710647055	0.62295082	0.001598535
tf-idf-no	0.81420765	0.728420895	0.626156482	0.00121756
tp-no-no	0.812227074	0.717346265	0.640890919	0.001239898
Grand Total	**0.81420765**	**0.718804738**	**0.62295082**	**0.001405713**
Row Labels	Accuracy max	Accuracy avg	Accuracy min	Accuracy varp
ewma20	0.81420765	0.71760567	0.62295082	0.001649284
sma20	0.77972973	0.720270267	0.640625	0.001104109
Grand Total	**0.81420765**	**0.718804738**	**0.62295082**	**0.001405713**

We demonstrated that it was possible to reveal an association between texts published in newspapers and on social networks and microblogging sites with the application of the machine learning-based classification. The content of the documents contributed to distinguishing between positive and negative stock price movements. All classifiers used were able to confirm the positive association between texts and stock price movements with all data sets prepared for the conducted experiments. Some of them, namely Linear SVC, Maximum Entropy, and multinomial Naïve Bayes classifiers outperformed the others in terms of the achieved accuracy. The difference between the maximal and minimal achieved accuracies for the same data was between about 20 and 30%. It was therefore obvious that the data preparation procedure had a substantial impact on the results. By further analysis of variable parameters, the values for which better results were accomplished were to be identified.

The chapter does not contain only the theoretical background, design and results of the experiments, but also a description of the technical solution of the entire process. A reader can thus understand what technological considerations needed to be done and what tools are available and can be successfully used.

Of course, there are many aspects that influence stock price movements and that are not included in online texts. It is, therefore, clear that the documents' content cannot explain or predict all movements. However, at least part of these movements is associated to the texts and can be used as part of a more complex model of economic phenomena.

Future research might include a tighter interconnection with other aspects of the financial markets domain, including, e.g., other external market and economy information and industry specifics. From the machine learning perspective, processing the data in a stream using, e.g., a moving window approach (Žižka & Dařena, 2015b), processing unbalanced data, or including additional features such as the dynamics of Facebook posts and comments likings, Yahoo! Finance articles sharing or tweets popularity are possible ways.

ACKNOWLEDGMENT

This research was supported by the Czech Science Foundation [grant No. 16-26353S "Sentiment and its Impact on Stock Markets."

REFERENCES

Ang, C. (2015). *Analyzing Financial Data and Implementing Financial Models Using R.* Springer. doi:10.1007/978-3-319-14075-9

Aski, A. S., & Sourati, N. K. (2016). Proposed efficient algorithm to filter spam using machine learning techniques. *Pacific Science Review A. Natural Science and Engineering, 18*(2), 145–149.

Benesty, J., Chen, J., Huang, Y., & Cohen, I. (2009). *Pearson Correlation Coefficient.* Springer. doi:10.1007/978-3-642-00296-0_5

Berry, M. W., & Kogan, J. (2010). *Text Mining: Applications and Theory.* Chichester, UK: Wiley. doi:10.1002/9780470689646

Blau, B. M., & Griffith, T. G. (2016). Price clustering and the stability of stock prices. *Journal of Business Research, 69*(10), 3933–3942. doi:10.1016/j.jbusres.2016.06.008

Bollen, J., Mao, H., & Zeng, X. (2011). Twitter mood predicts the stock market. *Journal of Computational Science, 2*(1), 1–8. doi:10.1016/j.jocs.2010.12.007

Borch, K. (1963). *Price movements in the stock market. Econometric research program, research paper no. 7.* Princeton University. doi:10.21236/AD0407934

Bray, T. (2014). *The JavaScript Object Notation (JSON) Data Interchange Format. Request for Comments: 7159, Internet Engineering Task Force.* IETF.

Breiman, L. (2001). Statistical modeling: The two cultures (with comments and a rejoinder by the author). *Statistical Science, 16*(3), 199–231. doi:10.1214s/1009213726

Bukovina, J. (2016). Social media big data and capital markets – An overview. *Journal of Behavioral and Experimental Finance, 11*, 18–26. doi:10.1016/j.jbef.2016.06.002

Caltech. (2017). *Historical Stock Data — Caltech Quantitative Finance Group.* Retrieved October 1, 2017, from http://quant.caltech.edu/historical-stock-data.html

Carvalho, G., de Matos, D. M., & Rocio, V. (2007). Document retrieval for question answering: a quantitative evaluation of text preprocessing. In *Proceedings of the ACM first Ph. D. workshop in CIKM* (pp. 125-130). ACM. 10.1145/1316874.1316894

Chen, C., Su, X., & Lin, J. (2016). The role of information uncertainty in moving-average technical analysis: A study of individual stock-option issuance in Taiwan. *Finance Research Letters, 18,* 263–272. doi:10.1016/j.frl.2016.04.026

Chisholm, E., & Kolda, T. G. (1999). *New term weighting formulas for the vector space method in information retrieval.* Computer Science and Mathematics Division, Oak Ridge National Laboratory. doi:10.2172/5698

Clark, E., & Araki, K. (2011). Text normalization in social media: Progress, problems and applications for a pre-processing system of casual English. *Procedia: Social and Behavioral Sciences, 27,* 2–11. doi:10.1016/j.sbspro.2011.10.577

Conway, M. (2010, April 01). Mining a corpus of biographical texts using keywords. *Literary and Linguistic Computing, 25*(1), 23–35. doi:10.1093/llc/fqp035

Eisenstein, J. (2017). Unsupervised Learning for Lexicon-Based Classification. In *Proceedings of the Thirty-First AAAI Conference on Artificial Intelligence* (pp. 3188-3194). Association for the Advancement of Artificial Intelligence.

Eldén, L. (2007). *Matrix Methods in Data Mining and Pattern Recognition.* Philadelphia: Society for Industrial and Applied Mathematics. doi:10.1137/1.9780898718867

Feldman, R., & Sanger, J. (2007). *The text mining handbook: advanced approaches in analyzing unstructured data.* Cambridge, UK: Cambridge University Press.

Go, A., Bhayani, R., & Huang, L. (2009). *Twitter Sentiment Classification using Distant Supervision.* Retrieved September 14, 2017, from http://s3.eddieoz.com/docs/sentiment_analysis/Twitter_Sentiment_Classification_using_Distant_Supervision.pdf

Gottschlich, J., & Hinz, O. (2014, March). A decision support system for stock investment recommendations using collective wisdom. *Decision Support Systems, 59,* 52–62. doi:10.1016/j.dss.2013.10.005

Granger, C. W. J. (1969). Investigating Causal Relations by Econometric Models and Cross-spectral Methods. *Econometrica, 37*(3), 424–438. doi:10.2307/1912791

Groth, S. S., & Muntermann, J. (2011). An intraday market risk management approach based on textual analysis. *Decision Support Systems, 50*(4), 680–691. doi:10.1016/j.dss.2010.08.019

Haddi, E., Liu, X., & Shi, Y. (2013). The role of text pre-processing in sentiment analysis. *Procedia Computer Science, 17,* 26–32. doi:10.1016/j.procs.2013.05.005

Hagenau, M., Liebmann, M., & Neumann, D. (2013). Automated news reading: Stock price prediction based on financial news using context-capturing features. *Decision Support Systems, 55*(3), 685–697. doi:10.1016/j.dss.2013.02.006

Huang, P., & Ni, Y. (2017). Board structure and stock price informativeness in terms of moving average rules. *The Quarterly Review of Economics and Finance, 63*, 161–169. doi:10.1016/j.qref.2016.04.012

Joachims, T. (2002). *Learning to classify text using support vector machines: Methods, theory and algorithms*. Kluwer Academic Publishers. doi:10.1007/978-1-4615-0907-3

Kearney, C., & Liu, S. (2014). Textual sentiment in finance: A survey of methods and models. *International Review of Financial Analysis, 33*, 171–185. doi:10.1016/j.irfa.2014.02.006

Kubat, M., Holte, R. C., & Matwin, S. (1998). Machine learning for the detection of oil spills in satellite radar images. *Machine Learning, 30*(2-3), 195–215. doi:10.1023/A:1007452223027

Lorica, B. (2015). *Six reasons why I recommend scikit-learn*. Retrieved February 14, 2017, from https://www.oreilly.com/ideas/six-reasons-why-i-recommend-scikit-learn

Lukebuehler. (2013). *Source of historical stock data – Stack Overflow*. Retrieved September 16, 2017, from http://stackoverflow.com/a/17263126

Matloff, N. (2017). *Statistical Regression and Classification: From Linear Models to Machine Learning*. Boca Raton, FL: CRC Press.

Mostafa, M. M. (2013). More than words: Social networks' text mining for consumer brand sentiments. *Expert Systems with Applications, 40*(10), 4241–4251. doi:10.1016/j.eswa.2013.01.019

NIST/SEMATECH. (2016). *e-Handbook of Statistical Methods*. Retrieved December 14, 2016, from http://www.itl.nist.gov/div898/handbook/

Pang, B., Lee, L., & Vaithyanathan, S. (2002). Thumbs up?: sentiment classification using machine learning techniques. In *Proceedings of the ACL-02 conference on Empirical methods in natural language processing* (vol. 10, pp. 79-86). Academic Press. 10.3115/1118693.1118704

Patel, J., Shah, S., Thakkar, P., & Kotecha, K. (2015). Predicting stock and stock price index movement using trend deterministic data preparation and machine learning techniques. *Expert Systems with Applications, 42*(1), 259–268. doi:10.1016/j.eswa.2014.07.040

Rao, T., & Srivastava, S. (2014). *Twitter sentiment analysis: How to hedge your bets in the stock markets. In State of the Art Applications of Social Network Analysis* (pp. 227–247). Springer.

Richardson, L., & Ruby, S. (2007). *RESTful Web Services*. Sebastopol, CA: O'Reilly.

Robertson, S. (2004). Understanding inverse document frequency: On theoretical arguments for IDF. *The Journal of Documentation, 60*(5), 503–520. doi:10.1108/00220410410560582

Salton, G., & McGill, M. J. (1983). *Introduction to Modern Information Retrieval*. McGraw Hill.

Schumaker, R. P., & Chen, H. (2009). Textual analysis of stock market prediction using breaking financial news: The AZFin text system. *ACM Transactions on Information Systems, 27*.

Shevlyakov, G. L., & Oja, H. (2016). *Robust Correlation: Theory and Applications*. John Wiley & Sons. doi:10.1002/9781119264507

Singhal, A. K. (1997). *Term Weighting Revisite* (Doctoral dissertation). Faculty of the Graduate School of Cornell University.

Sokolova, M., Japkowicz, N., & Szpakowicz, S. (2006). Beyond accuracy, F-score and ROC: a family of discriminant measures for performance evaluation. In *Australasian Joint Conference on Artificial Intelligence* (pp. 1015-1021). Academic Press. 10.1007/11941439_114

STATISTA. (2016). *Leading global social networks 2016*. Retrieved March 11, 2016, from http://www.statista.com/statistics/272014/global-socialnetworks-ranked-by-number-of-users/

Tumasjan, A., Sprenger, T. O., Sandner, P. G., & Welpe, I. M. (2011). Election forecasts with Twitter: How 140 characters reflect the political landscape. *Social Science Computer Review*, *29*(4), 402–418. doi:10.1177/0894439310386557

Wang, L., An, H., Xia, X., Liu, X., Sun, X., & Huang, X. (2014). Generating moving average trading rules on the oil futures market with genetic algorithms. *Mathematical Problems in Engineering*.

Weisstein, F. L., Song, L., Andersen, P., & Zhu, Y. (2017). Examining impacts of negative reviews and purchase goals on consumer purchase decision. *Journal of Retailing and Consumer Services*, *39*, 201–207. doi:10.1016/j.jretconser.2017.08.015

Witten, I. H., Frank, E., & Hall, M. A. (2011). *Data Mining: Practical Machine Learning Tools and Techniques*. Amsterdam: Elsevier.

Wong, F. M. F., Liu, Z., & Chiang, M. (2014). Stock market prediction from WSJ: text mining via sparse matrix factorization. In *2014 IEEE International Conference on Data Mining* (pp. 430-439). IEEE.

Wuthrich, B., Cho, V., Leung, S., Permunetilleke, D., Sankaran, K., & Zhang, J. (1998). Daily stock market forecast from textual web data. In *1998 IEEE International Conference on Systems, Man, and Cybernetics* (vol. 3, pp. 2720-2725). IEEE. 10.1109/ICSMC.1998.725072

Ye, Q., Law, R., & Gu, B. (2009). The impact of online user reviews on hotel room sales. *International Journal of Hospitality Management*, *28*(1), 180–182. doi:10.1016/j.ijhm.2008.06.011

Žižka, J., & Dařena, F. (2015a). Automated Mining of Relevant N-grams in Relation to Predominant Topics of Text Documents. In *International Conference on Text, Speech, and Dialogue* (pp. 461-469). Springer.

Žižka, J., & Dařena, F. (2015b). Revealing potential changes of significant terms in streams of textual data written in natural languages using windowing and text mining. In *Artificial Intelligence and Natural Language and Information Extraction, Social Media and Web Search FRUCT Conference* (pp. 131-138). Academic Press. 10.1109/AINL-ISMW-FRUCT.2015.7382982

KEY TERMS AND DEFINITIONS

Classification Accuracy: The rate between the sum of the number of true positives + true negatives (the objects that were correctly assigned to a class) and the sum of true positives + false positives

+ true negatives + false negatives (all objects that were classified), when answering questions (that is, classifying).

Correlation: A dependence or association (causal or not) between two random variables measuring the degree to which two variables move in relation to each other.

Machine Learning: Machine learning is a branch of artificial intelligence (subfield of computer science) that focuses on studying and developing algorithms that can learn from data. Machine learning enables making decisions that are not based on explicitly programmed instructions and thus improving performance of machines based on past experience. It covers a wide variety of tasks that can be distinguished according to the information that is available to the machine during learning.

Natural Language Processing: A field of computer science and linguistics concerned with the interaction between computers and human (natural) languages.

Stock Market: The collection of markets and exchanges where the issuing and trading of stocks of publicly held companies, bonds, and other sorts of securities take place.

Supervised Learning: A learning method (algorithm), which uses a feedback between a trainer and trainee. The trainer knows the right answers (data labels) while the trainee learns the correct answers using the feedback for corrections to eliminate its mistakes.

Text Mining: Text mining (sometimes also text data mining) is a discipline that focuses on extraction of useful knowledge from text data. It relies on the methods similar to those from data mining but includes also specialized methods that need to be applied to texts before employment of the data mining algorithms. Typical text mining tasks include document classification, information retrieval, document clustering, or information extraction. Text mining uses methods and techniques from artificial intelligence, machine learning, natural language processing, linguistics, statistics, and many others.

This research was previously published in Techno-Social Systems for Modern Economical and Governmental Infrastructures; pages 125-159, copyright year 2019 by Business Science Reference (an imprint of IGI Global).

Chapter 54

User–Generated Content and Consumer Purchase Intentions in the Cosmetic Industry:
Social Impact Perspective

Jemi Patel
Regent's University London, UK

ABSTRACT

Online retailers within the luxury cosmetics industry have grown in popularity due to a wider and more diverse catalogue of products. Beauty e-commerce has also seen an uplift due to the increase in blogs/vlogs and online YouTube tutorials which motivate customers to click through to brands and retailer sites through links and affiliate marketing. Given the importance of computer-mediated marketing environments, particularly the burgeoning Internet tapestry along with its various social networking platforms, it is fundamental for management to foster and understand how these emerging technologies impact on their marketing strategies. Drawing on social impact theory (SIT), this paper contends that user-generated content can provide the basis for brand managers in the cosmetic industry to re-evaluate their digital marketing strategies. The paper concludes with discussions about the value of social impact theory in the development of digital marketing strategies.

INTRODUCTION

Over the course of the last decade, the digital era has led to the evolution of marketing, and social media marketing in particular. Social media encompasses a broad range of online venues that facilitate interactions and collaboration through the sharing of content amongst users (Kim and Johnson, 2016; Stokinger & Ozuem, 2015). Social media has redefined the way in which consumers communicate to peers and with brands. Social media strategies have been adopted to deal with negative UGC circulated through various social platforms. UGC can be viewed in many formats, including via videos, reviews, blog posts, Facebook posts or Tweets. The growth in communities on blogs and YouTube has sparked a

DOI: 10.4018/978-1-7998-9020-1.ch054

frenzy within brands across industries (Momeni et al, 2015). Research conducted within the travel and tourism industry has identified the popularity of customer review sites amongst travellers, and there are implications for the impact such content has on individual choice regarding destination, location, hotel and dining (Hennig-Thurau et al, 2004; Fillieri et al, 2014; Ye et al, 2009). A study conducted by PhocusWright (2014) claimed that 53% of travellers would not book a hotel room that had not been reviewed (Piccoli and Ott, 2014). The fashion industry has also carried out extensive research into the impact of UGC on product sales, and these studies have indicated that UGC in the form of blogs, Instagram posts and various other social sharing platforms have had an effect on the purchase intentions of consumers. However, the quality of the content must be of a high standard in order for action to be taken (Zhou and Duan, 2015). It has taken luxury brands years to understand how the digital era can cater to their audience, for example, Prada only launched their website in 2007, this shows how reluctant brands can be to change, however, decisions like this leave brands in a vulnerable position and at the mercy of fake luxury goods hawkers. Brands such as Hermes and Channel have also resisted in integrating into e-retail (Okonkwo, 2010).

However, research conducted in both the Luxury Fashion and Travel & Tourism industries has yet to specifically examine the impact of UGC on the luxury cosmetics industry within the UK. However, key concepts such as consumer behaviour can be drawn from this research as it overlaps with the impact of UGC in the luxury cosmetics industry.

Halliday (2016) addresses user-generated content in the context of brands by seeking to understand its creators and consumers. The study reveals a number of consumer motivations for the creation of UGC, with a focus on service-dominant logic and consumer culture theory as key theoretical frameworks. These are used to investigate the particular motives that drive consumers to generate content. Halliday's study focuses primarily on young adults aged between 16 and 24 years. These are identified as the largest user group and the most typical consumers and creators of UGC. The study goes on to further unravel the key issue within UGC interactions by identifying how consumers trust source credibility. The results of the study indicate that the popularisation of UGC amongst young adults has meant that some companies/brands have lost control, authority and influence over their target audiences. The study also reveals that there was a higher level of engagement with sites that commentate on increased passion for brands, products or services (Halliday, 2016), However the study fails to mention platforms used by young adults in creating and sharing UGC, whether through Social Network Sites (SNS), blogs, review sites or YouTube. In spite of this in-depth literature devoted to understanding creators and consumers, other studies have examined the phenomenon of UGC on social media platforms (Tang et al, 2014; Zajc, 2015; Kumar, 2016; Kim 2016).

Tang et al's (2014) study describe how positive, negative and indifferently neutral opinions affect product sales both directly and indirectly. Positive UGC on blogs and YouTube along with other SNS sites increase product sales as they infer information about the reputation of the product, its usage and levels of satisfaction amongst its consumers. Such UGC also provides insight into experiences if and the enjoyment of products and services. It offers further insight into personal recommendations (Liu, 2006; DiRusso, Mudambi & Schuff, 2010; Tang et al, 2014). By the same token, negative UGC harms product sales as it implies that products fail to satisfy, and are disingenuous, Negative UGC reinforces the disappointment of consumers. Such consumers will gravitate towards positive UGC which communicates perceived quality, as opposed to negative UGC which would deem the purchase to be a risk (Berger, Sorensen, and Rasmussen, 2010; Liu, 2006; Tang et al, 2014). Halliday's (2016) study also identifies various levels of engagement. The effects of negative UGC on the luxury cosmetic industry can lead to decreases in sales and negative perceptions of brands or products.

Drawing on Social Impact Theory, the current paper examines how UGC impacts on consumer purchase intention in the UK luxury cosmetic industry. Social impact theory (SIT) has been identified as increasingly important in the fields of interpersonal influence and group behaviour. This theory describes social impact in terms of social force fields that lead us to behave in particular ways. Social impact felt by individuals should be a function of strength, immediacy, and the number of source persons should all directly affect the social force felt by the intended target. In the context of this study, SIT can be used to determine the strength, immediacy and number of source persons for YouTubers and Bloggers. YouTubers and bloggers have built communities in their millions with the power to influence behaviours within groups. Behaviours are influenced through attitudes and feelings towards a brand or product, which can directly influence purchasing decisions or the motivation to search for alternatives. Such platforms also influence consumer attitudes towards brands and products.

Risselada et al (2014) discuss the trust associated with consumers who choose to engage with UGC. The study reflects on how consumer purchase decisions are influenced by the number of sources with a similar opinion or the scale of key influencers on social media. This can be linked with SIT as one of the key components of this theory is the number of source persons which can influence the behaviour of a group or individual.

Several studies have indicated, identified and explained the importance of Web 2.0 in the context of the use of user-generated content (Riegner, 2007; Postigo, 2016, Berthon et al, 2012). Some have suggested that Web 2.0 is also referred to as a social web. Such a construct can help brands and organisations build personas and personal profiles from a consumer's online activities (Berners-Lee, 2010; Rainie & Wellman, 2013; Stokinger & Ozuem, 2016). The Social Web exploits the natural human desire to share, as SNS sites facilitate the sharing of content in real time with an unlimited number of users through various sites. As such, SNS sites represent an evolution from traditional WOM to eWOM. Research indicates that UGC, whether professionally created, or produced by ordinary users has an impact on the purchase intention of consumers. However, such research fails to link this kind of thinking to the UK luxury beauty industry. Studies conducted by these authors fail to identify the impact that user-generated content created by YouTubers and bloggers have on the purchase intentions of users who consume such data (Levy & Gvili, 2015; Lin & Heng, 2015; Halliday, 2016; Hajli, 2015).

With more than three billion consumers and seven billion devices connected to the Internet (The International Telecommunication Union, 2014), eWOM represents one of the most significant developments in contemporary consumer behaviour (Rosario et al, 2016). The motives for consumer engagement in eWOM have been identified as product involvement, self-enhancement, advice seeking, concern for others and dissonance reduction, amongst others (Hennig-Thurau et al, 2004). These motives have been identified as engagement triggers within the travel and tourism industry, however, have not been applied to the context of the UK beauty industry (Ye et al, 2009). Recent studies have identified the key concepts of user-generated content and the forms in which it takes such as SNS sites, YouTube and review sites (Lin & Heng, 2015; Henning-Thurau et al, 2004; Shen et al, 2016). With luxury cosmetic brands implementing strategies by using bloggers as brand ambassadors, this strategic move ensures that all parties receive value. Such value is represented by the brand, the blogger and the blogger's audience. Bloggers' recommendations spread further than they might if they were broadcast via more typical SNS' (Matthews, 2015).

BACKGROUND

The UK Luxury Beauty Industry consists of cosmetics and toiletries retailers both on- and offline. The major products and services in this industry are skincare products, cosmetics, toiletries, hair care products and fragrances. As of 2016, cosmetics account for 15.6% of revenue generation, and the segment is predicted to continue to grow within the next 5 years. Primarily female based consumers aged between 18 and 64 years old make up the vast majority of the industry's customers. However, there has been an increase in the demand from men, rising over the past 5 years. These numbers are expected to rise gradually between 2016 and 2017. The UK beauty industry's major market share holder is A S Watson (Health & Beauty UK) LTD with 15.2% of total market share. A S Watson owns a number of companies including the Perfume Shop, Savers, health & Beauty and Superdrug. Other companies within this industry include Prada (6.35% Market share), Polo Ralph Lauren (8.89% market share), Chanel (4.7% market share), Space NK (2.4% market share), L'Occitane Ltd (1.7%) and Estee Lauder Cosmetics Ltd (1.5% market share) (IBIS World, 2016; Mintel, 2015). Within the cosmetics manufacturing industry, there are three major key players; L'Oréal (9.9% market share), Unilever PLC (7.3% market share) and P&G (5.9% market share). These conglomerates include luxury brand names such as Kiehl's and Ralph Lauren (Carter, 2016).

Online retailers within the luxury cosmetics industry have grown in popularity due to a wider and more diverse catalogue of products. Beauty e-commerce has also seen an uplift due to the increase in blogs/vlogs and online YouTube tutorials which motivate customers to click through to brands and retailer sites through links and affiliate marketing. The luxury industry as a whole has been known to be late adopters of e-retailing. The way luxury presents itself has been challenged due to the digital era, this is due to the evolution of ideas, concepts, attitudes, behaviours, expectations and interpretations (Okonkwo, 2010). UGC on social media has led to a core user group comprising of 20% of Millennials and 22% of women aged between 16 and 24- years. These consumers view beauty content online through blogs and video content. YouTube is the second largest search engine and has become a key contender in the sharing and creating of beauty related UGC, in 2015. Some 43% of 16-24-year-olds watch beauty related content via this social media platform. UGC in the form of beauty blogs and YouTube tutorials has a strong reputation amongst its core user group. Videos have been highlighted as one of the main interest points. Bloggers use video capabilities on Instagram to showcase short tutorials, product swatches and makeup looks (Mintel, 2016). Brands present beauty bloggers/vloggers and YouTubers with a large community following with press releases and these are featured in videos such as "What's New" or "Monthly Favourites". Press releases include new product launches by brands. Based on these, consumers then create UGC and offer opinions on products including details such as packaging and usability. These create awareness of new products (Wiseman, 2014).

The beauty, and in particular, the luxury cosmetic industry is using user-generated content creators to reposition themselves within the market. Brands are collaborating with popular UGC creators by developing product ranges to attract a wider selection of audiences (Mintel, 2016). Popular collaborations include Kathleen Lights with the American brand Ofra, since the launch of the product it has received over 1,300 video reviews on YouTube (McClure, 2015). Another collaboration was prompted by a popular blogger; Jaclyn Hill and Becca Cosmetics. The collaboration broke the record for Sephora's most purchased product on its first day of release (Fraser, 2015). UK bloggers, vloggers and YouTubers such as Zoella and Tanya Burr have received great fame and success. They have capitalised on this momentum by launching their own beauty range ventures in retailers such as Superdrug and Feel Unique, these brands also stock luxury cosmetics such as Chanel and Armani (Superdrug, 2016) (Mintel, 2015).

User-generated content was first documented as early as the 18th century (Labato et al, 2011). The digital era has led to a migration of thoughts and conversations to the Internet in the form of blogs, review sites, social media networks and videos (Blackshaw, 2011). UGC can refer to professionally produced content, which is supported by commercial media, or content created by a user supported primarily by their experiences (Labato et al, 2011; Piccoli and Ott, 2014). The evolution of UGC started with oral communication and tangible images which led to the digitalisation of UGC through blogs, Facebook, Twitter, YouTube and review sites such as Trip Advisor. This transition has fed into the natural human need to share (Williams, 2015). With the evolution of UGC, many terms have been associated with the concept, such as Web 2.0, eWOM and SNS sites. The development in how UGC is shared has significantly changed due to the growing use of Web 2.0, eWOM and SNS sites. Sharing is no longer limited to friends and family but encompasses all users with or without an interest in the topic. This shift in technology has led to a powerful realignment from companies to consumers. With the large following and scale of communities that are built by consumers, affiliate codes and brand affiliation have emerged as phenomena amongst bloggers and YouTubers (Cesar and Avila, 2014). The launch of smartphones has made it increasingly convenient to upload content via apps. In the UK, some 76% of all adults now own a smartphone (Deloitte, 2015). Adults in general within the UK spend an average of 2 hours 26 minutes each day on their mobile devices. This has been a gradual increase over the past 5 years (eMarketer, 2015). As of March 2016, a report identified that the third most popular activity on the Internet in the UK is to visit sites for information regarding potential product purchases (Statista, 2016).

The issue of UGC is very important for marketers as many forms of UGC include product reviews and brand recommendations. There are an increasing number of consumers who are starting to trust final product reviews by peers, as opposed to brand-produced content (Morrison et al, 2013). The effects of brand-related UGC and its potential impact on consumer behaviour can be recognised as a characteristic of Computer-Mediated Communication (CMC). This is because social interactions between CMC differ from those that take place in Face-To-Face (FTF) settings, and through mass media. This is due to the high level of anonymity which pays less attention to the physical appearance in CMC, as opposed to FTF communication. However, YouTube, which can be classed a CMC also crosses over into FTF communication, as users are able to physically see and hear the content and its creator. FTF communication is categorised as WOM whereas CMC communication is categorised as EWOM, as it is able to reach audiences globally (Morrison, Cheong & McMillian 2013).

THEORETICAL CONTEXT AND PERSPECTIVES

The concept of UGC has recently gained prominence in several industries, including in the Travel & Tourism industry (Tang et al, 2014), (Del Chiappa et al, 2015) and in Luxury Fashion Retailing (Okonkwo, 2010). It is noted for its popularity and prevalence. Within the travel industry, UGC is created in the form of customer reviews on sites such as Trip Advisor, whereas in the fashion industry, UGC is created in the form of visual imagery on social media networks such as Instagram. User-generated content has been referred to as information and/or views that are shared with others with the power to influence the purchase behaviour of its readers. UGC can also be referred to as User-Created Content (UCC), user-generated publishing and self-publishing (Tang et al, 2014). Daugherty et al (2008) describe UGC as media content primarily distributed on the Internet. However, this interpretation is too broad in the current context as it does not take into consideration the various platforms used in the creation and sharing of UGC along with the lack of differentiation in eWOM and brand generated content.

The American Interactive Advertising Bureau (IAB) (2008, pp. 45) defined UGC as *"any material created and uploaded to the Internet by non-media professionals"*. Although this definition acknowledges the Internet, it fails to encompass UGC created as part of paid employment on behalf of brands (Christodoulides et al, 2012). The Organisation for Economic Co-operation and Development (OECD) (2007) have also echoed the IABs definition by including the creation of content outside professional routines and practises as one of three key characteristics of UGC. The other two are content that is made publically available over the Internet, and content that reflects a certain amount of creative effort. The report also identifies emerging and converging media which can be identified as mobile applications, satellite navigation services and games consoles (Christodoulides et al, 2012). Kaplan and Haenlein (2010 pp. 61) have identified UGC as content that is *"created outside of professional routines and practises, it may be individually or collaboratively produced, modified, shared and consumed and can be seen as the sum of all ways in which people make use of social media"*. This interpretation of UGC has prevailed in acknowledging the role of social media, sharing between communities and the production of content. Drawing from the above, Kaplan and Haenlein's (2010) interpretation will be used as the definition for UGC in this study.

Several authors including Tang et al (2014), Croteau (2006) and Morrison et al (2013) have referred to UGC in the marketing industry as content which has been created by users to share information, and/or their opinions with others. UGC is material that has not been created by a brand. However, in attempts to reposition themselves, brands are working with social influencers to increase their brand ranking (Yoo, 2014). This is through blogger outreach programmes as well as attaining bloggers as brand ambassadors (Daukas, 2013).

The digital era has led Web 2.0 to be more commonly associated with UGC. By implication, several authors have referred to Web 2.0 as sites and services that rely upon the generation of content by users, as opposed to editors or dedicated content creators (Newman et al, 2016; O'Reilly, 2005; Anderson, 2007). Recent studies have further identified and characterised Web 2.0 into the Social Web (Halliday, 2016; Hajli, 2015). The evolution of the Social Web has allowed consumers and brands to connect and communicate like never before. This is due to the social introduction of brands, interest groups and other entities within the social realms, allowing users to be able to link with others, which helps build a persona or profile of consumers (Berners-Lee, 2010; Rainie & Wellman, 2012; Stokinger & Ozuem, 2016). However, there is no definitive definition of what the social web is and how user-generated content impacts the way Web 2.0 is used.

Traditional word of mouth communication has been referred to by some authors as oral communication made person to person. This form of communication is also known as offline interpersonal interaction (Levy & Gvili, 2015; Lin & Heng, 2015). It is perceived as one of the most important means of influencing consumer buying decisions, due to the credibility and reliability of the message based upon personal use or experience (Levy & Gvili, 2015; Lin & Heng, 2015; Craig, Greene & Versaci, 2015; Baker, Donthu & Kumar, 2016; Chen & Berger, 2016; Alhidari, Iyer & Paswan, 2015). However, the Internet has placed a greater importance on WOM as it evolves in eWOM, making opinions and experiences for products and services available to everyone. EWOM is an acronym for Electronic Word of Mouth. It has been made possible as a result of the evolution of the Internet and technology. This evolution has changed the dynamics of communication by offering customers new ways to connect and share UGC (Lin & Heng,

2015; Henning-Thurau et al, 2004; Shen et al,2016). EWOM has been defined by Alhidari et al (2015) as any positive or negative statement made by actual, potential or former customers in regards to a product, company or service. The statements are available to a multitude of people and institutions via the Internet (Henning-Thurau et al, 2004). Extant studies have noted some distinctions between traditional WOM and eWOM. Traditional word of mouth only extends to friends, family or colleagues, and can sometimes be based on biased opinions, whereas the advent of the Internet has extended the consumer's options for gathering unbiased information regarding products or services. It has also allowed them to voice and share their own consumption-related advice by engaging in eWOM. The process of WOM no longer takes time in terms of delivering salient information. Instead, social media and the Internet have allowed for content to be shared simultaneously (Henning-Thurau et al, 2004; Levy & Gvili, 2015; Lin & Heng, 2015; Craig, Greene & Versaci, 2015; Bowmen & Ozuem, 2016).

Mobile devices allow consumers, brands and marketing professionals to easily share information with others anywhere, anytime. Content is becoming easier to upload, therefore the quantity of eWOM available to digital audiences increases significantly (Hennig-Thurau et al, 2004; Levi & Gvili, 2004; Oh, Animesh & Pinsonneault, 2016). A study conducted by Piccoli and Ott (2014) highlighted significant differences between reviews posted via mobile platforms and those posted through a website. The key differences identified were as follows:

- Reviews posted via mobile devices are shorter.
- Reviews from mobile devices are posted earlier.
- Reviews posted from mobile devices are more negative.

These findings are collected from users within the travel industry, however, this study has identified a lack of research into motivations for posting online reviews (Piccoli and Ott, 2014). This study focuses on UGC within the travel industry and it is, therefore, unable to explore how these results will vary across sectors.

User-generated content can be created on various platforms, such as; offline print publications (non-professional use), social media, blogs, articles and websites. A selection of authors has suggested that UGC in the form of EWOM across social media platforms are usually brand related and have the potential to shape consumer brand perceptions. Traditional WOM is a one to many monologues, where eWOM is considered as a one to many dialogue (Smith, Fischer & Yongjian, 2012; Levy & Gvili, 2015; Alhidari, Iyer & Paswan, 2015; Kim, 2012; Momeni et al, 2015; Cheung, 2014). The term social media incorporates formats such as blogs, social networking sites (SNS) and content communities (Smith et al, 2012; Schivinski et al, 2016; Kumar et al, 2016; Baker, 2016; Schaedel and Clement, 2010; Poch & Martin, 2015). Each social platform is used differently to the other. For example, UGC on Facebook will not look the same content on YouTube (Alhidari, Iyer & Paswan, 2015).

A 2010 report published in Mintel outlines which social platforms have the most UGC exposure. The most popular of these include Wikipedia, Twitter, Facebook YouTube and blogs and websites (Mintel, 2010). However, various studies published in 2013 have shown a prominent difference in the key SNS sites, evidencing that Instagram, Google Plus and Pinterest amongst others have been added to the list of those that are most exposed through UGC (Alhidari, Iyer & Paswan, 2015). These studies, however, fail to identify the rise of beauty bloggers via their blogs or YouTube channels, which are changing the platforms which influence customer purchase intent in the UK luxury beauty industry (Wiseman, 2014; Kim, 2010; Pozharliev et al, 2015). Due to the migration of social media into the mainstream, marketers have been left with no choice but to pay attention (Smith, Fischer & Yongjian, 2012). Many authors have documented that the role of SNS is set to spread eWOM (Tang et al, 2014; Goldsmith & Horowitz, 2006; Gruen, Osmonbekov, & Czaplewski, 2006; Jalilvand & Samiei, 2012; Moran & Muzellec, 2014; Wolny & Mueller, 2013; Alhidari, Iyer & Paswan, 2015). Social media in the digital era is one of the most popular tools used for UGC through for example the sharing of images, Tweets, videos and posts by consumers. However, social media is being used by brands for digital advertising and promotions, customer service platforms, mine innovation ideas and engagement with customers (Smith, Fischer & Yongjian, 2012).

Brands are now using marketing campaigns to direct consumers to their social media pages, where they may be asked to like, share on comment on posts. The phenomenon of brands asking consumers to share content on their behalf is called Professional Created Content (PCC) (Smith, Fischer & Yongjian, 2012; Kim, 2012). The creation of content from an organic consumer is called user-generated content. Social media incorporates formats such as blogs, Social Networking Sites (SNS) and content communities (Smith et al, 2012). User-generated content across these media platforms are usually brand related and have the potential to shape consumer brand perceptions (Smith, Fischer & Yongjian, 2012; Levy & Gvili, 2015; Alhidari, Iyer & Paswan, 2015; Christodoulides, 2012). A study conducted by Cheong and Morrison (2008) extensively explores the consumer's reliance on product information and recommendations found in UGC. The study investigates the importance of all social networks with particular emphasis on websites, blogs and YouTube. The only limitation to this study is that it has been conducted on a population in the Unites States of America so it has no implications for consumer behaviour in the UK, the study also lacks information on communities with large populations which are regularly engaging with UGC.

UGC has always been part of society through traditional means. This has been made clear through behavioural studies showing that it is human nature to share; whether these are experiences, stories or ideas. This in itself is a motivator to participate in eWOM (Hennig-Thurau et al, 2004). As humans we are typically known to share experiences that are negative, however, the way we share has changed which is also changing the content that is being generated (Williams, 2015). Anderson (1998) along with other authors have suggested that WOM communication mainly arises when consumer's consumption-related expectations are unsatisfied (Hennig-Thurau et al, 2004). However, others have suggested that motives may differ when it comes to engaging in positive WOM (Sundaram, Mitra & Webster, 1998; Hennig-Thurau et al, 2004). The last 25 years have seen an evolution in sharing. In 1990, sharing was undertaken through the development of tangible pictures to show friends and families. This has evolved to the stage where users are now able to share digitally on social platforms to masses. This is not only the case for images, but also for videos, thoughts and feelings (Williams, 2015). As previously mentioned, each social media platform is used for different reasons. There are different factors that motivate consumers to create UGC. For networking sites such as Twitter and Facebook, motivations for consumers include communicating with friends, status updates and in particular updating friends and family with photos. For audio-video users such as YouTube and Skype, motivations include updating oneself on news around the world, following up on personal interests and to alleviate boredom (Halliday, 2016). These motivations, however, do not include usage to attain product specific information.

Given the conceptual closeness of WOM and eWOM, the motivating factors for participation in traditional WOM can also be attributed to eWOM (Hennig-Thurau et al, 2004).

The most prominent study of WOM communication is by Ditcher (1996). This study has identified four main motivational categories of positive WOM communication. Due to the lack of detailed information about the development of his typology, Engel, Blackwell and Miniard (1989) modified Ditcher's work by renaming the categories and introducing an additional motive (Hennig-Thurau et al, 2004; Shen et al, 2016; Oh, Animesh & Pinsonneault, 2016). These motives include product-involvement, self-involvement, self-enhancement, dissonance reduction and advice seeking. Many of these motives are repeated in other studies conducted by Ditcher (1996), Engel, Blackwell & Miniard (1989) and Sundaram, Mitra & Webster (1998). However, these studies have failed to incorporate motives for eWOM since the Internet was not part of mainstream society for word of mouth communication (Hennig-Thurau et al, 2004).

Balasubramanian and Mahajan (2001) have provided a useful framework for the consideration of integrating economic and social activity within the context of a virtual community (Hennig-Thurau et al 2004). Balasubramanian and Mahajan (2001) focus on three types of social interaction utility: focus-related utility, consumption utility and approval utility. A focus-related utility is the value the consumer receives when adding value through their contributions (Balasubramanian and Mahajan, 2001; Hennig-Thurau et al, 2004). In the context of web-based platforms, such contributions include providing reviews or comments on products of interests to others within the community. On blogs and YouTube this can be done by leaving comments, opinions and suggestions against the video or blog post (Burmann, 2010; Pace, 2008). Within the umbrella of focus-related utility lies four motives based on the literature on traditional WOM. These motives are: concern for other consumers, helping the company, social benefits and exerting power. These can be transferred across to motives for participating and engaging in eWOM (Hennig-Thurau et al, 2004; Schaedel and Clement, 2010). Engel et al's (1989) work can also be applied to eWOM communication on web-based platforms for UGC creation, where eWOM on these platforms may be initiated due to a desire to help others with their purchase decisions in order to save others from negative experiences. In many cases, both are implicated (Hennig-Thurau et al, 2004). This communication can be both positive and negative in relation to consumer experiences with products or services. Hennig-Thurau et al (2004) have identified that one characteristic of eWOM behaviour on web-based platforms is that consumers become part of a virtual community through their affiliations with content creators. This affiliation can represent a social benefit to consumers for identification and social integration (McWilliam, 2000; Oliver, 1999). A selection of authors has articulated that eWOM communication provides a mechanism to shift power from companies to consumers. This is more so the case when criticism is articulated by many simultaneously and this is a regular occurrence on web-based opinion platforms. (Hennig-Thurau et al, 2004; Berthon et al, 2008).

In the context of web-based opinion platforms, consumption utility refers to consumers obtaining value through the direct consumption of the contributions of other community components (Balasubramanian and Mahajan, 2001). In this context, consumption takes place when consumers read product reviews and comments left in the shape of UGC. It is also expected that consumers may leave comments regarding their product experiences and ask others to submit information to help with their problems (Hennig-Thurau et al, 2004). In an opinion based platform, approval utility refers to "when other constitutes consume and approve of the constitutes own contributions". Feedback can be either formal or informal (Hennig-Thurau et al, 2004). This type of utility is commonly used on review sites such as TripAdvisor. For example, users are able to rate how useful they find comments. The information gathered on review sites is then used to create a ranking system which identifies the top reviewers (Hennig-Thurau et al, 2004). However, this utility largely only focuses on review sites, but elements of it can be transferred to prominent social media sites such as favourites on Twitter, Likes on Facebook posts and top comments on YouTube (Stoeckl et al, 2010). Hennig-Thurau et al's (2004) study have identified two motives that are closely associated with approval utility. These are self-enhancement and economic rewards. The self-enhancement motivation is driven by a need for positive recognition (Engel et al, 1989). In the context of web-based platforms, this may be in the form of the number of views the creator's comments receive. These utilities can be applied to user-generated content on social media platforms in the form of eWOM. However, there is no literature that applies these to the context of this research. It is important to understand what motivates consumers to create UGC.

Ryan and Deci (2000, pp. 54) have defined motivation as 'being moved to do something'. Their framework has been recognised for its simplicity and for its useful measurement of motivation (Ryan & Deci, 2000; Poch & Martin, 2014; Vallerand, 2011). Their study has acknowledged the complexities involved in studying motivation, but it also recognises the importance of different kinds of motivation. They have classified motivation into intrinsic and extrinsic forms (Ryan & Deci, 2000; Poch & Martin, 2014; Vallerand, 2011; Shen et al, 2016).

An intrinsically motivated activity is performed for no apparent reward (Deci, 1971). Consumers who are motivated intrinsically engage with content for personal enjoyment as opposed to receiving something in return. Intrinsic motivation comes from inside an individual, whereas extrinsic motivation is from the outside (Deci, 1971; Poch & Martin, 2014). On the other hand, extrinsic motivation refers to behaviour that is driven by reward (Deci, 1971; Poch & Martin, 2014). The characteristics of intrinsic and extrinsic motivation are displayed in table 1 below. Many of these characteristics link to those written in literature by Hennig-Thurau et al (2004), Engel et al (1989) and Ditcher (1996).

Table 1. Characteristics of intrinsic and extrinsic motivation

Intrinsic	Extrinsic
Products dis/satisfaction	Self-enhancement
Altruism	Anxiety reduction
Product involvement	Advice seeking
Vengeance	Social benefits
Customer loyalty	Economic incentives

THE MODERATING ROLE OF SOCIAL IMPACT THEORY (SIT)

SIT has been defined by Latane (1981 p. 343) as

Any of the great variety of changes in physiological states and subjective feelings, motives and emotions, cognitions and beliefs, values and behaviour, that occur in an individual, human or animal, as a result of the real, implied or imagined presence or actions of other individuals.

SIT explains how social influence causes changes in consumer behaviour, attitudes and the belief of individuals as a result of interactions with others (Latane, 1981; Perez-Vega et al, 2016). Social influence is defined by Venkatesh et al (2003, p.451) as "the degree to which an individuals perceives that important others believe he or she should use the new system". The new system in this definition could be referring to luxury cosmetic products, apps, games or devices. Cialdini and Goldstein (2014) identified three broad categories of social influence:

- **Social Norms:** Habitual custom or "the way we do things."
- **Compliance:** The actions to consent to a certain request, and all the motivations surrounding this behaviour.
- **Conformity:** The act of changing one's behaviour to match the response of others.

This shows the SIT addressing the influence of conformity (Perez-Vega et al, 2016; Chaouali et al 2016).

Conformity is referred to as moving from one opinion to a contradictory view (Nook et al, 2016). Confirming behaviour involves forming an opinion that may be a result of persistent pressure by externals. However, this opinion develops into an opposite perspective that can also mean remaining in the same position due to peer pressure. This is commonly known as conformity by omission (Nook et al, 2016; Perez-Vega et al, 2016; Sridhar and Srinivasan, 2012). SIT proposes that conformity is gained if external pressure has the following three keys; source strength, source immediacy and source numbers. These keys have a direct impact on SIT. The theory suggests that like attracts like, therefore the introduction of specific interest groups on SNS sites allows content to be created and shared amongst users with similar interests, making communities with like-minded people. There is an element of trust involved that makes consumers gravitate towards those who share similar preferences as themselves (Risselada et al, 2014). This theory has been applied to the modern day social culture. However, literature hasn't applied this theory to the impact UGC has on consumers purchase intentions for the UK beauty industry. Social Impact Theory is an expansion on Social Identity Theory, which suggests that people instinctively react positivity to in-groups and negatively towards outgroups. This theory starts with social force, which is the pressure put on consumers that lead to a change in behaviour. If this succeeds, it is called social impact. Social force is generated by influencers through persuasion, threats, humour and embarrassment. Social force is made up of the following elements (Latane, 1981):

- **Strength:** This is how much power a consumer believes the influencer has.
- **Immediacy:** This is how recent the influence is and how close the influencer is to you.
- **Numbers:** The number of people putting pressure on a consumer to do something.

SIT pays a great deal of attention to the characteristics of the person giving the orders, however, it fails to pay the same regard to the person receiving them. SIT also treats people as passive, and it proposes that any person is capable of doing anything with the right amount of social force. SIT assumes that as the number of people increases the impact on the intended audience attitudes and behaviour will also modify. This is due to users of SNS often sharing information regarding products, brands, experiences and events, as the number of users who share UGC increases so will the impact on the target users who are looking for information on specific topics. This assumption justifies the application of SIT to UGC and its importance and effect on consumer attitudes and purchase intention (Mir & Zaheer, 2012).

Due to the recent growth in the impact of UGC, there is very little literature that really delves into the influence of brand-related UGC on consumer purchase intentions. However, Bechtel & Ts'erts'man (2002) have explained the influence of UGC on consumer attitudes and behaviour through the Stimulus (S) – Organism (O) – Response (R) model (S-O-R) (Kim & Johnson, 2016). When this model is applied to consumer behaviour research, S-O-R can be utilised as a structure that demonstrates the effect of external influences on consumers (S), the internal processes responding to that influence (O) and the resulting behaviour (R) (Kim & Johnson 2016). External responses in this framework are information inputs, either controlled by professionals or through social pressures and economic conditions (Bagozzi, 1983). The internal processes reacting to the influences include the emotional responses that are triggered. These could include fear, happiness and cognitive responses such as perceived risk (Bagozzi, 1983). The final intention of response is the activity leading to the outcome or choice (Bagozzi, 1983). Since the introduction of this model in 1983, it has been used for various research purposes within marketing. However, this model has not been applied to the effect of user-generated content on the purchase intention of the UK beauty industry (Chang et al, 2011; Kim & Johnson, 2016). The SOR model could be applied to purchase intentions within the UK beauty industry. Since UGC is the stimulus created on social media platforms, consumers who encounter this content are expected to process this information and determine its quality. In the case of social media platforms, this may be determined due to the influential status of the content creator (Kim & Johnson, 2016). This then leads to emotional or cognitive responses, followed by a final response; whether that is further sharing of the stimulus, buying the product or future purchase intention.

The information adoption model explains the information on computer-mediated communication platforms. It has been applied to many eWOM studies (Cheung et al, 2008; Cheung et al, 2009; Erkan & Evans, 2016). Argument Quality and Source Credibility affect the usefulness of the information with ultimately has an impact on the adoption of the information. This model is appropriate for research which focuses on eWOM on social media. Cheung et al (2008) have applied this model to online discussion forums. This makes it relevant due to the research focus of eWOM on social media (Cheung et al, 2008; Shu & Scott, 2014; Erkan & Evans,2016). Although this model has been commonly used, it has also been criticised as it only focuses on the characteristics of information which are quality, credibility and usefulness. This model excludes consumer behaviour towards information. It can be argued that the influence of eWOM on social media not only depends on the characteristics of the information but also on the consumers' behaviour towards the information (eWOM). This argument has not been tested, but it is supported by Knoll (2015). The developed model, therefore, extends the Integrated Assessment Model (IAM) through considering the behaviours of consumers towards the information (Knoll, 2015; Erkan & Evans, 2016).

Industry reports have stated that, on average, there are 2.4 billion daily conversations that take place involving brands and this has led marketing managers to continuously invest heavily in ways to understand UGC and WOM patterns. Baker, Donthu and Kumar (2016) have investigated how WOM conversations about brands influence purchase and retransmission intentions. This study specifically looks at which types of WOM conversations are more or less likely to affect consumer purchase intentions. Baker et al (2016, pp. 226) define purchase intentions as "the WOM recipient's degree of motivation and willingness to eventually purchase the brand discussed in the WOM episode". Typically, consumer purchase intentions are influenced by calculations which refer to practical cost considerations such as price, along with other tangible resources required for purchase. Purchase intentions can also be formed based on the practical gain of making purchases, and how the purchase may help to achieve social goals such as self-preservation or conformance to social norms (Baker et al, 2016).

The results of this study indicate a significant relationship between WOM and consumer purchase intentions, however, it fails to explore this within a specific industry to show how the relationships may vary based on industry and the type of platform used.

Research conducted by Yang & Chen (2015) indicates the importance of scents in consumer purchases; specifically, in the cosmetics, personal health care, house cleaning and food industries. The research suggests that first impressions are obtained by visual observations, however, blogs and YouTube videos allow content creators to describe scents which allow the consumer to form a preconceived notion of what to expect. Kotler (1973) stated that odours affect customer purchase intentions, and this has been supported by other authors such as Wang et al (2012). These studies describe various industries and it, therefore, failed to provide detailed information into the customer's purchase intentions within the luxury cosmetic industry. As mentioned before UGC is affecting many industries and the luxury cosmetic industry is no expectation. The luxury industries reputation of being behind in regards to the adoption of the digital area is a vital player in why it is crucial for luxury cosmetic brands to take note of how UGC is being used by their consumers, what is being said about them and how this information can be used to reposition these brands amongst its target audience.

CONCLUSION

This study examines the impact of UGC on consumer purchase intentions in the UK beauty industry. In order to understand UGC it is crucial that the concept is broken down by organisations to ensure departments and managers fully understand why, how and who is creating the content, and through which platforms they are being shared. Within the luxury cosmetics industry, UGC has been most popularly created on blogs and on YouTube by product and service users. Content creators have taken traditional WOM and transformed it into EWOM. These creators have built communities in their millions and have become brands in their own rights, with book deals, sponsorships and endorsements. The power has shifted from companies to consumers in a way never seen before (Ozuem & Tan, 2016; Okonkwo, 2010). Therefore, brands and companies within the luxury cosmetic industry need to identify the top used SNS and the key content creators. This will act as a foundation for an outreach programme and the identification of creators will allow brands to understand what their customers are looking for, and how better to improve their products and ranges. Once the outreach programme has been developed this will lead to an increase in sales and brand awareness. The identification of creators and SNSs will provide direction for the marketing manager as to how much resources need to be allocated to these components. In order for this outreach programme to be successful, marketing teams will need to conduct research into the psychographics of online UGC users. This information will allow brands to see which content creators cater to their preferred target audience, whether these are luxury or high street brands/products. To ensure an increase in brand awareness and sales, organisations must understand the significant role digital media and UGC plays in the achievement of these goals. Organisations should seek to integrate social and digital strategy within their corporate strategy. A continuous budget will also need to be allocated, to ensure that members of the identified outreach programme are being given appropriate PR packages which include new product releases. Many organisations lack confidence within the digital revolution due to a lack of education or experience in this field. However, trial and error will allow marketing departments to adopt strategies that work for them. Inconsistencies in budget allocation or failure to understand digital marketing at a senior level are detrimental to the brands' image and digital existence

Social network sites have become an integral component of the creation and sharing of UGC. Within the UK, beauty industry platforms such as Snapchat, Twitter, Instagram, Facebook, YouTube and Blogs are being used to engage communities and share content. YouTube and Blogs have become primary search engines for consumers who are looking for product reviews, new product releases and general opinions on products and services. Other SNSs have become secondary drivers, which inform users of video/blog releases, quick mini-tutorials or simply an insight into the creator's daily life. Marketing departments need to be aware of changing trends within the YouTube world. For example, creators are regularly taking part in challenges such as "full face with only one product" or "full face using highlighters only". By identifying these trends, early brands will be able to send YouTubers products that could possibly be featured in these videos. Without understanding the link between SNS and UGC, brands are unable to engage with content creators. In order to form a relationship with these hugely influence creators marketing managers need to dedicate a team(s) that are able to keep updated with new videos and blog, this helps brands understand the persona of the creator. Halliday (2016) addresses the motives for taking part in UGC from the creators perceptive with a strong focus on who creates material and for what reason it is consumed. Through the rise of YouTube videos, less well-known brands have been given a platform to raise brand awareness through product features in "how to videos" as well as "monthly favourites". More well-known brands such as YSL, Tarte and Hourglass actively send new product releases to YouTubers in PR packages which are featured in video such as "unboxing haul" or "new product updates". Such collaboration between brands and content creators allows the company to reach a mass audience through a trusted source. Beauty brands can also invest in advertising on popular blogs and YouTube channels and this will allow for exposure in the marketplace.

Brands who are participating on social networking sites should be aware of the rate of growth, and must be vigilant and participate in social networks that their target audience partakes in. This will keep brands current with social trends, increase creativity and ensure marketing efforts are effective and resources are being used efficiently. For example, Snapchat started off as a consumer-based app, however, due to its popularity, luxury cosmetic brands harnessed the platform to engage with consumers. This is one example of the transition from WOM to EWOM which Hajli (2015) has explored through research conducted on Web 2.0. The aim of any beauty brand is to increase brand awareness and sales. Blogs and social networking sites have become a portal of information that can have positive or negative impact on brands through EWOM. Brands must ensure there are sufficient resources allocated to follow what consumers are saying about their products or services and deal with this accordingly, as negative EWOM spreads faster than positive. Lin & Heng (2015) discuss the evolution of WOM and how the Internet has facilitated this transition, and how that impacts on consumer decisions and perceptions of a product or brand.

Traditional online and offline advertising in the luxury cosmetic industry has been successful in increasing brand/ product awareness. Before digital media, the luxury cosmetic industry relied on WOM and offline advertising methods such as TV adverts, Billboards and magazine features to showcase products. However, the evolution of social media, blogging and YouTube has allowed for consumers to find information regarding products through a few clicks. The communities that have been created by influencers through UGC created on blogs, YouTube and social media have become hugely influential within the luxury cosmetic industry. UGC, therefore, impacts the luxury cosmetic industry by having a direct impact on sales, trends, product ranges and coverage and the pigmentation of products. Luxury cosmetic brands are using YouTube influencers such as Jaclyn Hill to test new products and suggest improvements which could be made in order to ensure their products are approved by regular users. This shows the shift from brand created UGC to the influence consumers are having on the luxury cosmetic industry. Another example is ensuring that brands cater to various skin tones from the fairest to the deepest. Different skin types including dry to oily and finally different skin types such as sensitive and acne prone are all catered towards.

ACKNOWLEDGMENT

Special acknowledgment is given to Professor Wilson Ozuem for his consultation in the research process for this chapter.

REFERENCES

Alhidari, A., Iyer, P., & Paswan, A. (2015). Personal level antecedents of eWOM and purchase intention, on social networking sites. *Journal of Customer Behaviour, 14*(2), 107–125. doi:10.1362/147539 215X14373846805707

Amaro, S., & Duarte, P. (2015). An integrative model of consumers intentions to purchase travel online. *Tourism Management, 46*, 64–79. doi:10.1016/j.tourman.2014.06.006

Anderson, P. (2007). What is Web 2.0? Ideas, technologies and implications for education. *JISC Technology and Standards Watch, 1*, 1–64.

Bagozzi, R. P. (1983). A holistic methodology for modelling consumer response to innovation. *Operations Research, 31*(1), 128–176. doi:10.1287/opre.31.1.128 PMID:10258411

Baker, A. M., Donthu, N., & Kumar, V. (2016). Investigating how word-of-mouth conversations about brands influence purchase and Retransmission intentions. *JMR, Journal of Marketing Research, 53*(2), 225–239. doi:10.1509/jmr.14.0099

Balasubramanian, S., & Mahajan, V. (2001). The Economic Leverage of the Virtual Community. *International Journal of Electronic Commerce, 5*, 103–138.

Bechtel, R., & Ts'erts'man, A. (2002). *Handbook of environmental psychology.* New York: J. Wiley & Sons.

Benady, D. (2014). How technology is changing marketing. *The Guardian.* Retrieved June 1, 2016, from http://www.theguardian.com/media-network/media-network-blog/2014/sep/29/technology-changing-marketing-digital-media

Berger, J., Sorensen, A., & Rasmussen, S. (2010). Positive Effects of Negative Publicity: When Negative Reviews Increase Sales. *Marketing Science, 29*(5), 815–827. doi:10.1287/mksc.1090.0557

Berners-Lee, T. (2010). Long Live the web. *Scientific American, 303*(6), 80–85. doi:10.1038cientifica merican1210-80 PMID:21141362

Berthon, P., Pitt, L., & Campbell, C. (2008). Ad Lib: When customers create the ad. *California Management Review, 50*(4), 6–30. doi:10.2307/41166454

Berthon, P. L., Pitt, K., Plangger, K., & Shapiro, D. (2012). Marketing meets Web 2.0, social media, and creative consumers: Implications for international marketing strategy. *Business Horizons, 55*(3), 261–271. doi:10.1016/j.bushor.2012.01.007

Blackshaw, P. (2011). User-Generated Content in Context. *Journal of Advertising Research,* 51, 108–111.

Bousquet, K. (2015). Everything We Know about Jaclyn Hill's Upcoming Beauty Collaborations. *Stylecaster.com.* Retrieved June 21, 2016, from http://stylecaster.com/beauty/jaclyn-hill-collaborations/

Bowen, G., & Ozuem, W. (2016). *Competitive Social Media Marketing Strategies.* Hershey, PA, United States: Business Science Reference.

Burmann, C. (2010). A call for user-generated Branding. *Journal of Brand Management, 18*(1), 1–4. doi:10.1057/bm.2010.30

Carter, B. (2016). The UK's richest source of business and industry information. *IBIS website.* Retrieved August 24, 2016, from http://clients1.ibisworld.co.uk/reports/gl/industry/default.aspx?entid=730

Cesar, P., & Avila, M. (2014). *User-Generated Advertising: The effects of consumer-created brand videos and self-construal on brand attitudes.* Birmingham Business School.

Chang, H.-J., Eckman, M., & Yan, R.-N. (2011). Application of The Stimulus-Organism-Response Model to The Retail Environment: The Role of Hedonic Motivation in Impulse Buying Behavior. *International Review of Retail, Distribution and Consumer Research, 21*(3), 233–249. doi:10.1080/0959 3969.2011.578798

Chaouali, W., Yahia, I., & Souiden, N. (2016). The interplay of counter-conformity motivation, social influence, and trust in customers intention to adopt Internet banking services: The case of an emerging country. *Journal of Retailing and Consumer Services,* 28, 209–218. doi:10.1016/j.jretconser.2015.10.007

Chen, Z., & Berger, J. (2016). How Content Acquisition Method Affects Word of Mouth. *The Journal of Consumer Research, 43*(1), 86–102. doi:10.1093/jcr/ucw001

Cheung, C. M. K., Lee, M. K. O., & Rabjohn, N. (2008). The Impact of Electronic Word-Of-Mouth. *Internet Research, 18*(3), 229–247. doi:10.1108/10662240810883290

Cheung, M., Luo, C., Sia, C., & Chen, H. (2009). Credibility of Electronic Word-Of-Mouth: Informational and Normative Determinants of On-Line Consumer Recommendations. *International Journal of Electronic Commerce, 13*(4), 9–38. doi:10.2753/JEC1086-4415130402

Cheung, R. (2014). The influence of eWOM on information adoption in online customer communities. *Global Economic Review, 42*(1), 42–57. doi:10.1080/1226508X.2014.884048

Christodoulides, G., Jevons, C., & Bonhomme, J. (2012). Memo to Marketers: Quantitative Evidence for Change. *Journal of Advertising Research, 52*(1), 53–64. doi:10.2501/JAR-52-1-053-064

Cialdini, R. B., & Noah, J. (2004). Social Influence: Compliance and Conformity. *Annual Review of Psychology, 55*(1), 591–621. doi:10.1146/annurev.psych.55.090902.142015 PMID:14744228

Collins, A. (2016). Latest Becca x Jaclyn Hill Collaboration Did $3.5 Million in Sales with Online Launch. *WWD website*. Retrieved June 21, 2016, from http://wwd.com/beauty-industry-news/color-cosmetics/latest-becca-x-jaclyn-hill-collaboration-did-3-5-million-in-sales-with-online-launch-10438768/

Craig, C., Greene, W. H., & Versaci, A. (2015). E-Word of Mouth: Early Predictor of Audience Engagement. *Journal of Advertising Research, 55*(1), 62–72. doi:10.2501/JAR-55-1-062-072

Croteau, D. (2006). The growth of self-produced media content and the challenge to media studies. *Critical Studies in Media Communication, 23*(4), 340–344. doi:10.1080/07393180600933170

Daugherty, T., Eastin, M., & Bright, L. (2008). Exploring consumers motivations for creating user-generated content. *Journal of Interactive Advertising, 8*(2), 1–24. doi:10.1080/15252019.2008.10722139

Daukas, K. (2013). Blogger outreach programs – what you need to know. *Atlantic Web Works*. Retrieved June 18, 2016, from http://atlanticwebworks.com/blog/blogger-outreach-programs-basics-to-know/

Deci, E. (1971). Effects of Externally Mediated Rewards On Intrinsic Motivation. *Journal of Personality and Social Psychology, 18*(1), 105–115. doi:10.1037/h0030644

Deci, E., Vallerand, R., Pelletier, L., & Ryan, R. (1991). Motivation and Education: The Self-Determination Perspective. *HEDP, 26*(3), 325–346. doi:10.120715326985ep2603&4_6

Del Chiappa, G., Lorenzo-Romero, C., & Alarcon-del-Amo, M. (2015). The Influence of User-Generated Content on Tourists' Choices. *Trziste/Market, 27*(2), 221-236.

Del Giudice, M., Della Peruta, M., & Carayannis, E. (2013). *Social media and emerging economies*. Cham: Springer.

Deloitte. (2015). Mobile Consumer. Retrieved June 16, 2016, from http://www.deloitte.co.uk/mobileuk/assets/pdf/Deloitte-Mobile-Consumer-2015.pdf

Dichter, E. (1966). How word-of-mouth advertising works. *Harvard Business Review*, 44(6), 147–166.

DiRusso, D., Mudambi, S., & Schuff, D. (2011). Determinants of prices in an online marketplace. *Journal of Product and Brand Management, 20*(5), 420–428. doi:10.1108/10610421111157946

eMarketer. (2015). UK Adults Spend More Time on Mobile Devices than on PCs. Retrieved June 22, 2016 from http://www.emarketer.com/Article/UK-Adults-Spend-More-Time-on-Mobile-Devices-than-on-PCs/1012356

Engel, J. F., Blackwell, R. D., & Miniard, P. W. (1989). *Engel consumer behavior* (6th ed.). Chicago: Thomson Learning.

Erkan, I., & Evans, C. (2016). The influence of eWOM in social media on consumers purchase intentions: An extended approach to information adoption. *Computers in Human Behavior, 61*, 47–55. doi:10.1016/j.chb.2016.03.003

Filleri, R., Alguezaui, S., & McLeay, F. (2014). Why do travelers trust TripAdvisor? Antecedents of trust towards consumer-generated media and its influence on recommendation adoption and word of mouth. *Tourism Management, 51*, 174–185. doi:10.1016/j.tourman.2015.05.007

Fraser, M. (2015). Jaclyn Hill announces makeup line to debut in 2016, so dry your eyes if you haven't snagged "Champagne Pop". *Bustle*. Retrieved August 23, 2016, from http://www.bustle.com/articles/101208-jaclyn-hill-announces-makeup-line-to-debut-in-2016-so-dry-your-eyes-if-you-havent

Goldsmith, R. E., & Horowitz, D. (2006). Measuring motivations for online opinion seeking. *Journal of Interactive Advertising*, 6(2), 2–14. doi:10.1080/15252019.2006.10722114

Gruen, T. W., Osmonbekov, T., & Czaplewski, A. J. (2006). eWOM: The impact of customer to-customer online know-how exchange on customer value and loyalty. *Journal of Business Research*, 59(4), 449–456. doi:10.1016/j.jbusres.2005.10.004

Hajli, N. (2015). Social commerce constructs and consumers intention to buy. *International Journal of Information Management*, 35(2), 183–191. doi:10.1016/j.ijinfomgt.2014.12.005

Halliday, S. (2016). User-generated content about brands: Understanding its creators and consumers. *Journal of Business Research*, 69(1), 137–144. doi:10.1016/j.jbusres.2015.07.027

Hennig-Thurau, T., Gwinner, K., Walsh, G., & Gremler, D. (2004). Electronic word-of-mouth via consumer-opinion platforms: what motivates consumers to articulate themselves on the internet? *Journal of Interactive Marketing*, 18(1), 38–52. doi:10.1002/dir.10073

Interactive Advertising Bureau. (2008). User-Generated Content, Social Media and Advertising—An Overview.

International Telecommunication Union. (2014). Facts. Retrieved May 15, 2016, from www.itu.int/en/ITU-D/Statistics/Documents/facts

Jackson, J. (1987). Social Impact Theory: A Social Forces Model of Influence. In *Theories of Group Behavior* (pp. 111-124). Springer. Retrieved June 22, 2016, from http://link.springer.com/chapter/10.1007%2F978-1-4612-4634-3_6#page-1

Jalilvand, M. R., & Samiei, N. (2012). The effect of electronic word of mouth on brand image and purchase intention: An empirical study in the automobile industry in Iran. *Marketing Intelligence & Planning*, 30(4), 460–476. doi:10.1108/02634501211231946

Jayaram, D., Manrai, A., & Manrai, L. (2015). Effective Use of Marketing Technology in Eastern Europe: Web Analytics, Social Media, Customer Analytics, Digital Campaigns and Mobile Applications. *Journal of Economics. Finance and Administrative Science*, 20(39), 118–132. doi:10.1016/j.jefas.2015.07.001

Jin, S., & Phua, J. (2016). Making reservations online: The impact of consumer-written and system-aggregated UGC in travel booking websites on consumers behaviour intentions. *Journal of Travel & Tourism Marketing*, 33(1), 101–117. doi:10.1080/10548408.2015.1038419

Kaplan, A., & Haenlein, M. (2010). Users of the World, unite! The challenges and opportunities of social media. *Business Horizons*, 53(1), 59–68. doi:10.1016/j.bushor.2009.09.003

Kim, A. J., Kim, K., & Johnson, P. (2016). Power of consumers using social media: examining the influences of brand-related user-generated content on Facebook. *Computers in Human Behavior*, 58, 98–108. doi:10.1016/j.chb.2015.12.047

Kim, J. (2012). The Institutionalization of YouTube: From User-Generated Content to Professionally Generated Content. *Media Culture & Society, 34*(1), 53–67. doi:10.1177/0163443711427199

Knoll, J. (2015). Advertising in social media: a review of empirical evidence. *International Journal of Advertising*.

Kotler, P. (1973). The major tasks of marketing management. *Journal of Marketing, 37*(4), 42–49. doi:10.2307/1250357

Kumar, A., Bezawada, R., Rishika, R., Janakiraman, R., & Kannan, P. (2016). From social to sale: the effects of firm-generated content in social media on customer behavior. *Journal of Marketing, 80*(1), 7–25. doi:10.1509/jm.14.0249

Latane, B. (1981). The psychology of social impact. *The American Psychologist, 36*, 343–356. doi:10.1037/0003-066X.36.4.343

Levy, S., & Gvili, Y. (2015). How credible is e-word of mouth across digital-marketing channels? *Journal of Advertising Research, 55*(1), 95–109. doi:10.2501/JAR-55-1-095-109

Lin, Z., & Heng, C. (2015). The paradoxes of word of mouth in electronic commerce. *Journal of Management Information Systems, 32*(4), 246–284. doi:10.1080/07421222.2015.1138572

Liu, Y. (2006). Word of mouth for movies: its dynamics and impact on box office revenue. *Journal of Marketing, 70*(3), 74–89. doi:10.1509/jmkg.70.3.74

Lobato, R., Thomas, T., & Hunter, D. (2011). Histories of user-generated content: between formal and informal media economies. *International Journal of Communication, 5*, 899–914.

London Beauty Blogger. (2016). British Beauty Blogger & Makeup Revolution Team Up: 'Fortune Favours The Brave' Palette. Retrieved June 21, 2016, from http://www.londonbeautyqueen.com/2016/03/british-beauty-blogger-makeup.html

Matthews, K. (2015). A killer strategy using bloggers as brand ambassadors: a detailed look with Bulu box. *Group High Website*. Retrieved June 18, 2016, from http://www.grouphigh.com/blog/killer-strategy-using-bloggers-brand-ambassadors-detailed-look-bulu-box/

McClure, E. (2015). 11 YouTube stars with makeup collections we can't get enough of. *Bustle*. Retrieved August 23, 2016, from http://www.bustle.com/articles/129682-11-youtube-stars-with-makeup-collections-we-cant-get-enough-of

Mintel. (2015). Retrieved August 23, 2016, from http://academic.mintel.com/display/746614/

Mintel. (2015). Retrieved June 21, 2016, from http://academic.mintel.com/display/716179/

Mintel. (2015). Retrieved June 21, 2016, from http://academic.mintel.com/display/741005/

Mintel. (2016). Retrieved June 21, 2016, from http://academic.mintel.com/display/759427/

Mir, I., & Zaheer, A. (2012). Verification of social impact theory claims in social media content. *Journal of Internet Banking and Commerce., 17*(1), 1–15.

Momeni, E., Cardie, C., & Diakopoulos, N. (2015). A survey on assessment and ranking methodologies for user-generated content on the web. *ACM Computing Surveys*, *48*(3), 1–49. doi:10.1145/2811282

Moran, G., & Muzellec, L. (2014). eWOM credibility on social networking sites: A framework. *Journal of Marketing Communications*.

Morrison, M., Hyuk Jun Cheong, A., & McMillan, S. (2013). Posting, Lurking, And Networking: Behaviors and Characteristics of Consumers in The Context of User-Generated Content. *Journal of Interactive Advertising*, *13*(2), 97–108. doi:10.1080/15252019.2013.826552

Newman, R., Chang, V., Walters, J., Wills, R., & Wills, B. (2016). Web 2.0 – The Past and the Future. *International Journal of Information Management*, *36*(4), 591–598. doi:10.1016/j.ijinfomgt.2016.03.010

Nook, E., Ong, D., Morelli, S., Mitchell, J., & Zaki, J. (2016). Prosocial Conformity: Prosocial Norms Generalize Across Behavior and Empathy. *Personality and Social Psychology Bulletin*, *42*(8), 1045–1062. doi:10.1177/0146167216649932 PMID:27229679

O'Brien, C. (2011). The emergence of the social media empowered consumer. *Irish Marketing Review*, *21*(1), 32–40.

O'Reilly, T. (2005). What Is Web 2.0. O'Reilly. Retrieved May 27, 2016, from http://www.oreilly.com/pub/a/web2/archive/what-is-web-20.html

OECD. (2007). Retrieved June 24, 2016, from http://www.oecd.org/sti/ieconomy/participativewebandusercreatedcontentweb20wikisandsocialnetworking.htm

Oh, H., Animesh, A., & Pinsonneault, A. (2016). Free Versus For-A-Fee: The Impact of a Paywall on the pattern and effectiveness of WOM via social media. *Management Information Systems Quarterly*, *40*(1), 31–56. doi:10.25300/MISQ/2016/40.1.02

Okonkwo, U. (2010). *Luxury online: Styles, strategies, systems*. Basingstoke: Palgrave Macmillan. doi:10.1057/9780230248335

Oliver, M. (2010). Retrieved May 31, 2016, from http://academic.mintel.com/display/539418/

Organisation for Economic Co-operation and Development. (2007). *Participative Web and User Created Content: Web 2.0, Wikis and Social Networking*. OECD Information Technologies.

Ozuem, W., & Tan, K. (2016). Reconciling Social Media with Luxury Fashion Brands: An Exploratory Study. In L. Aiello (Ed.), Handbook of Research on Management of Cultural Products: E-Relationship Marketing and Accessibility Perspectives (Vol. 1, pp. 257-285). Hershey, PA: IGI Global.

Pace, S. (2008). YouTube: An opportunity for consumer narrative analysis? *Qualitative Market Research: An International Journal*, *11*(2), 213–226. doi:10.1108/13522750810864459

Perez-Vega, R., O'Gorman, K., & Waite, K. (2016). Social Impact Theory: An examination of how immediacy operates as an influence upon social media interaction. *The Marketing Review*, *16*(4), 1–45.

PhocusWright. (2014). Travel Research. Retrieved May 27, 2016, from http://www.phocuswright.com/Travel-Research

Piccoli, G., & Ott, M. (2014). Impact of mobility and timing on user-generated content. *MisQuarterly Executive, 13*(3), 147–157.

Poch, R., & Martin, B. (2015). Effects of Intrinsic and Extrinsic Motivation On User-Generated Content. *Journal of Strategic Marketing, 23*(4), 305–317. doi:10.1080/0965254X.2014.926966

Postigo, H. (2016). The socio-technical architecture of digital labor: Converting play into YouTube money. *New Media & Society, 18*(2), 332-349.

Pozharleiv, R., & Verbeke, W. (2015). Merely Being with You Increases My Attention to Luxury Products: Using EEG to Understand Consumers Emotional Experience with Luxury Branded Products. *JMR, Journal of Marketing Research, 52*(4), 546–558. doi:10.1509/jmr.13.0560

Rainie, H., & Wellman, B. (2013). Networked. *International Journal of Communication, 7*, 954–959.

Riegner, C. (2007). Word of Mouth on the web: The impact of Web 2.0 on consumer purchase decisions. *Journal of Advertising Research, 47*(4), 436–447. doi:10.2501/S0021849907070456

Risselada, H., Verhoef, P., & Bijmolt, T. (2014). Dynamic effects of social influence and direct marketing on the adoption of high-technology products. *Journal of Marketing, 78*(2), 52–68. doi:10.1509/jm.11.0592

Rosario, A., Sotgiu, F., De Valck, K., & Bijmolt, T. (2016). The effect of electronic word of mouth on sales: A meta-analytic review of platform, products, and metric factors. *JMR, Journal of Marketing Research, 53*(3), 297–318. doi:10.1509/jmr.14.0380

Ryan, R., & Deci, E. (2000). Intrinsic and Extrinsic Motivations: Classic Definitions and New Directions. *Contemporary Educational Psychology, 25*(1), 54–67. doi:10.1006/ceps.1999.1020 PMID:10620381

Schaedel, U., & Clement, M. (2010). Managing the online crowd: motivations for engagement in user-generated content. *Journal of Media Business Studies, 7*(3), 17–36. doi:10.1080/16522354.2010.11073509

Schivinski, B., Christodoulides, G., & Dabrowski, D. (2016). Measuring consumers engagement with brand-related social-media content: development and validation of a scale that identifies levels of social-media engagement with brands. *Journal of Advertising Research, 56*(1), 64–80. doi:10.2501/JAR-2016-004

Shen, W., Huang, J., & Li, D. (2016). The research of motivation for word-of-mouth: based on the self-determination theory. *Journal of Business and Retail Management Research, 10*(2), 75–84.

Shu, M., & Scott, N. (2014). Influence of social media on Chinese students choice of an overseas study destination: an information adoption model perspective. *Journal of Travel & Tourism Marketing, 31*(2), 286–302. doi:10.1080/10548408.2014.873318

Smith, A., Fischer, E., & Yongjian, C. (2012). How does brand-related user-generated content differ across YouTube, Facebook, And Twitter? *Journal of Interactive Marketing, 26*(2), 102–113. doi:10.1016/j.intmar.2012.01.002

Sridhar, S., & Srinivasan, R. (2012). Social influence on effects in online product ratings. *Journal of Marketing, 76*(5), 70–88. doi:10.1509/jm.10.0377

Statista. (2016). Retrieved June 22, 206, from Statista website, http://www.statista.com/statistics/289048/online-activities-ranked-by-usage-penetration-great-britain-uk/

Stockinger, E., & Ozuem, W. (2016). Social Media and Customer Retention: Implications for the Luxury Beauty Industry. In G. Brown & W. Ozuem (Eds.), Computer-Mediated Marketing Strategies: Social Media and Online Brand Communities (1st ed., pp. 200–222). Hershey, PA: IGI Global. doi:10.4018/978-1-4666-9776-8.ch012

Stoeckl, R., Rohrmeier, P., & Hess, T. (2007). *Motivations to produce user generated content: differences between webloggers and videobloggers.* BLED.

Sundaram, D. S., Mitra, K., & Webster, C. (1998). Word-of-Mouth Communications: A Motivational Analysis. *Advances in Consumer Research. Association for Consumer Research (U. S.), 25*, 527–531.

Superdrug. (2016). Retrieved June 21, 2016, from Superdrug website, http://www.superdrug.com/microsite/meet-the-bloggers

Sussman, S., & Schneier Siegal, W. (2003). Informational influence in organizations: an integrated approach to knowledge adoption. *Information Systems Research, 14*(1), 47–65. doi:10.1287/isre.14.1.47.14767

Tang, T., Fang, E., & Feng, W. (2014). Is neutral really neutral? The effects of neutral user-generated content on product sales. *Journal of Marketing, 78*(4), 41–58. doi:10.1509/jm.13.0301

Vallerand, R. J., & Lalande, D. (2011). The MPIC model: the perspective of the hierarchical model of intrinsic and extrinsic motivation. *Psychological Inquiry, 22*(1), 45–51. doi:10.1080/1047840X.2011.545366

Venkatesh, V., Morris, M., Gordon, G., & Davis, F. (2003). User acceptance of information technology: Toward a unified view. *Management Information Systems Quarterly, 27*(3), 425–478.

Waite, K., & O'Gorman, K. (2016). Social impact theory: an examination of how immediacy operates as an influence upon social media interaction. *The Marketing Review.*

Wang, X., & Li, Y. (2014). Trust, psychological need, and motivation to produce user-generated content: a self-determination perspective. *Journal of Electronic Commerce Research, 15*(3), 241–253.

Wang, X., Yu, C., & Wei, Y. (2012). Social Media Peer Communication and Impacts on Purchase Intentions: A Consumer Socialization Framework. *Journal of Interactive Marketing, 26*(4), 198–208. doi:10.1016/j.intmar.2011.11.004

Williams, P. (2015). The Evolution of User Generated Content. *LinkedIn.* Retrieved May 27, 2016, from https://www.linkedin.com/pulse/evolution-user-generated-content-paige-williams

Wiseman, E. (2014). Lights, camera, lipstick: beauty vloggers are changing the face of the make-up industry. *The Guardian.* Retrieved May 31, 2016, from website, http://www.theguardian.com/fashion/2014/jul/20/beauty-bloggers-changing-makeup-industry

Wolny, J., & Mueller, C. (2013). Analysis of fashion consumers motives to engage in electronic word-of-mouth communication through social media platforms. *Journal of Marketing Management, 29*(5-6), 562–583. doi:10.1080/0267257X.2013.778324

IBIS World. (2016). The UK's richest source of business and industry information. Retrieved June 21, 2016, from http://clients1.ibisworld.co.uk/reports/uk/industry/industryoutlook.aspx?entid=3080#IO

Yang, L., & Chen, K. (2015). Cosmetic scents by visual and olfactory senses versus purchase intention. *International Journal of Market Research, 57*(1), 125–143. doi:10.2501/IJMR-2014-039

Ye, Q., Law, R., & Gu, B. (2009). The impact of online user reviews on hotel room sales. *International Journal of Hospitality Management, 28*(1), 180–182. doi:10.1016/j.ijhm.2008.06.011

Ye, Q., Law, R., Gu, B., & Chen, W. (2011). The influence of UGC on traveller behaviour an empirical investigation on the effects of eWOM to hotel online bookings. *Computers in Human Behavior, 27*(2), 634–639. doi:10.1016/j.chb.2010.04.014

Yoo, C. (2014). Branding Potentials of Keyword Search Ads: The Effects of Ad Rankings on Brand Recognition and Evaluations. *Journal of Advertising, 43*(1), 85–99. doi:10.1080/00913367.2013.845541

Zajc, M. (2015). The social media dispositive and monetization of user-generated content. *The Information Society, 31*(1), 61–67. doi:10.1080/01972243.2015.977636

Zhou, W., & Duan, W. (2015). An empirical study of how third-party websites influence the feedback mechanism between online WOM and retail sales. *Decision Support Systems, 76*, 14–23. doi:10.1016/j.dss.2015.03.010

KEY TERMS AND DEFINITIONS

Beauty Industry: Provides haircare, skin care, male grooming and make-up products, divided into subcategories to cater to specific needs.

Blogging: A website containing a collection of personal thoughts, observations, opinions, attitudes and experiences.

Cosmetics: A product that once applied alters the natural state of the customer, either used for the purpose of cleaning, enhancing, protecting, maintaining or perfuming the face and body.

Electronic Word of Mouth (EWOM): A positive or negative statement made by an individual(s) regarding a product, service or organisation, which is made available to a multitude of individuals and institutions through the Internet.

Purchase Intention: A dependent variable that depends on several external factors which can alter the willingness of a customer's decision to buy a product or service.

Social Media: A collection of various social platforms and channels which enables users to connect and engage with other users and content online.

User-Generated Content (UGC): Unbiased content which has been created by an individual(s), through personal experiences, who have not been paid on sponsored to create on behalf of brands.

This research was previously published in Digital Marketing Strategies for Fashion and Luxury Brands; pages 225-247, copyright year 2018 by Business Science Reference (an imprint of IGI Global).

Chapter 55
The Utilization of Social Media by Small and Medium Food Vendors in Brunei Darussalam

Meryeme Bouargan
University of Brunei Darussalam, Gadong, Brunei

Rabi'atul Adawiyah Haji Abd Halim
University of Brunei Darussalam, Gadong, Brunei

Nuruljannah Haji Husaini
University of Brunei Darussalam, Gadong, Brunei

Nor Azeem Jusniah
University of Brunei Darussalam, Gadong, Brunei

Nur Hazwani Masturah Haji Ahmad
University of Brunei Darussalam, Gadong, Brunei

Mohammad Nabil Almunawar
 https://orcid.org/0000-0001-5296-2576
University of Brunei Darussalam, Gadong, Brunei

ABSTRACT

This research examines the factors that contribute to the utilization of social media by the small and medium-sized enterprises (SMEs) operating in the food industry in Brunei Darussalam. It also investigates how social media provides opportunities to SMEs. This research was done using a quantitative method through primary research that was focused on small and medium-sized food vendors in Brunei Darussalam. Survey questions were distributed to food SMEs and vendors, who use social media to assist them in conducting their business, to serve as a guideline to understand how social media networks can lead to positive business outcomes and how understanding key factors may lead to optimizing product portfolios and to discover new opportunities for their business to expand. Based on the authors' research, cost effectiveness was found to influence social media usage among the small and medium food vendors in Brunei. Factors such as trust, interactivity and compatibility, however were not found to be the factors influencing the utilization of social media.

DOI: 10.4018/978-1-7998-9020-1.ch055

1. INTRODUCTION

Social media has been globally accepted as effective media for communication and collaboration as it provides many advantages which are not offered by other media such as cost-effective, many-to-many interactivity and rich in information content in various forms (multimedia) (Baruah, 2012). As such, it has become an important part of people's lives to connect and keep updated with their relatives and friends. It also opened up new opportunities for individuals to express their creativity in the virtual community. Not only social media has proven to play an essential part in individuals' lives, it also becomes significantly important for small and medium-sized enterprises (SMEs) in running their businesses (Dahnil et al., 2014). Given the limited resources and capacities of SMEs, social media is believed to help improve business performances by bringing in new opportunities.

In Brunei Darussalam, social media utilization for businesses seems to be no longer optional. Bruneians can access the Internet on a daily basis. According to the new Digital in 2017 Global Overview report, with the majority of the total population (86 percent) using the social media, Brunei Darussalam became the third highest in terms of social media penetration globally (Othman, 2017). Particularly in the food industry, there is an evidently growing interest in the adoption of social media. Businesses use social media as an alternative channel to promote and sell their products, to do research for their product development to optimize their product portfolios and to discover new opportunities for their business to expand. In such manner, it is important for SMEs food industry to have knowledge on the success factors on the utilization social media as this may enhance their ability to make decisions accurately. Learning from mistakes is important. Therefore, various factors that may stop some enterprises from utilizing social media in their business despite their potential benefits need to be properly studied.

The aims of this research are to identify and analyze social media adoption among SMEs in the food industry of Brunei Darussalam and to understand what influences the businesses to use social media in their businesses. The research was carried out with a quantitative method to analyze the responses, supported by other researchers' findings. The study focuses mainly on finding out the reasons why SMEs lean more toward social media to attract their customers and how customers respond to the marketing strategies implemented by these businesses especially now that we are in an era where customers prefer honesty and transparency especially when it comes to food as it is directly related to health and hygiene. Finally, this paper will explore the opportunities provided by social media that could be used by these small and medium enterprises for their growth. It also aims to discover the targeted customers and how the use of social networks such as Facebook and Instagram have become the solution to get new customers.

This paper is organized as follows. Literature review is presented in the next section followed by a discussion on the framework and hypotheses development. Next, we describe research methodology employed followed by data analysis and results of hypotheses testing. We then discuss the result and the final section is conclusions made from the study.

2. LITERATURE REVIEW

2.1. SMEs in Brunei

In the context of Brunei, SMEs is defined as enterprises having employees ranging from 1 to 100 (Polsaram et al, 2011). Small and medium enterprises (SMEs) play vital part in Brunei Darussalam economic development as a part to diversify the Brunei's economy and create employment. According to International Business Publications (2015), the SMEs in Brunei have contributed to the employment in the private sector for about 92% and 66% of the GDP in the non-oil sector. The government has been supporting the growth of SMEs to diversify Brunei's economy. SMEs are encouraged to be creative and exploring the business opportunities locally and outside country as expressed in various Sultan's speech, His Majesty wants his government to give support in the development of SMEs which will allow them to contribute to Brunei's economy (Thambipllai, 2008).

The government has made several actions on the development of SME such as the establishment of Resource Centre which now called as Resource and Standard Centre. It emphasizes on the development of SMEs and provide services to them such as counseling, workshops and others programme that are made specific for SME which are provided by Ministry of Industry and Primary Resources (International Business Publications, 2015). The government established a statutory body called Darussalam Enterprises (DARe) in 2016 to monitor and nurture the growth of local enterprises development. The majority of the board members (81%) are private sector representation which to ensure that private sector driven the direction and development of SME through DARe. Business Support Centre established by DARe in the same year which the centre will provide a single portal or venue for businesses such as give advice and information about business and application of SME programmes, grants and loans (Borneo Bulletin, 2016a).

Banks such as Bank Islam Brunei Darussalam also assists the development of SMEs. They introduced SME 360° which will assist SMEs and the bank also established one-stop agency which called SME 360° branch to serve their clients so they could do their businesses and also provide SME-related financial products (Mohammad, 2016). Local SMEs are increasing due to the cube stores where the stores provide small spaces for low rent. The cube stores encourage Bruneian vendors to start their own business with the cube shops as it removes the difficulty of renting the whole shop and it do not need a business license (Borneo Bulletin, 2016b). The cubes available for rent allow the vendors to sell their products such as food, clothes and beauty products. The cube stores can help unemployed people to gain income, as instrument to make their business grow further and make them less reliant on the government.

2.2. Social Media Adoption for Marketing Purposes

SMEs are a driving force for the economic growth of many countries such as Malaysia and Indonesia, as it has widely helped fight unemployment and enhanced development in these countries. (Ozigbo & Ezeaku, 2009). Unfortunately, some may not know how to utilize technology for marketing purposes (Vásquez and Escamilla, 2014). By concentrating on the right platform to campaign effectively, businesses can attract potential customers, influence them to purchase and increase their sales. Social media such as Facebook, Twitter, Snapchat, Instagram and YouTube can be used to expose their businesses for marketing purposes, publicity, and customer relations and market research purposes. Enterprises should keep their efforts manageable and their accounts regularly updated even if maintaining social media takes time (Niven, 2014).

Social media has the potential to be powerful media to engage with consumers and generate brand advocate (Hutter et al., 2009). However, to overcome potential consumers' reluctance, trust needs to be established and reinforced so online word of mouth marketing (e-WOM marketing) can be promoted. With the recent advances in technology, social media and marketing now work closely in the business environment. Using social media increases the search ability of the brand and creates two-way communication with customers, in other words, allows the company to do social network marketing (Öztamur and Karakadilar, 2014).

In Malaysia, the use of Facebook has become increasingly popular to sell products, advertising and marketing at a relatively low cost. Previous studies have found that it is good for businesses to embrace social media such as Facebook due its minimal cost and only requires low IT skills level (Derham et al, 2011). Hassan, S., Nadzim, & Shiratuddin, (2015) claimed in their studies that the use of social media not only saves money for the company but also impact the company positively by boosting their economic growth.

Another study by Kirtis and Karahan (2011) reveals that social media can strengthen the relationship with customers. Having an online presence makes it possible to reach a much larger audience in a shorter period than the traditional means of communication and all at a cost that is practically null. For many business leaders, social media are seen as a way to strengthen the reputation, visibility and reputation of their organisation (Kaplan & Haenlein, 2010).

A study developed by Ainin et al. (2015) found that Facebook usage positively impact on SMEs performance outcomes and they also identified factors such as interactivity, compatibility and cost effectiveness influence the SMEs to adopt Facebook for the business activities.

2.3. Influence of Culture on the Role of Social Media in the Consumer Decision-Making Process

Marketers can reach potential and current customers through social media, as social media provides the possibility of e-WOM. Goodrich and de Mooij (2013) found that Hofstede's cultural dimensions (Hofstede, 1983) could influence purchase decisions through the use of social media. Hofstede's cultural dimensions of individualism/collectivism (IDV/COL) and power distance (PDI) best explain differences in how consumers obtain information and the role of information in the decision-making process. Collectivists tend to acquire information passively through personal contacts and base their buying decisions on opinions of others, feelings, and company trust; whereas people of individualistic culture actively search for information through word of mouth or traditional media. According to the results of the study by Goodrich and de Mooij (2013), marketers in collectivistic culture should make use of social media more as their marketing strategy due to social media playing an important role in forming opinions They also found long/short-term orientation plays a role in differences regarding communication behavior between the businesses and the consumers in explaining variations in trust in online sources of information.

3. FRAMEWORK AND HYPOTHESES DEVELOPMENT

From the above literature review, it can be agreed that social media usage helps small businesses to grow through marketing (Neti, 2011). To better understand the factors influencing social media adoption, the research has been inspired by a framework developed by Ainin et al (2015). Ainin's study claimed that previous studies have focused on the impact of the adoption of social media in relation with trust, compatibility, cost effectiveness and interactivity as well as financial and non-financial performance. For that matter, they suggested investigating the extent to which these six factors are correlated with the use of social media by SMEs in the Malaysian market. In the same fashion, we have adapted Ainin's model and used it to explore how factors such as trust, compatibility, cost effectiveness and interactivity influence social media usage in this study in the context of Brunei (Figure 1).

Figure 1. The research model

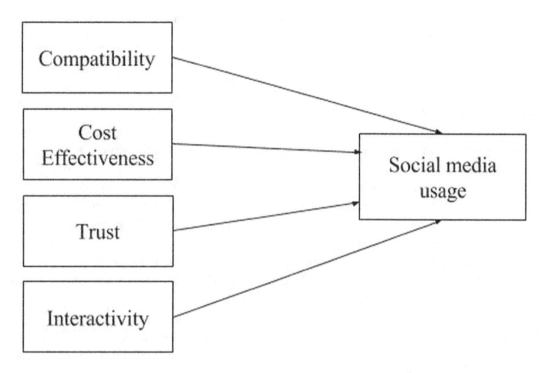

The four factors explored in this research are:

1. *Compatibility* refers to the degree to which innovation fits with the potential adopter's existing values, previous practices and current needs (Roger, 1983). Previous studies have investigated how compatibility may or may not influence firms to adopt technology in their businesses and have found mixed results regarding the factor compatibility influencing firms decision for technology adoption. The adoption of technology is usually affected by factors such as relative benefit, complexity, compatibility, testability, and observation (Rogers, 1995). Roger's study showed that a combination of these factors influences the adoption of technologies positively. Another study by Davis (1989) has showed that two psychological factors were found through their technology acceptance model (TAM). These factors would determine the adoption of technology ease of use has a greater impact on the adoption of technology: self-efficacy and instrumentality; which leads basically leads to determine the degree of compatibility of working with the said technology (Davis et al., 1989);

2. *Cost effectiveness* refers to the importance of cost in the adoption and utilization of the technology (Ernst and Young, 2001). Researchers have found that cost effectiveness has a significant influence towards businesses, especially SMEs, regarding technology adoption. In the same fashions, it was found out by Guariglia et al. (2011) that small sized businesses usually struggle with the

adoption of new technologies as it would be considered as an extra cost that they may not be able to handle. However, lately, many small companies have managed to improve their business using the Internet. Thanks to the cost effectiveness of Internet technologies. Through the Internet, especially social media, they can promote new products, locate new potential investors, manage their marketing and communications strategies, identify new customers and identify new market niche (Kaplan et al. 1997, Coccia 1997, Hawking, 1997). This only shows how the financial factor can be crucial to SMEs when it comes to adopting new technologies. As social media is relatively cheap to use, organizations are more likely to use social media for marketing and communication purposes (Michaelidou et al., 2011);

3. *Trust* refers to structural assurance and informational trust in using social media for work-related purposes. According to McKnight et al. (1998), structural assurances refer to the belief that favorable outcomes are likely because of contextual structures, such as contracts, regulations and guarantees. Whereas informational trust is defined as 'a user's belief about the reliability, credibility and accuracy of information obtained from Facebook (Chai et al., 2011). As businesses post information about their organizations, products and services they offer on social media, there is a possibility that there is a need for trust in adopting social media for work-related purposes. Being present on social media should represent a real guarantee of trust to customers. Trust helps increase the business reputation and attract more potential customers (Bauer, Grether & Leach, 2002). SMEs adoption of social media help them create a bond of trust with consumers. Trust can be achieved by being at the level of customer expectations for instance (Shih, 2009). All of this is the best way to build brand authority or expertise, build trust, and present the business in the best light (Michaelidou et al., 2011);

4. *Interactivity* refers to the interaction between human and technology regarding the design and implementation of the information systems (Lee and Kozar, 2012). Social media such as Facebook is considered as an interactive media as it enables two-way communication (Mayfield, 2008). Due to interactivity allowed by social media, it might have an influence towards businesses to use social media. In addition to having an Internet presence through a website, social media offers a level of interactivity. It's the fastest and most direct way of communicating with target businesses' goal is to differentiate themselves from the competition (Michaelidou, 2011), attract both suppliers and consumers and build solid relationships with them and finally transform the interactivity into a sale (Shih, 2009). (corrected). In fact, Businesses should interact with their target audience in order to help getting their brand noticed, they must be attracted to quality content. Social media can help collect more information about customers. The idea is to build brand awareness, and to acquire new customers. To do this, more than advertising in the strict sense, the preferred method is to deploy a content strategy. This method is the one that will allow you to position a business in the eyes of their targets, their customers and potential customers most of the time. (Breslauer & Smith 2009; eMarketer, 2010).

From the factors explained above, following hypotheses were developed to investigate how the above factors influence social media utilization amongst SMEs in Brunei's food sector (see Table 1).

Table 1. Null and alternative hypotheses for all the variables

Item	Hypotheses
H_1 $H_{0,1}$	Compatibility positively influences social media usage Compatibility negatively influences social media usage
H_2 $H_{0,2}$	Cost effectiveness of social media positively influences social media usage Cost effectiveness of social media negatively influences social media usage
H_3 $H_{0,3}$	Trust on social media positively influences social media usage Trust on social media negatively influences social media usage
H_4 $H_{0,4}$	Interactivity of social media positively influences social media usage Interactivity of social media negatively influences social media usage

4. RESEARCH METHODOLOGY

4.1. Sampling

Respondents aimed in this research were mainly the SMEs and local entrepreneurs who use social media such as Instagram, Facebook, WhatsApp, Twitter and Snapchat as their tools to conduct their business. This is because; it is believed that the targeted respondents have a better understanding and would be able to provide reliable data on food industry in Brunei. In this sense, we have handed out 60 questionnaires to be filled by the local entrepreneurs who use social media for their work-related transactions and deals. Questionnaires were distributed on and other were distributed through Google forms. It should be noted that the study aimed for a convenience sampling method which means that all possible subjects of the population have a chance of being included. It is relatively a cost-effective method of data collection.

4.2. Data Collection

The questionnaire was created using Google Form platform, which was then circulated through paper survey and social media platform from 7th of April to 16th of April in 2017. From these platforms, respondents could easily access the questionnaire and submit responses directly. These responses were then downloaded from Google Form into Excel and were then analyzed by using SPSS Statistics 20.

4.3. Instruments

Primary data collection instrument used for this research is in the form of a questionnaire, which was divided into two (2) sections. The first section looked into the details of respondents where questions such as gender, age, mode of running the business, types of social media used, frequency social media usage and also the reason for their choice of social media usage were asked. In the following section, it is where questions related to the constructs such as trust, interactivity, compatibility and cost effectiveness influencing social media adoption among SMEs in food industry in Brunei Darussalam were asked. As shown in Table 2, the statements were measured using five-point Likert scale items, ranging from 1 = "strongly disagree" to 5 = "strongly agree", and followed by comments section where respondents can give their comments regarding their social media adoption in their business.

Subsequently, secondary data was retrieved from the previous studies in the same area of interest, online journals, research papers and websites; in order to gather and strengthen all of the information needed also as our guidance in the research project.

Table 2. Operationalization construct

Construct	Construct Definition	Operational Definition
Social Media Usage	Social Media Usage refers to how social media help company to conduct their businesses.	Please indicate how likely you agree or disagree: 1. My business uses social media to advertise and promote product and services. 2. My business uses social media to create brand visibility. 3. My business uses social media to conduct marketing research. 4. My business uses social media to get referrals (word of mouth via likes, shares, and followers). 5. My business uses social media to communicate with customer. 6. My business uses social media to develop customer relations. 7. My business uses social media to conduct customer service activity (interactions with customer before, during and after purchase). 8. My business uses social media to feedback of product/services offered. 9. My business uses social media to reach new customers. 10. My business uses social media to search for competitor information.
Trust	Trust refers to structural assurance and informational trust in using social media for work-related purposes.	1. Social media provides my business with adequate measures to protect information posted by my company. 2. Social media provides my business with a safe environment to transact information. 3. Social media provides my business with adequate technological measures to deliver information. 4. Social media allows my business to be trusted. 5. Social media allows my business to give good quality service.
Interactivity	Interactivity refers to the interaction between human and technology regarding the design and implementation of the information systems	1. Social media provides my business with features for interactive communication with customers. 2. Social media provides my business with appropriate number of interactive features (e.g. graphics, music, etc.). 3. Social media provides my business with features for clear responses.
Compatibility	Compatibility refers to the degree to which innovation fits with the potential adopter's existing values, previous practice and current needs.	1. Social media usage is compatible with the company's IT infrastructure (devices, software, network, etc.). 2. Social media usage is consistent with the beliefs and values of your business. 3. Social media usage is consistent with your business strategy.
Cost Effectiveness	Cost effectiveness refers to the importance of cost in the adoption and utilization of Social Media	1. Social media is more cost effective than other types of marketing or customer service technologies. 2. My business can avoid unnecessary cost and time by using social media. 3. Social media saves seller's effort in marketing, branding and customer service.

5. DATA ANALYSIS AND RESULTS

This section presents the analysis of data and the test results for the hypotheses of the study. For this study, Descriptive Statistics and Multiple Regression Analysis were applied for statistical analysis.

5.1. Background of Respondents

The sample of this study would be those food vendors who use social media to do their business. About 20 paper-based questionnaires were distributed, but only 15 questionnaires returned. From the survey, we conduct online via Google Forms, we managed to get 45 respondents. Thus, for the data analysis, 60 respondents were selected as the sample size of this study, which gives a response rate of 92.3 percent. The following sections of data analysis will analyze the background of the respondents.

5.1.1. Gender

Based from the survey result, majority of the respondents of the sample population were female. 76.7 percent (or 46) respondents were female food vendors, while only 23.3 percent or 14 respondents are male. The data will be illustrated in Figure 2.

Figure 2. Respondents' gender

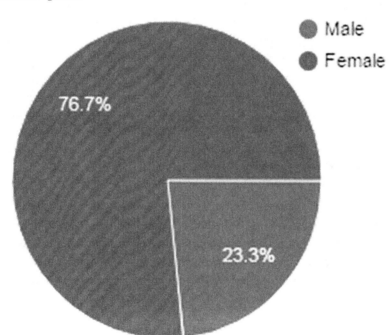

5.1.2. Age

From our survey results, a majority of the respondents are food vendors from age group 15-34 years old. Only a small number of 3.3% (or 2) respondents are from the age group 55 years old and above. A small percentage of 18.3% (or 11) respondents are from age group 18-24 years old, 23.3% (or 14) respondents are from age group 35-44 years old and 15% or (9 respondents) are from age group 45-54 years old). Summarised data is shown in Table 3.

Table 3. Respondents' age

	Frequency	Percentage (%)
18 years old and below	0	0
18 - 24 years old	11	18.3
25 - 34 years old	24	40.0
35 - 44 years old	14	23.3
45 – 54 years old	9	15.0
55 years old and above	2	3.3

5.1.3. Mode of Running Business

Based on the data analysis, 22 (36.7 percent) respondents run this business at a full-time basis and 38 (63.3 percent) respondents run this business at a part-time basis. This is as shown on Table 4.

Table 4. Respondents' mode of running business

	Frequency	Percentage (%)
Full-time	22	36.7
Part-time	38	63.3

5.1.4. Social Media Platform Used

Based on the data analysis, most respondents use more than one social media platform to assist their business. Most respondents use Instagram to assist their business with a percentage of 83.3 percent. 3.3 percent of the respondents use websites; 58.3 percent of the respondents use Facebook; 73.3 percent of the respondents use Whatsapp; 5 percent of the respondents use Twitter and only 1.7 percent of the respondents use Snapchat to assist their business. Table 5 below shows the social media platform that the food vendors are using.

Table 5. Respondents' choice of social media platform

	Frequency	Percentage (%)
Instagram	50	83.3
Website	2	3.3
Facebook	35	58.3
WhatsApp	44	73.3
Twitter	3	5
Snapchat	1	1.7

5.1.5. Frequency of Updating Social Media

Based on the data analysis, 25 (41.7 percent) of the respondents update their social media several times a day; 19 (31.7 percent) of the respondents update their social media about once a day; 14 (23.3 percent) of the respondents update their social media about 2-3 times a week and 2 (3.3 percent) of the respondents update their social media only once a week. Figure 3 below shows how often the respondents update or post on social media.

Figure 3. Respondents' frequency of updating social media

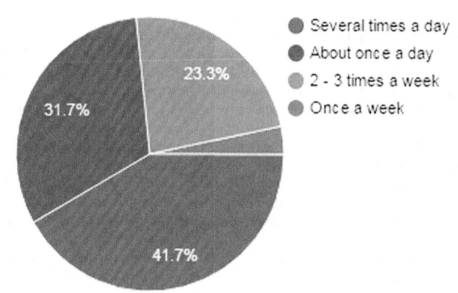

5.2. Descriptive Analysis of the Responses and Reliability

For this study, a reliability test was done to see if there is any item to be eliminated from each variable from the Likert-scale questions in the survey. From the test, as shown on Table 6, all five variables have good value of Cronbach's alpha, as the values are all ranging between 0.6 – 0.9. Thus, no items were eliminated and further data analysis were carried out.

Table 6 Summarized results from reliability test and minimum, maximum, mean and standard deviation values of constructs obtained from descriptive statistical analysis.

To calculate the values of minimum, maximum, mean and standard deviation of the scores, a descriptive analysis was done. The above table (Table 6) shows the dimension *Usage* (dependent variable) has a minimum score of 3.8 and maximum score of 5.0 which are the neutral and maximum score on the Likert-scale. The mean is 4.33 which indicates that most of the respondents gave agree as their answer regarding their social media usage. The standard deviation of the score is 0.399 which shows data are closely clustered around the mean, and are reliable.

Table 6. Reliability test results

Measure	No. of Items	Cronbach's Alpha, α	Min	Max	M	SD
Usage	10	0.888	3.80	5.00	4.33	0.399
Trust	5	0.882	3.00	5.00	3.87	0.555
Interactivity	3	0.774	3.00	5.00	4.11	0.461
Compatibility	3	0.889	3.00	5.00	3.74	0.615
Cost Effectiveness	3	0.845	3.00	5.00	4.54	0.559

For dimension *Trust* (independent variable), the minimum and maximum scores obtained were 3.0 and 5.0 respectively. The mean score was found to be 3.87, which indicates most respondents are positive with the *Trust* dimension. The high standard deviation (0.555) indicates high dispersion among the respondent's answers for the questions under *Tangibility* dimension.

For independent variable of *Interactivity,* it has a mean score of 4.11, a minimum value of 3.0 and a maximum value of 5.0, which shows that respondents gave a neutral to positive answer for this dimension. The low standard deviation of 46.1% shows that the dispersion among respondents' answers for questions under this variable is low.

For dimension *Compatibility*, the minimum and maximum scores obtained were 3.0 and 5.0 respectively, with the mean of 3.74, it shows that the *Compatibility* dimensions has positive score. The high standard deviation of 0.615 indicates high dispersion among the respondents' answers for questions under *Compatibility* dimension.

For dimension *Cost Effectiveness,* it has a mean score of 4.54, a minimum value of 3.0 and maximum value of 5.0. These values indicate that respondents gave a positive answer for questions under this dimension. The high standard deviation percentage of 55.9% shows the high dispersion of respondents' answers for questions under this independent variable.

From Figure 4, it can be seen that the dimension of *cost effectiveness* has the highest mean score, which indicates that food vendors in Brunei are adopting social media because of its *cost effectiveness.* For dimension *compatibility* on the other hand, it has the lowest mean score of 3.74, which indicates that respondents were mostly neutral about the *interactivity* of social media.

From the descriptive analysis on the survey responses, we have summarized the result on the frequency table (see Table 7). For *Usage,* it was found that food vendors who use social media as a platform to assist them in doing their businesses were either mostly positive or neutral regarding their social media usage. We have also found that most of the respondents were positive with the *Trust* dimension of the social media. As for the measure of *Interactivity*, a group of respondents felt that the social media platform is very interactive. Under the *Compatibility* dimension, more than half of the respondents are positive with the compatibility of the social media usage. For the measure of *Cost Effectiveness,* majority of the respondents are positive and agree that the use of social media is very cost effective in assisting them to conduct their business.

Figure 4. Mean scores of the five dimensions of the study

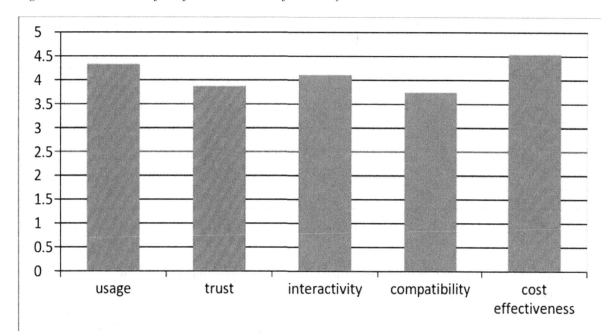

Table 7. Frequency table of responses for each variable used in the questionnaires

	Frequency		
	Strongly Disagree and Disagree	**Neutral**	**Strongly Agree and Agree**
Usage	0 (0.0%)	1 (1.7%)	59 (98.3%)
Trust	0 (0.0%)	5 (8.3%)	55 (91.7%)
Interactivity	0 (0.0%)	2 (3.3%)	58 (96.7%)
Compatibility	0 (0.0%)	19 (31.7%)	41 (68.3%)
Cost Effectiveness	0 (0.0%)	1 (1.7%)	59 (98.3%)

5.3. Multiple Regression Analysis

To examine the relationship between social media usage and its four dimensions, we have used multiple regression analyses. As seen from Table 8 of multiple regression data analysis, it was found that the adjusted R^2 of our model is 0.176 with the $R^2 = 0.232$ which indicates the variance in the data. Therefore, we can conclude that the low variance value of 23.2% shows that the independent variables are not capable in predicting our dependent variable, *Usage*.

From Table 8, it can be seen that only Cost Effectiveness has a significance value of less than 0.05. Thus, only independent variables of Cost Effectiveness were found to statistically significant. Also, Cost Effectiveness, valued at significance value of 0.025 [$F(4,55) = 4.149$, $p < .05$] has the most significant independent variable.

Table 8. Results from multiple regression analysis

	Unstandardized Estimates	Standard Error	Standardized Estimates	t	p-Level	Collinearity Statistics	
	B	SE	®			Tol	VIF
(constant)	2.053	.607		3.379	.001		
Trust	.177	.101	.246	1.746	.086	.704	1.421
Interactivity	.135	.119	.157	1.137	.261	.734	1.361
Compatibility	.035	.090	.054	.389	.699	.731	1.368
Cost Effectiveness	.200	.087	.281	2.297	.025	.935	1.069
R²	0.232			df		F	4.149
Adjusted R²	0.176		Regression	4			
* p<.05			Residual	55			

To strengthen the data found on the significance of the independent variables, we can look at the value of beta. The higher the value of beta, the more important the variable is. From the Table 8, it can be seen that Cost Effectiveness has the highest beta value of 28.1%, which strengthen the significance of the independent variable. This value also indicates that Cost Effectiveness is the largest contributor to our dependent variable, Usage.

From the findings obtained from multiple regression analysis conducted, we could now accept or reject the hypotheses for our study (Table 9). Therefore, hypotheses H4 (cost effectiveness) is accepted as we have enough evidence to support the hypothesis. However, for hypotheses H1, H2 and H3, due to not enough evidence to support the hypotheses, null hypotheses H0,1, H0,2 and H0,3 would have to be accepted:

H_1: There is a positive relationship between trust in social media and the social media usage (NOT SUPPORTED).

$H_{0,1}$: There is no relationship between trust in social media and the social media usage satisfaction (SUPPORTED).

H_2: There is a positive relationship between interactivity of social media and the social media usage (NOT SUPPORTED).

$H_{0,2}$: There is no relationship between interactivity of social media and the social media usage satisfaction (SUPPORTED).

H_3: There is a positive relationship between compatibility of social media and the social media usage (NOT SUPPORTED).

$H_{0,3}$: There is no relationship between compatibility of social media and the social media usage (SUPPORTED).

H_4: There is a positive relationship between cost effectiveness of social media and the social media usage (SUPPORTED).

Table 9. Conclusion for hypotheses testing using multiple regression analysis

Independent Variable	Conclusion From Hypothesis Testing
Trust	Hypothesis rejected
Interactivity	Hypothesis rejected
Compatibility	Hypothesis rejected
Cost Effectiveness	Hypothesis accepted

6. DISCUSSION

6.1. Cost Effectiveness

H_4: There is a positive relationship between cost effectiveness of social media and the social media usage (SUPPORTED).

Our results enabled us to understand that cost effectiveness is the only independent variable that is significant to our research. This conclusion is supported by the fact that the majority of respondents confirmed that social media saves them money and time while running marketing action plans as shown in Table 7. As a matter of fact, the cost effectiveness of social media plays an important role in improving SME Key Performance Indicators (KPIs). According to Eckerling (2014), Social media ROI is defined as "a measure of the efficiency of a social media marketing campaign." In fact, SMEs may use social media to improve their profitability through lead generation (leads) and direct sales (customers). In other words, SMEs' may use social media to boost their brand awareness metric while it can improve the turnover – especially when the company has financial constraint (Chong & Chan, 2012; Alam, 2009) through tackling the customer reach, which leads to a high probability of purchase. Opportunities are now on social networks and it could be a loss to consider omitting social media. Indeed, not all companies can already be present on social networks, but at least they must be concerned to integrate the tool in their communication strategy. The risk of using social media to boost a business performance is very low because social networks cost little, however, not being present can generate a potentially significant shortfall for businesses. Because social media costs only the time, and doesn't require high IT skills (Derham et al., 2011), that's why businesses should get out of their comfort zone and use it even more. In fact, they have to know that they are not supposed to stick to one social medium and that content must be posted regularly. Social networks are booming, undoubtedly. Many companies have chosen to use this new marketing mean to take advantage of its efficient impact. Facebook and its 1.35 billion active users or Twitter and its 284 million users show well that consumers can accept these platforms as marketing tool.

On the other hand, Trust, Interactivity and Compatibility were not significant enough to the importance of social media usage by SMEs. We could assume that low cost is what drives these SMEs to use social media.

6.2. Trust

H$_1$: There is a positive relationship between trust on social media and the social media usage (NOT SUPPORTED).

Our study found that trust is insignificant factor in social media usage in SMEs. This result is consistent with the results obtained by Wu and Liu (2007) and also Ainin (2015). As interpreted by Ainin, the possible reason for trust to be an insignificant factor is because social media service providers such as Facebook and Instagram are well known with millions of users globally. Due to that reputation, trust may not be an issue for organizations to use social media. Users may feel assured with social media service providers to keep their private information. It is also possible due to social media being cost effective; trust factor might be overlooked and not considered when adopting social media for marketing purposes. However, it should be noted that, trust factor may influence social media usage when businesses have to pay for a certain feature on social media such as the promotion feature. With the promotion feature, a business may be able to reach a certain audience with their advertisement with a cost involved. Then in that situation, trust may become an important factor as there is a possibility of credit card fraud (Wu & Liu, 2007).

Although our study does not give enough evidence to support the positive relation between trust and the usage of social media and its impact on business, it is considered to be one of the important factors for sustaining a business. It is a tool that helps SMEs build an online brand reputation in a profitable way (Gligorijevic & Leong, 2011). Trust in social media usually arises from the diversity and quality of information shared by the SME on a particular online platform. Social media allows SMEs to have the opportunity to build a relationship with their customers. It should be noted that they first would show interest in the product, then the business and will definitely share the information using either the tradition or the electronic word of mouth. Credible and transparent information about a business will likely make a customer share it especially if they find it interesting. Finally, it can be said that social networks make it possible to build a balanced relationship between the consumer and the company and because it is a win-win relationship which can lead to a long-term relationship. This could be done for example by selling a product or a service that solves customers' problems (Rust et al., 2010).

6.3. Interactivity

H$_2$: There is a positive relationship between interactivity of social media and the social media usage (NOT SUPPORTED).

The same goes for Interactivity hypothesis, which is rejected. Social networks are worth nothing if SMEs do not animate their community. The interaction could be in form of offers reserved for members, special events, invitations to events, etc. SMEs are advised to publish everything that makes the life of the company and to create interactivity. By asking questions, creating events, sending invitations and encouraging users to react to each publication, share them and give their opinions. This often allows SMEs to have relevant user experience feedback without resorting to costly and complicated surveys or panels to set up. Furthermore, it is believed that social networks change the way consumers express themselves to the company, as a result of their purchases. This leads us to think that companies should listen and respond to the conversations of Internet users and not ignore them (Rust et al., 2010). Interacting with customers on the Internet provides SMEs with a real-time source of information that can help them better serve their customers and increase their sale performance. To put it in different words, social networks are now an additional medium that companies must include in their business strategy and more specifically in their marketing strategy. A study has shown that this "electronic word-of-mouth" is seen as reliable by consumers and significantly affects a firm's perceived value" (Quesenberry, 2015).

Because social networks cost only the time, more efforts should be invested on social media. It is important to note that a few basic rules must be observed on social networks. Posting trustworthy content regularly and controlling the social media helps customers not to forget about the brand and keep it in their top of mind. That is where the role of a community manager is very significant: it will regulate and animate the community on social networks and ensure the exchanges that occur there. Moreover, it is necessary to be able to identify its target and its objectives to be attained on social media.

6.4. Compatibility

H₃: There is a positive relationship between compatibility of social media and the social media usage (NOT SUPPORTED).

As stated above, our findings did not support our hypothesis and rejected the idea that social media is compatible and easily adaptable to SMEs. On the other hand, it was stated by 68% of our respondents that social media is compatible with their organization, and that it has a positive impact on their business performance. A study stated that the use of Facebook has a significant relation with technology compatibility (Wang et al., 2010). In point of fact, social media platforms like Facebook are trying to attract small businesses by making them user-friendliness. Furthermore, the modern technology and social media also help direct consumers to a certain business, which means that SMES should just work harder to keep up with the up-to-date technological trends and integrate them in their business (Accion, 2016). As a matter of fact, it is believed that it is hard for SMEs to work without social media given the circumstances today. Indeed, companies have adapted their management and sales techniques to the opportunities offered by social media, and they would no longer be able to work without them. These media have become the spearhead of some companies. In addition to using these media tools as an advertising showcase, brands have the ability to interact very easily with Internet users via information, images or videos, thus enabling loyalty to be fast to earn.

7. CONCLUSION

Social media is widely used among small and medium enterprises for various reasons. As a matter of fact, Internet has shaken consumption patterns and challenged the functioning of most sectors.

Our aim was to investigate the use of social media within these small and medium entities. After reviewing and analyzing all the collected data and results, our research has revealed that the only factors that matters most to our sample that in Small and medium enterprises in Brunei is cost-effectiveness. Concerning trust, compatibility and interactivity, our research revealed that they had no positive correlation with our dependent variable. However, even though these above-mentioned variables were not supported by our study, this does not mean that our results are completely true because not all companies care mostly about making profit, but they can be driven by building a strong image and be closer to their employees and customers. As a matter of fact, this study can be expanded further by testing other sectors such as tourism and banking services for instance in order to gain a broader understanding about the use of these variables within these sectors.

Building up a strong marketing strategy through social media is an ever-ending process and it does not have a typical "how-to" manual that lets businesses learn how to use it over night. It thus appears that the image of SMEs is closely linked with the use of social networks due to its cost effectiveness. Without these networks, some companies would never have been able to make themselves known so quickly thanks to their interactivity on Facebook or Twitter, and other social media. We live in a world with a wide usage of mobile phones. Everything is done through Internet today. The world is radically changing and there is a need to create awareness among business owners that they have to embrace the digital transformation. This certainly requires being on track of what the regularly changing customer needs.

8. LIMITATIONS

One of the limitations encountered during this research was mainly during the data collection. In fact, many interviewees and respondents refused to give away some information for privacy or due to professional secrecy. Furthermore, some resources (business owners, business experts, social media experts) did not always have the opportune time to receive us, for various reasons.

On the other hand, surveys are always subject of bias. We opted to question both consumers and SMEs in order to have a broad view on impact of the social media on SMEs. The questionnaires used in this study were detailed in order to to prevent the reluctance of respondents to answer. One last difficulty was that older people are sometimes unfamiliar to responding to online questionnaires, which made the data collection take longer than expected. Finally, we've been only able to reach 60 SMEs to respond to our questionnaire. A larger sample could have been more useful to our research and enable us to achieve more accurate results,

REFERENCES

Adams, M. (2014). Three Ways To Build Customer Trust. *Forbes.com*. Retrieved from https://www.forbes.com/sites/yec/2014/04/22/three-ways-to-build-customer-trust/#4be1cf5822b8

Adapting To The Latest Technology Trends For Your Business. (2016). Accion. Retrieved from http://us.accion.org/business-resources/articles-videos/adapting-latest-technology-trends-your-business

Ainin, S., Naqshbandi, M. M., Moghavvemi, S., & Jaafar, N. I. (2015). Facebook usage, socialization and academic performance. *Computers & Education, 83*, 64–73. doi:10.1016/j.compedu.2014.12.018

Ainin, S., Parveen, F., Moghavvemi, S., Jaafar, N. I., & Mohd Shuib, N. L. (2015). Factors influencing the use of social media by SMEs and its performance outcomes. *Industrial Management & Data Systems, 115*(3), 570–588. doi:10.1108/IMDS-07-2014-0205

Alam, S. (2009). Adoption of internet in Malaysian SMEs. *Journal of Small Business and Enterprise Development, 16*(2), 240–255. doi:10.1108/14626000910956038

Baruah, T. D. (2012). Effectiveness of Social Media as a tool of communication and its potential for technology enabled connections: A micro-level study. *International Journal of Scientific and Research Publications*, *2*(5), 1–10.

Bauer, H. H., Grether, M., & Leach, M. (2002). Building customer relations over the Internet. *Industrial Marketing Management*, *31*(2), 155–163. doi:10.1016/S0019-8501(01)00186-9

Borneo Bulletin Yearbook. (2016a). Darussalam Enterprise (DARe). Retrieved from http://borneobulletinyearbook.com.bn/the-way-of-life-2/

Borneo Bulletin Yearbook. (2016b). SMEs Surging Ahead. Retrieved from http://2016.borneobulletinyearbook.com.bn/files/assets/basic-html/page-135.html#

Chai, S., Das, S., & Rao, H. R. (2011). Factors affecting bloggers' knowledge sharing: An investigation across gender. *Journal of Management Information Systems*, *28*(3), 309–342. Retrieved from http://www.tandfonline.com/doi/abs/10.2753/MIS0742-1222280309

Chong, A. Y.-L., & Chan, F. T. (2012). Structural equation modeling for multi-stage analysis on radio frequency identification (RFID) diffusion in the health care industry. *Expert Systems with Applications*, *39*(10), 8645–8654. doi:10.1016/j.eswa.2012.01.201

Coccia, S. M. (1997). Leveling the playing field. *Medical Marketing & Media*, *32*, 30–37.

Dahnil, M. I., Marzuki, K. M., Langgat, J., & Fabeil, N. F. (2014). Factors influencing SMEs adoption of social media marketing. *Procedia: Social and Behavioral Sciences*, *148*, 119–126. doi:10.1016/j.sbspro.2014.07.025

DanialNorjidi. (2016, March 24). DARe striving to improve business environment. *Borneo Bulletin*. Retrieved from http://www.borneobulletin.com.bn/dare-striving-to-improve-business-environment/

Davis, F. D. (1989). Perceived usefulness, perceived ease of use, and user acceptance of information technology. *Management Information Systems Quarterly*, *13*(3), 319–340. doi:10.2307/249008

Davis, F. D., Bagozzi, R. P., & Warshaw, P. R. (1989). User acceptance of computer technology: A comparison of two theoretical models. *Management Science*, *35*(8), 982–1003. doi:10.1287/mnsc.35.8.982

Derham, R., Cragg, P., & Morrish, S. (2011). Creating value: an SME and social media. In *PACIS 2011 Proceedings*. Academic Press. Retrieved from http://aisel.aisnet.org/pacis2011/53

Eckerling, D. (2014). How to Measure Social Media ROI. *Social Media ROI*. Retrieved from http://www.socialmediaexaminer.com/measure-social-media-roi/

Ernst and Young. (2001). Advancing with e-commerce. Retrieved from www.noie.gov.au

Gligorijevic, B., & Leong, B. (2011). Trust, Reputation and the Small Firm: Building Online Brand Reputation for SMEs. In *Proceedings of the Fifth International AAAI Conference on Weblogs and Social Media* (pp. 494-597). AAAI Press.

Goodrich, K., & de Mooij, M. (2013). How 'social' are social media? A cross-cultural comparison of online and offline purchase decision influences? *Journal of Marketing Communications, 20*(1/2), 1-14. Retrieved from https://www.mariekedemooij.com/articles/goodrich_demooij_2013_journal_marketing-communications.pdf

Guariglia, A., Liu, X., & Song, L. (2011). Internal finance and growth: Micro econometric evidence on Chinese firms. *Journal of Development Economics, 96*(1), 79–94. doi:10.1016/j.jdeveco.2010.07.003

Hassan, S., Nadzim, S. Z. A., & Shiratuddin, N. (2015). Strategic use of social media for small business based on the AIDA model. *Procedia: Social and Behavioral Sciences, 172*, 262–269. doi:10.1016/j.sbspro.2015.01.363

Hawking, P. (1997). The implications of Internet telephony to small businesses in Australia'. In *Conference Proceedings from SEAANZ Annual Conference.*

Hofstede, G. (1983). National cultures in four dimensions: A research-based theory of cultural differences among nations. *International Studies of Management & Organization, 13*(1-2), 46–74. doi:10.1080/00208825.1983.11656358

Hutter, K., Hautz, J., Dennhardt, S., & Füller, J. (2013). The impact of user interactions in social media on brand awareness and purchase intention: The case of MINI on Facebook. *Journal of Product and Brand Management, 22*(5/6), 342–351. doi:10.1108/JPBM-05-2013-0299

International Business Publications. (2016). *Brunei Investment and Business Guide*. Washington, DC: Author.

Kaplan, A. M., & Haenlein, M. (2010). Users of the world, unite! The challenges and opportunities of Social Media. *Business Horizons, 53*(1), 59–68. doi:10.1016/j.bushor.2009.09.003

Kaplan, T. E., Johnson, R. W., Pearce, C. G., & George, G. (1997). The strategic role of communication technology in small business: Where we are and where we should be going. *American Business Review, 15*(1), 86–91.

Kirtis, A. K., & Karahan, F. (2011) To be or not to be in Social Media arena as the most cost-efficient marketing strategy after the global recession. In the Proceeding of Social and Behavioral Sciences, pp. 260-268, 7 th International Strategic Management Conference. 10.1016/j.sbspro.2011.09.083

Lee, Y., & Kozar, K. (2012). Developing a theory of website usability: An exploratory study to identify constructs and nomological networks. *Decision Support Systems, 52*(2), 450–463. doi:10.1016/j.dss.2011.10.004

Mayfield, A. (2008). What is social media? Icrossing. Retrieved from http://www.icrossing.com/uk/sites/default/files_uk/insight_pdf_files/What%20is%20Social%20Media_iCrossing_ebook.pdf

McKnight, D. H., Cummings, L. L., & Chervany, N. L. (1998). Initial trust formation in new organizational relationships. *Academy of Management Review, 23*(3), 473–490. doi:10.5465/amr.1998.926622

Michaelidou, N., Siamagka, N. T., & Christodoulides, G. (2011). Usage, barriers and measurement of social media marketing: An exploratory investigation of small and medium B2B brands. *Industrial Marketing Management*, *40*(7), 1153–1159. doi:10.1016/j.indmarman.2011.09.009

Mohammad, L. (2016, September 23). BIBD launches first SME 360° branch. Retrieved from http://www.ei.gov.bn/Lists/Industry%20News/NewDispForm.aspx?ID=98&ContentTypeId=0x0100585AA17FA637114E870034FE25016A22

Neti, S. (2011). Social media and its role in marketing. *International Journal of Enterprise Computing and Business Systems*, *1*(2), 1–15.

Niven, R. (2014, April 16). *How small businesses are making the most of social media to grow*. Retrieved from https://www.theguardian.com/small-business-network/2014/apr/16/social-media-smes-growth

OECD. (2012). *Food and the Tourism Experience: The OECD-Korea Workshop*. Paris: OECD Publishing. doi:10.1787/9789264171923-

Othman, A. (2017, August 8). Surge in mobile phone, broadband penetration in Brunei. *Borneo Bulletin*. Retrieved from http://borneobulletin.com.bn/surge-mobile-phone-broadband-penetration-brunei/

Ozigbo, N. C., & Ezeaku, P. (2009). Adoption of information and communication technologies to the development of small and medium scale enterprises (SMEs) in Africa. *Journal of Business and Administrative Studies*, *1*(1), 1–20. doi:10.4314/jbas.v1i1.47894

Öztamur, D., & Karakadılar, İ. S. (2014). Exploring the role of social media for SMEs: As a new marketing strategy tool for the firm performance perspective. *Procedia: Social and Behavioral Sciences*, *150*, 511–520. doi:10.1016/j.sbspro.2014.09.067

Polsaram, P., Kulsiri, P., Techasermsukkul, L., Htwe, T. D., & Kwanchainond, K.(2011). A Survey Research Project on "Small and Medium Enterprises Development Policies of 4 ASEAN Countries": Brunei Darussalam, Cambodia, Lao PDR, Myanmar. ASEAN. Retrieved from http://www.asean.org/storage/images/documents/SME%20Policies%20in%204%20ASEAN%20Countries%20-%20Brunei%20Darussalam.pdf

Quesenberry, K. A. (2015, November). Conducting a Social Media Audit. *Harvard Business Review*. Retrieved from https://hbr.org/2015/11/conducting-a-social-media-audit

Rogers, E. M. (1983). *Diffusion of Innovations*. New York, NY: Free Press.

Rust, R. T., Moorman, C., & Bhalla, G. (2010, January). Rethinking Marketing. *Harvard Business Review*, 94–101. Retrieved from https://hbr.org/2010/01/rethinking-marketing

Shih, C. (2010). *The Facebook Era: Tapping Online Social Networks to Market. Sell, and Innovate*. Pearson Education.

Thambipillai, P. (2008). Brunei Darussalam: Making a Concerted Effort. *Southeast Asian Affairs*, 89-104.

Vásquez, G. A. N., & Escamilla, E. M. (2014). Best practice in the use of social networks marketing strategy as in SMEs. *Procedia: Social and Behavioral Sciences*, *148*, 533–542. doi:10.1016/j.sbspro.2014.07.076

Wang, Y. M., Wang, Y. S., & Yang, Y. F. (2010). Understanding the determinants of RFID adoption in the manufacturing industry. *Technological Forecasting and Social Change*, 77(5), 803–815. doi:10.1016/j.techfore.2010.03.006

Wu, J., & Liu, D. (2007). The effects of trust and enjoyment on intention to play online games. *Journal of Electronic Commerce Research*, 8(2), 128–140. Retrieved from https://www.researchgate.net/publication/228668939_The_effects_of_trust_and_enjoyment_on_intention_to_play_online_games

APPENDIX

Social Media Adoption in Food Industry Among SMEs in Brunei Darussalam

We are postgraduate students from University Brunei Darussalam (UBD) under the Faculty of School of Business and Economics. The purpose of conducting this survey is a part of our research, to gain an in depth understanding as well as to identify and analyse social media adoption in food industry among SMEs in Brunei Darussalam.

All responses will be kept confidential for academic purposes only. Your honest opinion and cooperation are highly appreciated. Thank you in advance for participating and helping us in our research.

Section A: Respondent's Background

1. Age *(please specify)*:
    _____

2. Gender *(please tick one)*:
    [ ] Female
    [ ] Male

3. Occupation *(you may tick more than one)*:
    [ ] Employed
    [ ] Unemployed
    [ ] Self-employed
    [ ] Student

4. Social media platform used *(you may tick more than one)*:
    [ ] Facebook
    [ ] Twitter
    [ ] Instagram
    [ ] Other
    (please specify): _____

5. How often do you use social media *(please tick one)*:
    [ ] Several times a day
    [ ] 2-3 times a week
    [ ] About once a day
    [ ] Once a week

Section B: Factors Influencing Social Media Adoption in Food Industry Among SMEs in Brunei Darussalam

Please rate your satisfaction according to the given situation.

1- SOCIAL MEDIA USAGE (refers to how social media help company to conduct business)

QUESTIONS	Strongly Disagree	Disagree	Neutral	Agree	Strongly Agree
1. My company use social media to advertise and promote product and services	1	2	3	4	5
2. My company use social media to create brand visibility	1	2	3	4	5
3. My company use social media to conduct marketing research	1	2	3	4	5
4. My company use social media to get referrals (word of mouths via shares and followers in social media)	1	2	3	4	5
5. My company use social media to communicate with customers	1	2	3	4	5
6. My company use social media to develop customer relations	1	2	3	4	5
7. My company use social media to conduct customer service activity (interactions with customers before, during and after a purchase)	1	2	3	4	5
8. My company use social media to receive feedback of products/services offered	1	2	3	4	5
9. My company use social media to reach new customers	1	2	3	4	5
10. My company use social media to search for competitor information	1	2	3	4	5

2- TRUST IN SOCIAL MEDIA (refers to the believe in the reliability, truth, ability and strength of social media)

QUESTIONS	Strongly Disagree	Disagree	Neutral	Agree	Strongly Agree
1. Social media provide my company with adequate measures to protect information posted by my company	1	2	3	4	5
2. Social media provide my company with a safe environment to transact information	1	2	3	4	5
3. Social media provide my company with adequate technological measures to deliver information	1	2	3	4	5
4. Social media allows my company to be trusted	1	2	3	4	5
5. Social media allows my company to give good quality of service	1	2	3	4	5

3- INTERACTIVITY THROUGH SOCIAL MEDIA (refers as a key and distinguished factor that impacts users' response to social media)

QUESTIONS	Strongly Disagree	Disagree	Neutral	Agree	Strongly Agree
1. Social media provides my company with features for interactive communication with customers	1	2	3	4	5
2. Social media provides my company with appropriate number of interactive features (eg: graphics, music, etc.)	1	2	3	4	5
3. Social media provides my company with features for vivid responses	1	2	3	4	5

4- COMPATIBILITY IN SOCIAL MEDIA (refers to the degree to which innovation fits with the potential adopter's existing values, previous practices and current needs)

QUESTIONS	Strongly Disagree	Disagree	Neutral	Agree	Strongly Agree
1. Social media usage is compatible with the company's IT infrastructure (devices, software, network, etc.)	1	2	3	4	5
2. Social media usage is consistent with the company's beliefs and values	1	2	3	4	5
3. Social media usage is consistent with the company's business strategy	1	2	3	4	5

5- COST EFFECTIVENESS OF SOCIAL MEDIA (refers to the importance of cost in the adoption and utilization of social media)

QUESTIONS	Strongly Disagree	Disagree	Neutral	Agree	Strongly Agree
1. Social media is more cost effective than other types of marketing or customer service technologies	1	2	3	4	5
2. My company can avoid unnecessary cost and time by using social media	1	2	3	4	5
3. Social media saves employees effort in marketing, branding and customer service	1	2	3	4	5

6- PERFORMANCE (refers to how social media can have an impact on businesses)

QUESTIONS	Strongly Disagree	Disagree	Neutral	Agree	Strongly Agree
1. Sales transactions increase with the help of social media	1	2	3	4	5
2. Sales volume increases with the help of social media	1	2	3	4	5
3. Number of customers increase with the help of social media	1	2	3	4	5

Section C: Comments

Any comments that you would like to add regarding the adoption of social media in food industry among SMEs in Brunei Darussalam?

Chapter 56
An Evaluation of Toronto's Destination Image Through Tourist Generated Content on Twitter

Hillary Clarke
Edinburgh Napier University, Edinburgh, UK

Ahmed Hassanien
Edinburgh Napier University, Edinburgh, UK

ABSTRACT

This study aims at evaluating the cognitive, affective, and conative components of destination image from the perception of tourists on social media. The netnography technique is used for data analysis and interpretation. Through a textual content analysis approach, an interpretation of meaning of content produced from tweets by tourists is conducted. The findings show that destination attractions were the most commented on component of the cognitive component. Throughout the travelling process, tourists assessed the affective destination image. It was found that tourists' evaluation was of favourable emotions towards Toronto as a destination. The conative component was assessed before, during, and after visiting Toronto. Tourists provided insight into their behaviour online through personal updates and information sharing. The research outcomes provide scholars and practitioners with greater insight into the dimensions of destination image formed by user-generated content from tourists and their usefulness for information exchange in various settings.

1. INTRODUCTION

Tourists' travel decision –making process is heavily influenced by destination image when planning a holiday and an integral component is the image that represents the destination (Cai, 2002; Morgan et al.; 2004, Iwashita, 2006). The destination image formation process takes place through a stimulus of media

DOI: 10.4018/978-1-7998-9020-1.ch056

including, official promotional campaigns, word-of-mouth, guidebooks, popular culture, and the media (Hammett, 2014). Additionally, Gunn (1988) proposes the seven-stage process that tourists use to form destination image: (1) accumulating mental images of the destination – organic level; (2) modifying the initial image after more information – induced level; (3) deciding to visit the destination; (4) visiting the destination; (5) sharing the destination; (6) returning home; and (7) modifying the image based on the experience. On the other hand, the emergence of social media is influencing how tourists assess destination image components. The study of social media relating to destination image is evolving as researchers seek to better understand what tourists expect and their behaviour online (Lange-Faria and Elliot, 2012). Few previous studies focused on the role of social media in the travel planning and destination marketing process (e.g. Chung and Buhalis, 2008; Hsu and Lin, 2008; O'Connor, 2008). However, there has been a gap in literature that explores tourists' evaluation of a destination image on social media despites its significance (Kladou and Mavragani, 2015; Zeng and Gerritsen, 2014).

Given the developments of new information sources, such as social media, and the influence of user-generated content on the customer's decision-making process (Jalilvand et al., 2012) it is consequently important to consider the evaluation of destination image from the tourists perspective. Accordingly, this study aims to assess tourists' evaluation of the destination image components of Toronto from tourist generated content on Twitter. This is assessed by exploring topics of destination image related information exchange on Twitter before, during and after travelling to Toronto so as to assess tourists' perceptions, experiences, and levels of satisfaction about the destination. In addition, the research will conclude with recommendations on how this evaluation of destination image components on social media can benefit destination-marketing organisations.

2. LITERATURE REVIEW

This section introduces and analyses previous research published about tourist generated online content on Twitter, destination image and the key topics that are connected to this area. This can be seen through the conceptual framework detailed in Figure 1.

Figure 1. Research conceptual framework

2.1. Tourist Generated Content on Twitter

User-generated content refers to, "the information that is digitalized uploaded by the users and made available through the Internet," (Munar, 2011, p. 292). It is created and used by users with the intent of sharing it with others (Kohli et al., 2015). Gretzel and Yoo (2008) found that more than 74% of travellers use the comments of other consumers as a source of information when planning their holiday. Tourists share their evaluation and perceptions of destination image on social media and these evaluations can influence the choice of the destination; not only friends and family but social media users from around the world (Kladou and Mavragani, 2015). Other tourists are seeking to gain authentic information, which is not always available from destination organisations; as a result, user-generated content is becoming the truth for destinations. Since user-generated content is out of the control of destination organisations their content appears to be more authentic to other tourists. Therefore, this becomes of special importance given the significance of social media and the influence of user-generated content on the tourists' decision-making process (Jalilvand et al., 2012).

User-generated content online has revolutionized the way in which tourists inform themselves and others on destination image, including methods of transportation, facilities, and other hospitality needs (Zheng and Gretzel, 2011). Tourists have the ability to quickly generate content of their experience and share it with the masses (Oliveira and Panyik, 2015). In this sense, consumers on social media not only have the ability to control the information they hear but also what they want to pass along (Kohli et al., 2015). Consequently, tourists are also creators and distributors of destination image on social media (Lim et al., 2012).

Twitter is one of the most popular online social networking services. It allows users to send and read 140 characters messages called "Tweets". There are over 300 million active users (Twitter, 2015a). Registered users are able to post and read Tweets, but unregistered users can only read others Tweets. Users can tweet through the Twitter website, compatible external applications (i.e. smartphones), or share message service (Twitter, 2015b). Users can subscribe to other people's Tweets by becoming followers, as well as pass on information by "retweeting" a message or mentioning it in a new post of their own. Within a tweet users can use a hashtag (#) before a relevant keyword or phrase (no spaces) to categorize their tweet and help them show more easily in a Twitter search (By clicking on a hashtag in any message it will show all results marked with that keyword (Twitter, 2015c). Twitter is a simple, accessible, yet powerful tool for social networking. Therefore, Twitter is becoming an integral component of marketing strategies.

Sreenivasan et al. (2015) investigated what users were discussing on Twitter to better understand travel-related opinions, and uncover the common themes of information exchange between users. Results showed that communication on Twitter was used for compliments, marketing, to provide personal updates, to share information, community support, information seeking, and to discuss grievances. These categories of topics of information exchange from user-generated content on Twitter will be used to see how tourists were communicating their evaluation of the destination image components.

2.2. Destination Image Components

A review of literature about the conceptualization of destination image proves that it is a multi-faceted, composite contract, which consists of interrelated cognitive and affective evaluation formed into an overall impression (Stepchenkova and Morrison, 2006). Milman and Pizam (1995) propose that destination image consists of three components: the product, the behaviour and attitude of the destination, and thirdly the environment. Gartner (1993) considers the concept of destination image as containing three main components: cognitive, affective and conative (Gartner 1993).

The cognitive component is related to awareness and what people know or may think they know about a destination (Baloglu, 1999; Pike and Ryan, 2004). Gartner (1993) notes that the type and amount of external information sources received by tourists will influence the formation of the cognitive component of image. Crompton (1979) states "the perceptual/cognitive evaluation of attributes is formed by external factors which include various information sources such as symbolic stimuli (promotional efforts of a destination through media) and social stimuli (friends' and relatives recommendation or word-of-mouth)." The cognitive component focuses on tangible physical attributes of the destination (Pike and Ryan, 2004).

Beyond beliefs and knowledge of the characteristics of a destination is the affective component that evolves around people's feelings toward the destination (Chen and Uysal, 2002; Kim and Richardson, 2003). The affective component can be favourable, unfavourable, or neutral in terms of feelings towards an object. It is proposed that 'affect' becomes active during the evaluation of the decision-making process (Gartner 1993). Baloglu and McCleary (1999) and Pike and Ryan (2004) demonstrate that four semantic differential scales can be applied to assessing affective component of a destination, which are: arousing-sleepy; pleasant-unpleasant; exciting-gloomy; and relaxing-distressing. This bi-dimensional model proposes that cognitive image is an antecedent of affective image (Gartner, 1993; Ryan and Cave, 2005). Baloglu and McCleary (1999) argue that affective image is the most influential factor, therefore is should be used more often by destinations to gain success.

Lastly, the conative dimension reflects the behavioural aspect of how people act on the information. This can be considered the action step and the likelihood of visiting or revisiting a destination, thus connected to tourist behaviour. In addition, San Martin and Rodriguez del Bosque (2008) suggested that these components can be factored into categories. The cognitive components can be factored into 'natural environment', 'cultural heritage', 'tourists' infrastructure' and 'atmosphere'. These categories can be broken down into sub-categories such as functional/tangible attributes (e.g. landscape, cultural attractions, infrastructure) and psychological/abstract landscape (e.g. hospitality, atmosphere). Following this framework, the cognitive component of Toronto will be evaluated based upon categories of attractions (infrastructure, natural environment, atmosphere, festival and events), facilities, food and drink, transportation, travel information. The affective component will assess attributes such as feelings and emotions that tourists may feel about the destination. Based on the tourists' evaluation of these components of destination image their behaviour towards the destination may be influenced whether they would recommend or visit the destination again (San Martin & Rodriguez del Bosque, 2008). Therefore, the connotative component will be determined based on tourists' comments on Twitter in regard to recommendations, feedback, and intentions to visit Toronto again. Comments could refer to more than one of the components.

2.3. Sentiments

Social media directly impacts electronic word of mouth (eWOM) communication because it allows people to share their experiences and sentiments to almost anyone anywhere in the world (Jansen et al., 2009). Baloglu and McCleary (1999) note that tourists tend to assess destination image through positive and negative traits. This transforms tourists' online interactions from a solitary experience into a social one by searching for relevant information and receiving recommendations from trusted sources (Akehurst, 2009; Chai and Kim, 2010; McDonnell and Shiri, 2011).

The way eWOM functions is based on social networking and trust; people rely on families, friends and others in their social network for reliable and trustworthy information (Jansen et al., 2009). Through information exchange with individuals who have experience of the destination, tourists are able to reduce uncertainty in their decision-making (Xiang and Gretzel, 2009).

3. METHODOLOGY

This study used "netnography" as a methodology to explore Toronto's Destination Image through Tourist Generated Content on Twitter. Netnography is a qualitative research technique that refers to the application of ethnography to online communities (Kozinets, 1998, 2002). It can be defined as a "written account of on-line cyber-culture, informed by the methods of cultural anthropology" Kozinets (1997, p. 3).

Data was collected through 'SoDash', a social media listening software that collects Tweets, in this case using keywords related to Toronto tourists. A textual content analysis is applied to nearly 2000 Tweets to use, "a systematic, replicable technique for compressing many words of text into fewer content categories based on explicit rules of coding," (Stemler, 2001). The above conceptual framework (Figure 1) is used to examine the interpretation of cognitive, affective, and conative destination image components from user-generated content, along with the used information exchange topics.

The software was used to set up a number of search criteria, including source, gender, date, location, device, number of followers/influenceto reveal the data that was relevant to the specific area of this study. The Tweets were collected and assigned custom tags, mimicking the framework being used for analysis. The custom tags on SoDash allowed Tweets to be categories into more relevant pieces of information. This allowed the researchers to gain more meaning from what tourists were saying about Toronto. The destination image components were categorized by the tags: attractions, facilities, travel information, transportation, price, food and drinks, and emotion (Gartner, 1993; San Martin and Rodriguez del Bosque, 2008). On the other hand, the information exchange topics had the custom tags of: compliments, information sharing, information seeking, marketing, community support, and grievance (Sreenivasan et al., 2015). An additional tag-set of 'before, during and after' were assigned to comments that were used to track the timeline of when tourists were tweeting. Therefore, the coding scheme followed the framework discussed in the previous section.

Another feature of SoDash is sentiment understanding. The software program is able to measure positive, negative, and neutral sentiments. This was done from measuring keywords in the comments, which the software recognized as either positive, negative or neutral. This allowed the author to gain insight and deeper meaning from what tourists were saying because the data collected revealed tourists' sentiments towards the destination in their comments.

4. FINDINGS AND ANALYSIS

Firstly, an overview of the data will be presented, including demographic information. Then, the findings and analysis will be presented under headings in accordance with the key themes of the above conceptual framework, in order to allow ease of comparison with the literature presented in the review.

4.1. Overview of Findings

From May 1 to August 1, 2015, 1922 tweets were collected. The tweets were from tourists around the world. The tweets were collected through keyword search relevant to Toronto as a destination for tourists. Some of the top keywords from user-generated content are Toronto, travel, vacation, tourists, and holiday. The number of messages per week increased more than 5 times from May to July, likely due to summer holidays commencing as well as the Pan American games that took place during the month of

July. A gender breakdown reveals that from the users that identified their gender on their profile, 53% of Tweets were made by females and 47% of tweets were by males. Throughout the time frame of 'before, during, and after' visiting, the percentage of females and males that were commenting about Toronto as a tourist destination remained relatively similar. Before visiting, 51% of users were females and 49% males and both during and after visiting Toronto it was found that 56% were by females and 44% by males.

The message proportion by country shows the top three countries: 33.8% of Tweets were from Canada, 27.2% from the United States and 12.2% from the United Kingdom. Other notable overseas visitors that were Tweeting about Toronto were from Australia, France, India, Ireland, Brazil and Mexico. However, Canadians, Americans and UK nationals are those who mostly commented on Twitter, which does not come as a surprise since most of the arrivals are from these countries.

Throughout the travelling process there were slight differences in the nationalities of those commenting. For instance, before, the largest number of overseas comments were from India and France Whereas, during visiting Toronto, users from Brazil, Germany, Japan and the United Arab emerged as the main users that were tweeting while on holiday. After visiting Toronto, Australians were amongst the nationalities that were commenting the most.

4.2. Topics of Tweets

Table 1 shows the frequency of the cognitive, affective and conative components of destination image that were mainly discussed by tourists on Twitter, through personal updates and information sharing.

Table 1. Tweet topics

Tweet Topic	Cognitive Frequency	Affective Frequency	Conative Frequency
Compliment	8	68	58
Personal Update	546	135	137
Information Sharing	423	98	117
Socializing	53	77	34
Grievance	1	32	27
Community Support	22	11	13
Information Seeking	17	10	8
Marketing	13	5	0

This high percentage of personal updates from tourists may highlight a bit of narcissism where users invest more time and energy in a virtual world to maintain their sense of importance and their self-esteem (Ong et al., 2011; Rosen, 2007).

Rather than using social media to gain awareness, users are using it to share their beliefs about a destination throughout the image formation process. It was surprising the lack of level of information seeking, community support and marketing being discussed before, during and after visiting the destination. This could imply a (high level of knowledge of customers due to their previous experience and the availability of online destination information. It also proves that users are not sharing a lot of marketing content from destination organisations on social media due to its bias (Jenkins, 1999). This finding demonstrated the idea that social media users have the control and can block out marketers (Kohli et al., 2015) and seek advice from more reliable sources of information (Dwivedi, 2009; Kozinets, 2002).

4.3. Sentiments Towards Destination Image

In line with validating previous literature, the data provides an assessment of user-generated content that includes whether tourists tended to share positive or negative evaluations and beliefs about the destination. Tourists' sentiments towards a destination, which represent their satisfaction of their experience, have been recognized as positive, negative or neutral Tweets.

The sentiments towards Toronto as a destination are overwhelmingly positive. Analysis indicates that there were 1498 (78%) positive comments, while only 303 (16%) of Tweets were negative. There were 121 (6%) comments that were neutral sentiment.

The comments that evaluated the affective component of destination image were 84% positive. Considering that affective image is the most influential factor (Baloglu and McCleary, 1999), this indicates that the destination of Toronto has a favourable image to gain success. Comments made by users that referred to the affective component, used words such as 'excitement', 'enjoy', 'blessed' to describe their feelings towards the destination.

The cognitive destination image had the second most positive sentiments by users when assessing the component. More specifically, positive comments referred to the landscape of Toronto that described it as 'beautiful', 'majestically', and 'awesome'. In terms of negative comments, the greatest number of comments were about the price of Toronto, for example, 'expensive', 'not cheap', and 'can't afford'. One user Tweets, "I'm poor just to think about how much my trip to Toronto will cost." As well, there were a large number of grievances towards facilities and transportations regarding delays, unfriendly staff, and inconveniences. For example, a user Tweets about the inconvenience of lost luggage "@anonymousX1 holiday spoilt only one day in Toronto now having to sit in a room, surely you can let us know when bags will arrive." By exploring tourists' sentiments towards Toronto they can highlight their strengths and address weakness in order to build a stronger destination image.

Throughout the travel process of before, during, and after visiting the destination the findings revealed that tourists' sentiments remained relatively the same. Before visiting Toronto there were 404 positive comments, 93 negative comments and 36 neutral comments. While visiting the destination there were 561 positive comments, 94 negative comments, and 36 comments that were neutral. After visiting Toronto there were 185 positive comments and 35 negative comments and 12 neutral comments. These findings suggest that the destination image generally met the expectations of the tourists.

4.4. Tourists' Assessment of Destination Image Components

4.4.1. Cognitive Destination Image

4.4.1.1. Description

The findings found that 1092/1922 (57%) assessed the cognitive component of Toronto as indicated in Table 2. The cognitive component is related to awareness and what people know or may think they know about a destination. The cognitive component focuses on tangible and psychological attributes (Pike and Ryan, 2004). According to San Martin and Rodriguez del Basque's (2008), cognitive destination image includes traits relevant to infrastructure, socioeconomic environment, atmosphere, the natural and the cultural environment. However, findings suggest traits such as festival and events and weather are relevant factors considered by tourists when assessing the cognitive component.

Table 2. Cognitive component findings

Cognitive Sub-Category	Frequencies
Infrastructure	758
Natural Environment	209
Atmosphere	100
Cultural Heritage	25

In terms of the cognitive components there were the most comments discussing the functional dimensions than the psychological and abstract dimensions, suggesting that this is a secondary component of cognitive. This reinforces Pike and Ryan's (2004) belief that cognitive component focuses on tangible physical attributes.

4.4.1.2. Time Frame

Before: Before traveling to Toronto there were 338 comments that assessed cognitive destination. There were the most Tweets that made reference to tourist infrastructure, mainly attractions before visiting Toronto. Apart of the comments that assessed infrastructure major tourists attractions were mention. For example, one user Tweets, "Half way done work. A little sleep after that off to Toronto Canada's wonderland #vacation #roadtrip #excited @anoymousX2 @anonymousX3." The attributes of the cognitive components being evaluated by tourists in the early stages of the destination image formation process are mostly of the functional and tangible aspects. This could suggest that the psychological and abstract cognitive dimensions are not as relevant to tourists when accumulating a mental image of a destination. This suggest that the mental image does not compromise of a holistic component, which disputes the findings of Echtner and Ritchie (1993). Rather, before visiting a destination tourists primarily evaluate destination image characteristics that are directly observable or measurable and attributes that are less tangible are an afterthought.

Amongst tourist attractions it was found that festivals and events were the most tweeted about aspect, for instance Pride, Pan Am Games, concerts (e.g. Shania Twain, Madonna), and sporting events. This trait of cognitive component was found to be a significant aspect of attractions that users were tweeting about. Festivals and events attract large number of visitors and are considered to be a motivator in tourism (Getz, 2008) and an effective enhancer of destination image (Hall, 1992; Ritchie, 1984). The fact that tourists were discussing this factor at the stage before visiting Toronto could imply that festivals and events were their motivation for visiting. A dominant theme of festivals and events being discussed was specifically sporting events, such as the Pan Am Games and Blue Jay (there was no mention of Toronto FC). One user Tweets, "Hitting Toronto back up for the pan am games July 11-22 then off to Newfoundland for 2 weeks for a week of work and a week of vacation."

During: While visiting Toronto there were 508 comments made by tourists that evaluated the cognitive component. Since it is argued that actual experience effectively modifies the destination image (Gunn 1988) it is important to assess image as the result of visiting a destination. During the visitation is the time frame when tourists are tweeting the most. It was found that 45% of Tweets happened during this time. While tourists are visiting Toronto, they are evaluating the cognitive component through a modified-induce process, which is significant given that by experiencing the destination, the image becomes more realistic, complex, and differentiated (Chon 1987).

The most tweeted about destination dimension took place during visits to Toronto tourist attractions. Comments referring to attractions were 86% positive. Results showed that the three most tweeted attractions are CN Tower (infrastructure), Niagara Falls (natural environment), and the Distillery District (infrastructure). One user commented on the CN Tower tweeting, "Top of the world @CN Tower." Additionally, many references to infrastructure include the skyline of Toronto, which includes the iconic CN Tower. These comments imply that Toronto is seen as a metropolitan city, where skyscrapers are the outstanding features. In line with Echtner and Ritchie (1993), infrastructure is a part of the functional dimension that makes up the tangible attributes of a destination. These findings suggest again that on social media, tourists tend to evaluate functional attributes rather than psychological ones.

When it comes to the less tangible attributes of the destination, weather was one of the most evaluated attributes of Toronto. As such, during tourists' time in Toronto there were mixed reviews of this factor. For instance, one tourist's comments, "Lovin the weather and lovin the city! #Toronto #vacation #selfie #summer #sunglasses #sun #warm". While another user shares their grievance, "Why is it raining like crazy in Toronto and Montreal the days we come and visit!! #britishweather #holiday #summer #canada." As, Milman and Pizam (1995) suggest the environment of the destination, including the weather is an essential component of destination image. As observed, the weather has the ability to make a positive or negative experience for tourists. Before travelling to Toronto, weather was a topic of information seeking or community support (ex. "what's the weather going to be like in Toronto? Getting clothes ready?"), whereas during the trip, weather is a discussion of compliments or grievance.

After: After visiting the destination there were 246 comments made by tourists when evaluating the cognitive destination image. The findings found that tourists use social media mainly for the travel planning and visiting process rather than a source for tourists to share their modified image based on experience (Gunn, 1988). This suggests that tourists' perceptions of destination image shared online are formed through layers of information and interactions that are socially constructed (Hammett, 2014).

The comments made after visiting Toronto about the cognitive destination image made reference to the hospitality and atmosphere more than the functional attributes. As a result, tourists assess the cognitive psychological component more after visiting the destination than before and during visiting the destination.

4.4.2. Affective Destination Image

4.4.2.1. Description

It was found that 436 of comments made by tourists' evaluated the affective destination image. The affective destination image revolves around people's feelings towards the destination (Chen and Uysal, 2002; Kim and Richardson, 2003). It is argued that the affective dimension is the most influential factor of destination image (Baloglu and McCleary, 1999). However, this study found that tourists evaluate the cognitive destination image more than the affective. As a result, cognitive factors should be used more often than affective by destinations to gain success. That being said, the tourists' perspective on the affective component plays a significant role in developing destination image and had the second most comments discussing this factor.

4.4.2.2. Time Frame

Before: It has been proposed that the affective component becomes active during the evaluation of the decision-making process (Chen and Uysal, 2002; Kim and Richardson, 2003). Specifically, before travelling to the destination, the affective component is when most users comments evaluated their feelings and excitement about visiting the destination. It was found that 206 comments that evaluated affective destination image were made before visiting.

One of the main themes found was that tourists updated their status about how 'excited' they were to visit the destination. For example, one user Tweets, "So excited for Toronto on Friday." The feelings of excitement imply that the tourists are aware of attributes of the destination that they are looking forward to seeing, which proposes the bi-dimensional model that 'cognitive image' is an antecedent of 'affective image' (Gartner, 1993; Ryan and Cave, 2005).

As previously mentioned, there was a high frequency of comments that discussed affective destination image by socializing with other users. Before visiting the destination, this provided insights for users' reasons for visiting, as they were often communicating with whom they were visiting and/or with whom they were travelling. For example, one user Tweets "Can't wait for holidays with my best ones! Majorca with [user name] and Toronto with [user name] #holiday #spain #canada." Another user Tweets, "Can't wait to go on vacation to Toronto and see my best friend [user name]." This indicates that users are more willing to share their emotions when it includes their friends and family.

Before visiting Toronto, it was found that there were many users expressing desire to visit the destination. An example is one user Tweets, "Canada looks like a nice place to vacation. Wouldn't mind staying in Toronto." Therefore, tourists hold high expectations of the destination that impact the emotions of tourists (San Martin and Rodriguez del Bosque, 2008). It was found that Toronto has a positive image held by those who have yet to experience it, which is likely to influence their decision to visit the destination.

Before even visiting Toronto, there was an overwhelmingly favourable emotion towards Toronto, which perhaps influenced the tourists' decision to visits the destination. According to Gunn (1988), the first two stages (of what?) are accumulating mental images of the destination and modifying the initial image after more information. Findings revealed that before visiting Toronto, the users were expressing positive feelings, which could imply that before experiencing the destination, the tourists anticipated visiting and held a positive image of Toronto.

During: While visiting Toronto it was found that tourists were not assessing this component as often as before travelling to the destination. However, it can be argued that experiencing the destinations strengthen tourist's perception of Toronto because there were 157 more positive comments during than before. Words used to describe tourist feelings were 'love', 'excited' 'wonderful', 'awesome'. One example is, "Oh #Toronto…I have such a crush on you! #GBFling #travel #visittoronto." The comments that were made by tourists to describe their feelings towards the destination demonstrate the semantic differential scales of the affective component (Baloglu and McCleary, 1999; Pike and Ryan, 2004). However, the majority of comments tended to be on the positive scale rather than the negative spectrum.

After: After visiting Toronto, there were 57 affective comments that referred to the psychological and abstract attributes of the destination and 38 comments about the functional traits. For example, one user Tweets, "TBH I'm glad I had @anonymousX4 and @anonymousX5 when I went to Toronto. By far my fav holiday." These findings suggest that when tourists return home from a destination their feelings are strongest towards the atmosphere and hospitality of the destination rather than the tangible attributes.

Destinations often attempt to present a positive image, which isn't always seen as credible. However, tourists are become trustworthy opinion makers (Oliveira and Panyik, 2015). It was found that tourists shared a favourable experience of Toronto after visiting, which has the ability to influence the choice of not only their friends and families but Twitter users from around the world (Kladou and Mavragani, 2015). Therefore, the influence of tourist-generated content could be used to highlight the affective component of Toronto as a favourable destination image.

4.4.3. Conative Destination Image

4.4.3.1. Description

There were 394comments made by users evaluating the conative destination image. The conative component of destination image is referred to as the 'action step'. It reflects the behavioural aspect of how people act on information. The conative dimension considers the probability of tourists visiting the destination or recommending it to others (Pike and Ryan, 2004).

Previous studies link consumer behaviour to demographics. However, Baloglu (1997) found no difference in whether socio-demographic variables influence destination image. No significant findings were made here to make an inference.

4.4.3.2. Time Frame

Before: Before visiting Toronto, tourists were assessing conative behaviour on Twitter. It was found that tourist shared their decision-making process online, which took place before experiencing the destination. For instance, users were tweeting about whether they would visit Toronto or not. These comments discussed their decision to visit the destination, sharing and seeking information, stating their intentions for wanting to visit the destination. This provides practitioners and researchers deeper-insights into tourist behaviour. A consumer's decision-making process is heavily influenced by user-generated content, which has become a way to build a positive destination image (Fotis et al., 2012).

During: Tourists' behaviour towards the destination is starting to take form on social media while visiting the destination. The connotative component is the action step of destination image formation. This is recognized when tourists' comments were connected with behaviour, for example, mentioning recommendation or intentions to revisit the destination (San Martin & Rodrigues del Bosque, 2008). Since social media promises a connection between space and time, tourists are simultaneously experiencing a destination while sharing it with others and adjusting their behaviour towards the destination accordingly. Beerli and Martin (2004, p. 677) argue that, "image development must be based on reality, otherwise the destination will not succeed in satisfying the tourists, which will in turn have a negative effect on the image they will transmit by word of mouth." This finding becomes of special importance, given the influence of user-generated content on the customers' decision-making process (Jalilvand et al., 2012).

Therefore, it can be argued that since user-generated content is a form of word of mouth that influences customer's decision-making process, it is an important dimension of the connotative component. Grice (1969) theorized that one could deduce meaning in comments by examining the underlying intentions; these intentions might include to share information, seek information, offer opinions, etc. As a result, tourists are simultaneously experiencing destination image through cognitive and affective components whilst transmitting it through (eWOM), thus influencing the connotative components.

After: Perhaps the most important component after visiting a destination is the connotative component; whether the tourists will revisit Toronto and/or recommend it to others. The significance of eWOM, as discussed before, implies that these comments may influence others in their behaviour towards the destination. There were 180 comments associated with the connotative component after visiting.

The recommendations generally are of specific cognitive components rather than general recommendations to visit Toronto. An example of a recommendation by one user is "@anoymousX6 the CN Tower is definitely worth visiting especially the glass floor and Chinatown is really interesting." Another recommendation made was " "Have you ever been on a helicopter tour of #Toronto? I highly recommend it #travel #tourism." An example of intentions of revisiting the destination an individual Tweets, "Bye for now Toronto – 'Til next time. #Sunset #Toronto #YYZ #aircanada #travel #exploreCanada."

Therefore, it was found that tourists' conative behaviour after visiting a destination is connected to the cognitive destination image.

5. CONCLUSION AND RECOMMENDATIONS

This study contributes new research to the conceptualization of destination image and formation process that is facilitated through users information exchange on Twitter. Additionally, this study implements a new framework to analyse destination image on social media. Based on the research findings, practical implications and recommendations can be made for both practitioners and scholars.

It is important for destination organisations to highlight the positive and monitor grievances and take measures to address negative comments. By tracking sentiments online, destination organisations can manage dissatisfied customers. The power and reach that social media has, as well as the real-time factor, means that organisations need to immediately address any complaints in a shorter turnaround time. In addition, destination organisations need to develop an effective way to communicate and influence consumers.

This study found that tourists use social media to share their personal experiences and socialize with friends rather than as a tool to seek information. This information is important for practitioners so they can tailor and collaborate on content that is more personal to the tourists' experience. As a result, this will add value to the consumer, while building their brand through direct communication.

Moreover, this study provides a timeline of the visitation of tourists to Toronto. Consequently, it is recommended that organisations response rates need to be most efficient while tourists are visiting the destination. The findings indicate that tourists are tweeting the most while visiting a destination, therefore destinations need to be engaged with tourists while they are experiencing the destination.

This study proposes that an adaptation of the destination image formation process model (Gunn, 1988) needs to be made to assess destination image on social media. That is because social media allows tourists to simultaneously experience, share, and modify their perception of destination image during the visitation stage.

Contradicting previous studies, this research recommends that organisations should leverage the cognitive destination image to gain success. This study found that tourists are assessing the cognitive components, specifically attractions and festivals and events, more than the affective and conative components. By understanding what it is that draws tourists to a destination, practitioners are able to better attract more visitors using this information. From a scholar's perspective, this study provides new knowledge into how the cognitive component is being assessed by tourists. The results found that before visiting a destination the functional aspect of cognitive component is being assessed online more than the psychological dimensions, which weakens the holistic impressions of destination image. However, after visiting the destination the psychological, specifically atmosphere and hospitality, are being assessed more. These findings suggest that tourists consider attributes that are directly observable when forming a mental image of a destination however, after experiencing the destination, tourists evaluate cognitive destination image based on the psychological aspects.

As this study reinforces the idea that the affective component is evaluated at the decision-making stage, this finding is useful information for organisations to attract loyal customers and repeat visitors. Tourists shared favourable comments about the destination, therefore Tourism Toronto could use the user-generated content to deliver the message that they want to disseminate regarding the destination image. Consequently, organisations need to monitor user-generated content and sentiments. As discussed before, negative feelings can have a backlash on organisations. As a result, organisations need to manage and identify potential problems and build messages that positively connect with tourists' emotions.

Practitioners need to use social media as a tool to influence tourists' demands for a destination. This study found that conative behaviour is taking form online before, during, and after visiting a destination. Findings suggest that social media is changing tourists' behaviour as they are simultaneously experiencing and sharing their experience via social media, which in return affects tourists' behaviour and those that receive this eWOM communication. Therefore, organisations need to understand tourists' needs, motives, and their decision-making process. Again, organisations need to market the destination based on different market segments of tourists' behaviour.

5.1. Future Research

As part of the limitations of this study, future studies are recommended to further develop knowledge of this area of study. Foremost, this study covers a wide range of issues including destination image, types of information exchange on Twitter, time frame, demographics, and sentiments, therefore a more focussed study of a particular dimension (e.g. attractions) could be conducted to gain a deeper understanding. Further analysis of user-generated content throughout the year, and as the evaluation of destination image components over time, would provide broader understanding of the tourists' attitudes, experiences, and level of satisfaction of the destination. This study only briefly touched on the demographics of nationalities of users. There is more research needed to examine cross-cultural difference in the context of social media.

5.2. Limitations

Furthermore, this study contributes to the literature to assess destination image from the tourist's perspective online. However, there are a few limitations to acknowledge. Firstly, it is difficult to conduct demographic research on social media, specifically Twitter, since it provides limited information of gender and nationality. Also, this information isn't verified to be correct (i.e. somebody could say they are somebody they are not). Secondly, the only social media site examined was Twitter, therefore, users of other social media sites might differ in their information exchange and usage, and this may require further investigation. Thirdly, this study only collected Twitter comments from May 2015 to August 2015, this limited the number of Tweets captured. As well, it only provides a snap of tourists that visited the destination. It is possible that Tweets differ from time period, more so, from season.

REFERENCES

Akehurst, G. (2009). User generated content: The use of blogs for tourism organisations and tourism consumers. *Service Business*, *3*(1), 51–61. doi:10.100711628-008-0054-2

Alonso, S., & Fonseca, S. (2012). Immigration, left and right. *Party Politics*, *18*(6), 865–884. doi:10.1177/1354068810393265

Anderson, E. W. (1998). Customer satisfaction and word of mouth. *Journal of Service Research*, *1*(1), 5–17. doi:10.1177/109467059800100102

Ayeh, J. (2015). Travellers' acceptance of consumer-generated media: An integrated model of technology acceptance and source credibility theories. *Computers in Human Behavior*, *48*, 173–180. doi:10.1016/j.chb.2014.12.049

Baloglu, S. (1997). The relationship between destination images and sociodemo-graphic and trip characteristics of international travelers. *Journal of Vacation Marketing*, *3*(3), 221–233. doi:10.1177/135676679700300304

Baloglu, S. (1999). A Path analytic model of visitation intention involving information sources, socio-psychological motivations, and destination image. *Journal of Travel & Tourism Marketing*, *8*(3), 81–90. doi:10.1300/J073v08n03_05

Baloglu, S., & McCleary, K. (1999). A model of destination image formation. *Journal of Tourism Research*, *26*, 868–897.

Bandaranayake, T. (2012). *Understanding Research Philosophies Approaches*. Slideshare. Retrieved from http://www.slideshare.net/thusharabandaranayake/understanding-research-philosophies

Beerli, A., & Martin, J. D. (2004). Factors influencing destination image. *Journal of Tourism Research*, *31*(3), 657–681.

Bigne, E., Sanchez, I., & Sanz, S. (2009). The Functional-psychological Continuum in the Cognitive Image of a Destination: A Confirmatory Analysis. *Tourism Management*, *30*(5), 1–9.

Blaxter, L., Hughes, C., & Tight, M. (2010). *How to research*. Maidenhead: Open University Press.

Bryman, A., & Bell, E. (2011). *Business Research Methods* (3rd ed.). Oxford: Oxford University Press.

Chai, S., & Kim, M. (2010). What makes bloggers share knowledge? An investigation on the role of trust. *International Journal of Information Management*, *30*(5), 408–415. doi:10.1016/j.ijinfomgt.2010.02.005

Chen, J. S., & Uysal, M. (2002). Market positioning analysis: A hybrid approach. *Journals of Tourism Research*, *29*(4), 987–1003. doi:10.1016/S0160-7383(02)00003-8

Chon, K.-S. (1987). An assessment of images of Korea as a tourist destination by American tourists. *Hotel and Tourism Management Review*, *3*, 155–170.

Chung, J. Y., & Buhalis, D. (2008). Web 2.0: A Study of Online Travel Community, In O'Connor, P., Hopken, W. & Gretzel, U. (Eds.), Information and Communication Technologies in Tourism (pp. 70-81). Vienna: Springer.

Crompton, J. L. (1979). An Assessment of the Image of Mexico as a Vacation Destination and the Influence of Geographical Location Upon that Image. *Journal of Travel Research*, *17*(4), 18–23. doi:10.1177/004728757901700404

Dwivedi, M. (2009). Online destination image of India: A consumer based perspective. *International Journal of Contemporary Hospitality Management*, *21*(2), 226–232. doi:10.1108/09596110910935714

Echtner, C. M., & Ritchie, J. R. B. (1993). The measurement of destination image: An empirical assessment. *Journal of Travel Research*, *31*(4), 3–13. doi:10.1177/004728759303100402

Fotis, J., Buhalis, D., & Rossides, N. (2012). Social media use and impact during the holiday travel planning process. In Fuchs, M., Ricci, F., & Cantoni, L., (Eds.), Information and communication technologies in tourism (pp. 13–24). Vienna: Springer. doi:10.1007/978-3-7091-1142-0_2

Gartner, W. (1993). Image formation process. In M. Uysal & D.R. Fesenmaier (Eds.), Communication and channel systems in tourism marketing (pp. 191–215). Routledge.

Getz, D. (2008). Event Tourism: Definition, Evolution, and Research. *Tourism Management*, *29*(3), 403–428. doi:10.1016/j.tourman.2007.07.017

Govers, R., Go, F. M., & Kumar, K. (2007). Virtual destination image a new measurement approach. *Journals of Tourism Research*, *34*(4), 977–997. doi:10.1016/j.annals.2007.06.001

Gretzel, U., & Yoo, K. (2008). Use and impact of online travel reviews. In: O'Connor, P., Höpken, W., & Gretzel, U. (Eds.), Information and Communication Technologies in Tourism (pp. 35–46). Vienna: Springer. doi:10.1007/978-3-211-77280-5_4

Grice, H. P. (1969). Utterer's Meaning and Intentions. *The Philosophical Review*, *78*(2), 86–116. doi:10.2307/2184179

Gunn, C. (1988). *Vacationscapes: Designing Tourist Regions*. New York: Van Vostrand Reinhold.

Hall, C. M. (1992). *Hallmark Tourist Events: Impacts, Management, and Planning*. London: Belhaven Press.

Hammett, D. (2014). Tourism Images and British Media Representations of South Africa. *Tourism Geographies*, *16*(2), 221–236. doi:10.1080/14616688.2012.762688

Hersberger, J. A., Murray, A. L., & Rioux, K. S. (2007). Examining information exchange and virtual communities: An emergent framework. *Online Information Review*, *31*(2), 135–147. doi:10.1108/14684520710747194

Hsu, C. L., & Lin, J. C. C. (2008). Acceptance of blog usage: The roles of technology acceptance, social influence and knowledge sharing motivation. *Information & Management*, *45*(1), 65–74. doi:10.1016/j.im.2007.11.001

Iwashita, C. (2006). Media Representation of the UK as a Destination for Japanese Tourists: Popular Culture and Tourism. *Tourist Studies*, *6*(1), 59–77. doi:10.1177/1468797606071477

Jalilvand, M. R., Samiei, N., Dini, B., & Manzari, P. Y. (2012). Examining the structural relationships of electronic word of mouth, destination image, tourist attitude toward destination and travel intention: An integrated approach. *Journal of Destination Marketing & Management*, *1*(1-2), 134–143. doi:10.1016/j.jdmm.2012.10.001

Jansen, B. J., Zhang, M., Sobel, K., & Chowdury, A. (2009). Twitter power: Tweets as electronic word of mouth. *Journal of the American Society for Information Science and Technology*, *60*(9), 1–20.

Jenkins, O. H. (1999). Understanding and measuring tourist destination images. *International Journal of Tourism Research*, *1*(1), 1–15. doi:10.1002/(SICI)1522-1970(199901/02)1:1<1::AID-JTR143>3.0.CO;2-L

Kim, H., & Richardson, S. L. (2003). Motion picture impacts on destination images. *Annals of Tourism Research*, *30*(1), 216–237. doi:10.1016/S0160-7383(02)00062-2

Kladou, S., & Mavragani, E. (2015). Assessing destination image: An online marketing approach and the case of TripAdvisor. *Journal of Destination Marketing & Management*, *4*(3), 187–193. doi:10.1016/j.jdmm.2015.04.003

Kohli, C., Suri, R., & Kapoor, A. (2015). Will Social Media Kill Branding? *Business Horizons*, *58*(1), 35–44. doi:10.1016/j.bushor.2014.08.004

Kozinets, R. V. (1997). 'I want to believe': A netnography of the X-Philes' subculture of consumption. *Advances in Consumer Research. Association for Consumer Research (U. S.)*, *24*, 470–475.

Kozinets, R. V. (1998). On netnography: Initial reflections on consumer research investigations of cyberculture. *Advances in Consumer Research. Association for Consumer Research (U. S.)*, *25*, 366–371.

Kozinets, R. V. (2002). The field behind the screen: Using netnography for marketing research in online communities. *JMR, Journal of Marketing Research*, *39*(February), 61–72. doi:10.1509/jmkr.39.1.61.18935

Lange-Faria, W., & Elliot, S. (2012). Understanding the role of social media in destination marketing *Tourism:* An International Multidisciplinary. *Journal of Tourism*, *7*(1), 193–211.

Lim, Y., Chung, Y., & Weaver, P. A. (2012). The Impact of Social Media on Destination Branding. *Journal of Vacation Marketing*, *18*(3), 197–206. doi:10.1177/1356766712449366

Matloka, J., & Buhalis, D. (2010). Destination marketing through user personalised content (UPC). In U. Gretzel, R. Law, & M. Fuchs (Eds.), Information and Communication Technologies in Tourism (pp. 519-530). Vienna: Springer.

McDonnell, M. & Shiri, A. (2011). Social search: a taxonomy of, and a user-centred approach to, social web search. *Program: electronic library and information systems*, *45*(1), 6-28.

Milman, A., & Pizam, A. (1995). The Role of the Awareness and Familiarity with a Destination: The Central Florida Case. *Journal of Travel Research*, *33*(3), 21–27. doi:10.1177/004728759503300304

Morgan, N., Pritchard, A., & Pride, R. (2004). *Destination branding: Creating the unique destination proposition*. Routledge.

Munar, A. M. (2011). Tourist-created Content: Rethinking Destination Branding. *International Journal of Culture, Tourism and Hospitality Research*, *5*(3), 291–305. doi:10.1108/17506181111156989

O'Connor, P. (2008). User-generated content and travel: a case study on Tripadvisor.Com. In P. O'Connor, W. Hopken, & U. Gretzel (Eds.), Information and Communication Technologies in Tourism (pp. 47-58). Vienna: Springer.

Oliveira, E., & Panyik, E. (2015). Content, context and co-creation: Digital challenges in destination branding with references to Portugal as a tourist destination. *Journal of Vacation Marketing*, *21*(1), 53–74. doi:10.1177/1356766714544235

Ong, E. Y. L., Ang, R. P., Ho, J. C. M., Lim, J. C. Y., Goh, D. H., Lee, C. S., & Chua, A. Y. K. (2011). Narcissism, extraversion and adolescents' self-presentation on Facebook. *Personality and Individual Differences*, *50*(2), 180–185. doi:10.1016/j.paid.2010.09.022

Pike, S., & Ryan, C. (2004). Destination positioning analysis through a comparison of cognitive, affective, and conative perceptions. *Journal of Travel Research*, *42*(4), 333–342. doi:10.1177/0047287504263029

Ritchie, J. R. B. (1984). Assessing the impacts of hallmark events: Conceptual and research issues. *Journal of Travel Research*, *23*(1), 2–11. doi:10.1177/004728758402300101

Rosen, C. (2007). Virtual friendship and the new narcissism. *New Atlantis (Washington, D.C.), 17*(Summer), 15–31.

Ryan, C., & Cave, J. (2005). Structuring destination image. A qualitative approach. *Journal of Travel Research, 44*(2), 143–150. doi:10.1177/0047287505278991

San Martin, H., & Rodriguez del Bosque, I. A. (2008). Exploring the cognitive– affective nature of destination image and the role of psychological factors in its formation. *Tourism Management, 29*(2), 263–277. doi:10.1016/j.tourman.2007.03.012

Sreenivasan, N. D., Lee, C. S., & Goh, D. H.-L. (2012). Tweeting the Friendly Skies: Investigating Information Exchange among Twitter Users about Airlines. *Program: Electronic Library and Information Systems, 46*(1), 21–42. doi:10.1108/00330331211204548

Stemler, S. (2001). An Overview of Content Analysis. *Practical Assessment, Research and Evaluation.* Pareonline. Retrieved from http://pareonline.net/getvn.asp?v=7&n=17

Stepchenkova, S., & Morrison, A. M. (2006). The destination image of Russia: From the online induced perspective. *Tourism Management, 27*(5), 943–956. doi:10.1016/j.tourman.2005.10.021

Twitter. (2015a). *Company About.* Retrieved from https://about.Twitter.com/company

Twitter. (2015b). *Getting Started with Twitter.* Retrieved from https://support.Twitter.com/articles/215585

Twitter. (2015c). *Using Hashtags on Twitter.* Retrieved from https://support.Twitter.com/articles/49309

Twitter. (2015d). *Twitter Privacy Policy.* Retrieved from https://Twitter.com/privacy?lang=en

Veal, A. J. (2011). *Research Methods for Leisure and Tourism: A Practical Guide (4th ed.).* Harlow: Pearson Education/Financial Times Prentice Hall.

Virkus, S. (2008). Use of Web 2.0 technologies in LIS education: experiences at Tallinn University, Estonia. *Program: electronic library and information systems, 42*(3), 262-74.

Walden, P., Carlsson, C., & Papageorgiou, A. (2011). Travel information search – the presence of social media. *Proceedings of the 44th Hawaii International Conference on System Sciences.* IEEE Computer Society. 10.1109/HICSS.2011.458

Xiang, Z., & Gretzel, U. (2009). Role of social media in online travel information search. *Tourism Management, 31*(2), 179–188. doi:10.1016/j.tourman.2009.02.016

Zeng, B., & Gerritsen, R. (2014). What do we know about social media in tourism? A review. *Tourism Management Perspectives, 10*(April), 27–36. doi:10.1016/j.tmp.2014.01.001

Zheng, X., & Gretzel, U. (2010). Role of social media in online travel information search. *Tourism Management, 31*(2), 179–188. doi:10.1016/j.tourman.2009.02.016

This research was previously published in the International Journal of Customer Relationship Marketing and Management (IJCRMM), 11(2); pages 1-16, copyright year 2020 by IGI Publishing (an imprint of IGI Global).

Section 5
Organizational and Social Implications

Chapter 57

An Empirical Evaluation of Adoption and Diffusion of New ICTs for Knowledge Sharing in IT Organizations

Srinivasan Vaidyanathan

VIT Business School, VIT University, Chennai, India

Sudarsanam S. Kidambi

VIT Business School, VIT University, Chennai, India

ABSTRACT

This article describes how knowledge is one of the most important assets in organizations which should be carefully managed and is continuously generated throughout an organization. Knowledge sharing is a process through which, one person is affected by the experiences of another. This involves more than simply acquiring or transmitting knowledge from one party to another, but is a process of exchanging and processing knowledge in a way that knowledge of one person can be integrated and used in by another person. Plenty of studies on knowledge sharing have been examined by numerous companies. However, not many empirical studies have been conducted in accordance with the framed model of ICT as a determinant and sharing of knowledge through social media within IT companies. This empirical study is aimed at identifying the critical ICT factors for enriching the knowledge sharing among employees through social media in IT organizations. The expected outcome of this study will be analyzing and establishing the causal relationships between the ICT influencing factors and knowledge sharing through social media.

INTRODUCTION

Knowledge sharing generates opportunities for an organization to maximize its capabilities and produces solutions and efficiencies that provide a business with a competitive advantage (Reid, 2003). Knowledge

DOI: 10.4018/978-1-7998-9020-1.ch057

sharing can be defined as a social interaction culture, encompassing the exchange of employee knowledge, experiences, and skills within the entire department or across various departments of the organization. Knowledge sharing embraces a set of shared understandings that are related to providing employees, access to relevant information and developing and leveraging knowledge networks within organizations (Hogel et al., 2003). Moreover, knowledge sharing occurs at the individual and organizational levels. From an individual employee perspective, knowledge sharing is communicating to other fellow colleagues to help them perform something better, more effectively, or more efficiently. At an organization level, knowledge sharing is capturing, organizing, reusing, and transferring experience-based knowledge that resides within and making that knowledge available to others in the business. Many a number of prior researches, have demonstrated that knowledge sharing is indispensable to organizations, because it supports them to enhance their innovation performance and cut down redundant learning efforts (Calantone et al., 2002; Scarbrough, 2003).

Knowledge is experience or information that can be transferred or disseminated. Knowledge, while made up of data and information, can be regarded of as much greater understanding of relationships, a situation, causal phenomena, and the rules and theories (both explicit and implicit) that underlie a given domain or problem. It is part of every business process. Therefore, the organizations in IT industry are supposed to build strengths and break barriers in establishing the participative environment of knowledge sharing to increase their efficiency and be more proactive in delivering utmost quality of work. Also IT corporates need to unearth the exact mechanisms by which knowledge and learning are institutionalized and embedded in corporate memory. They can successfully foster a knowledge sharing culture not only by promptly incorporating knowledge in its business strategy, but also by influencing positive employee attitudes and behaviors that will encourage willingness to share knowledge and be consistent in sharing knowledge (Connelly and Kelloway, 2003 & Lin and Lee, 2004). Furthermore, several past researches focused on the relationship between knowledge sharing enablers and processes (Van den Hooff and Van Weenen, 2004a, 2004b; Bock et al., 2005; Yeh et al., 2006), while others have focused on the relationship between knowledge sharing enablers and innovation performance (Calantone et al., 2002 & Syed-Ikhsan and Rowland, 2004).

However, there is inadequacy of empirical evidences that support and strengthen the critical concepts in ICT and Knowledge Sharing areas. This paper is targeted at empirically evaluating ICT as a key enabler of knowledge sharing through Social Media in IT industry. The research model that was followed is depicted in Figure 1.

MATERIALS AND METHODS

Materials (Literature Review)

Knowledge can be considered from several perspectives - as a state of mind, an object, a process, a condition of having access to information and a capability. First and foremost, the standpoint on knowledge being looked up as a state of mind, there is a distinctive focus on ever-increasing individual's personal knowledge, so individuals can effectively and efficiently apply it to the organization's requirements. Using the lens of knowledge as an object, knowledge can stand outside of human action, in which case storing, retrieving and manipulating it is feasible. Providing the viewpoint of knowledge as a process, there is a greater importance on applying the amassed expertise. It theorizes that knowledge and human action do not exist individually. Painting the picture as knowledge viewed as a condition of access to information provides for a logical extension to the object point of view. This view imparted that organizational knowledge must be organized in such a way that it is accessible and retrievable easily. The last and final perspective on knowledge when viewed as a capability, emphasizes that knowledge has the capability to influence future action (Wu and Zhu, 2012).

Figure 1. Research model

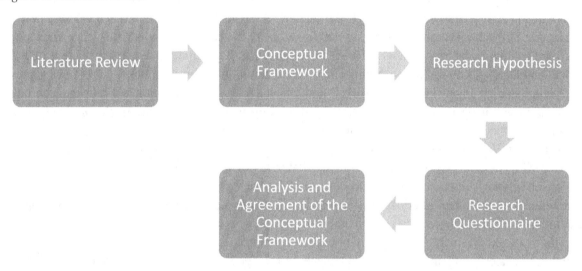

Srinivasan Vaidyanathan & Sudarsanam (2017) purported that centralized sets of repositories, organized around established business processes is the focus of Knowledge management (KM) systems today. They can be seen as a huge overhead and are expensive to implement. Most importantly the long-term commitment of the major resources of their deployment, maintenance, and daily operation is not sustainable. Consequently, even tailor-made solutions end up going unused, with the knowledge workers, being the custodians, and maintaining these custom KM solutions not having the Information Technology (IT) tools to provide support for their responsibilities. Rooted on these underutilized KM systems, the persistent evolution of Social Media technologies is providing a collaboration based KM solution which is state-of-the-art (Levy,2009). Social networking technologies provide immediate and alternative solutions to the large investments for the deployment, maintenance, and daily operations for today's Knowledge Management systems (Burrus, 2010; Diehl, Grabill, Hart-Davidson & Iyer, 2008). It is time for organizations to start looking at tomorrow's knowledge management solution and realize this new solution is a more efficient and effective model for today's enterprise knowledge management systems.

In the twenty-first century, knowledge emerged through interaction among employees and was meant to be a central part of continuous learning in organizations. (Szulanski, 2000) in due course defined this as "Organization Learning Theory", which is prevalently known in the current world. However, Nonaka (1994), formed the "Dynamic Theory of Knowledge Creation" one of the most renowned theories in the field of Knowledge Management. This theory acted as a linchpin for an influential and comprehensive academic basis on how to conceptualize the entire knowledge creation process which later rose to fame as the SECI model. In this model, Knowledge Sharing played a pivotal role for all knowledge conversions to succeed within the four modes of conversion, namely, Socialization, Externalization, Combination, and Internalization (Nonaka, 1994). Nonaka (1994) argued that the individual and organizational commitment was ultimately instrumental to the success of knowledge sharing. Research tradition in the 90s also emphasized on the technological aspect of KM where more focus was given on the KM systems (Gray, 2000).

IT can be defined as telecommunication systems, computers and software. It is believed that organizing, transmitting, storing and using many data and information at low cost, high-speed and with multiple deployments can be delivered through IT (Miranda & Tarapanoff, 2008). Empirical research tradition shows that IT has been studied in many researches as one of the key factors which influence knowledge sharing (Tohidinia and Mosakhani, 2010, Al-Ma'aitah, 2008, Tian et al., 2009; Al-Alawi et al., 2007). Sohail and Daud (2009) suggested thatinformation and communication technology (ICT) may improve knowledge sharing among knowledge workers and enhance access to information and knowledge through eliminating provisional and spatial barriers. Modern information and telecommunication technology facilitate knowledge sharing without taking into account time and distance.

Srinivasan Vaidyanathan& Sudarsanam (2017) observed that social media can be instrumental for tacit knowledge sharing through interaction and collaborative technology in business organizations. Their review on scholarly researches and evidences reveal that the knowledge is trapped in information silos as in emails or on human minds in the form of implicit knowledge. Either knowledge is not properly captured, codified and disseminated with others or knowledge is evaporated when a project is completed and the team gets dismantled. This lacuna becomes manifold in a virtual or distributed organization which is prevalent in IT industry. They advocate knowledge sharing through a suite of Social Media tools that could be used by IT corporates with a view to instill knowledge sharing among its employees. One must do a careful and balanced selection of such tools taking into consideration of their strengths and weaknesses.

Akhavan et al. (2012) attempted to test the relationship between Knowledge Sharing and Knowledge Creation. They applied the three mechanisms suggested by Sa'enz et al. (2009) as dimensions of knowledge sharing and the SECI model articulated by Nonaka and Takeuchi (1995) was used for knowledge creation. Sa'enz et al. (2009) in their research in the field of knowledge sharing and innovation performance suggested day-to-day management processes, IT-based knowledge sharing and people-focused knowledge sharing asthe three ways of sharing knowledge in organizations. While Sa'enzet al. (2009) examined the relation of knowledge sharing mechanisms with innovation, the study of Akkavan et al. (2012) was concentrated to study these mechanisms in relation to knowledge creation stages. Among the three mechanisms, namely, day-to-day management processes, IT and people focused knowledge sharing, the mechanism of importance to the current study is on IT.

Kokanuch and Tuntrabundit (2014) disclosed that knowledge sharing aspect can be illustrated by which organizational workers exchange, collaboratively create their knowledge, and amalgamate it into organizational knowledge. This study focused on three areas of knowledge sharing ability: dimensions of knowledge sharing competency, the antecedents of knowledge sharing in an organizational background, and their results that were built upon the review of earlier empirical studies. Three dimensions of knowledge sharing capability (i.e., knowledge sharing readiness, richness interchanging knowledge, and continuous knowledge integration) were accordingly developed for this study. It was concluded that knowledge sharing effects were analyzed by richness in knowledge sharing success and organizational performances. These three dimensions of knowledge sharing capability are of critical importance to the current study.

Within the scope of this study, "Adoption" implies that the selection of ICTs, that are chosen with a fine distinction of "new" and "path-breaking", for use by individuals and departments within IT organizations. "Diffusion" denotes the widespread implementation and application of such new ICTs for sharing knowledge within the IT organizations. Knowledge sharing using Social Media is defined as an effort to use tools that include Social Networking Sites, blogs, microblogs, chats, forums, communities, internet / intranet based interactivity and web tools like Wikis, applications to make voice / video calls like Skype for Business etc that enable participation, conversation, sharing and creation of knowledge among the fellow colleagues. The knowledge sharing literature has identified a wide range of factors that influence knowledge sharing behavior. These factors could be summarized into three broad dimensions - management processes, ICT and People Focused. However, this study is designed to seek the ICT factors that influence the behavior to share knowledge using social media.

Methods

Taking into consideration of the critical literature review of selected papers and the research framework, mostly based on Akhavan et al. (2012) & Kokanuch and Tuntrabundit (2014) studies, a survey questionnaire was designed with the help of previous research on ICT and Knowledge Sharing Capability dimensions as well as getting the mindshare of professional experts in the Knowledge Management discipline.

To assess the ICT factors of knowledge sharing and knowledge sharing using social media capability dimensions, survey respondents were asked to indicate the degree of various practices in their firms using a five-point Likert scale (1 = very low to 5 =very high). This research aimed to measure level of the two main variables, namely ICT and knowledge sharing and their relationship in the IT industry. The questionnaire consisted of two sections: The first section was intended tocollect socio-demographic information about the respondents. The second section involved 7 questions related to research variables as shown in Table 1.

The questionnaire was pre-tested with 10 experts in IT industry to evaluate the questionnaire's validity with regard to clarity, bias, ambiguous questions, and relevance to the business environment and operations of their respective companies. After pre-testing and revising, the survey instrument was distributed to200 respondents in IT industry, through an online survey tool, in which 154 questionnaires were completed and submitted. Only those IT companies at Chennai that had organizational practices of knowledge sharing through social media were selected as sample organizations for research. The response rate of questionnaires was 77%.

RESULTS AND DISCUSSION

Socio-Demographics of research respondents show that 56% of the sample were of age group > 35 years and about 64% were > 10 years of experience in IT industry. The profile of the research respondents were almost all at Middle to Senior levels with only a sparse 2.6% at Junior levels. Most of the research sample had Bachelor's degree and above with only a negligible 0.6% holding a Diploma certificate. A view of the Socio-Demographics of the research sample is provided in Table 2& 3:

Table 1. Survey questionnaire

	ICT	1	2	3	4	5
ICT_0001	Information Technologies are used to update and review data; and facilitate communication with other departments.	Strongly Disagree	Disagree	Neutral	Agree	Strongly Agree
ICT_0002	Individuals use social media to interact with one another.	Strongly Disagree	Disagree	Neutral	Agree	Strongly Agree
ICT_0003	Individuals use intranet network to transfer their information.	Strongly Disagree	Disagree	Neutral	Agree	Strongly Agree
ICT_0004	Systems and software that contribute to sharing information exist across the company.	Strongly Disagree	Disagree	Neutral	Agree	Strongly Agree
	Knowledge Sharing through Social Media	**1**	**2**	**3**	**4**	**5**
KS_SM_0001	Knowledge Sharing Readiness	Unsatisfactory	Fair	Satisfactory	Good	Excellent
KS_SM_0002	Richness in exchanging Knowledge	Unsatisfactory	Fair	Satisfactory	Good	Excellent
KS_SM_0003	Continuous Knowledge Integration	Unsatisfactory	Fair	Satisfactory	Good	Excellent

Table 2. Socio-demographics – AGE group and total years of service in IT

AGE Group (Years):		Frequency	Percent	Total years of service in IT:	Frequency	Percent
	<= 25	11	7.1	<= 5	23	14.9
	26-35	56	36.4	6-10	33	21.4
	> 35	87	56.5	> 10	98	63.6
	Total	154	100.0	Total	154	100.0

Table 3. Socio-demographics – education level and profile

	Education Level:	Frequency	Percent	Profile:	Frequency	Percent
	Diploma / Certificate	1	.6	Junior	4	2.6
	Bachelors' Degree	64	41.6	Middle	78	50.6
	Masters' Degree & Above	88	57.1	Senior	72	46.8
	Total	153	99.4	Total	154	100.0
Missing	System	1	.6			
Total		154	100.0			

Cronbach alpha values range from 0 to 1 and in social sciences; values approaching 1 denote very high reliability and internal consistency of research instrument. The preferred value is above 0.7 (Nunally, 1978). The Cronbach alpha of the questionnaire was measured for ICT and Knowledge Sharing through Social Media respectively, which validates their high reliability. Table 4 shows the reliability of ICT and knowledge sharing through Social Media questionnaire.

Table 4. Reliability statistics

	ICT	Knowledge Sharing Through Social Media
Cronbach's Alpha	0.831	0.926

Conceptual Model

As mentioned earlier, the prime focus of this research is to evaluate the impact and the influential relationship between ICT factors and knowledge sharing through social media.

Figure 2. Conceptual model

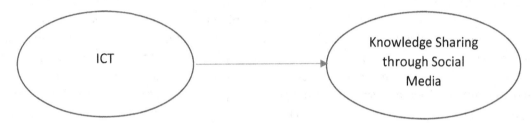

With reference to the conceptual model represented in Figure 2, the objective of this research was to empirically test the impact of ICT factors on knowledge sharing through social media and establish the influential relationship among them. The independent variable, ICT, was taken from Akhavan et al. (2012) research on the three mechanisms of knowledge sharing and ICT was one among them. The dependent variable, knowledge sharing through social media, was taken up based on the research by Kokanuch and Tuntrabundit (2014) on the three dimensions of knowledge sharing capability and all the three dimensions were taken into study. As a result of these relationship, the hypothesis of research for empirical testing is given below.

H1: ICT has a positive effect on Knowledge Sharing through Social Media
H0: ICT has no effect on Knowledge Sharing through Social Media

Data Analysis and Research Findings

To determine the sample size required for Confirmatory Factor Analysis, unfortunately, there is no easy way. There are some very rough guidelines for sample sizes. A broad brush painting of sample sizes would be that less than 100 is considered "small" and may only be appropriate for very simple models; 100 to 200 is "medium" and may be an acceptable minimum sample size if the model is not too complex; and greater than 200 is "large", which is probably acceptable for most models (Kline, 2005). Sample size of 154 is an acceptable minimum given the model assumed is straight forward and not too complex. Table 5 provides a summary of the Descriptive Statistics of the research sample.

Table 5. Descriptive statistics

	N	Minimum	Maximum	Mean	Std. Deviation
Information Technologies are used to update and review data; and facilitate communication with other departments.	154	1.00	5.00	3.7338	.89327
Individuals use social media to interact with one another.	154	1.00	5.00	3.2857	1.05232
Individuals use intranet network to transfer their information.	154	1.00	5.00	3.5974	1.00664
Systems and software that contribute to sharing information exist across the company.	154	1.00	5.00	3.6753	1.02825
Knowledge Sharing Readiness.	154	1.00	5.00	3.3831	1.03025
Richness in exchanging Knowledge.	154	1.00	5.00	3.2532	1.08201
Continuous Knowledge Integration.	154	1.00	5.00	3.1169	1.12574

From Table 5, it was noted that the minimum observed rating was "Strongly Disagree" and the maximum observed rating was "Strongly Agree" for the "ICT" variable and all the measurement items underneath. Also, it was interpreted that the Mean of all the "ICT" measurement items indicate that the majority of respondents opted to be "Neutral" to "Agree". Similarly, it was noted that the minimum observed rating was "Unsatisfactory" and the maximum observed rating was "Excellent" for the "Knowledge Sharing Through Social Media" variable and all the measurement items underneath. Also, it was interpreted that the Mean of all the "Knowledge Sharing Through Social Media" measurement items indicate that the majority of respondents opted to be "Satisfactory" to "Good". The Standard Deviation was observed to be relatively small hovering around 1 for both variables. It implied that the values in the dataset are normally distributed, pretty closely clustered around the mean, and with relatively few values tended to assume the extreme highs or lows.

SPSS AMOS 22.0 statistical software was used to examine the research hypothesis stated before. Confirmatory Factor Analysis was conducted to determine the ability of a predefined factor model to fit an observed set of data. Prior to validating the full structural model with all latent variables, it was required to validate the measurement model as a preliminary step. The measurement model deals with the latent variables and thei rindicators and is an integral part of SEM model. Like any other SEM model, the measurement model was evaluated for validity, using standard goodness of fit measures. Maximum likelihood (ML) estimation method was used in all analysis using AMOS 22. Maximum likelihood "aims to find the parameter values that make the observed data most likely (or conversely maximize the likelihood of the parameters given the data)" (Brown, 2006).The measurement model evaluated is given in Figure 3.

The 4 indicator variable model of "ICT" dimension was suggesting poor fitting model in the first estimate. The RMSEA was above the permissible level. On verification of modification indices, indicator variables "ICT_0004" was showing cross loadings to 1 other variable and was found to be a major cause for poor fit and hence were removed. A second estimate of "ICT" model showed good fit post the removal of "ICT_0004". The 3 indicator variable model "KS_SM" was suggesting good fit at the first stage. The resulting confirmatory measurement model was found to be a good fit with recommended indices as illustrated below in structural model. All the paths shown in the model are significant as critical ratio were above 1.96.

Figure 3. Measurement model

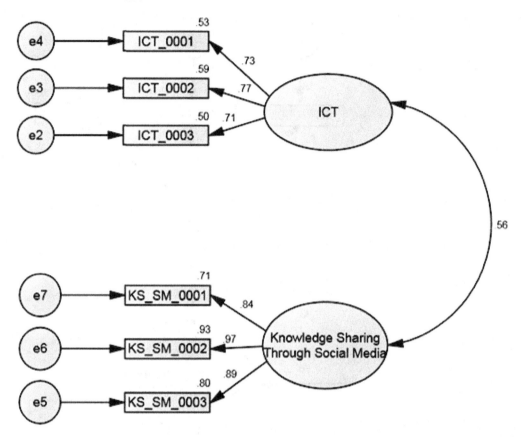

Then, validity of conceptual model and the relationship between ICT and knowledge sharing through social media was examined through Structural equation modeling. Figure 4 below depicts the output of research hmodel which accepted the relationship between variables. All model fit indices were in acceptable range.

The results of path analysis for the structural model is portrayed in Table 6.

It can be seen from Table 6 that the Standardized Regression Coefficient of ICT being 0.561 represents the effect of ICT on Knowledge Sharing through Social Media, holding other variables as constant. The p value is significant at 0.1% level. Hence the null hypothesis "H0: ICT has no effect on Knowledge Sharing through Social Media" is rejected.

The positive coefficient implies that for every 1 unit-increase in ICT, there will be 0.561 unit-increase in Knowledge Sharing through Social Media. Therefore, the alternative hypothesis "H1: ICT has a positive effect on knowledge sharing through social media" is accepted.

The model was examined along with following model-fit indices and error term magnitude estimates: General CMIN / df estimates, Goodness-of-fit index (GFI), Adjusted Goodness-of-fit index (AGFI), Normal Fit Index(NFI), Comparative fit index (CFI), Root Mean Square Residual (RMR) and Root Mean Square Error of Approximation (RMSEA).Fit statistics greater than or equal to .90 for GFI, NFI, and CFI indicate a good model fit (Bagozzi &Yi, 1988) and for RMSEA values ranging from .06 to.10 reflect acceptable to mediocre fit (Browneand Cudeck, 1993).

Figure 4. Structural model

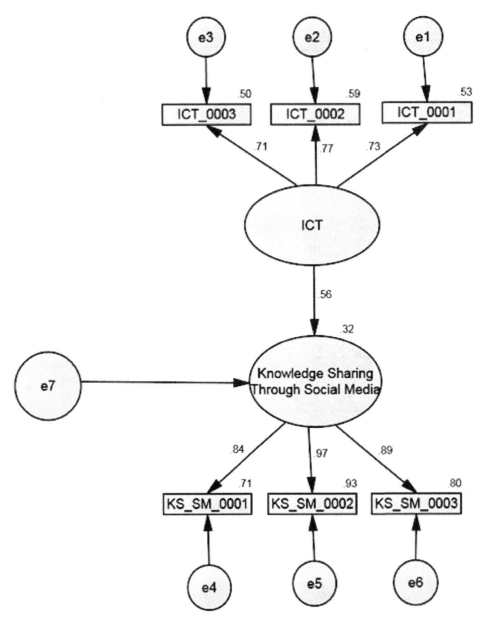

From the Major Model Fit Indices Summary shown in Table 7, the model fits indices were all found to be in statistically acceptable ranges. In addition, RMR indicated an appropriate model-data fit and RMSEA showed acceptable model fit.

Considering the validity of the path analysis and credibility of model indices, the conceptual model was adopted thus the positive influential relationship between the independent and dependent variable in conceptual model was substantiated.

Table 6. Path analysis (SEM)

Path	UE	SE	p value
Knowledge Sharing through Social Media <- ICT	0.868	0.561	***
ICT_0003 <- ICT	1.099	0.71	***
ICT_0002 <- ICT	1.238	0.765	***
ICT_0001 <- ICT	1	0.728	
KS_SM_0003 <- KSSM	1	0.894	
KS_SM_0002 <- KSSM	1.039	0.966	***
KS_SM_0001 <- KSSM	0.861	0.841	***

Table 7. Major model fit indices summary

Parameters	Acceptable values for Good Fit	Research Model values
CMIN/df	< 3.5	1.547
GFI	>0.9	0.974
AGFI	>0.9	0.931
NFI	>0.9	0.978
CFI	>0.9	0.992
RMR	<0.10	0.041
RMSEA	<0.06	0.060

CONCLUSION

This paper focuses mainly on the relationship of ICT as a key knowledge sharing mechanism with knowledge sharing capability dimensions through social media. This study concentrated on examining this influential relationship between ICT and knowledge sharing through social media in IT Companies within Chennai. Knowledge management and its role in the IT industry has been prevalent, however, new ICTs like social media for knowledge sharing is an emerging concept which have recently given renewed focus to the business strategies of the IT companies giving them competitive advantages.

Statistical results in this study proved that ICT has a positive impact on knowledge sharing through social media. IT Companies, by virtue of its very nature, should foster newer Information and Communication Technologies like Social Media to update and review data and facilitate communication with other departments. Within their internet / intranet networks, they will need to increasingly "adopt" tools that are in the spectrum of new ICTs, such as Social Networking Sites, Blogs, Wikis, Skype for Business etc, to name a few, but are not limited to, for use by its employees. Such a strong and committed advocacy by IT organizations will ensure "diffusion" of such tools for widespread participation, sharing and creation of knowledge among employees.

Having utmost capability dimensions of knowledge sharing readiness, richness of exchanging knowledge and integration of continuous knowledge, Social Media tools on IT companies' internet / intranet networks will motivate employees to "diffuse" such tools to interact with one another and transfer information and knowledge. Observed results of this study suggest that the IT companies may increasingly leverage new ICTs like Social Media for knowledge sharing which would place them in the leading edge of the market. Such an investment in knowledge management initiatives may benefit the companies in its sustenance of business and growth, with benefits outweighing the costs of such investments.

This research article contributes to the literature and research tradition on knowledge sharing using social media. This empirical study has attempted to establish the positive influential relationship and established the conduit between the key characteristics of ICTs and Knowledge Sharing, looking through the lens of Social Media, in IT industries.

FURTHER RESEARCH

Further research studies may be conducted in other non-service or core business industries to compare the results. This cross-sectional study can be carried out at different vantage points in time in future to test and validate the observed results. Also, future researches may carry out this study in other geographies and countries, in order to check the position of ICT and knowledge sharing in such regions.

REFERENCES

Akhavan, P., Ghojavand, S., & Roghayeh, A. (2012). Knowledge sharing and its impact on knowledge creation. *Journal of information and knowledge management*, *11*(2), 101-113.

Al-Ma'aitah, M. (2008). Using Electronic Collaborative Media in Knowledge Sharing Phases: Case Study in Jordan Hospitals. *Education and Information Technologies*, *2*(4), 238–247.

Bagozzi, R. P., & Yi, Y. (1988). On the evaluation of structural equation models. *Journal of the Academy of Marketing Science*, *16*(1), 74–94. doi:10.1007/BF02723327

Bock, G. W., Zmud, R. W., Kim, Y. G., & Lee. (2005). Behavioral intention formation in knowledge sharing: Examining the roles of extrinsic motivators, social-psychological forces, and organizational climate. *Management Information Systems Quarterly*, *29*(1), 87–111. doi:10.2307/25148669

Brown, T. A. (2006). *Confirmatory factor analysis for applied research*. New York: Guilford Press.

Browne, M. W., & Cudeck, R. (1993). Alternative ways of assessing model fit. In K. A. Bollen & J. S. Long (Eds.), *Testing structural equation models* (pp. 136–162). Newbury Park, CA: Sage. pp.

Burrus, D. (2010). Social networks in the workplace: The risk and opportunity of Business 2.0. *Strategy and Leadership*, *38*(4), 50–54. doi:10.1108/10878571011059674

Calantone, R. J., Cavusgil, S. T., & Zhao, Y. (2002). Learning orientation, firm innovation capability, and firm performance. *Industrial Marketing Management*, *31*(6), 515–524. doi:10.1016/S0019-8501(01)00203-6

Connelly, C. E., & Kelloway, E. K. (2003). Predictors of employees' perceptions of knowledge sharing culture. *Leadership and Organization Development Journal*, *24*(5), 294–301. doi:10.1108/01437730310485815

Diehl, A., Grabill, J. T., Hart-Davidson, W., & Iyer, V. (2008). Grassroots: Supporting the knowledge work of everyday life. *Technical Communication Quarterly*, *17*(4), 413–434. doi:10.1080/10572250802324937

Gray, P. H. (2000). The effects of knowledge management systems on emergent teams: Towards a research model. *The Journal of Strategic Information Systems*, *9*(2/3), 175–191. doi:10.1016/S0963-8687(00)00040-8

Hogel, M., Parboteeah, K. P., & Munson, C. L. (2003). Team-level antecedents of individuals' knowledge networks. *Decision Sciences*, *34*(4), 741–770. doi:10.1111/j.1540-5414.2003.02344.x

Ismail Al-Alawi, A., Yousif Al-Marzooqi, N., & Fraidoon Mohammed, Y. (2007). Organizational culture and knowledge sharing: Critical success factors. *Knowledge Management*, *11*(2), 22–42. doi:10.1108/13673270710738898

Kline, R. B. (2005). Principles and Practice of Structural Equation Modeling (2nd ed.). New York: The Guilford Press.

Kokanuch, A., & Tuntrabundit, K. (2014). Knowledge Sharing Capability and Organizational Performance: A Theoretical Perspective. In *Proceedings of the 10th International Academic Conference*, June 3, Vienna.

Levy, M. (2009). WEB 2.0 implications on knowledge management. *Journal of Knowledge Management*, *13*(1), 120–134. doi:10.1108/13673270910931215

Lin, H.-F., & Lee, G.-G. (2004). Perceptions of senior managers toward knowledge-sharing behaviour. *Management Decision*, *42*(Issue: 1), 108–125. doi:10.1108/00251740410510181

Miranda Silvania, V., & Tarapanoff Kira, M. A. (2008). Information needs and information competencies: A case study of the off-site supervision of financial institutions in Brazil. *Information Systems*, *13*(2), 1–24.

Nonaka, I. (1994). A Dynamic Theory of Organizational Knowledge Creation. *Organization Science*, *5*(1), 14–37. doi:10.1287/orsc.5.1.14

Nonaka, I., & Takeuchi, H. (1995). *The Knowledge-Creating Company: How Japanese Companies Create the Dynamics of Innovation*. New York: Oxford University Press.

Reid, F. (2003). Creating a knowledge-sharing culture among diverse business units. *Employment Relations Today*, *30*(3), 43–49. doi:10.1002/ert.10097

Sa'enz, J., Aramburu, N., & Rivera, O. (2009). Knowledge sharing and innovation performance A comparison between high-tech and low-tech companies'. *Intellectual Capital*, *10*(1), 22–36. doi:10.1108/14691930910922879

Scarbrough, H. (2003). Knowledge management, HRM and the innovation process. *International Journal of Manpower*, *24*(5), 501–516. doi:10.1108/01437720310491053

Sohail M.S., and Daud, S. (2009). Knowledge sharing in higher education institutions Perspectives from Malaysia. *Information and knowledge management systems*, Vol.39 No. 2, pp.125-142.

Srinivasan, V. & Sudarsanam, S.K. (2017). Social Media in Knowledge Management. In N. Raghavendra Rao (Ed.), *Social Media Listening and Monitoring for Business Applications* (pp. 94–114). PA: IGI Global; doi:10.4018/978-1-5225-0846-5.ch005

Syed-Ikhsan, S. O., & Rowland, F. (2004). Knowledge management in a public organization: A study on the relationship between organizational elements and the performance of knowledge transfer. *Journal of Knowledge Management*, 8(2), 95–111. doi:10.1108/13673270410529145

Szulanski, G. (2000). The process of knowledge transfer: A diachronic analysis of stickiness. *Organizational Behavior and Human Decision Processes*, 82(1), 9–27. doi:10.1006/obhd.2000.2884

Tian, J., Nakamori, Y., & Wierzbicki, A. (2009). Knowledge management and knowledge creation in academia: A study based on surveys in a Japanese research university. *Knowledge Management*, 13(2), 76–92.

Tohidinia, Z., & Mosakhani, M. (2010). Knowledge sharing behaviour and its predictors. *Industrial Management & Data Systems*, 110(4), 611–631. doi:10.1108/02635571011039052

Van den Hooff, B., & Van Weenen, F. D. L. (2004a). Committed to share: Commitment and CMC use as antecedents of knowledge sharing. *Knowledge and Process Management*, 11(1), 13–24. doi:10.1002/kpm.187

Van den Hooff, B., & Van Weenen, F. D. L. (2004b). Knowledge sharing in context: The influence of organizational commitment, communication climate and CMC use on knowledge sharing. *Journal of Knowledge Management*, 8(6), 117–130. doi:10.1108/13673270410567675

Wu, Y., & Zhu, W. (2012). An integrated theoretical model for determinants of knowledge sharing behaviours. *Kybernetes*, 41(10), 1462–1482. doi:10.1108/03684921211276675

Yeh, Y. J., Lai, S. Q., & Ho, C. T. (2006). Knowledge management enablers: A case study. *Industrial Management & Data Systems*, 106(6), 793–810. doi:10.1108/02635570610671489

This research was previously published in the International Journal of Web Portals (IJWP), 10(1); pages 1-14, copyright year 2018 by IGI Publishing (an imprint of IGI Global).

Chapter 58

Stakeholder Perceptions and Word–of–Mouth on CSR Dynamics:
A Big Data Analysis from Twitter

Andrée Marie López-Fernández
Universidad Panamericana, Mexico City, Mexico

Zamira Burgos Silva
Medstent, S.A. de C.V., Mexico City, Mexico

ABSTRACT

Corporate social responsibility is a strategy by which firms address social issues whilst tending to their profit enhancing objectives. However, is a socially responsible firm fulfilling its objectives if current and potential stakeholders perceive it to be unethical, engaging in poor and questionable practices? The article analyzes Big Data retrieved from Twitter related to five firms that have stated to be socially responsible but have yet to obtain stakeholders' legitimacy granted by the engagement in corporate social responsibility. The article contributes to the understanding and effects of firm dynamics in corporate social responsibility or lack thereof, on social networking sites by means of Big Data analysis.

INTRODUCTION

It has become clear that both firms and stakeholders have increased their interest in the effects of their actions on the environment and society. There is a vast amount of organizations around the world that have taken the ideals of social accountability to action by engaging in corporate social responsibility (CSR). Stakeholders have gradually become more aware of the existence of CSR and more knowledgeable of the implications of social responsibility. Furthermore, because stakeholders grant CSR a certain degree of importance, they are more inclined to exhort organizations to fulfill their objectives and strategies in the utmost responsible way, to be accountable for their actions, in other words, to do the right thing.

DOI: 10.4018/978-1-7998-9020-1.ch058

Therefore, the transparent communication of CSR is critical to stakeholders' perspectives and, for that matter, decision making.

Transparency is elemental to CSR (Crowther & Aras, 2008) because it provides the firm with legitimacy, fosters accountability and sustainability, and drives growth and development. Both internal and external stakeholders need to be knowledgeable in the firm's CSR related policies and actions in order to effectively consider them in their decision making. The communication of CSR has traditionally been achieved via the firm's annual reports (Patten, 1991; Nielsen & Thomsen, 2007) and/or with excerpts on the firm's website. Although the information is online, these means' reach is limited to those actively searching for the information in question.

Firms have increased their use of social networking sites to put forth their practices and accelerate their strategies (López Fernández, 2012). Therefore, today, a great deal of CSR related practices is also communicated through social media and widely discussed on social networking sites (SNSs). These sites connect people with same interests (Mejias, 2010) and may also connect those with contrasting interests. It used to be that people would use SNSs to socialize with others with similar profiles, objectives, ideals, values and beliefs; however, the increasing scope of networks has led to greater diversity and, in turn, controversy. Consider the last US Presidential election; many took to SNSs to offer their insights on the candidates' policies, resulting in impassioned dialogue and, in some cases, the reduction in network size. These types of interactions are also visible in regard to business practices and stakeholders' thoughts on them.

The activity on SNSs is viewed by millions of users (Bauer, 2014), who are firms' current and potential stakeholders (Fernández & Rajagopal, 2014). For instance, Twitter has over three hundred million active users each month (Twitter, 2016), and is, therefore, one of the most used SNSs worldwide. This means that the communication of CSR policies, practices and results, or lack thereof, may be potentiated via platforms such as Twitter. And, since word-of-mouth (WOM) on SNSs, like Twitter, is unlimited (Stauss, 1997) and mostly unrestricted, this practice fixes the limited reach problem of traditional means of communication; however, it does not come without its downside. The same massive audience that may appreciate the positive communication occurring between firms and stakeholders may also witness negative communication occurring among stakeholders and, stakeholders and firms. Therefore, firms should be aware that the use of SNSs may have both positive and negative impacts on stakeholders' perspectives.

The principal objective of the study is to evaluate the potential impact of the WOM retrieved through Big Data on stakeholders' perceptions and firms based on the latter being dynamic in CSR. In order to do so, content analysis has been implemented to evaluate Big Data retrieved via Twitter related to five different large firms. The paper is sectioned as follows: section two reviews previous literature, section three includes the study's design, section four encompasses the study's findings and discussion, and section five incorporates concluding remarks, limitations and future research directions.

LITERATURE REVIEW

Corporate social responsibility (CSR) is a concept that has many definitions (Frederick, 2006; Ismail, 2009) and, as such, may be understood and measured in various manners. It is still largely considered to be a voluntary practice (Van Marrewijk, 2003) as there are very few countries that have embraced laws related to social responsibility. It has been considered as a firm's active interest in the impact of their actions on internal and external stakeholders (Ismail, 2009). And the firm's active effort to minimize negative and maximize positive effects (Nicolae & Sabina, 2010) on society and the environment. CSR is, then, a strategy that enables firms to tend to environmental and social issues whilst effectively managing and fulfilling operational objectives and strategies.

Stakeholders have become aware of firm engagement in CSR, or lack thereof, and it is their invested concerns in social issues that have made them reluctant to associate with non-socially responsible firms. Furthermore, their expectations are well aligned with those of society regarding the firm's performance (Branco & Rodrigues, 2007), as such, firms should absolutely tend to them. The communication and transparency of CSR efforts is considered to be essential to a firms' image towards stakeholders and overall performance (Maguire, 2011) as all interested parties should be made aware of the firm's policies, actions and results to be able to accurately shape their decisions. CSR influences the way stakeholders perceive the firm. The awareness of socially responsible actions positively influences stakeholders' opinions while knowing that the firm is engaging in questionable or unethical practices creates a negative impression.

Social media is a set of applications that enable users to generate and share content (Kaplan & Haenlein, 2010). Although social media, per se, does not make people social, it does have the potential to influence behaviors. Social networking sites (SNSs) are services through which users may create profiles and connections with others (Boyd & Ellison, 2007). They are online platforms that allow firms and stakeholders to put forth their ideas, opinions, experiences, likes, and dislikes, among others, instantly and globally at the comfort of their various devices. SNSs have proven that everyone has a voice which can be translated into data (Oboler et al., 2012); such voice has the potential to drive innovation, improve time to market, inventory management, sales and marketing decisions, and collaboration among internal and external stakeholders (Brown et al., 2011).

Firms have rightly increased their use of social media to promote their endeavors; achieving and monitoring deeper insights into stakeholders' behavior, loyalty, perspective, and attitude toward a firm's products and/or services and brand protects the firm's overall financial interests and performance. The use of SNSs allows firms to influence stakeholders' opinions regarding their business dynamics (Snider et al., 2003). Therefore, the communication occurring on SNSs regarding a firm's engagement in CSR may actually shape stakeholder purchase decision making and, in turn, impact business growth. For instance, the communication of CSR practices via social media impacts stakeholders' trust and credibility towards a firm which, in turn, stimulates an increase in sales (Ashok, 2010) and growth.

The word-of-mouth (WOM) encountered via SNSs is considerably more powerful than traditional media because the information shared is most likely provided by close personal friends or even friends of friends; thus, it is granted significant validity, legitimacy and power, which is not obtained from traditional media (Fernández & Rajagopal, 2013). When such information is related to firms and their brands, both the positive and negative content has a potential impact on business growth and development Therefore, the content of the WOM should be carefully considered as to improve stakeholders' perspectives and ultimate satisfaction.

WOM, then, may impact stakeholders' perspectives regarding a brand and/or firm. For instance, stakeholders may potentially respond with sanctions as they become aware that a firm is engaging in poor practices. Further, depending on the severity and/or the perception of the severity of the action in question, stakeholders might engage in badmouthing, boycotting, or even make efforts stop the firm from operating (Godfrey et al., 2009). According to Werther & Chandler (2011) if stakeholders should choose to sanction a firm, the fulfillment of its strategic goals may be at risk. Hence, firms should be vigilant of their behavior and performance because the repercussions of their actions are now placed on a boundless platform, and stakeholders worldwide are 24/7 witnesses and commentators.

It has become clear that the long-term impact of SNSs will change firms' dynamics as they manage internal processes and procedures to improve product decisions, inventory alignment with various demands, market positioning, growth and development investments, and the various and complex relationships among stakeholders (Davenport et al., 2013), amongst others. Furthermore, because of the loop feedback that social media and Big Data create, firms may engage with current and potential stakeholders around the globe allowing the transformation of information technology's function to a customer centric innovation management (Asur & Huberman, 2010).

Twitter is a SNS that allows users to publish their thoughts, state of mind, what they are thinking the moment they are thinking it. The information posted on Twitter, also known as Tweets, may contain photos, videos, or just text. Each Tweet can be reposted which means that the number of users that can potentially see a Tweet is massive; the process is certainly similar to a ripple effect. As such, it should come to no surprise that millions of Tweets are shared in real time every day (Twitter, 2016). The WOM observed on Twitter has been enriched with the use of hashtags which highlight key words and categorize the content of the Tweet in question; a hashtag is accompanied by a pound or number sign to indicate the nature of the word or set or words (#Hashtags, 2012).

Big data is not just a revolutionary concept, it is exactly how it sounds; that is, large amounts of data whose size is beyond the ability of commonly used software tools to capture, manage, and process the data within a tolerable elapsed time (Manovich, 2011). It is a powerful tool that enables firms to procure insights and effectively manage prompt decision making. Big data may be retrieved from various sources, both internal and external, and including, for instance, customer surveys, massive surveys such as a census, an email list or analytics report from a social media page (Boyd & Crawford, 2012). Thus, the WOM occurring on SNSs, as informal as it may be, is valuable Big Data waiting to be retrieved. It, then, may be significantly beneficial to a firm's marketing endeavors and overall decision making by aiding in the better understanding of their stakeholders' characteristics and demographics.

Big Data offers the ability to obtain new information, create new value, and modify relationships, markets and organizations (Mayer-Schönberger & Cukier, 2013) at a larger scale than with traditional sources of data. Big Data includes information shared, posted and reposted, tweeted and retweeted on SNSs, obtained via devices' sensors and mobile phones, amongst others (McAfee & Brynjolfsson, 2012); therefore, the elements that characterize it are volume, variety and velocity (Zikopoulos & Eaton, 2011). Further, since Big Data is a network of information, there is much value to be obtained about stakeholders, their connections to others, the groups they are associated with, and the information's structure (Boyd & Crawford, 2011), amongst others.

A firm that is transparent in their socially responsible efforts, which are positively perceived by current and potential stakeholders, may have a positive effect on consumer behavior. Thus, users may tend to increase the positive WOM they put forth, or Tweet. However, as stakeholders perceive firms to be engaging in non-ethical practices, they will most likely increase the negative WOM Tweeted. Accordingly, communicating and not communicating on CSR practices have effects on the frequency and type of content of the WOM and on stakeholders' purchase decision making. Thus, the large amount of available information, although unstructured, contains significantly valuable data for firms' decision making (McAfee & Brynjolfsson, 2012). Therefore, the Big Data retrievable via SNSs, in reference to CSR may aid decision makers in shaping strategies, and the overall fulfillment of objectives.

STUDY DESIGN

The present study aims to determine the potential use of Big Data analytics to improve CSR practices whilst determining stakeholders' perspectives of firm engagement in CSR. The exploratory design model for the study has been developed taking firms that have a dynamic role in CSR at the center of analysis. The selection of the firms was based on the latter meeting three criterions. First, the firms should be well recognized amongst the general public; second, they should offer products and/or services that the general public could utilize on a daily basis and, third, the firms should have affirmed to be dynamic in CSR. As such, five firms were selected, hereinafter referred to as coffee company, pharmaceutical company, retail store, supermarket, and agriculture company. The nature of the analysis was qualitative as content analysis was implemented (Denskus & Esser, 2013; Leone & Paoli, 2015) to evaluate the WOM issued related to the firms and their engagement in CSR via Twitter. This type of analysis of data collected from Twitter enables the understanding of consumer behavior (Schwartz & Ungar, 2015), including their sentiment or feelings regarding products (Pang & Lee, 2008) services, brands, and firms, amongst others.

There are various reasons why Twitter was the selected source of data for the study, including that it (*i*) meets the criteria for Big Data analytics, and (*ii*) both the analyzed firms and current and potential stakeholders utilize the platform. Furthermore, Twitter, unlike other SNSs, is an open platform (Procter et al., 2013); meaning that, users may follow and Tweet others without having to be followed in return. This ultimately increases the potential Tweets and Retweets on a given subject matter. The use of hashtags, which is much more concentrated on said SNS, allows users to classify ideas (Procter et al., 2013) they are sharing according to the topic highlighted in the uninterrupted phrase headed by a pound sign (octo-thorpe). Also, as opposed to other SNS, Twitter limits each Tweet to 140 characters which compels users to be concise facilitating data analysis. As such, Tweets are effectively simultaneous updates (Hodder & Houghton, 2015) of users' thoughts, experiences, and opinions. According to Wang et al., (2011) the combination of the massive amount of messages generated everyday along with the users' tendency to be brutally honest make Twitter a solid data source for various areas of research, including branding and consumer behavior, amongst others. Additionally, since Big Data is not only about size, but also velocity, variety, and its value (Demchenko, et al; 2013), Twitter is a significant source of Big Data through which research questions may be effectively studied and answered (Wang et al., 2016).

Data collection and analysis required the use of various techniques to filter, code, classify, manage and analyze the data. The data was collected bimonthly over a period of two years, 2014 to 2016. The data was collected with computational methods by means of a software application; the SNS, Twitter, was essentially "swept" with only the firm (official account) as a variable. By doing so, the initial sample size resulted in 1,780,389 Tweets. The content analysis was performed both computationally and manually (Lewis et al., 2013) as the software aided in data collection and sorting for processing and further analysis. First, the collected data was filtered by only selecting the data that was written in English. The second step was to code the data to classify it with the aim of discovering patterns as well as to eliminate further outliers. For the third step, coding, the labels utilized were hashtags associated with CSR or lack thereof, including: #corporatesocialresponsibility, #csr, #boycott, and #ban. The first two hashtags were selected because they reveal users' grasp of CSR as a concept; the intention was to gather the data of those that have an integral understanding of the concept, as opposed to single variables such as ethics, transparency, sustainability, gender equality, amongst many others. The last two hashtags were selected because they suggest the users' utter dissatisfaction and disapproval with the firms' lack of CSR. As such, these hashtags represent the limits of the scope. By coding the data, the sample size was reduced to 2778; finally, the data was once more analyzed to determine repetition as to ensure that the data had been duplicated. Finally, it was found that eighteen Tweets associated with the hashtag #ban referred to other issues unrelated to the prohibition, veto, or sanction towards the firm. Thus, once the discrepant cases were removed, the sample size for the study resulted in 2760 Tweets.

Manual content analysis was implemented to determine the nature of each Tweet (Lewis et al., 2013) and the impact of the WOM on stakeholders' perceptions as was similarly carried out by Haigh et al., 2013). Tweets and retweets were coded by means of the hashtags and categorized in three different groups, these being, (*i*) positive WOM, (*ii*) neutral WOM, and (*iii*) negative WOM. Figure 1 illustrates the proposed model of the study. As can be seen, it is suggested that the WOM generated by Twitter users (i.e. the firm and its current and potential stakeholders) has a direct impact on stakeholders' perceptions regarding the firm, which leads to further WOM; and, the latter ultimately has a direct impact on business growth of the firm. Therefore, each Tweet and retweet, charged with positive, neutral or negative content, has the potential to influence stakeholders' ultimate purchase decision making which will, in turn, impact business growth and development. And, as stakeholders are directly associated with the firm's effective achievement of objectives and strategies, their perspectives will surely enhance or impede the latter's fulfillment.

Figure 1. Proposed model of the study

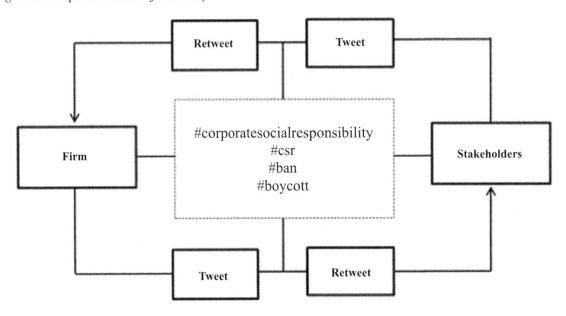

It is important to note that the type of WOM (i.e. positive, negative and neutral) is provided by the users; therefore, although the data may seem to have positive content, it is the overall intention of each Tweet that has been considered for their classification. For instance, many may believe that gun control is a positive notion, however, as was encountered in the data retrieved from the *coffee company*, some users consider gun control to be prejudicial, thus, the content of their Tweet is negative.

FINDINGS AND DISCUSSION

The analyzed hashtags' frequency of use is illustrated in Figure 2. The majority of the Tweets retrieved are associated with the hashtag #boycott, followed by #csr, #ban and, finally, #corporatesocialresponsibility. Although over two thousand tweets were analyzed, it does not mean that these are the only existing Tweets that are related to these firms and to their CSR or lack thereof; rather, these are the Tweets that have been related with the abovementioned hashtags. All firms have been associated with the four hashtags; the hashtag with the least amount of Tweets is #corporatesocialresponsibility which could be due to the actual size of hashtag. The Tweets' content ranges from: the description of best practices and social responsibility, to poor, questionable practices and lack of CSR.

Figure 2. Analyzed hashtags' frequency of use

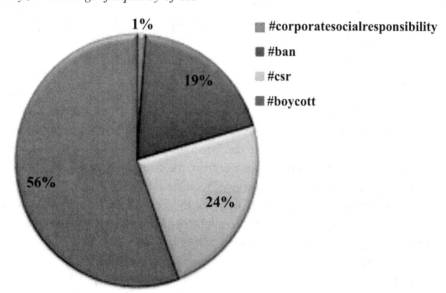

The number of Tweets associated with each hashtag per firm is exhibited in Table 1. The *coffee company* has been mostly associated with #csr, over 200 times, and #boycott with over 160 Tweets. This pattern, of most related hashtags, also occurs with the *pharmaceutical company,* the *retail store,* and the *supermarket.* Only the *agricultural company* had a much larger amount of Tweets associated with #ban and #boycott, with over 940 and 450 Tweets respectively. The latter include Tweets and retweets. Therefore, the data that can be retrieved by using #csr and #boycott is more significant than the other two hashtags.

Coffee Company

The *coffee company* has approximately 11,800,000 followers on Twitter, who Tweet and retweet ideas, opinions, experiences, images, and links to other sites regarding the firm in one hundred and forty characters or less. Out of all five firms analyzed, this firm showed the largest increase in followers, approximately

45 percent, throughout the study. Such increment could be due to the firm's growth and position in the marketplace. All four hashtags have been associated with the firm in question, resulting in 413 Tweets. The content of the data is positive, negative and neutral (Table 2 illustrates the type of content, WOM, found as the hashtags were associated with each of the analyzed firms). The vast majority of the Tweets, 78 percent, are negative, 17 percent are positive and only 5 percent are neutral.

Table 1. Tweet association with hashtags per firm

Firm	Hashtags				Total
	#corporatesocialresponsibility	#csr	#boycott	#ban	
Coffee company	13	203	168	29	413
Pharmaceutical company	6	87	94	24	211
Retail store	3	92	91	3	189
Supermarket	9	224	241	26	500
Agricultural company	1	50	942	454	1447
Total	32	656	1536	536	2760

The positive Tweets refer to the firm's practices that somewhat relate to its engagement in CSR. For instance, there are Tweets that make reference to the firm aiding the community, providing jobs, furthering education, best practices, sustainability, volunteerism, the firm's position against inequality, and a campaign to deter racism. The neutral Tweets retrieved relate to information provided on the firm's plans and intentions to be socially responsible, users "tips" for the firm to be more transparent in regards to their engagement in CSR, and the notion that Millennials (Millennial generation or Generation Y) seek to work for organizations that are dynamic in CSR.

The negative Tweets make reference to the firm's poor practices, less than ethical practices, and/ or lack of engagement in CSR; that is, the firm's stance on gun control (pro and anti-gun), same sex marriage, racism, food scandals, not being socially responsible or sustainable, greenwashing, socialwashing, just good marketing, tax evasion, stealing and the firm's industrial relations. Further, users offer information on the firm's lack of fair trade, unjust working conditions, unfair wages, and reduced benefits, discrimination and racism, and taking on a political role and misuse of lobbying. Meaning that, stakeholders are using the platform to educate the firm on better practices; thus, there is a clear intention to help improve the firm's business dynamics. A significant number of users have boycotted the firm because of its alleged support for Israel, genocide, and in pro of freeing Gaza, and for political association during last US Presidential campaign. Moreover, several users make reference to the firm by only stating the word "fail".

The expectation is that the content of the Tweets incorporating hashtags related to CSR would be of positive WOM. The majority of the Tweets associated with #corporatesocialresponsibility are positive and neutral; however, the vast majority of Tweets associated with #csr contain negative WOM. Therefore, current and potential stakeholders are utilizing #csr to promote the notion that the firm is lacking in CSR rather than endorsing good practices. Further, #boycott and #ban are used to promote their indignant stance on the firm's poor, questionable and unethical practices.

Pharmaceutical Company

The pharmaceutical company has approximately 125,000 followers on Twitter who are able to simultaneously receive information regarding the firm's activity in real time. It is noteworthy that the number of followers significantly increased, approximately 25 percent, during the time of the study. Although the reasons of the latter are not clear, as the number of followers increased so did the amount of Tweets highlighting the firm's questionable practices. 211 Tweets were analyzed which include the firm and the hashtags mentioned earlier. The company has been associated with all four hashtags, and positive, negative and neutral WOM was encountered within the retrieved Tweets (See Table 2). The majority, 85 percent of the Tweets, contains negative WOM, 11 percent includes positive WOM, and only 4 percent of the Tweets are neutral.

The positive Tweets make reference to the firm engaging in social programs, its foundation, donations, awards, focus on sustainability and association with the UNEP (United Nations Environment Programme). Neutral Tweets refer to the firm's report on sustainability. And, negative Tweets contain information related to the firm being racist, greedy, their lack of engagement in CSR and sustainability, unethical practices such as animal cruelty, use of pesticides, unverified quality in products, and the firm's industrial relations. Further, several users have decided to boycott the firm due to their alleged alliance to certain political figures and the disapproval of a former governor of Alaska.

The majority of Tweets associated with #csr include positive and neutral WOM; however, the vast majority of Tweets related to the firm are associated with #boycott and #ban where all Tweets contain negative WOM. There is much more negative data than positive data that is being associated with the firm. Thus, current and potential stakeholders are taking to the platform to express discontent with the firm's business dynamics and outmost disapproval of their lack of social responsibility.

Retail Store

The retail store has approximately 1,200,000 followers on Twitter, with less than a 1 percent increase throughout the study. The firm has been associated with all four hashtags, resulting in a total of 189 Tweets. Further, only positive and negative WOM was found in the content of the Tweets (See Table 2). A staggering 94 percent of the Tweets retrieved contain negative WOM, and only 6 percent of the Tweets contain positive WOM. Therefore, the firm is associated with poor, questionable, and unethical practices, rather than with social responsibility. The positive Tweets refer to the firm's sustainable practices, affirmation of being socially responsible and the obtainment of an award; whilst the negative Tweets mention the firm's lack of sustainability, ethics, and social responsibility. Moreover, users make mention of the firm's questionable actions related to intellectual property, labor exploitation (slave labor), sweatshops, animal cruelty, and indignant working conditions; the latter being associated with both #csr and #boycott and #ban. Therefore, current and potential stakeholders are utilizing the hashtag #csr to make reference to the firm's lack of CSR, and #boycott to further promote their indignant stance of the firm's processes and procedures.

Supermarket

The *supermarket* has approximately 480,000 followers on Twitter; throughout the study there was 2 percent increase in followers. 500 Tweets were analyzed by associating the firm with each of the four hashtags. The Tweets retrieved contain positive, negative and neutral WOM (See Table 2). 88 percent of the Tweets contain negative WOM, 8 percent contains positive WOM, and only 4 percent are neutral. Thus, the vast majority of Tweets associate the firm with questionable and unethical practices rather than the promotion of socially responsible actions.

The positive Tweets make reference to the firm's donations, attention towards the reduction of hunger, association with a foundation, stance on sustainability, the elimination of sweets in the stores' check-out lines, and action taken on food waste. The neutral Tweets offer information of the firm's plans and intentions to be socially responsible. And, the negative Tweets make reference to the firm not being socially responsible or sustainable, greenwashing, unethical practices such as modern day slavery, unjust working conditions, exploitation of labor, animal cruelty, tax evasion, excessive food waste, stealing, and misleading customers, and animal cruelty. Users noted experiences where employees harassed, bullied, and were rude to customers, and dissatisfaction due to the firm's industrial relations and political association, including the alleged support for Israel in pro of freeing Gaza.

The least amount of Tweets is associated with #corporatesocialresponsibility, as was the case with all analyzed firms; this hashtag included only one positive Tweet, and roughly 28 percent of the Tweets associated with #csr are positive and neutral. Therefore, as in the cases stated above, the hashtag #csr is mostly utilized to describe current and potential stakeholders' disapproval of the firm's lack of engagement in CSR, and #boycott and #ban are used to further promote outrage due to the firm's poor practices.

Agriculture Company

The *agriculture company* has approximately 100,000 followers on Twitter, accounting for less than a 1 percent increase in followers during the study. By far, the amount of data retrieved for this firm was the largest; all four hashtags were associated with the firm yielding a total of 1447 Tweets for analysis. The WOM of the Tweets contain positive, negative and neutral content (See Table 2). 93 percent of the Tweets contain negative WOM, 4 percent is neutral, and only 3 percent contains positive WOM. Therefore, the vast majority of communication occurring via Twitter, regarding this firm, is negative.

The positive Tweets utilized #csr and were mostly mentioned by the firm itself to promote socially responsible practices and company values, and the neutral Tweets include company information. The negative Tweets, however, clearly illustrate current and potential stakeholders' disapproval, anger, and frustration towards the firm. These make reference to the firm not being socially responsible or sustainable, its unethical practices, the endangerment of health, and animal cruelty. Users have taken to the platform to vigorously point out the firm's failure to comply with international quality standards and exhort others to join in the efforts to #ban and #boycott the firm. It is clear that the company's followers are determined to sanction the firm with efforts to revoke its right to operate.

Table 2. Tweet association according to content per firm [figures in percent]

	Coffee Company	**Pharmaceutical Company**	**Retail Store**	**Supermarket**	**Agricultural Company**
Positive	17	11	6	8	3
Neutral	5	4	0	4	4
Negative	78	85	94	88	93
Total	100	100	100	100	100

MANAGERIAL IMPLICATIONS AND CONCLUSION

Stakeholders are utilizing the SNS, Twitter, to put forth personal ideas, opinions, experiences, as well as hyperlinks to external reports, news, and blogs, among others. Stakeholders' perceptions are directly associated to the firms' policies, actions and overall outcomes, and the perceptions, in turn, are directly correlated with the firms' growth and development; that is, the process is cyclical. Stakeholders' perceptions are instantly placed on an online platform making each Tweet public and simultaneously accessible to a massive audience with Wi-Fi. Ultimately, stakeholders' perceptions influence purchase decision making which, in turn, impacts firms' growth and development. Therefore, the data retrievable from such stakeholders' Tweets is particularly important for firms' decision making.

The data obtained through the present study allows the understanding of stakeholders' (current and potential) perceptions of five firms' engagement, or lack thereof, in CSR. The content of the Tweets analyzed is, in general, negative. Such negative WOM is impacting other current and potential stakeholders' perceptions of the firms in question, which is visible through the action of retweeting, marking as favorite, and comments of support made to several Tweets. Furthermore, the negative WOM is ultimately impacting the firms' growth and development, as is visible by stakeholders' attitudes and position to boycott and/or ban them due to unethical practices, and/or their perception of questionable practices.

The data revealed that stakeholders are much less forgiving of bad or questionable practices when it comes to the pharmaceutical and agricultural company, while are more tolerant regarding the other firms. In fact, negative Tweets regarding the first two firms upheld throughout the duration of the study, while Tweets referring to the other firms were sporadic; that is, they perish almost as fast as they trend. It would seem that the greatest similarity amongst stakeholders is that there is no hesitation to Tweeting and Retweeting any and all negative information regarding business dynamics. The overall effect of perceptions remains unclear as, even though users praise CSR engagement and/or call for boycott, their actual consumption or lack thereof is uncertain.

Big Data, undeniably, is a very powerful tool that enables firms to create value and competitive advantage; in order to do so, firms need to analyze, measure, and add value to the available information to maximize their activity. As findings suggest, stakeholders' perceptions, attitudes, opinions, etcetera, generate large amounts of data that indicate clear patterns of behavior ranging from satisfaction, to dissatisfaction and even outrage towards the firms' processes and procedures. Stakeholders find each firm to be accountable for their actions, they not only consider them to be lacking in CSR but they even perceive them to be dishonorable and unprincipled.

The key to the successful use of Big Data, such as the data retrieved for the present study, is to be proactive, listen to and communicate with stakeholders (current and potential) as to bring the conversation closer to those in charge of decision making. It is outstanding that these firms have not addressed these issues on the SNS head-on; rather, they have left them there to be publically seen and shared by millions. Therefore, solely monitoring activity on SNSs will no longer suffice; it is important that firms elevate their communication and transparency efforts, especially when referring to strategies such as CSR. Big Data is, then, a profitable tool by which firms may obtain accurate information regarding stakeholders' needs, wants, values, principals, and even action plans that may positively or negatively impact them.

Data is pivotal for accurate and prompt decision making and, in this new paradigm, Big Data enables deeper and broader insights to stakeholders' perceptions and, ultimately, their decision making. Thus, the effective use of Big Data may potentially help firms shape their objectives and strategies as to better serve a broader audience (i.e. current and potential stakeholders). Finally, the study's findings suggest that the analyzed firms are either not socially responsible or are not fully engaging in CSR. Said firms should absolutely take advantage of such Big Data to improve their approach to both CSR and the communication and transparency of CSR. The latter may prove to be the difference between a boycotted and/or banned firm, from a successful firm that has achieved brand loyalty, and been granted legitimacy by stakeholders.

LIMITATIONS AND FUTURE DIRECTIONS

The study's limitations include the sample size. Although a total of 2760 Tweets were analyzed, the sample was restricted due to the hashtags incorporated and the number of firms selected for the analysis; therefore, the results may not be generalized. Future research could focus on firms' position on Big Data; that is, firms' decision making processes based on the procurement of Big Data. Moreover, future research could analyze firms' decision making based on retrieved Big Data to further execute CSR strategies. Finally, the implications of the stakeholders' perceptions and effects of trending WOM may be analyzed in future research.

REFERENCES

Ashok, K. (2010). Framing Corporate Social Responsibility on the websites of Fortune 10 Green Giants. San Jose State University.

Asur, S., & Huberman, B. A. (2010, August). Predicting the future with social media. In *Proceedings of the 2010 IEEE/WIC/ACM International Conference on* Web Intelligence and Intelligent Agent Technology (WI-IAT) (Vol. 1, pp. 492-499). Toronto, Canada: IEEE.

Bauer, T. (2014). The responsibilities of social networking companies: Applying political CSR theory to Google, Facebook and Twitter. In R. Tench, W. Sun, & B. Jones (Eds.), *Communicating corporate social responsibility: Perspectives and practices (Critical studies on corporate responsibility, governance and sustainability)* (pp. 259–282). Bingley: Emerald Group Publishing Limited. doi:10.1108/S2043-9059(2014)0000006005

Boyd, D., & Crawford, K. (2011, September 21). Six provocations for big data. *A decade in Internet time: Symposium on the dynamics of the Internet and society.* Retrieved from http://ssrn.com/abstract=1926431

Boyd, D., & Crawford, K. (2012). Critical questions for Big Data: Provocations for a cultural, technological, and scholarly phenomenon. *Information Communication and Society*, *15*(5), 662–679. doi:10.1080/1369118X.2012.678878

Boyd, D. M., & Ellison, N. B. (2007). Social network sites: Definition, history, and scholarship. *Journal of Computer-Mediated Communication*, *13*(1), 210–230. doi:10.1111/j.1083-6101.2007.00393.x

Branco, M. C., & Rodrigues, L. L. (2007). Positioning stakeholder theory within the debate on corporate social responsibility. *Electronic Journal of Business Ethics and Organization Studies*, *12*(1), 5–15.

Brown, B., Chui, M., & Manyika, J. (2011). Are you ready for the era of 'big data'? *Insights & Publications. The McKinsey Quarterly*, *4*, 24–35. Retrieved July 30, 2014 from http://www.mckinsey.com/insights/strategy/are_you_ready_for_the_era_of_big_data

Crowther, D., & Aras, G. (2008). *Corporate social responsibility.* Ventus Publishing ApS.

Davenport, T. H., Barth, P., & Bean, R. (2013). How "big data" is different. *MIT Sloan Management Review*, *54*(1), 22–24.

Dee, J. (2010). *Small Business, Big Opportunity, Sustainable Growth.* Melbourne: Sensis Pty Ltd.

Demchenko, Y., Grosso, P., De Laat, C., & Membrey, P. (2013). Addressing big data issues in scientific data infrastructure. In *Proceedings of the 2013 International Conference on* Collaboration Technologies and Systems (CTS) (pp. 48-55). San Diego, CA: IEEE.

Denskus, T., & Esser, D. E. (2013). Social media and global development rituals: A content analysis of blogs and tweets on the 2010 MDG Summit. *Third World Quarterly*, *34*(3), 405–422. doi:10.1080/01436597.2013.784607

Fernández, A. M., & Rajagopal, N. A. (2014). Convergence of corporate social responsibility and business growth: An analytical framework. *International Journal of Business Excellence*, *7*(6), 791–806. doi:10.1504/IJBEX.2014.065508

Fitch, G. H. (1976). Achieving corporate social responsibility. *Academy of Management Review*, *1*(1), 38–46. doi:10.5465/AMR.1976.4408754

Frederick, W. (2006). *Corporation, be good! The story of corporate social responsibility.* Indianapolis: Dog Ear Publishing.

Godfrey, P. C., Merrill, C. B., & Hansen, J. M. (2009). The relationship between corporate social responsibility and shareholder value: An empirical test of the risk management hypothesis. *Strategic Management Journal*, *30*(4), 425–445. doi:10.1002mj.750

Haigh, M. M., Brubaker, P., & Whiteside, E. (2013). Facebook: Examining the information presented and its impact on stakeholders. *Corporate Communications*, *18*(1), 52–69. doi:10.1108/13563281311294128

#Hashtags. (2012, June 12). *What is a (#) hashtag?* Retrieved July 28, 2014, from http://www.hashtags.org/how-to/history/what-is-a-hashtag/

Hodder, A., & Houghton, D. (2015, November). Union use of social media: A study of the University and College Union on Twitter. *New Technology, Work and Employment*, *30*(3), 173–189. doi:10.1111/ntwe.12055

Ismail, M. (2009). Corporate social responsibility and its role in community development: An international perspective. *Journal of International Social Research*, *2*(9), 199–209.

Kaplan, A. M., & Haenlein, M. (2010, February). Users of the world, unite! The challenges and opportunities of Social Media. *Business Horizons*, *53*(1), 59–68. doi:10.1016/j.bushor.2009.09.003

Leone, S., & Paoli, A. D. (2015). Public administrations in a digital public space. A framework for assessing participatory and multistakeholder models of relationship on Twitter. *Current Politics and Economics of Europe*, *27*(1), 86–122.

Lewis, S. C., Zamith, R., & Hermida, A. (2013). Content analysis in an era of Big Data: A hybrid approach to computational and manual methods. *Journal of Broadcasting & Electronic Media*, *57*(1), 34–52. doi:10.1080/08838151.2012.761702

López Fernández, A. M. (2012). *Social Networks as an approach to accelerate business strategy*. Mexico City: Congreso Internacional de Contaduría, Administración e Informática.

López-Fernández, A. M. (2014). Engaging stakeholders in co-creating corporate social responsibility: A study across industries in Mexico. *International Journal of Business Competition and Growth*, *3*(3), 241–253. doi:10.1504/IJBCG.2014.060316

Maguire, M. (2011, January). The future of corporate social responsibility reporting. *The Frederick S. Pardee center for the study of the longer-range future*.

Manovich, L. (2011). Trending: the promises and the challenges of Big social data. In *M.K. Gold. Debates in the Digital Humanities*. Minneapolis, MN: The University of Minnesota Press. Retrieved July 30, 2014, from http://www.manovich.net/DOCS/Manovich_trending_paper.pdf

Mayer-Schönberger, V., & Cukier, K. (2013). *Big data: A revolution that will transform how we live, work, and think*. Canada: Eamon Dolan/Houghton Mifflin Harcourt.

McAfee, A., & Brynjolfsson, E. (2012). Big Data. The management revolution. *Harvard Business Review*, *90*(10), 60–67. PMID:23074865

Mejias, U. A. (2010). The limits of Networks as models for organizing the sociality. *New Media & Society*, *12*(4), 603–617. doi:10.1177/1461444809341392

Nicolae, J. C., & Sabina, M. J. (2010). Dimensions and challenges of social responsibility. *Annales Universitatis Apulensis Series Oeconomica*, *12*(1), 1–23.

Nielsen, A. E., & Thomsen, C. (2007). Reporting CSR – what and how to say it? *Corporate Communications*, *12*(1), 25–40. doi:10.1108/13563280710723732

Oboler, A., Welsh, K., & Cruz, L. (2012, July 2). The danger of Big Data: Social media as computational social science. *First Monday*, *17*(7). doi:10.5210/fm.v17i7.3993

Pang, B., & Lee, L. (2008). Opinion mining and sentiment analysis. *Foundations and Trends in Information Retrieval*, *2*(1-2), 1–90. doi:10.1561/1500000011

Patten, D. (1991). Exposure, legitimacy, and social disclosure. *Journal of Accounting and Public Policy*, *10*(4), 297–308. doi:10.1016/0278-4254(91)90003-3

Procter, R., Vis, F., & Voss, A. (2013). Reading the riots on Twitter: Methodological innovation for the analysis of big data. *International Journal of Social Research Methodology*, *16*(3), 197–214. doi:10.1080/13645579.2013.774172

Schlusberg, M. (1969). Corporate Legitimacy and Social Responsibility: The Role of Law. *California Management Review, 12*(1), 65–76. doi:10.2307/41164207

Schwartz, H. A., & Ungar, L. H. (2015, May). Data-driven content analysis of social media: A systematic overview of automated methods. *The Annals of the American Academy, 659*(1), 78–94. doi:10.1177/0002716215569197

Snider, J., Hill, R. P., & Martin, D. (2003). Corporate social responsibility in the 21st Century: A view from the world's most successful firms. *Journal of Business Ethics, 48*(2), 175–187. doi:10.1023/B:BUSI.0000004606.29523.db

Stauss, B. (1997). Global Word of Mouth. *Marketing Management, 6*(3), 1–28.

Twitter. (2016, June). *Twitter usage/Company facts*. Retrieved January 15, 2016, from https://about.twitter.com/company

Utting, P. (2008, April). Corporate social responsibility, public private partnerships and human development. *HD Insights. Human Development Reports Networks,* (19).

Van Marrewijk, M. (2003). Concepts and definitions of CSR and corporate sustainability: Between agency and communion. *Journal of Business Ethics, 44*(2-3), 95–105. doi:10.1023/A:1023331212247

Wang, W., Hernandez, I., Newman, D. A., He, J., & Bian, J. (2016). Twitter analysis: Studying us weekly trends in work stress and emotion. *Applied Psychology, 65*(2), 355–378. doi:10.1111/apps.12065

Wang, X., Wei, F., Liu, X., Zhou, M., & Zhang, M. (2011). Topic sentiment analysis in Twitter: A graph-based hashtag sentiment classification approach. In *Proceedings of the 20th ACM international conference on Information and knowledge management* (pp. 1031-1040). Glasgow: AMC.

Werther, W. B. Jr., & Chandler, D. (2011). Part I. Strategic corporate social responsibility. In *W. B. Werther Jr., & D. Chandler, Corporate social responsibility. Stakeholders in a Global Environment* (2nd ed., pp. 1–19). California: SAGE Publications, Inc.

Zikopoulos, P., & Eaton, C. (2011). *Understanding big data: Analytics for enterprise class hadoop and streaming data.* McGraw-Hill.

This research was previously published in the International Journal of Business Data Communications and Networking (IJB-DCN), 14(1); pages 67-80, copyright year 2018 by IGI Publishing (an imprint of IGI Global).

Chapter 59

Investigating the Impact of Social Media on Gen Y Employees' Engagement:
An Indian Perspective

Mohammad Faraz Naim

Department of Management Studies, Indian Institute of Technology Roorkee, India

Usha Lenka

Department of Management Studies, Indian Institute of Technology Roorkee, India

ABSTRACT

The study examines the influence of social media on Gen Y employees' engagement. Hypotheses are developed to explain the influence of social media on Gen Y employees' engagement. A sample of 256 Indian Gen Y employees from IT industry participated in the survey. Structural equation modeling is used to test the research hypotheses. Findings reveal that social media has a significant positive effect on Gen Y employees' engagement. It is revealed that social media moderates the relationship of HR practices (communication, collaboration; knowledge sharing and recognition) and engagement in Gen Y employees. While the scope of this study is limited to IT industry and results may not generalize to different industries in different regions. Hence, future studies should test the given hypotheses in different industries of different regions. The findings suggest that organizations should incorporate social media into their HR strategy. The study is one of the first to date, to empirically test the effect of social media on Gen Y employee engagement.

INTRODUCTION

Over the last few years, employee engagement has become a key area of concern for organizations. One of the reasons behind this is the changing workforce dynamics, characterized by the multi-generational nature of the current workforce comprising of three generations namely Baby boomers (1946-1960), Gen

DOI: 10.4018/978-1-7998-9020-1.ch059

X (1961-1980) and Gen Y (1981-2000). This diverse workforce presents new challenges for organizations form the talent management perspective. While Baby boomers are approaching their retirement and Gen X also will follow within few years, by 2030, it is predicted that Gen Y will account for nearly three quarters of the global workforce. Therefore, Gen Y is both the present and future of the workforce; however, research suggests that Gen Y employees are tougher to engage than the earlier generations (Anderson, 2011). Hence, engaging Gen Y employees has become a grave talent management issue for organizations.

More importantly, there is growing evidence that Gen Y is different in terms of workplace attitude, values, and preferences; hence it is forcing organizations to re-think their working practices commensurate to the distinct psychological profile of Gen Y employees (Naim & Lenka, 2016). The extant research also indicates that different generations of employees tend to have unique engagement drivers (Gilbert, 2011). This builds a compelling case for organizations to design an effective engagement strategy. The past literature reveals that being grown up in technologically sophisticated era, Gen Y employees are techno-savvy and harbor a strong tendency for use of technology such as social media (Lowe, Levitt & Wilson, 2008). This has prompted us to explore the case of social media, which holds high influence in lives of Gen Y employees. In addition, social media (a class of online communication tools) possesses a remarkable ability of creating and sharing user-generated content. This has been shown to have a strong bearing on communication, information transfer, and collaboration within organizations (Vouri, 2012). Further, this study is a response to Bolton et al.'s (2013) call to examine the effect of organizational use of social media on engagement, commitment and loyalty. Additionally, social media has been studied to engage external stakeholders particularly, customers, but its potential to engage internal customers i.e. employees is still an unexplored territory. On this backdrop, this paper investigates the impact of social media use on engagement of Gen Y employees.

LITERATURE REVIEW

Social Media

Technological revolution has been the defining characteristic of the last few decades. The emergence of internet and social technologies has been the dominant force, in particular the rise of social media. The term 'social media' firstly appeared in press in 1997 (Bercovici, 2010). Social media comprises of online communication channels such as social networking sites (Facebook, Twitter, Linkedin), Blogs, discussion forums, Content sharing sites (Youtube, Flickr), Internal networking tools (Yammer). These tools primarily use ability to create user-generated content i.e. allowing users to create, edit, and share their content. Social media includes unique platforms that encourage active participation in the creation, modification, and communication of user-generated content (Universal McCann, 2008).

In academic literature, Kaplan and Haenlein (2010) have conducted the seminal work on conceptualizing the social media. They defined it as a group of internet based applications that build on the ideological and technological foundations of web 2.0 and that enable the creation and exchange of user generated content. According to Cavico et al. (2013), "social media consists of web-based internet networks where users can share information and communicate with other users in a collective manner" (p. 25). Smith (2012) conceptualized social media as "social interactions using technology (such as the internet and cell phones) with any combination of words, pictures, video, or audio" (p. 24). Social media is increasingly affecting the day-to-day organizational processes. It is transforming the way organizations communicate and connect with their stakeholders including employees, customers etc (Vuori, 2012). Although, academic research on social media is scant, few studies such as IBM's research on its internal networking tool called Beehive have reported positive impact of such tools on employee collaboration and communication (DiMiceo et al., 2008; Holtzblatt et al., 2013). In addition, prior literature on social media reveals its positive impact on tacit knowledge sharing, internal communication, collaboration and improving the interpersonal social ties and development of social capital (Lee, 2013; Paroutis & Al Saleh, 2009; Skeels and Grudin, 2009). To this end, employees utilize social media features of openness and community potential to build ties with colleagues and superiors leading to de elopement of social capital. In particular, internal networking tools and discussion forums offer avenues for effective dialogue, which assist in relationship building (Reitz, 2012).

It is apparent that social media offers capabilities to impact organizational processes. However, still there is a scope for designing a gestalt approach whereby social media features are integrated to serve Gen Y needs, leading to higher levels of engagement. Moreover, needs of this techno-savvy generation and functional capabilities of social media are in perfect fitment. Social media capabilities of free accessibility, pervasiveness, persistence and flexibility, make such tools to facilitate information exchange, collaboration recognition programs, and communication. Therefore, Gen Y's quest for public recognition, immediacy, techno-savvy nature, mobile and connected lifestyle, open feedback, desire for collaboration and knowledge sharing are facilitated by embracing social media at workplace. Further, contemporary industry surveys and practitioner literature indicates the expanding gravitation of Gen Y employees on social media. A case in point is Cisco Connected World Technology Report (2012), which indicates that nearly two-thirds of Gen Y employees exhibit a desire to use social media at workplace.

Employee Engagement

In current fast-paced and ever-changing business environment, organizations have turned their attention to the workforce to achieve competitive advantage and stay sustainable. However, the challenge lies in fully engaging Gen Y employees, capturing their minds and hearts, as they are least engaged workforce segment globally (Anderson, 2011; Kaye & Jordan-Evans, 2003). In recent years, employee engagement concept has attracted considerable academic and practitioner attention. A recent survey indicates that HR professionals consider engagement and retention to be the biggest challenge (Fallaw & Kantrowitz, 2013). In academic literature, the seminal work on employee engagement is done by Kahn (1990). He defines employee engagement as "the harnessing of organization members' selves to their work roles; in engagement, people employ and express themselves physically, cognitively, and emotionally during role performances." (p. 694). In his view, emotional engagement refers to being able to form ties with colleagues and superiors and to experience positive feelings of empathy, care and concern. While cognitive engagement means being aware of one's role and its linkage with organizational objectives. Engagement is also conceived as a positive, affective-cognitive state composed of vigor, dedication, and absorption (Schaufeli et al. 2002). For Macey and Schneider (2008) it is "a complex nomological network encompassing trait, state, and behavioral constructs, as well as the work and organizational conditions that might facilitate state and behavioral engagement" (pp. 23-4). According to Harter, Schmidt and Hayes (2002) employee engagement is "the individual's involvement and satisfaction with as well as enthusiasm for work" (p. 269). In accordance with Kahn's conceptualization, engagement has also been shown to comprise of cognitive, emotional, and behavioral components (Saks, 2006). In simplest terms, engaged employees are motivated, committed, and align themselves with their company's culture and business strategy (Coleman, 2005, p. 66).

The concept of employee engagement has received wide attention in the practitioner world. Most of the contemporary literature on engagement comes from leading consultancies including Aon Hewitt, CIPD, and Gallup, which conducts Employee Engagement Index surveys across the world. A recent Gallup (2013) study conducted in 142 countries reveals that just over 13% global employees are actively engaged at work. In other sense, about one in eight workers is actively engaged, while the bulk of employees worldwide about 63% are not engaged. Previous research suggests certain enablers of engagement including career development, feedback, co-worker support, working climate, job control, innovation, meaningful work, and appreciation (Bakker & Demerouti, 2007; Kahn, 1990). However, for Gen Y employees, supportive environment, developmental feedback, recognition of contributions, open and consistent communication, and sharing of ideas, knowledge, and views are key motivators to create engagement. One of the strategies to drive engagement of Gen Y employees is through integrating social media to facilitate HR practices such as communication, collaboration, knowledge sharing, and recognition. This in turn, satisfies affective needs (emotional support gained through network or connections), cognitive needs (knowledge sharing, information gathering and learning from others), tension release (leisure, fun, gamification), social needs (social interactions, networking) and personal interactive needs (personal/self branding or positive self marketing through increased visible recognition). When needs of Gen Y are served through HR practices facilitated by social media, it will result in higher engagement. Therefore, if an organization embraces social media it will promote HR practices, in turn satisfying the needs of Gen Y, which also happen to be enablers of engagement, thus translating into engagement.

Theoretical Background and Research Framework with Hypotheses Formulation

The present research framework investigates the relationship between HR practices and engagement with regard to the moderating role of social media use in organizations. Figure 1 outlines the proposed research framework, which includes a direct link between HR practices and employee engagement of Gen Y employees, moderated by social media use. The study uses HR practices of communication, collaboration, knowledge sharing, and recognition. From a conceptual perspective, HR practices have been shown to be strongly associated with employee engagement (Isa, 2011; Jose & Mampilly, 2012; Sardar et al, 2011).

HR Practices and Employee Engagement

HR practices are processes aimed at utilizing the firm's human resources to achieve its objectives. As Hannah and Iverson (2002, p. 339) assert "HRM practices are viewed by employees as a 'personalized' commitment to them by the organization which is then reciprocated back to the organization by employees through positive attitudes and behavior." These are considered as instrumental in shaping employees' perceptions, attitudes, and behaviors. This study measures employees' perceptions of four practices, namely, communication, collaboration, knowledge sharing, and recognition. These are selected because of their relevance with the objective of this study. They are known to be associated with employee engagement, and at the same time are influenced by social media.

Figure 1. Research framework

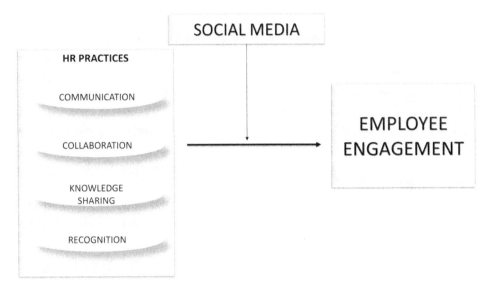

Engagement essentially follows the social exchange model, whereby employees evaluate employment relationships on cost-benefit terms and then reciprocate accordingly. To this end, HR practices such as communication, collaboration, knowledge sharing, and recognition, signals the organization's commitment and concern towards employees, which in turn generates reciprocal employee behaviors. Prior research has revealed the positive relationship of HR practices with employee behavioral outcomes of organizational commitment, motivation, job satisfaction, and intention to leave (Conway & Monks, 2009). However, the empirical research on linkage of HR practices and employee engagement is limited except for few studies (e.g. Isa, 2011; Jose & Mampilly; 2012, Sardar et al, 2011). Therefore, it is plausible to extrapolate from the above-noted studies, which reveal a relationship between HR practices and attitudinal or behavioral outcomes, that HR practices may impact employee engagement.

Communication and Employee Engagement

In simplest terms, internal communication involves information exchange among organizational members, with the objective to convey the values and goals of the organization. Prior literature strongly supports its positive impact on employee engagement (Hayase, 2009; Kahn, 1992; Welch, 2011). Specifically, open and effective senior management communication is shown to have a positive influence on employee engagement (Bakker et al., 2011). From Gen Y employees' perspective, they seek open and honest communication from top management, as they expect clear directions, well laid-out roles, and transparency in organizational policies and objectives. This can only be achieved through an efficient internal communication process, which satisfies Gen Y's informational needs and generates feeling of empowerment and involvement with the organization, in the process improving their engagement. Therefore, we hypothesize that:

H1: The effective communication offered by organization has a positive effect on engagement of Gen Y employees.

Collaboration and Employee Engagement

In present global business environment, even if employees have well-defined jobs and other resources at their disposal, they may still feel isolated and unaware about the latest happenings of the organization. Moreover, global nature of work makes working from different locations and interacting with geographically-distributed colleagues, it further makes collaboration important. Practitioner publications reveal several benefits of collaboration to organizations. However, there is dearth of academic research to investigate such benefits. A global survey by Randstand Workmonitor, has shown that more than 80% of Singaporean employees' desire to invest time in promoting workplace collaboration. Prior research also indicates that working in teams with good relationships and trust of fellow members has a positive effect on individual performance. Therefore, when employees feel being cared about by the organization, they have the tools and resources to interact with colleagues, build relationships, share their ideas and solve business problems; it improves their engagement levels (Crim & Seijts, 2006). A perception of being involved and cared for through support from team members, access to their knowledge; assist in Gen Y engagement. They are more likely to feel engaged, when they perceive an environment of collaboration and social relationships. Therefore, we hypothesize that:

H2: The extent to which organization practices collaboration has a positive effect on engagement of Gen Y employees.

Recognition and Employee Engagement

A timely and frequent recognition of employee performance is one of the strongest non-monetary rewards given to motivate employees. In accordance with Gallup (2012), employees need recognition at least a week to feel valued and motivated. In this vein, soft rewards such as pat on the back, a thank you card are effective to appreciate their contributions. Prior research confirms the positive relationship of recognition and employee engagement (Chughtai, 2013; Isa, 2011). Importantly, Gen Y employees desire to showcase their skills and harbor a feeling of being 'valued' and 'important (Hastings, 2008). Moreover, being attention-seekers, they seek open recognition of their contributions as a sign of acknowledgement. This in turn, satisfies their higher order need of appreciation and self-esteem, ultimately contributing to their engagement. Further, in line with SET, recognizing their contributions signals a return on their investment resulting in a reciprocal response of higher engagement (Kahn, 1990). Therefore, we hypothesize:

H3: The recognition programs offered by organization have a positive effect on engagement of Gen Y employees.

Knowledge Sharing and Employee Engagement

Gen Y employees display strong social tendencies i.e. they value building relationships with peers and supervisors. At the same time, they seek an environment open to sharing ideas, information, and knowledge. When an organization promotes a culture of knowledge sharing, it improves socialization process where employees engage in social interactions and build ties. Importantly, knowledge sharing will help Gen Y employees to learn and share resources, in the process leading to their development; which has been shown to be positively related with employee engagement. Therefore, knowledge sharing will foster

Gen Y development in terms of enhancement of their social and personal competencies and serve their cognitive developmental needs. Consequently, Gen Y employees will reciprocate by exhibiting positive behaviors of motivation and engagement. This factor is vital for Gen Y employees as they exhibit dominant growth needs and have a high learning orientation. As a result, they are more likely to feel engaged, when their sociocognitive needs are met. This is consistent with the prior literature, which reveals that knowledge sharing contributes to engagement (Macey et al., 2009). Therefore, we hypothesize that:

H4: The extent to which organization practices knowledge sharing has a positive effect on engagement of Gen Y employees.

Social Media, HR Practices and Employee Engagement

To study the role of a moderator, it is essential to first examine its significant interaction with other variables (i.e. communication, collaboration, knowledge sharing, and recognition) (Sharma et al., 1981). Social media possesses rich capabilities viz. user-generated content, sharing and participating elements with the dimensions of openness and pervasiveness. The extant social media literature corroborates that it improves organizational processes including, communication, collaboration, knowledge sharing, and recognition.

In context of communication, the openness, accessibility, visibility, and instantaneity enable social media to serve as a means of an open and transparent communication. In addition, multidirectional communication is also possible, where multiple employees can engage in a dialogue simultaneously. Social media platforms have been shown to improve internal communication, information and resource sharing (Lee & Xue, 2013). Tools like discussion forums, wiki have afforded a 'bottom-up' approach to communication, whereby employees of all levels can access, contribute and share resources (Rober & Cooper, 2011); while enterprise internal networks provide opportunities to employees to engage in formal and informal interactions with peers. The information-dissemination and community potential of social media provides opportunities for employees to connect and network easily, in turn, building social relationships often, with higher-level employees. This helps in identifying and using internal expertise for improved problem solving and decision making, therefore fueling collaboration (John & Seligman, 2006; Rothkrantz, 2015; Skeels & Grudin, 2009). Individual employees through their aggregate or collective knowledge creation and sharing activities in networks lead to collective intelligence (Mathews et al., 2011). Tools such as corporate wikis, internal networks like Yammer act as repositories of user-generated content to facilitate knowledge transfer which aids collaboration (Brozozowsky, 2009; Holtzbtat et al., 2013). Besides, social media facilitates organizing and sharing knowledge within an organization in particular, tacit knowledge (Paroutis & Al Saleh, 2009). It provides an open and accessible platform to share knowledge, experience, and expertise almost to anyone. Tools such as discussion forums, wikis and blogs facilitate dissemination of useful information and other resources, simultaneously make the search and discovery of new information easier (Holtzblatt et al., 2013; Zhao & Rosson, 2009). Furthermore, one area of significant social media impact is employee recognition. This is achieved by the visibility and openness of medium, allowing employee contributions visible to all; even contributions of lower-level employees are recognized and rewarded timely (Fraser & Dutta, 2008). Importantly, in present globalised business, geographically-distant managers can also recognize the accomplishments of their subordinates. This in turn, boosts their personal reputation by gaining acceptance and recognition from others (John & Seligman, 2006).

It is evident from afore-mentioned literature that social media facilitates HR practices. Further, prior research suggests a strong significant impact of, HR practices on employee engagement. Therefore, it is logical here to propose a moderating role of social media to strengthen the relationship between HR practices and engagement. Therefore, we argue that Gen Y employees' social media use will positively influence their perceptions of HR practices, which in turn positively influence their engagement. Thus, the following hypothesis is proposed:

H5: Gen Y employees' perception of HR practices will have a positive significant effect on their engagement.

H5a: Gen Y employees' social media use moderates the relationship between their engagement and their perception of HR practices (1a) Communication; (2a) collaboration; (3a) recognition; (4a) knowledge sharing.

METHODOLOGY

Sample and Questionnaire Design

A cross-sectional survey design was used to gather primary data. Data were collected by means of a structured questionnaire. Gen Y employees working in Indian multi-national IT organizations in Delhi-NCR region are selected as respondents. NCR is one of the biggest IT hubs in India and also a linchpin of India's economic growth. As per ASSOCHAM report, NCR has generated roughly 2.6 lakhs jobs doing first quarter of FY2016, the largest by any city in India (Dasgupta, 2016). The sample comprises of software development professionals born between 1980-2000 and possesses minimum working experience of six months. From the top 100 Indian IT companies list generated by NASSCOM (the Indian technology watchdog), all NCR-based firms were chosen owing to the convenience of data collection for authors. We contacted HR Managers to take their consent to participate in this research and to identify Gen Y employees based on their birth years. Respondents were selected randomly from the given list of employees that fall under Gen Y category.

In total eighteen organizations agreed to participate and hence we administered 390 online-questionnaires from August 2015 to November 2015 to survey Gen Y employees. Respondents were given two weeks to respond. After that time, a reminding mail was sent, again by the HR directors of the companies. In all, 256 completely-filled questionnaires were collected with a response rate of 65.64 per cent. In accordance with the recommendations of Kunce et al. (1975), sample size must be at least ten times the number of variables, hence the sample size of 256 is acceptable as our research model contains six variables, out of this sample 64 per cent are males and 36 per cent are females, with an age group of 20-24 represented by 27 per cent respondents, 25-29 by 57 per cent and 29-34 by 16 per cent. Out of the surveyed eighteen organizations, eight were large-sized organizations with an employee base of more than 5000, six were mid-sized organizations with an employee base of 500-5000, and four were small-sized with an employee base less than 500. All organizations were using social media tools for employees and have social media policy in place.

Measures

Questionnaire items were developed based on existing theoretical constructs and literature in the areas of social media use. The population born between 1980-2000 is defined as Gen Y employees. The five-point Likert scale (1 = strongly disagree; 5 = strongly agree) was used as the measurement method.

The questionnaire consists of five sections namely; first section is the brief introduction and instructions along with the purpose of research and assurance of establishing the anonymity of responses. Second includes the statements dealing with basic information of the respondents namely gender, years of experience, and age group, third section includes the statements on social media use. Fourth section includes the statements on HR practices, and last section includes the statements on engagement and the last one.

Social Media

Based on the extant social media literature a questionnaire is developed, as no suitable measure for social media existed. Based on this study, a questionnaire consisting of 5 items was developed (see the Appendix). Each item is a 5-point Likert type statement anchored at extreme poles ranging from 'strongly disagree' to 'strongly agree'. An example of an item is "It is good that social media is being used for working purposes." with a Cronbach's a value of 0.81. The mean value of social media use is 4.05 (SD = 0.489),

HR Practices

It includes statements on employees' perception of communication, collaboration, knowledge sharing and recognition. Questionnaires were developed for each of these HR practices. All items of the instrument follow Likert-type scale, ranging from 1 = strongly disagree to 5 = strongly agree. Communication has five items adapted from Meintjes and Steyn (2006). An example is "I communicate freely at workplace". Cronbach alpha found to be 0.96 and mean value is 3.99 (SD = 0.68). Collaboration has five items adapted from Davenport et al. (2006) and Svelby and Simons (2002). An example is "At work, it is easy for me to ask questions from others". Cronbach alpha found to be 0.78 and mean value is 3.85 (SD = 0.59). Recognition has 3 items adapted from Tremblay, Guay and Simard (2000a). An example is "I receive timely and frequent recognition of my achievements or contributions". Cronbach alpha found to be 0.72 and mean value is 3.34 (SD = 0.84). Knowledge sharing has 3 items adapted from Kim and Lee (2006). An example is "I feel comfortable sharing my knowledge and experiences." Cronbach alpha found to be 0.73 and mean value is 4.04 (SD = 0.76).

Engagement

It is measured by scale taken from Utrecht Work Engagement Scale (Schaufeli, and Bakker, 2003). This questionnaire has 17 items and measures work engagement on three dimensions- absorption, dedication, and vigor. An example is "Time flies when I am working." It is widely used scale of engagement. Cronbach alpha for engagement is 0.90 and mean value is 3.90 (SD = 0.68).

Analytical Techniques

Using AMOS 6.0, Structural Equation Modeling (SEM) is applied as the main analytical tool for this study. This study investigated the impact of HR practices on Gen Y employee engagement with moderating effect of social media use. Descriptive statistics [e.g. mean and standard deviation (SD)] were used for analysing the demographic data is presented in Table 1. The structural model was investigated using AMOS 6.0 with random maximum likelihood. Path analysis was performed on the model using standardized maximum likelihood estimation.

Measurement Model Assessment

Firstly, the instrument reliability and validity were examined. Secondly, the path coefficients of the structural model were determined for testing the hypotheses and conceptual model. To this end, in accordance with Fornell and Larcker (1981), the scales were examined for construct validity by estimating reliability, composite reliability (CR) and average variance extracted (AVE). Table 2 presents reliability and validity estimates and other metrics for the item measures.

Table 1. Construct means, standard deviations and correlations (N=256)

Variable	M	SD	1	2	3	4	5	6
1.Communication	3.9883	.68274	(.967)					
2.Collaboration	3.8488	.58608	.535**	(.782)				
3. Recognition	3.3398	.84596	.180*	.320*	(.722)			
4.Knowledge sharing	4.0415	.76183	.583**	.480**	.202*	(.732)		
5. Social media	4.0439	.4863	.136**	.107**	.183*	.127**	(.813)	
6.Employee engagement	3.9011	.67799	.773**	.526**	. 210*	.537**	.426**	(.906)

Notes: * p< 0;05; ** p<0;01; Reliability estimates (Cronbach's alphas) are in parentheses; N = 256 respondents

Table 2. Overall measurement model analysis

Sale	Standardized Loadingc	t values	R^2	Composite Reliability	AVE	α
Communication	0.79-0.96	16.287	.595	.978	.905	.967
Collaboration	0.72-0.88	12.454	.273	.872	.816	.782
Recognition	0.69-0.81	9.683	.103	.844	.742	.722
Knowledge sharing	0.69-0.85	11.256	.403	.876	.758	.732
Social media	0.71-0.88	10.258	.177	.892	.799	.813
Employee engagement	0.76-0.94	13.658	.270	.956	.901	.906
Overall Fit indices	χ^2= 218.764, χ^2/df =2.114, p<0.001, GFI (good-fit-index) = 0.928, AGFI (adjusted good-fit-index) = 0.871 RMR (root mean square residual) = 0.029, NFI (normed-fit-index) = 0.927 CFI(comparative-fit-index) = 0.982, IFI(incremental-fit-index) = 0.945 RMSEA(root mean square error of approximation) = 0.032						

Note; Fit statistics; χ^2= 116.9, p< 0;001; RMSEA = 0.04; GFI = 0.96; CFI = 0.99; All factor loadings are significant at p< 0;01

Table 3. Testing hypotheses by hierarchical moderated regression model

Variables	Hypotheses	Results (Supported)	Basic Model		Moderation Model		Extended Model	
			Std b	t-Values	Std b	t-Values	Std b	t-Values
COMM- EE	H1	Sup	0.62	15.9*	0.69	13.44**	0.61	9.24*
COMM*SM	H1a	Sup			0.71	2.8	0.78	10.84*
COLL-EE	H2	Sup	0.52	17.21*	0.49	14.31*	0.40	7.23*
COLL * SM	H2a	Sup			0.49	2.2	0.53	8.64*
RECOG-EE	H3	Sup	0.21	14.44**	0.17**	13.45**	0.12	4.43**
RECOG * SM	H3a	Sup			0.11	2.6	0.14	4.98**
KSHA-EE	H4	Sup	0.63	15.26*	0.61	13.89	0.54	8.67*
KSHA* SM	H4a	Sup	0.47		0.57	2.6	0.63	9.85**
HRI-EE	H5	Sup	0.58	19.38*	0.46	17.85*	0.33	6.91*
HRI*SM	H5a	Sup	0.11		0.18	2.9	0.22	5.67*
SM							0.11	4.15
R²			26.9%		29.1%		31.8%	
ΔR²				-	2.2		2.7	
Chi-square (df), Sig.			21.65		33.44		185.2	
GFI			0.97		0.96		0.95	
CFI			0.94		0.92		0.91	
RMSEA			0.05		0.04		0.03	

Notes; * p < 0;05; * * p < 0;01

RESULTS

Examination of Common Method Variance

As the data were gathered from same group of respondents at same point of time for all independent and dependent variables, therefore, there may be a threat of common method variance. To rectify this issue, we used Harman's single factor test to determine common method variance. In this regard, we ran exploratory factor analysis and constrained it to a single factor without selecting any rotation method. The result reveals a 39 percent explained variance, which was well within the prescribed limit of 50%, the minimum threshold in accordance with Harman's single factor test (Podsakoff et al. 2012), thereby indicating that common method variance is not a potential threat for the current study.

Construct Validation

All measures were subjected to confirmatory factor analysis (CFA) using AMOS 6.0 to provide support for the issues of dimensionality, convergent, and discriminant validity. As evident from Table 3, results of CFA indicates that this model has acceptable fit indices ($\chi^2 = 218.764$, $\chi^2 /df = 2.114$, p< .001, GFI (good-fit-index) = 0.928, AGFI (adjusted good-fit-index) = 0.871, RMR (root mean square residual) =

0.029, NFI (normed-fit-index) = 0.927 CFI(comparative-fit-index) = 0.982, IFI(incremental-fit-index) = 0.945 RMSEA (root mean square error of approximation) = 0.032). The magnitudes of standardized loadings ranged from 0.61 to 0.91, and *t*-values ranging from 9.683 to 16.287 were significant. All items had standardized loading greater than 0.60. Overall Goodness of fit statistics, magnitudes of standardized loadings and the t-values support for convergent validity (Anderson and Gerbing, 1988). Table 2 suggests that all reliability estimates were higher than 0.70 and the minimum value of the composite reliability of all the research constructs is 0.84 and the minimum average variance extracted (AVE) is 0.74. This indicates that each research construct possesses good internal consistency. Moreover, the factor loadings of all the items possess statistically significant levels. The factor loadings of all the items in the research model were > 0.5. In addition, the AVE values for all study variables were between 0.74 and 0.90, which were > 0.5. Thus, this measurement model possesses adequate convergent validity. The CFA results also shows that the square roots of all the AVE values of every research construct are higher than the pairwise correlation coefficients between the selected construct and all other variables. This constitutes the favorable discriminant validity of the measurement model (Hair et al. 2006; Kline, 2005).

Testing Hypotheses

To test H1-H4, we examined the factor loadings of the structural model with all parameters fixed across groups. As illustrated in Table 3, the model fit the data well, and all hypotheses are supported with a significance level of 5 percent and 10 percent. This study uses Ping's (1996) two-step estimation approach wherein, the origins of scales of the constructs are changed by mean-centering to reduce the correlations between the involved constructs and their interactions (Aiken and West, 1991). This is followed by multiplication of average scores of the indicators of latent variables to form interactions. Next, the factor loadings and the error variances of these interacting measures are fixed by particular values based on the formulas provided by Ping (1996) using parameter estimates from the measurement model.

Direct Effects

Results of the analysis of the model's direct effects using SEM provide fit indices of the structural model (Table 2). The results demonstrate that although χ^2 value (χ^2=218.764) is significant (p=0.001) and the ratio of the χ^2 to the degrees of freedom (χ^2/df=2.11) is below the cutoff value of 3, indicating that the model is acceptable. The values of the other fit indices such as the goodness-of-fit index (GFI), comparative fit index (CFI), normed fit index (NFI), and non-normed fit index (NNFI), root mean square residual (RMR) and root mean square error of approximation (RMSEA) are within the range of recommended values (Kline, 2005). Therefore, it is concluded that the overall fit of the model is good. The findings summarized in Table 3 indicate that HR practices – communication, collaboration, knowledge sharing, and recognition influence Gen Y employees' engagement positively at p<0.01. Among these four factors, communication shows the strongest (β. β 0.62) and recognition shows the weakest (although significant) impacts (β. β 0.21). As a whole, the model explains 29 percent of the variance in employee engagement.

Moderating Effects

Findings of moderating effect (Table 3) indicate that the moderating variable in the model social media use has clear moderating effects on the relationships between HR practices and employee engagement.

A hierarchical moderated regression analysis using structural equation modeling is used to estimate the effects of the variables and their interactions on engagement (Aiken & West, 1991). The first model (basic model) determines the impact of HR practices on Gen Y engagement. The second model estimates the moderating effect of social media use. The last model (extended model) examines the moderating effect after controlling for direct effects of social media use on Gen Y engagement. The results suggest that estimated models fits the data well and support H1a, H2a, H3a, and H4a by showing that the positive effect of communication, collaboration, recognition, and knowledge sharing respectively on Gen Y engagement, is strengthened through social media use. Importantly, addition of social media interaction terms increases the explained variance of engagement ($R2=$[3]1.8%).

Evaluation of Structural Model

Given the positive results for the analyses of discriminant validity, internal consistency reliability, and convergent validity, the structural model, in which the assumed relationships between latent variables are specified, can be evaluated. We estimated the R^2, path coefficients, and effect sizes. The R^2 and path coefficients provide information on the model efficiency. The R^2 indicates the portion of explained variance in relation to overall variance. The R^2 values may be between 0 and 1. Table 2 shows the values obtained for the R^2 and path coefficients. In general, the values should exhibit high scores to confirm whether the proposed model adequately represents the variance of an endogenous variable. However, all relevant parameters must be included in the model. The findings from Table 2 suggests a low R^2 value for recognition (RECOG), which is 0.103, indicating that the recognition measure is one of several determinants of employee engagement. Nevertheless, the high R^2 values for communication (COMM, $R^2 = 0.595$), collaboration (COLL, $R^2 = 0.273$), and knowledge sharing (KSHA, $R^2 = 0.403$), indicate that the model provides good explanations for their variance. The standardized path coefficients ranged from 0.210 to 0.773. See also Figure 2.

*Figure 2. Path analysis of structural model *P < 0.05, **P < 0.001*

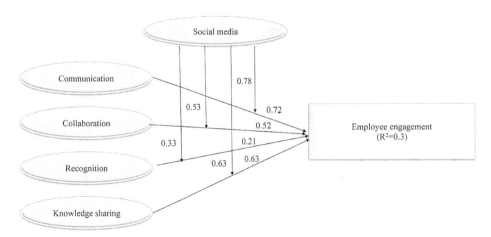

DISCUSSION

This study is focused on Indian Gen Y employees' social media use at the workplace and its impact on their engagement. India is one of the fastest growing economies around the world and its IT industry is one of the prime contributors to its GDP. The primary purpose of this study was to determine whether social media has an influence on engagement of Gen Y employees. In this vein, we indented to explore social media as a moderator that would strengthen the relationship between HR practices and employee engagement. In addition to this, the study investigates the relationship between HR practices and employee engagement.

The findings revealed that HR practices are a significant predictor of the engagement of Gen Y employees. The relationship between HR practices and Gen Y engagement was positive, which means that the availability of HR practices in the organization lead to Gen Y employees feeling more engaged. The multiple regression results are in agreement with research that found that HR practices lead to improvement in employee engagement (Jose & Mampilly; 2012; Sardar et al., 2011). Importantly the findings reveal that HR practices accounts for 29 per cent of the variance of employee engagement in the bivariate analysis. Of the four, HR practices, communication has the strongest impact and recognition programs have relatively low impact on employee engagement. This is perhaps due to the usage pattern of social media in the studied organizations. They communicate with their subsidiaries and offices at different locations through social media but do not make use of social media for conducting rewards and recognition.

The results showed a positive moderating effect of social media use on the relationship of HR practices and Gen Y engagement. This means that the social media use by Gen Y employees have a positive effect on their perceptions of HR practices. The findings further indicate that social media use in the organizations facilitates HR practices leading to the engagement of Gen Y employees. These results are in agreement with past studies, which suggests a role of social media in achieving employee engagement (Naim & Lenka, 2016; Naim & Lenka, 2016; Parry& Solidoro, 2013; Rai, 2012).

In this vein, Gen Y employees' perception of internal communication, collaboration and knowledge sharing opportunities offered by their organizations had a significant effect on engagement. Moreover, their perception towards HR practices is significantly affected by social media use. Overall, social media facilitates HR practices of communication, collaboration, recognition, and knowledge sharing to improve Gen Y engagement. Good people management that takes care of development, recognition, relationship building, and career management create a condition that is fulfilling and meaningful, resulting in the reciprocal behavior of higher engagement. This is consistent with the social exchange perspective, if Gen Y employees perceive a need satisfying experience in the organization, it creates a sense of belonging and organizational identity, and in turn they reciprocate with higher engagement.

Furthermore, Gen Y employees feel that HR practices when used properly direct them to do their job in an effective manner. The utilization of communication is an important part of the organization and makes them feel involved in key information flows and well-informed as well as updated. With this comes the facet of collaboration within the organization and it also improves the relationship with colleagues and superiors, and fosters team-work and identification of experts of a specific subject. An emphasis on knowledge sharing further helps in the learning and development of Gen Y employees, through acquisition of relevant skills and competencies. Recognition offered by the management inculcates a feeling of being valued and their performance is contributing to the bottom-line. In this view, by supporting aforementioned HR practices, social media use thereby, satisfies affective, cognitive needs of Gen Y employees. This in turn, helps in triggering higher levels of employee engagement. This is significant considering the nature of work of IT employees, whch has significant outcomes for their attitude and behaviors (Casado-Lumbreras et al., 2015; Colomo-Palacios et al., 2014).

Implications

Despite the growing interest in social media, no empirical study investigates its effect on employee engagement. Findings provide guidelines to help managers to better understand the significance of HR practices and social media use for Gen Y engagement. This study has numerous implications to theory and practice at large. From managerial standpoint, the study offers an approach to bolster the engagement strategy for Gen Y employees. The findings will encourage the management to adopt social media to satisfy Gen Y employees' needs to improve their engagement. The findings offer policy implications for organizations to incorporate social media into their strategy. In line with the findings, organizations can make use of social media to facilitate HR practices namely communication, collaboration, knowledge sharing, and recognition. Indian IT industry continues to be the forerunners of the economy in terms of employment generation. According to NASSCOM, (Indian IT trade association), IT industry has registered aggregated revenues of US$147 billion in 2015 and provided direct employment to 3.1 million people in 2013. Thus, it is prerequisite for hyper-competitive IT industry operating in globalized economy characterised by high talent mobility, to have an engaged workforce capable of completing projects within specified deadlines. Therefore, a significant implication of this study from the perspective of IT industry is a strategy to improve engagement rate as a valuable means to achieve competitive advantage. India's Union government has started 'Digital India' project to give IT industry a new impetus. This paper adds a new dimension of social media to the employer brand of organizations. More importantly, considering, Gen Y's desire for access of technology, organizations with social media will strengthen their Employee value proposition and make it more appealing to Gen Y employees. Thus, it will act as a talent magnet to attract as well as engage Gen Y employees.

From an academic standpoint, this study contributes to the literature on linkage between social media, HR practices, and Gen Y engagement. Past literature has suggested a link of social media with engagement and retention of Gen Y employees (Naim, 2014; Parry & Solidoro, 2013). However, to date, these suggested relationships are not empirically tested. In other words, this paper is first of its kind to empirically investigate the relationship between social media use in the organization and engagement of Gen Y employees. We believe that no study till date has examined the underlying association of social media and engagement of Indian Gen Y employees. This research is an attempt to take the topic of social media and employee engagement a step ahead by means of a quantitative analysis. Although employee engagement has attracted wide attention in scholar world, but its association with HR practices is largely missing in literature (Wollard & Shuck, 2011). This makes this research stand out as unique and exploratory. Further, another notable contribution is the development of scale on social media use in organizations, which further aids the future research. This study extends our understanding of employee engagement from Gen Y perspective by integrating social media with HR practices into a single model. Specifically, the study assesses the moderating effect of social media use in the same model to provide rich insights into its relationship with engagement.

Limitations and Future Scope of Research

Like any other research, this study is not devoid of any limitations. The first limitation is its relatively small sample size and cross-sectional nature. Hence, further research is needed to confirm our suggested relationships, as self-reported surveys are poor to establish cause-effect relationships. The research however confirmed the significance of social media in the context of employee engagement in Gen Y cohort. Importantly, even with a modest small size, the study is pertinent enough to serve as a stepping stone for future work. As this study was carried out in IT industry of India, empirical findings of the study could be more applicable in Asian countries as compared to Western ones. It is better to replicate this study in public sector organization or in other industries such as retail, pharmaceutical or in manufacturing sector, may be in a different country. Also, a comparative analysis could be undertaken involving Gen X and Gen Y employees to further confirm the research model. As quantitative research design has its obvious limitations so future studies should employ qualitative methods like focus interviews to further examine the results of this study. Further, it may not be a complete investigation of impact of social media on engagement as management perspective is not examined. Therefore, future research should interview both HR managers and Gen Y employees on their perception of the impact of social media on employee engagement. Further, this study will pave the way for future research work in this domain and will utilize longitudinal data.

CONCLUSION

This study was aimed at exploring a social media-based strategy to engage Gen Y employees. Findings demonstrated that use of social media has a significant moderating effect on the relationship between HR practices and employee engagement of Gen Y. It is suggested that if an organization implements social media for its employees' use, it will bolster employee engagement levels. Social media use positively influences communication, collaboration, knowledge sharing, and recognition practices in the organization, which ultimately evoke high engagement levels. Finally, we argue that the research framework of this study is a cornerstone to gain richer insights into social media value for organizations.

REFERENCES

Aiken, L. S. & Stephen, G. West (1991). *Multiple regression, Testing & interpreting interactions.*

Anderson, M. J. (2011). Six New Ways to Keep Gen Y Workers Engaged. *Evolvedemployer*. Retrieved from www.evolvedemployer.com/2011/07/13/six-new-ways-to-keep-gen-y-workers-engaged/

Bakker, A. B., Albrecht, S. L., & Leiter, M. P. (2011). Key questions regarding work engagement. *European Journal of Work and Organizational Psychology*, *20*(1), 4–28. doi:10.1080/1359432X.2010.485352

Bercovici, J. (2010). *Who coined "social media"? Web pioneers compete for credit.* Forbes. Disponível.

Bolton, R. N., Parasuraman, A., Hoefnagels, A., Migchels, N., Kabadayi, S., Gruber, T., ... Solnet, D. (2013). Understanding Generation Y and their use of social media, a review and research agenda. *Journal of Service Management*, *24*(3), 245–267. doi:10.1108/09564231311326987

Casado-Lumbreras, C., Colomo-Palacios, R., & Soto-Acosta, P. (2015). A vision on the evolution of perceptions of professional practice; the case of IT. *International Journal of Human Capital and Information Technology Professionals*, *6*(2), 65–78. doi:10.4018/IJHCITP.2015040105

Chughtai (2013). Role of HR Practices in Turnover Intentions with the Mediating Effect of Employee Engagement. *WSEAS Transactions on Business & Economics, 10*(2), 12-24.

Colomo-Palacios, R., Casado-Lumbreras, C., Misra, S., & Soto-Acosta, P. (2014). Career abandonment intentions among software workers. *Human Factors and Ergonomics in Manufacturing & Service Industries*, *24*(6), 641–655. doi:10.1002/hfm.20509

Conway, E., & Monks, K. (2008). HR practices and commitment to change, An employee-level analysis. *Human Resource Management Journal*, *18*(1), 72–89. doi:10.1111/j.1748-8583.2007.00059.x

Dasgupta. (2016). Delhi-NCR tops job creation among 8 cities in Q4 of FY16, says ASSOCHAM study. *India Times*. Retrieved from economictimes.indiatimes.com/articleshow/52477495.cms?utm_source=contentofinterest&utm_medium=text&utm_campaign=cppst

Davenport, D. L., Henderson, W. G., Mosca, C. L., Khuri, S. F., & Mentzer, R. M. Jr. (2007). Risk-adjusted morbidity in teaching hospitals correlates with reported levels of communication and collaboration on surgical teams but not with scale measures of teamwork climate, safety climate, or working conditions. *Journal of the American College of Surgeons*, *205*(6), 778–784. doi:10.1016/j.jamcollsurg.2007.07.039 PMID:18035261

DiMicco, J., Millen, D. R., Geyer, W., Dugan, C., Brownholtz, B., & Muller, M. (2008). Motivations for social networking at work. *Proceedings of the 2008 Conference on Computer Supported Cooperative Work* (pp. 711–720). New York, ACM.

Emerson, R. M. (1976). Social exchange theory. *Annual Review of Sociology*, *2*(1), 335–362. doi:10.1146/annurev.so.02.080176.002003

Fallaw, S. S., & Kantrowitz, T. M. (2013). *Global Assessment Trends Report*. SHL–The CEB Talent Measurement Solution.

Fornell, C., & Larcker, D. F. (1981). Structural equation models with unobservable variables and measurement error, Algebra and statistics. *JMR, Journal of Marketing Research*, *18*(3), 382–388. doi:10.2307/3150980

Fraser, M., & Dutta, S. (2008). *Throwing Sheep in the Boardroom, How Online Social Networking Will Transform Your Life, Work and World*. Chichester: John Wiley.

Gallup (2013). *State of the Global Workplace*. Gallup Consulting, Gallup, Washington, DC.

Gallup Organization. (2012). Employee Engagement, A Leading Indicator of Financial Performance. Retrieved from www.gallup.com/consulting/52/employee-engagement.aspx

Gerbing, D. W., & Anderson, J. C. (1988). An updated paradigm for scale development incorporating unidimensionality and its assessment. *JMR, Journal of Marketing Research*, *25*(2), 186–192. doi:10.2307/3172650

Gilbert, J., 2011, The Millennials, A new generation of employees, a new set of engagement policies The Workplace. *Ivey Business Journal*. Retrieved from iveybusinessjournal.com/topics/the-workplace/the-PGenY-a-new-generation-of-employees-a-new-set-of-engagement-policies

Hair, J. F., Black, W. C., Babin, B. J., Anderson, R. E. & Tatham, R. L. (2006). *Multivariate data analysis* (Vol. 6). Upper Saddle River, NJ, Pearson Prentice Hall.

Hannah, D. R., & Iverson, R. D. (2002). Employment Relationships in Context, Implications for Policy and Practice. In J. A. M. Coyle-Shapiro, L. Shore, S. Taylor, & L. Tetrick (Eds.), *The Employment Relationship, Examining Psychological and Contextual Perspectives* (pp. 332–350). Oxford: Oxford University Press.

Hayase, L. K. T. (2009). Internal communication in organizations and employee engagement [Unpublished doctoral dissertation]. University of Nevada, Las Vegas, USA.

Holtzblatt, L., Drury, J. L., Weiss, D., Damianos, L. E., & Cuomo, D. (2013). Evaluating the Uses and Benefits of an Enterprise Social Media Platform. *Journal of Social Media for Organizations*, *1*(1), 1–13.

Isa, S. N. B. (2011). The relationship between human resource practices and employee engagement, A case study in Nichias.

John, A., & Seligmann, D. (2006). Collaborative tagging and expertise in the enterprise. *Proceedings of the 15th International Conference on World Wide Web*. New York, NY; ACM. Press.

Jose, G., & Mampilly, S. R. (2012). Satisfaction with HR Practices and Employee Engagement, A Social Exchange Perspective. *Journal of Economics & Behavioral Studies*, *4*(7), 423–430.

Kahn, W. A. (1990). Psychological conditions of personal engagement and disengagement at work. *Academy of Management Journal*, *33*(4), 692–724. doi:10.2307/256287

Kaplan, A. M., & Haenlein, M. (2010). Users of the world, unite! The challenges and opportunities of Social Media. *Business Horizons*, *53*(1), 59–68. doi:10.1016/j.bushor.2009.09.003

Kaye, B., & Jordan-Evans, S. (2003). How to retain high-performance employees. *Proceedings of Annual* (Vol. 2, pp. 291-298).

Kim, H., Knight, D. K., & Crutsinger, C. (2009). Generation Y employees retail work experience, The mediating effect of job characteristics. *Journal of Business Research*, *62*(5), 548–556. doi:10.1016/j.jbusres.2008.06.014

Kim, S., & Lee, H. (2006). The impact of organizational context and information technology on employee knowledge-sharing capabilities. *Public Administration Review*, *66*(3), 370–385. doi:10.1111/j.1540-6210.2006.00595.x

Kline, R. B. (2005). Principles and Practice of Structural Equation Modeling (2nd ed.). New York, The Guilford Press.

Kunce, J. T., Cook, D. W., & Miller, D. E. (1975). Random variables and correlational overkill. *Educational and Psychological Measurement*, *35*(3), 529–534. doi:10.1177/001316447503500301

Lee, E., & Xue, W. (2013). How do online social networks drive internal communication and improve employee engagement? Retrieved from digitalcommons.ilr.cornell.edu/student/22/

Lockwood, N. R. (2007). Leveraging employee engagement for competitive advantage. *SHRM Research Quarterly, 52*(3), 1–12.

Macey, W. H., & Schneider, B. (2008). The meaning of employee engagement. *Industrial and Organizational Psychology: Perspectives on Science and Practice, 1*(1), 3–30. doi:10.1111/j.1754-9434.2007.0002.x

Matthews, T., Whittaker, S., Moran, T., & Yuen, S. (2011). Collaboration personas, A new approach to designing workplace collaboration tools. *Proceedings of CHI '11*, New York, NY; ACM Press.

Meintjes, C. & Steyn, B. (2006). A critical evaluation of the Downs-Hazen instrument (CSQ) by measuring employee communication satisfaction at a private higher education institution in South Africa.

Naim, M. F., & Lenka, U. (2016). Knowledge sharing as an intervention for Gen Y employees intention to stay. *Industrial and Commercial Training, 48*(3), 142–148. doi:10.1108/ICT-01-2015-0011

Naim, M. F., & Lenka, U. (2016). Mentoring, social media, and Gen Y employees' intention to stay, Towards a conceptual model. *International Journal of Business System & Research.*

Naim, M. F. (2014). Leveraging Social Media for Generation Y retention. *European Journal of Business & Management, 6*(23), 173–179.

Paroutis, S., & Al Saleh, A. (2009). Determinants of knowledge sharing using Web 2.0 technologies. *Journal of Knowledge Management, 13*(4), 52–63. doi:10.1108/13673270910971824

Parry, E., & Solidoro, A. (2013). Social media as a mechanism for engagement. In *Social Media in Human Resources Management* (pp. 121–141). Emerald Group Publishing Limited. doi:10.1108/S1877-6361(2013)0000012010

Ping, R. A. Jr. (1996). Latent variable interaction and quadratic effect estimation, A two-step technique using structural equation analysis. *Psychological Bulletin, 119*(1), 166–186. doi:10.1037/0033-2909.119.1.166

Reitz, A. (2012). Social media's function in organizations; A functional analysis approach. *Global Media Journal, 5*(2), 41–56.

Rober, M. B., & Cooper, L. P. (2011). Capturing knowledge via an "Intrapedia", A case study. *Proceedings of the 44th Annual Hawaii International Conference on System Sciences*. Los Alamitos, CA; IEEE Computer Society Press. 10.1109/HICSS.2011.94

Rothkrantz, L. (2015). How social media facilitate learning communities and peer groups around MOOCS. *International Journal of Human Capital and Information Technology Professionals, 6*(1), 1–13. doi:10.4018/ijhcitp.2015010101

Saks, A. M. (2006). Antecedents and consequences of employee engagement. *Journal of Managerial Psychology, 21*(7), 600–619. doi:10.1108/02683940610690169

Sardar, S., Rehman, A., Yousaf, U., & Aijaz, A. (2011). Impact of HR practices on employee engagement in banking sector of Pakistan. *Interdisciplinary Journal of Contemporary Research in Business*, *2*(9), 378–389.

Sashi, C. M. (2012). Customer engagement, buyer-seller relationships, and social media. *Management Decision*, *50*(2), 253–272. doi:10.1108/00251741211203551

Schaufeli, W. B., & Bakker, A. B. (2004). Job demands, job resources, and their relationship with burnout and engagement, a multi-sample study. *Journal of Organizational Behavior*, *25*(3), 293–315. doi:10.1002/job.248

Schaufeli, W. B., Salanova, M., Gonzalez-Roma, V., & Bakker, A. B. (2002). The measurement of engagement and burnout, a two sample confirmatory factor analytic approach. *Journal of Happiness Studies*, *3*(1), 71–92. doi:10.1023/A:1015630930326

Seijts, G. H., & Crim, D. (2006). What engages employees the most or, the ten C's of employee engagement. *Ivey Business Journal*, *70*(4), 1–5.

Sharma, S., Durand, R. M., & Gur-Arie, O. (1981). Identification and analysis of moderator variables. *JMR, Journal of Marketing Research*, *18*(3), 291–300. doi:10.2307/3150970

Skeels, M. M., & Grudin, J. (2009). When social networks cross boundaries, a case study of workplace use of Facebook and LinkedIn. *Proceedings of the ACM international conference on supporting group work* (pp. 95-104). New York, NY; ACM Press.

Smith, M. C. (2012). The interaction of social media and the law and how to survive the social media revolution. *New Hampshire Bar Journal*, *52*, 24–39.

Sveiby, K. E., & Simons, R. (2002). Collaborative climate and effectiveness of knowledge work-an empirical study. *Journal of Knowledge Management*, *6*(5), 420–433. doi:10.1108/13673270210450388

Tremblay, M., Guay, P., & Simard, G. (2000a). Organizational Commitment and Extra-behaviors, The Influence of Human Resource Practices.

Twenge, J. M., & Campbell, S. M. (2008). Generational differences in psychological traits and their impact on the workplace. *Journal of Managerial Psychology*, *23*(8), 862–877. doi:10.1108/02683940810904367

Universal McCann. (2008). *Power to the people social media tracker; Wave 3*. New York, NY: Universal McCann.

Walter, E., (2012), Number Crunching, The Top 51 Stats for Generation Y Marketers. Thenextweb. Retrieved from thenextweb.com/socialmedia/2012/01/21/number-crunching-the-top-51-stats-for-generation-y-marketers/

Welch, M. (2011). The evolution of the employee engagement concept, communication implications. *Corporate Communications. International Journal (Toronto, Ont.)*, *16*(4), 328–346.

Wollard, K., & Shuck, B. (2011). Antecedents of employee engagement, A structured review of literature. *Advances in Developing Human Resources, 13*(4), 429–446. doi:10.1177/1523422311431220

Zhao, D., & Rosson, M. B. (2009). How and why people Twitter, The role that microblogging plays in informal communication at work. *Proceedings of the International Conference on Supporting Group Work* (pp. 243–252). New York, NY. ACM Press.

This research was previously published in the International Journal of Human Capital and Information Technology Professionals (IJHCITP), 8(3); pages 29-48, copyright year 2017 by IGI Publishing (an imprint of IGI Global).

APPENDIX

Social Media Use

I feel that using social media, work for me has become more interesting.
It is good that social media is being used for working purposes.
I find social media easy to use and flexible.
My organization allows me to actively use social media (blogs, wiki, communities and internal networking tool (like Yammer, SharePoint, Chatter or any other own custom-build network) for work purposes.
My team leader and peers support me in using social media for work purposes.

Communication

I communicate freely at my workplace.
I have informal communication with my colleagues.
I feel better informed about ongoing activities in the organization.
I get timely and updated access of information.
My organization offers opportunities to connect and network with colleagues.

Collaboration

I find it useful to work in teams.
At work, I build relationships with others.
At work, I have the opportunities to create and discover new information and knowledge.
Facilitates search for like-minded members working in different departments or locations.
I feel comfortable asking questions from others.

Recognition

I can enhance my personal reputation by demonstrating my skills and expertise.
I receive timely and frequent recognition of my achievements or contributions.
I receive timely feedback of my performances.

Knowledge Sharing

At work, I feel comfortable sharing my professional knowledge and experiences.
My organization allows me free access to information and documents held within the organization.
I frequently collect knowledge from others.

Employee Engagement

At my work, I feel that I am bursting with energy.

I find the work that I do full of meaning and purpose.

Time flies when I'm working.

At my job, I feel strong and vigorous.

I am enthusiastic about my job.

When I am working, I forget everything else around me.

My job inspires me.

When I get up in the morning, I feel like going to work.

I feel happy when I am working intensely.

I am proud of the work that I do.

I am immersed in my work.

In continue working for very long periods at a time.

To me, my job is challenging.

I get carried away when I'm working.

At my job, I am very resilient, mentally.

It is difficult to detach myself from my job.

At my work, I always persevere, even when things do not go well.

Chapter 60
Examining Social Commerce Intentions Through the Uses and Gratifications Theory

Gokhan Aydin
Istanbul Medipol University, Istanbul, Turkey

ABSTRACT

Changes in consumer behavior enabled by social networking technologies is leading to a transformation in e-commerce. Consumers' use of social media sites and relevant technologies for different aspects of shopping has become an issue of utmost concern to retailers and related businesses. Adopting a uses and gratifications theory (UGT) perspective, the article aims to demonstrate motives of users utilizing social media in their purchase decisions. Drawing from digital marketing and e-commerce literature, relevant uses and gratifications for social commerce (s-commerce) were chosen as information access, escape, entertainment, passing time, cool and new trends, and socialization. The proposed model was analyzed and tested via OLS regression and ANOVA analysis using the data collected from a survey study on 361 subjects in Turkey. Information access, relaxing entertainment, and socialization motives emerged as significant antecedents of s-commerce intentions. No significant effect of demographics on social commerce intentions were observed in the analysis.

1. INTRODUCTION

Ease of access to information, products and services through Internet and information technologies, coupled with the rapid adoption of interactive technologies and social networks all over the world are transforming how business and commerce is conducted. As the number of users of social media sites such as Facebook, Twitter and Instagram grow, various businesses started using these platforms as an influential channel to reach and connect with potential and existing customers. Social networking sites can be leveraged to create trust and persuade consumers to choose products, however, control over the content published on these platforms is limited. To overcome these limitations e-commerce companies

DOI: 10.4018/978-1-7998-9020-1.ch060

started providing opportunities to comment, appraise and share content on their own platforms to create an interactive environment for users that is alike to social media. This transition to Web 2.0, which facilitates interaction between users and organizations, and provides participation and sharing opportunities to its participants has led to the emergence of social commerce (s-commerce) concept in 2005. It has become a hot topic since then (Curty & Zhang, 2011) and interest on it is expected to increase as it gains more significance (Chen & Shen, 2015; Lin, Li, & Wang, 2017). According to a systematic review of scholarly articles published between 2000 to 2014, "social media marketing", "online shopping & e-commerce" are among the Top-10 topics of online marketing research (Roy, Datta, & Basu, 2017). Two recent literature reviews on s-commerce that analyzed more than 100 and 400 studies respectively, stressed out the increasing significance of this concept (Busalim & Hussin, 2016; Lin et al., 2017). This phenomenon is highlighted by the increasing number of articles-11 in 2011 to 58 in 2016-appearing in Web of Knowledge database for "social commerce" or "s-commerce" terms in manuscript titles.

Social commerce (s-commerce) is considered as a new form of electronic commerce (e-commerce) which involves social networking systems that enable social interaction and user contributions (Liang, Ho, Li, & Turban, 2011). A significant majority of the relevant literature accepts social commerce as the use of social media sites in various stages of consumer decision process and s-commerce activities act as an enabler of online purchase process (Shen, 2012).

S-commerce is expected to become one of the most widely adopted electronic commerce platforms in the not-so-distant future (Zhang and Benyoucef 2016). Social networking sites and relevant tools provide abundant opportunities to browse products and to get comments and reviews provided by real users and peers. Consequently, several companies have made efforts to get a firm foothold and carry out actual sales transactions over social media. For instance, Dell claimed that it made $6.5 million by selling computers on Twitter between 2007 and 2010 and Disney allowed people to purchase tickets directly on Facebook without leaving the social network (Turban, Strauss, & Lai, 2015, p. 12). Facebook, not so long ago, launched Facebook Marketplace, a platform that facilitates buying and selling of goods. Furthermore, Facebook owned Instagram expanded its "shoppable posts" feature, which provide brands the ability to add e-commerce links within their Instagram posts to help drive transactions, to nine countries (Instagram, 2018).

Companies practicing e-commerce, especially retailers, want to leverage the benefits of social media to a greater extent. For instance, Instagram and Pinterest-the more visually attractive social platforms-have enticed the interest of businesses and entrepreneurs. These platforms are utilized for promotion and marketing communications as well as directly selling products to users (Instagram, 2018). To exploit the opportunities offered by Web 2.0 and social networking systems, it is imperative to study and understand consumer motivations in these environments. Within this dynamic environment, the present study offers two major contributions to the s-commerce literature. From a theoretical perspective, a model based on a well-established theory on consumer motives in social media use, namely UGT is utilized to enhance the classical utilitarian & hedonic motivation perspective that is used extensively in shopping literature. UGT is utilized by researchers in several context such as mobile app use behavior (Ha, Kim, Libaque-Saenz, Chang, & Park, 2015), social media use behavior (Gan & Li, 2018; Phua, Jin, & Kim, 2017), and online shopping use behavior (Lim & Ting, 2012) in addition to its original setting, mass media communications (Katz, Blumler, & Gurevitch, 1974). Up till this study, UGT's application to social commerce is limited to only a few studies (Sharma & Crossler, 2014; Yang & Li, 2014). This theoretical approach provides a novel perspective at the s-commerce use behavior compared to extant literature as the general hedonic motives constructs utilized in relevant literature is somewhat limited compared to detailed sub-categories provided by UGT. From a managerial perspective, the major contribution is confirming/refuting transferability of existing knowledge on e-commerce to s-commerce. This research is carried out in a developing country, Turkey, situated at the crossroads of Asia and Europe with consumers influenced by both Western and Eastern cultural aspects. Given that prior research on s-commerce consumer motives in developing countries is scarce, testing for the relevance of each gratification in new settings is crucial to arrive at valid conclusions. In addition, the effect of demographics that are becoming less meaningful in explaining differences in technology adoption consumer behavior in developed countries may not reflect to developing markets well. Considering the differing properties of Turkish culture in terms of demographics, especially in gender equality and women's social status, may lead to conflicting results with the current trends in developed countries.

In line with the research gap, the following research questions are aimed to be answered with the present study:

Q1: How different type of motives/gratifications affect social commerce intentions?
Q2: Do major demographics (age, gender, education and income) affect social commerce intentions?
Q3: Do major demographics (age, gender, education and income) affect user motivations/gratifications on social commerce intentions?

In order to answer the aforementioned research questions, e-commerce and s-commerce consumer behavior literature were examined. The research model was developed upon shopping values, UGT and relevant motivational studies. Hypotheses were developed and presented in Section 2, where the theoretical background is pondered in detail. This section is followed by methodology where sampling, data-collection and research model is described. In addition, operationalization of each relevant construct and the scales utilized are likewise presented in Section 3. Data analysis and results are provided in Section 4. The findings are discussed in Section 5 where theoretical and practical contributions of the present research are provided. The paper is concluded by highlighting the study's limitations and providing future research avenues.

2. THEORETICAL BACKGROUND

2.1. Social Networking Sites and Social Media

Social network sites, social media and Web 2.0 has been used interchangeably in the literature. Derived from the categorization by Constantinides and Fountain (2008), basic categories of social media can be listed as follows: blogs & microblogs (i.e. Wordpress, Blogger, Twitter), general social networking sites (i.e. Facebook), thematic and professional networking sites (i.e. Linked-in), content sharing sites & communities (i.e. Flickr, Youtube, 5oopx), forums/bulletin boards, content aggregators, social bookmarking sites & collaborative filtering sites (i.e. Stumbleupon or del.icio.us). As this categorization highlights, social networking sites are not limited to social media sites such as Facebook but encompass a wider range of sites such as forums, blogs, online communities and wikis. Consequently, use of social media in e-commerce / online shopping can be practiced in a wide-variety of platforms.

2.2. Consumer Motives in Shopping and E-Commerce

Consumer motives indicate the processes originated by needs aroused in an individual to achieve certain benefits or avoid unsought outcomes (Solomon, 2009). Human motives have been categorized in two basic categories, namely utilitarian and hedonic in consumer behavior literature (Hirschman & Holbrook, 1982). Thus, basically consumers shop online or offline with task-focused utilitarian motives or hedonic experiential motives (Büttner, Florack, & Göritz, 2013). These fundamental motives may be segmented into more detailed needs as well. Using various aspects of Web 2.0 technologies, e-commerce is becoming a medium that can provide hedonic experiences for consumers (Fang, George, Shao, & Wen, 2016). The extant literature that focuses on motivations have considered several types of gratifications under a larger hedonic motivations context. Hedonic or experiential aspects of shopping include adventure seeking, pursuing new experiences, sensory stimulation, and escape from daily life and boredom. Essentially, these sub-dimensions of hedonic value are considered in a multi-faceted way in the Uses and Gratifications Theory leading us to adopt it to investigate social commerce consumer behavior in a detailed way.

2.3. S-Commerce and E-Commerce

The differing approaches to define and operationalize social commerce is evident in the extant literature. In one hand, there are transactional approaches that define social commerce as "use of social media for transactions and activities that are driven primarily by social interactions and user contributions" (Zhang et al. 2014; Liang et al. 2011). A similar perspective ties the definition of s-commerce to e-commerce and accepts it as a sub-category of e-commerce (Turban, Bolloju, & Liang, 2010). Considering that e-commerce itself is defined in various ways (transactional-exchange of goods, services or a wider range of business activities including information exchange such as marketing, customer complaint management, supplier relations etc.), this perspective provides a broader range of operationalization that is not limited to transactions (Chaffey, 2009, p. 10; Turban et al., 2015). From a different point of view, s-commerce has been defined as "a form of Internet-based 'social media' that allow people to participate in the marketing and selling of products and services in online marketplaces and communities" (Stephen & Toubia, 2010; Turban et al., 2015, p. 12). This approach highlights social media's role and the integration of social network features into internet retailers' systems. Thus, s-commerce can be considered as an evolution of Web 2.0 technologies to online commerce operations as well (Busalim & Hussin, 2016; Turban & Liang, 2011). Web 2.0 technologies provide increased interactivity and lead to higher participation of consumers in various stages of e-commerce by means of writing and sharing blogs, commenting or rating systems and similar tools. Given the wide range of social networking systems available to consumers that facilitate two-way communication, social commerce is not limited to general social media sites such as Facebook. Other platforms and tools including forums, ratings, reviews sites, recommendations on e-commerce platforms, blogs and others enable social commerce (Kucukcay & Benyoucef, 2014). The majority of large e-commerce sites such as Amazon.com incorporate social networking tools (i.e. ratings, comment systems etc.) to their systems to enable social interaction within the system. Moreover, they are also offering new applications such as Spark by Amazon that aim users of sites such as Pinterest or Instagram that are becoming venues for shopping (Natanson, 2017).

2.3.1. Social Commerce Intentions

As discussed previously, s-commerce is defined in differing ways in the extant literature. It is usually considered as a type of electronic commerce activity (Turban & Liang, 2011). However, considering the proliferated types of social networking sites and the variety of tools each utilize it is hard to arrive at a globally accepted definition. Within the context of this study s-commerce concept is basically operationalized as "the use of social media in buying process of consumers". Intention to use social commerce is termed as s-commerce intentions for convenience throughout this study. S-commerce intentions are revealed via questioning the users' tendency to follow / give online recommendations on social media and their intentions to use social media in their shopping decisions. Despite the rising interest in this concept, the underlying motivations that affect s-commerce are not clear as there are several relevant studies with contradictory conclusions. The differences in motivating factors as well as variables such as demographics are evident in the literature. An overview of the literature on demographics' effects on e-commerce and relevant technology adoption is provided in the following section.

2.4. Uses and Gratifications

To explore consumer motivations in online shopping and s-commerce in more detail, Uses and Gratifications Theory (UGT) is adopted in the present study. The classical utilitarian and hedonic value/ motive framework is embraced from a wider perspective in UGT, a consumer-centric approach that was originally used to explain consumer motivations and effectiveness of mass-media use. According to UGT, "gratifications" are the perceived fulfillment of a need through an activity, for instance a particular media use. Consequently, UGT tries to explain and understand the psychological needs that are motivating individuals to use certain media and the resulting gratifications that fulfill these needs (Katz et al., 1974). In UGT, cognitive needs, affective needs, relaxation needs, personal and social integrative needs are considered as fundamental 'needs' categories. Similarly, to answer these basic needs, cognitive benefits, social-integrative benefits, personal-integrative benefits, and hedonic benefits are considered in the literature.

Cognitive gratifications or benefits, involve media's ability to deliver desirable information, whereas social integrative benefits indicate media's ability to enable social interaction and strengthening the consumer's ties with others. Personal integrative benefits are associated to the media's ability to enhance users' credibility, status, reputation and confidence. Finally, hedonic benefits refer to the aesthetic and pleasurable experiences obtained from using media (Katz, Blumler, & Gurevitch, 1973; Nambisan & Baron, 2007; Verhagen, Swen, Feldberg, & Merikivi, 2015).

Albeit originating from mass communication use behavior, UGT is a well-established approach that has been utilized to examine consumer behavior in several contexts. In its early applications main gratifications identified for media use were related to entertainment and information. Recent studies using UGT on new communication media such as social media and mobile devices also have identified similar motives. Internet / website use (Eighmey & McCord, 1998), mobile app use behavior (Ha et al., 2015), social media use behavior (Gan & Li, 2018; Joinson, 2008; Phua et al., 2017), and online shopping behavior (Joines, Scherer, & Scheufele, 2003; Lim & Ting, 2012) are among relevant contemporary application areas that obtained similar conclusions. Intriguingly, UGT can be considered a more suitable theory to apply to social media than traditional media in our current environment. UGT assumes active participation of users and an intentional purpose in consuming/using media. Unlike unwilling exposure to traditional media (outdoor, radio etc.) social media users willingly prefer and use these media (Ha et al., 2015; Xu, Ryan, Prybutok, & Wen, 2012).

Studies based on UGT identified several gratifications that an individual achieves from using social media, resulted in gratifications relevant in s-commerce context (Yang & Li, 2014). For instance, Papacharissi and Mendelson (2011)'s study on Facebook use behavior led to nine separate motives: information sharing, habitual pass time, relaxing entertainment, escapism, cool and new trend, companionship, professional advancement, social interaction and meeting new people. Other researchers have led to similar uses and gratifications of social media such as affection, coordination, disclosure, entertainment, escape, immediate access, relaxation, stylishness, leisure, social presence, following fashion, demonstrating sociability, and improving social knowledge (Papacharissi & Mendelson, 2011; Phua et al., 2017; Smock, Ellison, Lampe, & Wohn, 2011; Whiting & Williams, 2013; Xu et al., 2012).

Among the many gratifications put forward in the extant social media and s-commerce literature, the following were selected as they cover basic needs and offer the balance between parsimony and enough depth to uncover relevant motives:

- **Cognitive Needs**: information seeking
- **Affective/Hedonic Needs**: escape, entertainment, passing time
- **Social Needs:** Socialization gratification, Cool / new trend

2.4.1. Information

Information related gratifications are the major cognitive gratification of using media according to UGT. From a shopping-value perspective, this is the major component that reflects the utilitarian motives. Information related motives are operationalized in several ways in the literature focusing on UGT such as information seeking, information access and information quality. This gratification is related to satisfying the users' apparent or latent information needs. Depending on the context, the users may seek the information himself/herself, it may be provided by mass media or provided on web pages / shopping sites. In an online context, the search for information is one of the major reasons Internet and websites are used for (Papacharissi & Rubin, 2000; Peffers, 2001). In relevant studies on Internet use and e-commerce, seeking for and acquiring information was found to influence satisfaction of users (L. Chen, Gillenson, & Sherrell, 2002; Joines et al., 2003; Song, Larose, Eastin, & Lin, 2004). Likewise, obtaining information using social media sites is a cognitive gratification that was found to be among the main reasons to use social media (Hicks et al., 2012; Park, Kee, & Valenzuela, 2009). Acquiring information shared and understanding what other people-especially of significance-think of is a value specific to virtual communities such as social media sites. A similar concept defining the behavior of consumers to browse products for collecting information on new fashion trends is called idea shopping (Bloch, Ridgway, & Sherrell, 1989). Seeking information on fashion trends in itself is considered as a stand-alone gratification to browse products (Arnold & Reynolds, 2003). Information seeking gratification that is operationalized in this study is defined as "acquiring information to help in commerce activities and buying decisions on social networking sites" (Yang & Li, 2014). In the extant literature on social media use, information related gratifications were found to have a positive effect on relevant dependent variables such as use intentions (Bonds-Raacke & Raacke, 2010; Ha et al., 2015; Park et al., 2009). In addition, it was found to be a significant motivation for using virtual communities and social commerce sites (Teo, Chan, Wei, & Zhang, 2003; Yang & Li, 2014) and engaging in e-commerce (Liu & Forsythe, 2010).

In accordance with the established studies, information seeking gratification is hypothesized to have a positive effect on s-commerce intentions.

H1: Information seeking gratification will have positive effect on s-commerce intentions.

2.4.2. Entertainment

According to UGT, entertainment is one of the major factors that motivate users to use a particular media (Eighmey & McCord, 1998; Luo, 2002) such as social media (Xu et al., 2012). Entertainment is a relevant motive in retail and shopping literature, generally considered as hedonic or experiential motives. Hedonic motives has become as significant as utilitarian motives in purchase decisions, moreover, shopping in itself is a means to create joy and to entertain oneself (Babin, Darden, & Griffin, 1994; Childers, Carr, & Carson, 2001). In online shopping, consumers enjoy the shopping process itself and shopping behavior in general is perceived as a fun activity as opposed to being a tedious task or job to be finished (To, Liao, & Lin, 2007). Online shoppers pursue entertainment by using new technologies during online shopping (Kim & Forsythe, 2007). Research focusing on social networking site and general internet use indicated that entertaining websites provide higher satisfaction (Luo, 2002) and the entertainment gratification is among the most significant factors affecting attitudes towards websites (Hausman & Siekpe, 2009). Besides, it was also shown that entertainment affects users' participation behavior (Choi et al., 2016; Dholakia, Bagozzi, & Pearo, 2004). Similarly, in studies on e-commerce, entertainment factor was found to have a positive effect on commercial-oriented media usage (Hicks et al., 2012; Lim & Ting, 2012) and accepted as a significant predictor of behavior (Childers et al., 2001).

Based on extant literature, entertainment in social commerce context can be defined as "the extent to which the users perceive using social media for commerce as relaxing, fun and entertaining" (Hicks et al., 2012; Lim & Ting, 2012). It was found to be a major motivation for using social commerce sites (Yang & Li, 2014), therefore, we hypothesize entertainment gratification to have a positive effect on s-commerce intentions.

H2: Entertainment gratification will have positive effect on s-commerce intentions.

2.4.3. Passing Time

Internet and social media can be used in various ways. Social media, with its infinite scrolling, offers an effective way to utilize one's free time. The passing time gratification is grounded on this premise and can be defined simply as using social media to pass idle time. In several studies on social media, passing time gratification was found to be positively related to social media use behavior (Hicks et al., 2012; Sheldon, 2008). Consumers can see what their friends are using, buying, searching for and they can read and write relevant comments. Consequently, passing time gratification can be assumed to have a positive effect on s-commerce intention. The studies testing for this hypothesized effect found weak or insignificant effects. For instance passing time was found to be an insignificant predictor of social commerce in Yang and Li (2014)'s study but found to have a significant effect in certain others on social media (Hicks et al., 2012; Sheldon, 2008). Further studies in different contexts are needed to arrive at meaningful insights, thus we hypothesize pass time gratification to have a positive effect on s-commerce intentions.

H3: Passing Time gratification will have positive effect on s-commerce intentions.

2.4.4. Escape

Escape gratification is among the hedonic aspects of UGT and is considered to satisfy tension-free needs. Escape can be defined as participating in activities to get away from the real world, the problems and pressures of daily life (Xu et al., 2012). Considering that social media as a venue that promote easy communication, sharing and entertainment, it is an alternative to easily escape problems and pressures of daily life. However, studies incorporating escape gratification have led to contradicting results. Escape gratification was found to positively affect intentions and behavior in several studies on shopping and social media (Korgaonkar & Wolin, 1999; Papacharissi & Mendelson, 2011; Smock et al., 2011) whereas this effect was found to be insignificant in others (Xu et al., 2012; Yang & Li, 2014). It should be noted that escapism have been considered under a larger "entertainment" or "hedonic motivation" construct in certain motivational studies on shopping (Hirschman & Holbrook, 1982) and social media use (i.e. Ha et al., 2015; Smock et al., 2011). The limited number of studies that have incorporated this gratification separately limits the ability to justify the discrepancies. Therefore, to offer new evidence and test for the significance of this factor, escape gratification was hypothesized to have a positive effect on s-commerce intentions.

H4: Escape gratification will have positive effect on s-commerce intentions.

2.4.5. Cool & New Trend

The relevant literature on UGT in social media reveal "cool and new trend" gratification as a possible factor affecting user behavior. This gratification rests upon the belief that individuals use new media and technologies because it is the thing to do and everybody else is doing it. This gratification points to the symbolic benefits of using media and technologies as a way to achieve and sustain social acceptance. For instance, two studies, one by Sheldon (2008) and the other by Papacharissi and Mendelson (2011) on motives for using Facebook found coolness and new trend among other factors to be a significant motive. Cool and new trend gratification in social commerce context refer to users utilizing social commerce to look cool and fashionable. Given that users perceive social commerce as a reasonably new trend, it is possible to feel cool benefiting from s-commerce (Sharma & Crossler, 2014). Therefore, we hypothesize cool and new trend gratification to have a positive effect on s-commerce intentions.

H5: Cool and new trend gratification will have positive effect on s-commerce intentions.

2.4.6. Socialization

Another matter of debate is the significance of the "social" aspect of s-commerce. Both social media and shopping have "social" aspects. Apart from utilitarian benefits or pure enjoyment purposes, shopping can be used as a way to socialize as well. This phenomenon of shoppers' desire for social interaction with others of similar interests, and affiliating with reference groups was proposed by Tauber (1972) and Reynolds and Beatty (1999) highlighted social needs in shopping environments. These needs are conceptualized as social shopping in a separate study (Arnold & Reynolds, 2003). Consideration of social motives in e-commerce setting appeared in the form of a lack of socialization in early e-commerce operations that can deter consumers to shop online (Swaminathan, Lepkowska-White, & Rao, 1999). However, with the emergence of mobile technologies and Web 2.0 technologies, online shopping has inherited a social aspect as well. Accordingly, social shopping began to act as a significant factor influencing user behavior on m-commerce and s-commerce contexts (Åkesson, 2007; Parker & Wang, 2016). Social media-in itself-derives value from the communication and interaction it provides to users. Consequently, social interaction is a natural element of social media sites. Meeting the expectations, the studies on social media resulted in the notion that people use social network sites for socializing in addition to other needs such as self-status seeking or entertainment gratifications (Park et al., 2009; Whiting & Williams, 2013). It has been shown that social interactions on internet, whether they be on social media or websites, lead to higher engagement. For instance, it was found that social interaction motivation positively affects the time spent on a website (Ko, Cho, & Roberts, 2005). Using Web 2.0 technologies and social networking sites, consumers are able to connect with others of similar interests. These ties created over virtual environments are posited to be influential in consumer behavior and purchasing decisions (Choi et al., 2016). Studies considering "social" dimension of social networking sites in shopping contexts such as "social capital theory" (Nahapiet & Ghoshal, 1998) and "social identification" (Farivar, Turel, & Yuan, 2018) social interaction (J. Huang & Zhou, 2018) have led to conclusions that social interactions affect purchase intentions (i.e. L. T. Huang, 2016).

In the light of the studies on social media, e-commerce, and shopping value, we hypothesize socialization to have a positive effect on s-commerce intentions.

H6: Socialization gratification will have positive effect on s-commerce intentions.

2.5. Effect of Demographics on Gratifications & S-commerce

The existing literature examining the effects of demographics on technology and information systems use suggests that differences exist with regards to age, gender and income (Morris & Venkatesh, 2000). However, effect of demographics on use intentions were not covered in established consumer behavior theories and the lack of a well-founded framework presents a research gap. A summary of relevant studies on effect of demographics is provided in this section to offer insights on potential effects in social commerce setting.

The younger population have been exposed to Internet and social media at earlier ages and a digital divide between generations is evident in established studies on technology adoption (Korgaonkar & Wolin, 1999; Pfeil, Arjan, & Zaphiris, 2009; Viswanath Venkatesh & Morris, 2000). It has been found that older users have lower perceived technological skills (Chung, Park, Wang, Fulk, & McLaughlin, 2010) and lack of IT experience coupled with resistance to change creates barriers of adopting new technology and products (Trocchia & Janda, 2000). Several studies have considered age as a significant factor that affects online shopping / e-commerce behavior (Bigné, Ruiz, & Sanz, 2007; Hernández, Jiménez, & José Martín, 2011; Liébana-Cabanillas & Alonso-Dos-Santos, 2017; Stafford, Turan, & Raisinghani, 2004). It should be noted that not all research yielded differences among age groups in shopping. Insignificant relationships in commerce related technology use (Dabholkar, Michelle Bobbitt, & Lee, 2003; Hernández et al., 2011) or even negative relationships than expected (Joines et al., 2003) were also detected in shopping literature. This creates a research gap that further studies in differing contexts may shed light on.

Another significant demographic that is considered to have an effect on technology adoption and e-commerce use behavior is gender (Morris & Venkatesh, 2000; Sun & Zhang, 2006). It has been shown that behavioral intentions of men were affected to a greater extent by the usefulness of the technology than women (Venkatesh, Morris, and Ackerman 2000). Women, on the other hand, are more susceptible to external influence (i.e. social influence) than men (Haferkamp, Eimler, Papadakis, & Kruck, 2012; Muscanell & Guadagno, 2012; Sun & Zhang, 2006). The gratifications of social media users was found to vary with depending on gender as well (Park et al., 2009). Effect of gender on online decision making and shopping behavior has also been an area that have attracted researchers' interest (Hernández et al., 2011; Lin, Featherman, Brooks, & Hajli, 2018; Sun & Zhang, 2006). According to Sheldon (2008), women are more likely use social media for entertainment purposes and maintaining existing relationships, whereas, men are after developing new relationships. Interestingly new methodologies pave way to predict gender based on the data obtained from e-commerce websites (Duong, Tan, & Pham, 2016). Despite these findings, contradictory conclusions are present on gender's effect on technology use, media consumption and e-commerce. For instance, Nysveen, Pedersen, & Thorbjørnsen, (2005)'s study on personal motives for media consumption and (Faqih & Jaradat, 2015)'s study on mobile commerce indicated no differences between genders. The highly cited work of Venkatesh et al. (2000) demonstrated that medium to long-term decisions were not moderated by gender of users. It has been shown that if the respondents are familiar with the technology/service in question there are no significant differences between genders (Wong & Hanafi, 2007). On the other hand, according to the Turkish Statistical Institute statistics, there is a gender imbalance among internet shoppers in Turkey. The percentage of males shopping online (34%) are higher than that of females (25%) (Turkish Statistical Institute, 2018). These phenomena indicate a research gap aimed to be explored by this study.

In addition to age and gender, income can be considered an important demographic in e-commerce and s-commerce settings as it affects the ability of the consumers to purchase. Consumers with higher income are faced with less perceived financial risk when shopping online compared to consumers with lower income. Consumers with lower income may not easily access e-commerce (including mobile or social commerce) or may not be as experienced as higher-incomed counterparts. Consequently, it may be considered as an enabler of or barrier to e-commerce (Hernández et al., 2011). It has been considered as a significant factor in relevant technology adoption such as mobile payment systems (Shin, 2009) and mobile commerce (Zhang, Zhu, and Liu 2012). Researchers considered income as a factor that affects shopping behavior (Miyazaki & Fernandez, 2001; Valarezo, Pérez-Amaral, Garín-Muñoz, Herguera García, & López, 2018), yet not all findings are consistent. Income has been found as a significant factor affecting e-commerce use behavior (Valarezo et al., 2018) and its significance in emerging markets has been emphasized (Zhang et al., 2012). On the other hand, Bigné et al. (2007), Gibreel, AlOtaibi, and Altmann (2018) found no significant effect of income on mobile and social commerce intentions in their studies respectively.

Based on the findings in technology adoption and e-commerce literature, gender, age, education and income are accepted as major demographics that has potential effects on s-commerce intentions and gratifications, thus the following are hypothesized:

H7: Males will have higher social commerce intentions.

H8: Younger aged respondents will have higher s-commerce intentions.

H9: Higher education will lead to higher s-commerce intentions.

H10: Higher income will lead to higher s-commerce intentions.

H11: Females will have higher hedonic motives (entertainment, passing time, escape). whereas males will have higher cognitive (information) and social motives (socialization).

H12: Younger aged respondents will have higher hedonic motives (entertainment, passing time, escape) and social motives.

H13: Higher educated respondents will have higher cognitive motives (information) whereas lower educated people have higher hedonic motives.

2.6. Context: Social Media Use in Turkey

There are over 48 million Facebook accounts in Turkey, where more than 80 million people lives in a land on the intersection of Asia and Europe. This figure corresponds to nearly all the country's connected population, however due to multiple accounts, the number of unique users is estimated as 34 million (Statista, 2017; We Are Social & Hootsuite, 2017). Facebook is the second most popular site among internet users in Turkey after google.com in page views (IAB Turkey, 2017) and is the most popular social media site followed by Instagram and Twitter. The country, with its relatively young population is among the excessive users of the Internet and social media. Turkey is the 16th country in terms of time spent online and 2.8 hours of each day is devoted to social media (We Are Social & Hootsuite, 2017).

3. METHODOLOGY

The methodology in carrying out the present study is detailed in this section starting with the research model visualized in Figure 1, developed upon theoretical foundations. The model is followed by the sampling approach and measures employed in the study.

3.1. Proposed Model

Presented in Figure 1.

3.2. Measures

Each construct is designed by adapting existing scales of relevant studies. The gratifications are adapted from (Smock et al., 2011); socialization motivation from (Arnold & Reynolds, 2003; Tauber, 1972) and social commerce intentions from (Zhang et al. 2014; Liang et al. 2011). The draft version of the questionnaire was reviewed by three marketing academicians to ensure ease of understanding and contextual relevance in Turkish language. Moreover, a pilot test with 28 students was conducted to fine-tune the questionnaire.

Figure 1. Proposed model

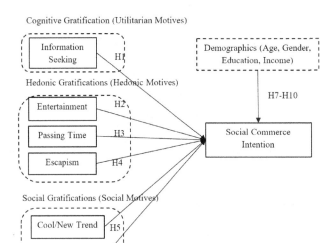

3.3. Sampling and Survey Administration

The target population is the social networking site users who benefit from social media and social networking technologies in their purchasing decisions. This population is defined as the social commerce users in a more compact form. In order to test the aforementioned hypotheses, a survey study was conducted in Turkey. Convenience sampling and snow-ball sampling are used to reach potential respondents. The survey was seeded through the researcher's, his colleagues', acquaintances', students' and ex-students' social media accounts (Facebook, LinkedIn and Twitter) and promoted in several online groups. Respondents of the questionnaire were asked to forward the questionnaire to a family member or friend who they believe may be interested in s-commerce activities. Participation in the survey was voluntary and the survey was kept online for two months during May and June 2017. Using two filter questions, one to validate social media use and the other to validate social media and relevant technologies use for shopping purposes, a total of 361 questionnaires were collected. The information on the total sample is provided in Table 1 and 2.

The information provided in Table 1 and Table 2 reveal that 91% of the respondents use social media actively. It should be noted that the nature of the survey was indicated beforehand to the potential respondents, so they were aware that study was on "social media". Among active users of social media, 42% specified that they use social media sites for periods longer than 3 hours each day. Moreover, 76% of active users indicated that they use social media in their purchases in several ways (looking for or reading product info or comments, doing actual transactions, etc.) 47% of the valid respondents were male and 25% of them held a master's or higher degree. The sample can be considered young, with almost half of the respondents aged within 18-21 bracket. Given the overall social commerce user details are unknown it is hard to get a representative sample. However, considering the profile of Internet users in Turkey, and Facebook & Instagram user statistics, the obtained sample reflects the overall users in terms of gender and age but skewed towards higher earners (Turkish Statistical Institute, 2018). Social media use duration per day reflects the published social media use statistics in Turkey (We Are Social & Hootsuite, 2017).

Table 1. Sample demographics

N=361	Frequency	%	Valid %		Frequency	%	Valid %
Monthly Income (USD equivalent)				**Education**			
<400	10	2.8	2.9	High School or Less	29	8.1	8.5
401-800	46	12.7	13.5	College Degree	46	12.7	13.5
801-1200	74	20.5	21.7	University Student	134	37.1	39.3
1201-1600	62	17.2	18.2	University Degree	51	14.1	15.0
1601-2000	39	10.8	11.4	Master's + Degree	86	23.8	25.2
2001-2400	33	9.1	9.7	*Missing*	*15*	*4.2*	-
2401-2800	25	6.9	7.3	**Age**			
2801+	52	14.4	15.2	18-21y	175	48.5	51.3
Missing	*20*	*5.5*	-	22-25y	46	12.7	13.5
Gender				26-30y	28	7.8	8.2
Male	162	44.9	46.8	31-39y	50	13.9	14.7
Female	184	51.0	53.2	40-49	33	9.1	9.7
Missing	*15*	*4.2*	-	50y+	14	3.9	4.1
				Missing	*15*	*4.2*	-
TOTAL	361	100		TOTAL	361	100	

Table 2. Sample SNS use info

Using Social Media	Frequency	Percent	Valid %	Cumulative %
Yes	329	91.1	91.1	91.1
No	32	8.9	8.9	100.0
Using Social Media for Shopping				
Yes	269	74.5	81.8	81.8
No	60	16.6	18.2	100.0
Missing (No SNS Use)	32	8.9	-	-
Social Media Use Per Day				
< 1 hour	41	11.4	12.5	12.5
1-2 hour	84	23.3	25.5	38.0
2-3 hour	66	18.3	20.1	58.1
3-4 hour	59	16.3	17.9	76.0
4-5 hour	29	8.0	8.8	84.8
5-6 hour	23	6.4	7.0	91.8
6+ hours	27	7.5	8.2	100.0
Missing	32	8.9	-	-
Total	361	100.0	100.0	100.0

4. DATA ANALYSIS AND RESULTS

Out of the total sample, 268 usable questionnaires with full demographics information were obtained after accounting for filtering questions, non-complete and low-quality questionnaires. First of all, the collected data was sorted and analyzed in SPSS 22.0 software. Descriptive statistics (means, std. deviations and medians) are calculated and provided in Table 3.

Table 3. Summary of scales and descriptive stats

N=268	Mean	Std. Dev.	Median	N=268	Mean	Std. Dev.	Median
ESC1	2.27	1.108	2	COL1	1.85	.916	2
ESC2	2.29	1.148	2	COL2	1.78	.895	2
ESC3	2.37	1.111	2	COL3	1.74	.897	2
INF1	3.46	1.056	4	INT1	3.03	1.070	3
INF2	3.45	1.080	4	INT2	2.96	1.137	3
INF3	3.75	.965	4	INT3	3.12	.966	3
REL1	3.06	1.033	3	INT4	3.38	.968	4
REL2	2.96	1.149	3	SOC1	2.67	1.12	3
REL3	3.03	1.167	3	SOC2	2.29	1.05	2
REL4	3.12	1.120	3	SOC4	2.69	1.07	3
PAS1	2.07	1.018	2	SOC5	3.09	1.17	3
PAS2	2.39	1.181	2	SOC6	2.14	.93	2
PAS3	2.72	1.278	3	SOC7	3.16	1.07	3

Among the variables tested as the predecessors of social commerce intention, the lowest scores were attained for the cool and new trend gratification and the escapism gratification (avg. means of 1.79 and 2.31 on a 5-point scale). The significant majority (94% and 91%) of the respondents answered the relevant questions in a negative or neutral way. Respondents answers to escapism gratification is similar to passing time gratification with an average mean score of 2.31 and 21% answering positively to the items in question. On the other hand, the highest scores are obtained in information seeking and entertainment factors (avg. means of 3.55 and 3.04 on a 5-point scale. Information seeking aspect of social commerce is perceived in a positive way by the 65% of the respondents (4&5 in 5-point scale) followed by entertainment (41% answered positively). However, the respondents' disposition towards the social aspect of shopping operationalized under social shopping factor is not positive. About 28% of the respondents answered the items relevant to this factor positively (4&5 on a 5-point Likert scale) and the average score was 2.67 (out of 5). Finally, the descriptive statistics on the dependent factor reveal that social commerce intentions are neutral with differing views throughout the sample (avg. mean score: 3.12; st.dev.1.04). These findings are elaborated together with the regression analysis findings in the discussions section.

4.1. Factor Analysis, Reliability and Validity

As a second step of the analysis, a confirmatory factor analysis was carried out and the resulting factor scores are used in a OLS regression analysis. Given that each question group is an established scale that has been previously validated in numerous studies, content and construct validity was considered to be supported. One item from socialization scale (SOC3) was left out of further analysis due to low factor loading. Composite reliability (CR) and Cronbach's alpha values were used to assess the internal consistency reliability of the model. The figures presented in Table 4, are all above 0.7 let alone information seeking factor (α=0.65). The findings indicate the scales have acceptable reliability (Carmines & Zeller, 1979; Fornell & Larcker, 1981). To test for the discriminant validity, indicators' loadings on their own constructs were compared to the loadings on the other constructs (cross-loadings). The cross-loadings were lower than items' loadings on their own constructs indicating discriminant validity. Convergent validity is evaluated using the outer loadings of the indicators and average variance extracted (AVE). The indicators' loadings on their own construct (outer loadings) were compared to loadings on other constructs (cross-loadings) to assess the discriminant validity. In addition, the square root of AVE was compared to the between-item-correlations (Fornell & Larcker, 1981). As illustrated in Table 5, the inter-variable correlations were lower than the square root of AVE and AVE values were greater than 0.50 threshold. Consequently, the convergent and discriminant validity conditions are satisfied (Hair, Hult, Ringle, & Sarstedt, 2013).

4.2. Regression Analysis

In this study, the effect of relevant uses and gratifications on social commerce intentions are evaluated using multiple regression analysis carried out in SPSS 22.0. The relationships between gratifications and social commerce intentions were tested utilizing the aforementioned hypotheses and the model presented as Equation (1).

$$Y = \beta_0 + X_1.\beta_1 + X_2.\ \beta_2 + X_3.\beta_3 + X_4.\beta_4 + X_5.\beta_5 + X_6.\beta_6 + \varepsilon \tag{1}$$

Y : Social commerce intention factor
$X_{1...6}$: Gratifications
β_m : Regression coefficients
ε : Error term

The results of the regression analysis revealed in Table 5 led to the acceptance of three hypotheses (H1, H2, H5) yet rejection of three others (H3, H4, H6). No significant effect of passing time, cool & new trend or escapism on social commerce intentions were detected in the analysis. According to the calculated beta coefficients, the largest effect on social commerce intentions originated from entertainment gratification followed by socialization and information seeking respectively.

Table 4. Factor analysis results

Item	Factor Loading	Variance Explained	KMO	χ^2	$p <$	Cronbach's α	AVE	CR
ESC1	.858							
ESC2	.952	81.91%	.668	527.766	.0001	0.889	0.819	0.931
ESC3	.903							
INF1	.668							
INF2	.838	59.62%	.610	121.519	.0001	0.648	0.591	0.811
INF3	.790							
ENT1	.703							
ENT2	.888	71.61%	.789	584.771	.0001	0.867	0.716	0.926
ENT3	.898							
ENT4	.880							
PAS1	.860							
PAS2	.947	81.12%	.673	493.222	.0001	0.880	0.811	0.928
PAS3	.893							
COL1	.875							
COL2	.938	82.54%	.720	503.007	.0001	0.893	0.826	0.934
COL3	.912							
SOC1	.778							
SOC2	,718							
SOC4	,778	54.25%	.816	544.419	.0001	0.830	0.543	0.877
SOC5	.737							
SOC6	.662							
SOC7	.741							
INT1	.845							
INT2	.648	61.09%	.704	357.632	.0001	0.778	0.611	0.861
INT3	.807							
INT4	.811							

The factor solutions for each variable explained variations ranging between 54-83%; (KMO= 0.610-0,816, χ^2 p< .0001).

Table 5. Inter-variable correlations

	SOC	ESC	INF	ENT	PAS	COL	INT
SOC	**.737***						
ESC	.401	**.905***					
INF	.358	.295	**.769***				
ENT	.462	.457	.465	**.846***			
PAS	.349	.427	.339	.544	**.901***		
COL	.378	.424	.246	.303	.492	**.908***	
INT	.361	.242	.317	.370	.183	.181	**.782***

* Square root of AVE is provided on the diagonal.

Table 6. Regression analysis results

Factors	Beta	Std. Err	Std. Beta	t	p <	Hypothesis
(Constant)	-5.69E-17	.055	-	.000	1.000	-
Information	.149	.064	.149	2.337	.020	H1 - Accept
Entertainment	.230	.075	.230	3.065	.002	H2 - Accept
Passing Time	-.095	.073	-.095	-1.305	.193	H3 - Reject
Escape	.038	.067	.038	.572	.568	H4 - Reject
Cool & New Trend	.026	.067	.026	.387	.699	H5 - Reject
Socialization	.210	.066	.210	3.165	.002	H6 - Accept

Adjusted R^2: 0.205; $F(6.262) = 11.232$, $p < 0.001$

4.3. Effect of Demographics: ANOVA and T-Tests

ANOVA and t-tests were carried with social commerce intentions as dependent variable and basic demographics-age, gender, education and income-as independent variables. Firstly, the tests were carried out for gender (2 groups), income (8 groups) age (6 groups) and education (5 groups). Levene's test for equality of variances for each group indicated that the variances can be considered equal. No differences were detected between genders (Women M = 3.25, SD =.79; Men M=3.27, SD=.69), age ($F(1, 267) = 0.260$, $p = .935$, partial $\eta^2 = .005$), income ($F(1, 267) = 0.412$, $p = .895$, partial $\eta^2 = .011$) and education ($F(1, 267) = 1.444$, $p = .249$, partial $\eta^2 = .003$) on social commerce intentions.

As a second step of this analysis, total sample was grouped into two in terms of age (18-25; 26+), income (<1,200 USD/month; >1,201 USD/month) and education (University graduate or above; high school degree or less) to provide easier interpretation and to increase the number of observations per group. A second round of "compare means" analysis (t-tests) was conducted with the demographics as grouping variables. Results indicated that there were no significant differences in social commerce intentions between income groups (Low M=3.21, SD=.79; High M=3.29, SD=.70), education groups (Low M=3.24 SD=72; High M=3,2979 SD=0,77) or age groups (Young M=3.24, SD=.74; Old M=3.29 SD=.74). Further t-test were carried out to test for the effect of demographics on each of the gratifications and all the results are presented in Table 6.

The results led to the rejection of hypotheses H7, H8, H9 and H10.

According to the t-test results, only a minority of the tests led to significant differences between groups. No differences in gratifications were attained in terms of income or gender. On the other hand, significant differences were detected in socialization factor between lower and higher education groups (Low M=2.75 SD=.72; High M=2.47 SD=0.80) and younger and older age groups (Young M=2.76, SD=.73; Old M=2.42 SD=.77). Older sample perceived less socialization gratification compared to younger sample in social commerce. Moreover, higher educated sample perceived less socialization gratification. In addition, similar differences were detected in escapism gratification between lower and higher education groups (Low M=2.40 SD=1.01; High M=2.15 SD=1.02) and younger and older age groups (Young M=2.39, SD=1.01; Old M=2.13 SD=1.01). Older sample has less escapism gratification compared to younger sample in social commerce. Similarly, higher educated sample has less escapism gratification. These results lead to the rejection of hypotheses H11 and partial acceptance of H12 and H13.

Table 7. T-tests based on demographic categories

	Income	N	Mean	Std. Dev.	Sig.	Mean Diff.	Gender	N	Mean	Std. Dev.	Sig.	Mean Diff.
SOC	Low	102	2.728	0.766	.175	.131	Men	124	2.720	0.801	.147	.135
	High	164	2.598	0.761			Women	145	2.585	0.720		
ESC	Low	102	2.235	1.013	.326	-.126	Men	124	2.371	1.051	.352	.116
	High	164	2.362	1.023			Women	145	2.255	0.984		
INF	Low	102	3.471	0.872	.154	-.143	Men	124	3.589	0.814	.522	.062
	High	164	3.614	0.743			Women	145	3.526	0.775		
REL	Low	102	3.076	1.002	.631	.058	Men	124	3.067	0.959	.704	.044
	High	164	3.018	0.918			Women	145	3.022	0.937		
COL	Low	102	1.837	0.882	.392	.089	Men	124	1.817	0.852	.591	.054
	High	164	1.748	0.777			Women	145	1.763	0.793		
INT	Low	102	3.208	0.789	.370	-.084	Men	124	3.242	0.795	.719	-.033
	High	164	3.291	0.705			Women	145	3.274	0.686		
Education		N	Mean	Std. Dev.	Sig.	Mean Diff.	Age	N	Mean	Std. Dev.	Sig.	Mean Diff.
SOC	Low	172	2.751	.722	**.003**	.285	Younger	183	2.756	0.730	**.001**	.339
	Higher	96	2.466	.797			Older	86	2.417	0.774		
ESC	Low	172	2.399	1.009	.057	.246	Younger	183	2.393	1.011	**.045**	.266
	Higher	96	2.153	1.017			Older	86	2.128	1.006		
INF	Low	172	3.578	.771	.553	.060	Younger	183	3.568	0.768	.692	.041
	Higher	96	3.517	.838			Older	86	3.527	0.847		
REL	Low	172	3.094	.964	.209	.152	Younger	183	3.090	0.941	.231	.148
	Higher	96	2.943	.910			Older	86	2.942	0.952		
COL	Low	172	1.806	.802	.615	.053	Younger	183	1.798	0.793	.777	.030
	Higher	96	1.753	.857			Older	86	1.767	0.878		
INT	Low	172	3.241	.720	.544	-.057	Younger	183	3.244	0.737	.610	-.049
	Higher	96	3.298	.771			Older	86	3.293	0.741		

4.4. Common Method Variance

The concern for common method variance is addressed in the design and administration of the survey study. First of all, anonymity of respondents is assured, a simple language without technical terms and short questions are preferred. Additionally, it was indicated to the respondents that there are no correct or incorrect answers. The severity of the common method variance is than tested using Harman's single-factor test. The Harman's single-factor test result is calculated as 32%. Variance explained by one factor solution is lower than 50% threshold indicating that common method variance is not a significant issue in the present study (Podsakoff, MacKenzie, Lee, & Podsakoff, 2003).

5. DISCUSSIONS

Findings suggest that both utilitarian and hedonic motivations in addition to socialization have significant effects on consumers' social commerce intentions. Namely, entertainment-a hedonic aspect-and the information seeking factor-a utilitarian gratification-emerged as significant factors affecting social commerce intentions.

The findings on basic descriptive statistics indicate that s-commerce is not perceived as a "cool and new trend" concept. It is evident that respondents are familiar with social media and its use in shopping and they do not perceive it as a novelty.

The finding that information seeking gratification, a utilitarian motive, have been found to affect social commerce intentions is in accordance with the extant literature. Whether it be on social media (Choi et al., 2016), mobile media (Aydin & Karamehmet, 2017) or e-commerce setting (Close & Kukar-Kinney, 2010) information provided by new technologies were deemed as a significant factor affecting intentions. However, not all the gratifications tested for their effects on social commerce intentions were found to be significant. The effect of two other hedonic gratifications-escapism and passing time-was found to be insignificant on social commerce intentions. In addition, the respondents scores to the relevant items indicate negative perceptions on these dimensions. S-commerce is not perceived as a tool to pass time and escape from daily life but as a general means to get entertained. The extant literature that have observed significant effects of these two constructs were on media usage (such as social media). These constructs-as aforementioned-highlight the opportunity provided by various media to easily get away from the burdens of daily life and use it to pass idle time. However, this ability of general media-and social media in particular-is not reflected to the social commerce context in the present study. Considering the nature of social commerce, actual purchase or browsing for purchase information requires more resources (time and /or money) and relevant desires that are to be satisfied. When using social media, users may not be interested in using this medium for shopping purposes to pass time or escape reality. There are probably better alternatives that suit the majority of users in differing ways to pass time. Using social media to pass idle time is a natural outcome of the new media (Hicks et al., 2012; Sheldon, 2008) but carrying out social commerce is not a necessity. The users can prefer watching entertaining content to get away from daily life. This premonition is confirmed in similar studies on e-commerce and s-commerce (Joines et al., 2003). In two recent studies on social commerce by Yang & Li (2014) and Gan and Li (2018) in China found no significant effect of passing time or escape gratification on social commerce and social media use intentions respectively.

Unlike the studies that identified information related gratifications as the most significant factor for social media use (Hicks et al., 2012), entertainment emerged as the most important factor in the present study. This finding is consistent with findings of Yang and Li (2014) in social commerce setting and Lim and Ting (2012) on e-commerce. Entertainment is among the significant aspects of media use (Eighmey & McCord, 1998; Luo, 2002; Xu et al., 2012) as well. Consequently, this outcome is in accordance with social media consumer behavior literature where similar constructs were found to affect use intentions (Gan & Li, 2018; To et al., 2007). The entertainment factor was followed by socialization and information seeking factors in terms of the effect sizes (unstandardized beta coefficients) on social commerce intentions.

Socialization motivation emerged as one of significant motivating factors in practicing social commerce. This finding is parallel to studies such as Parker and Wang (2016) but contrasts certain others on online shopping (Anderson, Knight, Pookulangara, & Josiam, 2014; Joines et al., 2003) and social media use (i.e. Gan & Li, 2018). Socialization, which was lacking or limited in classical e-commerce and online shopping contexts, (Swaminathan et al., 1999) is becoming a valid factor affecting user behavior in more recent applications of e-commerce such as m-commerce and s-commerce (Åkesson, 2007; Parker & Wang, 2016). Lack of extensive research to support or refute this finding is probably due to the operationalization of this factor under a larger "hedonic" or "experiential" motive construct in shopping literature (Anderson et al., 2014; i.e. Arnold & Reynolds, 2003; Wolfinbarger & Gilly, 2001). Nevertheless, it won't be wrong to propose that with the development of mobile technologies and Web 2.0 technologies, online shopping has inherited a social aspect as well. Accordingly, social motives began to act as a significant factor influencing user behavior on m-commerce and s-commerce contexts as also evidenced by (Åkesson, 2007; J. Huang & Zhou, 2018; Parker & Wang, 2016) if not in traditional e-commerce contexts.

One of the objectives of this study has been to validate or refute that, consumer demographics (age, gender, education and income) have significance in explaining social commerce intentions. In contrast to particular studies on shopping behavior and online commerce (Liébana-Cabanillas & Alonso-Dos-Santos, 2017; Sun & Zhang, 2006; Valarezo et al., 2018), no significant effects of demographics were detected on social commerce intentions. This finding is parallel to findings of recent studies on e-commerce and shopping (Bigné et al., 2007; Faqih & Jaradat, 2015; Gibreel et al., 2018; Hernández et al., 2011). Conflicting results observed in the literature regarding demographics such as income's significance may be related to differing cultures the studies were implemented in or how the s-commerce concept and use intentions were operationalized. Studies on actual transactions-buying of goods/services over Internet/ social media-may lead to significance of income as opposed to studies on intentions to use social media in shopping decision process.

A further analysis on demographics' effects on gratifications resulted in the finding that no effect of income or gender on each of the gratifications. On the other hand, significant differences were detected in socialization with regards age. Younger respondents were motivated less by socialization gratification compared to younger sample in social commerce. The lack of difference among younger and older sample indicates that regardless of age hedonic aspects motivate consumers in practicing social commerce.

The expected higher cognitive motive for higher educated group in terms of information gratification have not materialized according to the analysis results. Relatively high and low educated group both valued information aspects of s-commerce similarly. On the other hand, educated sample perceived less socialization gratification in s-commerce. Consequently, they are motivated to a lesser degree by the socialization offered through s-commerce.

6. CONCLUSION

This study contributes to the extant literature on social commerce, e-commerce and social media marketing in several ways. First of all, with few exceptions uses and gratification theory was not utilized in social commerce adequately. Secondly, s-commerce is defined in various ways and studies on this topic operationalize the relevant constructs in differing ways. This leads to a fragmentation and creates a need for further research that can provide comparable findings to accept/refute existing knowledge on online shopping behavior and e-commerce. Thirdly, the effect of demographics was found to vary in different cultures and contexts. It can even change for a particular context in the same culture in time as the underlying technology/service becomes more common and mainstream. Moreover, the particular context itself (social media and its tools) changes rapidly as the underlying systems evolve and algorithms and tools/services offered evolve.

Apart from theoretical contributions, the present study offers managerial implications for business owners, digital marketers and entrepreneurs vying to participate in social commerce. These implications are summarized in the following paragraphs.

No differences in social commerce intentions were detected in terms of gender, age, education or income. Given that all the data of participants used in analysis were obtained online and from social media users, at least a basic level of familiarity with the technology was already established. This may be counted among the major reasons of a lack of difference on demographics as indicated in the relevant studies (Venkatesh, Morris, and Ackerman 2000; Wong and Hanafi 2007). This leads to a significant conclusion for marketing practitioners that no easy segmentation can be made in terms of basic demographics (age, gender, education or income) to differentiate between users with differing s-commerce intentions. Alternatively, social commerce intentions may differ according to other constructs such as personality or lifestyle of the users. This suggestion should be tested in further studies.

Social media users that benefit from these mediums in their shopping process have not found this activity as cool or trendy. We can conclude that the novelty of social media and its use for online shopping is over. Users are motivated by other factors such as socialization, information seeking and hedonic aspects (i.e. entertainment) qualities offered by s-commerce. Digital / social marketing managers should focus on providing entertainment as a priority followed by easy access to information on their accounts and posts. The users' perceptions of entertainment gratification obtained by engaging in social commerce is neutral (3.06/5.00) but the variability is high. This leads to the conclusion that there are different segments among the users which find this activity entertaining and some not-so. The attitudes are not very strong and they can probably be swayed in either direction.

Perceptions on the information seeking benefit of using social media for shopping purposes is more positive compared to entertainment (3.55/5.00). The practitioners should continue providing informative content on their posts / platforms to cater to this gratification.

It was observed that social aspects of s-commerce affect motivations of younger consumers and less educated consumers more significantly. Companies targeting these demographic groups should take into account social aspects of commerce when developing/improving their systems.

Lastly, social interaction provided by the social networking sites and the social aspect of shopping should not be overlooked. This factor is found to affect social commerce intentions significantly as well. Offering tools offered by Web 2.0 technologies / social media on online commerce / shopping sites will be of benefit to the retailers. It should be noted that socialization gratification of s-commerce is perceived more positively by older sample compared to younger sample. Similarly, less-educated group perceived socialization gratification of s-commerce more positively.

6.1. Limitations and Future Research

This study is not without limitations. The conclusions that are drawn from the analyses are limited in several ways. First of all, the factors included in the model are not exhaustive as the buying process is a very complex phenomenon and there are numerous stimuli that affect decision-making (content, interaction, network characteristics, personality, lifestyles etc.). Second, the respondents were selected using a non-random sampling method, which is unfortunately the case in the majority of consumer behavior studies in literature.

A significant venue for further research is inclusion of further factors such as personality traits, lifestyles and working on a larger sample. In this way, it should be possible to carry out multi-group analysis to reveal different segments who value differing motives based on a wider range of personality traits. Moreover, a more representative sample may be obtained. Another research venue is carrying out a multi-cultural study to compare the social commerce motives in different cultures. Differences detected in user behavior and technology adoption between cultures may as well be evident in social commerce setting. Studies aiming to utilize clustering analysis based on social media use motivations and aforementioned factors may shed more light to differences in s-commerce intentions. As established in other studies certain users may be motivated by entertainment and others may be focused on carrying out s-commerce or other type of services provided by social media.

REFERENCES

Åkesson, M. (2007). Value proposition in m-commerce: exploring service provider and user perceptions. *Proceedings of 6th Annual Global Mobility Roundtable*, 1–19. Retrieved from http://www.diva-portal. org/smash/record.jsf?pid=diva2:239430

Anderson, K. C., Knight, D. K., Pookulangara, S., & Josiam, B. (2014). Influence of hedonic and utilitarian motivations on retailer loyalty and purchase intention: A facebook perspective. *Journal of Retailing and Consumer Services*, *21*(5), 773–779. doi:10.1016/j.jretconser.2014.05.007

Arnold, M. J., & Reynolds, K. E. (2003). Hedonic shopping motivations. *Journal of Retailing*, *79*(2), 77–95. doi:10.1016/S0022-4359(03)00007-1

Aydin, G., & Karamehmet, B. (2017). A comparative study on attitudes towards SMS advertising and mobile application advertising. *International Journal of Mobile Communications*, *15*(5), 514. doi:10.1504/ IJMC.2017.086366

Babin, B. J., Darden, W. R., & Griffin, M. (1994). Work and/or Fun: Measuring Hedonic and Utilitarian Shopping Value. *The Journal of Consumer Research*, *20*(4), 644. doi:10.1086/209376

Bigné, E., Ruiz, C., & Sanz, S. (2007). Key Drivers of Mobile Commerce Adoption. An Exploratory Study of Spanish Mobile Users. *Journal of Theoretical and Applied Electronic Commerce*, *2*(2), 48–60.

Bloch, P. H., Ridgway, N. M., & Sherrell, D. L. (1989). Extending the concept of shopping: An investigation of browsing activity. *Journal of the Academy of Marketing Science*, *17*(1), 13–21. doi:10.1007/ BF02726349

Bonds-Raacke, J., & Raacke, J. (2010). Myspace and facebook: Identifying dimensions of uses and gratifications for friend networking sites. *Individual Differences Research*, *8*(1), 27–33.

Busalim, A. H., & Hussin, A. R. C. (2016). Understanding social commerce: A systematic literature review and directions for further research. *International Journal of Information Management*, *36*(6), 1075–1088. doi:10.1016/j.ijinfomgt.2016.06.005

Büttner, O. B., Florack, A., & Göritz, A. S. (2013). Shopping Orientation and Mindsets: How Motivation Influences Consumer Information Processing During Shopping. *Psychology and Marketing, 30*(9), 779–793. doi:10.1002/mar.20645

Carmines, E. G., & Zeller, R. A. (1979). *Reliability and Validity Assessment.* Beverly Hills, CA: Sage Publications. doi:10.4135/9781412985642

Chaffey, D. (2009). *E-Business and E-Commerce Management: Strategy, Implementation and Practice* (4th ed.). Essex, UK: Pearson Education Limited.

Chen, J., & Shen, X. L. (2015). Consumers' decisions in social commerce context: An empirical investigation. *Decision Support Systems, 79,* 55–64. doi:10.1016/j.dss.2015.07.012

Chen, L., Gillenson, M. L., & Sherrell, D. L. (2002). Enticing online consumers: An extended technology acceptance perspective. *Information & Management, 39*(8), 705–719. doi:10.1016/S0378-7206(01)00127-6

Childers, T. L., Carr, C. L., & Carson, S. (2001). Hedonic and utilitrian motivations for online retail shopping behavior. *Journal of Retailing, 77*(4), 511–535. doi:10.1016/S0022-4359(01)00056-2

Choi, E., Fowler, D., Goh, B., Yuan, J., Choi, E.-K., & Wilson, K. (2016). Social Media Marketing: Applying the Uses and Gratifications Theory in the Hotel Industry companies toward improving their Facebook pages in order to meet the users' needs. *Journal of Hospitality Marketing & Management, 25*(7), 771–796. doi:10.1080/19368623.2016.1100102

Chung, J. E., Park, N., Wang, H., Fulk, J., & McLaughlin, M. (2010). Age differences in perceptions of online community participation among non-users: An extension of the Technology Acceptance Model. *Online Interactivity: Role of Technology in Behavior Change, 26*(6), 1674–1684. doi:10.1016/j.chb.2010.06.016

Close, A. G., & Kukar-Kinney, M. (2010). Beyond buying: Motivations behind consumers' online shopping cart use. *Journal of Business Research, 63*(9–10), 986–992. doi:10.1016/j.jbusres.2009.01.022

Constantinides, E., & Fountain, S. J. (2008). Web 2.0: Conceptual foundations and marketing issues. *Journal of Direct. Data and Digital Marketing Practice, 9*(3), 231–244. doi:10.1057/palgrave.dddmp.4350098

Curty, R. G., & Zhang, P. (2011). Social commerce: Looking back and forward. *Proceedings of the American Society for Information Science and Technology, 48*(1), 1–10. doi:10.1002/meet.2011.14504801096

Dabholkar, P. A., Michelle Bobbitt, L., & Lee, E. (2003). Understanding consumer motivation and behavior related to self-scanning in retailing. *International Journal of Service Industry Management, 14*(1), 59–95. doi:10.1108/09564230310465994

Dholakia, U. M., Bagozzi, R. P., & Pearo, L. K. (2004). A social influence model of consumer participation in network- and small-group-based virtual communities. *International Journal of Research in Marketing, 21*(3), 241–263. doi:10.1016/j.ijresmar.2003.12.004

Duong, D., Tan, H., & Pham, S. (2016). Customer gender prediction based on E-commerce data. In *Proceedings - 2016 8th International Conference on Knowledge and Systems Engineering, KSE 2016* (pp. 91–95). Academic Press. 10.1109/KSE.2016.7758035

Eighmey, J., & McCord, L. (1998). Adding Value in the Information Age: Uses and Gratifications of Sites on the World Wide Web. *Journal of Business Research, 41*(97), 187–194. doi:10.1016/S0148-2963(97)00061-1

Fang, J., George, B., Shao, Y., & Wen, C. (2016). Affective and cognitive factors influencing repeat buying in e-commerce. *Electronic Commerce Research and Applications, 19*, 44–55. doi:10.1016/j.elerap.2016.08.001

Faqih, K. M. S., & Jaradat, M. I. R. M. (2015). Assessing the moderating effect of gender differences and individualism-collectivism at individual-level on the adoption of mobile commerce technology: TAM3 perspective. *Journal of Retailing and Consumer Services, 22*, 37–52. doi:10.1016/j.jretconser.2014.09.006

Farivar, S., Turel, O., & Yuan, Y. (2018). Skewing users' rational risk considerations in social commerce: An empirical examination of the role of social identification. *Information & Management*, 1–33. doi:10.1016/j.im.2018.05.008

Fornell, C., & Larcker, D. F. (1981). Evaluating Structural Equation Models with Unobservable Variables and Measurement Error. *JMR, Journal of Marketing Research, 18*(1), 39–50. doi:10.1177/002224378101800104

Gan, C., & Li, H. (2018). Understanding the effects of gratifications on the continuance intention to use WeChat in China: A perspective on uses and gratifications. *Computers in Human Behavior, 78*, 306–315. doi:10.1016/j.chb.2017.10.003

Gibreel, O., AlOtaibi, D. A., & Altmann, J. (2018). Social commerce development in emerging markets. *Electronic Commerce Research and Applications, 27*, 152–162. doi:10.1016/j.elerap.2017.12.008

Ha, Y. W., Kim, J., Libaque-Saenz, C. F., Chang, Y., & Park, M.-C. (2015). Use and gratifications of mobile SNSs: Facebook and KakaoTalk in Korea. *Telematics and Informatics, 32*(3), 425–438. doi:10.1016/j.tele.2014.10.006

Haferkamp, N., Eimler, S. C., Papadakis, A.-M., & Kruck, J. V. (2012). Men Are from Mars, Women Are from Venus? Examining Gender Differences in Self-Presentation on Social Networking Sites. *Cyberpsychology, Behavior, and Social Networking, 15*(2), 91–98. doi:10.1089/cyber.2011.0151 PMID:22132897

Hair, J. F., Hult, G. T. M., Ringle, C. M., & Sarstedt, M. (2013). *A Primer on Partial Least Squares Structural Equation Modeling (PLS-SEM)* (1st ed.). Thousand Oaks, CA: Sage Publications, Inc.

Hausman, A. V., & Siekpe, J. S. (2009). The effect of web interface features on consumer online purchase intentions. *Journal of Business Research, 62*(1), 5–13. doi:10.1016/j.jbusres.2008.01.018

Hernández, B., Jiménez, J., & José Martín, M. (2011). Age, gender and income: Do they really moderate online shopping behaviour? *Online Information Review, 35*(1), 113–133. doi:10.1108/14684521111113614

Hicks, A., Comp, S., Horovitz, J., Hovarter, M., Miki, M., & Bevan, J. L. (2012). Why people use Yelp. com: An exploration of uses and gratifications. *Computers in Human Behavior, 28*(6), 2274–2279. doi:10.1016/j.chb.2012.06.034

Hirschman, E. C., & Holbrook, M. B. (1982). Hedonic consumption: Emerging concepts, methods and propositions. *Journal of Marketing, 46*(3), 92–101. doi:10.1177/002224298204600314

Huang, J., & Zhou, L. (2018). Timing of web personalization in mobile shopping: A perspective from Uses and Gratifications Theory. *Computers in Human Behavior, 88*, 103–113. doi:10.1016/j.chb.2018.06.035

Huang, L. T. (2016). Flow and social capital theory in online impulse buying. *Journal of Business Research, 69*(6), 2277–2283. doi:10.1016/j.jbusres.2015.12.042

IAB Turkey. (2017). *February 2017 Top 20 Lists*. Retrieved July 7, 2015, from http://www.iabturkiye. org/sites/default/files/internet_audience_toplist_02_2017.pdf

Instagram. (2018). *Bringing shopping on Instagram to more countries*. Retrieved March 22, 2018, from https://business.instagram.com/blog/shopping-on-instagram-goes-global/

Joines, J. L., Scherer, C. W., & Scheufele, D. A. (2003). Exploring motivations for consumer Web use and their implications for e-commerce. *Journal of Consumer Marketing, 20*(2), 90–108. doi:10.1108/07363760310464578

Joinson, A. N. (2008). Looking at, looking up or keeping up with people? In *Proceeding of the twenty-sixth annual CHI conference on Human factors in computing systems - CHI '08* (p. 1027). New York: ACM Press. 10.1145/1357054.1357213

Katz, E., Blumler, J. G., & Gurevitch, M. (1973). Uses and Gratifications Research. *Public Opinion Quarterly, 37*(4), 509. doi:10.1086/268109

Katz, E., Blumler, J. G., & Gurevitch, M. (1974). Utilization of mass communication by the individual. In J. G. Blumler & E. Katz (Eds.), *The Uses of Mass Communication* (pp. 19–32). Beverly Hills, CA: Sage Publication.

Kim, J., & Forsythe, S. (2007). Hedonic usage of product virtualization technologies in online apparel shopping. *International Journal of Retail & Distribution Management, 35*(6), 502–514. doi:10.1108/09590550710750368

Ko, H., Cho, C., & Roberts, M. S. (2005). Internet uses and gratifications: A structural equation model of interactive advertising. *Journal of Advertising, 34*(2), 57–70. doi:10.1080/00913367.2005.10639191

Korgaonkar, P. K., & Wolin, L. D. (1999). A multivariate analysis of Web usage. *Journal of Advertising Research, 39*(2), 53–68.

Kucukcay, I. E., & Benyoucef, M. (2014). Mobile Social Commerce Implementation. In *Proceedings of the 6th International Conference on Management of Emergent Digital EcoSystems - MEDES '14* (pp. 1–8). New York: ACM Press. 10.1145/2668260.2668276

Liang, T.-P., Ho, Y.-T., Li, Y.-W., & Turban, E. (2011). What Drives Social Commerce: The Role of Social Support and Relationship Quality. *International Journal of Electronic Commerce, 16*(2), 69–90. doi:10.2753/JEC1086-4415160204

Liébana-Cabanillas, F., & Alonso-Dos-Santos, M. (2017). Factors that determine the adoption of Facebook commerce: The moderating effect of age. *Journal of Engineering and Technology Management, 44*, 1–18. doi:10.1016/j.jengtecman.2017.03.001

Lim, W. M., & Ting, D. H. (2012). E-shopping: An analysis of the uses and gratifications theory. *Modern Applied Science*, *6*(5), 48–63. doi:10.5539/mas.v6n5p48

Lin, X., Featherman, M., Brooks, S. L., & Hajli, N. (2018). Exploring Gender Differences in Online Consumer Purchase Decision Making: An Online Product Presentation Perspective. *Information Systems Frontiers*. doi:10.100710796-018-9831-1

Lin, X., Li, Y., & Wang, X. (2017). Social commerce research: Definition, research themes and the trends. *International Journal of Information Management*, *37*(3), 190–201. doi:10.1016/j.ijinfomgt.2016.06.006

Liu, C., & Forsythe, S. (2010). Sustaining Online Shopping: Moderating Role of Online Shopping Motives. *Journal of Internet Commerce*, *9*(2), 83–103. doi:10.1080/15332861.2010.503848

Luo, X. (2002). *Uses and gratifications theory and e-consumer behaviors: A structural equation modeling study*. Retrieved from http://jiad.org/vol2/no2/luo/

Miyazaki, A. D., & Fernandez, A. (2001). Consumer Perceptions of Privacy and Security Risks for Online Shopping. *The Journal of Consumer Affairs*, *35*(1), 27–44. doi:10.1111/j.1745-6606.2001.tb00101.x

Morris, M. G., & Venkatesh, V. (2000). Age Differences in Technology Adoption Decisions: Implications for a Changing Work Force. *Personnel Psychology*, *53*(2), 375–403. doi:10.1111/j.1744-6570.2000.tb00206.x

Muscanell, N. L., & Guadagno, R. E. (2012). Make new friends or keep the old: Gender and personality differences in social networking use. *Computers in Human Behavior*, *28*(1), 107–112. doi:10.1016/j.chb.2011.08.016

Nahapiet, J., & Ghoshal, S. (1998). Social Capital, Intellectual Capital, and the Organizational Advantage. *Academy of Management Review*, *23*(2), 242–266. doi:10.5465/amr.1998.533225

Nambisan, S., & Baron, R. A. (2007). Interactions in virtual customer environments: Implications for product support and customer relationship management. *Journal of Interactive Marketing*, *21*(2), 42–62. doi:10.1002/dir.20077

Natanson, E. (2017). Amazon Spark - A Social Network for Product Discovery. *Forbes*. Retrieved from https://www.forbes.com/sites/eladnatanson/2017/09/05/amazon-spark-a-social-network-for-product-discovery/#14edd35791f9

Nysveen, H., Pedersen, P. E., & Thorbjørnsen, H. (2005). Explaining intention to use mobile chat services: Moderating effects of gender. *Journal of Consumer Marketing*, *22*(5), 247–256. doi:10.1108/07363760510611671

Papacharissi, Z., & Mendelson, A. (2011). Toward a New(er) Sociability: Uses, Gratifications, and Social Capital on Facebook. In S. Papathanassopoulos (Ed.), *Media Perspectives for the 21st Century* (pp. 212–230). New York: Routledge. doi:10.4324/9780203834077

Papacharissi, Z., & Rubin, A. M. (2000). Predictors of Internet Use. *Journal of Broadcasting & Electronic Media*, *44*(2), 175–196. doi:10.120715506878jobem4402_2

Park, N., Kee, K. F., & Valenzuela, S. (2009). Being Immersed in Social Networking Environment: Facebook Groups, Uses and Gratifications, and Social Outcomes. *Cyberpsychology & Behavior*, *12*(6), 729–733. doi:10.1089/cpb.2009.0003 PMID:19619037

Parker, C. J., & Wang, H. (2016). Examining hedonic and utilitarian motivations for m-commerce fashion retail app engagement. *Journal of Fashion Marketing and Management: An International Journal*, *20*(4), 487–506. doi:10.1108/JFMM-02-2016-0015

Peffers, K. (2001). The future of electronic commerce: A shift from the EC channel to strategic electronic commerce. *Journal of Information Technology Theory and Application*, *3*(4), 7–16. Retrieved from http://search.proquest.com/docview/200038024?accountid=8144%5Cnhttp://sfx.aub.aau.dk/sfxaub?url_ver=Z39.88-2004&rft_val_fmt=info:ofi/fmt:kev:mtx:journal&genre=article&sid=ProQ:ProQ%3Aabiglobal&atitle=The+future+of+electronic+commerce%3A+A+shift+from+the+E

Pfeil, U., Arjan, R., & Zaphiris, P. (2009). Age differences in online social networking - A study of user profiles and the social capital divide among teenagers and older users in MySpace. *Computers in Human Behavior*, *25*(3), 643–654. doi:10.1016/j.chb.2008.08.015

Phua, J., Jin, S. V., & Kim, J. (2017). Gratifications of using Facebook, Twitter, Instagram, or Snapchat to follow brands: The moderating effect of social comparison, trust, tie strength, and network homophily on brand identification, brand engagement, brand commitment, and membership intentio. *Telematics and Informatics*, *34*(1), 412–424. doi:10.1016/j.tele.2016.06.004

Podsakoff, P. M., MacKenzie, S. B., Lee, J.-Y., & Podsakoff, N. P. (2003). Common method biases in behavioral research: A critical review of the literature and recommended remedies. *The Journal of Applied Psychology*, *88*(5), 879–903. doi:10.1037/0021-9010.88.5.879 PMID:14516251

Reynolds, K. E., & Beatty, S. E. (1999). A relationship customer typology. *Journal of Retailing*, *75*(4), 509–523. doi:10.1016/S0022-4359(99)00016-0

Roy, G., Datta, B., & Basu, R. (2017). Trends and Future Directions in Online Marketing Research. *Journal of Internet Commerce*, *16*(1), 1–31. doi:10.1080/15332861.2016.1258929

Sharma, S., & Crossler, R. E. (2014). Intention to Engage in Social Commerce : Uses and Gratifications Approach. In *Twentieth Americas Conference on Information Systems* (Vol. 1, pp. 1–12). Retrieved from http://aisel.aisnet.org/cgi/viewcontent.cgi?article=1695&context=amcis2014

Sheldon, P. (2008). Student favorite: Facebook and motives for its uses. *Southwestern Mass Communication Journal*, *23*(October), 39–53. doi:10.1080/03634520216511

Shen, J. (2012). Social comparison, social presence, and enjoyment in the acceptance of social shopping websites. *Journal of Electronic Commerce Research*, *13*, 198–212.

Shin, D.-H. (2009). Towards an understanding of the consumer acceptance of mobile wallet. *Computers in Human Behavior*, *25*(6), 1343–1354. doi:10.1016/j.chb.2009.06.001

Smock, A. D., Ellison, N. B., Lampe, C., & Wohn, D. Y. (2011). Facebook as a toolkit: A uses and gratification approach to unbundling feature use. *Computers in Human Behavior*, *27*(6), 2322–2329. doi:10.1016/j.chb.2011.07.011

Solomon, M. R. (2009). *Consumer behavior: Buying, having, and being.* Upper Saddle River, NJ: Pearson- Prentice Hall.

Song, I., Larose, R., Eastin, M. S., & Lin, C. A. (2004). Internet Gratifications and Internet Addiction: On the Uses and Abuses of New Media. *Cyberpsychology & Behavior, 7*(4), 384–394. doi:10.1089/cpb.2004.7.384 PMID:15331025

Stafford, T. F., Turan, A., & Raisinghani, M. S. (2004). International and Cross-Cultural Influences on Online Shopping Behavior. *Journal of Global Information Technology Management, 7*(2), 70–87. doi:10.1080/1097198X.2004.10856373

Statista. (2017). *Forecast of social network user numbers in Turkey from 2014 to 2021.* Retrieved July 7, 2017, from https://www.statista.com/statistics/569090/predicted-number-of-social-network-users-in-turkey/

Stephen, A. T., & Toubia, O. (2010). Deriving Value from Social Commerce Networks. *JMR, Journal of Marketing Research, 47*(2), 215–228. doi:10.1509/jmkr.47.2.215

Sun, H., & Zhang, P. (2006). The role of moderating factors in user technology acceptance. *International Journal of Human-Computer Studies, 64*(2), 53–78. doi:10.1016/j.ijhcs.2005.04.013

Swaminathan, V., Lepkowska-White, E., & Rao, B. P. (1999). Browsers or Buyers in Cyberspace? An Investigation of Factors Influencing Electronic Exchange. *Journal of Computer-Mediated Communication, 5*(2), 1–19. doi:10.1111/j.1083-6101.1999.tb00335.x

Tauber, E. M. (1972). Why Do People Shop? *Journal of Marketing, 36*(4), 46–49. doi:10.2307/1250426

Teo, H.-H., Chan, H.-C., Wei, K.-K., & Zhang, Z. (2003). Evaluating information accessibility and community adaptivity features for sustaining virtual learning communities. *International Journal of Human-Computer Studies, 59*(5), 671–697. doi:10.1016/S1071-5819(03)00087-9

To, P. L., Liao, C., & Lin, T. H. (2007). Shopping motivations on Internet: A study based on utilitarian and hedonic value. *Technovation, 27*(12), 774–787. doi:10.1016/j.technovation.2007.01.001

Trocchia, P. J., & Janda, S. (2000). A phenomenological investigation of Internet usage among older individuals. *Journal of Consumer Marketing, 17*(7), 605–616. doi:10.1108/07363760010357804

Turban, E., Bolloju, N., & Liang, T.-P. (2010). Social Commerce: An E-Commerce Perspective. In *Proceedings of the 12th International Conference on Electronic Commerce: Roadmap for the Future of Electronic Business* (pp. 33–42). Honolulu, HI: IEEE. 10.1145/2389376.2389382

Turban, E., & Liang, T.-P. (2011). Introduction to the Special Issue Social Commerce: A Research Framework for Social Commerce. *International Journal of Electronic Commerce, 16*(2), 5–14. doi:10.2753/JEC1086-4415160201

Turban, E., Strauss, J., & Lai, L. (2015). *Social Commerce: Marketing, Technology and Management* (pp. 1–37). Springer. doi:10.1007/978-3-319-17028-2_7

Turkish Statistical Institute. (2018). *Household Information Technologies (IT) Use Research.* Retrieved from http://www.tuik.gov.tr/PreHaberBultenleri.do?id=27819

Valarezo, Á., Pérez-Amaral, T., Garín-Muñoz, T., Herguera García, I., & López, R. (2018, December). Drivers and barriers to cross-border e-commerce: Evidence from Spanish individual behavior. *Telecommunications Policy*, 1–10. doi:10.1016/j.telpol.2018.03.006

Venkatesh, V., & Morris, M. (2000). Why dont men ever stop to ask for directions? Gender, social influence, and their role in technology acceptance and usage behavior. *Management Information Systems Quarterly*, 24(1), 115–139. doi:10.2307/3250981

Venkatesh, V., Morris, M. G., & Ackerman, P. L. (2000). A Longitudinal Field Investigation of Gender Differences in Individual Technology Adoption Decision Making Processes. *Organizational Behavior and Human Decision Processes*, 83(1), 33–60. doi:10.1006/obhd.2000.2896 PMID:10973782

Verhagen, T., Swen, E., Feldberg, F., & Merikivi, J. (2015). Benefitting from virtual customer environments: An empirical study of customer engagement. *Computers in Human Behavior*, 48, 340–357. doi:10.1016/j.chb.2015.01.061

We Are Social & Hootsuite. (2017). *Digital in 2017 Global Overview: West Asia*. Retrieved from https://www.slideshare.net/wearesocial/digital-in-2018-in-western-asia-part-1-northwest-86865983

Whiting, A., & Williams, D. (2013). Why people use social media: A uses and gratifications approach. *Qualitative Market Research*, 16(4), 362–369. doi:10.1108/QMR-06-2013-0041

Wolfinbarger, M., & Gilly, M. C. (2001). Shopping Online for Freedom, Control, and Fun. *California Management Review*, 43(2), 34–55. doi:10.2307/41166074

Wong, S. L., & Hanafi, A. (2007). Gender Differences in Attitudes towards Information Technology among Malaysian Student Teachers: A Case Study at University Putra Malaysia. *Journal of Educational Technology & Society*, 10(2), 158–169.

Xu, C., Ryan, S., Prybutok, V., & Wen, C. (2012). It is not for fun: An examination of social network site usage. *Information & Management*, 49(5), 210–217. doi:10.1016/j.im.2012.05.001

Yang, X., & Li, G. (2014). Exploring social commerce adoption in China: A uses and gratification perspective. In *International Conference on Management Science & Engineering 21th Annual Conference Proceedings* (pp. 546–554). Helsinki, Finland: IEEE. 10.1109/ICMSE.2014.6930277

Zhang, H., Lu, Y., Gupta, S., & Zhao, L. (2014). What motivates customers to participate in social commerce? The impact of technological environments and virtual customer experiences. *Information & Management*, 51(8), 1017–1030. doi:10.1016/j.im.2014.07.005

Zhang, K. Z. K., & Benyoucef, M. (2016). Consumer behavior in social commerce: A literature review. *Decision Support Systems*, 86, 95–108. doi:10.1016/j.dss.2016.04.001

Zhang, L., Zhu, J., & Liu, Q. (2012). A meta-analysis of mobile commerce adoption and the moderating effect of culture. *Computers in Human Behavior*, 28(5), 1902–1911. doi:10.1016/j.chb.2012.05.008

This research was previously published in the International Journal of E-Business Research (IJEBR), 15(2); pages 44-70, copyright year 2019 by IGI Publishing (an imprint of IGI Global).

APPENDIX: SCALES AND ITEMS

Table 8. Scales and items

Code	Item	Construct & Source
SOC1	*I use social media in online shopping... (for all questions below)* to shop online with others as a way to socialize.	Socializing (Arnold & Reynolds, 2003; Tauber, 1972)
SOC2	.. to shop online with others having a social occasion.	
SOC3	to shop online with others as a way to have a bonding experience.	
SOC4	to shop online with others who have similar tastes/interests.	
SOC5	to communicate with other people who share similar shopping experiences.	
SOC6	to achieve a sense of belonging by shopping for the same products and brands that others purchase.	
SOC7	to observe what others are buying and using.	
INT1	I will consider the shopping experiences of my friends on social media when I want to shop.	Social Commerce Intention (Liang et al., 2011; H. Zhang et al., 2014)
INT2	I will ask my friends on social media to provide me with their suggestions before I go shopping.	
INT3	I am willing to buy the products recommended by my friends on social media	
INT4	I intend to recommend shopping using social media to my friends.	
ESC1	*I use social media in online shopping... (for all questions below)* To eliminate pressures (or responsibilities).	Escape (Smock et al., 2011)
ESC2	To forget about school, work, or other problems.	
ESC3	To get away from what I am doing.	
INF1	To seek useful information.	Information Seeking (Yang & Li, 2014)
INF2	To focus on fashion trends.	
INF3	To find favorable shops.	
REL1	Because it's interesting.	Entertainment (Smock et al., 2011)
REL2	Because it is a pleasant rest.	
REL3	Because it relaxes me.	
REL4	Because it's enjoyable.	
PAS1	When I have nothing better to do.	Passing Time (Smock et al., 2011)
PAS2	Because it gives me something to do to occupy my time.	
PAS3	Because it passes the time when I am bored.	
COL1	Because everybody else is doing it.	Cool and new trend (Smock et al., 2011)
COL2	Because it is the thing to do.	
COL3	Because it is cool.	

Chapter 61

Creating Consumer–Based Brand Equity With Social Media Content Marketing

Wolfgang Weitzl
University of Vienna, Austria

ABSTRACT

Due to the growing importance of company-initiated online brand communities (OBCs) like Facebook brand fan pages, details about consumers' perceptions of these sites need to be linked to their effects on customer-based brand equity. This research builds on Keller and Lehmann's brand value chain as the theoretical foundation and adopts the theory to fit the social media context. This approach enables the simultaneous evaluation of the impact of consumer online content perceptions on both fan-page engagement and consumers' brand mindset. Specifically, this research investigates the consumer-based outcomes of perceptions of content's vividness and interactivity as well as the effects of perceived information and entertainment value of brand posts. In addition, this empirical study evaluates the consequences of positive brand fans' comments for consumer online engagement (e.g., liking), brand awareness, image, and attitude. Results show that consumer-oriented brand pages can stimulate positive offline brand engagement such as loyalty and recommendation.

INTRODUCTION

Strong consumer-brand relationships produce positive outcomes for both relationship partners: While consumers benefit – amongst others – from satisfying their social needs, brands profit considerably from the loyalty and advocacy of their committed customers (e.g., Algesheimer, Dholakia, & Herrmann, 2005). 'Online brand communities' (OBCs) are one instrument to strengthen consumer-brand relationships and to increase relational bonds by fostering interaction with customers (e.g., Teichmann, Stokburger-Sauer, Plank, & Strobl, 2015). OBCs are "online aggregations of customers who collectively co-produce and consume content about a commercial activity that is central to their interest by exchanging intangible

DOI: 10.4018/978-1-7998-9020-1.ch061

resources" (Wiertz & de Ruyter, 2007, p. 349). In OBCs consumers gather together in sub-groups of the brand's clientele – sharing a common interest on a specific brand (Woisetschläger, Harleb, & Blut, 2008). Consumers participate in company-created OBCs in order to share their passion for a specific brand, to exchange consumption-relevant information and knowledge (e.g., brand stories), to provide recommendations and/or to simply express their affection for a specific brand.

Today, marketers regularly put much effort in the creation of maintenance of specific forms of OBCs: company-initiated 'brand fan-pages' on *Facebook*. Given *Facebook's* popularity, these brand-focused social media sites shall facilitate the interaction and information flow with and among consumers who are able to read, comment or 'like' brand posts (i.e., marketers' postings) and/or comments of fellow shoppers (i.e., consumers' postings) (McAlexander, Schouten, & Koenig, 2002; Muniz & O'Guinn, 2001). Within the last years, marketers have continued to invest both time and budget in social media outlets to foster dialogic communication with their customers online: Worldwide marketing spending on social media reached $31 billion in 2016 (Statista, 2017). Well-known examples include brand fan-pages hosted by *Coca-Cola* with 107m members (facebook.com/cocacola), *Starbucks* with 37m members (facebook.com/starbucks), and *Walmart* with 34m members (facebook.com/walmart). All these pages aim to promote companies' brands, services as well as products and – at the same time – seek to actively involve customers in the value creation process by providing the "right" content (Pagani, Hofacker, & Goldsmith, 2011).

Given its increasing marketing relevance, academic research has put much emphasis on the investigation of brand pages' effects on consumer reactions. For instance, Bagozzi and Dholakia (2006) find that members of brand fan-pages are more committed and loyal to the company. In addition, this consumer group is more susceptible to marketing messages. Simultaneously, positive consumer behavior seems to emanate to the non-online sphere as Royo-Vella and Casamassima (2011), amongst others, demonstrate: The scholars show that 'brand fans' (i.e., individuals who 'liked' the brand's official *Facebook* page) have higher satisfaction and affective commitment towards the brand in contrast to non-fans. Various studies support a positive relationship between the degree to which consumers are engaged in a brand's online community and consumer commitment (e.g., Kim, Choi, Qualls, &, Han, 2008), brand attachment and identification (e.g., Zhou, Zhang, Su, & Zhou, 2012), brand loyalty (Algesheimer, Dholakia, & Herrmann, 2005; Casalo, Flavian, & Guinaliu, 2007), and purchasing intentions (e.g., Hur, Ahn, & Kim, 2011).

Until today, however, only limited research addresses the direct effects of consumers' *Facebook* brand page content (i.e., brand posts) perceptions (i.e., subjective evaluations) on both (i) consumers' *brand page engagement* and (ii) consumers' *brand reactions*. Specifically, by developing a conceptual model, this research aims to investigate the diverse content factors driving community members' brand fan-page engagement (i.e., online community engagement or activities on the brand fan-page – e.g., 'liking', commenting, contributing) and consumers' brand mind set (i.e., brand-related attitudes). The conceptual model further assumes that both elements have an effect on consumers' *brand engagement* (i.e., loyalty and positive word-of-mouth). The framework of investigation is based upon current academic insights. This research contributes by investigating the role of consumer perceptions of various fan-page content characteristics (e.g., vividness; interactivity; information and entertainment value; valence of other brand fans' comments) in driving important social media outcomes. That is, consumer community and brand engagement as well as brand awareness, brand image and brand attitude. By doing so, this research develops a deep understanding of how consumers' perceptions of a brand-focused *Facebook* page can foster their relationships with the brand.

The remainder of the chapter is structured as follows: In the next section, brand communities and its online manifestation 'brand fan-pages' on social media will be discussed. This is followed by the development of the conceptual model and its research hypotheses. A description of the empirical study and its findings follows. This paper concludes with a discussion of the key findings, implications for scholars and practitioners as well as the limitations of this study. Possible routes for future scientific enquiry are discussed.

THEORETICAL BACKGROUND

Brand Communities and Brand Fan-Pages

The rise of the Internet enabled the development of communities that exist without physical, geographical and time constraints. In 'online communities' people can share information and interact with others entirely by means of computer-mediated communication. Such social groups are built around a common interest of its members (Bagozzi & Dholakia, 2002). Even more, a shared interest (e.g., a celebrity; topic) is both the defining feature of such communities and the basic prerequisite for their existence (Koh & Kim, 2003). This interest gives individuals a purpose to join a community, to interact and to create value (e.g., provide information; offering friendship) for others (Schau, Muniz, & Arnould, 2009; Seraj 2012).

Communities come in distinct forms. One of which are 'consumption communities', which can be defined as "affiliative groups whose online interactions are based upon shared enthusiasm for, and knowledge of, a specific consumption activity or related group of activities" (Kozinets, 1999, p. 254). 'Brand communities' are similar to consumption communities as they also have three ingredients that create a community: (i) shared consciousness, (ii) shared rituals and traditions, and (iii) member obligations to the society (Muniz & O'Guinn, 2001). However, in contrast to consumption communities, brand communities are based on a shared interest in and admiration for a specific *brand* (Muniz & O'Guinn, 2001). In addition, members are primary interested in other consumers' experiences with and thoughts on the brand in focus, its products, and its parent-company (McAlexander, Schouten & Koenig, 2002). Brand communities can be defined as a "specialized, non-geographically bound community based on a structured set of social relations among admirers of a brand" (Muniz & O'Guinn, 2001, p. 412). Brand communities perform many important tasks on behalf of the brand: For example, they support sharing of information, perpetuating the history and culture of the brand, and providing assistance to consumers as members can help each other by fixing each other's problems (Schau, Muniz, & Arnould, 2009). They further provide a social structure for consumer-brand relationships (Muniz & O'Guinn, 2001) and it enables its members to act as a brand's 'advocates' defending it against attacks and spreading enthusiasm (Habibi, Laroche, & Richard, 2014).

Brand communities can develop around different brands and products – including convenience goods (Cova & Pace, 2006) and can exist in different forms such as small or large (Bagozzi & Dholakia, 2006; McAlexander & Koenig, 2010), temporary, offline (Muniz & O'Guinn, 2001; Algesheimer, Dholakia & Herrmann, 2005; McAlexander, Schouten, & Koenig, 2002) as well as online (Adjei, Noble, & Noble, 2010; Muniz & Schau, 2007; Thompson & Sinha, 2008), which are here defined as 'online brand communities' (OBCs).

OBCs can be categorized according to their type of government in two distinct types: 'consumer-initiated' and 'company-initiated communities' (Jang, Ko, Koh, & Kim, 2008). While the former are unofficial communities built voluntarily by consumers without any initiative of the brand itself, the latter are created by marketers. Company-initiated communities attempt to initiate a dialogic conversation between marketers and a brand's customers as well as other stakeholders (e.g., general public), engage customers in the value creation process (e.g., enhancing the service experience and its aftermath), get direct feedback and to promote a brand's products in a positive environment where individuals love to spend their time (Adjei, Noble, & Noble, 2010).

Brand communities – whether they exist offline or online – can affect consumer behavior in favor of brands (e.g., Muniz & O'Guinn, 2001). For instance, from the beginning brand communities are understood as places for loyal consumers and that membership influences loyalty through different mechanisms including 'oppositional loyalty' (McAlexander, Schouten, & Koenig, 2002). This argument was later supported by various empirical findings. For instance, Casalo, Flavian, and Guinaliu (2007) found that, in the context of OBCs, participation in such communities enhances a consumer's brand trust as well as brand loyalty. Scholars widely agree that brand communities offer many advantages for both consumers and companies (e.g., Brown, Kozinets, & Sherry, 2003) and serve as an important instrument for building strong and lasting relationships with consumers (e.g., Algesheimer, Dholakia, & Herrmann, 2005). Earlier research suggests that the way brand communities are hosted (by consumer vs. company) also affects members' participation behaviors (e.g., Muniz & O'Guinn, 2001). For instance, Porter, Devaraj, and Sun (2013) provide some evidence that member-generated content influences participants' trust, information sharing, and word-of-mouth behavior. However, the impact of this driver diminishes in company-initiated communities. In addition, consumption-related outcomes including the willingness to re-purchase a brand can differ across platforms (e.g., Jang, Olfman, Ko, Koh, & Kim, 2008).

With the increasing popularity of social media, various companies are now using diverse online platforms to support the creation of brand communities. Brands such as *Harley Davidson* – with famous offline brand communities (McAlexander, Schouten, & Koenig, 2002) – try to connect with their customers beyond the offline sphere and enhance their brand community on *Facebook*. 'Brand fan-pages' are a specific type of a social network-based OBC. In the realm of this research, these pages are defined as company-initiated online communities that represents a brand's official channel to communicate and interact with its customers via *Facebook*.

On *Facebook*, consumers can "like" the brand and can easily become fans of brands – joining a group of consumers sharing a common interest for the brand. By doing so they can publicly share their enthusiasm, or even love for the brand (Albert, Merunka & Valette-Florence, 2008) with others. The reasons why consumer become 'brand fans' are, however, multifaceted: In line with earlier research, motives can be categorized as either utilitarian or hedonic. While *utilitarian motives* are goal-oriented, rational, driven by the consumer's peruse of effectiveness and instrumental values; *hedonic motives* are generally defined as a consumer's desire to seek fun, enjoyment and entertainment (Babin, Darden, & Griffin, 1994; Voss, Spangenberg, & Grohmann, 2003). This research suggests that consumers become 'brand fans' in order to achieve one or both of these two rudimental goals. Specifically, many consumer have joined a brand fan-page for obtaining useful information which enables them to make better and more efficient purchasing decisions. Such a desire is purely utilitarian. On the other hand, consumers strive for hedonic goals when thinking that visiting the fan-page is a good way to spend time, to be aroused, entertained and to have fun. Another main reason why consumers become fans on *Facebook* is their ability to become directly involved in the brand's communication: They can 'like' or comment directly on brand posts which empowers them to easily respond to brand messages (Kabadayi, & Price, 2014). This gives them the ability to influence others. This is an act of self-enhancement and therefore has a hedonic nature. In addition, consumers often join brand fan-pages for social reasons (e.g., finding new friends and similar others) and therefore out of more experiential than utilitarian reasons.

Communication Activities on Brand Fan-Pages

Brand fan-pages offer companies means to communicate with customers and foster interaction with and among brand enthusiasts. Basically, companies strive to fulfil both informational and social needs on social networking sites (e.g., Kozinets, 1999; Ridings & Gefen, 2004). They do so by delivering interesting, relevant, entertaining and engaging content in the form of 'brand posts'. On fan-pages companies often create a large proportion of the content themselves. The typical content therefore regularly includes a diverse set of promotional messages conveying product information, brand-related anecdotes, photos, links to other websites, videos, quizzes and other materials. As a result, brand fan-pages share some similarities with corporate blogs or even company websites. However, *Facebook* fan-pages also allow its members to initiate conversations, create content, make comments on brand posts and 'like' others' messages. As consumers can actively contribute in social media environments they should be considered active participants and co-creators of brand-related content. Unlike traditional media (e.g., static websites) where individuals absorb content passively, social media offers new ways to engage consumers with actively producing 'consumer posts'. This active creation of content shapes the character of the community and also determines the influences of users and participants on each other (Bagozzi & Dholakia, 2002). Community members, for instance, can post comments on their (positive/negative) personal experiences with the brand, their perceptions, thoughts and feelings. Consequently, consumer posts – together with brand posts – help to develop a unique brand image and meaning. Marketers have to recognize that brand meaning is not only influenced by their communication efforts, but it created with credible customers' statements voiced in OBCs.

CONCEPTUAL BACKGROUND AND HYPOTHESES

Figure 1 presents the conceptual framework. It builds on Keller and Lehmann's (2003) 'brand value chain' as the theoretical foundation and adopts it to the social media context. This adoption is required as the traditional value chain only takes company-controlled marketing communication into account (Aaker 1991; Keller & Lehmann, 2003). Communication content on brand fan-pages are, however, co-created by consumers. Hence, this study accounts for both marketer and consumer-generated content. The model at hand is comparable to the work of Bruhn, Schönmüller and Schäfer (2012). However, it incorporates, amongst other, the 'engagement' concept as well as de Vries, Gensler and Leeflang's (2012) grasp of the fan-page's key content determinants of consumer engagement. The basic structure of the model consists of the following key components: First, the diverse *fan-page perceptions* of the consumer: It is argued that the content of the brand posts (information, entertainment), along with perceived vividness, interactivity and valence of the page's user comments (i.e., consumer posts) are important criteria for consumers' evaluation of the brand fan-page. Second, 'consumer's fan-page engagement' (CFE) and 'consumers' brand engagement' (CBE) as two facets of *consumer engagement*. And finally, the consumer's *brand mindset* consisting of brand awareness, brand image and brand attitude. In the following section, the model's key components will be discussed and hypotheses about their relationships will be developed.

Figure 1.

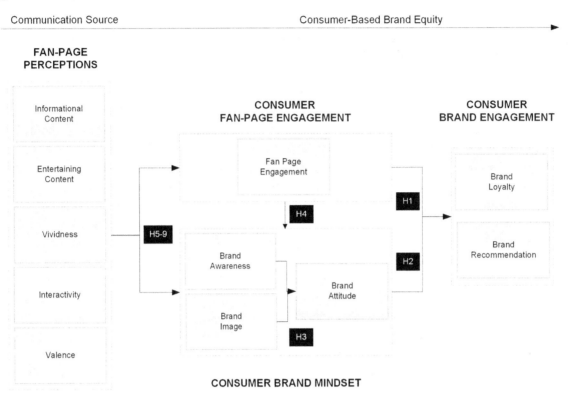

Consumer Engagement

Within the last years scholars from various disciplines including management, social psychology, marketing and information systems have made significant efforts to explore the nature of the 'engagement' concept (e.g., Bowden, 2009; Hollebeek, 2011; Vivek, Beatty, & Morgan, 2012). In marketing literature, academics strongly strive to understand 'consumer engagement', which is a sub-concept under the umbrella term of engagement. This literature stream is driven by the discussion of consumers' new role as actively involved contributors in brand communities which gained reasonable momentum. Given its importance, however, the engagement concept still suffers from a disagreement among scholars concerning the concept's definition, boundaries, dimensionality and operationalization. A literature review by Cheung, Shen, Lee and Chan (2015) reveals that in marketing three primary perspectives exist which differently define the concept: Accordingly, consumer engagement can be regarded as either (i) a psychological process, (ii) a motivational psychological state, or (iii) a behavioral manifestation.

For instance, O'Brien and Toms (2010) regard customer engagement as a psychological process that results in customer loyalty. Here, some researchers conceptualize consumer engagement as a psychological state which is mirrored by a degree of vigor, dedication, absorption and interaction. Cheung, She, Lee and Chan (2015) take a similar approach but identify vigor, absorption and dedication as its key dimensions. Hollebeek (2011, p. 790) defines customer engagement as "the level of an individual customer's motivational, brand-related and context-dependent state of mind characterized by specific levels of cognitive, emotional and behavioral activity in direct brand interactions". The third conceptual approach is to view consumer engagement as a behavioral manifestation: Here, customer engagement is regularly defined as "the intensity of an individual's participation in and connection with an organization's offerings and/or organizational activities, which either the customer or the organization initiate" (Vivek, Beatty, & Morgan, 2012, p. 127) and "a customer's behavioral manifestations that have a brand or firm focus, beyond purchase, resulting from motivational drivers" (van Doorn, et al., 2010, p. 254). In order to narrow discussion, this research focuses on the behavioral-intentional dimension of consumer engagement as it has been advanced by various researchers before (e.g., Dijkmans et al., 2015).

The concept of consumer engagement (as an act or behavioral intention) has been put forward to integrate a multitude of behavioral manifestations that go 'beyond the purchase' and have a company or brand focus (e.g., Vivek, Beatty, & Morgan, 2012). Some typical examples regularly surfacing in literature include referral/word-of-mouth (e.g., recommending a product to friends and family members), customer retention (e.g., regularly purchasing a company's products or services), support of other customers (e.g., assisting others with their shopping), after-sales services (e.g., helping complaining customers to solve their problem), co-creation (e.g., developing new product ideas for the company) and brand advocacy (e.g., protecting a brand against attacks like negative word-of-mouth) (e.g., Verhoef, Reinartz, & Krafft, 2010; Vivek, Beatty, & Morgan, 2012). This demonstrates the multifaceted nature of consumer engagement. However, one can derive two key notions from such behaviors: Firstly, engaged customers express themselves in interactions with both the involved *brand* and its existing and *fellow consumers* (Brodie, Ilic, Juric, & Hollebeek, 2013). And secondly, engaged customers promote a brand as well as its activities such as a brand fan-page's popularity (Vivek, Beatty, & Morgan, 2012). According to the latter insight it is reasonable to separate two different kinds of consumer engagement in the context of *Facebook* brand fan-pages: 'Consumer fan-page engagement' (CFE) vs. 'consumer brand engagement' (CBE).

CFE can be defined as a behavioral intention to continuously interact and get involved on a brand fan-page (Baldus, Voorhees, & Calantone, 2014). Hence, CFE explicitly refers to consumer engagement within an OBC and all intentions towards activities related to the member's interaction with this community (incl. the brand). Manifestations of such intentions are typically observed on brand fan-pages when consumer get actively involved by sharing their thoughts and opinions in posts (Hennig-Thurau, Gwinner, Walsh, & Gremler, 2004) or by helping other customers by providing a clarifying user comment. Within the conceptual framework the focus is on all facets of CFE, including a consumer's active and passive dedication to a specific brand page (e.g., participation in the community's activities such as his/her intention to share stories, photos, videos, 'liking' and to comment on related materials on the brand fan-page) (e.g., Habibi, Laroche, & Richard, 2014).

On the other hand, *brands* are another key object of consumer engagement regularly cited in literature (e.g., Sprott, Czellar, & Spangenberg, 2009). CBE is in this chapter understood as a consumer's positively valenced, brand-related behavioral intentions during or related to focal consumer/brand interactions. The concept denotes an interaction intention between the consumer and the brand, which can be manifested in various behaviors. Basically, the brand-engaged consumer is willing to invest effort in maintaining a degree of transactional/relational interaction with a specific brand (e.g., be loyal) and feels enthusiastic by communicating a brand's benefits to others (e.g., recommending the brand). Consequently, in this research two different kinds of CBE are investigated: *brand loyalty* (i.e., a consumer's intention to repurchase a brand) and *brand recommendation* (i.e., a consumer's willingness to recommend a brand to others).

Consumer Mindset

'Consumer-based brand equity' (or 'brand value') arises from the *consumer's mindset*, which consists of brand image, brand awareness and brand attitude (Aaker, 1991; Bruhn, Schoenmüller, & Schäfer, 2012) 'Brand awareness' signifies the presence of a brand in a consumer's memory. Hence, the concept indicates how well a consumer recalls or recognizes that specific brand (Rossiter & Percy, 1987). Keller (1993) views 'brand image' as the aggregation of different types of associations a consumer links to a specific brand as well as the favorability, strength and uniqueness of these associations. Brand associations are developed from a variety of sources (e.g., marketing communication) which can be classified in product-related and non-product related attributes. Product attributes, price information and packaging are examples for product-related attributes, while brand personality, user imagery and usage imagery are three key non product-related attributes according to Keller's (1993) framework of brand equity.

Most researchers (e.g., Helgeson & Supphellen, 2004) regard brand image and brand attitude as two distinct concepts. For instance, Keller (1993) states that 'brand image' is the perceptual belief about a brand's attributes, benefits and attitude associations which builds helps to develop consumer's overall evaluation or 'brand attitude'. The notion of brand attitude as a consumer's "internal evaluation of the brand" is also advanced, amongst others, by Mitchell and Olson (1981, p. 318). A person's attitude toward a brand hence depends on a consumer's own perceptions regarding a brand. The concept is recognized as a key component for valuing a brand's equity and as a reliable predictor of consumers' behaviors towards the brand. In this research's framework, the customer brand mindset is regarded as a key mediator that links consumer content perceptions of the brand page with CBE.

Hypotheses

Determinants of Consumer Brand Engagement: Scholars strongly argue for a positive and direct relationship between consumer online engagement and a number of brand relationship outcomes such as satisfaction, brand commitment and loyalty (e.g., Brodie, Ilic, Biljana. & Hollebeek, 2011). It seems appealing to argue that if a consumer participates on a brand fan-page by communicating and receiving messages from other fans this creates value. Such a value consequently fosters brand loyalty and customer advocacy (Algesheimer, Dholakia, & Herrmann, 2005). Thus, by engaging on the brand fan-page brand loyalty can be further strengthened (McAlexander, Schouten, & Koenig, 2002). The notion that (online) community engagement leads to positive brand engagement outcomes is strongly supported in literature: For instance, Thompson and Sinha (2008) find that active participants of a brand community are less likely to embrace competing products. Jang et al. (2008) study the effect of online brand community engagement on brand loyalty and discover a positive effect. Brand loyalty, in turn, is found to be a strong positive predictor of intentions to purchase the brand in future (e.g., Baldinger & Rubinson, 1996). Engagement towards a community is said to be reflected by the behavior of its members. Hence, active participation is considered a strong indicator of such a commitment (Casalo, Flavian, & Guinaliu, 2010; Jang, Olfman, Ko, Koh, & Kim, 2008). As a consequence, it seems that being a member of a company-initiated brand fan-page may be a good indicator of the person's commitment and loyalty towards the brand, which is considered to be a co-variate of consumer referral intent. Algesheimer, Dholakia and Herrmann (2005) find a generally positive impact of CFE on behavioral brand loyalty, defined as positive word-of-mouth and repeat purchase intention. Hence, the first hypothesis reads as follows:

H1: Fan-page engagement as a significant and positive effect on (a) brand loyalty and (b) brand recommendation.

The relationships between brand attitude, brand loyalty and word-of-mouth are well established and validated in consumer research. By following these insights and it can be expected that brand attitude has a strong, positive impact on repeat purchase intention as well as referral intention. A consumer's intention to repurchase is a psychological variable that mediates between brand attitude and actual repurchasing behavior (Miniard, Obermiller, & Page, 1983). This research follows Eagly and Chaiken's (1993) attitude-behavior-hypotheses which states that attitude (e.g., towards a brand) has a positive effect on repurchasing and referral intentions and propose the following hypothesis:

H2: Brand attitude as a significant and positive effect on (a) brand loyalty and (b) brand recommendation.

Relationships within the consumer brand mindset: This research defined brand attitude as an overall evaluation of the brand by the consumer. In line the 'theory of reasoned action' (Fishbein & Ajzen, 1975) it is here argued that a brand attitude is a multiplicative combination of brand-based associations of attributes, characteristics and benefits. And that the concept is itself influenced by both brand awareness and brand image (i.e., a consumer's *brand knowledge*). Therefore, it is hypothesized:

H3a: Brand awareness has a significant and positive effect on brand attitude.
H3b: Brand image has a significant and positive effect on brand attitude.

Relationship Between Consumer Community Engagement and the Consumer Brand Mindset: Being engaged on a brand fan-page means that a consumer is continuously experiencing the brand by actively interacting with it. While participating in the OBC, consumers are able to identify information that is relevant to them such as brand posts that convey a brand's identity (Aaker, 1991). 'Brand identity' is a unique set of brand associations that a company wants to create or maintain in the consumer's mind. Such posts remind the consumer about the brand's characteristics and include, amongst others, brand attributes, benefits and values. Based on such information consumers develop their own (cognitive/affective) brand associations (i.e., brand knowledge). Hence, information conveyed in brand posts is stored as brand associations in a consumer's memory. Consumers who are engaged in an OBC tend to have stronger brand commitment and they become vested in the success and failures of that brand (Ashforth & Mael, 1989). By considering this, one can assume that consumers who are continuously engaged on a brand fan-page are more likely to develop better brand knowledge and more positive attitudes towards the brand. Hence:

H4: Fan-page engagement has a significant and positive effect on (a) brand awareness, (b) brand image and (c) brand attitude.

Effects of Brand Fan-Page Content Perceptions: Researchers often apply the 'uses and gratifications theory' (Katz, 1959) to understand the goals and motivations of consumers engaged with different types of content. Previous applications of this theory on the context of brand communities and social media shows that information-seeking is an important factor for consumer engagement in, for instance, online brand communities (Raacke & Bonds-Raacke, 2008), social networking sites (Lin & Lu, 2011) and participation in Facebook groups (Valenzuela, Park, & Kee, 2009). Moreover, information was found to be the main reason for online engagement over brand-related content in the form of consumption, creation and contribution (Muntinga, Moorman, & Smit, 2011). Therefore, in case a brand fan-page conveys an adequate amount of informative brand posts, the brand fans' motivation to participate and consume such content are met. Informational brand posts contain consumption-relevant information about a specific brand, a product, a company or related marketing activities (de Vries, Gensler, & Lefflang, 2012). These posts also inform consumers about product alternatives which ultimately enables them to make better choices (Muntinga, Moorman, & Smit, 2011). One reason why consumers join brand fan-pages is their desire to have (positive) experiences with the brand. As a consequence, they are searching for information enabling such experiences (e.g., release dates, product descriptions) (Lin & Lu, 2011; Valenzuela, Park, & Kee, 2009) and are motivated to consume and interact with such brand posts (de Vries, Gensler, & Lefflang, 2012). If consumers pursue utilitarian goals, they are also more likely to respond to (informational) brand posts. This suggests that brand fans (particularly in a non-hedonic shopping context) have a more positive attitude toward informational brand posts compared to non-informational brand posts which leads to higher CFE. It is further argued that if consumers are successful in identifying informational brand posts which help them to build up their brand knowledge about the brand this also has a positive impact on the consumer brand mindset. This reasoning is supported by earlier research demonstrating that word-of-mouth (WOM) and communication originating from marketers (e.g., ads) have a significant effect on brand awareness (e.g., Godes & Mayzlin 2009) and brand image (e.g., Bruhn, Schoenmüller, & Schäfer, 2012). These considerations result in the following hypotheses:

H5: Informational content has a significant and positive effect on (a) fan-page engagement, (b) brand awareness and (c) brand image.

Dholakia, Bagozzi and Paero (2004) find that the 'enjoyment value' of OBC content has a positive impact on participation behavior such as engaging in conversations with others. Similarly, there is some evidence that consumers' information collection is an end in itself (Bloch, Ridgway, & Sherrell, 1989) and that they enjoy the information collection process (Mathwick & Rigdon, 2004). Thus, it seems that some consumers consider participating in a community as a good way to pass their time. In fact, various studies have shown that enjoyment-related benefits may function as a driver of customer engagement in communities (e.g., Dholakia Bagozzi, & Pearo, 2004), for example, demonstrate that entertainment causes people to consume, create and contribute to brand-related content online. *Entertainment brand posts* are messages that often do not refer to the brand or the product itself, but merely contain humorous videos, anecdotes, teasers, slogans or word play. Such posts furnish consumers with an opportunity to distract and divert themselves. They lead to aesthetic enjoyment and emotional release (e.g., fun). Earlier studies even claim that entertainment is the most crucial factor in determining social media users' behaviors. In addition, we can learn from advertising research that entertaining ads have a positive impact on the consumer's attitude towards advertising (Taylor, Lewin, & Strutton, 2011), positively influence the attitude toward the brand and lead to a higher intend to revisit a website (Raney, Arpan, Pashupati, & Brill, 2003). In sum, above discussion guides to the following hypothesis:

H6: Entertaining content has a significant and positive effect on (a) fan-page engagement, (b) brand awareness and (c) brand image.

Different media types entail different capacities for stimulating our senses. This is because of the 'vividness' of a message (de Vries, Gensler, & Leeflang, 2012). The idea of vividness is also often referred to as 'richness' of the (online) content. Typically, the concepts reflects the extent of a brand post's formal features or in other words: it describes the degree to which a brand post stimulates our different senses. A way to increase a message's (optical and audiovisual) vividness is, for example, the inclusion of dynamic animations, contrasting colors or pictures, and videos (Goldfarb & Tucker 2011). Currently, *Facebook* offers the possibility to share (1) status (text), (2) photo, (3) video and (4) links. These content types represent different levels of message vividness. For instance, a video post is more vivid than a status post because the former stimulates not only sight but also hearing (de Vries, Gensler, & Leeflang, 2012). Various studies found that the degree of vividness of a *Facebook* post impacts its popularity (e.g., Sabate, Berbegal-Mirabent, Canabate, & Lebherz, 2014). According to a study by Brookes (2010), images receive 54% more than text posts and videos receive 27% more engagement than text posts.

In addition, the degree of a fan-page's content vividness also determines the information about the involved brand. For example, compared with information in a status message, information combining text and photo formats can provide fans with more vivid information on a brand (van der Heide, D'Angelo, & Schumaker, 2012). As a result, consumer's brand knowledge is enhanced. According to previous research findings, a high degree of vividness appears is the most effective way to enhance attitudes toward a website (Fortin & Dholakia, 2005) as well as to increase 'click-through rates', which can be regarded as an engagement manifestation. These findings suggest that perceptions of a brand page's vividness are likely to lead to more positive attitudes toward the brand posts on this site. This favorable attitude should convince individuals to get engaged in the community. In addition, brand fans should consider vivid brand posts as more informative and relevant which increases brand awareness and stimulates specific brand associations. Therefore:

H7: Fan-page vividness has a significant and positive effect on (a) fan-page engagement, (b) brand awareness and (c) brand image.

Interactivity can be defined as the extent to which two or more communication parties can act on each other, on the communication medium and on the messages – as well as the degree to which such actions are synchronized. Accordingly, the concept of interactivity describes the level of two-way communication between the brand and its fans as well as the degree of interaction between the fans themselves. On *Facebook*, content creators can choose from various kinds of messages that differ in their level of interactivity in order to disseminate content. For instance, brand posts can include text only which is not interactive at all as it stimulates no direct reaction by the recipient. But message creators can also choose to include a link to another website which is considered to be more interactive (Fortin & Dholakia, 2005) since brand fans can get directly involved by clicking on the link. Other interactive forms include voting, direct calls to action (e.g., asking fans to click the 'like' button and comment on information), quizzes, contests and context questions begging direct answers from the fans (de Vries, Gensler, & Lefflang, 2012).

In academic literature, interactivity is regarded as a critical determinant of various affective, cognitive and behavioral outcomes including consumer satisfaction, attitude, decision making and involvement (e.g., Fortin & Dholakia, 2005). It has been shown that a high level of interactivity can stimulate favorable communication outcomes (Rafaeli & Ariel, 2007). Previous studies find a positive effect of interactivity on brand post's popularity and consumer online engagement (de Vries, Gensler, & Lefflang, 2012). Furthermore, consumer perceptions of interactivity are shown to be positively related to consumer attitudes towards a specific media products and their underlying brands. Therefore, by making an analogy between other forms of communication content and brand posts, one can expect a similarly positive effect of perceived interactivity. Consequently:

H8: Fan-page interactivity has a significant and positive effect on (a) fan-page engagement, (b) brand awareness and (c) brand image.

Valence refers to the extent to which the information reflects positively or negatively on the brand in question (Adjei, Noble, & Noble, 2010). As fans' brand posts (i.e., consumer word-of-mouth; WOM) are not generally amendable to marketing intervention nor to marketers' control, community member comments can either provide positive, neutral or negative information. Earlier research demonstrates that online discussions of positive brand experiences (positive WOM) can lead to empathy as well as positive feelings among participants (Bickart & Schindler, 2001). In contrast, negative comments (negative WOM) discourage people to adopt products (Dellarocas, Zhang, & Awad, 2007). In either way, positive/negative WOM can be particularly useful for consumers to make purchasing decisions and increasing consumers' brand awareness. Positively valenced consumer posts highlights the strengths of the brand and is associated with satisfying consumer experiences. This can encourage people to have more positive perceptions of the brand's value, to have more favorable brand associations, to consider purchasing it and to recommend the brand to others. In the context of OBCs, positive comments from community members are found to have a stronger effect than negative information (Adjei, Noble, & Noble, 2010) as it furnishes consumers with a much-needed confirmation of the suitability of their choice before they make the actual purchase. In addition, positive comments seem to have a complementary value to the company's brand posts (Bronner & de Hoog, 2010) and therefore have a positive effect on the attractiveness/correctness of the brand post. Positive comments on fan-page posts can hence increase the perceived value of this brand post and can create empathy among brand fans (de Vries, Gensler, & Leeflang, 2012). To sum up, it is reasonable to expect the following:

H9: Positive brand posts have a significant and positive effect on (a) fan-page engagement, (b) brand awareness and (c) brand image.

EMPIRICAL STUDY

Data Collection

For testing the hypotheses, an online survey was conducted. A total of 390 participants completed the standardized questionnaire. Specifically, data was collected from members of a *Facebook* brand page of a major Austrian grocery chain. The brand's fan-page existed over several years and was used by the retailer to disseminate a variety of different marketing messages to its clientele on a regular basis. The page was also used intensively by its community members to interact with each other, share their experiences and to provide customer feedback. At the time of research, the brand page had almost 300,000 fans. The decision to collect data from the retailing (grocery) industry was supported by the fact that particularly companies acting in highly competitive industries increasingly make use of OBCs in order to provided added value to their customers in order to keep them loyal (e.g., Ferguson & Brohaugh, 2008).

Survey data was collected within 14 days in April 2015. The survey was first pretested among ten university students in order to ensure its functionality and the comprehensibleness of its questions. After some minor changes to the online questionnaire's wording, respondents of the main study were invited with public website-links to the survey posted on the retailer's website as well as on its official brand fan-page. As an incentive, customers were encouraged to participate in the study by granting them the opportunity to enter a draw of 50 shopping vouchers (worth 20 Euros each). The survey attracted 425 respondents and after removing incomplete questionnaires, 390 responses were accepted for final analysis.

71% (n=278) of the respondents were women, which resembles roughly to the demographics of the retailer's *Facebook* fan community. Most respondents were aged between 20 and 39 years (67%; n=262). The vast majority of the respondents reported that they shop at the retailer on a weekly basis (80%; n=313).

Measurement

The online questionnaire consisted of several sections. Except for the socio-demographics and valence (which were measured with single-item measures) all constructs were measured with multiple items. More specifically, the measurement was based on a careful literature review, choosing the items from established scales validated in previous research in the context of (online) brand communities and consumer engagement. However, given the lack of appropriate measurement instruments in the context of *Facebook* fan-page perceptions (e.g., vividness, interactivity), the author had to adapt scales from studies conducted in other research contexts or had to introduce new items. For instance, the seven items for the brand fan-page's *interactivity* were adapted from de Vries, Gensler and Lefflang (2012) (e.g., 'The brand's *Facebook* page provides many links to other websites.'; 'The brand's *Facebook* page invites consumers to interact with <brand>.'), the five items on *vividness* were derived from de Vries, Gensler and Lefflang (2012) and self-constructed (e.g., 'The brand's *Facebook* page provides many images.'; '… many videos.'). These constructs were all formatively measured. Five items were used to assess content's *information value*. These items were taken from, amongst others, Lin and Lu (2011) (α=.91) and the items for content's *entertainment value* were derived from Dholakia, Bagozzi and Paero (2004) (α=.80). The scale for *brand awareness* was based on two sources: Bruhn, Schoenmüller and Schäfer, (2012) and Villajero-Ramos and Sanchez-Franco (2005) (α=.87). *Brand image* was based on five items from Bruhn, Schoenmüller and Schäfer, (2012), Villajero-Ramos and Sanchez-Franco (2005) and others (α=.86), while *brand attitude* was measured with items taken from Mitchel and Olsen (1981) (α=.91). *Consumer fan-page engagement* (CFE) was derived from Casalo, Flavian and Guinaliu (2010) (α=.86). Finally, *consumer brand engagement* (CBE) was measured as follows: *brand loyalty* was assessed with four items taken from Chaudhuri and Holbrook (2010) (α=.79), while the measurement of *brand recommendation* was based on Zeithaml (1986) (3 items; α=.87). To operationalize the items, 5-point Likert scales ranging from "strongly disagree" to "strongly agree and semantic differentials were used (see Table 1 for scale items).

Table 1. Scale items for construct measures

Construct	Items	Cronbach's α	Based on
Brand fan page's interactivity	The (Brand's) Facebook page provides … (i) many links to other websites; (ii) many consumer polls; The (Brand's) Facebook page invites consumers … (iii) to "like" its postings; (iv) to write comments; (v) to express one's opinions; (vi) to interact with the brand.	N/A (formatively measured)	De Vries, Gensler, and Lefflang (2012); Thorson and Rodgers (2006)
Vividness	The (Brand's) Facebook page postings include … (i) many images; (ii) many videos; (iii) sales promotions hints; (iv) event proclamations; (v) games	N/A (formatively measured)	De Vries, Gensler, and Lefflang (2012)
Content's informativeness	The (Brand's) postings … (i) provide information that is useful for my shopping. (ii) … are generally informative. (iii) … help me to know more about the brand. (iv) … increase my knowledge about the brand's products. (v) … give me purchase-relevant product information	.91	Chang, Yu and Lu (2014); Lin and Lu (2011)
Content's entertainment value	The (Brand's) postings … (i) are entertaining. (ii) are funny. (iii) help me to pass the time away when I am bored.	.80	Dholakia, Bagozzi, and Paero (2004)
Brand awareness	(i) I know the brand. (ii) Some characteristics of the brand come to my mind quickly. (iii) I have a very clear picture of (Brand). (iv) Several characteristics of (Brand) instantly come to my mind.	.87	Bruhn, Schönmüller, and Schäfer (2012); Villajero-Ramos and Sanchez-Franco (2005)
Brand image	(i) (Brand) has a strong personality. (ii) (Brand) has a strong image. (iii) (Brand) has a good reputation. (iv) (Brand) is credible. (v) (Brand) is a unique brand. (vi) (Brand) is a strong brand.	.86	Bruhn, Schönmüller, and Schäfer, (2012); Low and Lamb (2000); Villajero-Ramos and Sanchez-Franco (2005)
Brand attitude	(i) (Brand) is good. (ii) I like (Brand) very much. (iii) (Brand) is pleasant.	.91	Mitchel and Olsen (1981)
Community engagement	I regularly … (i) visit the (Brand's) Facebook community. (ii) "like" others' comments on this Facebook page. (iii) write comments on the (Brand's) Facebook page.	.86	Casalo, Flavian, and Guinaliu (2010)
Brand loyalty	(i) I feel loyal towards (Brand). (ii) I am committed to (Brand). (iii) I shop regularly at (Brand). (iv) I plan to shop at (Brand) more often in future.	.79	Chaudhuri and Holbrook (2010); Eisingerich and Rubera (2010)
Brand recommendation	(i) I say positive things about (Brand) to other people. (ii) I recommend (Brand) to others. (iii) I recommend (Brand's) products to other potential customers.	.87	Gruen, Osmonbekov and Czaplewski (2006); Zeithaml (1986)

Results

Consumer-based brand equity creation. A series of regression analyses was conducted to test the research hypotheses. With regard to the relationship between consumer fan-page engagement (CFE), customer brand mindset and brand engagement (CBE) (H1-2), results showed that the paths between CFE and brand loyalty (b=.25, t(187)=3.50, p<.001; R^2=.10, F(1,186)=12.25, p<.001), as well as between CFE and brand recommendation (b=.41, t(187)=6.21, p<.001; R^2=.17, F(1,186)=38.57, p<.001) were positive and significant. Hence, H1 was supported. Brand attitude had positive effects both on brand loyalty (b=.53, t(193)=8.71, p<.001; R^2=.28, F(1,192)=75.83, p<.001) and brand recommendation (b=.42, t(190)=6.34, p<.001; R^2=.18, F(1,189)=40.15, p<.001). These results supported H2a and H2b.

With regards to the relationship between brand awareness (b=.52, t(193)=8.35, p<.001; R^2=.27, F(1,192)=69.79, p<.001) and brand image (b=.74, t(192)=15.22, p<.001; R^2=.55, F(1,191)=231.76, p<.001) as drivers of brand attitude, empirical data revealed a significant positive relationship for both cases at the p=.001 level – which supported H3a and H3b. H4 proposes a positive relationship between CFE and the customer brand mindset. The data supported this hypothesis as CFE turned out to be significantly and positively related to brand awareness (b=.17, t(187)=2.41, p<.05; R^2=.04, F(1,186)=5.81, p<.001), brand image (b=.30, t(187)=4.30, p<.001; R^2=.09, F(1,186)=9.60, p<.001) and brand attitude (b=.19, t(187)=2.70, p<.01; R^2=.04, F(1,186)=7.30, p<.001).

Consumer reactions to Facebook content perceptions. H5 states that perceived informational fan-page content positively influences both CFE and the consumer brand mindset. The regression results showed that CFE (b=.33, t(186)=3.71, p<.001; R^2=.10, F(1,185)=22.18, p<.001), brand awareness (b=.29, t(191)=4.20, p<.001; R^2=.09, F(1,190)=17.67, p<.001), and brand image (b=.45, t(190)=6.70, p<.001; R^2=.20, F(1,189)=48.37, p<.001) were positively influenced by the perceived information value at a significance level of p<.001. Thus, the informational influence hypotheses (H5a-c) was accepted. Similarly, data supported the 'entertainment content hypotheses' (H6a-c) theorizing a positive relationship between perceived entertainment value of the fan-page's content and CFE (b=.41, t(185)=6.14, p<.001; R^2=.17, F(1,184)=37.74, p<.001), brand awareness (b=.41, t(190)=2.68, p<.01; R^2=.04, F(1,189)=7.17, p<.001), and brand image (b=.33, t(189)=4.71, p<.001; R^2=.11, F(1,188)=22.19, p<.001).

The empirical findings also supported the assumption that consumers' perception of a fan-page's vividness is positively related to his/her CFE (b=.21, t(184)=2.91, p<.01; R^2=.05, F(1,183)=8.46, p<.001), brand awareness (b=.17, t(189)=2.32, p<.05; R^2=.03, F(1,188)=5.39, p<.001), and brand image (b=.33, t(188)=4.71, p<.001; R^2=.11, F(1,187)=22.14, p<.001). Therefore, H7a-c were supported. Perceived interactivity had positive effects on CFE (b=.36, t(186)=5.29, p<.001; R^2=.13, F(1,185)=39.80, p<.001), brand awareness (b=.18, t(192)=2.45, p<.05; R^2=.03, F(1,191)=6.01, p<.05), and brand image (b=.39, t(191)=5.75, p<.001; R^2=.15, F(1,190)=33.10, p<.001), which supported H8.

Finally, H9 was partially supported: Here, respondents' perception that consumer comments express positive experiences with the brand (i.e., valence perception) increased CFE (b=.41, t(145)=3.61, p<.001; R^2=.08, F(1,144)=13.01, p<.001) and brand image (b=.31, t(149)=4.00, p<.001; R^2=.10, F(1,148)=15.90, p<.001). However, there was no effect on brand awareness (b=.14, t(150)=1.73, n.s.). Nevertheless, 23 out of 24 hypotheses were finally supported indicating the appropriateness of the underlying research model (Figure 2 summarizes the significant effects).

DISCUSSION

Marketers have put much emphasizes on creating and maintaining strong bonds with their customers by means of company-initiated online brand communities (OBCs). This research investigates consumer perceptions of content disseminated by marketers and other consumers on *Facebook* fan-pages and the arising consumer-based consequences. Specifically, the chapter at hand strives to evaluate the impact of diverse forms of consumer content perceptions on both 'consumer fan-page engagement' (i.e., online activities of community members; CFE) and the 'consumer brand mindset' (i.e., brand-related mental state consisting of community members' brand awareness, brand image and brand attitude). Empirical findings support the conceptual model (Figure 1), showing that consumers' positive evaluations of marketers-created brand posts (i.e., perceptions of its informational value, entertainment value, vividness, and its interactivity) as well as of the perceived valence of consumer-created posts all are strong predictors of fan-page engagement (i.e., online co-creation activities such as commenting, sharing and 'liking') and a favorable brand mindset (e.g., positive brand image). The results further demonstrate that a heightened CFE also affects consumers' brand mindset positively. The positive role of fan-page engagement is further fostered by providing empirical support that it – together with the brand mindset – has a stimulating impact on consumer brand engagement (i.e., favorable purchase-related and purchase-unrelated intentions to support the brand [CBE] – e.g., future brand loyalty, willingness to recommend the brand to others). This means that the current research has revealed the causal chain of effects that connects consumers' fan-page connections to consumer-based brand equity and in which community members' online activities as well as brand-related attitudes are important mediators.

Figure 2.

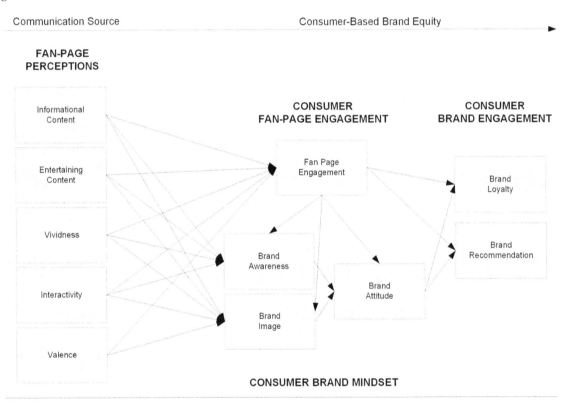

Note: Lines indicate significant, positive effects (at least on the p < .05 level).

This study contributes to the current state of OBC-related academic knowledge by investigating the determinants as well as the outcomes of consumer (active) online engagement (e.g., 'liking', commenting) on key brand-related consumer thoughts and intentions. Findings indicate that CFE should not be regarded as an end in itself, but rather as a key correlate of strong customer-brand relationships. For marketers, on the other hand, the chapter at hand conveys several important implications: First, marketers can steer consumer behavior by providing value-added content of *Facebook* sites. Brand fan-pages that adhere to principles such as interactivity and vividness are likely to lead to positive consumer reactions. Therefore, social media managers should provide brand posts that stimulate both the individuals' senses (e.g., by posting videos and emotion-eliciting pictures rather than simple text messages) and the individuals' willingness to interact with the brand (e.g., by posting quizzes, questions, votes). Second, even in a highly functional shopping context (e.g., grocery shopping), marketers should not only consider providing informational posts (i.e., content which provides information about promotions, sales, etc.), but they should also send posts that satisfy hedonic consumer motives to become an online community member and that entertain the audience. Positive perceptions of consumer-oriented brand posts seem to trigger both cooperative community activities (e.g., helping other shoppers), but also can contribute (to some extent) to customer loyalty as well as recommendation likelihood. Finally, the results imply that marketers should stimulate a community culture in which positive brand experiences are continuously shared among consumers. Favorable brand stories – or positive word-of-mouth – are valued by other consumers and encourages them to become active members of the community themselves and to think more positively about the brand, share its content, etc. Therefore, positively valenced consumer-created posts should be considered as an important form of online content on OBCs.

While providing several important insights for both scholars and marketers, the findings of this research and their implications should be interpreted by considering several limitations: First, this research only investigates a limited number of consumer content perceptions. Future research should consider additional forms (e.g., perception of the content sidedness) in order to derive a more complete picture of the key consumer evaluations and their consequences. Second, the hypothesized relationships among the model's key variables are only tested in a specific research context. Conducting an empirical study beyond the borders of grocery shopping would furnish scholars and marketers with additional, valuable insights about the validity of this research's findings. Third, future research should also consider the role of community members' characteristics (e.g., earlier relationship with the brand; motivation to become a member of the OBC) in order to investigate potential moderating effects pertaining the influence of different forms of online content. Lastly, the study at hand relies on survey data analyzed with a series of regression analyses in order to test the hypothesized relationships. More sophisticated methods, like structural equation modeling (SEM), should be applied to increase the confidence in the findings and to gain additional insights (e.g., relative importance of content perceptions). Experimental research should be conducted in order to ensure causality among variables – given the available data, causal claims are not appropriate in this research.

REFERENCES

Aaker, D. A. (1991). *Managing brand equity*. New York, NY: Free Press.

Adjei, M., Noble, S., & Noble, C. (2010). The influence of C2C communications in online brand communities on customer purchase behavior. *Journal of the Academy of Marketing Science*, *38*(5), 634–653. doi:10.100711747-009-0178-5

Albert, N., Merunka, D., & Valette-Florence, P. (2008). When consumers love their brands: Exploring the concept and its dimension. *Journal of Business Research*, *61*(10), 1062–1075. doi:10.1016/j.jbusres.2007.09.014

Algesheimer, R., Dholakia, U. M., & Herrmann, A. (2005). The social influence of brand community: Evidence from European car clubs. *Journal of Marketing*, *69*(3), 19–34. doi:10.1509/jmkg.69.3.19.66363

Ashforth, B. E., & Mael, F. (1989). Social identity theory and the organization. *Academy of Management Review, 14*(1), 20–39. doi:10.5465/amr.1989.4278999

Babin, B. J., Darden, W. J., & Giffin, M. (1994). Work and/or fun: Measuring hedonic and utilitarian shopping value. *The Journal of Consumer Research, 20*(4), 644–656. doi:10.1086/209376

Bagozzi, R. P., & Dholakia, U. M. (2002). Intentional social action in virtual communities. *Journal of Interactive Marketing, 16*(2), 2–21. doi:10.1002/dir.10006

Bagozzi, R. P., & Dholakia, U. M. (2006). Open source software user communities: A study of participation in Linux user groups. *Management Science, 52*(7), 1099–1115. doi:10.1287/mnsc.1060.0545

Baldiger, A. L., & Rubinson, J. R. (1996). Brand loyalty: The link between attitude and behavior. *Journal of Advertising Research, 36*(6), 22–34.

Baldus, B. J., Voorhees, C., & Calantone, R. (2015). Online brand community engagement: Scale development and validation. *Journal of Business Research, 68*(5), 978–985. doi:10.1016/j.jbusres.2014.09.035

Bickart, B., & Schindler, R. M. (2001). Internet forums as influential sources of consumer information. *Journal of Interactive Marketing, 15*(3), 31–40. doi:10.1002/dir.1014

Bloch, P. H., Ridgway, N. M., & Sherrell, D. L. (1989). Extending the concept of shopping: An investigation of browsing activity. *Journal of the Academy of Marketing Science, 17*(1), 13–21. doi:10.1007/BF02726349

Bowden, J. L.-H. (2009). The process of customer engagement: A conceptual framework. *Journal of Marketing Theory and Practice, 17*(1), 63–74. doi:10.2753/MTP1069-6679170105

Brodie, R. J., Hollebeek, L. D., Juric, B., & Ilic, A. (2011). Customer engagement: Conceptual domain, fundamental propositions, and implications for research. *Journal of Service Research, 14*(3), 252–271. doi:10.1177/1094670511411703

Bronner, A. E., & De Hoog, R. (2010). Consumer-generated versus marketer-generated websites in consumer decision making. *International Journal of Market Research, 52*(2), 231–248. doi:10.2501/S1470785309201193

Brookes, E. J. (2010). *The anatomy of a Facebook post*. Atlanta, GA: Virtue.

Brown, S., Kozinets, R. V., & Sherry, J. F. Jr. (2003). Teaching old brands new tricks: Retro branding and the revival of brand meaning. *Journal of Marketing, 67*(3), 19–33. doi:10.1509/jmkg.67.3.19.18657

Bruhn, M., Schoenmueller, V., & Schäfer, D. B. (2012). Are social media replacing traditional media in terms of brand equity creation? *Management Research Review, 35*(9), 770–790. doi:10.1108/01409171211255948

Casalo, L. V., Flavian, C., & Guinaliu, M. (2007). The role of security, privacy, usability and reputation in the development of online banking. *Online Information Review, 31*(5), 583–603. doi:10.1108/14684520710832315

Chaudhuri, A., & Holbrook, M. B. (2001). The chain of effects form brand trust and brand affect to brand performance: The role of brand loyalty. *Journal of Marketing, 65*(2), 81–93. doi:10.1509/jmkg.65.2.81.18255

Cheung, C., Shen, X., Lee, Z., & Chan, T. (2015). Promoting sales of online games through customer engagement. *Electronic Commerce Research and Applications*, *14*(4), 241–250. doi:10.1016/j.elerap.2015.03.001

Cova, B., & Pace, S. (2006). Brand community of convenience products: New forms of customer empowerment – the case "my Nutella The Community". *European Journal of Marketing*, *40*(9-10), 1087–1105. doi:10.1108/03090560610681023

De Vries, L., Gensler, S., & Leeflang, P. S. (2012). Popularity of brand posts on brand fan pages: An investigation of the effects of social media marketing. *Journal of Interactive Marketing*, *26*(2), 83–91. doi:10.1016/j.intmar.2012.01.003

Dellarocas, C., Zhang, X., & Awad, N. F. (2007). Exploring the value of online product reviews in forecasting sales: The case of motion pictures. *Journal of Interactive Marketing*, *21*(4), 23–45. doi:10.1002/dir.20087

Dholakia, U. M., Bagozzi, R. P., & Paero, L. K. (2004). A social influence model of consumer participation in network- and small-group-based virtual communities. *International Journal of Research in Marketing*, *21*(3), 241–263. doi:10.1016/j.ijresmar.2003.12.004

Dijkmans, C., Kerkhof, P., Buyukcan-Tetik, A., & Beukeboom, C. J. (2015). Online conversations and corporate reputation: A two-wave longitudinal study on the effects of exposure to the social media activities of a highly interactive company. *Journal of Computer-Mediated Communication*, *20*(6), 632–648. doi:10.1111/jcc4.12132

Eagly, A. H., & Chaiken, S. (1993). *The psychology of attitudes*. Orlando, FL: Harcourt Brace Jovanovich College Publishers.

Ferguson, R., & Broghaugh, B. (2008). Telecom's search for the ultimate customer loyalty platform. *Journal of Consumer Marketing*, *25*(5), 314–318. doi:10.1108/07363760810890543

Fishbein, M., & Ajzen, I. (1975). *Belief, attitude, intention, and behavior: An introduction to theory and research*. Reading, MA: Addison-Wesley.

Fortin, D., & Dholakia, R. R. (2005). Interactivity and vividness effects on social presence and involvement with a web-based advertisement. *Journal of Business Research*, *58*(3), 387–396. doi:10.1016/S0148-2963(03)00106-1

Godes, D., & Mayzlin, D. (2009). Firm-created word-of-mouth communication: Evidence from a field test. *Marketing Science*, *28*(4), 721–739. doi:10.1287/mksc.1080.0444

Goldfarb, A., & Tucker, C. (2011). Online display advertising: Targeting and obtrusiveness. *Marketing Science*, *30*(3), 389–404. doi:10.1287/mksc.1100.0583

Habibi, M. R., Laroche, M., & Richard, M.-O. (2014). The roles of brand community and community engagement in building brand trust on social media. *Computers in Human Behavior*, *37*, 152–161. doi:10.1016/j.chb.2014.04.016

Helgeson, J. G., & Supphellen, M. (2004). A conceptual and measurement comparison of self-congruity and brand personality: The impact of socially desirable responding. *International Journal of Market Research, 46*(2), 205–233. doi:10.1177/147078530404600201

Hennig-Thurau, T., Gwinner, K. P., Walsh, G., & Gremler, D. D. (2004). Electronic word-of-mouth via consumer-opinion platforms: What motivates consumers to articulate themselves on the internet? *Journal of Interactive Marketing, 18*(1), 38–52. doi:10.1002/dir.10073

Hollebeek, L. (2011). Exploring customer brand engagement: Definition and themes. *Journal of Strategic Marketing, 19*(7), 555–573. doi:10.1080/0965254X.2011.599493

Hur, W.-M., Ahn, W.-H., & Kim, M. (2011). Building brand loyalty through managing brand community commitment. *Management Decision, 49*(7), 1194–1213. doi:10.1108/00251741111151217

Jang, H., Olfman, L., Ko, I., Koh, J., & Kim, K. (2008). The influence of on-line brand community characteristics on community commitment and brand loyalty. *International Journal of Electronic Commerce, 12*(3), 57–80. doi:10.2753/JEC1086-4415120304

Kabadayi, S., & Price, K. (2014). Consumer-brand engagement on Facebook: Liking and commenting behaviors. *Journal of Research in Interactive Marketing, 8*(3), 203–223. doi:10.1108/JRIM-12-2013-0081

Katz, E. (1959). Mass communications research and the study of popular culture: An editorial note on a possible future for this journal. *Studies in Public Communication, 2*, 1–6.

Keller, K. L. (1993). Conceptualizing, measuring, and managing customer-based brand equity. *Journal of Marketing, 57*(1), 1–22. doi:10.2307/1252054

Keller, K. L., & Lehmann, D. R. (2003, May). How do brands create value? *Marketing Management*, 26-31.

Kim, J. W., Choi, J., Qualls, W., & Han, K. (2008). It take a marketplace community to raise brand commitment: The role of online communities. *Journal of Marketing Management, 24*(3-4), 409–431. doi:10.1362/026725708X306167

Koh, J., & Kim, Y. G. (2003). Sense of virtual community: A conceptual framework and empirical validation. *International Journal of Electronic Commerce, 8*, 75–93.

Kozinets, R. V. (1999). E-tribalized marketing?: The strategic implications of virtual communities of consumption. *European Management Journal, 17*(3), 252–264. doi:10.1016/S0263-2373(99)00004-3

Lin, K.-Y., & Lu, H.-P. (2011). Why people use social networking sites: An empirical study integrating network externalities and motivation theory. *Computers in Human Behavior, 27*(3), 1152–1161. doi:10.1016/j.chb.2010.12.009

Mathwick, C., & Rigdon, E. (2004). Play, flow, and the online search experience. *The Journal of Consumer Research, 31*(2), 324–332. doi:10.1086/422111

McAlexander, J. M., & Koenig, H. F. (2010). Contextual influences: Building brand community in large and small colleges. *Journal of Marketing for Higher Education, 20*(1), 69–84. doi:10.1080/08841241003788086

McAlexander, J. M., Schouten, J., & Koenig, H. F. (2002). Building brand community. *Journal of Marketing*, *66*(1), 38–54. doi:10.1509/jmkg.66.1.38.18451

Miniard, P. W., Obermiller, C., & Page, T. J. (1983). A further assessment of measurement influences on the intention behavior relationship. *JMR, Journal of Marketing Research*, *20*(2), 206–212. doi:10.2307/3151687

Mitchell, A. A., & Olson, J. C. (1981). Are product a beliefs the only mediator of advertising effects on brand attitude. *JMR, Journal of Marketing Research*, *18*(3), 318–332. doi:10.2307/3150973

Muniz, A., & Schau, H. J. (2007). The impact of market use of consumer generated content on a brand community. In G. Fitzsimons & V. Morwitz (Eds.), *NA - Advances in Consumer Research, 34* (pp. 644–646). Duluth, MN: Association for Consumer Research.

Muniz, A. M. Jr, & O'Guinn, T. C. (2001). Brand community. *The Journal of Consumer Research*, *27*(4), 412–432. doi:10.1086/319618

Muntinga, D. G., Moorman, M., & Smit, E. G. (2011). Introducing COBRA: Exploring motivations for brand-related social media use. *International Journal of Advertising*, *30*(1), 13–46. doi:10.2501/IJA-30-1-013-046

O'Brien, H. L., & Toms, E. G. (2010). The development and evaluation of a survey to measure user engagement. *Journal of the Association for Information Science and Technology*, *61*(1), 50–69.

Pagani, M., Hofacker, C. F., & Goldsmith, R. E. (2011). The influence of personality on active and passive use of social networking sites. *Psychology and Marketing*, *28*(5), 441–456. doi:10.1002/mar.20395

Porter, C. E., Devaraj, S., & Sun, D. (2013). A test of two models of value creation in virtual communities. *Journal of Management Information Systems*, *30*(1), 261–292. doi:10.2753/MIS0742-1222300108

Raacke, J., & Bonds-Raacke, J. (2008). MySpace and Facebook: Applying the uses and gratifications theory to exploring friend-networking sites. *Cyberpsychology & Behavior*, *11*(2), 169–174. doi:10.1089/cpb.2007.0056 PMID:18422409

Rafaeli, S., & Ariel, Y. (2007). Assessing interactivity in computer-mediated research. In A. N. Joinson, K.Y.A. McKenna., T. Postmes, & U.-D. Reips (Eds.), The Oxford Handbook of Internet Psychology. Oxford, UK: Oxford University Press.

Raney, A. A., Arpan, L. M., Pashupati, K., & Brill, D. A. (2003). At the movies, on the web: An investigation of the effects of entertaining and interactive web content on site and brand evaluations. *Journal of Interactive Marketing*, *17*(4), 38–53. doi:10.1002/dir.10064

Ridings, C. M., & Gefen, D. (2004). Virtual community attraction: Why people hand out online. *Journal of Computer-Mediated Communication, 10*(1).

Rossiter, J. R., & Percy, L. (1987). *Advertising and promotion management*. Singapore: McGraw-Hill.

Royo-Vela, M., & Casamassima, P. (2011). The influence of belonging to virtual brand communities on consumers' affective commitment, satisfaction and word-of-mouth advertising: The ZARA case. *Online Information Review*, *35*(4), 517–542. doi:10.1108/14684521111161918

Sabate, F., Berbegal-Mirabent, J., Carmona, A. C., & Lebherz, P. R. (2014). Factors influencing popularity of branded content in Facebook fan pages. *European Management Journal, 32*(6), 1001–1011. doi:10.1016/j.emj.2014.05.001

Schau, H. J., Muñiz, A. M. Jr, & Arnould, E. J. (2009). How brand community practices create value. *Journal of Marketing, 73*(5), 30–51. doi:10.1509/jmkg.73.5.30

Seraj, M. (2012). We create, we connect, we respect. Therefore we are: Intellectual, social and cultural value in online communities. *Journal of Interactive Marketing, 26*(4), 209–222. doi:10.1016/j.intmar.2012.03.002

Sprott, D., Czellar, S., & Spangenberg, E. (2009). The importance of a general measure of brand engagement on market behavior: Development and validation of a scale. *JMR, Journal of Marketing Research, 46*(1), 92–104. doi:10.1509/jmkr.46.1.92

Statista. (2007). *Social media marketing – Statistics and facts.* Available online: https://www.statista.com/topics/1538/social-media-marketing/

Taylor, D. G., Lewin, J. E., & Strutton, D. (2011). Friends, fans, and followers: Do ads work on social networks? *Journal of Advertising Research, 51*(1).

Teichmann, K., Stokburger-Sauer, N. E., Plank, A., & Strobl, A. (2015). Motivational drivers of content contribution to company- versus consumer-hosted online communities. *Psychology and Marketing, 32*(3), 341–355. doi:10.1002/mar.20783

Thompson, S. A., & Sinha, R. K. (2008). Brand communities and new product adoption: The influence and limits of oppositional loyalty. *Journal of Marketing, 72*(6), 65–80. doi:10.1509/jmkg.72.6.65

Valenzuela, S., Park, N., & Kee, K. F. (2009). Is there social capital in a social network site?: Facebook use and college students' life satisfaction, trust, and participation. *Journal of Computer-Mediated Communication, 14*(4), 875–901. doi:10.1111/j.1083-6101.2009.01474.x

Van der Heide, B., D'Angelo, J. D., & Schumaker, E. M. (2012). The effects of verbal versus photographic self-presentation on impression formation in Facebook. *Journal of Communication, 62*(1), 98–116. doi:10.1111/j.1460-2466.2011.01617.x

Van Doorn, J., Lemon, K. N., Mittal, V., Nass, S., Pick, D., Priner, P., & Verhoef, P. C. (2010). Customer engagement behavior: Theoretical foundations and research directions. *Journal of Service Research, 13*(3), 253–266. doi:10.1177/1094670510375599

Verhoef, P. C., Reinartz, W. J., & Krafft, M. (2010). Customer engagement as a new perspective in customer management. *Journal of Service Research, 13*(3), 247–252. doi:10.1177/1094670510375461

Villarejo-Ramos, A., & Sanchez-Franco, M. J. (2005). The impact of marketing communication and price promotion on brand equity. *Journal of Brand Management, 12*(6), 431–444. doi:10.1057/palgrave.bm.2540238

Vivek, S. D., Beatty, S. E., & Morgan, R. M. (2012). Customer engagement: Exploring customer relationships beyond purchase. *Journal of Marketing Theory and Practice, 20*(2), 122–146. doi:10.2753/MTP1069-6679200201

Voss, K. E., Spangenberg, E. R., & Grohmann, B. (2003). Measuring the hedonic and utilitarian dimensions of consumer attitude. *JMR, Journal of Marketing Research*, *40*(3), 310–320. doi:10.1509/jmkr.40.3.310.19238

Wiertz, C., & de Ruyter, K. (2007). Beyond the call of duty: Why customers contribute to firm-hosted commercial online communities. *Organization Studies*, *28*(3), 347–376. doi:10.1177/0170840607076003

Woitschläger, D. M., Hartleb, V., & Blut, M. (2008). How to make brand communities work: Antecedents and consequences of consumer participation. *Journal of Relationship Marketing*, *7*(3), 237–256. doi:10.1080/15332660802409605

Zeithaml, V. A., Berry, L. L., & Parasuraman, A. (1993). The nature and determinants of customer expectations of service. *Journal of the Academy of Marketing Science*, *21*(1), 1–12. doi:10.1177/0092070393211001

Zhou, Z., Zhang, O., Su, C., & Zhou, N. (2012). How do brand communities generate brand relationships? Intermediate mechanisms. *Journal of Business Research*, *65*(7), 890–895. doi:10.1016/j.jbusres.2011.06.034

This research was previously published in the Handbook of Research on Entrepreneurship and Marketing for Global Reach in the Digital Economy; pages 419-441, copyright year 2019 by Business Science Reference (an imprint of IGI Global).

Chapter 62

Leveraging Virtual Communities to Enhance Brand Equity:
A Case Study

Kelley A. O'Reilly
Western Michigan University, USA

Brett M. Kelley
Western Michigan University, USA

Karen M. Lancendorfer
Western Michigan University, USA

ABSTRACT

This chapter explores how one company leveraged motorsports to build brand credibility, establish powerful marketing relationships, and connect with distinctly different consumer groups via virtual brand communities. Companies with strong virtual communities may benefit from the case study suggestions that are provided and discussed based on the theoretical perspective of brand equity. Marketing scholars and practitioners alike may find this case study of interest due to the growing desire by companies to develop strong bonds with consumers and their interest in effectively leveraging virtual brand communities as a tool. Several practice recommendations for leveraging virtual communities to enhance brand equity are discussed.

INTRODUCTION

Integrated marketing communications (IMC) began generating interest in the early 1990s and has since been accepted by marketers as "...a natural evolution of traditional mass-media advertising, which has been changed, adjusted and refined as a result of new technology" (Schultz 1999, p. 337). IMC can be understood as a broader marketplace view that is sensitive to the impacts and effects of new technologies

DOI: 10.4018/978-1-7998-9020-1.ch062

and communication channels. In this way, IMC extends beyond traditional mass marketing communication which historically put the emphasis on mass media techniques for brand building efforts (Keller, 2009).

Typically driven by either strategy or efficiency, IMC planning focuses on various media mix elements as instrumental for branding efforts (Gabrielli and Balboni, 2010). Along these lines, marketers evaluate different communication options from a perspective of horizontal and vertical coordination, that is, both across and within media with particular focus on the coordination of consumer messaging. This highlights the essence of IMC planning which is a method for coordinating company communications in such a way as to *send* a clear and singular message regarding the company's unique value proposition. This viewpoint is still fairly traditional, with the company sending communications, and the consumer receiving the communication. However, Keller notes that these traditional techniques may be suboptimal in "...a marketplace where customers have access to massive amounts of information about brands, products and companies... (2009, p. 139). There is no doubt that technology, the Internet, and social networking sites have put consumers more in control than ever before as integrators and co-creators of brand meaning.

Considering this perspective, we consider a unique application of IMC that is consumer, rather than company, lead. Necessitated by a high degree of competition and lack of resources for more traditional market spending, the case company explored here focused on a little known motorsport in an attempt to build brand awareness. Consumer fans of the sport then guided the company to new alternative online environments which resulted in consumers, rather than the company, acting as integrators of promotional elements within the communication mix.

The case study explored here, as well as the phenomenon occurring, highlights the power that engaged current fans in virtual fan communities provide. It also furthers the idea that brand control and communication may be well-placed in the hands of online fans. Done properly, virtual communities can act as a conduit to new consumers (e.g. the network of friends and followers of fans). As demonstrated by the case company, tapping into the power of consumer-driven virtual communities resulted in brand "likes" driving as much brand equity as did brand "buys." Marketing scholars and practitioners alike may find this case study of interest due to the growing desire by companies to develop strong bonds with consumers and their interest in effectively using social media as a marketing tool.

BACKGROUND LITERATURE

Key Literature on Brand Equity

In simple terms, brand equity is the value that originates from the brand's customers, rather than from the product or service the brand represents. Brand equity is of interest to marketers due to the financial implications of value, but also because brand equity is positively correlated to favorable responses from consumers to an element of the marketing mix (Keller, 1993). Understanding how to build brand equity is of practical value to managers since it aids in refining the marketing mix elements. Defined as, "the differential effect of brand knowledge on consumer response to the marketing of the brand" (p. 8), it is desirable to establish strong connections and involvement between the consumer and the brand. These connections often start at consumer engagement whereby marketers attempt to influence and encourage consumers to interact with and about the brand (Schultz & Peltier, 2013), with often positive results. A number of brands have shown an improvement in business performance as a result of consumer engagement. According to the ENGAGEMENTdb Study by Wetpaint/Altimeter Group (Li, 2009), "the most valuable brands in the world are experiencing a direct correlation between top financial performance and deep social media engagement" (p. 1). In this way, we can view consumer engagement as the first step towards building brand equity. It should be noted that consumer loyalty and retention are often positively correlated with increased levels of consumer engagement (Vivek, Beatty, & Morgan, 2012).

To create and build brand equity requires brand familiarity and brand strength that yields positive unique brand associations in the minds of consumers (Keller, 1993). Considering that many marketing programs have been traditionally crafted to drive consumer purchases of the product or service, managing brands more holistically is particularly salient against the backdrop of the social media landscape and phenomenon of virtual brand communities. As means of example, Facebook is currently the dominant social-networking site, with an audience of over 200 million users (Statista, n.d). Facebook leads all other social networking sites when it comes to time spent, with 53 percent of Facebook users logging in multiple times a day (Morning Consult, n.d.). To remain successful in these virtual communities, marketers must acknowledge the role of the consumer as a co-creator of brand meaning if they hope to establish strong associations between the consumer and brand (Brown, Kozinets, & Sherry, 2003; Fournier & Avery, 2011). Brand communities give consumers a place to share content, and ultimately express their identity (Wang, Ma & Li, 2015). Chou suggests that, "establishing an online brand community is an effective way to enhance a company's brand equity as long as customer relationships are strengthened" (Chou, 2014, p. 137).

However, this cannot be done with a traditional marketing mindset of "capturing, driving, and convincing" consumers to take a certain action (O'Reilly & Lancendorfer, 2013). Authenticity is a vital ingredient in building and maintaining a successful brand because it forms a unique brand identity and provides a strong, favorable association (Gundlach & Neville, 2012)., Algesheimer, Dholakia, and Herman (2005) suggest that brand community members various behavioral intentions translate into actual behaviors – empirical support for advocates favoring the building of brand communities.

Key Literature on Social Media

Social media is best understood as a digital platform for creating content, sharing ideas, and connecting with companies and other customers. Its importance to marketers is fast-outstripping that of traditional media since it is relatively inexpensive and can quickly get marketing messages to prospects through interactive discussions and rapid word-of-mouth (Owyang, 2009). Social media tools are moving into a golden time as more and more consumers, born into the "Internet generation" reach their 20s, 30s and beyond. Research tells us that this generation enjoys using social media to socialize with friends, stay in touch with family, connect with old acquaintances, connect with people via shared interests, make new friends, follow celebrity posts, and find romance (Pew Internet, 2011). Indeed, it seems this is "…a generation [that] is growing up in an era where digital media are part of the taken-for-granted social and cultural fabric of learning, play, and social communication" (Ito, Davidson, Jenkins, Lee, Eisenberg & Weiss, 2008, p. vii).

"In the social media environment, every time a person uses an application designed by or about the company, the company gains increased exposure to its brand, often in highly relevant contexts" (Hoffman & Fodor, 2010, p. 46). This creates a distinct shift in control of brands across contexts whereby, "Consumers are now the individuals broadcasting personal or second-hand stories to their social networks and the world. They are a brand's storytellers and the new brand ambassadors" (Booth & Matic, 2011,

p. 185). Menachem et al. suggest that managers should actively empower customers to become brand advocates, and thus be a voice for the company (Menachem, Sujata, Padman, Bishnoi, & Upadhye, 2016). Interestingly, a consumer's relationship with a specific brand has been shown to be an "antecedent to his or her identification with the brand community" (Algesheimer et al., 2005, p. 30).

Companies who take a proactive stance to social media commonly empower employees to talk, listen, and respond to what consumers post on social media (Smith, Fischer, & Yongjian, 2012). Because marketer created content may encourage more sharing online, user-generated content can be indicative of brand engagement and word-of-mouth. Therefore, these co-created brand environments (Fournier & Avery, 2011) reward social media marketing strategies that "put the brand to work for the customers by satisfying their needs to create, consume, connect and control in the social Web" (Hoffman & Fodor, 2010, p. 49, italics in original). New technologies have made this very easy as, "... new low-cost digital production tools mean that amateur and casual media creators can author, edit, and distribute video and other rich media forms that were once prohibitively expensive to produce and share with others" (Ito et al., 2008, p. viii).

Key Literature on Virtual Communities

Brand communities can best be described as a "group of ardent consumers organized around the lifestyle, activities, and ethos of the brand" (Fournier & Avery, 2011, p. 133). In the online environment, the communication between members is virtual with groups coalescing through self-selection. Typically formed around a specific brand, members share values, practices, feedback, and have a strong sense of member identity with each other (Fournier & Lee, 2009).

Virtual brand communities are of interest to academics and practitioners alike since they have the ability to influence community members, speed up communications between members, provide robust access to member opinions and evaluations, and provide opportunities for interaction (Algesheimer et al., 2005). Virtual brand communities attract millions of users daily, so once consumers are aware and engaged with a brand they are in a position to communicate their opinions to other consumers (Habibi, Laroche, & Richard, 2014). In the age of social media marketing, it is common to determine the strength of these brand associations by quantifying the number of reviews, "likes", new member sign-ups, and the number of comments and quantity of user-generated content. Therefore, highly engaging social media campaigns involving user-generated content [will] likely generate commitment on the part of the consumer, reinforcing loyalty to the brand and making the customer more likely to commit additional effort to support the brand in the future (Hoffman & Fodor, 2010, p. 46).

This suggests that the traditional top-down approach to marketing should be abandoned in favor of more participatory and interactive cooperation between marketer and consumer (Christodoulides, Jevons, & Bonhomme, 2012). When marketers encourage online community participation, this strengthens relationship quality which in turn generates brand loyalty (Hajli, Shanmumgam, Papagiannidis, Zahay, & Richard, 2016). This will then create stronger brand associations, thereby improving consumer-based brand equity. In addition, consumers' experiences with brands can be shared and communicated more effectively through interactive environments than through traditional media outlets (Kim & Yu, 2016). Therefore, it seems that we are now faced with a new truth that "...corporate marketing never had control of the brand" (Booth & Matic, 2011, p. 185).

BACKGROUND ON CASE COMPANY

In 1983, Falken Tire Corporation (FTC), a subsidiary of Sumitomo Rubber Industries, launched the Falken brand in its native country of Japan. Two years later the brand was introduced in the North American market. The Falken brand was originally perceived in the U.S. market as a niche tire within the ultra-high performance replacement market. During its first two decades in the U.S., FTC's market share remained stagnant at less than 1%, with first tier brands such as Goodyear, Michelin, and Bridgestone controlling the market as shown in Table 1.

Table 1. 2016 US Performance Replacement Market Brands by Tier (Listed in order of market share)

Tier One	Tier Two	Tier Three
1 Goodyear	6 Toyo	11 Firestone
2 Michelin	7 BF Goodrich	12 Nexen
3 Bridgestone	8 Continental	13 Cooper
4 Yokohama	**9 Falken**	14 Pirelli
5 Hankook	10 Kuhmo	15 Dunlop

Source: Modern Tire Dealer
http://www.moderntiredealer.com/uploads/stats/MTD-Hi-Perf-chart.jpg

Positioned as a mid-range second tier tire, FTC sells through the wholesale and retail aftermarket channels. Most of FTC's marketing focus is business-to-business with promotional support and trade incentives targeted at the retail channel in the hope that retail salespeople will recommend the Falken brand during their interactions with customers. Over the years, this strategy had proven limited and FTC struggled to make head-way against larger competitors who had substantial budgets for marketing and advertising directed at both the business-to-business and business-to-consumer channels. One of the reasons was that most of FTC's top competitors had control over retail outlets giving them a competitive advantage and better control over the "retail sales floor." For example, Goodyear owned its own chain of retail stores and other competitors exerted influence in the retail aftermarket by offering associate dealer contracts providing signage, merchandising, and other incentives for retailers. In these cases, the tire manufacturer exerts some control over which brands a retailer carries, promotes, and ultimately recommends to customers.

In 2003, in an effort to improve their market share, FTC's President challenged the management team to deliver more exposure to the Falken brand in the performance market. From this challenge, one of FTC's managers suggested the motorsport of Drifting as a way to showcase the company's products. From a technical perspective, Drifting is a driving technique where the driver intentionally over steers, causing loss of traction in the rear wheels, while maintaining control through tight corners on small racetracks. Often the front wheels are pointing in the opposite direction of the turn (e.g., car is turning left, wheels are pointed right or vice versa) when Drifting. Drifting is best known today from Hollywood releases such as "The Fast and the Furious: Tokyo Drift", but at the time, the sport was relatively obscure, affordable, and exciting.

Using Motorsports to Establish Brand Credibility

Drift brought several elements to bear that were not true for other motorsports. First, Drifting uses relatively inexpensive street-legal vehicles that are within the reach of enthusiasts. Second, the tires and automotive components on the cars are the same that consumers can purchase at tire retailers or online. And third, it put the fans next to the track and up close to the action. To test whether this new sport would have broad enough appeal, FTC decided to host the first-ever Drift Show-off in southern California[1]. Massive positive fan response from this first event fueled FTC's desire to use the sport to build the credibility of its ultra-high performance tires. Although FTC had no experience managing a motorsports racing team, the opportunity seemed like a good strategic fit for the company – the sport was affordable and no other tire brand was dominant. Likewise, FTC was open to following their racing fans online in a move that would later create unexpected opportunity and benefit.

Developing Consumer-Based Brand Equity at the Track

When FTC first entered motorsports, the sales and marketing groups were not performing optimally. Interestingly, the track proved to be fertile ground for recruiting. This grassroots building of the management team proved to be a key element of the company's culture and passion for sport and more importantly, the fans of the sport. This motivation to "stay connected, approachable, and authentic" is evident throughout marketing decisions that FTC made in regard to racing and non-racing activities at the track and online. Reflecting on FTC's choice to be an active sponsor and participate in Drift, the VP of Marketing compared that decision to competitor moves into more formal sports such as Major League Baseball and explained, "…just because your brand is in the outfield doesn't mean they [consumers] are going to understand what you do or what you're about… but because we're out there in the dirt with enthusiasts, we became relevant." Adding to this "relevance" is the fan community that began to gather online to disseminate videos, blogs, and other brand-related information to an even broader audience. FTC noticed and began "follow" their fans online to learn what worked, and what didn't.

Following Online Brand Communities to New Media

While brand equity was being built through FTC's sponsorship efforts at the track, it was secondary to the impact of FTC's growing online virtual brand community. From the first Drifting event, photos, videos, and comments popped up online. In the early days, this was typically youtube.com videos posted by fans that attended the event. As FTC's success at the track continued, the company invested in personnel and equipment to document events making them a pioneer in "consistent video messaging" of their events and results. What is perhaps most interesting, is that the majority of racing fans and brand fans online were not active purchasers of the company's brand. This finding contradicts the linear cycle we expect from customer-based brand equity (Keller, 1993). From that theory we expect that customers will form some memory of the brand, the memory will hopefully build a positive and strong association, and that this association leads to brand loyalty as measured by sales turnover of the product or service. In this case study, loyalty seems to exist as evidenced by the willingness of customers to actively promote the brand, yet this is occurring before their first purchase. This suggests that consumer activation (rather than turnover) may be an alternative measure of loyalty, making the power of "likes" online a valuable metric of success and worthy of securing.

Leveraging Online Relationships

Perhaps recognizing that the most loyal are not active brand purchasers, the management team focused more on driving fan engagement and "likes" on social media sites. As part of this strategy, FTC used a combination of tools and techniques such as online video messaging, QR promo codes, promotional giveaways, and online marketing tactics to solicit user-generated content and engagement in the company's web assets. In essence, they created a culture of encouragement for the brand's fans to create the brand's stories online. As more participation evolved in the virtual brand community, FTC began to fine-tune messages, graphics, and imagery based upon the feedback they secured through their online presence. From this early online success, the company experienced collateral benefits of their strong online presence when new opportunities were created for additional online exposure among a new consumer segment: gamers.

One of the earliest marketing relationships that FTC established was with the digital gaming company, EA Games. The EA relationship gave the Falken brand a unique consumer branding opportunity with customers at a very early age. This relationship also helped to solidify the viability of the brand in the minds of B2B retail personnel and customers. Understanding the power of the retailer and crafting programs to best serve this unique market segment continues to be a focus of FTC; extending their success in Drift into other motorsports events such as Super Cross and American Le Mans Racing.

BEST PRACTICES FOR LEVERAGING VIRTUAL COMMUNITIES

This case study has shown how FTC engaged fans online, at motorsports events, and at retail. However, it is the virtual fan communities online that helped steer them to additional online venues, into new relationships, and into new consumer segments. It is this same online community that comprises one of the best and relatively untapped opportunities for many companies today.

It's important to remember that in the deployment of any virtual brand community strategy, a combination of both strategic actions and organizational capabilities must be considered. According to the consulting firm, Aberdeen Group (2008), a virtual brand community strategy requires "not only the need to create new cross-functional, enterprise-wide business processes to collect, manage, and share information with relevant stakeholders, as well as to measure success, but also the need to educate employees about the value …and why it should matter to them in the context of their specific areas of accountability" (p. 9). Accordingly, to aid companies and help them identify their firms' likelihood of success in leveraging virtual communities to enhance brand equity, the following suggestions are offered.

Tip 1: Be a Good Follower

Companies ensconced in traditional marketing mindsets tend to use online social media like advertising; focusing on creating compelling messages that draw interested potential buyers to the brand. In this way, the media is used as a draw to the brand. Interestingly, the results from the case company and academic research suggests that the reverse may be more effective in expanding online brand communities – that is, follow consumers to their choice of media. The tools (e.g. Facebook, Twitter, Snapchat, etc.) are dynamic while the practice recommendation is constant: the decision is not what tool to use, but rather where fans of our brand are having conversations, and what is being said. Secondarily, companies can then look to fans to help them improve the environment so that consumers loyal to the brand can draw others to the online medium of choice. As highlighted in previous research, "Enroll existing, long tenured customers who already have an affirmative relationship with the brand" (Algesheimer et al., 2005, p. 30), and then drive them to the online experience. In the instance of this case study, FTC used the motorsport event to create the desire for customers to use online channels for further interaction. Then FTC followed their customers to where the conversations were taking place online.

Tip 2: Community First, Brand Second

Increased brand exposure is a top benefit of social media (Social Media Examiner, 2013). From the same report, other benefits include increasing traffic, providing marketplace insight, and developing loyal fans - in fact, most marketers now recognize that developing loyal brand fans ranks higher in importance that generating leads. In fact, "when a brand focuses on acquiring and engaging fans, it can benefit from a significant secondary effect – exposure among friends of fans that often surpasses reach among fans" (Lipsman, Mudd, Rich, & Bruich, 2012). Because one of the primary benefits of social media is increasing exposure, virtual communities can have a significant positive effect on driving fan exposure → engagement → loyalty → influence → equity. In the case of FTC, the company found that many of their most avid brand fans were "virtually loyal." Meaning, they had a high degree of engagement on FTC's web assets, explicitly "liked" the brand, but had not yet purchased the product. These fans are the easiest to reach, and may indeed be the most valuable online asset of the company since recent research has shown that "Friends of fans typically represent a much larger set of consumers (34 times larger, on average, for the top 100 brand pages) and can receive social-media brand impressions by way of their friends" (Lipsman et al., 2012, p. 40). So for each "like" on FTC's brand pages, 34 additional potential customers are waiting in the wings to be enticed, motivated, or incentivized to communicate and interact with the company. For FTC, this was a central idea moving forward – driving the friends of fans since it appears that "like" may in fact be as good as buy. To drive "likes" research suggests including vivid and interactive posts such as videos or contests and avoiding the posting of questions or unrelated entertainment content (de Vries, Gensler, & Leeflang, 2012). Additionally, the creation of materials that encourage member embeddedness and engagement are recommended (Porter & Donthu, 2008; Porter, Donthu, MacElroy, & Wydra, 2011).

Tip 3: Get Comfortable With Conflict

The strength of a brand's virtual community is often borne from the ashes of conflict (Fournier & Lee, 2009). Because these groups are formed around their common shared commitment to the brand and what it stands for, strong opinions are often the norm. Combine this strength of conviction with the "keyboard courage" that accompanies online communication and incendiary conditions may prevail. This is good. In order for a group of like-minded folks to coalesce around the brand online, there must be a group who does not share the same view. This creation of an "in-group" versus an "out-group" is vital for the health and sustainability of the community. Think Ford vs. Chevy, i-Phone vs. Samsung, or Coke vs. Pepsi. Without battle-lines being drawn, your virtual community is more likely to be weak and fragmented. But, a virtual community that fans the flames of why their brand is better than the other brand, signals a stronger, more entrenched avid group of followers and shows that the brand's strength and loyalty is building brand equity. The key is not to feel as though conflicts should be regulated, monitored, or smoothed over. In fact, companies should consider reinforcing rivalries head-on and/or encouraging others to fan the flames.

Tip 4: Follow Aspirant Brands

Because of the velocity of trends and proliferation of virtual communities, marketers may be leery of their own ability to interact effectively with virtual communities of brand fans. One way to help companies leverage their presence in virtual brand communities is for companies to identify a group of peer com-panies outside of their own industry. In this way, marketing managers can identify with peer-companies who are targeting similar customers and positioning their brands in a complementary manner to their own brand. By watching these peer-companies, marketing managers can observe, learn, and expand their own approaches to virtual community interactions that might help further brand-building within their own firms. By selecting and "following/liking" a peer-group of firms and paying attention to their iterative marketing efforts both offline and online, companies can more easily monitor marketplace changes and develop new ideas to improve their own efforts. This strategy can be particularly helpful for companies that have traditionally only followed their own industry closely, but have not looked beyond their core industry. We recommend that marketers expand their view in order to recognize broader marketplace changes, virtual community trends, and audience preferences.

Tip 5: Fund It

As mentioned, virtual community trends, platforms, and audience preferences are changing at an amazing pace. With this rate of change it can be difficult to stay on top of virtual communities. While it was sug-gested earlier in this chapter to follow aspirant peer companies that you identify with and that are doing a good job targeting the same customer groups as your firm; likewise, you must take action to keep your own firm abreast of new online developments. This can sound daunting and expensive, but remember: online efforts are quickly outstripping that of traditional media. As such, online efforts, data collection and analysis, and strategic initiatives need to be funded with the same commitment of the company's more "mainstream" media. No longer can companies rely on the summer intern or recent grad to simply pump out Google Analytics and make some basic recommendations. Instead, consider the online data as valuable to the firm as any consultant's research report. Therefore, hiring analysts who can connect the dots between the raw consumer data and the behaviors that accompany each data point is vital.

Tip 6: Create a Web Policy

As soon as your company ventures into virtual communities, you will notice a curious thing – you will begin to hear the chatter of your customers more clearly, more loudly, and often more critically. The Internet is the great liaison between companies and the customers they serve, and therefore, virtual communities will activate customer feedback that is typically faster, harsher, and less private. Because it is recommended that you have a team of marketers monitoring all of your web assets as they relate to the brand's virtual presence, it is vital that these individuals know how to handle critical feedback and what actions they should take when they come across an inaccuracy in an online customer review of your product/service (Bastone, 2010, Brogan & Bastone, 2014). When a customer publicly posts a story about a gross-injustice experienced at the hands of your firm or brand, should you react? If misinformation is posted about your firm or brand, should you reply? These questions and dozens more like it must be contemplated in advance and captured via a web policy for your employees so they know how to monitor user-generated content on your site and across related social media sites. Don't assume your employees will know how to handle customer inquiries, complaints, and viral misinformation on the web. Ensure that your employees know what is expected, what they should do, and who they should contact if something pops up that they do not know how to handle.

Tip 7: Understand Your Own Bias for Control

Commonly senior management determines strategic corporate direction. While this is not inherently problematic, consideration must be given to the decision-makers own characteristics and biases. For instance, managers in their 40s or 50s may not appreciate the value of mobile marketing or a virtual brand community strategy which gives full control to the customers online. Therefore, leaders should understand their own biases and invite the views of customers and/or employees into the dialogue so that a wide range of feedback is received regarding how best to interact with customers online. To truly build brand value for the firm and equity from customers, requires a give-and-take that will likely reward balanced approaches to how and where these interactions take place.

Tip 8: Determine If the Organizational Culture Is Open to Honest Feedback

Because virtual brand communities typically involves open dialogue with customers, organizations will quickly begin to harvest both positive and negative input from the marketplace. For some organizations this will be received positively and viewed as a means to develop improvement strategies that focus on the cares and concerns of its current customers. For other firms, negative feedback may be met with a less open culture. Make sure your firm is ready for 'honest' feedback from consumers. Consider the current processes and procedures that are in place to receive, respond, and act on suggestions from customers. Research tells us that the quickest way to shut down customer feedback is to do nothing or worse yet, delete feedback from your own forums or threaded discussion boards that don't meet your own version of the brand's strengths. Firms should be ready for the good, the bad, and the ugly of online communications since for many customers, the Internet provides a large dose of "keyboard courage" which may be a jagged pill for some marketing managers to swallow. If you are not ready for negative feedback, you are not ready for a virtual brand community strategy.

FUTURE RESEARCH DIRECTIONS

The nature of e-Business applications, like virtual brand communities, will continue to hold great promise as well as challenge for practitioners in regard to creating stronger connections with consumers and enhancing brand-building efforts. Understanding the role that people, business processes, and technology play as a conduit between firm and customer, and customer to customer, is key. Therefore, we suggest that future research on virtual brand communities should be viewed from a cross-disciplinary lens that considers research from information systems, marketing, management, and psychology to name but a few. To effectively bridge this research divide requires a holistic look at the combination of people, processes, and technology as key drivers of online innovation and change.

CONCLUSION

Overall, this case has demonstrated that brands can be positively affected through virtual fan communities. From this view, companies may stand to experience positive market share gains by refining their online social media efforts to improve fan engagement online. By doing so, companies may broaden their appeal through the unique strategy of driving "likes" and leveraging 'friends of fans'. In this way, "likes" are indeed as good as "buys." The advent of social media requires practitioners today to shift their thinking; away from a one-way, push model, to a scenario where consumers are actively involved with companies and increasingly connected to other consumers through a variety of channels. The locus of control has now shifted to the consumer, and firms must both actively listen to consumers and agree to engage in open, two-way conversations to succeed (Stone & Woodcock, 2013). In order to utilize the opportunities provided by new media, managers must thoroughly understand the tools available to them.

This chapter has highlighted an approach for enhancing brand equity via virtual brand communities. Virtual communities offer companies the opportunity to become a more active partner "in the conversation" with empowered consumers through social media exposure, the engagement of loyal fan and brand advocate networks, and tapping into valuable market intelligence via social listening and crowdsourcing. With only 20% of U.S. companies focusing marketing efforts on consumer-centric social media strategies (Forrester, 2011), the time is right for insightful practitioners to commit to the deeper interactions with consumers through virtual communities that correlate with increased brand equity and better financial performance.

REFERENCES

Aberdeen Group. (2008). *Social media monitoring and analysis: Generating consumer insights from online conversation.* Retrieved September 1, 2013 from: http://robertoigarza.files.wordpress.com/2008/10/rep-social-media-monitoring-and-analysis-aberdeen-group-2008.pdf

Algesheimer, R., Dholakia, U. M., & Herrmann, A. (2005). The social influence of brand community: Evidence from European car clubs. *Journal of Marketing, 69*(3), 19–34. doi:10.1509/jmkg.69.3.19.66363

Bastone, J. (2010). Evaluate social media by listening, leveraging and engaging. *Direct: Magazine of Direct Marketing.* Retrieved February 12, 2014 from http://www.chiefmarketer.com/web-marketing/evaluate-social-media-by-listening-leveraging-and-engaging-17082010

Booth, N., & Matic, J. A. (2011). Mapping and leveraging influencers in social media to shape corporate brand perceptions. *Corporate Communications, 16*(3), 184–191. doi:10.1108/13563281111156853

Brogan, C., & Bastone, J. (2014). Acting on customer intelligence from social media. *AMA Marketing Effectiveness Online Seminar Series.* Retrieved February 12, 2014 from https://www.sas.com/offices/NA/canada/en/resources/whitepaper/wp_21122.pdf

Brown, S., Kozinets, R. V., & Sherry, J. F. Jr. (2003). Teaching old brands new tricks: Retro branding and the revival of brand meaning. *Journal of Marketing, 67*(3), 19–33. doi:10.1509/jmkg.67.3.19.18657

Chou, C. (2014). Social media characteristics, customer relationship and brand equity. *The Journal of Applied Business and Economics, 16*(1), 128–139.

Christodoulides, G., Jevons, C., & Bonhomme, J. (2012). Memo to marketers: Quantitative evidence for change. How user-generated content really affects brands. *Journal of Advertising Research*, *52*(1), 53–64. doi:10.2501/JAR-52-1-053-064

de Vries, L., Gensler, S., & Leeflang, P. S. H. (2012). Popularity of brand posts on brand fan pages: An investigation of the effects of social media. *Journal of Interactive Marketing*, *26*(2), 83–91. doi:10.1016/j. intmar.2012.01.003

Forrester Research, Inc. (2011). *Listening and engaging in the digital marketing age*. Retrieved August 31, 2013 from: http://i.dell.com/sites/content/corporate/secure/en/Documents/listening-and-engaging-in-the-digital-marketing-age.pdf

Fournier, S., & Avery, J. (2011). The uninvited brand. *Business Horizons*, *54*(3), 193–207. doi:10.1016/j. bushor.2011.01.001

Fournier, S., & Lee, L. (2009, April). Getting brand communities right. Harvard Business Review, 1-10.

Gabrielli, V., & Balboni, B. (2010). SME practice towards integrated marketing communications. *Marketing Intelligence & Planning*, *28*(3), 275–290. doi:10.1108/02634501011041426

Habibi, M. R., Laroche, M., & Richard, M. (2014). The roles of brand community and community engagement in building brand trust on social media. *Computers in Human Behavior*, *37*, 152–161. doi:10.1016/j.chb.2014.04.016

Hajli, N., Shanmugam, M., Papagiannidis, S., Zahay, D., & Richard, M. (2016). Branding co- creation with members of online communities. *Journal of Business Research*, *70*, 136–144. doi:10.1016/j. jbusres.2016.08.026

Hennig-Thurau, T., Malthouse, E., Friege, C., Gensler, S., Lobschat, L., Rangaswamy, A., & Skiera, B. (2010). The impact of new media on customer relationships. *Journal of Service Research*, *13*(3), 311–330. doi:10.1177/1094670510375460

Hoffman, D. L., & Fodor, M. (2010). Can you measure the ROI of your social media marketing? *MIT Sloan Management Review*, *52*(1), 41–49.

Ito, M., Davidson, C., Jenkins, H., Lee, C., Eisenberg, M., & Weiss, J. (2008). Youth online authorship. In D. Buckingham (Ed.), *Youth, identity, and digital media. The John D. and Catherine T. MacArthur Foundation Series on Digital Media and Learning (pp. vii-ix)*. Cambridge, MA: The MIT Press.

Keller, K. L. (1993). Conceptualizing, measuring, and managing customer-based brand equity. *Journal of Marketing*, *57*(1), 1–22. doi:10.2307/1252054

Keller, K. L. (2009). Building strong brands in a modern marketing communications environment. *Journal of Marketing Communications*, *15*(2), 139–155. doi:10.1080/13527260902757530

Kim, J., & Yu, E. (2016). The holistic brand experience of branded mobile applications affects brand loyalty. *Social Behavior and Personality*, *44*(1), 77–87. doi:10.2224bp.2016.44.1.77

Li, C. (2009). *The world's most valuable brands. Who's most engaged? ENGAGEMENTdb: Ranking the top 100 global brands.* Retrieved February 9, 2014 from: http://www.altimetergroup.com/2009/07/engagementdb.html

Lipsman, A., Mudd, G., Rich, M., & Bruich, S. (2012). The power of "like": How brands reach (and influence) fans through social media. *Journal of Advertising Research, 52,* 40–52. doi:10.2501/JAR-52-1-040-052

Menachem, D., Sujata, J., Padman, A., Bishnoi, K., & Upadhye, R. (2016). Online Brand Communities and Their Impact on Brand Equity of Indian Telecommunication Industry. *International Conference on Qualitative and Quantitative Economics Research. Global Science and Technology Forum,* 16–24.

Morning Consult. (n.d.). Frequency of Facebook use in the United States as of October 2017. *Statista - The Statistics Portal.* Retrieved October 22, 2017, from https://www.statista.com/statistics/199266/frequency-of-use-among-facebook-users-in the-united-states/

O'Reilly, K., & Lancendorfer, K. M. (2013). Consumers as "integrators" of marketing communications: When "like" is as good as "buy". *International Journal of E-Business Research, 9*(4), 1–15. doi:10.4018/ijebr.2013100101

Owyang, J. (2009). *The future of the social web: In five eras.* Retrieved April 24, 2012 from: http://www.web-strategist.com/blog/2009/04/27/future-of-the-social-web/

Pew Internet. (2011). Why Americans use social media. *Pew Research Center.* Retrieved October 25, 2017, from http://www.pewinternet.org/2011/11/15/why-americans-use-social-media/

Porter, C. E., & Donthu, N. (2008). Cultivating trust and harvesting value in virtual communities. *Management Science, 54*(1), 113–128. doi:10.1287/mnsc.1070.0765

Porter, C. E., Donthu, N., MacElroy, W. H., & Wydra, D. (2011). How to foster and sustain engagement in virtual communities. *California Management Review, 53*(4), 59–73. doi:10.1525/cmr.2011.53.4.80

Schultz, D. E. (1999). Integrated marketing communications and how it relates to traditional media advertising. In J.P. Jones (Ed.), The Advertising Business: Operations, Creativity, Media Planning, Integrated Communications (pp. 325-338). London, UK: Sage. doi:10.4135/9781452231440.n34

Schultz, D. E., & Peltier, J. (2013). Social media's slippery slope: Challenges, opportunities and future research directions. *Journal of Research in Interactive Marketing, 7*(2), 86–99. doi:10.1108/JRIM-12-2012-0054

Smith, A. N., Fischer, E., & Yongjian, C. (2012). How does brand-related user-generated content differ across YouTube, Facebook, and Twitter? *Journal of Interactive Marketing, 26*(2), 102–113. doi:10.1016/j.intmar.2012.01.002

Social Media Examiner. (2013). Retrieved January 3, 2014 from: http://www.socialmediaexaminer.com/social-media-marketing-industry-report-2013/

Statista. (n.d.). Number of Facebook users in the United States from 2015 to 2022 (in millions). *Statista - The Statistics Portal.* Retrieved October 20, 2017, from https://www.statista.com/statistics/408971/number-of-us-facebook-users/

Stone, M., & Woodcock, N. (2013). Social intelligence in customer engagement. *Journal of Strategic Marketing, 21*(5), 394–401. doi:10.1080/0965254X.2013.801613

Vivek, S. D., Beatty, S. E., & Morgan, R. M. (2012). Customer engagement: Exploring customer relationships beyond purchase. *Journal of Marketing Theory and Practice, 20*(2), 127–145. doi:10.2753/MTP1069-6679200201

Wang, Y., Ma, S., & Li, D. (2015). Customer participation in virtual brand communities: The self-construal perspective. *Information & Management, 52*(5), 577–587. doi:10.1016/j.im.2015.04.003

ADDITIONAL READING

Castronovo, C., & Huang, L. (2012). Social media in an alternative marketing communication model. *Journal of Marketing Development and Competitiveness, 6*(1), 117–134.

Grimes, S. (2013). The rise and stall of social media listening. *Information Week, 1361* (March 25), 5-6.

Hennig-Thurau, T., Malthouse, E., Friege, C., Gensler, S., Lobschat, L., Rangaswamy, A., & Skiera, B. (2010). The impact of new media on customer relationships. *Journal of Service Research, 13*(3), 311–330. doi:10.1177/1094670510375460

Kaplan, A. M., & Haenlein, M. (2010). Users of the world, unite! The challenges and opportunities of social media. *Business Horizons, 53*(1), 59–68. doi:10.1016/j.bushor.2009.09.003

LaPointe, P. (2011). The rock in the pond: How online buzz and offline WOM can make a strong message even more powerful. *Journal of Advertising Research, 51*(3), 456–457. doi:10.2501/JAR-51-3-456-457

LaPointe, P. (2012). Measuring Facebook's impact on marketing: The proverbial hits the fan. *Journal of Advertising Research, 52*(3), 286–287. doi:10.2501/JAR-52-3-286-287

McAlexander, J. H., Schouten, J. W., & Koenig, H. F. (2002). Building brand community. *Journal of Marketing, 66*(January), 38–54. doi:10.1509/jmkg.66.1.38.18451

Morgan, R. M., & Hunt, S. D. (1994). The commitment-trust theory of relationship marketing. *Journal of Marketing, 58*(July), 20–38. doi:10.2307/1252308

Naylor, R. W., Lamberton, C. P., & West, P. M. (2012). Beyond the "like" button: The impact of mere virtual presence on brand evaluations and purchase intentions in social media settings. *Journal of Marketing, 76*(6), 105–120. doi:10.1509/jm.11.0105

Nelson-Field, K., Riebe, E., & Sharp, B. (2012). What's not to "like?" Can a Facebook fan base give a brand the advertising reach it needs? *Journal of Advertising Research, 52*(2), 262–269. doi:10.2501/JAR-52-2-262-269

Pomirleanu, N., Schibrowsky, J. E., Peltier, J. W., & Nill, A. (2013). Internet marketing research: A review of the literature. *Journal of Research in Interactive Marketing, 7*(3), 166–181. doi:10.1108/JRIM-01-2013-0006

Quinton, S., & Harridge-March, S. (2010). Relationships in online communities: The potential for marketers. *Journal of Research in Interactive Marketing*, *4*(1), 59–73. doi:10.1108/17505931011033560

Trueman, M., Cornelius, N., & Wallace, J. (2012). Building brand value online: Exploring relationships between company and city brands. *European Journal of Marketing*, *46*(7/8), 1013–1031. doi:10.1108/03090561211230179

Weiss, A. M., Lurie, N. H., & MacInnis, D. J. (2008). Listening to strangers: Whose responses are valuable, how valuable are they, and why? *JMR, Journal of Marketing Research*, *45*(August), 425–436. doi:10.1509/jmkr.45.4.425

KEY TERMS AND DEFINITIONS

Brand Ambassador: A person recruited by an organization to advocate its products or services.

Brand Equity: Is the idea that having a well-known and well-received brand creates more monetary value for an organization than a lesser known brand.

Social Media Marketing: Refers to the practice of using social media sites to draw attention to a brand. The emphasis in social media marketing is to create interesting content that will attract readers and encourage them to share content on their own social media pages.

Top-Down Marketing: Is a traditional advertising structure where an idea is generated by an organization then broadcasted to the consumer.

User-Generated Content: Any online content such as photos, videos, tweets, pages, and other forms of media that is created by users of online services and generally shared through social media.

Virtual Communities: A group that forms online, typically on social media websites, where community members join on the basis of loyalty to a particular brand.

Word-of-Mouth: Is defined as the oral communication of brand or product information from one consumer to another that is encouraged by the organization selling the product.

ENDNOTE

[1] A fan-filmed video from this first event is available online at: http://www.youtube.com/watch?v=zwQk4YzRH90.

Chapter 63
Social Media, Interfacing Brands in Relation to the Social Media Ecosystem

Ze Zook
Regents University, UK

Ben Salmon
Wearecrank.com, UK

ABSTRACT

Much of the existing research in social media has been directed at examining the consequences of the interactive nature of the evolving medium and communication issues, with little to say about the impact of this medium on brands. Drawing on Fiske's relational model, this current chapter examines the interface between social media and brands, particularly on the breadth and the dimensions of the level of engagement. Social networks, such as Facebook and Twitter, are revolutionising the way companies market their products. New means of interaction and dialogue are used in part because of the inherent structure and features of these social media platforms. The chapter concludes by discussing the implications of the analysis for understanding of new terminology in the evolving marketing environment.

INTRODUCTION

Social media interfacing brands in a synchronous and asynchronous ecosystem addresses elements of consumer culture from an interdisciplinary perspective, with special reference to commercial exchanges. This exploratory chapter questions what kind of online social tendencies brands should execute to express their core values and engage with customers in the future.

The question addresses the nature and dimension of social interaction on brand-oriented social media platforms (Thackeray, Neiger, Hansson, & McKenzie, 2008), and it is explored with special reference to Facebook and to a lesser extent Twitter. Whether we can categorise 'this type of social interaction'

DOI: 10.4018/978-1-7998-9020-1.ch063

to our notion of brand communities (Kaplan & Haenlein, 2010) will be addressed by redefining what brand communities connote.

Understanding brands as symbols within an offline and online space intersects various disciplines. This chapter considers a postmodern approach that challenges marketing as a practice and concept bridging earlier critiques by academics, in particular. Brown (1993) surmised that postmodern marketing is a breakdown of the grand narratives. Brown also stated that marketing on the whole has been based on modernist principles of analysis, implementation planning, and control, yet the process and drive behind the 'postmodernism condition' is a challenge of the established institutional pillars and the dismantling of grand narratives. From this, Brown further questioned the whole evolution of marketing as a modernist concept from its Fordist-production, sales, and marketing orientation eras. He questioned the foundations of this belief.

Brown discussed two key components that are of relevance to this chapter in questioning and establishing the nature of marketing within the new media paradigm. The first component concerns the reproach between marketing theory and practice, of which social media explicitly exemplifies this wedge. The second component addresses the issue of terminology. This theoretical study argues for social media analysis to incorporate an anthropological approach at its centre to amalgamate the ever-changing phraseology in marketing terminology, such as cybermarketing and multichannel marketing, as well as nondefinable issues, such as ethics, privacy, and data (Brown, 1993).

Marketing scholarship has moved to the centre of concurrent discussions of postmodernity in the humanities and the social sciences (Gould & Lerman, 1998). The amorphous function of marketing, defined by the British Chartered Institute of Marketing (CIM) as a 'management process identifying, anticipating and satisfying customer needs for profit' (CIM, 2009), has grown since is inception in 1911, when modernist tendencies were becoming transformative (for example, the Wright brothers in 1903). However, the implications for how marketing processes and phenomena are researched and studied have a bearing on theory and practice.

To further this discussion, an interdisciplinary approach with an anthropological leaning is posited as being central to understanding consumerism and consumer-oriented brands through the social process (Horst, 2014). More so, that the nature of goods and services, available in an information-driven society through social networks with brand interface social media Web 2.0 platforms sits central to the discussions that critically address the schism between marketing and media. This chapter argues that marketing should be studied because the sociocultural process defines postmodern society (Firat, Dholakia, & Venkatesh, 1995). The marketing function, when broken down, cannot be captured solely by empirical positivist analysis, and it is this relational approach to the subject that enables brands to come alive and become 'experienceable' (Firat & Schultz, 1997).

That brands play on symbolism and allude to more than their sum of parts (Berry, Smith, & Pulford, 1999) as meaning culturally, is discussed within the remit as what to social media encompasses, including its and functions and ever-expanding remit and capabilities. The principles of eWoM, which is defined by Shu-Chuan and Kim (2011) as a distinctive derivate of social media, are applied to discussions relating to brand engagements with symbolism at the centre of this interaction. Analytical insight is applied on social processes through symbolic interactionism and Johari's window in relation to the Facebook ecosystem. This is continued in greater depth when the need is stated to understand normative values and groups in related contexts (Fiske, 1992) from a macro perspective so that these groups can be understood within and beyond geopolitical proximities, with defining indices.

Building on these precedents, this chapter then progresses towards the discussion on phraseology and concepts, notably the terminology, online communities, or virtual communities, related to symbolic brand interaction.

The various key concepts raised are then addressed from a management perspective with insight as to its implications. The element of the chapter is not finite and should be not be addressed as such prior to the conclusion.

Theoretical Context and Framework

Social networks, such as Facebook and Twitter, are revolutionising the way companies market their products (Frazier, 2010). New means of interaction and dialogue (Edwards et al., 2014) are used in part because of the inherent structure and features of these social media platforms (Seltzer & Mitrook, 2007). Hence, social media becomes the ideal platform for marketing-related activities, such as brand building, with particular brand channels, for example Twitter, favouring particular nuances such as high degrees of narcissim amongst the generation Y target group (Davenport et al., 2014), which ultimately encourages large swathes of the 'content' created, being fuelled by the participants who use the ecosystem. Thus, the next question is, what is 'social media'? Although multifarious definitions exist, social media can be defined as 'a group of Internet-based applications that build on the ideological and technological foundations of Web 2.0, and that allow the creation and exchange of User Generated Content' (Kaplan & Hanelein, 2010). Although debates regarding the ethics of the commercialisation of the Internet abound (Negrophonte, 1995), market-led economies become the de facto model for emerging economies around the globe. Thus, companies are interested in the social media space.

Two explicit reasons are provided (Kozinets, 2002): First is the inherent importance of 'consumers' being online. The word 'consumers' is used deliberately because it implies their intention and acceptance to purchase. Second is social media opens up new possibilities for marketing researchers to get close to the consumers and understand how symbols are ascribed meaning culturally (Barthes, 1997).

The interconnection of brands amongst themselves and through individuals and customers has altered our ever-increasing interconnected world. Our globalised world was given the term 'network society' (Castell, 2002), which was thought of as characterising and heralding key social structures and activities, organised around electronically processed information networks. The emphasis Castell maintained was on information and speed at fractions of a second. The use of Twitter bots is a phenomenon that distinquishes the network and simultaneously catapults it, in terms of advancement and progression. Having stated this, studies indicate that a human as opposed to a bot response achieves higher credibility (Edwards et al., 2014). Whilst this is at the heart of more immediate and prevalent issues concerning social networking sites and big data today (Zikopoulos, Lightstone, Matthew, Sachedina, & Baklarz, 2013), this chapter makes extensive use of discussions pertaining to Facebook and Twitter, which are currently the most popular networking platforms in relation to size, clout, and reach.

Facebook as a social media platform, from the individual and micro level to the dyadic, triadic, and actor levels, focuses on analysing network characteristics, such as size, relationship strength, density, centrality, prestige, and roles, such as isolates, liaisons, and bridges (Wasserman & Faust, 1994). Homophily and critical analysis of sociograms from real-time feeds can indicate levels of trust (Granovetter, 1973) and are attributes that are prerequisite for network formation on higher scales and volumes towards the formation of power law-oriented networks (free scale) and hubs (ibid.). The relevance and influence of Facebook on groups and group behaviour are pivotal to understanding the catalysts of the social process.

Nevertheless, these elements, which have more in common with the perceived usefulness of technology, can be insightful to understanding online behaviour through a theoretical analysis called the technology acceptance model, which is beyond the scope of this study (Chuttur, 2009).

Global emphasis is placed on Facebook because of its 1.65 billion users (Protalinski, 2016). If it were a geographical country, it would be the third largest on the planet. This is an important starting point to critically understand social networking transglobal behaviour. Facebook sits alongside other social media platforms, such as YouTube, with 1 billion unique users that visit the site per month; Twitter, the 140-character microblogging social platform with its 320 million users (Chaffey, 2016); Vkontakte, the Russian social media platform with is 95 million users (Smith, 2016); and QQ, with 853 million users in China (Chaffey, 2016).

Facebook should be seen as a communication platform. It owns WhatsApp, Instagram and Oculus Rift. Its portfolio of companies cover the breadth of desktop and mobile communications (BBC, 2014). Since its floatation in 2012, Facebook has heavily invested in the mobile sphere. Between 2013 and 2014, its mobile-only users nearly doubled to 341 million (TechCrunch, 2014). Facebook mobile ads contributed to 59% of all ad sales, equivalent to $1.4 billion, and users in the United States spend more than 40 minutes per day on Facebook (The Verge, 2014). Social networking sites (SNSs), such as Facebook, has changed the way we not only communicate and relate to each other but also market goods and services to one another implicitly and explicitly. With the ubiquity of computers and the proliferation of apps, the ability to be permanently interconnected is now greater than ever. This phenomenon has been called the 'martini effect' (Quinn & Oldmeadow, 2013).

Marketing and branding became joined at the hip when it emerged as a clear business strategy in 1931 (McCraw, 2000). Neil McElroy (1904–1972), an Account manager from Procter and Gamble wrote an internal memorandum when he was working on the advertising campaign for Camay soap. From this point onwards, brand management addressed the social, emotional, and identity values of users (Kotler & Gertner, 2002).

Whether individuals trust their neighbours and whether they consider their neighbourhood a place where people help one another describe the pattern and intensity of networks amongst people and the shared values that arise from those networks, and this situation ostensibly builds social capital (Champniss & Vila, 2011). Greater interaction between people generates a greater sense of community spirit, which is one attribute most brands want to be centred around. In marketing parlance, this is termed electronic word of mouth (eWoM) (Shu-Chuan & Kim, 2011). Definitions of social capital vary, but the main aspects include citizenship, 'neighbourliness', social networks, and civic participation. The definition used by the Office for National Statistics, taken from the Organisation for Economic Co-operation and Development, is 'networks together with shared norms, values and understandings that facilitate co-operation within or among groups'. Coca-Cola during their 2011 Australian Share-a-Like Coke campaign, which witnessed Coke cans bearing personalised local names, such as 'Bob', 'Sheila', etc., made extensive use of social capital by adapting to a changing environment and encouraged people to connect with the brand both online and offline. As a result, the consumption of Coca-Cola increased over the 2011 summer period (Marketing Magazine, 2012). Coke was successful by not only obtaining 7% revenue that season but also interestingly encouraging individuals to talk favourably about the brand, and their interaction was extended to Coke's online dynamic community. The question then beckons, should we address participants of this campaign as individuals, customers, or fans?

Symbolic Representation of Brands

What is a brand? A brand has been stated as being a promise (Riezebos, 1994). Expounding this question further, linguistically, a brand can become a symbolic noun and verb. The influence and resonance as to how a brand comes to life and what it means to people are reflected through social networks and on social media platforms. Brands have to craftfully work out what kind of customers they have in order to work out what kind of approximate media message, content and type should be uitiised (Kim et al., 2015). The social media agency 'We Are Social' claimed that 40% of the population in Europe are active social media users in 2014.

Exploring the social media space as a platform where goods and services interchange, implicitly embracing the places where culture, commerce, and economics meet most often (McCracken, 1990) through the lens of an interdisciplinary approach, is not so novel, as it may initially be conceived as such. The field of anthropology can be used as a starting point, with the hindsight that more and more marketers have been exploring anthropological methods in relation to consumption since the late 1990s (Holt, 1998). Consumer behaviour is explored with alternative methods and perspectives, leaning towards a theoretical conceptual bias rather than a methodologically one, focusing on case studies (Tian, 2001).

Accepting behaviour on social media platforms from the social science perspective provides credence to the participants on an individual as well as cultural level (Mooij, 2004). It is through this cultural prism that clearer insight on the multifaceted way brands engage and interact is highlighted before addressing the brand communal question (McCracken, 1990). An increasing number of people spend time in communities, and thus, investigating consumers' reasons for participation and involvement becomes meaningful (Kaplan & Haenlein, 2010; Ouwersloot & Odekerken-Schröder, 2008).

Social media has direct relevance to organisations when they are planning their marketing strategies. Organisations should be efficient with the available resources, including that sole finite elemental resource that can spell critical competitive advantage, and the execution of events should be speedy. The Internet condenses these elements (Negroponte, 1995), and business models are persistently morphing as the space-time and place continuum alternates into new formats. Tim O'Reilly (2007) from O'Reilly Media defined Web 2.0 as 'the platform being the network where the players connect'. The exposition of rich media, primarily video and images, has been a revolution in global communication, particularly pertaining to social media platforms, where brands need to ensure they are making use of the right channel (Levy & Gvilis, 2015).

Facebook Element

In 2011, Facebook, in conjunction with Yahoo, reconstructed Stanley Milgram's 1967 six-degree-of-separation small-world experiment; as the name implies, the ethos behind the experiment was the understanding and acknowledgement that the world was a small place. The focus of the research was to examine the average path length for social networks of people in the United States. However, the aim of the reconstruction was to make use of social networking to assess the degree of connectedness by taking an individual with an intended target and outcome within a network on the Facebook platform and work out mathematically whether such an individual would have accomplished the goals he set out to achieve through connecting with every sixth person (Telegraph, 2011).

Whilst the conclusion of the 2011 experiment was that the degree of connectivity was down to four as opposed to six, the Facebook ecosystem still prided itself on its 'connectability.'

The basis of connecting with people on Facebook through 'similarity', aspirations, or some other intention leans towards viral capability, built within the structure of the platform, rendering its seamless intuitive integration inherently attractive. Interfaces and desirable usability make the platform attractive with high stickability. These are unconscious triggers that reinforce usage (Kananukul et al., 2015). The key commodity that the platform and context have, is the potential to reinforce 'trust', executed implicitly by WOM and verified into action as 'likes' and proactive behaviour (Kabadayi & Price, 2014)

Lorenzo-Romero, Constantinides, and María del Carmen's (2011) summative work concluded that SNSs are the interface in a network hub and that communications and customer engagements are influenced and modified as a result of these interactions. This distinct feature of social media is caused by the level of engagement that can be narrowcast on a one-to-one or multiple basis, and this can be mapped out as four core attributes: intimacy, influence, involvement, and interaction (Haven, 2007). These attributes will be instrumental in exploring the individual and group dimensions of interpersonal and intrapersonal approaches of this study and will be adopted with the added element of brand interaction. Speed, frequency, and level of communication that is undertaken and their allegiance to the symbols and brands that facilitate this congregation, such as sites, are also considered, thereby transcending a nation's geographical boundaries. This situation affects the individual and group interaction (Tuten & Soloman, 2013).

Given that social networks process and manage information and are using microelectronic-based technologies (Castells, 2000), pending the programming and structure of the network, the question is, what is the function and remit of social media? Four functions have clearly been delineated, and these are publishing, entertainment, community, and social commerce (Tuten & Soloman, 2013). All these actions are social and part of the cultural processes that glue the network together (Castells, 2000). In social networks, the speed of communication shifts from traditional WOM, which involves personal communications amongst family, friends, and others, to eWOM and power law characteristics. Whilst symbolism sits at the heart of this, cultural dimensions (for example, individualist vs. collectivist societies) of different value indices and geopolitical economic frameworks invariably influence decision making, attitudes, and behaviour on social media network platforms pre- and postpurchasing (Goodrich & Mooij, 2014)

An example of cultural habits being synonymous with a culture and with the ability to influence and change other cultures is when back in 2011, Centryc Solutions, an Australian theme park, was way ahead of the curve looking to better connect with their customers and offer an innovative, social interactive experience. Research showed that their customers enjoyed themselves at the theme park but had little or no inclination to post about their experiences. The majority of the customers shared their experiences with friends back home verbally. Once customers opted in, what Centryc Solutions provided was a mechanism for the customers to connect their experiences within the theme park by providing those who were about to go on rides with radio-frequency identification tags. By swiping these tags, Centryc Solutions could identify the location of the customers within the park. Photos were taken during the customers' rides. As a fair-value exchange, the customers' photographs were automatically posted onto the theme park's Facebook page. A branded and an unbranded version was given to the customer together with a summarised e-mail, which contained all the events of the day and aggregated the customer's status and ranked them against their friends (Luna Park Sydney, YouTube, 2011).

Social media websites, such as Facebook, YouTube, and Twitter, provide unlimited means for Internet users to interact, express, share, and create content about anything, including brands. Such consumers' online brand-related activities (COBRAs) have significant consequences for firms. To effectively anticipate and direct these consequences, understanding people's motivations to engage in brand-related social media use is imperative.

Facebook Ecosystem

Although charting and navigating the ecosystem of Facebook are impossible, some indication of its reach, depth, and breadth is explored (Figure 1).

Figure 1. Facebook lights up the globe in 2016
Source: (Protalinski, 2016)

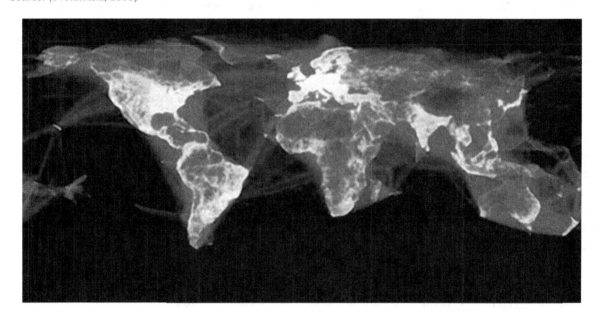

Given endless APIs, partnerships (Facebook and Amazon), and shared advertising networks, the ecosystem is multifaceted, agile, and amorphous, and consumer engagement sits at the heart of the Facebook ecosystem. This embraces and incorporates strength ties, homophily, eWOM, trust, and both normative and informational influences (Shu-Chuan & Kim, 2011).

Whilst behaviour is the end result of engagement, these are processes that follow through leading up to engagement (Kabadayi & Price, 2014). Loyalty lies at the centre of customer engagement (Roberts & Alpert, 2010), as it is one of the core drivers that motivational factors trigger elicit action. With the electronic medium being at the centre of this dynamic relationship, interactive experiences enhance the richness of the relationship, enabling a much more meaningful connection (Brodie et al., 2011). Brands with symbols and idents that convey meaning more than their face value sit at the nexus of this, fostering added value (Van Doorn et al., 2010).

Engagement, just like brand engagement, is based around homophilic tendency for the members of the cliques to be attracted together in the first place. However, to find new information or insights, members of the clique and self-interest groups have to look beyond the clique to others outside of the network hub, triggering 'the strength of weak ties' theory (Granovetter, 1973).

Meanwhile, COBRAs in relation to social media vary in accordance with different organisations and categories of organisations. For example, Red Bull on social media has a different method from Kingfisher public limited company. At the core of the consumer engagement principle is the very essence of what marketing is about: understanding customers and fulfilling their wants and needs in the relationship with an organisation (Brodie et al., 2011). The ethos of relationship marketing is the basis and driver of the interaction, the platform of trust and commitment to the process, and the willingness to interact. Companies are able to listen and enact on customers' preferences, such as including them within the product development and value chain creation cycle so that they become brand advocates (Sashi, 2012). The emotions have a clear instrumental role in fostering relational bonds (Brodie et al., 2011) between organisations and customers. Gummerus et al. (2012) emphasised the importance of these relationships being high quality, thought through and long-term media engagement on social networks sites, such as Facebook and Twitter, since they incorporate interactive experiences. This rich ecosystem consists of apps; rich media assets, such as video, audio, and text; and, increasingly important, analytical software (Kabadayi & Price, 2014).

An example is the leading entertainment retailer, Play.com. Lenskold Group (2013) conducted a study on analytical software tools and their ability to measure the effectiveness of social media campaigns year on year. To increase the level of engagement with customers making use of their social media engagement platform, Play.Com promoted their products to existing and new fans directly through their Facebook page, which is a platform to capture customer details from all incoming marketing channels but more importantly track their behaviour. After six months, data showed that the value of existing Play.com customers increased by over 24% within six months of rolling out the promotional program, whereas new customers increased an incremental 30%, and this value is from customers who directly visited their Facebook page, not through other traffic-driving sources (EngageSciences, 2012). This almost-continuous 24/7 connectivity, also called 'engagement', has consequential effects for brands (Irene & Lewis, 2010). This phenomenon concerning how social media is altering the way citizens globally interact with products and services in a brand-conscious world virtually and physically shifts the paradigm of the marketing curriculum in education, addressing the dichotomy of theory and practice.

A distinct approach to understanding human behaviour and determining what welds together relationships on agile technological infrastructure is promoted by Facebook and adapted in the work of Alan Fiske, an anthropologist, who devised a relational model (1992) on how people in different cultures through different epochs relate to one another socially as they evolve. Relational theory considers biosocial dimensions on how a society may have developed and evolved different values and institutions based on its geography, environment, culture, and context (Fiske, 2009). This model is adopted to generate greater understanding of human behaviour, users, customers, and potential on social media platforms.

Fiske's four-grid model posits that societies can be broken down into the following models of interaction: communal sharing (CS), authority ranking (AR), equality matching (EM), and market pricing (MP) (Figure 2). Numerous studies have demonstrated that people in all cultures integrate these models in their day-to-day encounters. However, societies at different stages of their evolution may go through biases, leaning towards one quadrant of the model as opposed to another. For example, theories have been proposed that in the Neolithic Age, society focused on being more communal and sharing (Sahlins, 1974), whereas the postmodern Western society leans towards the MP model (Firat, Nikhilesh, Dholakia, Alladi, & Venkatesh, 1995), which is taken to imply that relationships are being measured and evaluated on a cost-benefit analysis basis, with behaviours and actions being oriented towards a specified goal. The MP model is not inherently selfish or individualistic (Fiske, 2009). Although 'price' functions as a key lingua franca and barometer, it need not be exploitative because it can benefit social enterprises, for example, Oxfam organising a campaign on the Facebook platform to raise donations (MP).

Figure 2. Fiske Relational Model
Source: (Fiske, 1992)

Relational Model	Description	Examples
Communal Sharing (CS)	People treat each other as equivalent and undifferentiated in terms of contribution to community	•Using a "Commons" or shared resource •People intensely in love •Shared suffering for common well being
Authority Ranking (AR)	People have asymmetric positions in a linear hierarchy in which subordinates defer, respect and obey while superiors take precedence and control	•Military hierarchies •Ancestor worship •Monotheistic religious moralities •Class or ethnic rankings •Sports team standings
Equality Matching (EM)	Relationships keep track of the balance or difference among participants and know what is required to restore balance	•Turn-taking •One-person, one vote elections •Equal share distributions •"Eye for an Eye" vengeance
Market Pricing (MP)	Relationships are oriented to socially meaningful ratios or rates such as prices, wages, interest, rents, tithes, or cost-benefit analysis	•Property/Stock values •Arranged Marriage value •Standards of equity in judging entitlements

Hence, Fiske's model made use of addressing a new typology that operates like a rotating helicopter, funnelling its way through the prism of macrosocietal lens. It rotates because it mixes and matches in accordance with different segments of society and different epochs.

The other three relational models work harmoniously with one another. EM focuses on trying to keep relationships in balance with one another by minimising differences. In this respect, the old pre-Gorbachev Soviet era was an example of an intended EM. For example, in a hypothetical household with a couple, she takes out the garbage, and he brings the bins back in. People in relationships keep track of the balance or difference amongst those within the team, organisation, neighbourhood, or society. EM can be complex, pending an array of factors, such as the environment and the culture or subculture concerned. It highlights wider issues, such as trust and fairness, values and a sense of right and wrong, of which digital and social media are always fluid.

AR is all about relationships in relation to a hierarchical power, for example, in connection with the military, prestige, religion (monotheistic), or sports teams. Communication is usually top-down, and commonly, there is a threat of punishment should one not obey. In essence, these are relationships based on perceptions of legitimate asymmetries. For example, the social networking platform Diamond Lounge only allows persons of a certain category of income to be able to join them. This show of prestige is an exposition on power. This has vast implication for luxury brands on SNS. A critical component of this is the tone of voice (Tagg & Seargeant, 2013) used to communicate on these social media platforms, which for brands raises certain critical questions. Firstly, should communication be consistent across all social media platforms? Secondly, should this follow through on all social media devices? Thirdly, how does a brand ensure these are all integrated and consistent on other mediums?

The final quadrant from this model, the CS aspect, concerns treating people, or groups of people, in a manner that is not different from how they would treat anyone else in a relationship. It stems from a sense of collective responsibility, a respect and empathy for others. An example would be people from different countries, different cultures, and different ethnicities falling in love with each other and treating each other in a loving and nurturing way that if further along in the relationship, if they were to marry (with respect to their social selves), they would set up a family—encouraging communal well-being.

Communal well-being has recently been a core focus of the strategist guru Michael Porter, in a concept he has named corporate shared value. It stems from a 2011 paper he wrote in Harvard Business Review, whereby the organisational focus is on social (societal) value being transferred and transmitted to economic value. The concept can be thought of as the antithesis of corporate social responsibility. The essence of the theory is that organisations and corporations should focus on communal elements in their business conduct, considering the value chain and everything else (Porter, 2011). Coca-Cola champions this ethos (Forward Marketingtv, 2012), and an example is their global 2012–2014 Share-a-Coke campaign, as previously mentioned. The question of sharing items, opinions, comments, or reviews brings forward the question of reliability and credibility. It has been put forward that consumers perceive social media as a more reliable source of information about brands than marketer-generated content communicated (Mangold & Faulds, 2009). In an age where the distinction between online and offline is becoming much more blurred, the social media channel is changing its function and remit. Facebook capitalised on this element in a myriad of ways but most consciously through its advertising. Aside from the distinct pay per clip and associated methods, Facebook also shares advertising, as brands promote 'content', which in several instances may be information not directly related to a product or brand, on their site. For example, Red Bull Stratos (Marketing Magazine, 2012) is known as 'branded content' material through what is known as 'sponsored stories.' A 2012 study found that fans of brands on Facebook (those who have explicitly 'liked' a brand) are the easiest to reach with social-media brand impressions (Lipsman, Mudd, Rich, & Bruich, 2012). Whilst research findings in 2015 found that socializing and information seeking were the primary reasons for initially joining a Facebook brand page community (Shao & Ross, 2015). The essential question is, can such persons, fans, individuals, citizens, or customers be considered or consider themselves as a community?

What Is an Online Community? Is It a Service?

Before discussing concepts and attributes of a branded community, communities in general need to be understood from an online and virtual perspective. Traditionally, the word 'community' has been considered to be a closed system, with demarcations from one point to another with relatively stable membership and linkage to other communities (Anderson, 1999). Online communities share this attribute, but they are through groups of people who communicate with one another through electronic media, rather than face-to-face (Romm & Clarke, 1995). A branded community exhibits both characteristics (Cova & Pace, 2006), but this beckons the question, 'What is a virtual community?'

The word 'virtual', from the Latin word *virtus*, meaning 'strength,' 'manliness,' or 'virtue', has come to mean 'in essence' or 'effect' (TechTarget, 2014). Professor Benedict Anderson referred to a community as 'imagined', perceptions of togetherness, and not necessarily on actual interactions (1999), whereas Van Dijk maintained that communities are man-made (1997).

Hagel and Armstrong (1997) focused on the content and communication aspects of community with special emphasis on member-generated content, that is driven by the users of that content and how this accumulates as data which then gets recycled as communication when users send links and abbreviated content that has to comply with internet protocols prior to being transmitted.

As previously mentioned, brand communities can refer to groups that possess common interests in specific brands and form a social universe constructed upon their own myths, values, rituals, languages, and hierarchies (Cova & Pace, 2006). In this sense, brand communities are not necessarily about social relations or even feelings of community, but a sense of collective affiliation and ownership over shared cultural elements, whether communal interactions are enacted or collectively imagined.

The last definition came from Jones and Rafaeli (2000), who used the term 'virtual public' instead of virtual community. The use of the word 'public' brings us back to our linguistic limitations and references in connection with the new typography introduced by Fiske (1992).

Howard Rheingold, one of the most flamboyant and significant commentators on virtual communities, acknowledged the anthropological thesis that goods and services are by and large the by-product of any community, albeit in different shapes or forms.

In Rheingold's 2000 book, *The Virtual Community: Homesteading On*, he defined virtual communities as consisting of three core ingredients:

1. Social network capital. This ties in with Grovenwetter's weak ties (1973) syndrome and is related to the building of social capital. Porter (2011) asserted that this implicitly leads to economic capital.
2. Knowledge capital, which has to do with expertise.
3. Communion and conviviality, relating to close relationships between people.

At the centre of communal debates and trends are several unanswered questions related to big data, such as datasets as identities, differential privacy, and global citizenship. As Eric Schmidt famously said in 2010, 'Every two days now we create as much information as we did from the dawn of civilization up until 2003, that's something like five exabytes of data' (TechCrunch, 2010).

Any discussion on branded communities should consider that social media activity takes place online and offline. The defining characteristics of brand communities have so far struggled to identify the genuinely unique properties that separate brand communities from other types of social figurations.

Muniz and O'Guinn (2001) defined brand community as 'a specialized, non-geographically bound community, based on a structured set of social relationships among admirers of a brand'.

Studies have shown that consumer participation in brand communities affects customer loyalty positively and strengthens relationships (Kaplan & Haenlein, 2010).

In brand communities, members identify with a collectivity even though they may be geographically separated (Muniz & O'Guinn, 2001), thereby possessing a stability that is not dependent on the continuity of the social groups that form around it.

Specifically relating brand communities to social media are two distinct characteristics (Kaplan & Heinlein, 2010). One concerns degrees of exhibitionism, driven by groups, as well as narcissistic dynamics (Cova & Pace, 2006), which have deeper consequences relating to social identity and value (Bagozzi & Dholakia, 2006). The other concerns the element sum of the interaction and what it produces, otherwise known as 'social presence', or third space', a concept developed by Ray Oldenburg in 1991. The concept addresses the asynchronous and almost-synchronous dimensions of social media platforms. The unknown element as to who will be online when a user logs on and how this will shape and tailor the nature of any conversation leads to the other characteristic, that is, the richness of the media as an entity assists in amplifying the message and source origin into a new hybrid product labelled in some quarters as 'transmedia storytelling' (Pratten, 2011).

What is the future of social media? Why not look at a customer journey and try to mimic this using free social media networks?

The schism between social media as a platform for interacting, entertaining, fostering communal themes and engaging on one's own terms or as a service centres the focus on social customer relationship management (CRM) software, such as Salesforce.com and Bloomfires. Platforms such as these are expected to be higher in demand, as social media platforms become more interoperable by allowing CRM systems to be bolted on integrated into the existing architecture, which will alter the very nature of social media as opposed or in conjunction with call centres (Reader, 2014). The latter fosters one-to-one private conversations, whereas social media offers potentially an unlimited audience, and the responses are publicly visible (Econsultancy, 2010). Always-on brands such as Amazon, which achieved a massive 98% in responding to customers' social posts, Netflix, and Sony, which also had an acknowledgement rate of over 90% (Social Media Examiner, 2013), are exemplars in this arena. Response times to customers and helpfulness are expected to be critical Key Performance Indicators (KPIs) in critical decisions relating to whether organisations will opt for either call centre or social media or merge the two. Whist privacy may have been one of the key drivers in call centre promotions as big data and private social media channels become much more integrated, costs will be one of the deciding factors of the shape of the call-centre-versus-social-media outlook (Social Media Examiner, 2013).

Interaction Issues: The Social Process

Although the distinct nature of flows and brand interaction is not the core focus of this study, envisioning a brand community as a triad of customer–customer–brand has become residual (McAlexander, Schouten, & Koenig, 2002; Muniz & O'Guinn, 2001). A shift in perspective has been eminent with hybrid CRM systems, such as Conversocial, integrating into social media platforms.

Nevertheless, brand communities are significant in their own right. They are first and foremost symbols around which communities form as a secondary development, in contrast to the way that symbols are typically identified by communities that already exist in some form. This is the reverse of the centrifugal concept of the community being at the heart of community constructs (Cohen, 1985). Branded communities confirm the validity of the symbol, as an entity itself with meaning. This relates to Firat's assertion (Gould & Lerman, 1998) of the individual being devoid of ideology, translated as a means to an end whereby the prevalent ideology is commonly not challenged and is accepted without question (Stratton & Northcote, 2014). Confusion over the source of the symbol arises when vocalised participants of these communities are depicted as fluid and individualistic. Harley-Davidson as a brand community in relation to other motorcycle enthusiasts is a case in point (Schouten & McAlexander, 1995). Nevertheless, confusion becomes much more complex when brands want to come across as cool. In these instances, brand communities, for example, early Apple computing products, displayed characteristics of resistance to the mainstream (Muniz & O'Guinn, 2001).

Whilst the previous mention of social identity in relation to social media is an object of study beyond the remit of this paper, anthropological research seeks clarification in terminology because it has some bearing on definitions concerning tribes and 'consumer tribes' (O'Reilly, 2011, 2012, pp. 239–249). An earlier definition stated that consumer tribes are not united by the brand but by the passion or emotional tie that concerns the act of consumption (Cova & Cova, 2001, 2002; Cova et al., 2007). The need for clarification, O'Reily emphasised, is its overlap and confusion with the definition of 'neotribe', which was defined by Maffesoli in his 1996 publication 'as being fluid, occasional groups that are effervescent, ascetic, oriented toward the past or the future; they have as their common characteristic on the one hand, a breaking with the commonly held wisdom and, on the other, an enhancing of the organic aspect of the social aggregation'. The tribes existed as the antithesis of consumer tribes, for example, because of the emotional investment by the participants. An example of a neotribe is a nightclub venue, with the crowd, community, alternating with the music theme and event (Goulding et al., 2002). The best distinction between the concepts of neotribe and brand community is understood as the distinction between a social grouping (similar to a tribe) and a cultural grouping (similar to a subculture).

The relationship between an earlier raised theme of self and social awareness can be a toxic ingredient relating to the governance of the social platforms, with privacy and data ownership being areas of national and international contention (The Guardian, 2013). Brand communities are explicit in their exhibition of self-awareness and relationship to the community's relationship to commercial activity (Muniz & O'Guinn, 2001). Although it is not unique solely to branded communities, the nature and values of the brand will determine this covenant. For example, the fan base on social media for the Hunger Games franchise is likely to be a different constituent (Muniz & O'Guinn, 2001) and motivation of interaction.

Challenges in the Social Media Space: Is the Individual the Business?

Where does one start, and what is the future of social media? Why not look at a customer journey and try to mimic this using free social media networks? Some of these questions can be addressed within the social media ecosystem.

A significant book titled *Symbolic Interactionism* (Blumer, 1969) attempted to understand qualitatively what goes on within the individual prior to and during interaction as opposed to an action-monitored, aggregated response amongst thousands or millions of a large data samples. Criticisms of this approach to understand human relationships have been put forward because of their inherent lack of objectivity (Gouldner, 1964). This chapter argues for this awareness to be scooped into any analysis and that inter-actionism is more an approach that can be used in tandem with the relational model structure (Fiske, 1992), because the approach is more of a framework than a theory (Stryker & Vryan, 2006).

In 2012, Facebook was criticised when it was revealed a study was conducted without the knowledge of its users. The study focused on how interpersonal communication moods could be influenced (Kramera et al., 2014) in relation to positive or negative stimulus Facebook users received as input. Examples of such communication was directed at recipients through their newsfeed, which users generally sign up for when requesting specific information on certain themes or topics.

The findings from Facebook with approximately 700,000 data sample revealed that when individuals were less exposed to negative messages with emotional content, they were less likely to write negatively on their personal profile page (Kramera et al., 2014). Although a number of central principles, championed by Joel M. Charon, such as humans being understood as thinking, social beings, remain relevant to interactionism today, it is his critique and observation in relation to humans understanding how their senses worked in relation to their direct environments and from these situations the consequence of social thinking. This leads us to think about interaction in relation to communities (Charon, 2009).

Symbolic interactionism takes a strong onus from intrapersonal communications, concerning how individuals feel about messages and symbols and how brands position themselves on social network platforms (Straker et al., 2015) to be engaged with and interacted upon within the ecosystem of the digital arena. A critical tool of analysis that could be integrated into future social media research and assist reflection would be the analysis on how an individual sees himself and others and how he wants to be seen. Elements of this analysis are addressed in a theoretical framework model called the 'Johari window', developed in 1955 by Joseph Luft and Harrington Ingham. This model provides a visual representation of a person's character by interlacing the visual on a two-dimensional grid. From any axis along this grid, trust could be mapped, analysed, and understood when an individual or group was addressed.

Symbolic interaction with brands depending on the nuance, timing, offer, and mode of interaction can lead to the Pygmalion effect (Rosenthal & Jacobson, 2003). In other words, a self-fulfilling prophecy, implying a brand, for example, Lynx, whose brand message is around the rites of passage of gender attraction amongst teens and early twenty-somethings, projects usage of its anti-deodorant spray as increasing attraction with the opposite sexing correlation with increased frequency of use. This framework can be made clearer analytically by integrating the use of 'the Johari window' (Luft & Ingham, 1955) to social media profiles, such as Facebook (Table 1). An example is a 20-year-old male (known as 'X'), who looks, feels, and dresses good (open area 1), announces on social media that he would be venturing on a night out. Unknown to him, a girlfriend of a friend knows the venue and is likely to frequent it (open area 2). X has just started dating his female boss at his workplace (open area 3), but he has kept this clandestine. Despite male X having not placed any date of birth details on his social media status, X in seven days' time will receive a job offer as a shop manager from a progressive retail company (open area 4). From here on, should this information go on X's public profile, then the essence of communication, the ability to attract the opposite sex as a mate, will increase several-fold.

Table 1. Johari Window

1. Open / Free	2. Blind Area
3. Hidden Area	4. Unknown Area

1. Open area: what is known by the person about himself/herself and is also known by others

2. Blind area: what is unknown by the person about himself/herself but which others know

3. Hidden area: what the person knows about himself/herself that others do not know

4. Unknown area: what is unknown by the person about himself/herself and others (Luft, 1969)

Consumer Motivations to Participate in a Brand Community

Substantial bodies of academic research have addressed the motivation for joining branded communities. Sticking with the notion of Facebook, Dholakia, Bagozzi, and Pearo (2004) identified two clear benefits—informational and instrumental—that are often achievable through companies' Facebook sites. Practical benefits are embedded in the former when the community functions as a channel for customer feedback and questions.

Social benefits can also be informational. They come about from the interaction between the company through friendship (Gwinner, Gremler, & Bitner, 1998). This raises the question: what appropriate terminology should participants on social networks be addressed? Social benefits address the customers' need to feel useful, recognised, and needed in the community (Hars & Ou, 2002). Instrumental benefits are options that act as a conduit to achieving a greater target and focus, prominently from this entertainment and economic feature. The former benefits are derived from relaxation and fun (Dholakia, Bagozzi, & Pearo, 2004) and could motivate community participation in many ways. They operate as mood enhancers as people spend their time browsing the community page and apps, games, etc. Economic benefits (Gwinner, Gremler, & Bitner, 1998) refer to people joining brand communities for tangible reasons. It may be in order to gain discounts and time savings, competitions, etc. (McAlexander, Schouten, & Koenig, 2002).

Although the present study explores how brands interface with social media, motivational factors are simply one element out of several and are not summative. In 2002, McAlexander, Schouten, and Koenig's branded community study with jeep and Harley-Davidson found that even if a community is made up of its members and the relationships between the community elements (i.e., brand, community members, product, and marketer), the members are more interested in the brand than in each other. This relates to Pine and Gilmore's (1998) analysis of the experience economy, where the levels of engagement cover the immersive, active, passive, or absorptive levels of engagement.

The big question is should a global user join an online community, branded or not, if an important factor is the level of active participation on the platform network? In 2009, the research group Forrester produced a social technograph ladder with the following distribution (Figure 3):

Implications of Management

Marketing that considers the advancements in social media is still expanding and needs to be explored. This ties in with a postmodern approach to the subject whereby the relevance and dichotomy between theory and practice are consistently shifting. The assertion by Firut that customers and consumers are immune from ideology within their consumption habits is a testimony to this. The logic of this is that ideology exists within the technology per se. Hence, the way academics and practitioners need to analyse the subject has moved on from old frameworks. Technology heralds hegemony, and whoever wields control is the winner.

Correct phraseology is also an issue for contemporary marketing/branding because conflicting and contradictory terminologies are used interchangeably, making it difficult for practitioners and theorists to know when to use what (Brown, 1993). For example, social media makes use of a gamut of terms: friends, fans, customers, users, participants, etc., but what do all these terms mean? Do symbols imply varying degrees of sacredness so we can ascribe them as totems? Can an item be sacred in a consumerist-oriented society? An anthropological approach to the subject, nevertheless, acknowledges that symbols are representations greater than the sum of itself; therefore, an exploration into what they refer to expands the parameters, as well as the function, of the marketing concept.

Table 2. The social media engagement and stakeholder marketing

CS	AR
(Gwinner, Gremler, & Bitner, 1998)	(Cova & Pace, 2006).
Key Characteristics	**Key Characteristics**
• Economic benefits	• Groups possess common interests
• Browse for benefits	• Tone of voice is important
• mood enhancers	• They constructed upon their own myths
Examples	**Examples**
• Zappos	• Diamond Lounge (SNS)
• John Lewis	• Manchester United
• Coca Cola	• The London Metropolitan Police
EM	**MP**
(Dholakia, Bagozzi, & Pearo, 2004) and could motivate community participation in many ways.	Economic benefits (Gwinner, Gremler, & Bitner, 1998). (McAlexander, Schouten, & Koenig, 2002).
Key Characteristics	**Key Characteristics**
• Relaxation and fun	• They join for tangible reasons
• Instrumental benefits	• Economic benefits are paramount
Examples	• Price is the linqua Franca
• Apple	**Examples**
• Zara	• Oxfam
• Tesla	• Natwest
	• Ford motor car

Source: (Adapted from Fiske, 1992; Zook and Salmon, 2016)
- CS = Communal Sharing
- AR = Authority Ranking
- EM = Equality Matching
- MP = Market Pricing (Table 2)

Branding in essence in today's media-savvy ecosystem is marketing whereby the expectation is to be able to access and acquire products and services 24/7 on a global scale through the Internet; implicitly, social media platforms, such as Facebook and Twitter, become marketplaces. This ongoing change requires much more in-depth research as to the repercussions of global online consumption, but more significantly, this study argues that an anthropological approach is the most suitable model to address the phenomenon in its entirety. The divergent business models amidst different time zones and geographical spaces that intersect social media platforms are changing the way brands not only present themselves but also relate to users, who in marketing parlance become prospects and prosumers.

With technology structurally being one of the drivers of innovation, new business models and the marketing function, creation, and development of brands morph into new realms and territories driven by user-generated content. The relay and creation of messages in relation to brands by members on the platform, part of the brand community, become the funnel from which marketers can then drive forth their message (e.g., Coke). Messages created through conversation (comments) become the marketing message per se. The message is deemed credible because of this bottom-up approach (Levinson, 1997) and hence more trustworthy.

Marketers can purchase space, attention, and messages, but trust cannot be bought. Therefore, it is the currency of which whoever can win is bound to have the option to take the greater part of the spoils.

Figure 3. Social technographics
Source: Forrester: http://bit.ly/2fxdZKG

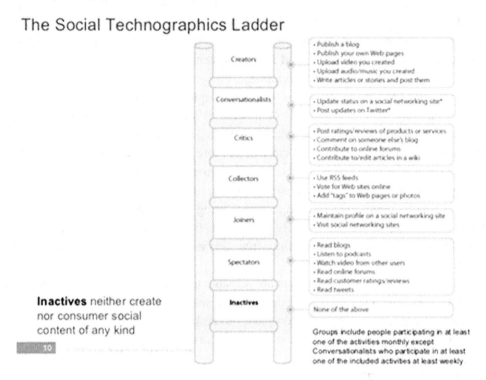

The marketing machine, integration, and array of goods, services, and information are beyond the construct of the old transactional model of mass marketing. Relationship marketing and its niche of segmentation development, made easier because of the digitalisation of data and CRM systems, propel beyond the intersection of zeros and ones but come to life through experience, in what Pine and Gilmore (1998) termed the 'experience economy'. The realms they identified, pertained to, such as edutainment, aesthetic, escapist, and entertainment tendencies, are strands they identified as the nuts and bolts of an online community. The branding component addresses elements of this, but as Dholakia, Bagozzi, and Pearo (2004) identified, what glues the community together as a centrepiece are normative and informational values that revert and overlap economic, entertainment, and other utility and symbolic attributes. Symbolic interactionism should be integrated into future research fields with the use of the Johari window framework to enable qualitative data to come to life.

However, given their pervasiveness in contemporary consumer-oriented lives, brands remain central because of their primary function of reducing uncertainties and minimising risks. Paradoxically, given the human cognitive construct, overstimulation, and big data syndrome, informational and Internet addiction 'narratives' are crucial in disseminating information (Kozinets, Valck, Wojnicki, & Wilner, 2010) to users, participants, and community members regarding what is different and what is relevant through storytelling. Coke, Nike, Red Bull, and a host of fast-moving consumer goods get community members to share stories, which may be through the 'Like' button (in the case of Facebook) or through the newsfeed of members, warranted through permission-based marketing.

The differences between online and virtual communities need to be acknowledged. Virtual communities as defined by Rheingold, as well as Armstrong and Hagel, have certain inherent qualities that pertain to an overall engaged, even if disembodied adjunction to larger bodies/entities that have come together for a mutual interest or a particular focus. The word 'virtual' in this context implies that another version of the original exists, that is, the community. Hence, it can be taken as being a derivative of something wider, physically real, or a tangible community. Although none of the case studies directly addressed this issue, as brands become more integrated into ecosystems, virtual platforms, such as Second Life, are likely to play a greater role in brand integration.

Conversations, branded content messages that can masquerade the originator of a message, be they from a brand or an individual, who may also duplicate as a consumer, elicit awkward questions that lead to the terrain of customer engagement and loyalty. The Forrester social technograph identified that certain actors within a social network platform will be more vocal and active than others. This may be effortless and at times an empty symbol. An example is when someone with a large following on Twitter is retreating specific messages simply to garner a larger following. Loyalty is difficult to qualify and define because it depends persistently on competitive offerings, what customer or individual expectations are and elements of synchronous offerings. As technology, from which social media depends, changes, so will the dimensions of loyalty. The certainty from this analysis is that fostering loyalty will be the mainstay of the battleground in the future.

Community and company announcements are possible to duplicate with social platforms, such as Facebook and Twitter, which are capable of dual roles. Since 2013, when the US Securities Exchange Commission announced that it is legal for companies to make use of social media platforms, this level playing field has led towards what one can call 'stakeholder marketing'.

Limitations of the Research

A more in-depth longitudinal study that will address some of the core issues mentioned in this chapter needs to be undertaken. Some of these issues pertain to the amalgamation of the different strands of research through a mixed-method approach over a duration of one to three years, targeted towards different demographic groups. Such a body of research would enable a realistic snapshot of the breadth and depth and behavioural tendencies of individuals and brands on social networks, such as Facebook. A mixed-method research approach is advocated whereby some of the themes introduced in this chapter should be integrated as a large sample frame from big data networks.

Such a body of work should address and overcome the issue of privacy by asking for the consent of the participants prior to the study. The use of big data should be incorporated. Already Internet behemoths, such as Netflix and Amazon, are aggressively enabling their content to be available through a multiplicity of devices and networks. Amazon's relationship with gaming to reinforce a much more sticky engagement is bound to upshoot. This study should be considered as a precursor, setting the tempo and template for a succeeding research that will shed light to issues. An exploratory analysis of the multifaceted dimension should still be used to determine how brands interact with users on social media networks, which would lead us more towards complexity theory. This latter subject area should be incorporated into any future study of magnitude to give it the best balance in the context of big data.

CONCLUSION

This chapter has explored the evolution and concept of marketing as we have come to know it, to its future antennas in the 21st century. Given that marketing is continually evolving, an interdisciplinary approach to the subject has been advocated, and this approach primarily focuses on an anthropological strand to understand the relationship of goods and services in consumer-oriented environments. The relationship of online marketing from which social media sits at the hub identifies how the communicators of brands, representing consumer goods and services, symbolically interface global citizens as prospects, potential customers, and prosumers. The natures of these online relationships are multidimensional, and dimensions of these engagements are clarified with the use of Fiske's relationship model and can be analysed in a much more meaningful way by incorporating symbolic interactionism and the Johari window. Whether these relationships can be classified as leading towards a branded or online or virtual community is inconclusive because further exploration and studies need to be conducted and much greater clarity of terminology generally accepted. Nevertheless, social media appears to certainly continue to alter marketing frameworks and concepts. This study is a firm advocate of the term 'stakeholder marketing'.

REFERENCES

Agichtein, E., Castillo, C., Donato, D., Gionis, A., & Mishne, G. (2008, February). Finding high-quality content in social media. *Proceedings of the 2008 International Conference on Web Search and Data Mining* (pp. 183-194). ACM.

Algesheimer, R., Dholakia, U. M., & Herrmann, A. (2005). The social influence of brand community: Evidence from European car clubs. *Journal of Marketing, 69*(3), 19–34. doi:10.1509/jmkg.69.3.19.66363

Anderson, B. (1983). *Imagined Communities: Reflections on the Origin and Spread of Nationalism.* London: Verso.

Anderson, C. (2007). *The Long Tail.* London: Random House.

Armstrong, A., & Hagel, J. (1997). Net Gain: Expanding Markets Through Virtual Communities (First Printing ed.). Harvard Business School Press.

Bagozzi, R. P., & Dholakia, U. M. (2006). Antecedents and purchase consequences of customer participation in small group brand communities. *International Journal of Research in Marketing, 23*(1), 45–61. doi:10.1016/j.ijresmar.2006.01.005

Barker, M., Bormann, N., Neher, K., & Barker, I. D. (2012). Social Media Marketing (Int'l ed.). Tennessee: South-Western College Publishing.

Barthes, R. (1997). *Elements of Semiology* (Reissue ed.). Atlantic Books.

Baudrillard, J. (1988). Selected Writings. California: Stanford University Press

BBC. (2013). Facebook social graph search results limited for teens. Retrieved from http://www.bbc.co.uk/news/technology-21472219

BBC News. (2013, April 3). SEC clears use of social media for company announcements. Retrieved from http://www.bbc.co.uk/news/business-22011563

Berger, J., & Milkman, K. L. (2013). Emotion and Virality: What makes online content go viral? *Insights*, *5*(1), 18–23.

Berry, C., Smith, P., & Pulford, A. (1999). *Strategic Marketing Communications: New Ways to Build and Integrate Communications*. London: Kogan Page.

Blumer, H. (1969). *Symbolic Interactionism: Perspective and Method*. New Jersey: Prentice-Hall, Inc.

Botsman, R., & Rogers, R. (2011). *What's Mine Is Yours: How Collaborative Consumption is Changing the Way We Live*. London: HarperCollins Business.

Brech, E., Thomson, A., John, F., & Wilson, J. F. (2010). *Management Pioneer: A Biography*. OUP Oxford. doi:10.1093/acprof:oso/9780199541966.001.0001

Brodie, R. J., Hollebeek, L. D., Biljana, J., & Ilic, A. (2011). Customer engagement: Conceptual domain, fundamental propositions and implications for research. *Journal of Service Research*, *14*(3), 252–271. doi:10.1177/1094670511411703

Brown, S. (1993). *Postmodern Marketing*. Boston: Cengage.

Brown, S. (2001). Torment Your Customers (They'll Love It). *Harvard Business Review*, (October), 82–88.

Campbell, S. (2010). How Does Facebook Work? The Nuts and Bolts [Technology Explained]. Makeuseof. Retrieved from http://www.makeuseof.com/tag/facebook-work-nuts-bolts-technology-explained/

Govani, T., & Pashley, H. (2005). Student Awareness of the Privacy Implications When Using Facebook. Carnegie Mellon University. Retrieved from http://lorrie.cranor.org/courses/fa05/tubzhlp.pdf

Castells, M. (2000). *The Rise of The Network Society: The Information Age: Economy, Society and Culture*. John Wiley & Sons.

Champniss, G., & Vila, R. F. (2011). *Brand Valued: How Socially Valued Brands Hold the Key to a Sustainable Future and Business Success*. New York: Wiley.

Charon, M. J. (2009). *Symbolic Interactionism: An Introduction, an Interpretation, an Integration* (10th ed.). Pearson.

Chu, S.-C., & Kim, Y. (2011). Determinants of consumer engagement in electronic word-of-mouth (eWOM) in social networking sites. *International Journal of Advertising*, *30*(1), 47–75. doi:10.2501/IJA-30-1-047-075

Chuttur, M.Y. (2009). Overview of the Technology Acceptance Model: Origins, Developments and Future Directions. Sprouts: Working Papers on Information Systems, Indiana University, USA.

Claritaslux, M. (2008). Vkontakte the new dating game for Russian girls. Retrieved from http://claritaslux.com/girls/vkontakte/

Coca-Cola (n. d.). Coca Cola and Olympic Games history. Retrieved from http://www.coca-cola.co.uk/olympic-games/coca-cola-and-olympic-games-history.html

Cohen, A. P. (1985). The Symbolic Construction of Community, London: Tavistock.

Emarketer.com. (2012, June). Companies Use Social to Track and Follow Up on Brand Mentions. Retrieved from http://www.emarketer.com/Article/Companies-Use-Social-Track-Follow-Up-on-Brand-Mentions/1009104

Constine, J. (2011). Facebook's Sponsored Stories Turns News Feed Posts Into Home Page Ads http://www.insidefacebook.com/2011/01/24/sponsored-stories-feed-ads/

Constine, J. (2013). Facebook Reveals 78% of US Users Are Mobile As It Starts Sharing User Counts by Country http://techcrunch.com/2013/08/13/facebook-mobile-user-count/

Conversocial. (2014). Social CRM.

Cook, K. S., & Rice, E. (2003). Social Exchange Theory. In J. Delamater (Ed.), *The Handbook of Social Psychology* (pp. 53–76). New York: Kluwer Academic.

Cook, S. K., Emerson, M. R., Gillmore, R. M., & Yamagishi, T. (1983). *The Distribution of Power in Exchange Networks: Theory and Experimental Results*. Chicago: University of Chicago.

Cova, B., & Cova, V. (2001). *Tribal Marketing: the Tribalisation of Society and its Impact on the Conduct of Marketing (r evised paper)*. *European Journal of Marketing*.

Cova, B., & Pace, S. (2006). Brand community of convenience products: New forms of customers empowerment – the case of my Nutella community. *European Journal of Marketing*, *40*(9), 1087–1105. doi:10.1108/03090560610681023

Daye, D. (2009). Great Moments in Branding: Neil Mcelroy Memo. Branding strategy insider. Retrieved from www.brandingstrategyinsider.com/2009/06/great-moments-in-branding-neil-mcelroy-memo.html

de Mooij, M.K. (2004). *Global Marketing and Advertising: Understanding Cultural Paradoxes*. Sage Publications.

Dholakia, U. M., Bagozzi, R. P., & Pearo, L. K. (2004). A social influence model of consumer participation in network-and small-group-based virtual communities. *International Journal of Research in Marketing*, *21*(3), 241–263. doi:10.1016/j.ijresmar.2003.12.004

Easley, D., & Kleinberg, J. (2010). *Networks, Crowds, and Markets: Reasoning about a Highly Connected World*. Cambridge: Cambridge University Press. doi:10.1017/CBO9780511761942

Economist, The. (2005, July 7). Can Netflix's Reed Hastings succeed in the battle to deliver movies online? Retrieved from http://www.economist.com/node/4149765

EngageSciences. (2012, October 18). EngageSciences customers talk about the platform (YouTube video). Retrieved from http://www.youtube.com/watch?feature=player_embedded&v=oyptdA5i-qg

Erickson, D. (2013). Top eTailers' Social Customer Service Performance. *e-Strategy Trends*. Retrieved from http://trends.e-strategyblog.com/2013/07/17/top-etailers-social-customer-service-performance/

Firat, A., Dholakia, N., & Venkatesh, A. (1995). Marketing in a postmodern world. *European Journal of Marketing*, *29*(1), 40–56. doi:10.1108/03090569510075334

Firat, A., & Schultz, C. J. (1997). From segmentation to fragmentation. Markets and marketing strategy in the postmodern era. *European Journal of Marketing, 31*(3/4), 183–207. doi:10.1108/EUM0000000004321

Fiske, A. (1992). The Four Elementary Forms of Sociality Framework for a Unified Theory of Social Relations. *Psychological Review, 99*(4), 689–723. doi:10.1037/0033-295X.99.4.689 PMID:1454904

Fiske, A. (2009). Civilizations and Relational Models Theory. *Culture and Civilization matters*. Retrieved from https://fuquaccl.wordpress.com/tag/alan-fiske/

Fox, Z. (2012). How Social Media Is Helping Colorado Wildfire Relief. *Mashable*. Retrieved from http://mashable.com/2012/06/29/colorado-wildfire-social-media/

Frazier, E. (2010). Bringing new buzz to Super Bowl ads. On Twitter and Facebook, the Super Bowl has already begun. *Charlotteobserver*. Retrieved from http://www.charlotteobserver.com/2010/02/06/1228342/bringingnew-buzz-to-big-game.html

Gaudin, S. (2012, December). Vote ends on Facebook privacy changes, for good Apathetic users mean vote falls far short of forcing Facebook to keep old rules. *Computerworld.com*. Retrieved from http://www.computerworld.com/s/article/9234561/Vote_ends_on_Facebook_privacy_changes_for_good

Godin, S. (1999). Permission Based Marketing. New York: Simon & Schuster

Godin, S. (2008). *Tribes: We Need You to Lead Us*. Essex: Platkus.

Goodrich, K., & Mooij, M. (2014). How social are social media? A cross-cultural comparison of online and offline purchase decision influences. *Journal of Marketing Communications, 20*(1-2), 2014. doi:10.1080/13527266.2013.797773

Gould, J. S., & Lerman, D. B. (1998). Postmodern versus long-standing cultural narratives in consumer behaviour: An empirical study of NetGirl online. *European Journal of Marketing, 32*(7/8), 644–654. doi:10.1108/03090569810224047

Goulding, C., Saren, M., & Follett, J. (2002). Working Weeks, Rave Weekends; Identity Fragmentation and the Emergence of New Communities. *Consumption Markets & Culture, 5*(4), 261–284. doi:10.1080/1025386022000001406

Gouldner, W. A. (1964). *Anti-Minotaur: The Myth of Value; in (1971) The Coming Crisis of Western Sociology*. Heinemann.

Graham, F. (2013). Can big data help fight fires and save lives? *BBC News*. Retrieved from http://www.bbc.co.uk/news/business-21902070

Granovetter, M. (1973). The strength of weak ties. *American Journal of Sociology, 78*(6), 1360–1380. doi:10.1086/225469

Guadagni, D. (2010). Social media case study: how Comcast is winning the battle for perception. *Activerain*. Retrieved from http://activerain.com/blogsview/1664971/social-media-case-study-how-comcast-is-winning-the-battle-for-perception#sthash.luH5AzHO.dpuf

Gummerus, J., Liljander, V., Weman, E., & Pihlstrom, M. (2012). Customer engagement in a Facebook brand community. *Management Research Review, 35*(9), 857–877. doi:10.1108/01409171211256578

Gwinner, K., Gremler, D. D., & Bitner, J. M. (1998). Relational Benefits in Services Industries: The Customers Perspective. *Journal of the Academy of Marketing Science*, 26(Spring), 101–114. doi:10.1177/0092070398262002

Hamburger, E. (2014) Facebook's new stats: 1.32 billion users, 30 percent only use it on their phone. *The Verge*. Retrieved from http://www.theverge.com/2014/7/23/5930743/facebooks-new-stats-1-32-billion-users-per-month-30-percent-only-use-it-on-their-phones

Hars, A., & Ou, S. (2002). Working for Free? Motivations for Participating in Open-Source Projects. *International Journal of Electronic Commerce*, 6(3), 25–39.

Haven, B. (2007). Marketing's New Key Metric: Engagement, for Marketing Leadership Professionals.

Hofstede, G., Hofstede, J. G., & Minkov, M. (2010). *Cultures and Organizations: Software of the Mind. Revised and Expanded* (3rd ed.). Columbus: McGraw-Hill.

Holloman, C. (2012). *The Social Media MBA: Your Competitive Edge in Social Media Strategy Development and Delivery. New York*: Wiley Publishers.

Holt, B. D. (1998). Does Cultural Capital Structure American Consumption? *The Journal of Consumer Research*, 25(1), 1–25. doi:10.1086/209523

Homans, G.C. (1987). Certainties and Doubts: Collected Papers, 1962-1985. New Brunswick, New Jersey: Transaction Books.

Hongxiu, L., Mäntymäki, M., & Zhang, X. (Eds.). (2014). Digital Services and Information Intelligence. *Proceedings of the 13th IFIP WG 6.11 Conference on e-Business, e-Services and e-Society*.

Horst, J.J.H. (2014). *The Social Thought of Georg Simmel (Social Thinkers Series)*. Sage Publications.

Irene, J. D., & Lewis, F. W. (2010). The Evolution (Revolution) of Social Media and Social Networking as Necessary Topic in the Marketing Curriculum: A Case for Integrating Social Media into Marketing Classes. *Proceedings of the Society for Marketing Advances conference* (p. 140).

Jones, Q., & Rafaeli, S. (2000). Time to split, virtually: Discourse architecture and community building create vibrant virtual publics. *Electronic Markets*, 10(4), 214–223. doi:10.1080/101967800750050326

Jordan, T. A. (2012). *Business Anthropology* (2nd ed.). Illinois: Waveland Pr Inc.

Kabadayi, S., & Price, K. (2014). Consumer – brand engagement on Facebook: Liking and commenting behaviors. *Journal of Research in Interactive Marketing*, 8(3), 203–223. doi:10.1108/JRIM-12-2013-0081

Kadushin, C. (2012). *Understanding social networks: Theories, concepts, and findings Oxford*. Oxford University Press.

Kaplan, A. M., & Haenlein, M. (2010). Users of the world, unite! The challenges and opportunities of social media. *Business Horizons*, 53(1), 59–68. doi:10.1016/j.bushor.2009.09.003

Keen, A. (2012). *Digital Vertigo*. London: Constable.

Keesing, M. R., & Strathern, J. A. (1997). *Cultural Anthropology: A Contemporary Perspective* (3rd ed.). Kentucky: Wadsworth Publishing Co Inc.

Kemp, N. (2012). Six marketing lessons from Red Bull Stratos. *Campaign.co.uk*. Retrieved from http://www.brandrepublic.com/news/1155718/

Koch, R. (2001). *The 80/20 Principle: The Secret of Achieving More with Less*. London: Nicholas Brealey Publishing.

Kotler, P., & Armstrong, G. (2014). *Principles of Marketing* (15th ed.). New Jersey: Pearson.

Kotler, P., & Gertner, D. (2002). Country as a brand, product and beyond: a place marketing and brand management perspective. In N. Morgen, A. Pritchard, & R. Pride (Eds.), *Destination Branding: creating the unique destination proposition*. Oxford: Elsevier Butterworth- Heinemann. doi:10.1057/palgrave.bm.2540076

Kotler, P. and Zaltman, G. (1971). Social marketing: an approach to planned social change. *Journal of Marketing, 35*, 3-12.

Kozinets, R. V. (2002). The field behind the screen: Using netnography for marketing research in online communities. *JMR, Journal of Marketing Research, 39*(1), 61–72. doi:10.1509/jmkr.39.1.61.18935

Kozinets, V., de Valck, K., Wojnicki, A. C., & Wilner, S. J. S. (2010). Networked Narratives: Understanding Word-of-Mouth Marketing in Online Communities. *Journal of Marketing, 74*(2), 71–89. doi:10.1509/jmkg.74.2.71

Kramera, I.D.A., Guillory, E.J., & Hancock, T.J. (2014). Experimental Evidence of Massive-Scale Emotional Contagion through social networks (Fiske, S.T. ed.). Cornell University.

Lake, C. (2010) The horror, the horror: @VodafoneUK's social media balls up. *eConsultancy.com*. Retrieved from http://econsultancy.com/blog/5401-the-horror-the-horror-vodafoneuk-s-social-media-balls-up

Lawler, E. J. (2001). An Affect Theory of Social Exchange. *American Journal of Sociology*, 107.

Leadfindr. (2013, May). Finding new customers for a gym (YouTube video). Retrieved from http://www.youtube.com/watch?v=MhRqHHdJ8yo

Leonardi, P. M., Huysman, M., & Steinfield, C. (2013). Enterprise social media: Definition, history, and prospects for the study of social technologies in organizations. *Journal of Computer-Mediated Communication, 19*(1), 1–19. doi:10.1111/jcc4.12029

Levi-Strauss, C. (1974). Structural Anthropology. New York: Basic Books

Levinson, C., & Levinson, J. (2007). *Guerilla Marketing: Easy and Inexpensive Strategies for Making Big Profits from Your Small Business Paperback* (4th ed.). Boston: Houghton Mifflin.

Licino, H. (2013). Succeeding At Social Media ROI Measurement. Benchmarkmail.com. Retrieved from http://www.benchmarkemail.com/blogs/detail/succeeding-at-social-media-roi-measurement

Lipsman, A., Mudd, G., Rich, M., & Bruich, S. (2012). How Brands Reach (and Influence) Fans Through Social-Media Marketing. *Journal of Advertising, 52*(1), 40–52. doi:10.2501/JAR-52-1-040-052

Lorenzo-Romero, C., Constantinides, E., & María-del-Carmen, A. (2011). Consumer adoption of social networking sites: Implications for theory and practice. *Journal of Research in Interactive Marketing, Volume, 5*(2/3), 2011.

Luft, J. (1969). *Of Human Interaction*. Palo Alto, CA: National Press.

Luft, J., & Ingham, H. (1955). The Johari window, a graphic model of interpersonal awareness. *Proceedings of the western training laboratory in group development,* UCLA, Los Angeles, CA.

Luna Park Sydney. (2011, June). My Experience (YouTube video). Retrieved from http://www.youtube.com/watch?v=Md8iAatlqhY

Lunden, I. (2012). Night Of The Living Social Network: Friends Reunited Relaunches Tomorrow As A Digital Scrapbook. *Techrunch.com*. Retrieved from http://techcrunch.com/2012/03/26/night-of-the-living-social-network-friends-reunited-relaunches-tomorrow-as-a-digital-scrapbook/

Lunden, I. (2014) Facebook Passes 1B Mobile Users, 200m Messenger Users In Q1. *Techcrunch*. Retrieved from http://techcrunch.com/2014/04/23/facebook-passes-1b-mobile-monthly-active-users-in-q1-as-mobile-ads-reach-59-of-all-ad-sales/

MacAskill, E. (2013) Edward Snowden: how the spy story of the age leaked out. *The Guardian*. Retrieved from http://www.theguardian.com/world/2013/jun/11/edward-snowden-nsa-whistleblower-profile

Maffesoli, M. (1996). *The Time of the Tribes: The Decline of Individualism in Mass Society*. London: Sage.

Mangold, W., & Faulds, D. (2009). Social media: The new hybrid element of the promotion mix. *Business Horizons, 52*(4), 357–365. doi:10.1016/j.bushor.2009.03.002

Market Sentinel. (2007). Responding to crisis using social media; Updating the "Dell Hell" case study - are Dell turning opinion round? Retrieved from www.marketsentinel.com

Marketing and the 7P's. (2015). Retrieved from http://www.cim.co.uk/files/7ps.pdf

Marketingmag.com. (2012). Campaign: Share a Coke. Retrieved from https://www.marketingmag.com.au/hubs-c/share-a-coke-campaign-post-analysis/

ForwardMarketingtv. (2012). Coca-Cola Content 2020 Initiative Strategy Video - Parts I & II (YouTube video). Retrieved from http://www.youtube.com/watch?v=G1P3r2EsAos

Maslow, A. (1954). *Motivation and Personality*. New York: Harper.

McAlexander, J. H., Schouten, J. W., & Koenig, H. F. (2002). Building brand community. *Journal of Marketing, 66*(1), 38–54. doi:10.1509/jmkg.66.1.38.18451

McCarthy, J. E. (1960). *Basic Marketing. A Managerial Approach*. Homewood, IL: Richard D. Irwin.

McCracken, G. (1990). *Culture and Consumption: New Approaches to the Symbolic Character of Consumer Goods and Activities*. New Jersey: John Wiley & Sons.

McCraw, K. T. (2000). *American Business, 1920-2000: How It Worked - P&G: Changing the Face of Consumer Marketing*. Harlan Davidson Publishers.

McLuhan, M. (1964). *Understanding Media: The Extensions of Man* (1st ed.). New York: McGraw Hill.

Meekar, M. (2012, December). 2012 internet trends. Retrieved from http://www.kpcb.com/insights/2012-internet-trends-update

Meekar, M. (2013, May). 2013 internet trends. Retrieved from http://www.kpcb.com/insights/2013-internet-trends

Mescall, J. (2013, June 26). John Mescall on making shareable advertising. Vimeo. Retrieved from http://vimeo.com/68842157

Michael, P. (2010). Creating Shared Value. (YouTube video). Retrieved from http://www.youtube.com/watch?v=z2oS3zk8VA4

Michelle, D.H. (2010) Sentiment Analysis, Hard But Worth It! Customer Think. Retrieved from http://customerthink.com/sentiment_analysis_hard_but_worth_it/

Muniz, A. M. Jr, & OGuinn, T. C. (2001). Brand community. *The Journal of Consumer Research*, *27*(4), 412–432. doi:10.1086/319618

Muniz, A. M. Jr, & OGuinn, T. C. (2001). Brand community. *The Journal of Consumer Research*, *27*(4), 412–432. doi:10.1086/319618

Negroponte, N. (1995). *Being Digital*. Alfred A. Knopf, Inc.

O'Reilly, D. (2011). Leisure tribe-onomics. In S. Cameron (Ed.), *Handbook on the Economics of Leisure* (pp. 239–249). Cheltenham: Edward Elgar Publishing. doi:10.4337/9780857930569.00021

OECD. (2014). What is Social Capital. Retrieved from http://www.oecd.org/insights/37966934.pdf

Ogilvy, J. (1990). This postmodern business. *Marketing and Research Today*, February, 4-20.

Oldenburg, R. (1991). *The Great Good Place*. New York: Marlowe & Company.

Olsen, B. (1995). *Brand loyalty and consumption patterns*.

OReilly, D. (2012). Maffesoli and consumer tribes: Developing theoretical links. *Marketing Theory*, *12*(3), 341–347. doi:10.1177/1470593112451801

Ouwersloot, H., & Odekerken-Schroder, G. (2008). Whos who in brand communities – and why? *European Journal of Marketing*, *42*(5/6), 571–585. doi:10.1108/03090560810862516

Pakhomova, E. (2013) What next for social networking site. *Calvert Journal*. Retrieved from http://calvertjournal.com/articles/show/894/what-next-for-social-networking-site-vkontakte

Papacharissi, Z. (2010). *A Networked Self: Identity, Community, and Culture on Social Network Sites*. London: Routledge.

Petty, R., & Cacioppo, J. (1996). *Attitudes and Persuasion: Classic and Contemporary Approaches (New ed.). Colorado: Westview Press.*

Pew Research Center. (2013). 72% of Online Adults are Social Networking Site Users Social networking sites remain most popular among young adults, but other age groups continue to increase their engagement. Retrieved from http://www.pewinternet.org/~/media//Files/Reports/2013/PIP_Social_networking_sites_update_PDF.pdf

Pew Research Center. (2013, December). Social media update 2013. Retrieved from http://www.pewinternet.org/~/media//Files/Reports/2013/Social%20Networking%202013_PDF.pdf

Pine, J., & Gilmore, J. (1999). *The Experience Economy*. Boston: Harvard Business School Press.

Porter, M. E. (1980). *Competitive Strategy*. New York: Free Press.

Pratten, R. (2011). *Getting Started in Transmedia Storytelling: A Practical Guide for Beginners*. CreateSpace Independent Publishing Platform.

Protalinski, E. (2016) Facebook passes 1.65 billion monthly active users, 54% access the service only on mobile. *VentureBeat.com*. Retrieved from http://venturebeat.com/2016/04/27/facebook-passes-1-65-billion-monthly-active-users-54-access-the-service-only-on-mobile/

Protalinski, E. (2016, April 16). Facebook passes 1.65 billion monthly active users, 54% access the service only on mobile. *VentureBeat.com*. Retrieved from http://venturebeat.com/2016/04/27/facebook-passes-1-65-billion-monthly-active-users-54-access-the-service-only-on-mobile/

Qualman, E. (2011). *Socialnomics: How Social Media Transforms the Way We Live and Do Business*. Hoboken: John Wiley & Sons.

Quinn, S., & Oldmeadow, J. (2013). The martini effect and social networking sites: Early adolescents, mobile social networking and connectedness to friends. *Mobile Media & Communication, 1*(2), 237–247. doi:10.1177/2050157912474812

Rangun, V. K., & Karim, S. (1991). *Teaching note: Focusing the concepts of social marketing*. Cambridge: Harvard Business School Press.

Reader, R. (2014). Conversocial integrates with Instagram to give customers some love. *VentureBeat. com*. Retrieved from http://venturebeat.com/2014/07/29/coversocial-now-integrates-with-instagram-to-give-potential-customers-some-love/

Rheingold, H. (1993). Virtual Community. Massachusetts: MIT Press.

Riezebos, H. J. (1994). *Brand-added value: Theory and empirical research about the value of brands to consumers*. Eburon Publishers.

Rifkin, J. (2000). *The Age of Access*. London: Penguin.

Roberts, C., & Albert, F. (2010). The total customer engagement: Designing and aligning key strategic elements to achieve growth. *Journal of Product and Brand Management, 19*(3), 198–209. doi:10.1108/10610421011046175

Romm, C., & Clarke, R. J. (1995). Virtual communities research themes: A preliminary draft for a comprehensive model. *Proc. Australian Conference on Information Systems*, Perth, Australia (pp. 26–29, 57–66).

Rosenthal, R., & Jacobson, L. (2003). *Pygmalion in the Classroom: Teacher Expectation and Pupils' Intellectual Development* (new ed.). Crown House Publishing.

Rouse, M. (2010, September). Social graph. Retrieved from http://whatis.techtarget.com/definition/social-graph

Safko, L. (2010). *The social media bible: tactics, tools, and strategies for business success.* John Wiley & Sons.

Sahlins, M. (1974). *Stone Age Economics.* Aldine: *Trans-Action.*

Sashi, C. M. (2012). Customer engagement, buyer-seller relationships and social media. *Management Decision, 50*(2), 253–272. doi:10.1108/00251741211203551

Schiller, D. (2012). Web Economics: The Product is You! *Socialmediatoday.com.* Retrieved from http://socialmediatoday.com/daniel-schiller/625921/web-economics-product-you

Schiller, D. (2012). Web Economics: The Product is You! *Socialmediatoday.com.* Retrieved from http://socialmediatoday.com/daniel-schiller/625921/web-economics-product-you

Schouten, J. W., & McAlexander, H. J. (1995). Subcultures of Consumption: An Ethnography of the New Bikers. *The Journal of Consumer Research, 22*(June), 43–61. doi:10.1086/209434

Sernovitz, A. (2012). *Word of Mouth Marketing: How Smart Companies Get People Texas.* Greenleaf Book Group Press.

Shankar, A., Cova, B., & Kozinets, R. (2007). *Consumer Tribes.* Routledge.

Shu-Chuan, C., & Kim, Y. (2011). Determinants of consumer engagement in electronic word-of-mouth (eWOM) in social networking sites. *International Journal of Advertising, 30*(1), 47–75. doi:10.2501/IJA-30-1-047-075

Simons Institute. (2013) Big Data and Differential Privacy. Retrieved from http://simons.berkeley.edu/workshops/bigdata2013-4

Smith, C. (2016) Russian Social Networks Stats, Digital Marketing ramblings (DMR). *Expandedramblings.com.* Retrieved from http://expandedramblings.com/index.php/russian-social-media-stats-yandex-vkontakte/

Smith, P., & Zook, Z. (2011). *Marketing Communications: Integrating Offline with Social Media.* London: Kogan Page.

Smith, P. R., Berry, C., & Pulford, A. (1999). *Strategic Marketing Communications: New Ways to Build and Integrate Communications.* London: Kogan Page.

University of Roehampton. (2013) Social Sales Case Study (YouTube video). Retrieved from http://www.youtube.com/watch?v=7TbC5buIgBE

Spencer-Oatey, H. (2012). What is Culture? A Compilation of Quotations. Warwick University. Retrieved from http://www2.warwick.ac.uk/fac/soc/al/globalpad/openhouse/interculturalskills/global_pad_-_what_is_culture.pdf

Stambor, Z. (2013). Best Buy is best at resolving shoppers' complaints on social media. *Internetretailer. com*. Retrieved from http://www.internetretailer.com/mobile/2013/07/02/best-buy-best-resolving-complaints-social-media

Statisticbrain (2014). Total number of active registered Twitter users 645,750,000. Retrieved from http://www.statisticbrain.com/twitter-statistics/

Statisticbrain.com. (n. d.). YouTube company statistics. Retrieved from http://www.statisticbrain.com/youtube-statistics/

Stryker, S., & Vryan, D.K. (2006). Handbooks of Sociology and Social Research.

Stuart, H. (2014) Coke Marketing Campaign 'Share A Coke' Slammed For Alleged Anti-Gay Discrimination. *Huffington Post*. Retrieved from http://www.huffingtonpost.com/2014/01/26/share-a-coke_n_4669957.html

Sukhraj, R. (2013, August 29). 10 Social Media KPIs You Should Track and Monitor. *Impact*. Retrieved from http://www.impactbnd.com/blog/8-social-media-kpis-you-should-track-and-monitor

Tagg, C., & Seargeant, P. (2013). *The Language of Social Media: Identity and Community on the Internet*. London: Palgrave Macmillan.

Tasner, M. (2010). *Marketing in the Moment – The Practical Guide to Using Web 3.0 Marketing to Reach Your Customers First*. New Jersey: Pearson.

Techtarget. (2014). Archive for the Tech Marketing Archive topic. Retrieved from http://mktr2mktr.com/

Thackeray, R., Neiger, B. I., Hanson, C. L., & McKenzie, J. F. (2008). Enhancing Promotional Strategies Within Social Marketing Programs: Use of Web 2.0 Social Media. *Health Promotion Practice*, 9(4), 338–343. doi:10.1177/1524839908325335 PMID:18936268

Schmidt, E. (2013). Eric Schmidt's 2014 predictions: big genomics and smartphones everywhere. *The Guardian*. Retrieved from http://www.theguardian.com/technology/2013/dec/31/eric-schmidts-2014-predictions-big-genomics-and-smartphones-everywhere

The Guardian. (2014). Two jailed for Twitter abuse of feminist campaigner. Retrieved from http://www.theguardian.com/uk-news/2014/jan/24/two-jailed-twitter-abuse-feminist-campaigner

Barnett, E. (2011). Facebook cuts six degrees of Separation to Four. *The Telegraph*. Retrieved from http://www.telegraph.co.uk/technology/facebook/8906693/Facebook-cuts-six-degrees-of-separation-to-four.html

The Well. (1974). Community Memory. Retrieved from http://www.well.com/~szpak/cm/

Tian, G. T. (2001). Anthropological Approach to Consumer Science: A Practical Teaching Case Study. High Plains Applied Anthropologist, 2(21).

Tian, R. (2010). Anthropological Approach to Consumer Behavior: A Marketing Educational Case of Teaching and Learning.

Trent, S., & Mitrook, A. M. (2007). The Dialogic Potential of Weblogs in Relationship Building. *Public Relations Review*, (March), 16, 33, 227–229.

Rose, B. (2008) Zappos pays to weed out uncommitted workers. *Chicago Tribune*. Retrieved from http://articles.chicagotribune.com/2008-06-16/business/0806140083_1_zappos-litmus-works

Tuten, T. L., & Soloman, M. R. (2013). *Social media marketing*. Upper Saddle River, New Jersey: Pearson Education, Inc.

UCLA. (n. d.). Relational Models Theory. Retrieved from http://www.rmt.ucla.edu/

Urwick, F. L. (1947). The Elements of Administration (2nd ed.). London.

US Security Exchange Commission. (n. d.). SEC Says Social Media OK for Company Announcements if Investors Are Alerted, Press Release; For Immediate Release 2013-51. Retrieved from http://www.sec.gov/News/PressRelease/Detail/PressRelease/1365171513574

Van Dijk, J. A. G. M. (1997). The Reality of Virtual Communities. In J. Groebel (Ed.), *Trends in Communication I* (pp. 39–63). Amsterdam: Boom Publishers.

Van Doorn, J., Lemon, K. N., Mittal, V., Nass, S., Doreen, P., Pirner, P., & Verhoef, P. C. (2010). Customer engagement behavior: Theoretical foundations and research directions. *Journal of Service Research*, *13*(3), 252–266. doi:10.1177/1094670510375599

Warner, C., Clay-Warner, J., & Robinson, D. T. (Eds.). (2008). *Social Structure and Emotion, Wasserman, S & Faust, K (1994) Social Network Analysis: Methods and Applications*. Cambridge University Press.

Watts, D.J., & Peretti, J. (2007). Viral Marketing for the Real World. Retrieved from http://hbr.org/2007/05/viral-marketing-for-the-real-world

We Are Social. (2014). *Digital*. Social and Mobile Worldwide.

Why VK Lets Users Search For Pirated Movie. (n. d.). Retrieved from http://www.socialnetworkingwatch.com/2014/01/why-vk-lets-users-search-for-pirated-movies-.html

Zappos. (2013). About Zappos. Retrieved from http://about.zappos.com/our-unique-culture/zappos-core-values/build-open-and-honest-relationships-communication

Zikopoulos, P., Sam Lightstone, S., Matthew, H., Sachedina, A., & Baklarz, G. (2013) *Understanding Big Data: Analytics for Enterprise Class Hadoop and Streaming Data* (1st ed.). McGraw-Hill Osborne Media.

KEY TERMS AND DEFINITIONS

Consumer Oriented: Commonly implies the wants and needs of the end user of a product or service. Businesses and enterprises are encouraged to build the wants and needs of their offerings to customers. This however presumes customers are rational and know what they want. Certain schools of thought do not take this premise.

eWoM: Electronic Word of Mouth, in essence, conversations of social networks, individual conversations via devices that have the capability to scale because of the usability, platform structure, and habitual disposition of cultural habits as to how we use them on social media platforms within networks.

New Media Paradigm: Nontraditional broadcast mediums and devices that enable synchronous and asynchronous communication on multifaceted levels, adhering to different dimensions.

Social Networking Transglobal Behaviour: Behaviour on social networks that transcends national geographical boundaries.

Social Presence: Is there a dichotomy between private and social spaces? What are the asynchronous and synchronous dimensions of platforms that embody social spaces?

Symbolic Interactionism: Whereby perspective becomes the key funnel as to how and when entities engage. Commonly, this pertains to people. There is usually some visual cue functioning as a representation that anchors one to be drawn towards an item, object, or principle.

Virtual Community: A cluster of individuals in concert together with specific shared values and opinions through some connection, communicating primarily through electronic communications.

This research was previously published in Key Challenges and Opportunities in Web Entrepreneurship; pages 132-170, copyright year 2017 by Business Science Reference (an imprint of IGI Global).

Chapter 64
Role of Personalization in Shaping Attitudes Towards Social Media Ads

Gökhan Aydin
Istanbul Medipol University, Istanbul, Turkey

ABSTRACT

The present article aims to understand attitudes towards social media ads, one of the most recent and rapidly growing forms of digital advertisements. So far, little attention has been paid in developing countries to the most rapidly growing type of advertising and the present study aims to contribute to fill this research gap. A survey study was carried out to understand the attitudes using Ducoffe's advertising value model and extending it by the inclusion of "rewards" and "personalization" constructs. Facebook ads are used as a proxy for social media ads and a total of 327 questionnaires were collected from Turkish consumers, which were filtered down to 281 and analyzed using structural equation modelling. The findings indicate that credibility, personalization, informativeness and entertainment have direct positive effects on advertising value and have indirect effects on attitudes towards social media ads. Personalization emerged as a significant factor affecting all other related constructs.

INTRODUCTION

Internet has become an important tool and integral part of daily life. In line with rapidly growing population with access to the internet, new economic systems are devised, and current ones are transformed. In marketing communication, advertisements carried out through digital channels have the highest growth rates among all channels. Digital advertising spending increased by 23% in the first half of 2017 exceeding 40 billion USD according to the Interactive Advertising Bureau (IAB, 2017). This new medium is used more frequently as social media irreversibly changes the way individuals communicate. Turkey, the focal point of the present study, also experienced such growth. Digital advertising became the second largest channel with an annual growth rate of 14% in 2016 according to IAB Turkey (IAB Turkey, 2016). From a fundamental perspective, digital advertising is only a part of larger digital mar-

DOI: 10.4018/978-1-7998-9020-1.ch064

keting activities, which may be carried through the media that is owned, earned or paid for (Strauss & Frost, 2013). Organizations' reach on owned media, the channels they directly control is currently on decline (Delo, 2013). For instance, depending on the type of the content shared on its Facebook pages, a brand can only reach between 2% and 8% of its followers (DeMers, 2015). This figure was 16% on average in 2012 (O'Reilly, 2015). Modifications that social media sites such as Facebook have made to relevant algorithms in recent years are among the main reasons that have led to a decrease in organic reach (DeMers, 2015). This decrease has been directing organizations towards using digital advertising and advertisements (Sloane, 2015). Accordingly, Facebook promoted posts almost doubled to 17% of all posts in 2014 compared to 9% in 2013 (O'Reilly, 2015). The forecasts of Zenith Media indicate that social media advertising spending will grow by 20% annually till the end of 2019, when it will be worth 50 billion USD (Zenith, 2016). Among other factors, increasing spending on social media may also be attributed to the emergence of native advertising. Native advertising is defined as a type of advertising that is designed to blend into page content and is consistent with the general aspect of the page and the media platform (IAB, 2013). Native advertising holds promise and is considered superior to display ads in terms of avoidance and engagement (Cho & Cheon, 2004; FTC, 2013; Pophal, 2014). In a study by online marketing firm HubShout, 66% of internet users preferred to click on sponsored articles over banner ads (Pophal, 2014). Consequently, the spending on native ads are on the rise. The State of the News Media 2014 report by Pew Research Center reported an increase of 43% in native advertising spending from 2012 to 2013 (Mitchell, 2014).

In line with rapidly growing and changing digital marketing environment, the present study aims to understand attitudes towards social media ads and to reveal the factors affecting attitude formation. The relevant literature is analyzed to set a framework for this study and define the predecessors of attitudes towards digital ads.

THEORETICAL FRAMEWORK

Most of the relevant studies on digital advertising have utilized traditional advertising models and tested their validity in various digital channels (Haghirian, Madlberger, & Tanuskova, 2005; Tsang, Ho, & Liang, 2004). Despite an increase in the number of the studies on these issues, fragmentation of digital media have been continually creating new areas of interest (Schlosser, Shavitt, & Kanfer, 1999; Wolin, Korgaonkar, & Lund, 2002). In terms of cultural and geographical coverage, the extant literature is predominantly focused on developed countries with strong technological infrastructures and large proportions of consumers have already been exposed to digital channels and advertisements (Wang & Sun, 2010). Developing countries on the other hand, lag behind developed counterparts in terms of infrastructure, internet penetration levels and previous experience with digital media (United Nations Development Programme, 2013). Furthermore, differences between Western and Eastern cultures may lead to differing attitudes towards ads as experienced in the previous studies (Ferle & Lee, 2003; Zhou, Zhang, & Vertinsky, 2002). This creates an important research gap in the literature focusing on developing countries and different cultures. New studies in this rapidly growing field will contribute to the understanding of consumer attitudes in different settings as well as providing ways to improve attitudes by revealing significant antecedents for marketing practitioners.

Social Media Sites

Traditional social networks, which preceded their virtual counterparts focused on face-to-face relationships between friends or parties with potential mutual interests. Currently, social networks (social media sites) refers to web-based services that offer online virtual communities interacting with each other by computer mediated communication tools. Social media and web-based social media can be briefly defined as "a group of internet-based applications that were built on the ideological and technological foundations of Web 2.0 and that allow creation and exchange of user generated content" (Kaplan & Haenlein, 2010).

The increasing popularity of social media sites and their use for marketing purposes has multiple basis. First of all, interactivity is among the major benefits offered by these sites over traditional media that utilize one-way communication. Interactivity is found to affect user attitudes towards websites (McMillan, Hwang, & Lee, 2003). Differing from other types of digital ads such as web and email ads, social media advertising messages such as Facebook ads/promoted messages are harder to block by users (Frier & Stone, 2015). There are only a limited number of ad-blocking tools that claim to block Facebook ads (i.e. Facebook AdBlock). Targeting different customer groups are also easier in social media sites such as Facebook and Twitter, which offer several filtering options. For instance, Facebook offers targeting opportunities by providing hundreds of options organized under four basic categories (demographics, place, interests and use behavior) that can lead to thousands of unique consumer groups (Facebook, 2015). Moreover, by offering promoted pages or ads to users by displaying names of their friends who have previously interacted (liked, commented etc.) with, social media sites can provide higher credibility for the content they promote.

Among social media sites, Facebook is currently the most popular in the world with more than 1.4 billion active members, 82% of whom are from outside the U.S. (Socialbakers, 2015). Its members use Facebook to connect, communicate, interact and stay in touch with their friends and family accessing it from PCs or mobile devices (Steinfield, Ellison, & Lampe, 2008). In addition to multi-platform accessibility, high adoption rates in the developing and developed countries make it a unique medium to reach consumers in a wide range of regions. In Turkey, there are over 35 million Facebook accounts corresponding to more than 90% of the country's connected population (Gemius, 2014; Kara, 2015). Facebook is the second most popular site among internet users in Turkey after google.com in page views (IAB Turkey, 2017).

In addition to its popularity among users, Facebook is also the most popular social media site for advertisers. As of June 2015, there are more than 2.5 million advertisers on Facebook, which demonstrates a 25% increase experienced just in 6 months (Sterling, 2015). Facebook is increasing its share of online advertising spending especially in the mobile segment. According to the projections by eMarketer, Facebook will realize strong growth and reach 20.3% of the rapidly growing mobile advertising market by 2017 in the U.S. (Marshall, 2015). In 2014, 19 billion USD was spent on mobile advertising, which corresponds to an increase of 78% since 2013 (Olmstead & Lu, 2015). The popularity among users and advertisers makes Facebook a good platform for social media related marketing studies. Accordingly, Facebook was chosen as the setting of the present study to reveal attitudes towards social media ads.

Advertising Value and Attitudes Towards Ads

Despite the increased interest in digital advertising in the last decade, empirical research focusing on different forms of this type of advertising is limited due to an increasing fragmentation of advertising mediums (Karson, McCloy, & Bonner, 2006). There are studies that focus on SMS ads (Barwise & Strong, 2002; Tsang et al., 2004), email ads (Cheng, Blankson, Wang, & Chen, 2009; Martin, Van Durme, Raulas, & Merisavo, 2003), e-advertising (Cho & Cheon, 2004; Wolin & Korgaonkar, 2003) and banner ads (Hong, Thong, & Tam, 2004). Social media advertising, which is the focus of the present study, is a relatively new field in advertising where the literature is currently proliferating (Alalwan, Rana, Dwivedi, & Algharabat, 2017; Chang, Chen, & Tan, 2012; De Keyzer, Dens, & De Pelsmacker, 2015; Duffett, 2015; Ha, Park, & Lee, 2014; Jung, Shim, Jin, & Khang, 2016; Knoll, 2016; Lin & Kim, 2016; Lukka & James, 2014; Stavrianea & Kavoura, 2015; Tran, 2017).

Among the existing advertising literature, Ducoffe's (1995, 1996) advertising value model is among the more popular models utilized in explaining consumer beliefs and attitudes towards various forms of digital advertising. This model was developed for analyzing web advertising by Ducoffe (1995) and focused on the value created by advertising rather than attitudes. Advertising value was defined as *"the subjective evaluation of the relative worth or utility of advertising to consumers"*. Satisfaction for consumers (recipients of the advertisement) can only be provided if perceived value of the advertisement itself is high enough to meet consumers' expectations. Several researchers adopted this approach to reveal relevant factors creating value for customers (Jung et al., 2016; Kim & Han, 2014). This model was developed upon the Uses and Gratifications Theory (UGT), a consumer-centric approach that was originally established by Katz et al. (1973) to explain consumer motivations and effectiveness of mass communication media. In UGT, cognitive needs, affective needs, personal and social integrative needs and relaxation needs are considered as fundamental 'needs and gratification' categories. The model developed by Ducoffe (1995) incorporated cognitive needs through informativeness and credibility constructs and affective needs through entertainment and irritation constructs. This approach suggesting affective needs and experiences for measuring individual's judgments of advertising is in harmony with the popular tripartite attitude theory by Rosenberg and Hovland (Eagly & Chaiken, 1998; Rosenberg & Hovland, 1960; Schlosser et al., 1999). This theory accepts affective, cognitive and behavioral experiences as the antecedents of attitude. The third dimension of this attitudinal model, lacking in Ducoffe's model, which incorporates behavioral experiences, was also found to affect attitude formation by Schlosser et al. (1999). This dimension was operationalized using the "advertising utility" construct in Schlosser et al.'s study. Likewise, "tangible rewards" are introduced to incorporate behavioral experiences factor in the present study.

A separate line of research on this field utilizes the well-known Technology Acceptance Model, and usefulness factor which can be considered similar to ad value in advertising context was found to affect user attitudes in the literature (Lin & Kim, 2016).

Attitudes Towards Digital Advertisements

The studies focused on consumer behavior in digital advertising literature provide mixed results in terms of overall attitudes. Various studies focusing on e-mail, banner, web and mobile advertising contexts (Cho & Cheon, 2004; Korgaonkar, Silverblatt, & Becerra, 2010; Luna Cortés & Royo Vela, 2013; Martin et al., 2003; Mehta & Sivadas, 1995; Tsang et al., 2004; Usta, 2009; Wolin et al., 2002) found the attitudes towards these types of advertising to be negative. However, two studies in Turkey (Barutçu, 2007; Ünal, Ercis, & Keser, 2011) found more favorable attitudes towards this new medium of advertising. Some of these differences may be explained by the inclusion of both push and pull type ads under one digital advertising category. Web-based ads basically pull consumers towards the marketers' content, whereas email, SMS and similar advertisements push the marketers' message to consumers (Schlosser et al., 1999; Wolin & Korgaonkar, 2003). From this perspective, it is natural to have varying consumer attitudes in different categories of digital advertising.

Moreover, related studies show that overall attitudes are usually slightly favorable or slightly unfavorable. Consequently, we can assume that users have no strong opinions against these advertisements. In this setting, it is indispensable to understand and analyze the antecedents of attitude to manage ads successfully.

Social media advertising has similarities to other digital advertising mediums, especially mobile advertising. The internet and social media sites including Facebook are accessed through mobile devices more frequently in developed countries and regions such as the U.S.A. and Europe (Chaffey, 2016; ComScore, 2014). According to a recent earnings announcement, over half of all Facebook users access the service exclusively on mobile devices (Facebook, 2016). Moreover, limited fixed line infrastructure in underdeveloped countries leads to greater use of mobile communication systems (United Nations Development Programme, 2013). Consequently, the probability of encountering social media ads on mobile devices is increasing every day (Hoelzel, 2014).

Personalization options are more abundant in mobile and social media ads compared to other digital marketing alternatives. Consequently, studies on mobile advertising may offer good insights to researchers of social media advertising. Another similar research area is internet ads (banner etc.), where the medium is also suitable for interactivity and two-way communication. Given the similarities, there are also differences, the basic one being the way messages are delivered. The use of quickly distinguishable elements as advertisements (i.e. static banners, roll-over banners etc.) is more common in traditional media. Conversely, the advertisement content is usually hard to distinguish from user generated content in social media. The high number of (over 1,700 per month) banner ads shown to consumers creates a so-called banner-blindness (Benway & Lane, 1998). On the contrary, social media sites offer a more subtle way of presenting ads among newsfeeds (Morrissey, 2013). In practice, only about 40% of the users can distinguish native ads and real news (Pogue, 2015). This lack of recognition is demonstrated even more clearly by the findings of Wojdynski and Evans (2016) where only 8% of the participants recognized the native advertisements they are shown in an experimental study. Consequently, the attitudes towards Facebook promoted ads (a native advertisement) and their antecedents may be dissimilar to the other digital channels (Duffett, 2015).

In the present study, Ducoffe's advertising value (ad value) model was adopted and extended by the inclusion of personalization and tangible rewards constructs. The factors incorporated into the study as the antecedents of ad value and attitudes are discussed in the following sections.

Personalization

Currently, consumers are bombarded by ad messages every day and the number of these messages can reach to several thousand if labels and similar visual cues are considered as ad messages (Johnson, 2014; Smith, n.d.). The high number of messages received can be considered as one of the factors that have led to overall negative attitudes towards ads (Mittal, 1994). On the other hand, digital channels provide abundant opportunities for personalization of the messages. It should be noted that the significance of personalization is not limited to the advertising industry. Personalization was found to be a critical factor for e-retailers and appears as a significant factor in persuasion of the consumers (Pappas, Kourouthanassis, Giannakos, & Chrissikopoulos, 2017). Focusing on advertisements, personalization of the message content or the delivery can both create value. There are several ways to personalize messages using demographics, interests and behavior data in social media sites (Facebook, 2015; Tran, 2017), which are mediums that collects and stores noteworthy amounts of personal data. In experimental and survey studies carried out on personalization, consumers are found to be more receptive to ads personalized for them and provide a more positive response (De Keyzer et al., 2015; DeZoysa, 2002; Kim & Han, 2014; Robins, 2003; Walrave, Poels, Antheunis, Van den Broeck, & van Noort, 2016). Consequently, customized and targeted messages can offer superior value to the receiver and sender of the message with less frequent but customized deliveries. Personalization of the ad can make it more informative, less irritating and more entertaining for the consumer. Furthermore, the personalization may create trust in the receiver and can affect the credibility of the ad. These effects are tested and verified in mobile advertising by Kim and Han (2014) and in social media (Facebook) context by Tran (2017). In accordance with the literature, the following hypotheses are proposed:

H$_1$: Personalization has a positive effect on ad credibility
H$_2$: Personalization has a positive effect on perceived entertainment
H$_3$: Personalization has a positive effect on informativeness
H$_4$: Personalization has a positive effect on irritation risk mitigation

It was intuitively expected that a message tailored to specific users taking into account their demographics, interests and use behavior will lead to higher perceived value and positive attitudes among consumers, which was also corroborated in the related literature (Kim & Han, 2014; Xu, 2006; Xu, Liao, & Li, 2008).

H$_5$: Personalization has a positive effect on Facebook advertising value

Credibility

Credibility is among the primary factors affecting the ad value and attitudes towards ads in the existing literature (Ducoffe, 1995; MacKenzie & Lutz, 1989). Mackenzie and Lutz (1989) defined advertisement credibility as "the extent to which the consumers perceive the claims about the brand/product advertised in the advertisement to be truthful and believable". The credibility of an advertisement incorporates the credibility of the advertisement source (institution) as well as the credibility of the ad message itself (MacKenzie & Lutz, 1989). The degree of reliability, accuracy and trustworthiness of the advertisement itself and the advertisement source as perceived by the consumers affect their attitudes towards the ad and the perceived ad value (Brackett & Carr, 2001; Goldsmith, Lafferty, & Newell, 2000). This effect was detected in various settings including web-based ads and mobile ads (Altuna & Konuk, 2009; Brackett & Carr, 2001; Choi, Hwang, & McMillan, 2008; Chowdhury, Parvin, Weitenberner, & Becker, 2006; Okazaki, 2004; Xu et al., 2008). Consequently, the credibility factor was incorporated into the model and the following hypothesis was proposed:

H$_6$: Credibility has a positive effect on Facebook advertising value

Entertainment

The enjoyment obtained from the advertisements is considered as one of the antecedents of advertising value and studied under entertainment construct in the literature. Enjoyment of media is considered as a significant intrinsic motivation element (Davis, Bagozzi, & Warshaw, 1992). According to McQuail, (1983) perceived entertainment of an ad represents the ability to satisfy consumers' need for escapism, diversion, aesthetic enjoyment or emotional release. This motivational factor analyzed in empirical studies was found to have a positive effect on acceptance, adoption and use intention of new technologies such as internet, mobile devices and social media (Agrifoglio & Black, 2012; Lee, Xiong, & Hu, 2012; Leng & Lada, 2011; Thong, Hong, & Tam, 2006; Venkatesh & Davis, 2000). In the context of advertising, consumers develop positive attitudes towards the ads they perceive as entertaining and their interest and loyalty may be increased through the use of entertaining ads (Haghirian et al., 2005; Shavitt, Lowrey, & Haefner, 1998; Xu, 2006). These effects on attitudes and intentions were witnessed in digital advertisements including web banners, email, mobile and social media ads (Choi et al., 2008; Haghirian et al., 2005; Liu, Sinkovics, Pezderka, & Haghirian, 2012; Tsang et al., 2004; Zhang & Mao, 2016) and in particular studies the entertainment factor appeared as the most important factor affecting overall attitudes towards digital advertisements (Petrovici & Marinov, 2010; Shavitt et al., 1998; Tsang et al., 2004; Xu et al., 2008). Consequently, it is assumed that:

H$_7$: Perceived entertainment has a positive effect on Facebook advertising value

Informativeness

Depending on UGT, information delivery of a medium is considered as a need-satisfying function. Information provided in advertisements should be timely, relevant and accurate to be of value (Milne & Gordon, 1993; Siau & Shen, 2003). Informativeness provides the content utility of an advertisement to consumers (Tsang et al., 2004). This factor as one of the cognitive dimensions of Ducoffe's advertising value model was found to affect consumer attitudes towards ads in various contexts (Bauer, Barnes, Reichardt, & Neumann, 2005; Choi et al., 2008; Ducoffe, 1996; Tsang et al., 2004; Zhang & Mao, 2016). The informativeness factor was incorporated into the proposed model with the following hypothesis:

H$_8$: Informativeness has a positive effect on Facebook advertising value

Irritation

The advertising messages that consumers receive may be perceived as confusing, distracting, manipulative or even offensive (Ducoffe, 1995), which is likely to irritate receivers. Consequently, irritation dimension is considered an important factor in diminishing advertising value and in developing negative attitudes towards advertisements (Ducoffe, 1996; Liu et al., 2012; Schlosser et al., 1999). Irritation factor may be particularly important for messages received on Facebook, which is a medium used for sharing and viewing personal content. Studies on traditional and digital advertising found irritation as a significant element affecting attitudes towards advertisements negatively. For instance, in mobile advertising, which is a similar digital and personal medium, irritation was found to diminish advertising value (Altuna & Konuk, 2009; Luna Cortés & Royo Vela, 2013; Okazaki, 2004; Tsang et al., 2004; Ünal et al., 2011;

Wong, 2010). In a recent study controversial adverts was fund to irritate consumers and lead to avoidance of ads on social media (Ferreira, Moraes, Michaelidou, & McGrath, 2017). Therefore, irritation was incorporated into the model in the present study and is predicted to adversely affect advertising value and attitudes towards Facebook ads.

H$_9$: Irritation has a negative effect on Facebook advertising value
H$_{10}$: Irritation has a negative effect on attitudes towards Facebook ads

Tangible Rewards

It was seen that consumers' concentration on ads increases when advertising message includes tangible benefits that can fulfill their needs (Kim & Han, 2014). Consumers are eager to try to obtain these benefits, which can be presented as discount coupons, free sample gifts, competitions or sweepstakes. These incentives that relate to behavioral experiences create value for consumers by increasing usefulness of advertisement messages through the presentation of tangible benefits (Kim & Han, 2014; Varnali, Yilmaz, & Toker, 2012). This construct compliments the utility obtained by customers through informativeness and entertainment dimensions. With this perspective, tangible rewards construct was incorporated into the study with the following hypothesis:

H$_{11}$: Tangible rewards have a positive effect on Facebook advertising value

RESEARCH OBJECTIVES AND METHODOLOGY

The objective of the present research is to address the following questions that were contemplated in the theoretical framework section:

- Are overall attitudes towards social media advertising favorable?
- What are the significant antecedents of social media ad value and attitudes towards social media advertising?
- Does personalization play an important role in ad value and attitude formation?

The present study focuses on Facebook in Turkey, the 7th largest country in the world in terms of Facebook membership (BoomSocial, 2015). Turkey with a population of roughly 80 million is situated at the crossroads of Asia and Europe and despite being majorly Muslim has a secular administrative and legal system. Turkish consumers are under the influence of the Western modern society and values as well as traditions and mysticism of the Middle Eastern cultures creating a unique setting for consumer behavior studies.

Facebook sponsored ads were chosen as the focus of this study. These advertisements are presented in users' newsfeed labeled as promoted messages. Explanations provided in the questionnaire were devised to make social media advertisement clear for all respondents.

The model that was developed based on the relevant literature to address the research questions is visualized in Figure 1.

Figure 1. Proposed Model

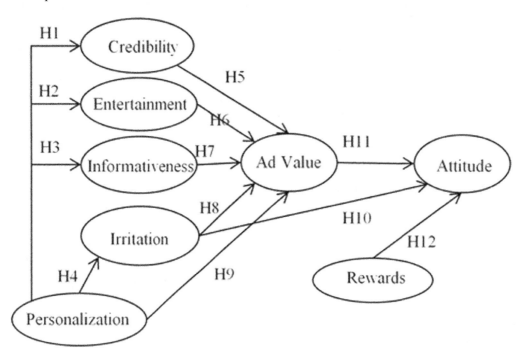

Sampling and Measurement

Convenience and snowball sampling methods were used in the selection of respondents. No demographic quotas were used in sampling except for excluding users younger than 18 years of age. The questionnaire that is presented in Table 5 in Appendix was posted and promoted on Facebook pages of the researcher, researcher's connections and on various group pages.

As can be derived from the sample demographics provided in Table 1, more than half of the respondents were members of Generation-Y followed by 38% from Generation-Z and Generation-X and older generation making up the remaining 10%. Internet penetration rate in Turkey is 70% among the 12-24 age group and the highest rate (76%) is seen in the 18-24 group (Gemius, 2014). Consequently, we can assume that age distribution of the sample is similar to the overall Turkish internet users' age distribution. One demographic that deviates from the overall internet user base is the education level. Almost half of the respondents indicated that they have a university or a higher degree, while university degree holders make up only 14% of all Turkish internet users (Gemius, 2014).

Analysis and Results

Before the path analysis, descriptive statistics of the collected data presented in Table 6 in Appendix were examined. It was seen that only 12% of the respondents answered the entertainment items favorably (4 and 5 on 5-point Likert scale). The same figure for informativeness and credibility were 14% and 11%, respectively. The advertising value and attitude constructs have similar unfavorable respondent feedback with only 10% of the respondents answering favorably. Of irritation items, 42% were answered favorably indicating an irritation towards social media ads. The average scores barely above 2 for attitudes and advertising value revealed the negative disposition of users towards SNS advertisements. Personalization construct that reflects the degree of ads' perceived personalization was again unfavorable but to a lesser extent than other constructs with average item score of 2.60.

Table 1. Sample Demographics and Facebook Use Experience

Demographic	Value	Frequencies	Percent
Gender	Female	143	50.9%
	Male	138	49.1%
Age	18-21 (Gen Z)	107	38.1%
	22-29 (Gen Y)	62	22.1%
	30-37 (Gen Y)	84	29.9%
	38-49 (Gen X)	23	8.2%
	50+	5	1.8%
Education	Elementary School	2	0.7%
	High School	140	49.8%
	University	67	23.8%
	Graduate / PhD	72	25.6%
Income (USD Equivalent)	0-1000$	69	24.5%
	1,001$-2,000$	104	37.0%
	2,001$-3,000$	50	17.8%
	3,001$+	57	20.3%
Facebook Member Since	Less Than 3 Years	17	6.1%
	3-6 Years	97	34.5%
	More Than 6 years	167	59.4%

Another important finding of the descriptive analysis was that 23 out of 33 items showed significant Kurtosis and 19 items significant skewness. Consequently, a SEM technique that can work with non-normal distributions, namely partial least squares structural equation modelling (PLS-SEM) was selected to carry out path analysis. Validity and reliability of the measures are discussed below and assessment results are provided in Table 2.

To test the internal consistency reliability of the model, Cronbach's alpha (CA) and composite reliability (CR) criteria were used. As seen in Table 2, CA and CR for all the variables were higher than 0.7 threshold (Nunnally, 1978). Indicators' loadings on their own constructs were compared to the loadings on the other constructs to test whether validity was established. As can be seen in Table 6 in Appendix, the cross-loadings were lower than outer loadings for all the items. Following this confirmation, an approach proposed by Fornell and Larcker (1981) that compares the correlations between the items with the square roots of average variance extracted (AVE) was utilized. The inter-item correlations were lower than square root of AVE (Hair, Hult, Ringle, & Sarstedt, 2013). In addition, all the loadings and AVE were above the recommended levels (>0.5). In the light of these findings, the validity and reliability conditions were considered satisfied and the PLS-SEM model (Figure 2) was evaluated using coefficients of determination (R²), significance of path coefficients and predictive relevance (Q²) values (Hair et al., 2013, 169). R² values of 0.667 for attitudes and 0.716 for advertising value coupled with significant path coefficients indicate high prediction power. Stone-Geisser's Q² value calculated by using blindfolding procedure was also used to assess the predictive power of the model (Geisser, 1974; Stone, 1974). Q² values of 0.49 for advertising value and 0.47 for attitudes constructs, both above the 0.35 threshold, suggest large predictive relevance for the model (Hair et al., 2013; Henseler, Ringle, & Sinkovics, 2009). It can be concluded that the utilized model was able to explain the attitude formation towards social media ads.

Table 2. Validity and Reliability Analysis

Latent Variable	AVE	CR	CA	Avg. IIC.	ADV	ATT	CRE	PER	ENT	INF	IRT	REW
ADV	0.710	0.880	0.796	0.553	**0.842***							
ATT	0.725	0.888	0.809	0.547	0.806	**0.852**						
CRE	0.538	0.821	0.710	0.415	0.719	0.686	**0.734**					
PER	0.580	0.845	0.781	0.276	0.520	0.500	0.470	**0.762**				
ENT	0.606	0.857	0.780	0.441	0.723	0.681	0.542	0.373	**0.779**			
INF	0.654	0.883	0.823	0.472	0.726	0.703	0.667	0.428	0.668	**0.808**		
IRT	0.629	0.870	0.805	-0.250	-0.383	-0.386	-0.363	-0.192	-0.413	-0.346	**0.793**	
REW	0.777	0.913	0.857	0.471	0.653	0.604	0.581	0.387	0.568	0.532	-0.272	**0.881**

* The square root of average variance extracted is provided on the diagonal. Avg. IIC: Average inter-item correlations.

Figure 2. Path Analysis Results

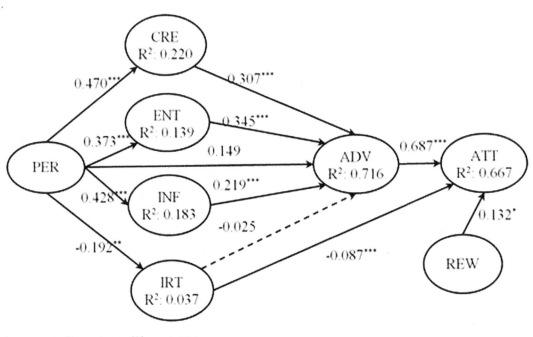

ᵖp ≤ 0.05; ᵖᵖp ≤ 0.01; ᵖᵖᵖp ≤ 0.001

As indicated in Table 3, all the hypotheses were supported except for irritation's effect on advertising value. Among the antecedents of advertising value, entertainment construct had the largest direct effect followed by credibility, informativeness and lastly personalization. Similar significant effects of entertainment factor on advertising value were corroborated previously in other studies (Jung et al., 2016; Tsang et al., 2004; Xu et al., 2008; Zhang & Mao, 2016). Informativeness factor appeared to be one of the factors with the weaker effects on ad value. This finding may be attributed to the wealth of information available to consumers resulting from increasing availability and accessibility of internet and communication devices.

Table 3. Inner Model Results and Hypothesis Testing

Hypothesis	Path	Path Coeff.	Std. Error	t- stat.	H-Supported?	Sign.
H_1	PER->CRE	0.4695	0.0546	8.599	Yes	<0.001
H_2	PER->ENT	0.3731	0.0529	7.053	Yes	<0.001
H_3	PER->INF	0.4275	0.0480	8.906	Yes	<0.001
H_4	PER->IRT	-0.1921	0.0629	3.054	Yes	<0.01
H_5	PER->ADV	0.3072	0.0514	5.977	Yes	<0.001
H_6	ENT->ADV	0.3450	0.0540	6.389	Yes	<0.001
H_7	INF->ADV	0.2190	0.0538	4.071	Yes	<0.001
H_8	IRT->ADV	-0.0248	0.0258	-0.961	No	-
H_9	IRT->ATT	0.1485	0.0361	4.114	Yes	<0.001
H_{10}	PER->ADV	0.1485	0.0361	4.114	Yes	<0.001
H_{11}	ADV->ATT	0.6868	0.0461	14.898	Yes	<0.001
H_{12}	REW->ATT	0.1318	0.0527	2.501	Yes	<0.05

Notes: PER: Personalization, CRE: Credibility, INF: Informativeness, ENT: Entertainment, IRT: Irritation, ADV: Ad value, ATT: Attitudes, REW: Rewards

Another finding attained in the analysis was the strong effect of advertising value on attitudes. As the perceived value of advertising increases, consumer attitudes towards ads improve considerably.

In addition to testing of hypotheses via direct effects, total effects were also calculated and the results are provided in Table 4. Total effects incorporate indirect effects through other constructs in addition to the direct effects between variables. In this way, it is possible to reveal the total effect of a variable on another construct in complex models and assess relationships more clearly.

When the total effects are analyzed, the ad value appeared as the most significant factor affecting attitudes towards social media ads. Among the predecessors of attitude, this construct was followed by personalization, entertainment, informativeness and rewards constructs in terms of effect size. All the aforementioned constructs positively affected the attitudes towards social media ads. The irritation factor had a negative effect on attitudes as expected. Ad value was affected by all its predecessors in most of the ways proposed by Ducoffe (1995, 1996) and demonstrated by several researchers (Haghirian, Madlberger, & Inoue, 2008; Liu et al., 2012) apart from irritation. Irritation's theoretical effect on advertising value was not detected in this study, which was also observed in the recent studies on similar digital media (Choi et al., 2008; Chowdhury et al., 2006; Xu et al., 2008). This phenomenon may be attributed to users' increased power and higher control over advertisements on digital media. Users can easily skip the advertisements on Facebook, which is not always possible in traditional channels such as advertisements presented in movie theaters. In addition, social media ads are personalized to a certain extent according to their users' demographics and interest areas, which can also lead to lower significance of irritation for the consumers. Excluding irritation's effect on advertising value, the findings corroborated all the expected relationships proposed in the relevant theories. Consequently, personalization, credibility, entertainment and informativeness were found to be significant antecedents of ad value and or attitudes towards Facebook ads. Theoretical and practical implications of these findings are discussed in the next section.

Table 4. Total Effects

Path	Total Effects	Std. Error	t-statistics	Sign.
ADV -> ATT	0.6868	0.0461	14.898	<0.001
CRE -> ADV	0.3072	0.0514	5.977	<0.001
CRE -> ATT	0.2110	0.0384	5.495	<0.001
PER -> ADV	0.5198	0.0427	12.173	<0.001
PER -> ATT	0.3737	0.0410	9.115	<0.001
PER-> CRE	0.4695	0.0546	8.599	<0.001
PER -> ENT	0.3731	0.0529	7.053	<0.001
PER -> INF	0.4275	0.0480	8.906	<0.001
PER -> IRT	-0.1921	0.0631	3.044	<0.01
ENT -> ADV	0.3450	0.0540	6.389	<0.001
ENT -> ATT	0.2369	0.0405	5.849	<0.001
INF -> ADV	0.2190	0.0538	4.071	<0.001
INF -> ATT	0.1504	0.0380	3.958	<0.001
IRT -> ADV	-0.0248	0.0352	0.705	-
IRT -> ATT	-0.1038	0.0420	2.471	<0.05
REW -> ATT	0.1318	0.0528	2.496	<0.01

THEORETICAL AND MANAGERIAL IMPLICATIONS

The present study provides findings and insights that are consistent to relevant literature in terms of the influence of personalization on consumer attitudes and responses (De Keyzer et al., 2015; Tran, 2017; Walrave et al., 2016). As can be seen from the findings, when the indirect effects were incorporated, personalization factor affected all the other constructs it is related to. These results demonstrate that perceived personalization of advertisements plays a critical role in improving customers perception of ads on social media sites. We can infer that personalized advertising on social media sites leads to more positive consumer attitudes and responses than non-personalized advertising. Personalization factor has the ability to lower negative effects (as seen in personalization's negative effect on irritation) and to improve positive factors (i.e. entertainment, credibility) that lead to advertising value and attitudes. In fact, the personalization construct had the largest total effect on advertising value considering the indirect effect. This can mainly be attributed to the fact that personalized ads are perceived as more relevant by the consumers. Another relevant factor is the increasing power and control of consumers on digital channels. Consumers demand seamless experiences tailored to their needs. Advertisements that are catered to their needs, values, lifestyles and use behavior were perceived as more valuable. Advertisers should carefully develop personalized ad messages to create accordance between the target consumers' interests /characteristics and the advertisement. If this relevancy cannot be perceived by the receiver of the message, ad value will not increase and attitudes and will not improve. The shift in digital advertising towards social media advertising may be partly attributed to the personalization opportunities provided by these networks. Marketing practitioners are encouraged to prefer customizable channels and personalize advertising message content to reach smaller segments with more targeted ads.

The second largest effect on ad value was created by the entertainment factor. The perceived entertainment of the advertising messages was considered as a more significant factor for the respondents than other factors such as the perceived informativeness. This indicates that consumers find more value in entertaining messages than informative messages provided in Facebook ads. This phenomenon was observed in other relevant studies as well (Choi et al., 2008; Haghirian et al., 2005; Liu et al., 2012; Tsang et al., 2004). The credibility, which also appeared as a significant factor that positively affects ad value, had only a moderate effect on this construct. Credibility of the message and the institution providing the message was an important factor affecting ad value and attitudes towards the ads in social media. Misleading messages that appear in the newsfeeds of consumers can diminish the credibility and result in negative attitudes. Improving the personalization helps in improving the credibility of the message, which is an important finding for companies and brands yet to establish high brand awareness in target markets.

The rewards construct also had a significant positive effect on attitudes, however this effect was limited (path coefficient: 0.132). Respondents' attitudes can only be changed slightly using tangible rewards in social media advertisements. Tangible rewards can be used to increase click-thru rates as consumers want to obtain these benefits however they alone are not strong enough to change attitudes. Marketing practitioners are encouraged to use them sparingly and concentrate on more significant factors mentioned in the previous paragraphs.

CONCLUSION AND LIMITATIONS

The present study investigates the attitudes towards social media ads based on findings from Turkey, a country ranking among the leading use frequency and membership of Facebook. By using well established scales, this study offers replication opportunities for researchers.

First, overall attitudes towards social media ads were found to be unfavorable in the present study. Only 10% of the respondents held positive attitudes towards social media ads. The largest effect on the attitudes originated from advertising value. Advertising value and attitude constructs have common foundations, thus this finding is in accordance with the theoretical framework.

Among the antecedents of ad value, only the effect of irritation was found to be insignificant. All the other factors affected advertising value positively. On the other hand, irritation affected the attitudes towards advertising directly as also observed in literature (Logan et al., 2012; Luna Cortés and Royo Vela, 2013). Informativeness factor emerged as the construct with the smallest effect on ad value. Originally, this factor was one of the two major factors affecting ad value in Ducoffe's (1996) study along with entertainment factor. On the other hand, more recent studies support the weak effect of informativeness on ad value and attitudes (Choi et al., 2008; Tsang et al., 2004) or even lack of it (Jung et al., 2016). This may be attributed to readily available and easily accessible information on brands and products enabled by the internet and advancing communication technologies. Alternative ways to access information at the time of consumers' choice decrease the informative value of advertisements for consumers. We can conclude that perceived informativeness of an advertisement is still a significant factor for consumers; however perceived value of this factor has decreased in the previous decades. The diminishing information value of advertisements may be offset by offering fun and entertaining content in advertising messages to attract target audience's interest. This is especially important on a social media site that is used frequently for entertainment purposes in addition to communication and sharing content. Marketers should be aware that in order to draw an audience, away from their personal business to watch and interact with a message, that message must be entertaining (Fox-Davies, 2016).

Social media sites have emerged as promising mediums to channel digital marketing communication efforts by offering good personalization opportunities. The expected significant role of personalization in attitude formation was validated in the present study. According to the findings, personalizing advertisements can lead to higher information and entertainment value for consumers. Moreover, advertisements' / advertisers' credibility can also be improved by personalization as seen in literature (Tran, 2017). In accordance with these outcomes, personalization appeared as the most important factor affecting ad value and the second most important factor affecting attitudes towards social ads. This effect on attitude was indirect and created through ad value antecedents and advertising value itself. Similarly, a significant portion of the effect of personalization on advertising value was indirect and observed through other constructs (advertising value antecedents).

Rewards construct's effect on attitude formation was also found to be positive and significant. Offering tangible benefits to consumers may improve their attitudes towards social media ads. Tangible rewards are frequently promoted in advertisements by marketers, but their effectiveness on shaping attitudes is limited according to the findings. Relying solely on tangible rewards in marketing communication may not be sufficient to improve attitudes to a large extent.

Finally, we can conclude that Facebook ads have not been embraced by consumers yet. Most of the respondents in the present study found advertisements on their newsfeed irritating and developed negative attitudes. Social media ads were found neither informative nor entertaining by majority of the respondents. Consequently, consumers cannot obtain significant value from these ads that lead to low perceived advertising values. Credibility of the ads was also questioned by the respondents. The ads promoted on Facebook in Turkey occasionally include deceptive offers and misleading messages. This may lead to credibility issues for the institutions and their advertising messages on this medium. Not dissimilar to banner ads, this may pose a problem for Facebook in terms of calling consumers to action in the long run. The low credibility of ads promoted on this medium may be attributable to the previous unpleasant experiences of the users and to poor control mechanisms in operation on Facebook's part. Among the analyzed factors, personalization probably offers the best promise for advertisers that are eager to utilize social media ads. Customizing advertisements according to interest areas, activities, demographics and behavior of the consumers can lead to improvements in ad value and attitudes towards social media ads.

Limitations and Future Research Avenues

Application of non-random sampling method in the present study resulted in a sample reflecting internet using population in Turkey in terms of gender and age distribution, however with a higher education level. For future studies, working with larger samples reflecting the point of view of a wider range of consumer segments may offer valuable insights.

The present study is limited to Facebook and ads provided on this platform. Albeit it is the largest social media site throughout the world, there are also several alternative platforms for advertisers. This creates a limitation in the scope of the study and the findings may not be generalized to all social networking sites.

Another limitation is due to the ever-changing nature of social media advertising. Social media sites such as Facebook are frequently changing their advertising policies and algorithms. These changes are not limited to but include the way advertising messages are presented to consumers. Future research on this dynamic topic is needed to provide up-to-date information and insights to marketing academicians and practitioners. Comparing results of studies carried out in previous years with more recent ones may provide insights into the effects of changes in Facebook's advertising policies.

The present study has revealed various factors' effects on attitudes on social media sites utilizing a questionnaire. In this type of self-evaluation studies, respondents' perceptions and previous experiences are evaluated by themselves. Another future research avenue may be providing insights into each factor's effect on behavior by conducting experimental designs. For instance, the studies on personalization by De Keyzer et al. (2015) and Walrave et al. (2016) may shed light to prospective researchers in this area. Utilizing different methodologies to confirm the findings will help establishing generalizability of the present and similar studies' implications.

REFERENCES

Agrifoglio, R., & Black, S. (2012). Extrinsic vs. Intrinsic Motivation in Continued Twitter Usage. *Journal of Computer IS*, *53*(1), 33–41.

Alalwan, A. A., Rana, N. P., Dwivedi, Y. K., & Algharabat, R. (2017). Social media in marketing: A review and analysis of the existing literature. *Telematics and Informatics*, (May). doi:10.1016/j.tele.2017.05.008

Altuna, O. K., & Konuk, F. A. (2009). Understanding Consumer Attitudes Toward Mobile Advertising and its Impact on Consumers' Behavioral Intention: A ross-market comparison of U.S. and Turkish Consumers. *International Journal of Mobile Marketing*, *4*(2), 43–51.

Barutçu, S. (2007). Attitudes Towards Mobile Marketing Tools: A study of Turkish Consumers. *Journal of Targeting. Measurement and Analysis for Marketing*, *16*(1), 26–38. doi:10.1057/palgrave.jt.5750061

Barwise, P., & Strong, C. (2002). Permission-based mobile advertising. *Journal of Interactive Marketing*, *16*(1), 14–24. doi:10.1002/dir.10000

Bauer, H., Barnes, S., Reichardt, T., & Neumann, M. (2005). Driving consumer acceptance of mobile marketing: A theoretical framework and empirical study. *Journal of Electronic Commerce Research*, *6*(3), 181–192.

Benway, J. P., & Lane, D. (1998). Banner Blindness: Web Searchers Often Miss "Obvious" Links. *Internetworking*, *1*(3), 1–11.

BoomSocial. (2015). Country Stats. Retrieved September 8, 2015, from http://www.boomsocial.com/ EN/Facebook/Countries

Brackett, L. K., & Carr, B. N. Jr. (2001). Cyberspace advertising vs. other media: Consumer vs. mature student attitudes. *Journal of Advertising Research*, *41*(5), 23–32. doi:10.2501/JAR-41-5-23-32

Chaffey, D. (2016). Global social media research summary 2016. Retrieved May 4, 2016, from http://www. smartinsights.com/social-media-marketing/social-media-strategy/new-global-social-media-research/

Chang, K. T. T., Chen, W., & Tan, B. C. Y. (2012). Advertising Effectiveness in Social Networking Sites: Social Ties, Expertise, and Product Type. *IEEE Transactions on Engineering Management*, *59*(4), 634–643. doi:10.1109/TEM.2011.2177665

Cheng, J. M. S., Blankson, C., Wang, E. S. T., & Chen, L. S. L. (2009). Consumer attitudes and interactive digital advertising. *International Journal of Advertising*, *28*(3), 501–525. doi:10.2501/S0265048709200710

Cho, C., & Cheon, H. J. (2004). Why Do People Avoid Advertising on the Internet? *Journal of Advertising*, *33*(4), 89–97. doi:10.1080/00913367.2004.10639175

Choi, Y. K., Hwang, J., & McMillan, S. J. (2008). Gearing up for mobile advertising: A cross-cultural examination of key factors that drive mobile messages home to consumers. *Psychology and Marketing*, *25*(8), 756–768. doi:10.1002/mar.20237

Chowdhury, H. K., Parvin, N., Weitenberner, C., & Becker, M. (2006). Consumer Attitude Toward Mobile Advertising in an Emerging Market: An Empirical Study. *International Journal of Mobile Marketing*, *1*(2), 33–41.

ComScore. (2014). *The US Mobile App Report*.

Davis, F. D., Bagozzi, R. P., & Warshaw, P. R. (1992). Extrinsic and intrinsic motivation to use computers in the workplace. *Journal of Applied Social Psychology*, *22*(14), 1111–1132. doi:10.1111/j.1559-1816.1992. tb00945.x

De Keyzer, F., Dens, N., & De Pelsmacker, P. (2015). Is this for me? How Consumers Respond to Personalized Advertising on Social Network Sites. *Journal of Interactive Advertising*, *15*(2), 124–134. do i:10.1080/15252019.2015.1082450

Delo, C. (2013). Facebook Admits Organic Reach Is Falling Short, Urges Marketers to Buy Ads. Retrieved May 1, 2016, from http://adage.com/article/digital/facebook-admits-organic-reach-brand-posts-dipping/245530/

DeMers, J. (2015). Why Your Organic Facebook Reach Is Still Falling -- And What To Do About It. Retrieved July 27, 2015, from http://www.forbes.com/sites/jaysondemers/2015/05/13/why-your-organic-facebook-reach-is-still-falling-and-what-to-do-about-it/

DeZoysa, S. (2002). Mobile advertising needs to get personal. *Telecommunications International*, *36*(2), 8.

Ducoffe, R. (1995). How consumers assess the value of advertising. *Journal of Current Issues and Research in Advertising*, *17*(1). doi:10.1080/10641734.1995.10505022

Ducoffe, R. (1996). Advertising value and advertising on the web. *Journal of Advertising Research*, *36*(5), 21–35.

Duffett, R. G. (2015). The influence of Facebook advertising on cognitive attitudes amid Generation Y. *Electronic Commerce Research*, *15*(2), 243–267. doi:10.100710660-015-9177-4

Eagly, A., & Chaiken, S. (1998). Attitude Structure and Function. In D. T. Gilbert, S. T. Fiske, & G. Lindzey (Eds.), *Handbook of Social Psychology* (pp. 269–322). New York, USA: McGraw Hill.

Facebook. (2015). What are my targeting options? Retrieved September 8, 2015, from https://www.facebook.com/business/help/mobile-basic/207847739273775

Facebook. (2016). Facebook Q4 2015 Results. Retrieved May 5, 2016 from investor.fb.com

Ferreira, C., Moraes, C., Michaelidou, N., & McGrath, N. (2017). Social Media Advertising: Factors Influencing Consumer Ad Avoidance. *Journal of Consumer Behaviour*, *16*(2), 183–201. doi:10.1362/147539217X14909733609398

Fox-Davies, T. (2016). Communications Outlook. Retrieved May 1, 2016, from http://www.canvas8.com/content/2016/01/06/expert-outlook-2016.html

Frier, S., & Stone, B. (2015). Facebook Ads Are All-Knowing, Unblockable, and in Everyone's Phone. Retrieved October 1, 2015, from http://www.bloomberg.com/news/articles/2015-09-28/facebook-ads-are-all-knowing-unblockable-and-in-everyone-s-phone

FTC. (2013). Blurred Lines: Advertising or Content? – An FTC Workshop on Native Advertising. Retrieved from https://www.ftc.gov/news-events/events-calendar/2013/12/blurred-lines-advertising-or-content-ftc-workshop-native

Geisser, S. (1974). A predictive approach to the random effect model. *Biometrika*, *61*(1), 101–107. doi:10.1093/biomet/61.1.101

Gemius. (2014). Digital Maps Turkey Russia. Retrieved October 10, 2015, from http://www.iabturkiye.org/sites/default/files/dijital_haritalar-turkiye_rusya.pdf

Goldsmith, R. E., Lafferty, B., & Newell, S. J. (2000). The Impact of Corporate Credibility and Celebrity Credibility on Consumer Reaction to Advertisements and Brands. *Journal of Advertising*, *29*(3), 43–54. doi:10.1080/00913367.2000.10673616

Ha, Y. W., Park, M.-C., & Lee, E. (2014). A framework for mobile SNS advertising effectiveness: User perceptions and behaviour perspective. *Behaviour & Information Technology*, *33*(12), 1333–1346. doi:10.1080/0144929X.2014.928906

Haghirian, P., Madlberger, M., & Inoue, A. (2008). Mobile advertising in different stages of development: A cross-country comparison of consumer attitudes. In *Proceedings of the Annual Hawaii International Conference on System Sciences*, Sophia University, Vienna University of Economics and Business Administration, Keio University. 10.1109/HICSS.2008.318

Haghirian, P., Madlberger, M., & Tanuskova, A. (2005). Increasing advertising value of mobile marketing-an empirical study of antecedents. In *38th Hawaii International Conference on System Sciences.* 10.1109/HICSS.2005.311

Hair, J. F., Hult, G. T. M., Ringle, C. M., & Sarstedt, M. (2013). *A Primer on Partial Least Squares Structural Equation Modeling (PLS-SEM)* (1st ed.). Thousand Oaks: Sage Publications, Inc.

Henseler, J., Ringle, C. M., & Sinkovics, R. R. (2009). The use of partial least squares path modeling in international marketing. *Advances in International Marketing*, *20*, 277–320.

Hoelzel, M. (2014). The Social-Media Advertising Report. Retrieved September 8, 2015, from http://www.businessinsider.com/social-media-advertising-spending-growth-2014-9

Hong, W., Thong, J. Y. L., & Tam, K. Y. (2004). Does animation attract online users' attention? The effects of flash on information search performance and perceptions. *Information Systems Research*, *15*(1), 60–86. doi:10.1287/isre.1040.0017

IAB. (2013). *The Native Advertising Playbook.*

IAB. (2017). Digital Ad Spend Increases 23% Year-Over-Year in First Half of 2017. Retrieved January 2, 2018 from https://www.iab.com/news/digital-ad-spend-increases-23-year-year-first-half-2017-hitting-record-breaking-high-40-1-billion-according-iab-internet-advertising-revenue-report/

Johnson, S. (2014). New Research Sheds Light on Daily Ad Exposures. Retrieved September 9, 2015, from http://sjinsights.net/2014/09/29/new-research-sheds-light-on-daily-ad-exposures/

Jung, J., Shim, S. W., Jin, H. S., & Khang, H. (2016). Factors affecting attitudes and behavioural intention towards social networking advertising: A case of Facebook users in South Korea. *International Journal of Advertising*, *35*(2), 248–265. doi:10.1080/02650487.2015.1014777

Kaplan, A. M., & Haenlein, M. (2010). Users of the world, unite! The challenges and opportunities of Social Media. *Business Horizons*, *53*(1), 59–68. doi:10.1016/j.bushor.2009.09.003

Kara, M. (2015). Facebook'un Türkiye'deki aylık kullanıcı sayısı 40 milyona dayandı. Retrieved October 8, 2015, from http://webrazzi.com/2015/09/03/facebook-turkiye-aylik-kullanici-sayisi/

Karson, E. J., McCloy, S. D., & Bonner, P. G. (2006). An Examination of Consumers' Attitudes and Beliefs towards Web Site Advertising. *Journal of Current Issues and Research in Advertising*, *28*(2), 77–91. doi:10.1080/10641734.2006.10505200

Katz, E., Blumler, J. G., & Gurevitch, M. (1973). Uses and Gratifications Research. *Public Opinion Quarterly*, *37*(4), 509. doi:10.1086/268109

Kim, Y. J., & Han, J. (2014). Why smartphone advertising attracts customers: A model of Web advertising, flow, and personalization. *Computers in Human Behavior*, *33*, 256–269. doi:10.1016/j.chb.2014.01.015

Knoll, J. (2016). Advertising in social media: A review of empirical evidence. *International Journal of Advertising*, *35*(2), 266–300. doi:10.1080/02650487.2015.1021898

Korgaonkar, P. K., Silverblatt, R., & Becerra, E. P. (2010). The Hispanic View of E-mail, Popup, and Banner Advertising. *International Journal of E-Business Research*, *6*(2), 45–58. doi:10.4018/jebr.2010040103

La Ferle, C., & Lee, W.-N. (2003). Attitudes toward advertising: A comparative study of consumers in China, Taiwan, South Korea and the United States. *Journal of International Consumer Marketing*, *15*(2), 5–23. doi:10.1300/J046v15n02_02

Lee, W., Xiong, L., & Hu, C. (2012). The effect of Facebook users' arousal and valence on intention to go to the festival: Applying an extension of the technology acceptance model. *International Journal of Hospitality Management*, *31*(3), 819–827. doi:10.1016/j.ijhm.2011.09.018

Leng, G., & Lada, S. (2011). An Exploration of Social Networking Sites (SNS) Adoption in Malaysia Using Technology Acceptance Model (TAM), Theory of Planned Behavior (TPB) And Intrinsic Motivation. *Journal of Internet Banking and Commerce*, *16*(2), 1–27.

Lin, C. A., & Kim, T. (2016). Predicting user response to sponsored advertising on social media via the technology acceptance model. *Computers in Human Behavior*, *64*, 710–718. doi:10.1016/j.chb.2016.07.027

Liu, C.-L., Sinkovics, R. R., Pezderka, N., & Haghirian, P. (2012). Determinants of Consumer Perceptions toward Mobile Advertising — A Comparison between Japan and Austria. *Journal of Interactive Marketing*, *26*(1), 21–32. doi:10.1016/j.intmar.2011.07.002

Logan, K., Bright, L. F., & Gangadharbatla, H. (2012). Facebook versus television: Advertising value perceptions among females. *Journal of Research in Interactive Marketing*, *6*(3), 164–179. doi:10.1108/17505931211274651

Lukka, V., & James, P. T. J. (2014). Attitudes toward Facebook advertising. *Journal of Management and Marketing Research*.

Luna Cortés, G., & Royo Vela, M. (2013). The Antecedents of Consumers' Negative Attitudes Toward SMS Advertising: A Theoretical Framework and Empirical Study. *Journal of Interactive Advertising*, *13*(2), 109–117. doi:10.1080/15252019.2013.826553

MacKenzie, S. B., & Lutz, R. J. (1989). An Empirical Examination of the Structural Antecedents of Attitude Toward the Ad in an Advertising Pretesting Context. *Journal of Marketing*, *53*(April), 48–65. doi:10.2307/1251413

Marshall, J. (2015). Facebook to Boost Mobile-Ad Market Share, as eMarketer Reverses Forecast. Retrieved October 8, 2015 from http://blogs.wsj.com/cmo/2015/09/08/facebook-projected-to-narrow-mobile-ad-gap-with-google-as-emarketer-reverses-forecast/

Martin, B. A. S., Van Durme, J., Raulas, M., & Merisavo, M. (2003). Email Advertising: Exploratory Insights from Finland. *Journal of Advertising Research*, *43*(3), 293–300.

McMillan, S. J., Hwang, J. S., & Lee, G. (2003). Effects of structural and perceptual factors on attitudes toward the website. *Journal of Advertising Research*, *43*(4), 400–409. doi:10.2501/JAR-43-4-400-409

McQuail, D. (1983). *Mass Communication Theory: An Introduction*. London: Sage Publication.

Mehta, R., & Sivadas, E. (1995). Direct marketing on the internet: An empirical assessment of consumer attitudes. *Journal of Direct Marketing*, *9*(3), 21–32. doi:10.1002/dir.4000090305

Milne, G., & Gordon, M. E. (1993). Direct Mail Privacy - Efficiency Trade - Offs within an Implied Social Contract Framework. *Journal of Public Policy & Marketing*, *12*(2), 206–216.

Mitchell, A. (2014). *State of the News Media 2014.*

Mittal, B. (1994). Public assessment of TV advertising: Faint praise and harsh criticism. *Journal of Advertising Research*, *34*(1), 35–53.

Morrissey, B. (2013). 15 Alarming Stats About Banner Ads. Retrieved May 3, 2016, from http://digiday. com/publishers/15-alarming-stats-about-banner-ads/

Nunnally, J. C. (1978). *Psychometric theory* (2nd ed.). New York: McGraw-Hill, c.

O'Reilly, L. (2015). Posting a photo is the worst way to get people to see your Facebook posts. Retrieved July 27, 2015 from http://www.businessinsider.com/facebook-photos-worst-for-organic-reach-socialbakers-video-text-2015-2

Okazaki, S. (2004). How do Japanese consumers perceive wireless ads? A multivariate analysis. *International Journal of Advertising*, *23*(4), 429–454. doi:10.1080/02650487.2004.11072894

Olmstead, K., & Lu, K. (2015). State of the news Media 2015. Retrieved from http://www.journalism. org/2015/04/29/digital-news-revenue-fact-sheet/

Pappas, I. O., Kourouthanassis, P. E., Giannakos, M. N., & Chrissikopoulos, V. (2017). Sense and sensibility in personalized e-commerce: How emotions rebalance the purchase intentions of persuaded customers. *Psychology and Marketing*, *34*(10), 972–986. doi:10.1002/mar.21036

Petrovici, D., & Marinov, M. (2010). Determinants and antecedents of general attitudes towards advertising - A study of two EU accession countries. *European Journal of Marketing*, *41*(3–4), 307–326. doi:10.1108/03090560710728354

Pogue, D. (2015). Truth in Digital Advertising. *Scientific American*, *312*(5), 32. doi:10.1038cientifica merican0515-32 PMID:26336708

Pophal, L. (2014). Consumers coming to accept native advertising done right. *EContent (Wilton, Conn.)*, *37*(6), 1.

Robins, F. (2003). The marketing of 3G. *Marketing Intelligence & Planning*, *21*(6), 370–378. doi:10.1108/02634500310499239

Rosenberg, M., & Hovland, C. (1960). Cognitive, Affective, and Behavioral Components of Attitudes. In Attitude Organization and Change: An Analysis of Consistency among Attitude Components. doi:10.2307/3319768

Schlosser, A., Shavitt, S., & Kanfer, A. (1999). Survey of Internet users' attitudes toward Internet advertising. *Journal of Interactive Marketing*, *13*(3), 34–54. doi:10.1002/(SICI)1520-6653(199922)13:3<34::AID-DIR3>3.0.CO;2-R

Shavitt, S., Lowrey, P., & Haefner, J. (1998). Public attitudes toward advertising: More favorable than you might think. *Journal of Advertising Research*, *38*(4), 7–22.

Siau, K., & Shen, Z. (2003). Building Customer Trust in Mobile Commerce. *Communications of the ACM*, *46*(4), 91–94. doi:10.1145/641205.641211

Sloane, G. (2015). Facebook Ad Prices Are Rising Amid Organic Reach Squeeze. Retrieved July 27, 2015, from http://www.adweek.com/news/technology/facebook-ad-prices-are-rising-amid-organic-reach-squeeze-156888

Smith, J. W. (n.d.). The Myth of 5,000 Ads. Retrieved September 9, 2015 from http://cbi.hhcc.com/writing/the-myth-of-5000-ads/

Socialbakers. (2015). Facebook statistics directory. Retrieved September 8, 2015 from http://www.socialbakers.com/statistics/facebook/

Stavrianea, A., & Kavoura, A. (2015). Social media's and online user-generated content's role in services advertising. In AIP Conference Proceedings (Vol. 1644, pp. 318–324). doi:10.1063/1.4907853

Steinfield, C., Ellison, N. B., & Lampe, C. (2008). Social capital, self-esteem, and use of online social network sites: A longitudinal analysis. *Journal of Applied Developmental Psychology*, *29*(6), 434–445. doi:10.1016/j.appdev.2008.07.002

Sterling, G. (2015). Up a half million in six months, Facebook says it now has 2.5 million advertisers. Retrieved October 8, 2015, from http://marketingland.com/up-a-half-million-in-six-months-facebook-says-it-now-has-2-5-million-advertisers-144426

Stone, M. (1974). Cross-validatory choice and assessment of statistical predictions. *Journal of the Royal Statistical Society. Series A (General)*, *36*, 111–147.

Strauss, J., & Frost, R. (2013). *E-Marketing: Pearson New* (International ed.). Essex, UK: Pearson Education Limited.

Thong, J. Y. L., Hong, S.-J., & Tam, K. Y. (2006). The effects of post-adoption beliefs on the expectation-confirmation model for information technology continuance. *International Journal of Human-Computer Studies*, *64*(9), 799–810. doi:10.1016/j.ijhcs.2006.05.001

Tran, T. P. (2017). Personalized ads on Facebook: An effective marketing tool for online marketers. *Journal of Retailing and Consumer Services*, *39*(March), 230–242. doi:10.1016/j.jretconser.2017.06.010

Tsang, M., Ho, S., & Liang, T. (2004). Consumer attitudes toward mobile advertising: An empirical study. *International Journal of Electronic Commerce*, *8*(3), 65–78.

Turkey, I. A. B. (2016). AdEx Turkey. Retrieved January 5, 2018, from http://www.iabturkiye.org/adex-detay_adex-tr-2016

Turkey, I. A. B. (2017). February 2017 Top 20 Lists. Retrieved July 7, 2015, from http://www.iabturkiye.org/sites/default/files/internet_audience_toplist_02_2017.pdf

Ünal, S., Ercis, A., & Keser, E. (2011). Attitudes towards Mobile Advertising – A Research to Determine the Differences between the Attitudes of Youth and Adults. *Procedia: Social and Behavioral Sciences*, *24*, 361–377. doi:10.1016/j.sbspro.2011.09.067

United Nations Development Programme. (2013). *Mobile Technologies and Empowerment*. NY.

Usta, R. (2009). Understanding attitudes towards mobile advertising. *Doğuş Üniversitesi Dergisi, 10*(2), 294–309. (in Turkish)

Varnali, K., Yilmaz, C., & Toker, A. (2012). Predictors of attitudinal and behavioral outcomes in mobile advertising: A field experiment. *Electronic Commerce Research and Applications, 11*(6), 570–581. doi:10.1016/j.elerap.2012.08.002

Venkatesh, V., & Davis, F. D. F. (2000). A theoretical extension of the technology acceptance model: Four longitudinal field studies. *Management Science, 46*(2), 186–204. doi:10.1287/mnsc.46.2.186.11926

Walrave, M., Poels, K., Antheunis, M. L., Van den Broeck, E., & van Noort, G. (2016). Like or dislike? Adolescents' responses to personalized social network site advertising. *Journal of Marketing Communications, 22*. doi:10.1080/13527266.2016.1182938

Wang, Y., & Sun, S. (2010). Assessing beliefs, attitudes, and behavioral responses toward online advertising in three countries. *International Business Review, 19*(4), 333–344. doi:10.1016/j.ibusrev.2010.01.004

Wojdynski, B. W., & Evans, N. J. (2016). Going native: effects of disclosure position and language on the recognition and evaluation of online native advertising. *Journal of Advertising, 45*(2), 157–168. doi:10.1080/00913367.2015.1115380

Wolin, L. D., & Korgaonkar, P. (2003). Web advertising: Gender differences in beliefs, attitudes and behavior. *Internet Research, 13*(5), 375–385. doi:10.1108/10662240310501658

Wolin, L. D., Korgaonkar, P., & Lund, D. (2002). Beliefs, attitudes and behaviour towards Web advertising. *International Journal of Advertising, 21*(1), 87–113. doi:10.1080/02650487.2002.11104918

Wong, M. T. M. (2010). *Consumers' Attitude Towards Mobile Marketing*. Hong Kong Polytechnic University.

Xu, D. J. (2006). The Influence of Personalization in Affecting Consumer Attitudes Toward Mobile Advertising in China. *Journal of Computer Information Systems, 47*(2), 9–19.

Xu, D. J., Liao, S. S., & Li, Q. (2008). Combining empirical experimentation and modeling techniques: A design research approach for personalized mobile advertising applications. *Decision Support Systems, 44*(3), 710–724. doi:10.1016/j.dss.2007.10.002

Zenith. (2016). Social media ads to hit US$50bn in 2019, catching up with newspapers. Retrieved February 27, 2017 from https://www.zenithmedia.com/social-media-ads-hit-us50bn-2019-catching-newspapers/

Zhang, J., & Mao, E. (2016). From Online Motivations to Ad Clicks and to Behavioral Intentions: An Empirical Study of Consumer Response to Social Media Advertising. *Psychology and Marketing, 33*(3), 155–164. doi:10.1002/mar.20862

Zhou, D., Zhang, W., & Vertinsky, I. (2002). Advertising Trends in Urban China. *Journal of Advertising Research, 42*(3), 73–81. doi:10.2501/JAR-42-3-73-81

This research was previously published in the International Journal of E-Business Research (IJEBR), 14(3); pages 54-76, copyright year 2018 by IGI Publishing (an imprint of IGI Global).

APPENDIX

Table 5. Survey form

Item	Dimension	Source(s)
Facebook advertising is entertaining	Entertainment	(Ducoffe, 1995, 1996; Wang & Sun, 2010)
Facebook advertising is enjoyable		
Facebook advertising is pleasant		
Facebook advertising is interesting		
Facebook advertising is a good source of product information	Information	(Ducoffe, 1995, 1996; Liu et al., 2012)
Facebook advertising provides timely information on products		
Facebook advertising supplies relevant product information		
Facebook advertisements is a good source of up to date products or services information		
Facebook advertising is irritating.	Irritation	(Ducoffe, 1995, 1996)
Facebook advertising is annoying.		
Facebook advertising insult's people's intelligence.		
Facebook advertising is intrusive.		
Facebook advertising is convincing.	Credibility	(Liu et al., 2012; MacKenzie & Lutz, 1989)
Facebook advertising is credible.		
Facebook advertising is believable.		
Facebook advertising is truthful.		
Facebook advertising is useful.	Ad. Value	(Ducoffe, 1995, 1996)
Facebook advertising is valuable.		
Facebook advertising is important.		
Overall, I like Facebook advertising.	Attitude	(Tsang et al., 2004; Wolin et al., 2002)
Generally, I find Facebook advertising a good thing.		
I consider Facebook advertising essential.		
I feel that Facebook advertisements are tailored to me.	Personalization	(Ünal et al., 2011; Xu et al., 2008)
I feel that contents in Facebook advertisements are personalized.		
I feel that Facebook advertising is personalized for my usage.		
I feel that Facebook advertising is delivered to me in a timely way.		
I am satisfied to get Facebook advertisements that offer rewards.	Incentives / Rewards	(Kim & Han, 2014; Ünal et al., 2011)
I take action to get Facebook advertisements that offer rewards.		
I respond to Facebook advertising to obtain incentives.		

Table 6. Descriptive statistics and loadings

N=281	Range:1-5		Cross Loadings & Outer Loadings							
Items	Mean	Std. Dev.	ADV	ATT	CRE	CUS	ENT	INF	IRT	REW
ADV1	2.14	.994	**0.865**	0.714	0.652	0.471	0.660	0.706	-0.354	0.594
ADV2	1.83	.918	**0.834**	0.618	0.566	0.422	0.603	0.556	-0.326	0.581
ADV3	2.02	1.005	**0.827**	0.701	0.594	0.417	0.561	0.564	-0.286	0.475
ATT1	2.07	1.021	0.629	**0.789**	0.578	0.346	0.568	0.582	-0.326	0.572
ATT2	2.11	.979	0.712	**0.872**	0.560	0.471	0.596	0.597	-0.346	0.448
ATT3	2.15	1.031	0.716	**0.891**	0.611	0.457	0.574	0.616	-0.314	0.524
CRE1	2.12	1.014	0.594	0.577	**0.764**	0.342	0.476	0.528	-0.227	0.492
CRE2	2.21	.981	0.596	0.559	**0.828**	0.398	0.412	0.527	-0.305	0.473
CRE3	2.46	1.121	0.411	0.358	**0.590**	0.260	0.350	0.374	-0.387	0.271
CRE4	2.46	.971	0.486	0.489	**0.732**	0.366	0.346	0.514	-0.178	0.440
PERS1	2.63	1.259	0.210	0.212	0.182	**0.607**	0.139	0.110	-0.137	0.118
PERS2	2.82	1.272	0.332	0.344	0.328	**0.805**	0.226	0.278	-0.058	0.195
PERS3	2.73	1.306	0.320	0.332	0.276	**0.807**	0.213	0.210	-0.040	0.247
PERS4	2.23	1.011	0.555	0.505	0.495	**0.807**	0.418	0.502	-0.261	0.452
ENT1	1.93	.948	0.708	0.643	0.491	0.367	**0.905**	0.580	-0.362	0.506
ENT2	1.92	.936	0.577	0.550	0.442	0.330	**0.841**	0.531	-0.340	0.522
ENT3	2.46	1.295	0.305	0.288	0.250	0.103	**0.553**	0.283	-0.422	0.266
ENT4	2.19	1.085	0.570	0.558	0.456	0.286	**0.770**	0.619	-0.244	0.425
INF1	2.12	.948	0.621	0.555	0.527	0.334	0.598	**0.773**	-0.310	0.449
INF2	2.47	1.021	0.544	0.512	0.561	0.396	0.492	**0.797**	-0.264	0.394
INF3	2.47	1.032	0.571	0.577	0.525	0.343	0.530	**0.826**	-0.239	0.420
INF4	2.43	1.135	0.608	0.626	0.544	0.309	0.533	**0.836**	-0.303	0.453
IRT1	3.35	1.290	-0.355	-0.340	-0.315	-0.181	-0.441	-0.323	**0.855**	-0.274
IRT2	3.36	1.240	-0.356	-0.331	-0.346	-0.170	-0.353	-0.280	**0.873**	-0.261
IRT3	3.02	1.143	-0.298	-0.341	-0.304	-0.126	-0.287	-0.312	**0.775**	-0.189
IRT4	3.08	1.264	-0.138	-0.157	-0.117	-0.129	-0.158	-0.127	**0.649**	-0.080
REW1	1.98	1.061	0.591	0.540	0.509	0.397	0.523	0.475	-0.267	**0.897**
REW2	1.80	1.027	0.558	0.476	0.498	0.254	0.464	0.431	-0.178	**0.853**
REW3	1.84	1.036	0.578	0.575	0.530	0.363	0.512	0.495	-0.267	**0.894**

Bold text on the diagonal refers to outer loadings.

Chapter 65

Consumer Behavior, Trust, and Electronic Word–of–Mouth Communication:
Developing an Online Purchase Intention Model

Francesca Di Virgilio
University of Molise, Italy

Gilda Antonelli
University of Sannio, Italy

ABSTRACT

Social media platforms have become a major forum for consumers to interact with firms and other individuals. Drawing on both the customer-dominant logic and the theory of planned behavior, the present chapter aims to advance understanding and encourage research on the variables that drive consumers' online purchase intention. Although there is a general agreement in recognizing the importance of social media platforms as a source of information about consumer behavior, a complete theorization of the variables that affect the relation between behavioral intention and online purchase intention is still lacking. The proposed theoretical model is an extension of the theory of planned behavior and incorporates trust and electronic word-of-mouth communication as part of the customers' online purchase intention. Finally, the theoretical and managerial implications are further discussed.

DOI: 10.4018/978-1-7998-9020-1.ch065

INTRODUCTION

Social media are dramatically changing the relationship among individuals, firms, and societies (Leung, 2013; Oakley & Salam, 2014). Web 2.0 technologies, as the basis of social media platforms and social networking sites (e.g. Alibaba, eBay), enable the acquisition of products through supporting users' interactions and contributions (Liang & Turban, 2011).

A growing number of companies recognizes the significant role that social media play as a means of communication and as a driving force in creating new business opportunities (Kim & Ko, 2012; Sashi, 2012). They enable consumers and firms to interact and exchange different categories of information, including comments, evaluations, images, photos and videos.

Hence, consumer's behavior information allows firms to strategically position themselves ahead of their competitors. The capability of managing information becomes a core competence of the firm in creating competitive long term strategies. Since social media websites are powerful tools used to expand one's network and help in connecting with acquaintances and strangers (Chang et al., 2015), as the proliferation and the use of social media apps improve, firms have a great opportunity to determine consumers' requirements and needs by involving consumers in panel questionnaires and interviews. A broad variety of social media tools enable firms to connect with a wide range of potential and existing customers (Briones, et al., 2011; Chang, Yu, & Lu, 2015; Wu, 2016; Bianchi & Andrews, 2015; Curran & Lennon, 2011), to post contents, share ideas, learn and fulfill social needs (Ferreira, et al, 2014). In particular, a growing number of companies recognize that social media provide a means to communicate and change the business model while creating new opportunities (Kim & Ko, 2012; Sashi, 2012, Wu, 2016; Chang et al., 2015; Culnan et al., 2010). Specifically, through social media information, it becomes possible to describe the customer's buying behavior (Culnan, et al., 2010; Zaglia, 2013).

In the context of high rather than low customer involvement in social media, consumers that are more involved and believe that social media are important and interesting will be more dependent on them in searching for suggestions and sharing information on products and services.

From a customer-dominant logic perspective, understanding how social media obtains maximum benefits is still a research gap. The literature attributes this research gap to a combination of factors such as cost, time and lack of top management knowledge, unproven success metrics, and the company's perceived loss of control (Whelan, et al., 2011). Because of a number of technology-related challenges, firms are slow in adopting social media as a strategy to leverage business opportunities (Kaplan & Haenlein, 2010).

To address these research gaps, we have designed a theoretical model based on the theory of planned behavior (TPB) (Ajzen, 1991; Fishbein & Ajzen, 1975) in order to identify the underlying factors and conditions that drive consumers to engage in social media so that they purchase online.

In particular, our chapter aims to fill the research gap in consumer behavior on purchase intention on social media platforms and adopts a customer-dominant logic perspective with its integration of the following important approach: TPB (Ajzen, 1991; Fishbein & Ajzen, 1975).

Our theoretical model of consumer behavior intention analyzes the direct effects of two important factors on consumers' purchase intentions: trust and Electronic word-of-mouth communication (eWOM). Trust – a belief in the reliability, truth, and ability of the exchange party – is recognized as one of the main variables that refrain customers from electronic purchases (Gefen, 2000; Liang & Turban, 2011; Kim & Pak, 2013; Hajli, et al., 2016). However, given the context of social media, users acquire knowledge of a specific product from social media and may engage in a purchase. Thus, in the context of the social media and embedded content provided by peers, trust may increase the users' purchase intentions from an e-vendor (Kim & Park; 2013).

Electronic word-of-mouth eWOM is the exchange of product or service evaluations among people who meet, talk, and text each other within a variety of online environments (King et al., 2014; Yoon, 2012; Barreto, 2014).

In this scenario, we organized the chapter in different parts. In the first part we make a contribution to the body of literature by examining first the role of social media platforms for the improvement of decision making as compared to more traditional methods; second, the customer-dominant logic as an innovative way of interpreting the relationship between consumers and firms; and last, the theory of planned behavior. In the second part, we analyze trust in social platforms and e-word-of-mouth communication as important variables which may mediate the effect of consumers' behavior intentions for online purchasing; and then we identify four directions which are the results of the literature review and the observation of real consumers' behaviors. Finally, we construct a theoretical model based on digital consumer purchase intention. We close the chapter by discussing future research directions for this work.

BACKGROUND

Social Media

The literature defines social media as a group of Internet-based applications that build on the ideological and technological foundations of Web 2.0 technology, and that allow the creation and exchange of user-generated content (Bianchi & Andrews, 2015; Chang et al., 2015; Kaplan & Haenlein, 2010). Kaplan and Haenlein (2011) and Sashi (2012) define social media marketing as electronic-word-of-mouth (Di Pietro et al. 2013) and as a sort of marketing message of a firm, brand, or product. Despite buyers' strong enthusiasm, many firms remain skeptical about embracing social media to assist the marketing function (Ferreira et al., 2014; Sashi, 2012; Bruhn et al., 2012).

Social media have changed the classic business dynamics. Through more efficient communication means, such as weblogs, social networks, social bookmarking sites, wikis, and virtual worlds (Curran & Lennon, 2011), social media facilitate promotion among dispersed individuals with seemingly, marginal concerns (Rodriguez, Peterson, & Krishnan, 2012), they foster mutual enrichment through conversation, exchange, and participation (Whelan et al., 2011) and they reduce transaction and coordination costs. In addition, social media platforms allow salespeople to coordinate internal value-creating functions and deliver superior value in customer relationships (Bharadwaj, 2000; Kaplan & Haenlien, 2009). In doing so, they represent an important marketing strategy in which organizations build relationships with customers (Agnihotri et al., 2012; Culnan et al., 2010). Social media also capture the attention of managers. A recent global survey of managers has found that almost half of the buyers pay attention to social media's role when involved in the buying process (Agnihotri, et al., 2012).

This expanded role of social media platforms can better contribute to improving decision making than traditional methods (Bruhn, et al., 2012) on purchase intention. Consequently, firms can adopt a customer-dominant logic and become involved in consumers' lives and businesses (Cheung & To, 2015; Heinonen & Strandvik, 2015; Heinonen et al., 2010).

The Customer-Dominant Logic

Customer-dominant logic is an innovative way of interpreting the relationship between consumers and firms (Heinonen & Strandvik, 2015; Heinonen et al., 2010; Cheung & To, 2016). This kind of management perspective is dominated by consumer-related aspects rather than by a focus on services, products, systems, profits, and costs. Customer-dominant logic is grounded in an understanding of consumers' lives and their use of services or products (Heinonen & Strandvik, 2015; Cheung & To, 2016).

Following the neo-institutionalism theory, institutional logics define the content and meaning of institutions (which are believed to exert some kind of 'pressure' at firm level in order to gain endorsement from important referent audiences) providing means both of understanding the social world and of acting confidently within it (Greenwood et al., 2011; Tolbert et al., 2011). As useful constructs for the organizational studies, the institutional logic concept was introduced by Jackall (1988), Friedland and Alford (1991) who defined it as a set of material practices and symbolic construction that surely influence individual or collective actors but that, in turn, may be also modified by them. For Jackall (1988) an institutional logic is the way a particular social world works; for Friedland and Alford (1991) it provides social actors with vocabularies of motive and sense of self. The main institutions, namely, the capitalist market, the bureaucratic state, families, democracy, and religion, which have a central logic, while constraining both the means and ends of individual behavior and being constitutive of individuals, organizations, and society, also provide sources of agency and change. Moreover, institutional complexity becomes an opportunity for transforming individual identities, organizations and society.

By putting together the structural and normative approach of Jackall (1988) and the structural and symbolic approach of Friedland and Alford (1991), Thornton and Ocasio defined the institutional logics as "the socially constructed, historical patterns of material practices, assumptions, values, beliefs, and rules by which individuals produce and reproduce their material subsistence, organize time and space, and provide meaning to their social reality" (1999, p. 804).

As a result, the interests, identities, values, and assumptions are embedded within prevailing institutional logics. Moreover, to locate behavior in a context requires theorizing an inter-institutional system of societal actors in which each sector represents a different set of expectations and human and organizational behavior, allowing sources of heterogeneity and agency coming from the contradictions between the logics of different institutional orders. Each of the institutional orders in society has both material and cultural characteristics so that institutions develop and change as a result of the interplay between both of these forces. In addition, institutional logics may develop at a variety of different levels (i.e. organizations, markets, industries, inter-organizational networks, geographic communities, and organizational fields), and in order to apply the institutional logics approach it is critical that the level of analysis at which institutionalization occurs be clearly specified.

Actors may transform social relations within and among institutions, in order to create new practices and models of actions, obviously if they loosen their embeddedness into the social context. This in other words, as taken-for-granted assumptions and practices, institutional logics are strongly embedded in individual and organizational actors' cognition and give appropriateness and meaningfulness to what should be preferred, also, influencing the perceptive, attentive, evaluative and responsive processes to environmental stimuli of actors (Almandoz, 2014).

While Friedland and Alford (1991) pointed to such societal logics as 'capitalism', 'democracy', 'family', and 'religion'; currently, the major types of rationalized institutional logics are 'family', 'religion', 'state', 'market', 'profession', 'corporation', and 'community' (Thornton et al., 2012; Thornton & Ocasio, 2008).

Institutional logics become, over time, both a theory and a method of analysis which enable researchers and scholars to understand the role that societal-level culture has on individual and organizational actors' cognition and behavior (DiMaggio, 1997).

According to this, organizational forms, managerial practices, and individual behaviors are the result of existing institutional logics so that they may become a way to interpret tensions and change dynamics observed in contemporary organizations and organization fields due to the competition and struggle among various categories of actors committed to constraining institutional logics (Scott, 2014; Thornton, 2004).

Components of Theory of Planned Behavior

The theory of planned behavior (TPB) (Ajzen, 1991; Fishbein & Ajzen, 1975) posits that an individual's intention to engage in a behavior is shaped by his or her attitudes toward the behavior, the subjective norms and the perceived behavioral control; whereas his or her intentions and perceived behavioral control have an impact on actual behavior. The TPB has been used to explore the acceptance of computer and ICT technologies since the 1980s (Davis et al., 1989; Jiang et al., 2016; Kim, et al., 2016; Mou & Lin, 2015; Taylor & Todd, 1995). Cho et al. (2015) suggested that the TPB is useful for exploring the influence of social and psychological variables on consumers' behavioral intention.

When consumers perceive social media to have a high rather than a low level of usefulness in terms of obtaining updated information and suggestions on products and services, they may tend to spend more time and effort in learning about the products and the services and rely more directly on social media websites. Increased participation in online purchasing provides a viable means for consumers to develop a favorable attitude toward service firms testified by a more active involvement in the improvement of the features and perceived benefits of products and services (Cheung & To, 2016). A growing body of literature published over the last three decades underlines the importance of consumer behavior as an avenue of research worthy of attention from the research community. The same literature, however, suggests that it is extremely complex to analyze consumer's behavior, and that traditional research measures may catch only a portion of its richness (Myers, et al., 1979; Pfeffer, 1993; Summers, 2001; McInnis, 2004; Levy, 2006). Consumer's behavior is a complex topic that includes different perspectives and uses several disciplinary approaches such as consumer culture theory research, transformative consumer research, social cognition research stream, motivation research area, behavioral decision theory.

Nevertheless, the evolution of consumer's behavior shows that a "theory of consumer" (Teas & Palan, 1997; Summers, 2001) is still not available and many scholars are trying to build a more comprehensive theory.

Several articles published in top-tier management journals have focused primarily on intra-individual behaviors and, in particular, on measuring cognitive processes by studying individuals' performance when purchasing consumptions goods (Bagozzi, 2000; Briley & Wyer, 2002; Thomas-Hunt, et al., 2003; Cummings, 2004). The general premise of the TPB is that an individual is more likely to adopt a behavior when he or she holds a favorable attitude towards it; he or she perceives what other individuals think about his or her behavior, with the result of taking more control over the expected barriers (Ajzen, 1991). According to the TPB (Ajzen, 1991; Fishbein & Ajzen, 1975), an individual's attitude toward a particular behavior is one of the most significant predictors of an individual's intention to engage in that behavior and as well as of his/her actual behavior. The attitude toward the behavior is defined as the degree to which the individual has a positive evaluation of the behavior in question.

Fishbein and Ajzen (1975) identified two other important factors that affect behavioral intention: subjective norms that can be seen as the perceived social pressure on the individual to engage in a specific behavior; perceived behavioral control, which refers to the individual's perception of the ease of engaging in a behavior. In addition, an individual's behavioral intention and perceived behavioral control directly influence his or her actual behavior. Bai, Tang, Yang and Gong (2014) highlighted that subjective norms or perceived pressure from significant others have a great impact on an individual's intention to make choices more freely.

As stated above, attitude is a strong predictor of behavioral intention (Ajzen,1991; Mou & Lin, 2015). When consumers develop a favorable attitude toward social media, they may be interested in initiating a strong intention of fulfilling their beliefs.

Studies of the acceptance of computer or information and communication technologies (ICT) suggest that attitudes toward the use of a computer/ICT technology are determined by its perceived usefulness and ease of use (Davis, Bagozzi, & Warshaw, 1989; Porter & Donthu, 2006; Taylor & Todd, 1995; Di Virgilio et al. 2017). Perceived usefulness is defined as the degree to which an individual believes that the use of a particular system may increase his or her performance (Davis et al., 1989). Perceived usefulness has a much stronger effect on consumers' attitudes toward the use of a new technology than perceived ease of use (Davis et al., 1989; Porter & Donthu, 2006; Taylor & Todd, 1995; Di Pietro et al. 2013). When consumers trust that using social media will broaden their understanding of the products and services, they have a more favorable attitude toward their engagement in social media platforms. In addition, consumers may recognize social media as an effective channel for sharing their opinions on products and services with friends and relatives as well as a helpful resource to aid the decision-making process for the purchasing of products and services they are interested in. Thus, a high level of perceived usefulness will lead consumers to develop a favorable attitude toward engaging in social media. Indeed, perceived usefulness represents a key determinant of consumer attitudes and behavioral intention toward online shopping (Childers, et al., 2002; O'Cass & Fenech, 2003).

In the present study, we focus on consumer attitudes toward engaging in social media purchasing. Since social media are pervasive in people's daily lives (Midyette, et al., 2014; Yan, et al., 2014), we drop the variable of perceived ease of use and retain perceived usefulness as an antecedent of the attitude construct.

MAIN FOCUS OF THE CHAPTER

Purchase Intention: The Effects of Trust and Ewom

Trust

In the theoretical model we present here, we consider trust in social media platforms and eWOM as important variables which may mediate the effect of individuals' behavior in online purchasing intentions. Purchase intentions in social media contexts refer to the customers' intentions to engage in online purchases from e-vendors in social media platforms. Intentions are the determinants of behavior and are defined as "the strength of one's intentions to perform a specific behavior" (Fishbein & Ajzen, 1975, p.288).

Ba & Pavlou (2002) posit that trust is an individual's belief that an exchange will happen in a manner consistent with one's confident expectations. Trust is a unidimensional or a multidimensional concept

(Gefen, 2002). However, a better understating of trust comes from the recognition of its dimensions. Cognitive and affective trust are the main types of trust (Aiken & Boush, 2006): cognitive trust is the customer's belief in and willingness of dependency on an exchange partner's ability and consistency. Affective trust is a customer's belief about a firm's level of care and concerns based on emotions (Kim & Park, 2013). Both cognitive and affective trust contain dimensions of credibility (one's belief that the exchange party is reliable) and benevolence (beliefs that the exchange partner is motivated by seeking joint gain) (Aiken & Boush, 2006).

For the purpose of the present study, trust is used as the sense of trusting beliefs, referring to the beliefs that "one can rely upon a promise made by another and that the other, in unforeseen circumstances, will act toward oneself with goodwill and in a benign fashion" (Suh & Han, 2003, p. 137). In online contexts, trust is based on beliefs in the trustworthiness of an exchange party and the characteristics of competence, integrity, and benevolence (McKnight, et al., 2002). Given the context of social media platforms, uncertainty is usually higher due to the high level of user-generated contents and the lack of face-to-face interactions (Featherman & Hajli, 2015). Despite this, the enhancement of experience with exchange parties could reduce the uncertainty and increase tendencies for online commerce adoption through the increase in trust (Gefen & Straub, 2004).

The lack of face-to-face interactions could result in customers' suspicion of truthfulness in online exchanges and the paucity of knowledge about the e-vendors could further heighten the adverse influence of risk in online shopping (Kaiser & Müller-Seitz, 2008). Kim & Park (2013) investigate the antecedents of trust and its direct effects on purchase intentions and word-of-mouth intentions on social commerce platforms. Seven social commerce characteristics are identified as the key antecedents of trust: reputation, size, information quality, transaction safety, communication, economic feasibility, and word-of-mouth referrals. It is noteworthy that customer reviews and experiences posted in forums and communities can improve trust in a specific website.

Previous literature found that the purchase from an e-vendor depends on customer trust in the e-vendor (Gefen, et al., 2003). We propose that trust in a social media platform could increase customers' purchase intentions. Social media platforms bring customers into contact with e-vendors and provide the facilities for the value exchange between the parties. Within social media platforms, customers see advertisements, pictures/videos/news, recommendations and Likes related to the e-vendors. However, according to Hajli et al. (2016), trust in the social media platforms could determine the customer's reliance on the credibility of the contents and of the e-vendors' activities. Credibility encompasses integrity and ability of the platform in providing the expected outcomes, which in turn, increases intentions to buy on the platform (Kaiser & Müller-Seitz, 2008).

As suggested by McKnight and Chervany (2001), there could be four variables that affect consumers' trust in social media platforms: 1) competence or power of the social media platforms to fulfill a successful exchange or the provision of recovery if the failure occurs from the e-vendor side; 2) benevolence, indicating the concern of the social media platforms to favor users regardless of the profit utilitarian aim; 3) integrity, related to ethical behavior of the social media platforms and their fulfillment of promises; 4) predictability, as the consistency of the action of the social media platforms, enabling users to forecast future exchanges. These variables enhance customer's reliance on the user-generated contents, reducing the uncertainty of exchanging outcomes and extending the duration of the relationship between SMP and consumers (Suh & Han, 2003). Kim and Park (2013) indicated that users who trust social commerce sites are more likely to spread positive word-of-mouth and purchase on these platforms.

Electronic Word-of-Mouth Communication

Electronic word-of-mouth (eWOM) is defined as the exchange of product or service evaluations among people who meet, talk and text each other in the virtual world (King et al., 2014; Yoon, 2012; Barreto, 2014). EWOM is emerging as a more influential knowledge sharing tool than traditional word-of-mouth (WOM) (Katz & Lazarsfeld, 1955). Social media have become among the most prevalent eWOM channels because of their ubiquity, mobility, and interactivity (French & Read, 2013; Zmuda, 2013). These characteristics enable social media users to communicate and connect with each other more frequently and more closely (Laroche et al., 2013; Kleina et al., 2015).

Despite the benefits of using social media to improve eWOM effectiveness, the effects of network closeness and network strength on the diffusion of eWOM remain unclear (Wang et al., 2016).

Relevant studies have investigated the key drivers (Cheung & Lee, 2012; Chu & Kim, 2011) of eWOM and their impact on sales (Chevalier & Mayzlin, 2006), on the consumer decision-making process (De Bruyn & Lilien, 2008), and on the attitude toward both brands and websites (Lee et al., 2009). In particular, through the social digital media, *ad hoc* virtual communities and blogs, eWOM provides additional and highly-customized information related to the research on social media platform. Then, it measures the popularity and the inclinations for a specific brand, when a product or service are concerned (Casaló et al., 2010; Chan & Li, 2010; Park & Kim, 2008). As a consequence, in the process of choosing what to buy, consumers are compelled to use social media to search for information on possible product or service, to visualize images, and access other's opinions in order to gain a larger amount of info to make a more effective choice. According to Bickart and Schindler (2001), eWOM has the potential to reduce the risk, uncertainty, and ambiguity associated with a product or service.

Potential consumers thus depend on referrals from their friends, family members, and social networks. In this sense, eWOM becomes a powerful tool for catching consumers' attention and influencing their behaviors (Litvin et al., 2008; Chan & Li, 2010).

THE THEORETICAL MODEL

Considering the research literature and the above description of individuals' actual behavior in online purchases, we have constructed a theoretical model of the online customer purchase intention. The TPB states that there is a direct effect of the customers behavioral intention on their purchase intention. When we come to purchasing on social media platforms, this occurrence becomes even more apparent since the use of the web is pervading everyday life and online transactions are increasing at an exponential rate. Beside the specific application of the relation to the specific channel, we add some value to the model considering the mediation effect which is played on the purchase intention by trust in the specific platform and the availability of eWOM communication. The latter propositions come from the following statements which are the results of the literature review and the observation of the concrete consumer's behaviors:

- *Trust in the social media platform affects the perceived usefulness of the channel as supporting tool for purchase intentions.*
- *Trust has a direct influence on the attitude towards the online purchase intention that can reinforce the customer behavioral intention.*

- *E-word-of-mouth communication has a direct influence on the perceived usefulness of the social media platform in online purchasing, therefore, amplifying the online purchased intention.*
- *E-word-of-mouth communication affects the perceived trust in the social media platform and therefore influences online purchase intention.*

Figure 1 describes our theoretical model to enlighten the mediation effect of the variables on online purchasing intention

Figure 1. The Theoretical Model of Online Purchase Intention

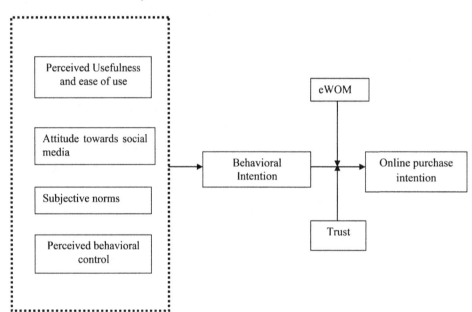

CONCLUSION AND FUTURE RESEARCH

The theoretical model that we propose will accomplish an important goal with respect to consumer's behavior. Using the theory of planned behavior interpretation and customer-dominant logic and guided by the theoretical approaches from related research in consumer behavior, this chapter provides an analytical framework to explore the consumer's online purchase intention. It introduces the mediation effect of trust in social media platform and eWOM communication on the direct effect performed by the customers' behavioral intentions on the purchase intention and it expands the area of effect to the social media platform. This study is one of the first that examine the antecedents and boundary condition of the TPB in the context of social media platforms. We found that perceived usefulness was a key determinant of attitudes toward engaging in social media and that consumer behavior was a moderator of the link between perceived usefulness and attitudes toward engaging in social media. Moreover, using TPB theory and dominant logic literature, we speculate that the trust in social media platform and eWOM communication has a mediating effect on online purchase intention.

Practitioners can use our theoretical model to increase purchase intention of consumers and better target future marketing strategies to increase the online amount of transactions. In fact, the outcome of this study is of benefit to both, the consumers and the firms. From a better understanding of the variables that influence the consumer's purchase intention a company will have a greater understanding of consumers' expectations and will be able to implement social media platforms and to improve the support of the purchasing decision-making process.

In addition, the consumer's attitudes toward purchasing on social media platforms could be implemented by improving trust and eWOM communication, which in turn, can lead to a higher level of engagement in online purchasing. Trust is a critical issue in a social commerce contexts and specifically, it plays an important role in increasing purchase intentions. The more customers trust the platform, the more they engage in the purchasing process. Social media platform designers are able to increase customers' trust by enhancing the characteristic of the platforms, including reputation, size, information quality, transaction safety, communication, economic feasibility, and word-of-mouth referrals (Kim & Park, 2013). However, trust is not the only factor and other elements are also important in increasing purchase intentions.

These studies open a new path of research on how consumer behavior can take place through the combined effect of trust and eWOM on behavioral intentions.

This study contributes to the development of research on consumer's online behavior. Since only a few analysis on customer-dominant logic have been carried out in the field of consumer's research, this study can act as a catalyst for future scientific inquiries in this important area.

Today the development and use of eWOM for supporting and influencing consumers on their online purchasing intentions play a key role for both managers and researchers. EWOM could be quite effective in helping a customer to make decisions about purchasing. It should be interesting to introduce digital content and technologies that understand consumers behavior, to facilitate the decision making process through a user-friendly interface, by giving information related to products, promotions, new arrivals. In order to achieve an efficient, flexible and meaningful feeling of human-computer interaction, the main features to develop are the interactivity and the multimodality. The quality of interactions affects the knowledge creation, which is capable of influencing the decision-making process (Yoo et al., 2010).

The issue of how to effectively design and deploy social media platforms in this approach is most certainly an additional future research direction. It is clear that the social media platforms offer companies many opportunities to interact with consumers along with the entire decision-making process.

A future research direction can assess the model empirically by targeting a panel of online buyers in order to observe them in their purchasing process. It should increase the number of different control variables to explore the effect of the decision-making unit on other information acquisition variables, such as the content and sequence of the information acquired. Findings from the alternative models indicate that those who use social media information to a greater extent (information seekers) tend to more likely engaged in online relationships with e-vendors independently of their trust in that specific social media platform. Future studies may also examine our model in different cultural contexts and generations, in which consumers will have different orientations (Bilgihan, 2016); it is possible that some consumers may place higher values on some preferred networks because they better fit their needs. Such differences in individual network value may affect the intensity of consumers' intentions to purchase. Finally, future studies could test whether and to what extent the degree of customer engagement moderates the link between perceived usefulness and attitude toward co-creation in social media (Chathoth, et al., 2016; Zhang, et al., 2015)

REFERENCES

Agnihotri, R., Kothandaraman, P., Kashyap, R., & Singh, R. (2012). Bringing social into sales: The impact of salespeoples social media use on service behaviors and value creation. *Journal of Personal Selling & Sales Management, 22*(3), 333–348. doi:10.2753/PSS0885-3134320304

Aiken, K. D., & Boush, D. M. (2006). Trustmarks, objective-source ratings, and implied investments in advertising: Investigating online trust and the context-specific nature of internet signals. *Journal of the Academy of Marketing Science, 34*(3), 308–323. doi:10.1177/0092070304271004

Ajzen, I. (1991). The theory of planned behavior. *Organizational Behavior and Human Decision Processes, 50*(2), 179–211. doi:10.1016/0749-5978(91)90020-T

Almandoz, J. (2014). Founding teams as carriers of competing logics: When institutional forces predict banks risk exposure. *Administrative Science Quarterly, 59*(3), 442–473. doi:10.1177/0001839214537810

Ba, S., & Pavlou, P. A. (2002). Evidence of the effect of trust building technology in electronic markets: Price premiums and buyer behavior. *Management Information Systems Quarterly, 26*(3), 243–268. doi:10.2307/4132332

Bagozzi, R. P., & Dholakia, U. (1999). Goal Setting and Goal Striving in Consumer Behavior. *Journal of Marketing, 63*, 19–32. doi:10.2307/1252098

Bai, L., Tang, J., Yang, Y., & Gong, S. (2014). Hygienic food handling intention: An application of the theory of planned behavior in the Chinese cultural context. *Food Control, 42*, 172–180. doi:10.1016/j.foodcont.2014.02.008

Barreto, A. M. (2014). The word-of-mouth phenomenon in the social media era. *International Journal of Market Research, 56*(5), 631–654.

Benbasat, I., & Weber, R. (1996). Research Commentary: Rethinking Diversity in Information System Research. *Information Systems Research, 7*(4), 389–399. doi:10.1287/isre.7.4.389

Bharadwaj, A. S. (2000). A resource-based perspective on information technology capability and firm performance: An empirical investigation. *Management Information Systems Quarterly, 24*(1), 169–196. doi:10.2307/3250983

Bianchi, C., & Andrews, L. (2015). Investigating marketing managers perspectives on social media in Chile. *Journal of Business Research, 68*(12), 2552–2559. doi:10.1016/j.jbusres.2015.06.026

Bickart, B., & Schindler, R. M. (2001). Internet forums as influential sources of consumer information. *Journal of Interactive Marketing, 15*(3), 31–40. doi:10.1002/dir.1014

Bickart, B., & Schindler, R. M. (2001). Internet forums as influential sources of consumer information. *Journal of Interactive Marketing, 15*(3), 31–40. doi:10.1002/dir.1014

Bilgihan, A. (2016). Gen Y customer loyalty in online shopping: An integrated model of trust, user experience, and branding. *Computers in Human Behavior, 61*, 103–113. doi:10.1016/j.chb.2016.03.014

Briones, R. L., Kuch, B., Liu, B. F., & Jin, Y. (2011). Keeping up with the digital age: How the American Red Cross uses social media to build relationships. *Public Relations Review*, *37*(1), 37–43. doi:10.1016/j. pubrev.2010.12.006

Bruhn, M., Schoenmueller, V., & Schafer, D. B. (2012). Are social media replacing traditional media in terms of brand equity creation? *Management Research Review*, *35*(9), 770–790. doi:10.1108/01409171211255948

Casaló, L. V., Flaviàn, C., & Guinlalìu, M. (2010). Determinants of the intention to participate in firm-hosted online travel communities and effects on consumer behavioural intentions. *Tourism Management*, *31*(6), 898–911. doi:10.1016/j.tourman.2010.04.007

Chan, K. W., & Li, S. Y. (2010). Understanding consumer-to-consumer interactions in virtual communities: The salience of reciprocity. *The Journal of Business*, *63*, 1033–1040.

Chan, K. W., & Li, S. Y. (2010). Understanding consumer-to-consumer interactions in virtual communities: The salience of reciprocity. *The Journal of Business*, *63*, 1033–1040.

Chang, Y., Yu, H., & Lu, H. (2015). Persuasive messages, popularity cohesion, and message diffusion in social media marketing. *Journal of Business Research*, *68*(4), 777–782. doi:10.1016/j.jbusres.2014.11.027

Chathoth, P. K., Ungson, G. R., Harrington, R. J., & Chan, E. S. (2016). Co-creation and higher order customer engagement in hospitality and tourism services: A critical review. *International Journal of Contemporary Hospitality Management*, *28*(2), 222–245. doi:10.1108/IJCHM-10-2014-0526

Cheung, C. M. K., & Lee, M. K. O. (2012). What drives consumers to spread electronic word of mouth in online consumer-opinion platforms. *Decision Support Systems*, *53*(1), 218–225. doi:10.1016/j. dss.2012.01.015

Cheung, M. F. Y., & To, W. M. (2015). Do task- and relation-oriented customers co-create a better quality of service? An empirical study of customer-dominant logic. *Management Decision*, *53*(1), 179–197. doi:10.1108/MD-05-2014-0252

Chevalier, J. A., & Mayzlin, D. (2006). The effect of word of mouth on sales: Online book reviews. *JMR, Journal of Marketing Research*, *43*(3), 345–354. doi:10.1509/jmkr.43.3.345

Childers, T. L., Carr, C. L., Peck, J., & Carson, S. (2002). Hedonic and utilitarian motivations for online retail shopping behavior. *Journal of Retailing*, *77*(4), 511–535. doi:10.1016/S0022-4359(01)00056-2

Cho, S. H., Chang, K. L., Yeo, J. H., Head, L. W., Zastrow, M., & Zdorovtsov, C. (2015). Comparison of fruit and vegetable consumption among Native and non-Native American population in rural communities. *International Journal of Consumer Studies*, *39*(1), 67–73. doi:10.1111/ijcs.12153

Choi, B., & Lee, I. (2016). *Trust in open versus closed social media: The relative influence of user- and marketer generated content in social network services on customer trust*. Telematic Information. doi:10.1016/j.tele.2016.11.005

Chu, S. C., & Kim, Y. (2011). Determinants of consumer engagement in electronic word-of-mouth (eWOM) in social networking sites. *International Journal of Advertising*, *30*(1), 47–75. doi:10.2501/ IJA-30-1-047-075

Culnan, M., McHugh, P., & Zubillaga, J. (2010). How large U.S. companies can use twitter and other social media to gain business value. *MIS Quarterly Executive, 9*(4), 243–259.

Curran, J., & Lennon, R. (2011). Participating in the conversation: Exploring usage of social media. *Academy of Marketing Studies Journal, 15*(1), 21–38.

Davis, F. D., Bagozzi, R. P., & Warshaw, P. R. (1989). User acceptance of computer technology: A comparison of two theoretical models. *Management Science, 35*(8), 982–1003. doi:10.1287/mnsc.35.8.982

De Bruyn, A., & Lilien, G. L. (2008). A multi-stage model of word-of-mouth influence through viral marketing. *International Journal of Research in Marketing, 25*(3), 151–163. doi:10.1016/j.ijresmar.2008.03.004

Di Maggio, P. J. (1997). Culture and cognition. *Annual Review of Sociology, 23*(1), 263–287. doi:10.1146/annurev.soc.23.1.263

Di Pietro L., Di Virgilio F. & Pantano E. (2013). Negative eWOM in user-generated contents: recommendations for firms and organizations. *International Journal of Digital Content Technology and its Applications, 7*(5), 1-8.

Di Virgilio, F., Camillo, A. A., & Camillo, I. (2017). The Impact of Social Network on Italian Users Behavioural Intention for the Choice of a Medical Tourist Destination. *International Journal of Tourism and Hospitality Management in the Digital Age, 1*(1), 36–49. doi:10.4018/IJTHMDA.2017010103

Featherman, M. S., & Hajli, N. (2015). Self-service technologies and e-services risks in social commerce era. *Journal of Business Ethics*, 1–19.

Ferreira, J. B., da Rocha, A., & Ferreira da Silva, J. (2014). Impacts of technology readiness on emotions and cognition in Brazil. *Journal of Business Research, 67*(5), 865–873. doi:10.1016/j.jbusres.2013.07.005

Fishbein, M., & Ajzen, I. (1975). *Belief, attitude, intention and Behavior: An introduction to theory and research*. Reading, MA: Addison-Wesley.

French, A. M., & Read, A. (2013). My moms on Facebook: An evaluation of information sharing depth in social networking. *Behaviour & Information Technology, 32*(10), 1049–1059. doi:10.1080/0144929X.2013.816775

Friedland, R., & Alford, R. R. (1991). Bringing society back in: Symbols, practices, and institutional contradictions. In W. Powell & P. J. DiMaggio (Eds.), *The New Institutionalism in Organizational Analysis* (pp. 232–263). Chicago: University of Chicago Press.

Gefen, D. (2002). Reflections on the dimensions of trust and trustworthiness among online consumers. *The Data Base for Advances in Information Systems, 33*(3), 38–53. doi:10.1145/569905.569910

Gefen, D., Karahanna, E., & Straub, D. W. (2003). Trust and TAM in online shopping: An integrated model. *Management Information Systems Quarterly, 27*(1), 51–90.

Gefen, D., & Straub, D. (2000). The relative importance of perceived ease of use in IS adoption: A study of E-commerce adoption. *Journal of the Association for Information Systems, 1*, 1–30.

Gefen, D., & Straub, D. W. (2004). Consumer trust in B2C e-commerce and the importance of social presence: Experiments in e-products and e-services. *Omega, 32*(6), 407–424. doi:10.1016/j.omega.2004.01.006

Greenwood, R., Raynard, M., Kodeih, F., Micelotta, E. R., & Lounsbury, M. (2011). Institutional Complexity and Organizational Responses. *The Academy of Management Annals, 5*(1), 317–371. doi:10.10 80/19416520.2011.590299

Hajli, N., & ... . (2016). A social commerce investigation of the role of trust in a social networking site on purchase intentions. *Journal of Business Research*. doi:10.1016/j.jbusres.2016.10.004

Heinonen, K., & Strandvik, T. (2015). Customer-dominant logic: Foundations and implications. *Journal of Services Marketing, 29*(6/7), 472–484. doi:10.1108/JSM-02-2015-0096

Heinonen, K., Strandvik, T., Mickelsson, K. J., Edvardsson, B., Sundström, E., & Andersson, P. (2010). A customer-dominant logic of service. *Journal of Service Management, 21*(4), 531–548. doi:10.1108/09564231011066088

Jackall, R. (1988). *Moral Mazes: The World of Corporate Managers*. New York: Oxford University Press.

Jiang, C., Zhao, W., Sun, X., Zhang, K., Zheng, R., & Qu, W. (2016). The effects of the self and social identity on the intention to microblog: An extension of the theory of planned behavior. *Computers in Human Behavior, 64*, 754–759. doi:10.1016/j.chb.2016.07.046

Kaiser, S., & Müller-Seitz, G. (2008). Leveraging lead user knowledge in software development: The case of weblog technology. *Industry and Innovation, 15*(2), 199–221. doi:10.1080/13662710801954542

Kaplan, A. M., & Haenlein, M. (2009). Consumers, companies, and virtual social worlds: A qualitative analysis of Second Life. *Advances in Consumer Research. Association for Consumer Research (U. S.), 36*(1), 873–874.

Kaplan, A. M., & Haenlein, M. (2010). Users of the world, unite! The challenges and opportunities of social media. *Business Horizons, 53*(1), 59–68. doi:10.1016/j.bushor.2009.09.003

Katz, E., & Lazarsfeld, P. F. (1955). *Personal Influence: The Part of Played by People in The Flow of Mass Communications*. Free Press.

Kim, A. J., & Ko, E. (2012). Do social media marketing activities enhance customer equity? An empirical study of luxury fashion brand. *Journal of Business Research, 65*(10), 1480–1486. doi:10.1016/j. jbusres.2011.10.014

Kim, E., Lee, J. A., Sung, Y., & Choi, S. M. (2016). Predicting selfie-posting behavior on social networking sites: An extension of theory of planned behavior. *Computers in Human Behavior, 62*, 116–123. doi:10.1016/j.chb.2016.03.078

Kim, S., & Park, H. (2013). Effects of various characteristics of social commerce (s-commerce) on consumers trust and trust performance. *International Journal of Information Management, 33*(2), 318–332. doi:10.1016/j.ijinfomgt.2012.11.006

King, R. A., Racherla, P., & Bush, V. D. (2014). What we know and dont know about online word-of-mouth: A review and synthesis of the literature. *Journal of Interactive Marketing, 28*(3), 167–183. doi:10.1016/j.intmar.2014.02.001

Kleina, A., Ahlfb, H., & Sharmac, V. (2015). Social activity and structural centrality in online social networks. *Telematics and Informatics*, *32*(2), 321–332. doi:10.1016/j.tele.2014.09.008

Laroche, M., Habibi, M. R., & Richard, M. O. (2013). To be or not to be in social media: How brand loyalty is affected by social media? *International Journal of Information Management*, *33*(1), 76–82. doi:10.1016/j.ijinfomgt.2012.07.003

Lee, M., Rodgers, S., & Kim, M. (2009). Effects of valence and extremity of eWOM on attitude toward the brand and website. *Journal of Current Issues and Research in Advertising*, *31*(2), 1–11. doi:10.108 0/10641734.2009.10505262

Leung, L. (2013). Generational differences in content generation in social media: The roles of the gratifications sought and of narcissism. *Computers in Human Behavior*, *29*(3), 997–1006. doi:10.1016/j. chb.2012.12.028

Levy, S. J. (2006). How New, How Dominant? In R. F. Lusch & S. L. Vargo (Eds.), *The Service-Dominant Logic of Marketing. Dialog, Debate, and Directions*. Armonk, NY: M.E. Sharpe.

Liang, T. P., & Lai, H. J. (2002). Effect of store design on consumer purchase: An empirical study of online bookstores. *Information & Management*, *39*(6), 431–444. doi:10.1016/S0378-7206(01)00129-X

Liang, T. P., & Turban, E. (2011). Introduction to the special issue, social commerce: A research framework for social commerce. *International Journal of Electronic Commerce*, *16*(2), 5–14. doi:10.2753/ JEC1086-4415160201

Litvin, S. W., Goldsmith, R. E., & Pan, B. (2008). Electronic word-of-mouth in hospitality and tourism management. *Tourism Management*, *29*(3), 458–468. doi:10.1016/j.tourman.2007.05.011

McInnis, D.J. (2004). Where Have All the Papers Gone? Reflections on the Decline of Conceptual Articles. *ACR News*, 1-3.

McKnight, D. H., & Chervany, N. L. (2001). What trust means in e-commerce customer relationships: An interdisciplinary conceptual typology. *International Journal of Electronic Commerce*, *6*(2), 35–59.

McKnight, D. H., Choudhury, V., & Kacmar, C. (2002). Developing and validating trust measures for e-commerce: An integrative typology. *Information Systems Research*, *13*(3), 334–359. doi:10.1287/ isre.13.3.334.81

Midyette, J. D., Youngkin, A., & Snow-Croft, S. (2014). Social media and communications: Developing a policy to guide the flow of information. *Medical Reference Services Quarterly*, *33*(1), 39–50. doi:10. 1080/02763869.2014.866482 PMID:24528263

Millissa, F. Y. (2016). Service co-creation in social media: An extension of the theory of planned behavior. *Computers in Human Behavior*, *65*, 260–266. doi:10.1016/j.chb.2016.08.031

Mou, Y., & Lin, C. A. (2015). Exploring podcast adoption intention via perceived social norms, interpersonal communication, and theory of planned behavior. *Journal of Broadcasting & Electronic Media*, *59*(3), 475-493.

Myers, J. G., Greyser, S. A., & Massy, W. F. (1979). The Effectiveness of Marketings R&D for Marketing Management: An Assessment. *Journal of Marketing*, *43*(1), 17–29. doi:10.2307/1250754

Oakley, R. L., & Salam, A. F. (2014). Examining the impact of computer-mediated social networks on individual consumerism environmental behaviors. *Computers in Human Behavior*, *35*, 516–526. doi:10.1016/j.chb.2014.02.033

OCass, A., & Fenech, T. (2003). Web retailing adoption: Exploring the nature of internet users web retailing behavior. *Journal of Retailing and Consumer Services*, *10*(2), 81–94. doi:10.1016/S0969-6989(02)00004-8

Park, D. H., & Kim, S. (2008). The effects of consumer knowledge on message processing of electronic word-of-mouth via online consumer reviews. *Electronic Commerce Research and Applications*, *7*(4), 399–410. doi:10.1016/j.elerap.2007.12.001

Pfeffer, J. (1993). Barriers to the Advance of Organizational Science: Paradigm Development as a Dependent Variable. *Academy of Management Review*, *18*(4), 599–620.

Porter, C. E., & Donthu, N. (2006). Using the technology acceptance model to explain how attitudes determine Internet usage: The role of perceived access barriers and demographics. *Journal of Business Research*, *59*(9), 999–1007. doi:10.1016/j.jbusres.2006.06.003

Rodriguez, M., Peterson, R. M., & Krishnan, V. (2012). Social medias influence on business-to-business sales performance. *Journal of Personal Selling & Sales Management*, *32*(2), 365–378. doi:10.2753/PSS0885-3134320306

Sashi, C. M. (2012). Customer engagement, buyer–seller relationships, and social media. *Management Decision*, *50*(2), 253–272. doi:10.1108/00251741211203551

Sashi, C. M. (2012). Customer engagement, buyer–seller relationships, and social media. *Management Decision*, *50*(2), 253–272. doi:10.1108/00251741211203551

Scott, W. R. (2014). *Institutions and Organizations: Ideas, Interests, and Identities*. Los Angeles, CA: Sage.

Suh, B., & Han, I. (2003). The impact of customer trust and perception of security control on the acceptance of electronic commerce. *International Journal of Electronic Commerce*, *7*(3), 135–161.

Summers, J. O. (2001). Guidelines for Conducting Research and Publishing in Marketing: From Conceptualization Though the Review Process. *Journal of the Academy of Marketing Science*, *29*(4), 405–415. doi:10.1177/03079450094243

Taylor, S., & Todd, P. A. (1995). Understanding information technology usage: A test of competing models. *Information Systems Research*, *6*(2), 144–176. doi:10.1287/isre.6.2.144

Teas, K. R., & Palan, K. M. (1997). The Realms of Scientific Meaning Framework for Constructing Theoretically Meaningful Nominal Definitions of Marketing Concepts. *Journal of Marketing*, *61*(4), 52–67. doi:10.2307/1251830

Thornton, P. H. (2004). *Markets From Culture: Institutional Logics and Organizational Decisions in Higher Education Publishing*. Stanford, CA: Stanford University Press.

Thornton, P. H., & Ocasio, W. (1999). Institutional logics and the historical contingency of power in organizations: Executive succession in the higher education publishing industry, 19581990. *American Journal of Sociology*, *105*(3), 801–843. doi:10.1086/210361

Thornton, P. H., & Ocasio, W. (2008). Institutional logics. In R. Greenwood, C. Oliver, K. Sahlin, & R. Suddaby (Eds.), *The Sage Handbook of Organizational Institutionalism* (pp. 99–129). Los Angeles, CA: Sage. doi:10.4135/9781849200387.n4

Thornton, P. H., Ocasio, W., & Lounsbury, M. (2012). *The Institutional Logics Perspective: A New Approach to Culture, Structure, and Process*. Oxford, UK: Oxford University Press. doi:10.1093/acprof:o so/9780199601936.001.0001

Tolbert, P. S., David, R. J., & Sine, W. D. (2011). Studying choice and change: The intersection of institutional theory and entrepreneurship research. *Organization Science*, *22*(5), 1332–1344. doi:10.1287/ orsc.1100.0601

Wang, T., Keng-Jung Yeh, R., Chen, C., & Tsydypov, Z. (2016). What drives electronic word-of-mouth on social networking sites? Perspectives of social capital and self-determination. *Telematics and Informatics*, *33*(4), 1034–1047. doi:10.1016/j.tele.2016.03.005

Whelan, E., Parise, S., De Valk, J., & Aalbers, R. (2011). Creating employee networks that deliver open innovation. *MIT Sloan Management Review*, *53*(1), 37–44.

Wu, C.-W. (2016). The performance impact of social media in the chain store industry. *Journal of Business Research*, *69*(11), 5310–5316. doi:10.1016/j.jbusres.2016.04.130

Yan, G., He, W., Shen, J., & Tang, C. (2014). A bilingual approach for conducting Chinese and English social media sentiment analysis. *Computer Networks*, *75*, 491–503. doi:10.1016/j.comnet.2014.08.021

Yoon, S. J. (2012). A social network approach to the influences of shopping experiences on E-WOM. *Journal of Electronic Commerce Research*, *13*(3), 213–223.

Zaglia, M. E. (2013). Brand communities embedded in social networks. *Journal of Business Research*, *66*(2), 216–223. doi:10.1016/j.jbusres.2012.07.015 PMID:23564989

Zhang, T. T., Kandampully, J., & Bilgihan, A. (2015). Motivations for customer engagement in online co-innovation communities (OCCs): A conceptual framework. *Journal of Hospitality and Tourism Technology*, *6*(3), 311–328. doi:10.1108/JHTT-10-2014-0062

Zmuda, N. (2013). *Pepsi Beverage Guru Unveils His Plan to Win the World Over*. Retrieved from <http:// adage.com/article/news/pepsi-beverage-guruunveils- plan-win-world/228641>

KEY TERMS AND DEFINITIONS

Co-Creation: Is a management initiative, or form of economic strategy, that brings different parties together (for instance, a company and a group of customers), in order to jointly produce a mutually valued outcome.

Customer-Dominant Logic: Is grounded in an understanding of consumers' lives and the use they make of services or products.

Embeddedness: Refers to the degree to which economic activity is constrained by non-economic institutions.

E-Vendor: Is an individual or company that sells goods or services to someone else in the economic production chain through the Internet as well as networking systems.

EWOM: Is defined as the exchange of product or service evaluations among people who meet, talk and text each other in the virtual world.

Intention: Purpose or attitude toward the effect of one's actions or conduct.

Social Media Platform: (Also social networking site or social media) is an online platform that is used by people to build social networks or social relations with other people who share similar personal or career interests, activities, backgrounds or real-life connections, and where can purchase online.

This research was previously published in Social Media for Knowledge Management Applications in Modern Organizations; pages 58-80, copyright year 2018 by Business Science Reference (an imprint of IGI Global).

Chapter 66
Facebook eWOM:
Self–Shared Versus System–Generated Credibility Cue

Payal S Kapoor
FORE School of Management, New Delhi, India

K R Jayasimha
Indian Institute of Management Indore, Indore, India

Srinivas Gunta
Indian Institute of Management Indore, Indore, India

Ashish Sadh
Indian Institute of Management Indore, Indore, India

ABSTRACT

The study examines how consumers, in a Facebook eWOM context, perceived source and message credibility by utilizing self-shared and system-generated cues. It investigates:(1) to what extent source and message credibility derived from these cues may lead to significant attitudinal responses and intentions to purchase; (2) and to what extent attitudinal responses are likely to vary with different levels and combinations of these credibility cues. Data was collected from 246 respondents who were exposed to Facebook eWOM scenarios. The structural model results confirm that the perceived source and message credibility derived from self-shared and system-generated cues are significant antecedents to purchase-related consideration for a brand. The results further confirm that these cues have an overall balancing effect: one compensates for the low level of the other leading to a significant persuasive response. The study evaluates traditional antecedents of WOM adoption, namely, perceived source and message credibility derived from unique interface-related features.

DOI: 10.4018/978-1-7998-9020-1.ch066

1. INTRODUCTION

Social media has enabled consumers the world over to share and access the personal experiences, thoughts, and opinions of others with ease. A great deal of brand-related information which is not marketer generated, or electronic word of mouth (eWOM), can be transferred via social media with the click of a few buttons. Prior studies suggest that eWOM shared or received via social media is changing the consumer decision-making process (Edelman, 2010; Schultz and Peltier, 2013). Consumers are connected in a network of brand-related conversation, and while this may facilitate the widespread dissemination of information, the downside is that eWOM on social media may be shared between those who have no prior relationship with the user in question. Furthermore, the interface may ensure significant anonymity to users, and very limited or no real personal information may be available about the users; in some cases, users may even be susceptible to identity deception (Moran and Muzellec, 2017). The interface itself is devoid of interpersonal and social context cues (Walther, 1996; Walther, 2007). Therefore, a critical question regarding this widespread medium of communication is: how do consumers perceive the credibility of brand-related information on social media? In other words, how do consumers form judgments about what to believe, and what information may lead to persuasive results? What types of interface-related information, heuristics, and cues are more impactful, and how much influence will translate to attitude formation or consumption-related behavior?

Consumers process information either systematically or based on heuristics. According to the heuristic-systematic model of information processing, users of social media, bounded by rationality, are likely to rely more on heuristics than systematic information processing (Hlee et al., 2018; Metzger et al., 2010). Prior research has examined source and message related credibility, and their influence in eWOM adoption along with which heuristics enable perceptions of credibility to form. For instance, Kim et al. (2016) found that messages with high "argument quality" and high perceived source credibility result in greater perceived usefulness of eWOM (Hur et al., s2017, p. 171). Cheung et al. (2008) evaluated credibility and information adoption with respect to online review comments and found messages and reviews that rated high in terms of comprehensiveness and relevance led to greater information adoption. Along similar lines, Baek et al. (2012) established that review ratings, perceived credibility, and actual content all help in credibility judgement. Reichelt et al. (2014, p. 65) have suggested that both "perceived credibility of relatively anonymous online comments" (message) and its "contributors" (source) influence the utility users derive from the eWOM. Interestingly, Mudambi and Schuff (2010) found more detailed and extensive reviews to be more believable. However, this may differ between search and experience goods. Finally, Ghose and Ipeirotis (2011) have concluded that subjectivity, readability, and linguistic correctness of reviews is useful for credibility judgment. These studies illustrate how the traditional indicators of credibility (source and message) are constructed in online customer communities and retail markets and how consumers establish overall credibility judgments. Present work investigates the heuristics that enable judgments of credibility specifically with respect to the Facebook eWOM context.

The focus of the present research is on the user's credibility evaluation of eWOM generated between weak connections on the social networking site (SNS) Facebook. Facebook, with 2.23 billion monthly active users,[1] is a "dominant social media format" most popular among consumers and marketers (Kim et al., 2015, p. 13; Schivinski and Dabrowski, 2015). Being the most popular SNS of current times, it has empowered users with easy access to social information and impression management of self. Facebook's interactive and static features that allow for user description, status updates, photos sharing, likes, comments, shares, check-ins, and recommendations, among other features, have created a unique platform for eWOM behavior. However, unlike product review sites, the influence of Facebook eWOM is not straightforward since the interface is embedded with several combinations of heuristics and information (Tong et al., 2008; Antheunis and Schouten, 2011). After reviewing the available literature, the study addresses how source credibility and message credibility are assessed in the Facebook eWOM context when the strength of the relation between users is weak. This experimental investigation focuses on answering the following critical questions: (1) To what extent do source and message credibility, as perceived in the Facebook eWOM context, lead to significant attitudinal responses to certain brands and the intention to purchase; and (2) to what extent are attitudinal responses likely to vary due to the distinctive Facebook interface credibility cues (self-shared and system-generated credibility cues).

2. THEORETICAL BACKGROUND

2.1. eWOM in a Computer Mediated Environment

The significance of face-to-face (FtF) WOM in consumer decision-making processes has been well researched in the marketing literature. It is found to be more influential than other forms of persuasive communication as it is received from familiar and trustworthy sources. Web 2.0 and the new media now provide many virtual avenues for consumers to continue such conversations, leading to the revision of terms from WOM to eWOM. Consumers can share their brand-related opinions via product review websites (e.g., mouthshut.com), online retailers' websites (e.g., amazon.com; flipkart.com), brands' websites (e.g., forums.us.dell.com), personal blogs, message boards, and SNS (e.g., Facebook, Instagram and Twitter) (Hennig-Thurau et al., 2004).

eWOM is defined as "any positive or negative statement made by potential, actual, or former customers about a product or company, which is made available to a multitude of people and institutions via the Internet" (Hennig-Thurau et al., 2004, p. 39). eWOM may be exchanged as a Twitter tweet (microblog), a blog post, a review or rating, or a Facebook post, among many other means. With the spread of internet and changing media consumption habits, several studies have found eWOM to be more influential than traditional marketer-generated communication (Triantafillidou and Siomkos, 2014).

eWOM has attracted significant research interest in the recent times for a number of reasons. Firstly, the computer mediated environment (CME), also defined as screen-mediated, significantly differs from FtF communication. Users in the CME are diverse and the environment "opens up the WOM network from one's immediate contacts to the entire Internet world" (Cheung et al., 2009, p. 9). Therefore, eWOM may be shared between users who have no significant prior relationship. Secondly, in the absence of non-verbal or social context cues, the overall influence and perception of eWOM is not straightforward. According to the "Social Information Processing Model" (Walther, 1996), despite the lack of non-verbal or social context cues, studies have concluded that increased intimacy and liking is possible in interactions tested in the CME if time is not a constraint. In other words, an eventual parity is observed between the impact of FtF interactions and interactions that take place in CME because, irrespective of the medium, individuals are driven by the "same overarching relational goals when interacting with others" (Edwards et al., 2013, p. A13; Yuksel and Labrecque, 2016). It is therefore likely that users adjust to the new environment with a lack of information and use alternative linguistic cues embedded in the interface for judgment (Walther, 1996; Walther, 2007). Therefore, in an environment where there is primarily an absence of nonverbal cues in addition no prior knowledge of the other, users of new media often rely on "different strategies to reduce uncertainty and to form impressions" (Antheunis et al., 2012, p. 758; Reichelt et al., 2014).

2.2. Facebook eWOM Among Weak Ties

Facebook and other SNSs offer several opportunities for users to indulge in eWOM behavior (Hennig-Thurau et al., 2004; Svensson, 2011; Humphrey et al., 2017). Facebook, being a social networking site, encourages "social interactions through profile-based user accounts" (Keenan and Shiri, 2009, p. 439). Users can indulge in Facebook eWOM, brand-related exchange of information, on Facebook by updating, commenting, liking, or sharing posts. As depicted in Figure 1, the influence of Facebook eWOM, just like any other form of WOM, is moderated by its perceived credibility. Being the biggest social media site, it has users connected across demographics and nationalities by providing tools and features that allow for the convenient spread of WOM. In fact, 62% of the "share of influence impressions" for eWOM were generated on Facebook (Svensson, 2011, p. 2). Not all posts on Facebook are private and not all friends (Facebook connections) are those who are known to the users in reality. Unlike other CMEs, apart from a user's profile-based information, Facebook also provides social context cues like mutual friends or shared interests through which total strangers often become friends on Facebook (Ellison et al., 2011). Recently, the Facebook interface has added an aggregated-information-based feature called trending. Brand-related topics are often found to be trending, targeting users who can read brand-related information in addition to other users whom they may not be friends with on Facebook (and otherwise). Hence the network's strength in terms of relationships and connections may fall anywhere on the continuum between very weak to strong. Tie strength refers to "the intensity of social relationship between customers," and on Facebook it may range from "strong primary ties—those with close friends and family members—to weak secondary ties (those with acquaintances rarely seen to non-existent ties with complete strangers)" (Chahal and Rani, 2017). Consequently, brand-related conversations are also taking place between users who have had no prior significant relationship. In fact, as Facebook eWOM is generated, it may get shared or receive engagement from others in the network; this allows for a "greater number of acquaintances (weak ties) to receive information instead of just close friends (strong ties)" (Svensson, 2011, p. 2). According to Gladwell (2010), weak ties are more significant and relevant than strong ties on social networking sites (this statement may be truer for microblogging sites like Twitter); with new features being added on Facebook, like trending, recommendations, and marketplaces, a network of users is enabled to connect with each other online without necessarily being connected with each other offline.

2.3. Source and Message Credibility Evaluation for the Facebook eWOM Context

Perceived credibility is an important antecedent to eWOM adoption (Cheung et. al., 2009). WOM will generally have a significant influence if the information is perceived as credible, both in FtF interaction and CME (Hovland and Weiss, 1951; Dholakia and Sternthal, 1977; Fan et al., 2013). However, social media has made the determination of credibility significantly complex, and, as suggested, this is largely due to the fact that the "standard conventions of determining credibility break down in cyberspace" (Metzger et al., 2010, p. 413). There are several reasons for this. To begin, as has already been explained, interactions may take place between total strangers or those with whom there has been a limited prior relationship. In other words, tie strength between users may be predominantly weak. Additionally, the rationality of users may be bounded due to limitations of time or information and the user's judgement approach satisficing, whereby "people do not use all their cognitive resources to obtain optimal outcomes, but instead use just enough to provide a sufficiently optimal outcome for the context" (Metzger et al., 2010, p. 417). Furthermore, as per the heuristic-systematic model of information processing, people process information systematically or based on heuristics. Users of social media, bounded by rationality, are likely to rely extensively on heuristics than systematic information processing (Hlee et al., 2018) Lastly, unlike with FtF interactions, identity deception in CME is possible as different social media sites permit different degrees of anonymity to their users (Donath, 1999; Hollenbaugh and Everett, 2013). Therefore, it is posited that reliance on conventional methods of credibility determination may be unsuitable in the CME (Cheung et al., 2009; Metzger and Flanagin, 2013) and, more specifically, on social media.

Figure 1. Perceived credibility of Facebook eWOM

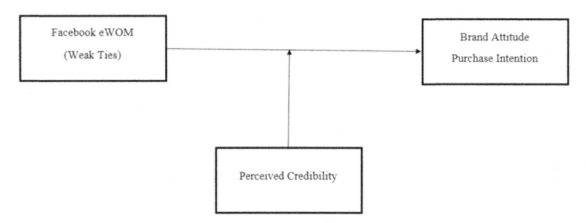

Traditionally, credibility evaluation involves the assessment of the source, message, and receiver characteristics (Wathen and Burkell, 2002). The importance of source credibility, assessed in terms of a source's characteristics such as attractiveness, physical appearance, familiarity, expertise, knowledge, and power, has been studied and validated in past research. The higher the source's perceived expertise, the higher the perceived trustworthiness in the overall assessment of credibility (Hovland and Weiss, 1951; Sundar et al., 2007; Todd and Melancon, 2018). Expertise refers to a source's ability or qualifications to accurately convey a message, and trustworthiness refers to the source's "integrity, reputation and motivation to tell the truth" (Hovland and Weiss, 1951; O'Keefe, 2002; Borah and Xiao, 2018, p. 2). Even though source credibility is one of the "fundamental predictors of a consumer's acceptance of a message in WOM," on social media platforms such as Facebook eWOM with weak ties, it is more difficult to make judgements of a source's expertise and trustworthiness (Hu and Kim, 2018, p. 126). Perceived expertise and trustworthiness on social media on the part of the consumer is fraught with complexity and ambiguity, specifically with respect to the use of both official and unofficial self-generated and system-generated information (Borah and Xiao, 2018).

Source credibility theory asserts that greater the perception of source credibility, the more likely it is that the receiver will develop a positive attitude toward the brand along with the intention to purchase.

If the perceived credibility is weak, it may not lead to any attitudinal outcomes. Attitude is "an overall persistent evaluation towards people, things, or goods", including "favourable or unfavourable evaluation, emotional feeling, and behavioural tendency" (Wu and Wang, 2011, p. 453). Brand attitude refers to a consumer's "evaluative judgement about a given object" (Crites et al., 1994, p. 619). It is further defined as the "predisposition to respond in a favourable or unfavourable manner to a particular brand after the advertising stimulus has been shown to the individual" (Phelps and Hoy, 1996, p. 80). A positive or negative brand attitude may be a consequence of the persuasiveness of the communication (Reichelt et al., 2014). Attitude has three components: cognition, affect, and conation. The current research focuses on the affective (brand attitude) and conative (intention to purchase). Intention to purchase refers to the behavioral response in the form of the likelihood of a consumer purchasing the brand. Brand attitude plays a crucial role in motivating the consumer's purchase intentions (Phelps and Hoy, 1996). However, attitudes toward the brand and the subsequent intentions to purchase vary significantly with changes in the perceptions of credibility (Hovland and Weiss, 1951; Dholakia and Stemthal, 1977). In other words, Facebook eWOM as generating insignificant source credibility may have a persuasive effect on cultivating positive attitudes toward the brand and intentions to purchase. Therefore, the first set of hypotheses of the study evaluates the attitudinal responses based on consumers' perceived credibility in the Facebook eWOM context:

H1: For the Facebook eWOM context, perceived source credibility will be significantly related to (a) a consumer's attitude towards the brand; and (b) the intention to purchase.

H2: For the Facebook eWOM context, a consumer's attitude toward the brand will mediate the relationship between perceived source credibility and the intention to purchase.

Furthermore, the perceived quality of the message content also plays a significant role in establishing consumer trust (Jin and Lee, 2014). Message credibility refers to the perceived believability of the written or spoken words of the message based on the argumentative quality, clarity, factuality, and perceived accuracy. Attribute ambiguity and language abstraction are the relevant factors for consideration. Attribute ambiguity is based on the "reasons put forth by consumers as to why they loved or hated the branded experience," and language abstraction can range from concrete to abstract (Moran and Muzellec, 2017, p. 8). Attribution theory (Kelley 1973) is useful here for clarification in the sense that content that is strongly "attributed to stimulus level characteristics (i.e. product quality or functionality)" will lead to greater message credibility than those "perceived to be based on non-stimulus attributes such as incentives or personal satisfaction" (Moran & Muzellec, 2017, p. 8). In other words, eWOM messages that focus extensively on highlighting facts like product attributes, also referred to as attribute-value messages, are found to be more believable than emotional recommendations (Lee and Youn, 2009; Cheung et al., 2009; Luo et al., 2013). However, to what degree these assessments of message credibility are important for judgments of Facebook eWOM, specifically regarding attitudinal responses, is unclear. Therefore, the following are hypothesized:

H3: For the Facebook eWOM context, perceived message credibility will be significantly related to (a) a consumer's attitude toward the brand; and (b) the intention to purchase.

H4: For the Facebook eWOM context, the consumer's attitude toward the brand will mediate the relationship between perceived message credibility and the intention to purchase.

H5: Consumers' attitudes toward the brand will be significantly related to their intentions to purchase in the Facebook eWOM context

Figure 2 displays the conceptual model.

Figure 2. Conceptual model

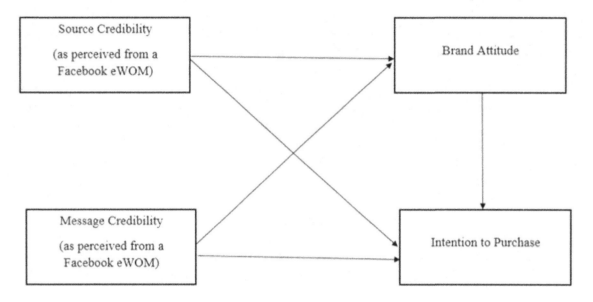

2.4. Self-Shared and System-Generated Credibility Cues

According to Walther and Parks (2002, p. 538), FtF interactions have the benefit of several "visual, auditory and verbal cues" that help in source and message credibility judgments. A lack of visual, auditory, and verbal cues will have to be compensated for by "information cues afforded by the channel" for credibility judgments (Edwards et al., 2013, p. A15). Hence, in the absence of FtF interactions, credibility judgment in a CME is predominantly based on all the stored-information cues embedded in the interface. Kang (2010), using Metzger's measurements of online credibility (source, message/content, and medium), conducted focus group discussions to understand how users perceive the credibility of blogs. Participants of the focus group confirmed the source's (blogger's) perceived "knowledge, passion, transparency, [and] reliability" influenced their judgments along with how "authentic, insightful, informative, consistent, accurate, timely, popular, fair, and focused" the content appeared to be (Edwards et al., 2013). Along the same lines, different social media sites offer a "variety of stored information of others" or cues that are accessible to users for credibility judgments including interface-related features, user profile details, user's likes and dislikes, user shared posts (messages), network strength, and user photographs, among others (Walther et al., 2009, p. 230). This variety of "interactive and static" cues, which enable overall credibility assessment, are categorized as self-shared and system-generated credibility cues (Tong et al., 2008; Antheunis and Schouten, 2011, p. 392). While the self-shared cues are owned and controlled by the user by self-selectively sharing information, system-generated cues are those "that the computer system chooses to show on a user's profile, such as the number of friends the profile owner has gathered" (Antheunis & Schouten, 2011, p. 392; Utz, 2010). In the following sections, these two types of cues are explained in greater detail.

2.4.1. Self-Shared Cues – Source Related – Facebook eWOM Context

A Facebook user's personal characteristics, knowledge, and expertise can be deciphered from his or her self-shared public or semi-public profiles (Castillo et al., 2011; Luo et al., 2013). Most social media sites "provide identity information" such as user names, location, and even display photos (fake or real). According to Hlee et al., "The identity cue is a self-created cue showing their private information" (2018, p. 5). The "About" section allows the user to self-describe himself or herself by providing information on work experience, education, places lived, life events, hobbies, interests, and also an "Intro" description. Self-shared user profile details enable source credibility assessment and are therefore described as self-shared source credibility cues (Walther et al., 2009; Walther, 2011; Castillo et al., 2011)

2.4.2. Self-Shared – Message Related - Facebook eWOM Context

As has already been explained, eWOM messages or Facebook posts, self-shared by users, which are high on product "attribute value," well-structured, factual, and overall informative are perceived as more credible than simple recommendations. In other words, Facebook eWOM messages articulated in a detailed and informative manner with significant information on product attributes enable message credibility assessment and are therefore described as self-shared message credibility cues (Eastin, 2001; Lee and Young, 2009).

2.4.3. System-Generated Credibility Cues

A social media interface has a significant amount of system-generated information regarding users' "network and interaction structure" which becomes the basis for credibility assessment (Edwards et al., 2013). System-generated cues are defined as "pieces of information that are system or machine rendered" (Wang et al., 2018, p. 106). These cues, such as the number of Facebook friends, are a machine-generated value and are hence considered as unbiased and accurate, unlike self-shared information. Hlee et al. suggest that the "number of reviews, friends, fans or elite badge etc." are system-generated information that strengthen the reputation of a user, like a "collective endorsement by peers" (2018, p. 6). Some recent studies have tested system-generated cues in the context of credibility assessment. A study by Westerman et al. (2012) suggests that there is a curvilinear effect of the number of followers; that is, either too many followers or too few can lead to lower credibility perception. Another study by Tong et al. (2008) examined this effect specifically for Facebook, examining how the number of Facebook friends leads to source attractiveness. Similar results were observed. Therefore, system-generated cues ought to influence the overall credibility of the user and user-generated Facebook eWOM. Thus, the system-generated cues tested in the present research include the number of Facebook friends in addition to the number of likes, comments, and shares that a particular post has gathered (Sundar, 2008; Westerman et al., 2012). Figure 3 shows the credibility in the social media setting.

Figure 3. Credibility in the social media setting

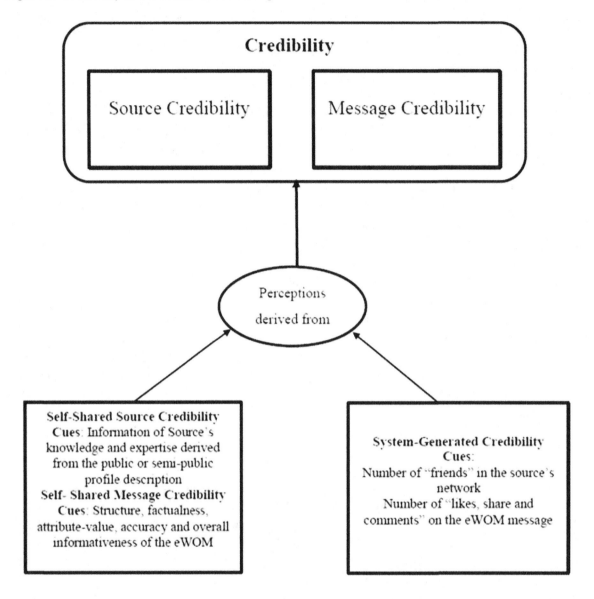

2.5. Self-Shared Versus System-Generated Credibility Cues

Self-shared information on Facebook is derived from content created by the user. This content could be a "self-selective presentation" allowing the user to create a more desirable profile. It is suggested that self-shared information can be "more selective, malleable, and subject to self-censorship" (Walther, 1996, p. 20; Edwards et. al., 2013). Since identity is distinct from one's physical self, "One can have as many electronic personas as one has time and energy to create," leading to increased possibilities for online deception (Donath, 1999, p. 2; Hollenbaugh and Everett, 2013). Furthermore, as posited by the MAIN model (Sundar, 2008), system-generated cues are perceived as more credible since the information has been "verified and/or chosen by a non-human entity (i.e., machine or computer)". Machine-generated heuristics are assumed to be free of subjective bias and possible deceptions. System-generated cues offer heuristics appeal, and people may perceive them as more credible simply "because technology is presumed free of subjective bias, [and thus] consumers tend to trust machine-generated information more than information provided by human agents" (Edwards et al., 2013, p. A13).

Studies suggest that on social media, the "average Joes" are perceived as more credible than high achievers in the offline world. In other words, users with "average" Facebook profile descriptions (self-shared) having high system-generated credibility cues may be perceived as more credible than those who have glamorous self-shared profile information (Aral et al., 2013). However, "both types of cues are heuristic information" and they are both likely to play uniquely influential and critical roles in the establishment of credibility (Hlee et al., 2018, p. 6) Hence the attitudinal response is likely to vary significantly with respect to Facebook eWOM messages having different combinations (high and low) of system-generated and self-shared credibility cues. Since it is impossible to separate system-generated from self-shared credibility cues on Facebook, especially in the eWOM context, there are four possible combinations (**Table 1**).

Table 1. Credibility cue combinations in Facebook eWOM

Credibility cue combinations in Facebook eWOM			
		System Generated Cues	
		High	Low
Self Shared Cues	High	High System High Self (1)	Low System High Self (2)
	Low	High System Low Self (4)	Low System Low Self (3)

Thus, the next set of hypotheses concern group-level differences in attitudinal responses to self-shared versus system-generated credibility cues:

H6: The influence of the consumer's attitude toward the brand on the intention to purchase will significantly differ for credibility cue Combination 1 and Combination 4.

H7: The influence of the consumer's attitude toward the brand on the intention to purchase will significantly differ for credibility cue Combination 1 and Combination 2.

H8: The influence of the consumer's attitude toward the brand on the intention to purchase will significantly differ for credibility cue Combination 1 and Combination 3.

H9: The influence of the consumer's attitude toward the brand on the intention to purchase will significantly differ for credibility cue Combination 2 and Combination 4.

H10: The influence of the consumer's attitude toward the brand on the intention to purchase will significantly differ for credibility cue Combination 2 and Combination 3.

H11: The influence of the consumer's attitude toward the brand on the intention to purchase will significantly differ for credibility cue Combination 3 and Combination 4.

3. METHODOLOGY

3.1. Research Design

This study was structured as a 2 X 2 between-subject factorial design experiment where two treatment variables at two levels each were manipulated to observe the impact on the dependent variables. The treatment variables were self-shared creditability cues (high and low) and system-generated credibility cues (high and low). The self-shared credibility cues were considered to be high when both source and message credibility cues were manipulated to high, and they were considered to be low when both source and message credibility were manipulated to be low. A manipulation check was conducted for the dependent variables of perceived source credibility and perceived message credibility. The factorial experiment design has four treatment conditions, as shown in Table 2 (Appendix). Three stimuli were used in the experiment: a mock Facebook profile; a mock Facebook post (eWOM message), and a fictitious brand in the mobile phone category (Zingbel 1.1).

3.2. Experiment Description, Stimuli Pre-Testing and Selection

A replicate of a typical Facebook timeline was developed upon which a Facebook user shared his opinion about a recently acquired mobile phone in the form of a Facebook post. Respondents were exposed to a static webpage displaying the Facebook interface. The mock Facebook profile and mock Facebook post were manipulated with self-shared source and message credibility cues and system-generated credibility cues. All stimuli were subject to extensive pre-testing before final selection. Only the results found to be statistically significant were used for the main study. Details of the stimuli and pre-testing are below:

3.2.1. System-Generated Cues

Based on previous studies, system-generated cues are manipulated as high when there is a very high number of friends, post likes, shares, and comments, and low when there is very low number of these same activities (Tong et al., 2008; Castillo et al., 2011; Westerman et al., 2012).

3.2.2. Self-Shared Cues

Self-shared source credibility cues were manipulated as high or low on the basis of the mock Facebook user's educational background, attractiveness of the display picture, work experience, and self-description in "About Me." Forty-five respondents were exposed to six mock Facebook profiles with varying self-shared source credibility cues; those perceived as most and least credible were selected (Willemsen et al., 2012). A source credibility scale was used to measure each stimulus (Ohanian, 1990). Pre-testing helped in selecting mock Facebook profiles that were perceived as either highly credible or not credible ($\bar{X}_{Credibility}$ = 55.52 & 39.26 (High vs. Low), p < .05)

Self-shared message credibility cues were manipulated as either high or low on the basis of attribute level information, message factuality, accuracy, message structure, informativeness, and argument strength (Eastin, 2001). Again, forty-five respondents were exposed to six mock Facebook brand-related posts with varying self-shared message credibility cues; those perceived as most and least credible were selected (Willemsen et al., 2012). Pre-testing helped in selecting mock Facebook posts that were perceived as having either high or low message credibility ($\bar{X}_{Message\ Credibility}$ = 13.5, 7 (High vs. Low), p < .05). As mentioned, high self-shared credibility cues are a combination of high source and high message credibility cues, and low self-shared credibility cues are a combination of low source and low message credibility cues. For all the four treatment conditions (Table 2, Appendix), positive message framing was used (Grewal et al., 1994).

3.2.3. Fictitious Brand

The fictitious brand selected was in the "smart mobile phone" product category. This product category was chosen because familiarity and ownership with respect to this category are very high, which are important selection criteria for any experiment-based study (Low and Lamb, 2000). Moreover, the mobile phone category is also one of the most frequently discussed online. "Zingbel 1.1" was chosen as the brand name so as to follow a similar naming strategy of all other popular brands in the market. Most of the existing brands found in the market follow a "nonword brand name" or "irrelevant word brand name" strategy (Lerman and Garbarino, 2002). This enabled category familiarity and at the same time prevented the influence of an existing brand.

An amalgamation of mock Facebook profiles and posts regarding the fictitious mobile phone brand Zingbel 1.1 was displayed on a static webpage for all treatment conditions. Respondents could click on the tab "About", that would lead to the full profile of the source. The webpage appeared to be exactly like any Facebook timeline (**Appendix – Figure 4 and 5** are examples of treatment conditions 1 and 4).

3.3. Experiment Procedure

The experiment was conducted with undergraduate, graduate, and executive students of a leading public-state funded institution of higher studies. A total of 275 respondents participated in the study, and 246 responses were considered for analysis as the rest did not clear the qualifying questionnaire. All measures were selected from existing literature and were found to be reliable (**Appendix – Table 3. Construct details & reliability; Table 4. Control variables; sample description**). Each experiment was conducted individually; the respondents were sequentially allotted one of the four experiment conditions. Instructions were given so that respondents would assume that the mock Facebook profile was an acquaintance and friend of his or her Facebook network (weak-tie relationship). Respondents were told to view the experimental Facebook timeline carefully, including the full profile. Each respondent viewed the stimulus for three to four minutes, after which a pen-and-paper-based questionnaire was administered.

3.4. Manipulation Check

Respondents were asked about their perception of source credibility, message credibility, and credibility derived from system-generated cues across treatment conditions (Dholakia and Sternthal, 1977; Har-mon and Koney, 1982; Perdue and Summers, 1986; Grewal et al., 1994; Bone, 1995; Liu et al., 2017). All stimuli were found to be significantly accurate, confirming that the manipulation was accurately perceived, details of the same in the below section.

3.4.1. Self-Shared Source Credibility

Manipulation check results confirmed self-shared source credibility cues manipulated as high and low were accurately perceived as high and low, with source credibility as the only grouping variable used ($\bar{X}_{High\ Self-shared\ Source\ Credibility}$ = 53.72, SD = 7.716; $\bar{X}_{Low\ Self-shared\ Source\ Credibility}$ = 43.59, SD = 8.32, p < .05).

3.4.2. Self-Shared Message Credibility

Manipulation check results confirmed that the self-shared message credibility cues manipulated as high and low were accurately perceived as high and low, with message credibility as the only grouping variable used ($\bar{X}_{High\ Self-shared\ Mource\ Credibility}$ = 14.12, SD = 3.13; $\bar{X}_{Low\ Self-shared\ Mource\ Credibility}$ = 12.46, SD = 3.37, p < .05).

3.4.3. System-Generated Cues

One limitation this study has is that there is no measure to capture system-generated cues. There was an insignificant difference in the mean of the self-shared source credibility and self-shared message credibility cues when system-generated cues were manipulated as high and low, which can be attributed to the accurate manipulation of system-generated cues. The results of the manipulation check confirmed the same ($\bar{X}_{High\ Self-shared\ Source\ Credibility}$ = 49.00, SD = 9.52; $\bar{X}_{Low\ Self-shared\ Source\ Credibility}$ = 48.30, SD = 9.46; $\bar{X}_{High\ Self-shared\ Mource\ Credibility}$ = 13.20, SD = 3.29; $\bar{X}_{Low\ Self-shared\ Mource\ Credibility}$ = 13.34, SD = 3.43, p > .05).

4. RESULTS

As mentioned above, data was collected for 275 respondents, and 246 responses were considered for final evaluation. Partial least squares structural equation modeling (PLS-SEM) using SmartPLS 3.0 was used to study the relations between measures. PLS-SEM is considered useful to study causal-predictive analyses (Hair et al., 2012). The measurement model assesses the necessary validity and reliability of all the constructs. Convergent validity is studied by observing the significance of factor loadings, average variance extracted (AVE), and reliability measures (Appendix – Table 5, Figure 6). All loadings were satisfactory (> .60) except for one item, but since all the AVE were satisfactory (> .50) and reliability was greater than 0.70 for all the constructs, the item was retained (Hair et al., 2012).

The structural model results are presented in Table 6 and Figure 7. The first set of hypotheses (H1 to H5) of the study evaluate the attitudinal responses to consumers' perceived source credibility and perceived message credibility for the Facebook eWOM context. H1a was not supported, as the path coefficient from source credibility to brand attitude was not significant (β = 0.12, t = 1.48, p > 0.05). However, H1b was supported, as the path coefficient from source credibility to purchase intention was significant (β = 0.16, t = 2.30, p < 0.05). Mediation of brand attitude in the relationship with source credibility was also not established since the special indirect effect was not significant. Therefore, H2 was not supported ($\beta = 0.02$, t = 1.15, p > 0.05). H3a and H3b were supported, as the path coefficients from message credibility to brand attitude and purchase intention were significant ($\beta = 0.33$, t = 3.87, p < 0.05; $\beta = 0.37$, t = 5.29, p < 0.05). Mediation of brand attitude in the relationship with message credibility was established since the special indirect effect was significant. Therefore, H4 was supported ($\beta = 0.06$, t = 1.99, p > 0.05). Finally, H5 was supported since the coefficient from brand attitude to purchase intention was significant ($\beta = 0.18$, t = 2.66, p > 0.05).

For the second set of hypotheses (H6 to H11) which investigate the difference in the attitudinal responses of consumers to self-shared and system-generated credibility cues, multi-group analysis using PLS-SEM was conducted for the different treatment conditions. The results of the multi-group analysis are presented in Table 7. The difference in the path coefficients was evaluated using parametric tests and the Welch-Satterthwaite T-Test. H7 and H10 were not supported, while the remaining hypotheses were supported (**Table 7**).

5. DISCUSSION

Research on Facebook eWOM has paid little attention to interface-related cues that may influence attitudinal responses. The current study focused on three critical questions: (1) How can source and message credibility be assessed for the Facebook eWOM context when the strength of the relation between users is weak? (2) To what extent do source and message credibility, as perceived in the Facebook eWOM context, lead to significant attitudinal responses in form of consumers' attitudes to the brand and intentions to purchase? and (3) How will attitudinal responses vary with respect to different Facebook interface-related source and message credibility cues (self-shared and system-generated)? Based on the review of the extant literature, the current study systematically argues that consumers are likely perceive credibility based on the source and message, which is useful since the information is being exchanged between people in a CME, and those who are involved may not be part of a physical social network. More specifically, perception of source and message credibility were found to deviate significantly on the Facebook interface, and more so when the connection was a weak tie.

Perceived credibility is an important antecedent to eWOM adoption, and the first set of hypotheses tested to what extent source and message credibility, as perceived in the Facebook eWOM context, may lead to significant attitudinal responses. H1a was not supported, suggesting consumers' perceptions of source credibility did not lead to significant attitudes toward the brand. However, H1b was supported, confirming that perception of source credibility significantly leads to intentions to purchase. This result is confusing, considering that the affective component of attitude leads to the conative component. The relationship could be insignificant due to some aspect of the sample and data. However, the p-value of β ($\beta = 0.12$) was .139, although certainly not sufficient to be significant but not large enough to completely dismiss the role of source credibility as an antecedent to attitudinal responses considering that intention to purchase was significant. In other words, perceived source credibility, derived from the Facebook profile information of the source, was a significant antecedent to induce purchase-related consideration for the brand. Furthermore, H3a and H3b were both supported, suggesting that consumer perception of message credibility does cultivate significant attitudes toward the brand and intentions to purchase. The results strongly confirm that perceived message credibility, derived from a Facebook post, is a significant antecedent to induce attitudes toward the brand as well as purchase-related considerations. Furthermore,

H5 was supported, confirming that a general attitude toward the brand, as influenced by the source and message credibility cues, will lead to significant intentions to purchase. In sum, the present study sought to contribute to theory and practice by shedding light on how consumers perceive credibility and its subsequent influence, and this is demonstrated in the empirical results of H1 to H5.

H6 to H11 investigate to what extent attitudinal responses vary with respect to self-shared and system-generated credibility cues. The overall results support the conclusion that different combinations of self-shared and system-generated cues will result in varying attitudinal responses. It is interesting to note that H6, H8, H9, and H11 were supported, but H7 and H10 were not supported. H6 compares the influence of consumer attitudes toward the brand on purchase intentions between treatment conditions 1 and 4. The only difference between the two treatment conditions is the low level of self-shared credibility cues for treatment condition 4. H6 was supported, and the difference in β was significant. Furthermore, β was higher for Condition 1 (treatment condition 1: $\beta = 0.263$, treatment condition 4: $\beta = -0.177$), suggesting a stronger combined influence when both types of credibility cues were manipulated to be high versus another with low self-generated cues. However, the same was not true for H7 and H10. H7 compares treatment conditions 1 and 2. With self-shared cues manipulated as high, the only difference between the two treatment conditions was the low level of system-generated cues for treatment condition 2. H7 was not supported, and the difference in β was not significant, suggesting that the influence of brand attitudes on purchase intentions is not significantly different when the only difference between the two conditions is the level of the system-generated cue. H10 compares treatment conditions 2 and 3. With system-generated cues manipulated to be low, the only difference between the two treatment conditions was the high level of self-generated cues for treatment condition 2. H10 was not supported, and the difference in the β coefficient was not significant, suggesting that the influence of brand attitudes on purchase intentions was not significantly different when the only difference between the two conditions was the level of the self-shared cue. However, H8 was supported, and it compared treatment conditions 1 and 3. Treatment condition 3 was based on low levels of both self-shared and system-generated cues, and the difference in β was significant. It is interesting to observe that β was lower for treatment condition 1 than treatment condition 3 (treatment condition 1: $\beta = 0.263$, treatment condition 3: $\beta = 0.652$), suggesting that the influence of an unfavorable attitude towards the brand is stronger on unfavourable purchase intentions with both self-shared and system-generated credibility manipulated to be low. H9 was also supported in comparing treatment conditions 2 and 4. The difference between the two treatment conditions is that while treatment condition 2 had high levels of self-shared cues with system-generated cues as minimal, treatment condition 4 was the reverse. The difference in β was significant given that it was higher for treatment condition 2 than treatment condition 4 (treatment condition 2: $\beta = 0.450$, treatment condition 4: $\beta = -0.177$), suggesting that the high self-shared credibility cues, despite being combined with low system-generated cues, had a stronger influence of brand attitudes on intentions to purchase compared with treatment conditions with low self-generated cues and high system-generated cues. Lastly, H11 compared treatment conditions 4 and 3. H11 was supported, and the difference in β was significant. It is interesting to observe that, just like with H8, β was lower for treatment condition 4 than treatment condition 3 (treatment condition 4: $\beta = -0.177$, treatment condition 3: $\beta = 0.652$), once again suggesting the influence of unfavourable attitudes toward the brand being stronger on unfavourable purchase intentions with both self-shared and system-generated credibility manipulated to be low.

These results indicate that, in general, when both self-shared and system-generated cues were high, the influence of brand attitudes on purchase intentions were significantly different for two out of the three combinations of treatment conditions. Similarly, when both self-shared and system-generated cues were low, the influence of brand attitudes on purchase intentions was significantly different for two out of three treatment conditions. Clearly, self-shared and system-generated cues have a balancing effect on the overall adoption of the Facebook eWOM. The lower level of the one compensates for the higher levels of another, allowing the consumer to make an overall judgment based on the information available. In other words, system-generated credibility cues like the number of friends a user has may be able compensate for a lack of self-shared expertise of the source and believability of the content; at the same time, for another Facebook eWOM, high levels of self-shared expertise of the source and believability of content may be able to compensate for low system-generated cues.

6. IMPLICATIONS FOR THEORY AND PRACTICE

The context of inquiry of the current study warrants deeper consideration. SNSs like Facebook are immensely popular, allowing users to create and share eWOM with ease, with such content being shared and re-shared multiple times, thus allowing for the secondary dissemination of brand-related information to the friends of friends network. Therefore, understanding how users assess credibility in a weak-tie Facebook eWOM context is of significant importance to marketers. The higher the perception of credibility, the greater will be the consumer's disposition toward the brand. This study presents how different sets of cues, embedded in the Facebook interface, have a variable influence on users. Specifically, different levels and combinations of self-shared and system-generated credibility cues were observed to influence the consumers' attitudes toward the brand and intentions to purchase differently, confirming that the adoption of the Facebook eWOM is likely to differ depending on the nature of the self-shared and system-generated credibility cues. In general, this research brings to fore how traditional measures of credibility judgment are changing. The importance of system-generated credibility cues, a unique set of heuristics of CME for overall credibility judgment, cannot be stressed enough. Even self-shared information can have a confounding effect on the overall judgment that is made. Current research contributes to theory as it allows for a deeper understanding of online consumer and eWOM behavior, and both areas are of critical importance in the new media age.

Marketers often utilize "exogenously-created WOM" or WOM marketing (WOMM) as a promotional tool, often referred to as "intentional influencing of consumer-to-consumer communications by professional marketing techniques" (Kozinets et al., 2010, p. 71). Before the rise in popularity of digital platforms, such practices were restricted by geography and context, but in recent times, "influencer marketing" is a critical component of the promotional mix of brands. Influential users of SNSs are identified, and marketers may share brand-related information through "seeding campaigns." Users on SNSs are perceived as credible by measuring their "social score;" in other words, their credibility is evaluated using "new tactics and metrics" (Kozinets et al., 2010, p. 73). The current research is a study in this direction; it will help marketers understand the various sources of credibility and their respective influential power. Therefore, it is insightful for the effective development of WOMM campaigns and influencer-based marketing research.

There are many ways marketers are using Facebook as a promotional medium. Brands with Facebook pages are very common and important from a consumer point of view. Some of these pages can also be consumer created (Kabadayi and Price, 2014). The credibility of the brand increases if the users engaging with it are perceived as credible. The present research provides insight into this issue. Marketers can determine which user is more influential than others, and certain posts shared by users which have the potential of being perceived as credible can be pinned or prominently posted on the brand's Facebook wall.

"Trending" is a recent feature that has been added to the Facebook interface. Very often, brand-related topics are found to be trending. Users can read what other users have shared even if they may not be connected as friends. The same is true for other features like "Recommendations" and "Marketplaces," or user generated public posts that may go viral via hashtags; in these cases, information can be shared without users being friends, and thus this is a legitimate source of brand related information. However, to what extent users are influenced by these trending messages or recommendations will significantly depend on their perceived credibility derived from system-generated and self-shared cues. The present study is therefore helpful to marketers in effectively using WOMM to co-create positive brand narratives.

7. LIMITATIONS AND FUTURE RESEARCH

Credibility assessment is a receiver-based judgment. Receiver-based traits, including characteristics like susceptibility to informal influence, the need for uniqueness, the capability of empathy, or narcissism may further moderate the responses to Facebook eWOM. The current study did not examine receiver-based factors. Furthermore, treatment condition 3, which had both self-shared cues and system-generated cues manipulated to be low, indicated a high β of brand attitude to purchase intention. While this does not change the result, a high β is intriguing. Authors intuitively conclude this to be a receiver-based influence. It is possible the response is influenced by the "underdog effect." The low self-shared source credibility cues and low system-generated cues possibly created a strong feeling of sympathy for the mock Facebook profile (Paharia et al., 2010). Hence, future studies focused on the influence of receiver-based traits could help validate the results.

This study attempts to facilitate understanding of credibility assessment and its influence in the limited context of Facebook eWOM being shared between weak ties. Hence, another limitation is the applicability of the results to other SNSs like Instagram or Twitter. Both SNSs have their own unique interfaces with distinctive embedded self-shared and system-generated cues. Further generalization can be made only once the other sites are tested. Moreover, strong ties have also been found to have a significant influence in social media; further studies should focus on eWOM being shared between strong ties.

Another limitation of the study is the use of a fictitious brand. A fictitious brand was used to enable control for each respondent's prior brand knowledge and brand-related information being shared by alternative sources. In reality, consumers are simultaneously exposed to multiple brand-related messages from numerous sources. Hence, further studies can focus on existing brands, especially when additional marketer generated promotions are part of the context.

Despite these limitations, the current research has brought to the several directions of further study. Other product categories can be explored such that the influence of the category of product may be further determined. In addition, the role of credibility with respect to eWOM related to low-priced products and experienced goods may be different for high-priced products and searched goods. Furthermore, the role of anonymity and identity deception can be further explored. With social media becoming a critical platform for brand-related conversations, further research can only benefit marketers.

ACKNOWLEDGMENT

The infrastructural support provided by FORE School of Management, New Delhi to Prof Payal S Kapoor is gratefully appreciated.

REFERENCES

Antheunis, M. L., & Schouten, A. P. (2011). The effects of other-generated and system-generated cues on adolescents' perceived attractiveness on social network sites. *Journal of Computer-Mediated Communication*, *16*(3), 391–406. doi:10.1111/j.1083-6101.2011.01545.x

Aral, S., Dellarocas, C., & Godes, D. (2013). Introduction to the special issue-social media and business transformation: A framework for research. *Information Systems Research*, *24*(1), 3–13. doi:10.1287/isre.1120.0470

Baek, H., Ahn, J., & Choi, Y. (2012). Helpfulness of online consumer reviews: Readers' objectives and review cues. *International Journal of Electronic Commerce*, *17*(2), 99–126. doi:10.2753/JEC1086-4415170204

Borah, P., & Xiao, X. (2018). The Importance of 'Likes': The Interplay of Message Framing, Source, and Social Endorsement on Credibility Perceptions of Health Information on Facebook. *Journal of Health Communication*, *23*(4), 399–411. doi:10.1080/10810730.2018.1455770 PMID:29601271

Castillo, C., Mendoza, M., & Poblete, B. (2011). Information credibility on Twitter. In *Proceedings of the 20th International Conference on the World Wide Web* (pp. 675-684). ACM. 10.1145/1963405.1963500

Chahal, H., & Rani, A. (2017). How trust moderates social media engagement and brand equity. *Journal of Research in Interactive Marketing*, *11*(3), 312–335. doi:10.1108/JRIM-10-2016-0104

Cheung, C. M., Lee, M. K., & Rabjohn, N. (2008). The impact of electronic word-of-mouth: The adoption of online opinions in online customer communities. *Internet Research*, *18*(3), 229–247. doi:10.1108/10662240810883290

Cheung, M. Y., Luo, C., Sia, C. L., & Chen, H. (2009). Credibility of electronic word-of-mouth: Informational and normative determinants of on-line consumer recommendations. *International Journal of Electronic Commerce*, *13*(4), 9–38. doi:10.2753/JEC1086-4415130402

Crites, S. L. Jr, Fabrigar, L. R., & Petty, R. E. (1994). Measuring the affective and cognitive properties of attitudes: Conceptual and methodological issues. *Personality and Social Psychology Bulletin*, *20*(6), 619–634. doi:10.1177/0146167294206001

Dholakia, R. R., & Sternthal, B. (1977). Highly credible sources: Persuasive facilitators or persuasive liabilities? *The Journal of Consumer Research*, *3*(4), 223–232. doi:10.1086/208671

Donath, J. S. (1999). *Identity and deception in the virtual community. Communities in Cyberspace* (pp. 29–59). Routledge.

Eastin, M. S. (2001). Credibility assessments of online health information: The effects of source expertise and knowledge of content. *Journal of Computer-Mediated Communication, 6*(4).

Edwards, C., Spence, P. R., Gentile, C. J., Edwards, A., & Edwards, A. (2013). How much Klout do you have... A test of system generated cues on source credibility. *Computers in Human Behavior, 29*(5), A12–A16. doi:10.1016/j.chb.2012.12.034

Ellison, N. B., Steinfield, C., & Lampe, C. (2011). Connection strategies: Social capital implications of Facebook-enabled communication practices. *New Media & Society, 13*(6), 873–892. doi:10.1177/1461444810385389

Fan, Y. W., Miao, Y. F., Fang, Y. H., & Lin, R. Y. (2013). Establishing the adoption of electronic word-of-mouth through consumers' perceived credibility. *International Business Research, 6*(3), 58–65. doi:10.5539/ibr.v6n3p58

Ghose, A., & Ipeirotis, P. G. (2011). Estimating the helpfulness and economic impact of product reviews: Mining text and reviewer characteristics. *IEEE Transactions on Knowledge and Data Engineering, 23*(10), 1498–1512. doi:10.1109/TKDE.2010.188

Gladwell, M. (2010). Small change. *The New Yorker*, October 4, pp. 42-49.

Hollenbaugh, E. E., & Everett, M. K. (2013). The effects of anonymity on self-disclosure in blogs: An application of the online disinhibition effect. *Journal of Computer-Mediated Communication, 18*(3), 283–302. doi:10.1111/jcc4.12008

Hur, K., Kim, T. T., Karatepe, O. M., & Lee, G. (2017). An exploration of the factors influencing social media continuance usage and information sharing intentions among Korean travelers. *Tourism Management, 63*, 170–178. doi:10.1016/j.tourman.2017.06.013

Hlee, S., Lee, H., & Koo, C. (2018). Hospitality and Tourism Online Review Research: A Systematic Analysis and Heuristic-Systematic Model. *Sustainability, 10*(4), 1141–1168. doi:10.3390u10041141

Hovland, C. I., & Weiss, W. (1951). The influence of source credibility on communication effectiveness. *Public Opinion Quarterly, 15*(4), 635–650. doi:10.1086/266350

Hu, Y., & Kim, H. J. (2018). Positive and negative eWOM motivations and hotel customers' eWOM behavior: Does personality matter? *International Journal of Hospitality Management, 75*, 27–37. doi:10.1016/j.ijhm.2018.03.004

Humphrey, W. F. Jr, Laverie, D. A., & Rinaldo, S. B. (2017). Brand choice via incidental social media exposure. *Journal of Research in Interactive Marketing, 11*(2), 110–130. doi:10.1108/JRIM-04-2016-0025

Jin Ma, Y., & Lee, H. H. (2014). Consumer responses toward online review manipulation. *Journal of Research in Interactive Marketing, 8*(3), 224–244. doi:10.1108/JRIM-04-2013-0022

Kabadayi, S., & Price, K. (2014). Consumer–brand engagement on Facebook: Liking and commenting behaviors. *Journal of Research in Interactive Marketing, 8*(3), 203–223. doi:10.1108/JRIM-12-2013-0081

Keenan, A., & Shiri, A. (2009). Sociability and social interaction on social networking websites. *Library Review, 58*(6), 438–450. doi:10.1108/00242530910969794

Kim, D. H., Spiller, L., & Hettche, M. (2015). Analyzing media types and content orientations in Facebook for global brands. *Journal of Research in Interactive Marketing*, 9(1), 4–30. doi:10.1108/JRIM-05-2014-0023

Kim, M. J., Chung, N. H., Lee, C. K., & Preis, M. W. (2016). Dual-route of persuasive communications in mobile tourism shopping. *Telematics and Informatics*, 33(2), 293–308. doi:10.1016/j.tele.2015.08.009

Kozinets, R. V., De Valck, K., Wojnicki, A. C., & Wilner, S. J. (2010). Networked narratives: Understanding word-of-mouth marketing in online communities. *Journal of Marketing*, 74(2), 71–89. doi:10.1509/jmkg.74.2.71

Lee, M., & Youn, S. (2009). Electronic word of mouth. *International Journal of Advertising*, 28(3), 473–499. doi:10.2501/S0265048709200709

Lerman, D., & Garbarino, E. (2002). Recall and recognition of brand names: A comparison of word and nonword name types. *Psychology and Marketing*, 19(7-8), 621–639. doi:10.1002/mar.10028

Liu, X., Hu, J., & Xu, B. (2017). Does eWOM matter to brand extension? An examination of the impact of online reviews on brand extension evaluations. *Journal of Research in Interactive Marketing*, 11(3), 232–245. doi:10.1108/JRIM-02-2016-0012

Low, G. S., & Lamb, C. W. Jr. (2000). The measurement and dimensionality of brand associations. *Journal of Product and Brand Management*, 9(6), 350–370. doi:10.1108/10610420010356966

Luo, C., Luo, X. R., Schatzberg, L., & Sia, C. L. (2013). Impact of informational factors on online recommendation credibility: The moderating role of source credibility. *Decision Support Systems*, 56, 92–102. doi:10.1016/j.dss.2013.05.005

Metzger, M. J., & Flanagin, A. J. (2013). Credibility and trust of information in online environments: The use of cognitive heuristics. *Journal of Pragmatics*, 59, 210–220. doi:10.1016/j.pragma.2013.07.012

Metzger, M. J., Flanagin, A. J., & Medders, R. B. (2010). Social and heuristic approaches to credibility evaluation online. *Journal of Communication*, 60(3), 413–439. doi:10.1111/j.1460-2466.2010.01488.x

Mudambi, S. M., & Schuff, D. (2010). What makes a helpful review? A study of customer reviews on Amazon.com. *Management Information Systems Quarterly*, 34(1), 185–200. doi:10.2307/20721420

Moran, G., & Muzellec, L. (2017). eWOM credibility on social networking sites: A framework. *Journal of Marketing Communications*, 23(2), 149–161. doi:10.1080/13527266.2014.969756

Paharia, N., Keinan, A., Avery, J., & Schor, J. B. (2010). The underdog effect: The marketing of disadvantage and determination through brand biography. *The Journal of Consumer Research*, 37(5), 775–790. doi:10.1086/656219

Perdue, B. C., & Summers, J. O. (1986). Checking the success of manipulations in marketing experiments. *JMR, Journal of Marketing Research*, 23(4), 317–326. doi:10.1177/002224378602300401

Phelps, J. E., & Hoy, M. G. (1996). The Aad-Ab-PI relationship in children: The impact of brand familiarity and measurement timing. *Psychology and Marketing*, 13(1), 77–105. doi:10.1002/(SICI)1520-6793(199601)13:1<77::AID-MAR5>3.0.CO;2-M

Reichelt, J., Sievert, J., & Jacob, F. (2014). How credibility affects eWOM reading: The influences of expertise, trustworthiness, and similarity on utilitarian and social functions. *Journal of Marketing Communications, 20*(1-2), 65–81. doi:10.1080/13527266.2013.797758

Sundar, S. S. (2008). *The MAIN model: A heuristic approach to understanding technology effects on credibility. In Digital Media, Youth, and Credibility* (pp. 73–100). .

Sundar, S. S., Knobloch-Westerwick, S., & Hastall, M. R. (2007). News cues: Information scent and cognitive heuristics. *Journal of the American Society for Information Technology, 58*(3), 366–378. doi:10.1002/asi.20511

Schivinski, B., & Dabrowski, D. (2015). The impact of brand communication on brand equity through Facebook. *Journal of Research in Interactive Marketing, 9*(1), 31–53. doi:10.1108/JRIM-02-2014-0007

Schultz, D. E., & Peltier, P. (2013). Social Media's Slippery Slope: Challenges, Opportunities and Future Research Directions. *Journal of Research in Interactive Marketing, 7*(2), 86–99. doi:10.1108/JRIM-12-2012-0054

Svensson, A. (2011). *Facebook – the Social Newspaper that Never Sleeps – A study of Facebook eWOM's persuasiveness on the receivers.* University of Gothenburg.

Todd, P. R., & Melancon, J. (2018). Gender and live-streaming: Source credibility and motivation. *Journal of Research in Interactive Marketing, 12*(1), 79–93. doi:10.1108/JRIM-05-2017-0035

Triantafillidou, A., & Siomkos, G. (2014). Consumption experience outcomes: Satisfaction, nostalgia intensity, word-of-mouth communication and behavioural intentions. *Journal of Consumer Marketing, 31*(6/7), 526–540. doi:10.1108/JCM-05-2014-0982

Utz, S. (2010). Show me your friends and I will tell you what type of person you are: How one's profile, number of friends, and type of friends influence impression formation on social network sites. *Journal of Computer-Mediated Communication, 15*(2), 314–335. doi:10.1111/j.1083-6101.2010.01522.x

Walther, J. B. (1996). Computer-mediated communication impersonal, interpersonal, and hyperpersonal interaction. *Communication Research, 23*(1), 3–43. doi:10.1177/009365096023001001

Walther, J. B. (2007). Selective self-presentation in computer-mediated communication: Hyperpersonal dimensions of technology, language, and cognition. *Computers in Human Behavior, 23*(5), 2538–2557. doi:10.1016/j.chb.2006.05.002

Walther, J. B., & Parks, M. R. (2002). Cues filtered out, cues filtered in. In Handbook of Interpersonal Communication (pp. 529-563).

Walther, J. B., Van Der Heide, B., Hamel, L. M., & Shulman, H. C. (2009). Self-generated versus other-generated statements and impressions in computer-mediated communication a test of warranting theory using Facebook. *Communication Research, 36*(2), 229–253. doi:10.1177/0093650208330251

Wathen, C. N., & Burkell, J. (2002). Believe it or not: Factors influencing credibility on the Web. *Journal of the American Society for Information Science and Technology, 53*(2), 134–144. doi:10.1002/asi.10016

Westerman, D. W., Spence, P. R., & Van Der Heide, B. (2012). A social network as information: The effect of system generated reports of connectedness on credibility and health care information on Twitter. *Computers in Human Behavior*, *28*(1), 199–206. doi:10.1016/j.chb.2011.09.001

Wang, L., Qian, D., & Zhu, L. (2018). The effect of system generated cues on microblog rewarding repost behavior – A source credibility perspective. *Journal of Electronic Commerce Research*, *19*(1), 104–118.

Wu, P. C., & Wang, Y. C. (2011). The influences of electronic word-of-mouth message appeal and message source credibility on brand attitude. *Asia Pacific Journal of Marketing and Logistics*, *23*(4), 448–472. doi:10.1108/13555851111165020

Yuksel, M., & Labrecque, L. I. (2016). Digital buddies': Parasocial interactions in social media. *Journal of Research in Interactive Marketing*, *10*(4), 305–320. doi:10.1108/JRIM-03-2016-0023

ENDNOTE

[1]   https://www.statista.com/statistics/264810/number-of-monthly-active-facebook-users-worldwide/

This research was previously published in the International Journal of Online Marketing (IJOM), 9(3); pages 23-48, copyright year 2019 by IGI Publishing (an imprint of IGI Global).

APPENDIX

Table 2. Factorial experiment design

Credibility cue combinations in Facebook eWOM - Treatment Conditions			
		System Generated Cues	
		High	Low
Self Shared Cues	High	High System High Self (1) - 61 respondents	Low System High Self (2) - 60 respondents
	Low	High System Low Self (4) - 62 respondents	Low System Low Self (3) - 63 respondents

Table 3. Construct details and reliability

Construct	Scale Source	No. of Items	Items	Cronbach α
Brand attitude	Lutz, 1989	3	Zingbel 1.1 is a good product; Zingbel 1.1 is a favourable product; Zingbel 1.1 is a pleasant product	0.841
Purchase intention	Lutz, 1989	2	I would like to buy Zingbel 1.1; I would like to own Zingbel 1.1	0.843
Message credibility	Eastin,2001	3	The Facebook post was not at all accurate/very accurate; not at all factual/very factual; not at all believable/very believable	0.792
Source credibility	Ohanian, 1990	10	The Facebook profile was Inexpert/expert; inexperienced/experienced; unqualified/qualified; unknowledgeable/knowledgeable; undependable/dependable; dishonest/honest; unbelievable/believable; insincere/sincere; untrustworthy/trustworthy	0.895

Table 4. Measurement model results

Measurement Model Results				
Construct	Factor Loading	CA	CR	AVE
Brand Attitude		0.841	0.904	0.759
BA1	0.869			
BA2	0.875			
BA3	0.870			
Purchase Intention		0.843	0.927	0.864
PI1	0.927			
PI2	0.932			
Source Credibility		0.895	0.913	0.514
SC1	0.742			
SC2	0.745			
SC3	0.741			
SC4	0.774			
SC5	0.764			
SC6	0.702			
SC7	0.594			
SC8	0.698			
SC9	0.669			
SC10	0.722			
Message Credibility		0.792	0.878	0.705
MC1	0.855			
MC2	0.809			
MC3	0.855			

Table 5. Sample description and control variables

Demographics		Count	Percentage
Gender	Male	180	74.38
	Female	62	25.62
Age	18-22	88	36.36
	23-27	102	42.15
	28-32	29	11.98
	33-40	15	6.20
	41-45	12	4.96
	46 and above	0	0.00
Average Facebook Usage per Week	1 to 2 hours	75	30.99
	2 to 5 hours	67	27.69
	More than 5 hours	104	42.98

Screening Questions	Qualifier Question	Selection Criterion
eWOM Behaviour	In the last six months, while browsing Facebook, have you ever come across any post where your Facebook friend has shared information, opinion or experience related to any product or service?	"Yes" to at least one of them
	In the last six months, while browsing Facebook, have you ever shared some information, opinion or experience related to any product or service with your Facebook friends?	
	In the last six months, while browsing Facebook, have you yourself ever recommended a information, opinion or experience to your Facebook friends through a post?	
Social Media Usage	On an average how many hours do you spend on Facebook in a week?	Minimum 1 - 2 hours

Table 6. SEM results

Hypothesis	Path	Original Sample (O)	Standard Deviation (STDEV)	T Statistics	p Values	Decision
H1a	Source credibility -> Brand Attitude	0.123	0.083	1.480	0.139	Not supported
H1b	Source credibility -> Purchase Intention	0.169	0.073	2.304	0.021	Supported
H2	Source credibility -> Brand Attitude -> Purchase Intention	0.023	0.020	1.157	0.248	Not supported
H3a	Message Credibility -> Brand Attitude	0.332	0.086	3.874	0.000	Supported
H3b	Message Credibility -> Purchase Intention	0.370	0.070	5.295	0.000	Supported
H4	Message Credibility -> Brand Attitude -> Purchase Intention	0.063	0.031	1.993	0.046	Supported
H5	Brand Attitude -> Purchase Intention	0.189	0.071	2.661	0.008	Supported

Table 7. SEM results

Hypothesis	Treatment Conditions	Path Coefficient Difference	p-Value (Welch-Satterthwait Test)	p-Value (Parametric Test)	Decision
H6	1 vs 4	0.440	0.021	0.019	Supported
H7	1 vs 2	0.188	0.304	0.302	Not supported
H8	1 vs 3	0.390	0.020	0.018	Supported
H9	2 vs 4	0.628	0.001	0.001	Supported
H10	2 vs 3	0.202	0.222	0.222	Not supported
H11	4 vs 3	0.829	0.000	0.000	Supported

Figure 4. Mock source profile and eWOM (experiment condition 1, screenshot of the webpage) (Full mocked profile displayed upon clicking About)

Figure 5. Mocked source profile and eWOM (experiment condition 4, screenshot of the webpage)

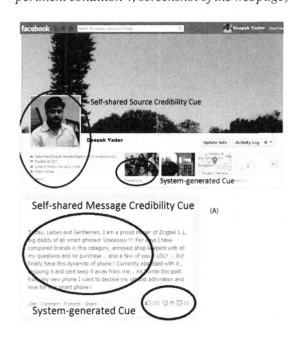

Figure 6. PLS Algorithm resultsi

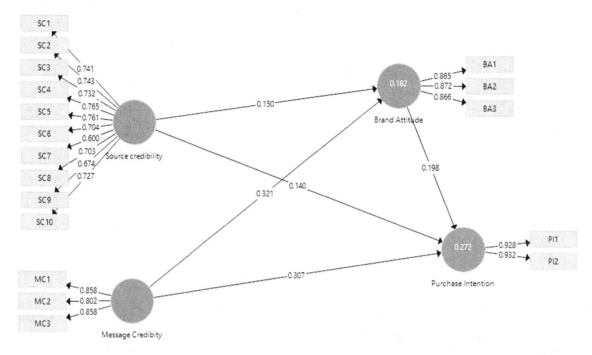

Figure 7. Bootstrapping results

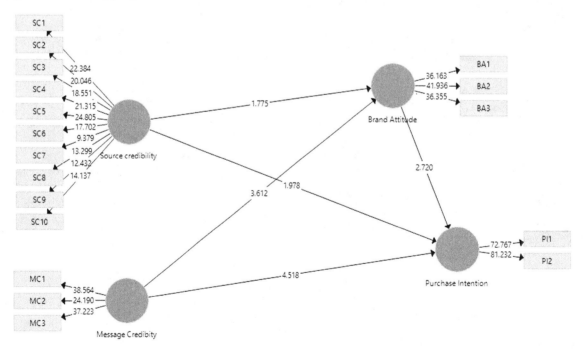

Chapter 67
Storytelling as an Approach to Voice Complaints and eWOM on Social Media/Facebook

Xiang Ying Mei
Inland Norway University of Applied Sciences, Norway

Ingrid K. Bagaas
Inland Norway University of Applied Sciences, Norway

Erling K. L. Relling
Inland Norway University of Applied Sciences, Norway

ABSTRACT

Customer complaints are unavoidable in any businesses and how firms handle such complaints will affect the public's perception of the company's brand and reputation. While storytelling is being embraced by an increasing number of companies as a different way to communicate their brand, many customers are now also using storytelling as an approach to voice their unfavourable experiences on the social media in regards to a particular unsatisfactory purchase as part of electronic word-of-mouth (eWOM). Such creative and humorous complaints serve as a way to cut through the clutter in order to gain the company's attention. Those companies that embrace such complaints by responding in an equally humorous and creative manner as part of their service recovery process will manage to recover their customers as well as their employees. As such posts are often shared publicly on the Internet, they may become viral and thus can create great positive effect on the company's reputation. Hence, it is important to empower the employees to recover the services using untraditional responses.

DOI: 10.4018/978-1-7998-9020-1.ch067

INTRODUCTION

Grégoire, Salle, and Tripp (2015) stress that with the possibilities of social media; a new world of Wild West has been created, where angry citizens and customers take the law into their own hands. Studies have shown that angry customers turn to social media channels such as Facebook as part of eWOM as they believe that the traditional channels are not as effective anymore. While eWOM can be both positive and negative, it is the negative eWOM that has detrimental effects on companies and firms. As complaints and negative eWOM have become more common in the recent years, customers who complain on social media have also become more creative as many unsatisfied customers are using stories and storytelling as ways to capture the attention of the companies. From the customers' point of view, storytelling as an approach can be used consciously or unconsciously as it is regarded an easy way to reach out and capture the listeners' attention through sympathy or humour. Such mindset is supported by the essence of storytelling, as human beings are able to remember stories better than pure facts, and stories are something that fascinate people (Lundqvist, Liljander, Gummerus, & van Riel, 2012). As explained by Woodside (2010, p. 535), "if you can harness imagination and the principles of a well-told story, then you get people rising to their feet amid thunderous applause instead of yawning and ignoring you". Furthermore, in many cases when storytelling as a complaint approach was initiated by the customers, some proactive companies also manage to recover the service by responding with stories as part of storytelling rather than providing standardised responses and apologies. Hence, storytelling can be used by a customer to voice a complaint, as well as by a company to subsequently respond to the complaint as part of its service recovery. Such approach creates elements of positive surprises, which turn the entire negative experience to something humorous and fun for both parties (Ferrari, 2015).

This chapter explores eWOM in the context of Facebook and customers' use of storytelling to voice their complaints as well as the companies' subsequent responses with storytelling in order to recover the service. While some of the examples are based on the retail sectors, Tronvoll (2012) argues that customer complaints in any sectors should consider the Service Dominant Logic (SD-Logic) approach. The SD-logic advocates that a service or a product does not have any value until it is being used by the customer (Vargo & Lusch, 2004). Customer complaint thus cannot be considered as an after-purchase behaviour but rather as a phenomenological, unfavourable service experience. Hence, service recovery is equally important in any sectors, not just service industries. Additionally, the retail industry is highly susceptible to service failure due to the number of people involved. Despite being a major industry in revenue generation, the study of service failures and recovery in the retail sector is still limited (Koc, 2018). Topics to be explored in this chapter includes storytelling, eWOM, word-of-mouse, service recovery, social media and Facebook as well as examples of creative complaints voiced as storytelling. While numerous studies have investigated customer complaints and service recoveries, investigating this topic through the lens of storytelling is still rather new (Black & Kelley, 2009) as the topic of storytelling in regards to marketing is still relatively under-researched (Mei, Hågensen, & Kristiansen, 2018).

BACKGROUND

Storytelling as an Approach to Voice Complaints

With roots in oral traditions, storytelling has been a natural way of communication between people (Kent, 2015). It is essentially a narrative form of telling everyday occurrences (Fog, Budtz, & Yakaboylu, 2005), although it is difficult to find one universal definition due to the complexity of the concept (Howison, Higgins-Desbiolles, & Sun, 2017). Human beings have always been fascinated by stories as stories influence people and help them to perceive and act in the world they live in (Weick, 1995). The more entertaining and dramatic the story is, the more popular the person or persons in the story will become (Mossberg & Johansen, 2006). Storytelling is also linked with memorability, as "human memory is story-based" (Schank, 1999, p. 12). When stories are stored in the memories, it is more likely for people to remember and relate to them. The power of story and storytelling is evident due to their significance in various field of research including human behaviour, psychology, history and other social studies (e.g. Green & Brock, 2000; McAdams, 2001; Scott, 2011; Singer & Bluck, 2001). There are various forms of storytelling including written or spoken as well as told through pictures, moving images, live audio or videos. While stories usually have a beginning, middle and an end, they do not necessary occur in that order or the story may simply convey a time and place (Lundqvist, Liljander, Gummerus & van Riel, 2012; Quesenbery & Brooks, 2010). Stories can also be used to describe a situation or context to illustrate a problem (Quesenbery & Brooks, 2010), an explanation which is relevant to this current chapter.

In business and marketing, storytelling is a type of content marketing, which has gained more attention in the recent years. While stories have existed as long as human beings have existed, using storytelling as a marketing approach or as a way to build a company's brands is rather recent. Explained by Woodside, Sood, and Miller (2008, p. 97) "...lectures tend to put people to sleep, stories move them to action. People relate to each other in terms of stories - and products and brands often play both central and peripheral roles in their stories". Hence, storytelling is now used by many companies to share their values and brands (Mossberg, 2008). Additionally, due to the development of the technology and changes in communication channels, it has also become easier for consumers to share their buying experiences. Many customers thus use their stories to reach and gain attention from the companies as well as other customers. Subsequently, it can be argued that customers are using storytelling as a tool to promote their opinions. This is also referred to as consumer narratives when WOM is structured as a story (Delgadillo & Escalas, 2004). For instance, Woodside et al. (2008) observe that many consumers are motivated to share their lived and buying experiences of brands online on various blogs and other types of personal journals. Although documenting buying experiences in such journals are not new, with the development of the Internet and social media, such experiences can be shared with the whole world (Kluth, 2006), which can create both opportunities and challenges for companies. Moreover, there are also some essentially differences between WOM and storytelling, as WOM may merely consist of facts or informative contents whereas storytelling is regarded as communication of both information and experiences, with stories that have the power to integrate cognitive and emotional elements, to engage listener and to produce a discourse about a particular experience (Howison et al., 2017; Minazzi, 2014; Solnet, Kandampully, & Kralj, 2010).

To determine whether a WOM communication is a message or a story, the structure is an important indicator (Howison et al., 2017). A story consists of two very important elements; that it is chronological and causal. In the case of chronology, the story takes place over time and it has a beginning, middle and end as discussed. Furthermore, causality defines relationships between story elements, meaning there should be a series of events that trigger a psychological reaction in the main character in order to explain the character's subsequent actions (Delgadillo & Escalas, 2004; Pennington & Hastie, 1986). Essentially, consumers who act as the protagonist, tell a story to their listener by relating their experiences with products, services and brands to others (Delgadillo & Escalas, 2004). There are also various types of eWOM communication stories. Narrative poems are for instance a type of poetry that tells a story. The story is usually written in verses and they may have rhymes, although it is not always necessary. The story may be short or long, simple or complex but it is normally dramatic, with objectives (Meyer, 2005). The following section further explores the topic of WOM and eWOM.

CUSTOMER OPINIONS AND CONVERSATIONS

Word-of-Mouth (WOM)

There are several definitions of what WOM is. One of the first to look at the impact of WOM on customer behaviour was Arndt (1967) who explains it as an oral person-to-person communication between a sender and a recipient. Such communication must not be considered by the recipient as advertisement about a brand, product or service (Buttle, 1998). Additionally, Bone (1992) argues that WOM must be regarded as a group phenomenon, where comments, thoughts and ideas are shared between two or more individuals and none of the individuals represents a source of marketing. According to Buttle (1998) however, such definitions are not satisfactory, as WOM can also be a business strategy as companies are increasingly offering incentives or rewards for customers to spread positive WOM to others.

Delgadillo and Escalas (2004) argue that although there is not much a company can do to influence WOM communication, it is important for marketers to understand how such process works as WOM can be both positive and negative. A positive WOM can increase the likelihood that a customer chooses to purchase the product or service, while a negative WOM has the opposite effect (Litvin, Goldsmith, & Pan, 2008). Tronvoll (2012) explains that if someone receives negative WOM from a source they regard as credible, this could have a greater impact on the customer than information from the company itself. Negative WOM has also been shown to have a greater impact on customer perceptions than a positive WOM (Tronvoll, 2012). This indicates that negative WOM can be very damaging to a business, its brands and reputation, and it may take a lot of effort to correct a negative WOM. Some of the reasons for a negative WOM to occur may be dissatisfaction with a product or service, and a company's failed attempts to provide proper complaint handling to recover the service as well as inadequate responses to complaints (Bruhn, Schoenmueller, & Schäfer, 2012). There is also greater likelihood that customers who are dissatisfied with the way that company handles their complaints will spread negative WOM and are less likely to want to use the company again in the future (Tronvoll, 2007).

Electric Word-of-Mouth (eWOM) and Word-of-Mouse

While it was common in the past to ask friends and acquaintances about experiences in regards to various products and services, consumers are now seeking information from strangers and customer reviews from different websites (Gelb & Sundaram, 2002). As discussed, customers are no longer just passive users as they also create and share content online (Edvardsson, Tronvoll, & Gruber, 2011). This requires businesses to adapt and ideally contribute to this new reality. With the new Web 2.0 era, new concepts have also occurred such as eWOM and Word-of-Mouse. According to Gelb and Sundaram (2002, p. 22), the biggest difference between face-to-face communication such as traditional WOM and eWOM including Word-of-Mouse is that eWOM is primarily "dominated by those eager to volunteer facts, opinions, warnings, and experiences to strangers". Hence, in the era of Internet and social media, Carl (2006, p. 605) further defines WOM as "informal, evaluative communication (positive or negative) between at least two conversational participants about the characteristics of an organisation and / or a brand, product, or service that could take place online or offline". Thus, while WOM has traditionally occurred between recipients face-to-face, it is now also occurring online over-the-air as eWOM has become the norm.

eWOM can bring both challenges and opportunities, including lower costs for accessing and exchanging information (Litvin et al., 2008). However, a challenge may be that it is very easy to be anonymous in conversations, which enables people to communicate statements that can be both misleading and out of context (Litvin et al., 2008). Anonymity can also lead to more customers willing to share all of their negative experiences of companies because they do not have a personal connection with the person who is reading the complaint (Gelb & Sundaram, 2002). Anonymity thus encourages more people to complain and many may choose to share things with others that they would not normally share with someone (Gelb & Sundaram, 2002). However, a negative side of anonymity and eWOM is that customers do not need any experience to write a negative review because no one can actually check if the customers have the basis to write the complaint (Gelb & Sundaram, 2002). Black and Kelley (2009) used in their survey of customer reviews from Yahoo!, and one of the major weaknesses of this survey as pointed out, is that anyone could write these reviews. For instance, there may be an employee or competitor trying to spread negativity about the company. Thus, in the context of social media in general, anonymity can thus be a challenge. Furthermore, another challenge of eWOM is the issue of private versus public. Both positive and negative eWOM including complaints can be public and private. Public eWOM includes customers voicing their views directly to the retailer by posting positive or negative eWOM on the retailer's Facebook page for instance. Private eWOM on the other hand involves customers voicing their opinions to other customers, friends and acquaintances through various social media platforms (Day & Landon, 1977; Harrison-Walker, 2001), and such opinions and subsequent conversations usually remain largely undetected by companies (Balaji, Jha, & Royne, 2015). However, the traditional understanding of private complaint may not be relevant in the era of social media as although customers can voice their opinions privately to friends and acquaintances, the post can be made publicly available to anyone. Hence, making it difficult to maintain a separation of private and public (Tronvoll, 2012).

eWOM on Facebook

Facebook, which is the most popular social media platform on the Internet worldwide followed by Youtube and Whatsapp (see figure 1), is the main platform explored in this book chapter. Anyone over the years of 13 can create an account on the platform with the exception of few countries such as China (except Hong Kong and Macau), Iran and North Korea where Facebook is fully banned while there may be restricted access in few other countries (Kirkland, 2014). As per October 2018, Facebook has approximately 2.2 million registered active users worldwide (Statista, 2018).

While anonymous eWOM is a recognised challenge on social media in general, such challenge is also dependent on the type of social media platform. In regards to Facebook, a user account is required to post and share information on the platform. Moreover, customers who post genuine complaints on

Facebook often use real accounts to do so as they are concerned with seeking response and understanding from other customers and the company rather than merely spreading negative eWOW (Mei, Bagaas, Relling, 2018). Nevertheless, fake accounts are also commonly found on the platform with an estimated of 116 million fake accounts as per third quarter of 2018 (Nicas, 2019). Fake accounts can be used to share information as well as to comment posts such as to fuel the initial complaints. Hence, although anonymity may not be an issue in regards to genuine complaints on Facebook, other people who join the conversation may be anonymous if fake accounts are used, especially if the posts are public. The following section discusses creative complaints in the context of social media.

Figure 1. Social media users worldwide
Source: (Statista, 2018)

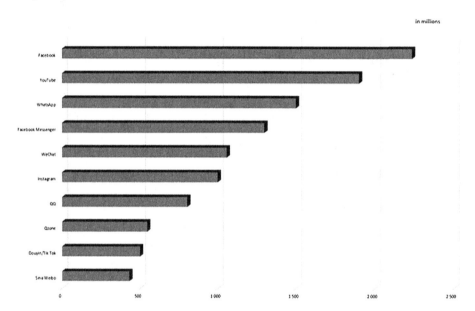

CREATIVE COMPLAINTS AND RESPONSES ON THE SOCIAL MEDIA

Complaints Voiced as Storytelling

Many creative complaints have been found on various social media platforms as social media is a great place to attract attention. There are numerous examples of creative customer complaints and negative eWOM on the Internet such as posting humorous YouTube videos as complaints, creating a Website for visual complaints and publishing e-mail addresses of company executives to get their attentions (Tuggle, 2015) as well as using poem or rhyme as discussed. One common characteristic is that such creative complaints are shared rapidly and then become viral. For instance, a customer complaint presented as a story told through a PowerPoint presentation became spread worldwide on the Internet despite the complaint not being initially intended to be shared in public (Shea, Enghagen, & Khullar, 2004).

One way to create creative complaints is using humour. Humour in complaints as a way to turn something negative into somewhat positive, may not be new phenomenon (McGraw, Warren, & Kan,

2015). However, although humorous complaints are creative, they are not synonymous with storytelling because as discussed, stories need to have some specific elements in order to be categorised as stories. For instance, a complaint can be humorous without featuring a story. Hence, using humour together with a compelling story may provide additional beneficial outcomes for both the complainant and the company dealing with the complaint. Similarly while consumer narrative, WOM and eWOM in general have become common in the era of social media, using storytelling to tell compelling stories together with rhymes or poems in a humorous, fun and even sarcastic manner to voice unfavourable and negative buying experiences may be a less conventional approach. With the jungle of information available on the Internet and social media, customer complaints just like any other information may be lost, easily ignored and buried. Hence, creative complaints are one way to attract the attention of the receiver.

Creative Responses by the Company

With any negative eWOM including customer complaints, companies need to have a proper service recovery system and such process is even more critical due to the speed and impact of the social media. What is interesting in this new reality is that some companies are realising that they need to be at the forefront when dealing with customer complaints by adapt their service recovery process accordingly. Hence, rather than providing standardised replies, apologies and compensation, proactive companies are attempting to recover the service by replying the customers in a similar humorous and fun manner. Hence, while a creative complaint was initiated as storytelling by the customer to voice their opinion regarding an unfavourable experience, many companies have been equally creative to respond to the customers with storytelling. This leads to positive surprises for both parties as well as other customers as the creative, humorous and unique posts or stories can also be shared by other users. The following section further explores the importance of service recovery as well as service recovery strategies in details.

HANDELING CUSTOMER COMPLAINTS

Service Recovery

Hart, Heskett, and Sasser (1990) argue that in the delivery of service, mistakes and failures are inevitable as customer complaints cannot be fully avoided. While service may be the core product in some industries such as tourism, banking and transport, customer service is still an important part in other sectors such as retails selling physical goods and products, particularly when a SD-Logic as discussed by Tronvoll (2012) is adapted. Hence, a proper service recovery process should exist in any businesses. Grönroos (1988) believes that service recovery is needed when the customer discovers that something negative occurs or when something unexpected happens and the company has to take immediate corrective action. Tax and Brown (2000, p. 272) define service recovery as "... a process that identifies service failure, effectively resolves customer problems, classifies their root causes and yields data that can be integrated with other measures of performance to assess and improve the service system". Michel, Bowen, and Johnston (2009) have expanded such definition by proposing that service recovery is the integrative action that a company takes to re-establish customer satisfaction and loyalty after a service failure (customer recovery). This is to ensure that failure incidents encourage learning and process improvement (process recovery) and to train and reward employees for this purpose (employee recovery) (Michel et al., 2009).

For new customers, a single error can have larger consequences than existing customers (Stone, 2011). This is because new customers have not had any previous positive experiences with the company that can outweigh an unfavourable experience. Existing customers may also have a good relationship with the company and will therefore be more tolerant if one error should occur. On the other hand, existing customers will have higher expectations for the recovery process because they have a greater commitment to the business than new customers do. Thus, there may be major consequences for the long-term relationship if a proper service recovery system does not exist (Stone, 2011).

Recovery Strategies

According to Dwyer, Schurr, and Oh (1987) and Stone (2011) compensation and listening to the customer are important in a recovery process in order to maintain a good buyer-seller relationship. When companies receive customer complaints, they have both had the opportunity to restore customer confidence and they can find out which service teams have failed (Berry, Wall, & Carbone, 2006). Although service recovery systems can add more costs to the business including staff and communication costs, there are also benefits such as gaining information to improve the practice and products, loyalty and positive WOM (Stone, 2011). Tax and Brown (1998) suggest a four-step service recovery process; identify errors (teach the customer how to complain, communicate the importance of recovery and use technical support), solve customer problems (be fair to the customer and give fair outcomes), communicate and classify errors (for example, use internal complaint forums) and introduce the data and improve service. Key strategies for a good recovery process are, according to Tax and Brown (1998) training the employees in the frontline and empowering them to make good choices to solve customer problems, create guidelines and make solutions readily available and effective.

Although the literature has argued that service recovery is an important process in any businesses to regain loyalty and trust among the customers as in customer recovery, many companies are still hopeless when dealing with unsatisfied customers. This is evident in the numerous customer complaints found on Facebook for instance where the customers turn to the social media in order to vent their frustration (Mei, et al., 2018). Additionally, the focus of service recovery studies has been on customer recovery, and less attention has been devoted to the employees (Johnston & Michel, 2008). Arguably, dealing with customer complaints as well as improper service recovery policies in the organisation may lead to much difficulties and stress not only for the customers but also for the frontline employees dealing with the complaints (Bowen & Johnston, 1999). Consequently, this would lead to employee turnover, negative attitudes and absenteeism (Johnston & Michel, 2008). Hence, organisations that empower their frontline employees to deal with creative and humorous customer complaints with the same creative and humorous responses, may be able to recover their customers as well as their employees leading to loyal customers and less turnover and stress among the employees. The following section explores some of the creative complaints voiced as storytelling, which have been posted on Facebook as well as subsequent creative and humorous responses by the company's representatives. Facebook was chosen due to the popularity of the platform as discussed while cases were chosen due to storytelling being used as an approach to voice complaints and companies that subsequently choose to respond with storytelling. Customers' written consents have been attained prior to publishing their original Facebook post.

CASES AND EXAMPLES

Case 1 – Freia Chocolate

The first case involves a customer who purchased several chocolate bars. The customer explained that after purchasing the chocolate bars, he believed that they all felt too light, as they should have contained 100 grams each. When the chocolate bars were weighted on the kitchen scale, it only indicated approximately 84 grams each. Believe that voicing his unfavourable experience in a creative way was the way to capture the company's attention; the customer decided to post the unfavourable experience or complaint as a rhyme/poem on the chocolate manufacturer's public Facebook page. Unfortunately, some of the humour and content as well as rhyme are lost when translating the original poem from Norwegian to English.

Table 1. Case 1

Authors' Own Translation	Customer's Original Facebook Post in Norwegian
A woman from the north decided to bake. Now the old man should have his favourite taste. Ingredients were taken from drawers and cupboards, no time to waste. The man was sent to Coop Market to trade what she wanted to transform to delicatessen. The chocolate from Freia was a matter of course when the cream on the top would wave. When the old man returned, Mrs Kauka was at her most frustrated, "you have bought too little chocolate". Then I thought "I'm running to the bathroom". Now I'm behind wondering if I should scream or laugh, the 100 grams bar only weighed 84. Fortunately, I can safely arrive, but Freia may have to hide. When the lady blows her mind, it can soon be moonlit inside. But we up in the north are of the calm stroke and do not want to send a complaint in anger. We just want to inform all of you so this does not happen to others. So when you get the machines adjusted, the guy can finally get a cake served.	En kvinne i fra nord bestemte seg for å bake. Nu skulle gubben få favoritten sin smake. Ingredienser ble hentet fra skuffer og skap, her skulle ingen tid gå til tap. Mannen ble sendt til Coop Marked for å handle, det som hun til en delikatesse skulle forvandle. Selskaps-sjokolade fra Freia var en selvfølge, når kremen på toppen skulle bølge. Når gubben fra butikken returnerte, frua kauka på sitt mest frustrerte "du har jo kjøpt for lite sjokolade". Da tenkte æ "no rømme æ på badet" No sitt æ bak do å lure på om æ skal skrike eller flire, den 100 grams plata den veide bare 84. Heldigvis kan no æ trygt komme frem, men Freia må kanskje gjemme seg dem. Når fruen blåser ut sitt sinne, da kan det fort bli månelyst inne. Men vi opp i fra nord er av det rolige slage, å ønsker ikke å sende i sinne en klage. Vi vil bare informere alle dere, så dette ikke hender med flere. Så når dere maskinene får justert, kan gubben endelig få kake servert.

As the original post has been removed, it is not possible to specify the number of shares. However, the post was picked up by several newspapers as it captured people's attention and interest not only due to the creative and humorous complaint, but also because the response from the chocolate manufacturer Freia was a humorous rhythm as well. Below is the response from the company.

Table 2. Case 1

Authors' Own Translation	Original Facebook Response From the Company
Once the damage has occurred and the chocolate is sunken. Then we understand that the atmosphere at home gets lukewarm! The product must be replaced - no doubt about it. That way, at home, it will be peace on it!	Når skaden er skjedd og sjokoladen er slunken. Så forstår vi at stemningen hjemme blir lunken! Varen skal erstattes - ingen tvil om det Sånn kan det i hjemmet endelig bli fred!

As the result, the customer was satisfied with the reply and outcome of his complaint. The whole episode was turned into a positive experience for both parties.

Case 2 – Mill Caviar on Tube

The second case involves a dissatisfied customer and some caviar that he had purchased. The nature of the complaint involves the poor quality of the packaging. Similar to case 1, the customer posted the complaint through storytelling and poem/rhythm on the company's public Facebook page.

Table 3. Case 2

Authors' Own Translation	Customer' Original Facebook Post
Dear Mills	Kjære Mills
Now I hope you take us on our word,	Nå håper jeg at dere tar oss på ordet,
For today, our vision is sad.	for i dag beskuet vårt syn noe trist.
The Caviar we have on the breakfast table,	Kaviaren vi har på frokostbordet,
Enamel was loose (why is uncertain).	emaljen var løs (hvorfor er uvisst).
It's on the food. "So lame", I thought,	Den drysset på maten. "Så kjipt", tenkte jeg,
and tried to remove most of it.	og prøvde å fjerne det meste.
But there was a lot of sprinkle, and I was quickly bored, and that was the worst.	Men det var masse av dryss, og jeg gikk raskt lei, og det var det aller verste.
Bread and tube went right in the "bucket",	Skive og tube gikk rett i "spannet",
We didn't even get to say goodbye.	vi fikk ikke engang tatt riktig farvel.
So after standing here a little, trampled and cursing,	Så etter å stått her litt, trampet og bannet,
I write to you, hoping for some luck.	skriver jeg til dere, i håp om litt hell.
We've always been faithful to you	Vi har alltid vært trofast mot dere
with remoulade, caviar, mayonnaise, liver pate, dressing and much more,	med remulade, kaviar, majones, leverpostei, dressing og mye mere,
and don't want to give you hassle.	og ønsker ikke å gi dere pes.
But the situation has occurred,	Men situasjonen har oppstått,
we feel depressed.	vi kjenner oss deppa.
The impression we have now received,	Det inntrykk vi nå har fått,
makes us hang with the lips.	får oss til å henge med leppa.
So please, don't let others struggle	Så vær så snill, ikke la andre slite
like us here at the breakfast table!	slik som oss her ved frokostbordet!
Fix the tube quickly, it costs so little,	Fiks tuben raskt, det koster så lite,
So we'll be happy, and take our word.	så vi blir fornøyd, og ta oss på ordet.
With friendly greeting	Med vennlig hilsen
N.N.	N.N
Sad family man	Trist familiefar

Also, as case 1, an equally humorous poem/rhythm was replied by the company. The response from the caviar company Mills is provided below.

Following the first incident, the service was recovered, and the customer was satisfied with the outcome and continued to be a loyal customer. Nevertheless, another unfavourable incident occurred again after some time involving the same customer and product, the customer once again voiced his complaints on Facebook through storytelling.

Following the successful service recovery at the previous incident, the company also followed up the complaint with a similar response.

Table 4. Case 2

Authors' Own Translation	Original Facebook Response From the Company
Dear N. N. It's very unfortunate and we apologise so much, Unfortunately, you're not alone to experience that the tube can peel off. We recently changed the supplier on our tube paint, but it has also created frustration and stomach pain. We compensate of course for your lost money, and we hope you no longer Mills repress. For new tubes with better paint is right around the corner, since July 1 we've got new crops in the mayonnaise container. I also have to mention that the paint that hits your hands, absolutely is not bad for your family or friends but it sucks that this affects you and yours, I'm really sorry and I feel like crying. I hope we can fix the mistake we've done, Send me your account number and we'll transfer money reasonably fast. We don't want you to have your lips hanging, it also does us in Mills depressing.	Kjære N. N. Det er svært uheldig og vi beklager så masse, du er dessverre ikke alene om at tuben kan flasse. Vi har nylig byttet leverandør på tubelakken vår, men det har heller skapt frustrasjon og magesår. Vi kompenserer selvfølgelig for dine tapte penger, og vi håper du ikke lenger Mills fortrenger. For nye tuber med bedre lakk er rett rundt svingen, siden 1. juli har vi fått nye avlinger i majones-bingen. Jeg må også nevne at lakken som treffer dine hender, absolutt ikke er helsefarlig for hverken din familie eller venner. Men dritkjip er det at dette rammer deg og dine, Jeg blir oppriktig lei meg og føler for å grine. Jeg håper vi kan rette opp feilen vi har gjort, send meg ditt kontonummer så overfører vi penger rimelig fort. Vi ønsker ikke at dere skal henge med leppa, det gjør også oss i Mills deppa.

Table 5. Case 2

Authors' Own Translation	Complainer's Original Facebook Post
Hey Mills, it's just me. In 2015, I complained. When the caviar tube-enamel crumbled? Do you remember that? The media rumbled The breakfast table was clear once again, covered with good food and children's song. We sat there and hummed to good music, when I (once again) got a good idea; "Mills caviar on my bread I'll have!", and I could not say better, for my daughter had just finished it, and it could another round again. But as I squeeze out the 'gold' on the bread, then get that constipation!?? The wife says "toss it". But I breathed and pestered, squeezed and hugged. Then it appeared ... we were all a little scared; "Fishbone!", "Fishbowl?", "Snot or something?" The children's suggestions were reasonably good, but the vision cannot deceive this lad; "Cartilage after the fish!", says the desperate dad So once again my bread went into the bucket. I yell "Is nothing perfect here in this country anymore!!??" I sat down, the cheerfulness was gone. Nobody at the breakfast table said a word. Now I write again about my sorrow to you. I hope there are no more, who experience what I experienced today. Neither should this be a big deal. Such things may happen, we can all make mistakes. What may have happened, I have no clue? But next time I know that the tube is tight, I'd rather let it lie rather than getting a sweat. With best regards N. N. Even sadder family father than before.	Heisann Mills, det er bare meg. I 2015 så klaget jeg. Da kaviartube-emaljen smuldret? Husker dere det? Mediene buldret. Frokostbordet var klart nok en gang, oppdekket med god mat og barnesang. Vi satt der og nynnet til god musikk, da jeg (nok engang) en god idé fikk; "Mills kaviar på min skive skal jeg ha!", og jeg kunne ikke sagt bedre ifra, for min datter var nettopp ferdig med den, og den kunne gå på rundgang igjen. Men idet jeg klemmer ut 'gullet' på skiven, så får den forstoppelse!?? Kona sier "hiv den". Men jeg pustet og peste, trykket og klemte. Så dukket det opp...vi ble alle litt skremte; "Fiskebein!", "Fiskebæsj?", 'Snørr eller noe?'. Barnas forslag var jo rimelig gode, men synet kan ikke bedra denne karen; "Brusk etter fisken!", sier den fortvilende faren. Så nok en gang gikk min skive i spannet. Jeg roper "Er ingenting lenger perfekt her i landet!!??" Jeg satte meg ned, munterheten var vekk. Ingen ved frokostbordet sa et kvekk. Nå skriver jeg igjen om min sorg til dere. Jeg håper at det ikke finnes flere, som opplever det jeg opplevde i dag. Ønsker heller ikke at det skal bli en stor sak. Slike ting kan jo skje, vi kan alle gjør feil. Hva kan ha skjedd, jeg har ikke peil? Men neste gang jeg kjenner at tuben er tett, vil jeg heller la den ligge enn at jeg blir svett. Med vennlig hilsen N. N. Enda tristere familiefar enn før.

Table 6. Case 2

Authors' Own Translation	Original Facebook Response From the Company
Hi dear N.N, Of course, we remember you! We have thought about how often it goes with the family father, who was so unlucky with the flaky caviar. Since 2015, much has changed in Mills. Communication in the factory is now happening in rhyme, it is a bit slower, but the atmosphere is fine Your attached picture has been carefully investigated, and our quality manager looks with his well-trained eye that it was a bit of the roe sack that has sneaked in. It is completely harmless, but it should not happen. We understand well that this broke the idyll. It is certainly not fine, and we blame ourselves. We would like to give you a compensation, if you send us your account number, we will transfer money to new caviation. Thank you N.N. for telling us. The routines are sharpened - the rules are tightened - in the hopes that you will be happy!	Hei kjære N.N, Det klart vi husker deg! Vi har tenkt titt og ofte på hvordan det går med familiefaren, som var så uheldig med den flassende kaviaren. Siden 2015 har nemlig mye endret seg i Mills. Kommunikasjon i fabrikken skjer nå på rim, Det går litt tregere, men stemningen er fin. Ditt vedlagte bilde er undersøkt nøye, og vår kvalitetssjef ser med sitt veltrente øye, at det var en bit av rognsekken som har sneket seg med. Det er helt ufarlig, men det skal ikke skje. Vi forstår godt at dette tok knekken på idyllen. Det er absolutt ikke stas, og vi tar på oss skylden. Vi vil gjerne få lov å gi dere en kompensasjon, om du sender oss ditt kontonummer setter vi over penger til ny kaviarrasjon. Tusen takk N.N., for at du sa ifra. Rutinene skjerpes – reglene terpes – i håp om at du skal bli glad!

At the end, the customer was content because the service was once again recovered and he continues to remain a loyal customer. The posts as well as other newspaper articles that reported on the incidents had more than 3000 shares on Facebook. The caviar company's responses and approaches to service recovery were also well received and appraised by the public. As discussed, while these two examples are industries where "services" are not the core product, by applying a SD-Logic approach, customer complaints in any industries should be considered as a phenomenological and unfavourable service experience rather than an after-purchase incident (Tronvoll, 2012). Hence, means to recover the service is equally relevant and important in any industries, particularly in the era of social media when unfavourable experiences can be easily shared with unlimited number of people openly in the public.

Case 3 – Norwegian Air

Evidently, service recovery in industries where "service" is the core product, is even more crucial due to the characteristics of inseparability, heterogeneity and perishability of services, as well as the interactions between service employees and customer (Koc, 2018). The following example involves a negative incident that a customer had experiences with the airline Norwegian Air. Due to an issue with the misspelling of the customer's name, the airline wanted to charge an extra fee. In addition, there were some other issues with the flight, including a delay. Hence, the customer wanted to voice his unfavourable experiences. The complaint which was voiced as a story that rhymes was responded in the same manner by representatives of the airline, with the promise to wave the extra fee.

While the original Facebook post did not generate numerous shares on the platform, the post was picked up by Australian newspapers, Norwegian newspapers as well as American newspapers including Fox news and British newspapers such as BBC news and the Independent in addition to numerous other newspapers. Also similar to the previous cases, the story captured people's attention, turning this to an incident with positive outcomes for both the customer and the company. Moreover, the reason why this particular post generated international attention was because the complaint was posted in English whereas the previous two cases were in Norwegian.

Table 7. Case 3

Customer's Original Facebook Post	Original Facebook Response From the Company
Why can't you be fair Norwegian Air No headphones do you include Nine hours with no free food The stress of a sixty quid bag Would make the plumpest of memories sag. Aviational scandals from Scandinavian vandals. You're a disgrace to the Norwegian flag. And <u>Kiwi.com</u> you're just as bad. Helping these rogues as there's money to be had. Is it hard to operate with decency? To cooperate and offer leniency? I admit it was wrong to put his first name as Bill William Edward Gabriel, the seat who's bum will fill. One hundred and twenty euros for what? For two minutes of typing that's rather a lot. Why can't you be fair Norwegian Air Just skip that amendment fee And just let us change it for free	We understand all the fuzz We try our best to reduce all the buzz But fear not because' we do not throw anyone under the buss especially not a person like you since diamonds in this world are so few We are sorry for any inconvenience that may have occurred. It can seem like our vision is sometimes blurred. But I can promise you that we try to fly like a bird. We thank you for your rhyme We had a really great time You thank us for being fair We thank you for joining us up in the air We wish you a great trip With us the world is on your finger tip Just be sure to follow the landing strip We wish you an awesome day! Best regards, Mats & Natacha

Other Examples of Creative Complaints

There are two additional examples of customers who have used storytelling as an approach to voice their unfavourable experiences. However, as their posts have since been deleted, it is not possible to include the original posts at this point. One of the complaints involved a typo in the printed chocolate wrapping paper. The concept of the chocolate wrapping paper was fairy tales with packaging containing stories of traditional folk adventure such as plot twists and emotions. Hence, the customer decided to post her complaint on the chocolate company Freia's public Facebook page also formulated as a traditional folk adventure. The post started with "once upon a time" and adjectives were used, along with traditional folk adventure such as plot twists and emotions. The message was that there was a typo in the printed fairy tales chocolate wrapping. When asking the customer about the reason she decided to create such a post, she explained that she wanted an answer from the company but at the same time she did not want to be perceived as a customer who would complain about the smallest matter. She believed that in order for the message to be well received by the company, it should be written in a fun humorous way in order to be receive more positively. This concurs with the studies of (McGraw et al., 2015) as some customers are reluctant to complaint in fear of being labelled as difficult customers. Hence, humour is used to counterweigh a negative incident. As discussed, customer complaints and service failure cannot only create stress and unfavourable situations for the customers, but also for the service employees. By using a humorous and untraditional approach to voice complaints, the complaints may also be more positively received by the frontline employees handling the complaints.

Another example involved a broken washing machine. The complaint was also formulated as a story starting by explaining the situation where the washing machine had broken and the need for a new one. Furthermore, the purchase process was described, from when the customer went to the store until the new washing machine was in the house. Among other things, the values for product selection were explained and that the customer wanted to choose an expensive alternative with the expectation of quality. The seller's attitude and mood were also described in detail. Halfway through the story, the customer came to the point of the story, namely to describe how little help and poor service he had received when the new product was broken and should be repaired. The conclusion was that he had waited for the repairer to come back with the right tool for several months, as well as made a number of inquiries to customer service over the phone. The whole complaint was concluded with a sarcastic suggestion of using the washboard and the nearest river as a washing method, and sarcastic thanks for expensive phone calls and empty promises from the company. The story thus contained a beginning, middle and end, with a climax and a turning point (Lundquist et al, 2012).

DISCUSSION

The previous section illustrated five cases in total where the first three are similar in nature and the latter two are alike. Evidently, the first three cases achieved more success. It has been argued that virality on social media is shown by the number of shares. In order for people to share posts and contents on the social media, they have to be something out of the ordinary and fascinating, making it worthwhile to share (Moriuchi, 2016). While the number of shares cannot be determined for all the cases, the fact that the first three cases were all picked by several local, national and international newspapers, does provide a certain confirmation on their virality. Furthermore, sharing on Facebook is not as common compared with other social media platforms, especially among millennials, as although many of them have Facebook accounts, very little is shared on this platform in particular (Dooley, 2017). Hence, the number of shares does not necessarily illustrate the virality.

The first three cases also illustrate the importance of employee empowerment in regards to service recovery as emphasised by Tax and Brown (1998), by training and empowering the frontline employees to make good choices to solve customer problems. The cases showcase that the frontline employees or the employees responsible of responding to customer complaints on Facebook, were empowered to make decisions to recover the service. They were authorised to respond to the complaints in an equally humorous and creative manner through storytelling. This led to positive outcomes and success for the companies. This also suggests that the companies listened to the complainant by acknowledging the error and the importance of recovery, and they were concerned with solving customer problems and improving the service, which are all key recovery strategies (Tax & Brown, 1998). Additionally, how fast the companies manage to solve the issue is also a vital part of successful service recovery as this will determine the level of satisfaction of the complainant (Harris, Grewal, Mohr, & Bernhardt, 2006). In the first three cases, all three companies managed to respond to the customer in timely manner, which is also vital especially when the complaints are posted on social media and Facebook. The cases thus achieve success due to the creative complaints and the timely subsequent unconventional responses by the companies to recover the services.

The main difference between the first three cases and the latter two is that in the latter two, the customers did not receive any story or storytelling as responses by the companies' representatives. Hence, their creative complaints voiced as storytelling on Facebook were not as eagerly shared or they did not manage to capture the attention of the general public as they were not perceived as interesting enough. While the service was recovered, it was nothing out of the ordinary to capture people's attention. Hence, although there may be numerous examples of creative and humorous customer complaints voiced as storytelling on the social media, it is also the companies' unconventional responses that contribute to make the entire incident interesting and worthwhile to capture people's attention and interest by turning the situation into positive experiences and outcomes for both parties involved.

CONCLUSION AND FUTURE RESEARCH DIRECTIONS

Complaints will exist as long as human beings exist as they are part of the social life, hence it is impossible to avoid them completely (McGraw et al., 2015). In the new era of social media, complaints can also be rapidly shared to a large number of people, causing numerous challenges for companies. While most companies have some sort of systems of service recovery, many are still hopeless in dealing with complaints, as many customers believe that they are not being heard. Hence, using storytelling to voice customer complaints and unfavourable experiences is one way for the customer to capture the company's attention. Arguably, it may take more effort from the customer's side to voice the complaint as a compelling story either through humour, rhyme or poem rather than an ordinary complaint. For managers, they must train and empower their frontline employees or employees dealing with complaints to be on the lookout for creative complaints. Fast respond is also vital especially when dealing with complaints posted on social media. Employees must thus be trained to be confident to respond and recover the service in the same manner. This may serve as a way to prevent the customer from complaining further and before the post garners too much negative attention on the social media. The examples provided in this chapter suggest that by empowering the frontline employees to respond to untraditional customer complaints with untraditional responses, the outcome may be positive for both parties. However, it would be important to note that creative and untraditional responses should merely be used to respond to creative complaints and that serious complaints should not be recovered using untraditional responses as this may be interpreted as mockery or unserious respond from the company's side.

Furthermore, the cases provided in this chapter derived from Northern Europe involving Nordic companies. Customer complaints and approach to service recoveries may be affected by cultural factors (Gordon & Patterson, 2009) as behaviour is influenced by the cultural background since culture is the framework for social interactions in general (Hofstede, 2001; Triandis, 1989). In such sense, customers' behaviour, expectations and perceptions during any service encounters also vary from culture to culture. Hence, the approach to voicing complaints as storytelling in a humorous and creative manner may not be as common or acceptable in a different cultural context. Future scientific studies should investigate the topic of applying storytelling as an approach in complaint behaviour as well as focusing on other countries with different cultural context.

REFERENCES

Arndt, J. (1967). Role of Product-Related Conversations in the Diffusion of a New Product. *JMR, Journal of Marketing Research*, *4*(3), 291–295. doi:10.1177/002224376700400308

Balaji, M. S., Jha, S., & Royne, M. B. (2015). Customer e-complaining behaviours using social media. *Service Industries Journal*, *35*(11-12), 633–635. doi:10.1080/02642069.2015.1062883

Berry, L. L., Wall, E. A., & Carbone, L. P. (2006). Service Clues and Customer Assessment of the Service Experience: Lessons from Marketing. *The Academy of Management Perspectives*, *20*(2), 43–57. doi:10.5465/amp.2006.20591004

Black, H. G., & Kelley, S. W. (2009). A storytelling perspective on online customer reviews reporting service failure and recovery. *Journal of Travel & Tourism Marketing*, *26*(2), 169–179. doi:10.1080/10548400902864768

Bone, P. F. (1992). Determinants of Word-Of-Mouth Communications During Product Consumption. *Advances in Consumer Research. Association for Consumer Research (U. S.)*, *19*, 579–583.

Bowen, D. E., & Johnston, R. (1999). *Internal service recovery: developing a new construct*. Academic Press. doi:10.1108/09564239910264307

Bruhn, M., Schoenmueller, V., & Schäfer, D. B. (2012). Are social media replacing traditional media in terms of brand equity creation? *Management Research Review*, *35*(9), 770–790. doi:10.1108/01409171211255948

Buttle, F. A. (1998). Word of mouth: Understanding and managing referral marketing. *Journal of Strategic Marketing*, *6*(3), 241–254. doi:10.1080/096525498346658

Carl, W. J. (2006). WHAT'S ALL THE BUZZ ABOUT? Everyday Communication and the Relational Basis of Word-of-Mouth and Buzz Marketing Practices. *Management Communication Quarterly*, *19*(4), 601–634. doi:10.1177/0893318905284763

Day, R. L., & Landon, E. L. J. (1977). Toward a theory of consumer complaining behavior. In A. G. Woodside, J. N. Sheth, & P. D. Bennett (Eds.), *Consumer and Industrial Buying Behavior* (pp. 425–437). New York, NY: North-Holland Publishing.

Delgadillo, Y., & Escalas, J. E. (2004). Narrative Word-of-Mouth Communication: Exploring Memory and Attitude Effects of Consumer Storytelling. *Advances in Consumer Research. Association for Consumer Research (U. S.)*, *31*(1), 186–192.

Dwyer, F. R., Schurr, P. H., & Oh, S. (1987). Developing Buyer-Seller Relationships. *Journal of Marketing*, *51*(2), 11–27. doi:10.1177/002224298705100202

Edvardsson, B., Tronvoll, B., & Gruber, T. (2011). Expanding understanding of service exchange and value co-creation: A social construction approach. *Journal of the Academy of Marketing Science*, *39*(2), 327–339. doi:10.100711747-010-0200-y

Ferrari, S. (2015). Storytelling and Narrative Marketing in the Era of Social Media. In I. Deliyannis, P. Kostagiolas, & C. Banou (Eds.), *Experimental Multimedia Systems for Interactivity and Strategic Innovation* (pp. 1–15). Hershey, PA: IGI Global.

Gelb, B. D., & Sundaram, S. (2002). Adapting to "word of mouse". *Business Horizons*, *45*(4), 21–25. doi:10.1016/S0007-6813(02)00222-7

Gordon, P. J., & Patterson, T. E. (2009). Using the Transparency Index to Categorize European Countries. *Journal of International Business Research*, *8*(1), 69–77.

Green, M. C., & Brock, T. C. (2000). The role of transportation in the persuasiveness of public narratives. *Journal of Personality and Social Psychology, 79*(5), 701–721. doi:10.1037/0022-3514.79.5.701 PMID:11079236

Grégoire, Y., Salle, A., & Tripp, T. M. (2015). Managing social media crises with your customers: The good, the bad, and the ugly. *Business Horizons, 58*(2), 173–182. doi:10.1016/j.bushor.2014.11.001

Grönroos, C. (1988). Service quality: The six criteria of good perceived service quality. *Review of Business, 9*(3), 10–13.

Harris, K. E., Grewal, D., Mohr, L. A., & Bernhardt, K. L. (2006). Consumer responses to service recovery strategies: The moderating role of online versus offline environment. *Journal of Business Research, 59*(4), 425–431. doi:10.1016/j.jbusres.2005.10.005

Harrison-Walker, L. J. (2001). E-complaining: A content analysis of an Internet complaint forum. *Journal of Services Marketing, 15*(5), 397–412. doi:10.1108/EUM0000000005657

Hart, C. W. L., Heskett, J. L., & Sasser, W. E. (1990). The profitable art of service recovery. *Harvard Business Review*, (July/August): 148–156. PMID:10106796

Hofstede, G. H. (2001). *Culture's Consequences: Comparing Values, Behaviors, Institutions, and Organizations Across Nations* (2nd ed.). Thousand Oaks, CA: Sage Publications.

Howison, S., Higgins-Desbiolles, F., & Sun, Z. (2017). Storytelling in tourism: Chinese visitors and Māori hosts in New Zealand. *Anatolia, 28*(3), 327–337. doi:10.1080/13032917.2017.1318296

Johnston, R., & Michel, S. (2008). *Three outcomes of service recovery: Customer recovery, process recovery and employee recovery.* Academic Press. doi:10.1108/01443570810841112

Kent, M. L. (2015). The power of storytelling in public relations: Introducing the 20 master plots. *Public Relations Review, 41*(4), 480–489. doi:10.1016/j.pubrev.2015.05.011

Kirkland, A. (2014). *10 countries where Facebook has been banned.* Retrieved from https://www.indexoncensorship.org/2014/02/10-countries-facebook-banned/

Kluth, A. (2006). Among the audience: A survey of new media. *The Economist, 22*, 3-20.

Koc, E. (2018). Service failures and recovery in hospitality and tourism: A review of literature and recommendations for future research. *Journal of Hospitality Marketing & Management*, 1–25. doi:10.1080/19368623.2019.1537139

Litvin, S. W., Goldsmith, R. E., & Pan, B. (2008). Electronic word-of-mouth in hospitality and tourism management. *Tourism Management, 29*(3), 458–468. doi:10.1016/j.tourman.2007.05.011

Lundqvist, A., Liljander, V., Gummerus, J., & van Riel, A. (2012). The impact of storytelling on the consumer brand experience: The case of a firm-originated story. *Journal of Brand Management, 20*(4), 283–297. doi:10.1057/bm.2012.15

McAdams, D. P. (2001). The psychology of life stories. *Review of General Psychology, 5*(2), 100–122. doi:10.1037/1089-2680.5.2.100

McGraw, A. P., Warren, C., & Kan, C. (2015). Humorous Complaining. *The Journal of Consumer Research*, *41*(5), 1153–1171. doi:10.1086/678904

Mei, X. Y., Bagaas, I. K., & Relling, E. K. L. (2018). Customer complaint behaviour (CCB) in the retail sector: Why do customers voice their complaints on Facebook? *International Review of Retail, Distribution and Consumer Research*, 1–16. doi:10.1080/09593969.2018.1556179

Mei, X. Y., Hågensen, A.-M. S., & Kristiansen, H. S. (2018). Storytelling through experiencescape: Creating unique stories and extraordinary experiences in farm tourism. *Tourism and Hospitality Research*, *0*(0). doi:10.1177/1467358418813410

Meyer, M. (2005). The Bedford Introduction to Literature. St. Martin.

Michel, S., Bowen, D. E., & Johnston, R. (2009). Why service recovery fails; Tensions among customer, employee, and process perspectives. *Journal of Service Management*, *20*(3), 253–273. doi:10.1108/09564230910964381

Minazzi, R. (2014). *Social Media Marketing in Tourism and Hospitality*. Berlin: Springer.

Moriuchi, E. (2016). *Social Media Marketing: Strategies in Utilizing Consumer-Generated Content*. New York: Business Expert Press.

Mossberg, L. (2008). Extraordinary Experiences through Storytelling. *Scandinavian Journal of Hospitality and Tourism*, *8*(3), 195–210. doi:10.1080/15022250802532443

Mossberg, L., & Johansen, E. N. (2006). *Storytelling: Marknadsföring i Upplevelseindustrin*. Göteborg: Studentlitteratur AB.

Nicas, J. (2019). *Does Facebook really know how many fake accounts it has?* Retrieved from https://www.nytimes.com/2019/01/30/technology/facebook-fake-accounts.html

Pennington, N., & Hastie, R. (1986). Evidence evaluation in complex decision making. *Journal of Personality and Social Psychology*, *51*(2), 242–258. doi:10.1037/0022-3514.51.2.242

Quesenbery, W., & Brooks, K. (2010). *Storytelling for User Experience: Crafting Stories for Better Design*. New York: Louis Rosefeld.

Schank, R. C. (1999). *Dynamic Memory Revisited*. Cambridge University Press. doi:10.1017/CBO9780511527920

Scott, J. W. (2011). Storytelling. *History and Theory*, *50*(2), 203–209. doi:10.1111/j.1468-2303.2011.00577.x

Shea, L., Enghagen, L., & Khullar, A. (2004). Internet Diffusion of an E-Complaint. *Journal of Travel & Tourism Marketing*, *17*(2-3), 145–165. doi:10.1300/J073v17n02_12

Singer, J. A., & Bluck, S. (2001). New perspectives on autobiographical memory: The integration of narrative processing and autobiographical reasoning. *Review of General Psychology*, *5*(2), 91–99. doi:10.1037/1089-2680.5.2.91

Solnet, D., Kandampully, J., & Kralj, A. (2010). Legends of service excellence: The habits of seven highly effective hospitality companies. *Journal of Hospitality Marketing & Management, 19*(8), 889–908. do i:10.1080/19368623.2010.514562

Statista. (2018). *Most popular social networks worldwide as of October 2018, ranked by number of active users (in millions).* Retrieved from https://www.statista.com/statistics/272014/global-social-networks-ranked-by-number-of-users/

Stone, M. (2011). Literature review on complaints management. *Journal of Database Marketing & Customer Strategy Management, 18*(2), 108–122. doi:10.1057/dbm.2011.16

Tax, S. S., & Brown, S. W. (1998). Recovering and learning from service failures. (includes appendix). *Sloan Management Review, 40*(1), 75.

Tax, S. S., & Brown, S. W. (2000). Service Recovery: Research Insights and Practices. In T. Schwartz & D. Iacobucci (Eds.), *Handbook of Services Marketing and Management* (pp. 271–285). Thousand Oaks, CA: Sage Publications.

Triandis, H. C. (1989). The self and social behavior in different cultural contexts. *Psychological Review, 96*(3), 506–520. doi:10.1037/0033-295X.96.3.506

Tronvoll, B. (2007). Customer complaint behaviour from the perspective of the service-dominant logic of marketing. *Managing Service Quality, 17*(6), 601–620. doi:10.1108/09604520710834966

Tronvoll, B. (2012). A Dynamic Model of Customer Complaint Behaviour from the Perspective of Service-Dominant Logic. *European Journal of Marketing, 46*(1/2), 284–305. doi:10.1108/03090561211189338

Tuggle, B. (2015). *10 Funniest & Most Creative Consumer Complaints Ever.* Retrieved from http://time.com/money/3965118/funny-effective-consumer-complaints/

Vargo, S., & Lusch, R. (2004). The Four Service Marketing Myths: Remnants of a Goods-Based, Manu-facturing Model. *Journal of Service Research, 6*(4), 324–335. doi:10.1177/1094670503262946

Weick, K. E. (1995). *Sensemaking in Organizations.* Thousand Oaks, CA: Sage.

Woodside, A. G. (2010). Brand-consumer storytelling theory and research: Introduction to a Psychology & Marketing special issue. *Psychology and Marketing, 27*(6), 531–540. doi:10.1002/mar.20342

Woodside, A. G., Sood, S., & Miller, K. E. (2008). When consumers and brands talk: Storytelling theory and research in psychology and marketing. *Psychology and Marketing, 25*(2), 97–145. doi:10.1002/mar.20203

ADDITIONAL READING

Beitelspacher, L. S., Richey, R. G., & Reynolds, K. E. (2011). Exploring a new perspective on service efficiency: Service culture in retail organizations. *Journal of Services Marketing, 25*(3), 215–228. doi:10.1108/08876041111129191

Bharadwaj, A., Sawy, O. A. E., Pavlou, P. A., & Venkatraman, N. (2013). Digital business strategy: toward a next generation of insights.(Special Issue: Digital Business Strategy)(Report). *Management Information Systems Quarterly*, *37*(2), 471–482. doi:10.25300/MISQ/2013/37:2.3

Black, H. G., & Kelley, S. W. (2009). A storytelling perspective on online customer reviews reporting service failure and recovery. *Journal of Travel & Tourism Marketing*, *26*(2), 169–179. doi:10.1080/10548400902864768

Castronovo, C., & Huang, L. (2012). Social Media in an Alternative Marketing Communication Model. *Journal of Marketing Development and Competitiveness*, *6*(1), 117–131.

Crié, D. (2003). Consumers' complaint behaviour. Taxonomy, typology and determinants: Towards a unified ontology. *Journal of Database Marketing & Customer Strategy Management*, *11*(1), 60–79. doi:10.1057/palgrave.dbm.3240206

Heskett, J. L., Sasser, W. E. Jr, & Schlesinger, L. J. (2003). *The Value-Profit Chain: Treat Employees Like Customers and Customers Like Employees*. New York: The Free Press.

Kelley, S. W., Hoffman, K. D., & Davis, M. A. (1993). A typology of retail failures and recoveries. *Journal of Retailing*, *69*(4), 429–452. doi:10.1016/0022-4359(93)90016-C

Mattila, A. S., & Wirtz, J. (2004). Consumer complaining to firms: The determinants of channel choice. *Journal of Services Marketing*, *18*(2), 147–155. doi:10.1108/08876040410528746

Susskind, A. M. (2000). Efficacy and Outcome Expectations Related to Customer Complaints About Service Experiences. *Communication Research*, *27*(3), 353–378. doi:10.1177/009365000027003004

Tripp, T. M., & Gregoire, Y. (2011). When unhappy customers strike back on the Internet. *MIT Sloan Management Review*, *52*(3), 37–44.

KEY TERMS AND DEFINITIONS

Creative Complaints: Unconventional manners of voicing complaints using humor and other creative ways such as rhymes and poems.

Customer Complaints: Customers' way of expressing dissatisfaction of an unfavorable buying or service experience.

eWOM: Communication for the purpose of information sharing between individuals through the Internet and electronic media.

Facebook: A social media platform and application that enables users to share information including photos, videos, and experiences for the purpose of social networking.

Service Recovery: A process to respond to complaints as a way to recover the failed service experiences.

Social Media: Involves applications and platforms on the Internet that enable sharing of information such as eWOM.

Storytelling: Describes the activity of sharing through stories.

WOM: Oral communication for the purpose of information sharing between individuals.

This research was previously published in Exploring the Power of Electronic Word-of-Mouth in the Services Industry; pages 49-68, copyright year 2020 by Business Science Reference (an imprint of IGI Global).

Index

A

Absorptive Capacity Theory 202, 204, 207-208, 212, 215-216, 219, 221, 225-226

Academic Library 1001-1003, 1460-1461, 1466, 1473, 1475-1477, 1479

Accessibility 20, 111, 152, 169, 194, 224, 237, 307, 338, 340, 342, 349-350, 360, 691, 729, 817, 854, 860, 865, 951, 1103, 1182, 1186, 1230, 1304, 1313, 1578, 1585, 1617, 1667, 1669-1670, 1672-1677, 1694, 1742, 1860

Ad Audience 1027

ad optimization 607

ad placement 599, 605, 623-624, 672, 686-687

Ad Targeting 599, 624

Advertising Effectiveness 195, 582, 601-602, 610, 620-621, 642, 649, 665, 683, 685, 1318-1319, 1661, 1833, 1844

Advertising Media 134, 138, 149, 604, 626, 1005

advertising value model (AVM) 647-648, 651, 653, 661

affective components of destination image 284, 286, 289-290, 303

affective-based 357, 359, 364

Analytic Tools 406

Apis 41, 408, 417-419, 518, 551, 1277, 1521, 1731

Artificial Intelligence 143, 152-153, 315, 374, 379, 382, 403, 417, 539-540, 555-556, 585, 595-596, 598, 705, 707, 710, 720, 722, 725, 736, 763, 790, 859, 867, 1080, 1082-1083, 1694, 1696

Automatic Personalization 582

Avatar 707, 709, 725

B

Ban 400, 807, 1169-1175

bandwagon effect 1014, 1027

Beauty Industry 952, 1084, 1086-1087, 1090, 1094-1096, 1105-1106, 1604

Big Data 27, 34-41, 43, 110, 115, 127, 160, 229, 233, 243, 245-246, 248-251, 253, 255-256, 260, 263, 289-290, 293-294, 296, 298, 415-416, 418-419, 538-539, 541-542, 551, 553, 555, 644-645, 736, 767, 788-789, 792-794, 796, 798, 802-805, 808, 850-851, 855-856, 858-859, 865, 868, 870-872, 1003, 1027, 1079, 1165-1166, 1168-1169, 1175-1179, 1273, 1281-1282, 1287-1288, 1292, 1298, 1300, 1517-1518, 1521, 1536-1537, 1635, 1688, 1833, 1841, 1863

Big Data Analysis 249, 294, 415, 767, 793, 796, 798, 802-805, 858, 1165, 1517

Blogging 22, 34, 47, 51, 56, 59, 143, 194-195, 206, 408, 411, 752, 810, 815, 821, 823, 827, 830, 936, 1084, 1097, 1106, 1413, 1417, 1588, 1615, 1617, 1787, 1793, 1806

Blogs 3, 33, 46, 53, 64, 78, 87-88, 114, 143, 145, 159, 164, 173-175, 185, 190, 198, 206, 224, 271, 279-280, 287, 289, 299, 301, 379, 385, 418-419, 422, 425, 429, 431, 442, 455, 544, 603, 646, 693, 740, 808, 815, 821, 851-852, 855, 868, 875, 880, 895, 920-921, 936-938, 941, 945, 1028, 1049, 1053-1054, 1084-1085, 1087-1088, 1090-1092, 1096-1097, 1145, 1155, 1161, 1175, 1177, 1181, 1186, 1201, 1205-1206, 1237, 1261, 1294, 1321, 1335, 1348, 1352, 1364, 1375, 1394, 1440, 1452, 1462, 1485, 1487, 1521, 1573, 1587-1589, 1600, 1610, 1612, 1618, 1631, 1655, 1660, 1668, 1688, 1690, 1694, 1700, 1702, 1715, 1721, 1723, 1733, 1743-1744, 1747-1748, 1755, 1770, 1775, 1777, 1828

Bollywood 1497-1498, 1501, 1508-1510, 1512

Boycott 53, 795, 1165, 1169, 1171-1175, 1723

Brand Ambassador 56, 1270, 1587

Brand Associations 68, 80, 161, 177-178, 183, 200, 1240-1241, 1243-1244, 1258-1259, 1365

Brand Attitude 184, 199, 606, 640, 665-666, 1053, 1234, 1237, 1240-1241, 1245-1247, 1253, 1351, 1358-1359, 1362, 1367, 1543, 1611

Brand Awareness 49, 51-52, 83, 91-93, 95, 98, 100, 167, 176-177, 189, 326-327, 457, 483, 498, 588, 594,

G

U

V

W

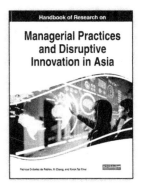
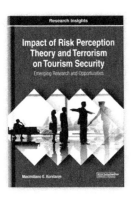

Become an Evaluator for IGI Global Authored Book Projects

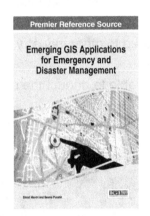

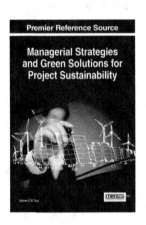

The overall success of an authored book project is dependent on quality and timely manuscript evaluations.

Applications and Inquiries may be sent to:
development@igi-global.com

Applicants must have a doctorate (or equivalent degree) as well as publishing, research, and reviewing experience. Authored Book Evaluators are appointed for one-year terms and are expected to complete at least three evaluations per term. Upon successful completion of this term, evaluators can be considered for an additional term.

If you have a colleague that may be interested in this opportunity, we encourage you to share this information with them.

IGI Global Author Services

Providing a high-quality, affordable, and expeditious service, IGI Global's Author Services enable authors to streamline their publishing process, increase chance of acceptance, and adhere to IGI Global's publication standards.

Benefits of Author Services:

- **Professional Service:** All our editors, designers, and translators are experts in their field with years of experience and professional certifications.
- **Quality Guarantee & Certificate:** Each order is returned with a quality guarantee and certificate of professional completion.
- **Timeliness:** All editorial orders have a guaranteed return timeframe of 3-5 business days and translation orders are guaranteed in 7-10 business days.
- **Affordable Pricing:** IGI Global Author Services are competitively priced compared to other industry service providers.
- **APC Reimbursement:** IGI Global authors publishing Open Access (OA) will be able to deduct the cost of editing and other IGI Global author services from their OA APC publishing fee.

Author Services Offered:

English Language Copy Editing
Professional, native English language copy editors improve your manuscript's grammar, spelling, punctuation, terminology, semantics, consistency, flow, formatting, and more.

Scientific & Scholarly Editing
A Ph.D. level review for qualities such as originality and significance, interest to researchers, level of methodology and analysis, coverage of literature, organization, quality of writing, and strengths and weaknesses.

Figure, Table, Chart & Equation Conversions
Work with IGI Global's graphic designers before submission to enhance and design all figures and charts to IGI Global's specific standards for clarity.

Translation
Providing 70 language options, including Simplified and Traditional Chinese, Spanish, Arabic, German, French, and more.

Hear What the Experts Are Saying About IGI Global's Author Services

"Publishing with IGI Global has been *an amazing experience* for me for sharing my research. The *strong academic production* support ensures quality and timely completion." – **Prof. Margaret Niess, Oregon State University, USA**

"The service was *very fast, very thorough, and very helpful* in ensuring our chapter meets the criteria and requirements of the book's editors. I was *quite impressed and happy* with your service." – **Prof. Tom Brinthaupt, Middle Tennessee State University, USA**

Learn More or Get Started Here:

For Questions, Contact IGI Global's Customer Service Team at cust@igi-global.com or 717-533-8845

IGI Global
PUBLISHER of TIMELY KNOWLEDGE
www.igi-global.com

www.igi-global.com

Publisher of Peer-Reviewed, Timely, and Innovative Academic Research Since 1988

IGI Global's Transformative Open Access (OA) Model:
How to Turn Your University Library's Database Acquisitions Into a Source of OA Funding

Well in advance of Plan S, IGI Global unveiled their OA Fee Waiver (Read & Publish) Initiative. Under this initiative, librarians who invest in IGI Global's InfoSci-Books and/or InfoSci-Journals databases will be able to subsidize their patrons' OA article processing charges (APCs) when their work is submitted and accepted (after the peer review process) into an IGI Global journal.

How Does it Work?

Step 1: **Library Invests in the InfoSci-Databases:** A library perpetually purchases or subscribes to the InfoSci-Books, InfoSci-Journals, or discipline/subject databases.

Step 2: **IGI Global Matches the Library Investment with OA Subsidies Fund:** IGI Global provides a fund to go towards subsidizing the OA APCs for the library's patrons.

Step 3: **Patron of the Library is Accepted into IGI Global Journal (After Peer Review):** When a patron's paper is accepted into an IGI Global journal, they option to have their paper published under a traditional publishing model or as OA.

Step 4: **IGI Global Will Deduct APC Cost from OA Subsidies Fund:** If the author decides to publish under OA, the OA APC fee will be deducted from the OA subsidies fund.

Step 5: **Author's Work Becomes Freely Available:** The patron's work will be freely available under CC BY copyright license, enabling them to share it freely with the academic community.

Note: This fund will be offered on an annual basis and will renew as the subscription is renewed for each year thereafter. IGI Global will manage the fund and award the APC waivers unless the librarian has a preference as to how the funds should be managed.

Hear From the Experts on This Initiative:

"I'm very happy to have been able to make one of my recent research contributions *freely available* along with having access to the *valuable resources* found within IGI Global's InfoSci-Journals database."

— **Prof. Stuart Palmer,** Deakin University, Australia

"Receiving the support from IGI Global's OA Fee Waiver Initiative *encourages me to continue my research work without any hesitation.*"

— **Prof. Wenlong Liu,** College of Economics and Management at Nanjing University of Aeronautics & Astronautics, China

For More Information, Scan the QR Code or Contact: IGI Global's Digital Resources Team at eresources@igi-global.com.

Printed in the United States
by Baker & Taylor Publisher Services